An Anthology of Canadian
Native Literature
in English

THIRD EDITION

EDITED BY

Daniel David Moses
& Terry Goldie

OXFORD
UNIVERSITY PRESS

OXFORD
UNIVERSITY PRESS

70 Wynford Drive, Don Mills, Ontario M3C 1J9
www.oup.com/ca

Oxford University Press is a department of the University of Oxford.
It furthers the University's objective of excellence in research, scholarship,
and education by publishing worldwide in

Oxford New York
Auckland   Cape Town   Dar es Salaam   Hong Kong   Karachi
Kuala Lumpur Madrid   Melbourne   Mexico City   Nairobi
New Delhi   Shanghai   Taipei   Toronto

With offices in
Argentina   Austria   Brazil   Chile   Czech Republic   France   Greece
Guatemala   Hungary   Italy   Japan   Poland   Portugal   Singapore
South Korea   Switzerland   Thailand   Turkey   Ukraine   Vietnam

Oxford is a trade mark of Oxford University Press
in the UK and in certain other countries

Published in Canada
by Oxford University Press

Copyright © Oxford University Press Canada 2005

Library and Archives Canada Cataloguing in Publication
An anthology of Canadian native literature in English / edited by
Daniel David Moses & Terry Goldie. — 3rd ed.
Includes index.

ISBN–13: 978–0–19–542078–4.–   ISBN–10: 0–19–542078–0

1. Canadian literature (English)—Native authors.   2. Native peoples—Literary collections.
I. Moses, Daniel David, 1952–   II. Goldie, Terry

PS8235.I6A56 2005   C810.8'0897   C2004–907129–7

Cover design: Brett J. Miller

1 2 3 4 – 08 07 06 05
This book is printed on permanent (acid-free) paper ∞.
Printed in Canada

Contents

Preface to the Third Edition

TERRY GOLDIE: There was a Newfoundland book at the end of the 19th century that had a great title: *Where Are We and Whither Tending?* So my first question about Native Canadian literature is, 'Where are we and whither tending?'

DANIEL DAVID MOSES: Your metaphor makes me think too much about explorers and frontiers. But rather than a journey of discovery, I would suggest human life as the measure and that Native literature is almost past its youthful idealistic and angry stage. Adolescents tend to be so hopeful: all they can experience is disappointment in this world. Partly this means Native literature is no longer shouting loudly, 'Look at me!', but is now also taking time to consider just what it can do to heal its community. (Do other literatures have to be so conscious of their audience?) Native literature is doing this quietly and more artfully than ever before, and perhaps a bit too introvertedly.

But that is understandable if we consider what young people must go through before they decide how to use the voice they come to realize they have—yes, yes, you do use this English language as well as any in the world!—with some sense of justice as well as beauty and clarity. All this happens despite the reflex of cynicism that any smart young person develops just to get through those teenage years. If we have not already heard that voice make a statement that the rest of the country and the world can and must hear, then it will happen soon.

TG: I like that. Is it true of individual writers as well? We have deleted and added selections for many writers. Do you think the individual oeuvres show this growth beyond cynicism? Or?

DDM: It can be true of the individual writer. Look at the new work we read by the more senior people in this writing community, things we do not have space to excerpt. Basil Johnson's *Crazy Dave* comes to my mind as a work of great understanding and compassion. But some people just cannot be healed. Their wounds—or at least the wounds in their community—are so deep and abiding. Think of having a place like Davis Inlet as a permanent part of your soul and imagination, the anguish and shame: the whole town is the bad part of town. Not to mention your life. And such writers, living in Canada 'on reserve'—at least in their minds—never really expect to have the opportunity to find health and so don't have the energy or the skills to achieve it. Young artists have the strength to bear it. Some of our new writers are articulating that 'same old story' but with fascinating new vocabularies. At a certain time of life, however, you either find your way out of life or grow up and out and move on. But all these writers together have prepared the way for the next generation. We bless our parents for this. Fewer of the next generation will need to spend their precious lifetime talking to the hand that so poorly fed us. More of us will be in control of our own lives. Cynicism will become once more the province of the young.

TG: So are you saying that the writers have less need for resistance but instead can concentrate on consolidation and healing? And that this is more possible than when we began this project fifteen years ago?

DDM: Yes, this is where we are tending, at least as I perceive or maybe dream it. Think about the number of new writers whose work we've included, add that to the number we already had, think about the number we did not have room to recognize—or those who are learning their art and craft and are not quite ready—and you get this impressionist picture. If you're used to looking at beadwork, the Impressionists are just so real. They create a portrait of a growing community of voices, voices that tell stories from places all across the country, from different experiences of colonialism, from different traditions. More and more in the decade-and-a-half since we started this project, the tellers of those stories have begun to hear each other, thanks to this project and other projects like it, and to recognize each other and themselves and all they have in common and in difference. The White Man needed this mystification, 'The Indian', for his own version of the story of the country, and it got in the way of our versions of who we are. But now it can do that less and less often. More and more we are all doing as I remember my parents doing. This may be just a story, but I do remember it: whenever the Lone Ranger got credit for Tonto's heroism we would roll our eyes and change the channel to the one with the Indians on it. We can do that now, thanks to APTN [the Aboriginal Peoples' Television Network]. We are realizing we can be busy making our own mistakes and then we shall have a reason to fix them, because they belong to us.

TG: So there is a community of Native writers that goes across Canada. It often seems as if there are two Native communities, the local one of your own nation and the 'pan-Indian', or at least Canadian pan-Indian, as in the Assembly of First Nations. Is this another newer community, 'pan-Indian' artists? Is APTN an important symptom of this community? Does this exist in a way that it didn't when Native Earth Performing Arts began? Is it an especially strong nail in the Lone Ranger's coffin? Too many questions, but I hope they connect.

DDM: I think that is true if you remember the complexity of community and the unofficial ways community can function. The moccasin telegraph today sends important messages across the country by phone and e-mail. Did you hear Maria Campbell won the Molson Prize this year? We are not yet the artistic AFN because we have not had the money to organize any long-lasting organization. It is hard enough getting the dollars to live and work without creating a bureaucracy. But someday we shall all be middle-class, if the middle-class continues to exist. There was at least one national meeting sponsored by the Canada Council, I believe, for the Aboriginal arts in general, and a couple of others for the Aboriginal theatre community. Those meetings served mostly to put faces to names and to encourage those working in isolation— which on a certain level is each and every one of us—that we are not alone. The energy of those meetings took me back to the early days at Native Earth. The little-theatre-that-could turned into a focus of hope for so much of the First Nations artistic energy in the country. It got noticed, coming to the fore just as Oka erupted.

But most artistic production and publication and teaching and learning happen in the local community. An organization like the Association for Native Development in the Performing and Visual Arts was most effective when its small projects took on lives of their own; that is where the Centre for Indigenous Theatre came from. And the Six Nations Writers Group in my home community, for another instance, clearly see the opportunity that organizing, training, and publication offer. Didn't APTN evolve out of a local project?

This is feeling like too many answers.

I hope the Lone Ranger doesn't have to die. A grown man who spent all those years acting out a dream of male friendship for the entertainment of little boys deserves the chance to grow up and have some sort of adult relationship, don't you think?

TG: I realize you are joking about the Lone Ranger, but it is interesting you ended that message with a hope for an 'adult relationship'. Do you think Native writing has now reached an adulthood it didn't have fifteen years ago?

DDM: Adulthood? I would suggest that like all goals worth one's while, maturity is a process, and that if we approach it as a destination—the 'journey of discovery' metaphor rearing its head again!—we are in for frustration because, like the proverbial mirage, it recedes as we approach. What if we mix the two metaphors—'human life' and 'journey of discovery'—into one: the 'life path and/or life journey'? Then I think we can assert that a lot of us who make up the body literate of First Nations societies are on the right path(s), are finding the ways our individual human voices can tell the old stories again as we see and hear and re-imagine and know them, the ways that include a braiding together of what forms and content we've retained of our traditions and of what we find of use (ever practical, us!) in the culture of the globalizers.

The pitch of the voice of a new or young adult, after the voice breaks or shifts timbre, can have a beauty even those globalizer-types find of value, even if they can only talk about it with metaphors of precious metals and gems. I'm thinking now of my visit last month to St Petersburg, Russia, where I saw both the treasures in the Winter Palace (a horse blanket sparkling with thousands of diamonds!) and talked to students of the Canada College of the State University, kids who are even newer to capitalism than we are but so full of energy and curiosity! But the value of material things, I remind myself, is also a metaphor.

The voice that tells a story gives actuality to the metaphysical. Or at least that is the adult-ish idea. We're getting there. Mother Earth out of the mouths of babes?

Preface to the First Edition: Two Voices

We were concerned as we discussed an appropriate introduction for this book not to conceal the differences between our perspectives as a Native writer and a white academic. The process of selecting an anthology is like a long discussion and, in keeping with a body of work so rooted in the oral tradition, we decided a dialogue would be the best format. What follows is a transcription of one such conversation, edited to improve its focus.

TERRY GOLDIE: A good place to start might be why we wanted to do this project.

DANIEL DAVID MOSES: I guess I thought that Oxford as a world-sized company would be a useful place to do one of these anthologies. There's a lot of writing going on inside the country that just doesn't get heard about outside the country.

TG: Did you feel a sense of collective responsibility to do something for the Native writing community in general?

DDM: That's one way of putting it. But also I think the ideas presented by Native people are particularly important. I think Native people have a sense of a larger responsibility to the planet, whether we come at it just from the idea that Native traditions honour the environment as a mother, or whether we come at it from the idea that we're looked at as people who should have those ideas and therefore we're allowed to have them.

TG: I guess my reason to do the project was that in my own book *Fear and Temptation* I looked only at representations of Native peoples in white literature. I had not in any sense responded to what Native people were saying. But I didn't want to write about Native writing because that would have been just one more white version of Native culture. I thought that to create an anthology would not give my comments about a Native voice but rather do a little bit to get the Native voice heard. However, there are still problems. One that both you and I have had is just selection, what goes in and what doesn't and how to decide. But I think you are a bit more comfortable with that than I am. Is that true?

DDM: Well, I try to be practical about getting the job done. I think if we'd had more time we probably could have dealt with your discomfort, but we had just a little over a year.

TG: An even more important element of timing is that the material we both seem most interested in has been published since 1985. Rightly or wrongly, we are capturing things at a point when there is more than enough material to justify the project but at a point where no one has sifted through that material. I don't think that we are in any sense really responding to a canon, including the authors and the stories and the poems that people expect to be in, because I don't know that anybody's made that decision yet. No community, whether it's the Native writers themselves or Native communities or the literary community, or whatever, has made the decision about what should go in.

DDM: Yes, the decisions on what should go in something that you might call the canon can be easily disguised as aesthetic decisions, but if we are making a canon the decisions are definitely political, especially with a literature that is emerging even as we speak. What we've collected might seem to come from all areas along a scale of 'good writing'. But the actual impact of the stories also has to be part of the decision making. We are in history and this writing is very involved in that history. It seems foolish to try to take it out of life and put it in a separate canon. Why worry about the immortals?

TG: I certainly want people to respect this anthology and find it interesting, but I would feel personally a bit of a failure if people thought that it therefore establishes what is the best in Native writing, or even establishes what is the best in Native writing in 1992. I would like the book to get the material out, get people to read it. If aesthetic evaluation has to be done—and I'm not sure it has to be done—it can wait for a long time yet.

You have a good point too, about the stories themselves. I don't think we've tried to be perfectly culturally representative, but I think that the value of selections at this historical point has been a major concern. *Princess Pocahontas and the Blue Spots* is very much of this time and that gives it unusual power. The anthology is by no means just for a white audience, but a part of our purpose is to provide a space in which Native writers can present to outsiders their view of this time.

DDM: I'm always getting phone calls from people who want me to come and tell Native legends. I know Native legends but I really have a feeling that it's not my right to go traipsing around, telling other people's stories. This image of traditional Native storytelling places Native people in the museum with all the other extinct species. We're living now, in this world, and like everyone else we have to deal with mass media, everything from video to paperback books. Of course our ways of expressing ourselves are no longer only oral storytelling. We have seen other media and some of us know them intimately enough to use them to express whatever we need to express. Some Native people make brilliant speeches for the media and some people write poems and some do those things that over the last twenty-five years or so we've come to call performance. And the example of traditional Native storytelling, its orality or whatever you would call it, has been for me a freeing thing. The pieces I write look like plays or poems or short stories, but I'm interested in how they sound and how they work when they're spoken.

TG: Do you think that there is more interest in formal innovation by Native writers than by others?

DDM: I'm not really sure I can judge that. From my perspective, the Native tradition allows you the freedom to do things that people respond to. You are dealing with your own life, with your own stuff intimately, and looking to formal innovation not as an end in itself, but as part of the story. Mainstream writers are constantly told to be original, but if you spend your time trying to be original you end up just doing the same sort of thing all the time.

TG: I think one reason why Native literature is so interesting is that while it is based on very old traditions, as a literature it is quite young. As are the authors. A high percentage of the writers that we've included are under fifty, many under forty. That contributes to the feeling of innovation and yet always with a sense of tradition.

Yet I don't think we have included any authors who are in any sense iconoclasts of their own culture, although they might be iconoclasts of the mainstream culture. For example, the Métis have been told they didn't have a culture, neither a traditional nor a new culture. Instead writers like Maria Campbell and Duke Redbird have found that culture and reasserted it—unlike innovative and mainstream writers, who often seem to be tearing things down.

We've been referring to 'mainstream writers'. Do you think of Native writing as a separate stream? Is it something that could not or should not be subsumed by the mainstream? For instance, it's been argued that if Margaret Atwood is placed on a shelf of Canadian books, she is ghettoized and is not given the proper stature that she deserves as a world author.

DDM: My image of that mainstream is that it is pretty wide but it's spiritually shallow. I don't think we are worried about being 'subsumed'. If we become part of that mainstream we're going to be the deep currents.

TG: You were referring before to limited white views of what Native literature is. I have trouble with anyone who says that any category of human, whether it's Germans or short people, writes in a certain way. Yet I agree with you that the majority of Native writing has something that can be called spiritual. That is quite constant even though it appears in many forms. Do you find that?

DDM: Oh, yes. I think that that is one of the reasons our theatre has become so strong, because everyone needs a spiritual life, I mean spiritual just in the sense of knowing the meaning of your life, what you are doing and why you are doing it. The mainstream god got killed a while back and a lot of people are desperately holding on to the corpse. Meanwhile Native peoples' traditions, the meanings of their life, are intimately connected to the actual physical world they live in, so they don't have to hold on desperately to their sense of who they are. Unless, of course, they come to the city and believe what's going on here, but then they are just partaking of the mainstream dilemma.

TG: Your own play *Big Buck City* shows that urban mainstreaming, but the presence of a trickster figure on stage maintains certain Native values. The trickster seems to be a concern for contemporary Native writers from a variety of cultures. Is it because of the many spiritual dimensions it suggests, or is it also theatrical? I guess theatrical, because the trickster extends both verbal and visual possibilities.

DDM: The trickster is the embodiment of our sense of humour about the way we live our lives. It's a very central part of our attitude that things are funny even though horrible things happen.

TG: Like the irony of that old joke that when the missionaries came they had the bibles and the Native peoples the land, and now the Native peoples have the bibles and the white people have the land. It's an ironic take on a horrible situation. But I think the humour you are talking about is something much more wide-ranging.

DDM: It's also a response to existential problems, of being conscious and aware of the limits of our life. It's really a balanced philosophy.

TG: It is interesting how many extraordinarily different writers use trickster figures. Beth Brant and Tom King, who in most ways have an extremely different take on the world, both use coyote. It seems to explain things in a non-reductive way for both of them, and for you and for many other writers.

DDM: Well, it is an archetypical figure in the human imagination. Mainstream society doesn't like it, but it does pop up in mainstream culture here and there, either denigrated or turned into a nightmare, just because it seems so irrational.

TG: Yes, but mainstream ancient Greek culture had tricksters, mainstream ancient Roman culture had tricksters, mainstream European culture in the middle ages had tons of tricksters. It seems to be the Christian church in the post-Renaissance age that really tried to defeat the trickster. There are some trickster saints in the Roman Catholic traditions, but nobody ever talks about them. It's as though modern Europe wanted to get rid of anything that couldn't be reduced to good and bad. You're never sure what the trickster is going to do next, whether what he's going to do might be perceived by the audience or the characters involved as good or bad. As you've said, Dan, Native culture isn't concerned with good or bad, it's concerned with harmony. Yet the trickster is part of that spirituality that white people are always turning to Native cultures for. A Native leader from the West Coast once said that he didn't see why white people were so obsessed with staring at other people's navels. There is a sense that white appropriation of Native voice is trying almost to swallow Native culture and have it inside. I'm thinking of even the best and most sophisticated white writing on Native people. Rudy Wiebe's 'Where is the Voice Coming From?', a beautiful, wonderfully sensitive story, demonstrates the desire of the white culture to somehow package Native culture so that it can be swallowed and the voice can be found.

DDM: There's a big emptiness there that has to be filled.

TG: It's a sad thing to say but I think it's true.

DDM: It can't be filled by eating. People are fooling themselves if they think that just by taking someone else's stuff they are going to be happy. They have to find their own. The whole structure of mainstream society prevents that from happening. Someone will come up to me at a conference and ask me how to get in touch with the earth, when two feet away from us there's a flower bed. All you've got to do is look and see the life that's going on in that flower bed. There are things growing, there are things crawling, there are things breathing, the sun's on them, the air's through them, there's a whole complex system of physics and pleasure going on there. It's not really that hard to get into if you just remember that when mainstream society talks about human beings and nature, it's a false dichotomy: we're part of nature.

TG: It seems to take a major shift in perspective. In Newfoundland there's still a tradition of the fairies. If you find yourself in a place you've often been and suddenly you have a sense that the whole is transformed and you are looking at it totally differently, then you say that you've been taken by the fairies. Even though your physical self does not move, somehow the whole world is transformed. I think that's what a lot of these white writers are looking for. As you say, they don't need the fairies, they don't need to take Native culture, if they would just try to seek the transformation in a direct way. Many white writers who use Native stories, Native legends, and Native voices justify it by saying they have this extraordinary empathy for Native culture. The simple answer seems to be that if you have that empathy why not let it live on its own? Why not let it be?

DDM: I have a lot of friends, white writers, who don't feel the need to hijack my stuff because they are not afraid of their own experience, when they have those experiences that are non-linear, non-rational, that are mystical experiences. That's the part of the mind where their work as creative writers is being done. You hook into the way the mind makes sense other than logic. But our culture is so obsessed with everything making sense, being straightforward, being hooked into time lines and bottom lines.

TG: I think there is a global problem with the 'fourth world'. That is George Manuel's term, the fourth world being indigenous peoples' cultures that are controlled by the non-indigenous, like Canada or New Zealand or Australia. The non-indigenous often speak as though they own the Native people, although they don't put it this way. As a Canadian I might refer to 'our Native people'; regardless of my intention, the patronizing assumption is there. The non-indigenous assume that the true fourth world is only that which was there when their ancestors arrived. The fourth world is not allowed to develop: witness your observation that people expect you to tell traditional stories.

Although we might not be totally positive about Native people who become totally urbanized, yet they are in the contemporary world and adapting to the world in accord with their own views of necessity. The opposition to that is the society depicted in the first part of Anne Cameron's *Daughters of Copper Woman*. She presents an earlier Native culture that is pure and matriarchal and full of all of the things that Anne Cameron believes to be good. And then it's packaged in that book for transmission to a generally non-indigenous feminist audience who feel alienated from masculinist culture. They want a pure feminist past so they create a pure feminist fourth world.

DDM: If the mainstream culture seeks to maintain the Native past, does this mean mainstream culture needs to maintain its own guilt?

TG: Oh, yes. There's no question about that. There is a desire to package that guilt. It seems to me that guilt is a stronger, clearer thing in Newfoundland than it is in many other of the Canadian white cultures simply because of the genocide, the absolute extermination of the Beothuks. The Beothuks can be packaged as a pure prehistorical entity. They can be maintained as a source of guilt but without dealing with the present.

Newfoundlanders don't have to deal with any of the social problems that might be related to contemporary white treatment of Native people. This seems at least part of the reason why Newfoundlanders are so averse to accepting the contemporary Mi'kmaq population of the southern coast as indigenous. Because they still exist, they cannot be a source of pure past guilt.

DDM: So what's the use of guilt?

TG: For the most part probably nothing, but might white guilt have potential to do some good for land rights?

DDM: Maybe something else. One of the words that always comes up in Native gatherings, and particularly among Native artists, is that it is part of our jobs as Native artists to help people heal. Whether we're talking about Native people taught by residential schools or whether we're talking about white people who've just been in a car accident, that's what we see as our job: we're looking for the meaning of life to explain the injustices of reality. To me it sounds as if this guilt is the opposite thing: it seems that you don't want to heal, you want to keep the wound. In romanticism you're dancing around a wound. You have these great desires, these great idealistic possibilities, and then they're cut down and things end in death and it's very sad and beautiful. I've seen the attraction of it, because I've grown up partially in the mainstream culture, but it strikes me as really sick. I think maybe the reason for keeping the wound open is that alienation from yourself that the mainstream mindset creates. Up in your head you're separate from your animal self. Even if you're creating art that isn't healing, at least you can feel something.

TG: As an outsider I hesitate to say this, but I think white society has caused Native people so much pain that they feel forced to look for healing. Women who have been abused as children have gone through similar stages. Through this and other examples of pain that white people have themselves felt, they have gained more and more respect for and interest in Native powers. I suspect that many are reading this anthology in search of that healing. But some Native writers seem to emphasize white guilt. I don't know if that's an accurate assumption on my part or not. Take Lenore Keeshig-Tobias's piece that confronts the Canadian response to the Oka situation. I totally agree with what she has to say, but it does seem to assert white guilt. Is that an inaccurate reading on my part?

DDM: No, I think that's true of her response to that specific situation.

TG: Don't white people have a reasonable amount to be guilty about? Still, guilt in itself doesn't get you anywhere.

DDM: Well, feeling guilty is a fuzzy state of mind. You're aware of the problem but not really focusing on it. I think Lenore was trying to get people to focus. Maybe to feel ashamed, which is an active, public way of feeling guilty. One of the differences between Native culture and the mainstream one is the use by Native culture of shame as a social control. If you're ashamed of your behaviour you might face up to it. To conquer your demons you have to face them.

TG: A lot of anthologies are seen as competitions—who gets in and who doesn't get in. But I think that in most Native cultures there is a tradition of consensus and of allowing the voices to be heard. So for this anthology, instead of having to include twenty poems by William Wordsworth and ten by T.S. Eliot because they are the big ones that won the competition, we've included many texts of value in their own contexts. That is one of the prime reasons to include so much orature. And even to use the term 'orature', which unlike 'oral literature' or 'oral poetry' does not denote the oral as inferior to the formally written. The constitution of the Six Nations Confederation is an oral document that is really prose history, but it is also an important text of orature, representing in itself that kind of consensus process in a traditional culture. I don't think that the historical material in the anthology is representative of the variety of Native cultures, but it gives a sense of some of the bases of contemporary Native culture, such as the spirituality, the collectivity, and the oral.

DDM: It's a strange technology we're dealing with, this writing our words down on paper and alienating the best parts of ourselves into books. I mean, we started out using that technology as a storage medium, and instead we've become oppressed by it.

TG: How is it oppressive, do you think?

DDM: Well, I think that's one of the actual physical ways that the alienation, the separation between the person and their thought, happens.

TG: Do you mean that somebody owning your book of poetry and reading it separately from yourself is alienating to both of you? Do you think that attitude would be more common among Native writers?

DDM: A lot of Native people have been working with words without publishing. It's not this horrible painful need that so many white writers have when they spend a couple of years working on something and can't get it published. If the material is working orally within the community, that's enough.

TG: Many Native politicians have been recognized as orators. But fifteen years ago there were few Native writers recognized as such. The dominant sense that I had of contemporary Native verbal culture was through political speeches, and through political documents such as Harold Cardinal's that connect directly to those speeches. It's something that I've always found a bit surprising, but I'm beginning to see good reasons for that. Mudrooroo Narogin talks about the difficulty in that the white population of Australia assumes that Aboriginal writers are writing for them. As he said, it's strange enough to write for a culture that is not your own but it's even stranger to write for it when it is the culture of those who have conquered you. But from what you're saying about the oral form and about the writer's role in the community, the Native people in Canada have been creating their verbal performance very much for their own community.

DDM: I did one piece based on an Oneida story and afterwards this poet asked, 'Now does that represent us white guys?' I said, 'This is precontact, it has nothing to do with you.' It was as if he really wanted an in to the story, but there are times when you just have to sit back and watch.

TG: As a Native person would you have more right to write a story using an Inuit voice, for example?

DDM: I would have to find some reason to do it. It would have to be something that was very important to me, but I really doubt that I would try it. I don't know the culture intimately enough to do it properly and I'd rather not fall on my face unless I have to.

TG: The primary culture that Tom King is using, for example, in *Medicine River* is not his own culture. It's a culture that he presumably knows mainly as an academic and as a teacher of Native students from Alberta. I think the justification is Wayne Keon's suggestion of pan-Native similarity. Perhaps one example is that spirituality you were mentioning.

DDM: Well, I go into Native groups all over the country and I always feel comfortable with them. I feel that I can go to any Native events. Whereas I've lived in Toronto for many years and there are places here I feel strange.

TG: I think that all our selections are written with some Native context. Some writers, like Lee Maracle, are not departing from a Native voice but ranging out in their subject matter. She is looking at a variety of cultural interactions. I suppose that relates in some way to what you were saying about overcoming limitations in genre. It's the opposite of something like W.P. Kinsella's Silas Ermineskin stories, which are highly limited by genre. Kinsella creates humour by showing Silas's failure to understand the majority culture, and the almost unconscious wisdom with which Silas perceives the inadequacies of the majority culture. That pattern is a part of comic storytelling throughout the world. It's really a more highly developed version of an ethnic joke. I suppose Kinsella has been a focus for discussion of the appropriation of voice because the ethnic joke always presents such a false view of ethnicity.

DDM: The few of Kinsella's stories I've read really did seem like a bad ventriloquist's act. I hope he keeps working on the baseball stuff.

TG: When we originally started working on this anthology it was suggested to us that we include some white writing on Native people, and we both agreed that we didn't want to do that. But what about the very sensitive responses to Native culture that you get in something like *The Temptations of Big Bear*? Many years ago at a Native Studies conference I found the response of Native undergraduate students to that book was phenomenal. They really believed it to be an empowering book for them.

DDM: I would have to assume that the aesthetics that are being used also relate to the traditions of healing. I mean that's why it would empower. I can't argue with healing.

TG: It becomes a two-part question. On the one hand, Native cultures have certain values and certain powers that can to a certain extent be acquired by a sensitive and creative representation of those cultures, as in the case of *Big Bear*. But could they be acquired to the degree that they can be presented from the Native culture itself? Also, all of the stories and poems and plays in this anthology are owned, whether one sees them as owned by the writer or owned by the culture. They are things of value. Kinsella is a different sort of problem, but the sensitive reworking of legends, like Cameron's *Daughters of Copper Woman*, is still something being taken from the culture.

DDM: Most of the pieces in this anthology are original pieces so we don't need to question ownership in that case. But in Native traditions of storytelling, if you make the story it belongs to you. Stories can also be given away or traded for. I think the concern with appropriation has more to do with the fact that most people aren't sensitive listeners, so they are not sensitive transmitters of stories, partly because the cultures have different values. When someone from another culture hears a story I tell, they perceive only the things that relate to their values. If they try to retell my story they are going to emphasize those things that are important to them. That only makes sense. So all we're saying is don't retell our stories, change them, and pretend they are what we're about, because they are not.

TG: One of the things that's often missed in this discussion is that in most cases a writer is first a reader, or at least a hearer or viewer. Then that reader becomes the writer. I think a lot of writers fail to see their political responsibility. The African National Congress called South African writers and visual artists 'cultural workers'. They had a duty to respond to the political values of that culture. The individual writers are not free to respond in any way to anything. The individual writer must be responsible to his or her own culture and to the other cultures that impinge on that. Still, I get the impression that you aren't very comfortable with politically labelled approaches to literature.

DDM: I am uncomfortable with any jargon that will separate the strands of my story into their different categories. We can talk psychology, we can talk economics, but my job is to integrate those concerns. I don't find it useful for what I do to talk about the political ramifications of one character's behaviour, although they are certainly part of what I'm doing.

TG: But wouldn't you say that there is more overt politics in this anthology than you would find in a lot of others?

DDM: Oh, yes. But that's other people's tastes, other people's experience. Some of the people in this anthology have actually made political jargon seem like real language to me again.

TG: That sounds good. One of the reasons for my getting involved in this was certainly the political agenda. The choices have been made by both of us, although I chose a lot of the early material and you most of the contemporary. But when I first heard it I immediately thought we had to have Lenore Keeshig-Tobias's piece on Oka. First, simply for its political value. The other thing is, as you say, its language. Its rhetorical flourishes gain power from its substance, but the substance is not everything. The same thing is true of autobiographical material. The substance is important, but so is the form.

DDM: I think our cultures probably allow us to be more autobiographical than the mainstream. In the mainstream markets, editors want to know what one alienated individual thinks. Our culture is suspicious of that. We want to know where the opinion is coming from. Who are his or her people?

TG: Is that from a belief in experience, a belief that you have knowledge because of your experience and therefore your knowledge should be related to your experience?

DDM: I think it comes from the attitude that everyone is an individual spirit with something unique to say that is important in the life of the entire community. And most Native writers are, as I said before, speaking first to their own community.

TG: Still, there is a tradition of minority cultures in a variety of contexts writing to explain themselves to the rest of the world. Chinua Achebe in Nigeria writes in a way that explains a lot of ethnography. He claims that his target audience is pan-African, yet much seems to be shaped for European consumption. But Native writers are writing first for their own. That is one reason some people reject certain Native texts. When people said Tomson Highway's *Dry Lips Oughta Move to Kapuskasing* was misogynist, it seemed to be because they weren't trained by the culture to understand it. Perhaps that's the answer; rather than appropriating the voice, educate yourselves so you are ready to read, ready to watch. That's what the white audience should be doing.

DDM: I can tell my story as well as I can, but I can't do the audience's job for them. In that case it's not going to be art, it's going to be education in its more uncomfortable forms. Certainly, art does educate but in a way that is so much fun nobody minds.

The variety that results, the different ways this English language is being nuanced and danced about on these pages, is fascinating. I've come across things that I didn't think were possible with this language. It's really encouraging.

TG: Did you ever have any questions about whether we should do something like this for Oxford University Press, a symbol of empire?

DDM: Well, it's only a symbol. No, I mean I feel sorry for those guys now. It'll probably help them a bit, you know.

Toronto
June, 1991

The sources for the various selections are listed on the acknowledgements page but we would like to acknowledge specifically the anthologists whose work has been most helpful to us: Penny Petrone, Thomas King, John Robert Colombo, and Robin McGrath. Various libraries were used, but we would like to mention especially the Metropolitan Toronto Reference Library; the Scott Library, York University; and the Newfoundland Studies Centre, Memorial University of Newfoundland. Last but first, the founder of this project, our former editor, Richard Teleky, and the person who did far more than her share of work, our present editor, Phyllis Wilson.

Traditional Orature

SOUTHERN FIRST NATIONS

While the majority of pieces collected here are writings by Native authors, the cultural roots of this literature are in traditional orature. The term 'orature' is chosen as a parallel to the term 'literature'. 'Orature' indicates that body of knowledge usually referred to as 'oral literature'. The latter term is problematic, including as it does the words 'literature', with its implications of reading and books, and 'oral', with implications of the spoken and heard. 'Oral literature' seems a debased version of a true written literature. The term 'orature' allows this body of knowledge its own validity.

It is tempting to emphasize authenticity in a consideration of traditional material, but this is generally counterproductive. If 'authentic' implies without change through white contact, there is no such account of traditional cultures from southern Canada. The first considered white accounts of Native cultures long postdate the first contact.

We have used early versions of poems and songs as they were recorded, usually by amateur folklorists, to suggest the cultural and aesthetic roots of this collection. All the examples here come from John Robert Colombo's *Songs of the Indians*, which provides interesting notes and comments about the material, both general and specific. The verse forms and word usage more likely reflect English literary values than Native ones, but their provenance gives them clear historical positions. They are also of interest as demonstrations of various cultural tensions. As an example, here are some comments made by the famous American folklorist and collector Charles G. Leland, in *The Algonquin Legends of New England*, on a piece provided by Mrs W. Wallace Brown of Calais, Maine:

The old woman ended this story by saying abruptly, 'Don't know any more. Guess they all eat up by *mooin*' (the bear). She said it was only a fragment. 'If you could

have heard her repeat this', adds Mrs Brown, 'in pieces, stopping to explain what the characters said, and describing how they looked, and anon singing it again, you would have got the *inner sense* of a wonderfully weird tale. The woman's feet-covering and the man's dress *like* a rainbow, yet not one, which made their bodies invisible, seemed to exercise her imagination strangely; and these were to her the most important part of the story.' The fragment is part of a very old myth; I regret to say a very obscure one. The poem, 'declared to be very ancient', is given here as 'Fragment of a Passamaquoddy song'.

The section given here from 'Traditional History of the Confederacy of Six Nations' is a different example of the problem of authenticity. As Colombo notes, 'This official version of the oral tradition was prepared by a Committee of the Chiefs at the Six Nations Reserve, Grand River, at the turn of the century.' Like the material presented by traditional storytellers today, it has the authenticity of all oral material that is reaffirmed through its transmission within a cultural tradition.

While authenticity might be impossible, contemporary scholarship continues to work to find ways to improve the representation of orature. In the present volume, we draw your attention to the selections from Ghandl and Harry Robinson. For a more general view, see the anthonolgy *Voices from Four Directions: Contemporary Translations of the Native Literatures of North America* (2004), edited by Brian Swann. Robert Bringhurst's collection of translations, *A Story Sharp as a Knife: The Classic Haida Mythtellers and Their World* (1999), is an excellent introduction to orature in general, and the bibliography offers many possibilities for research.

Song for Medicine Hunting

Now I hear it, my friends, of the Metai, who are sitting about me.
Who makes this river flow? The Spirit, he makes this river flow.
Look at me well, my friends; examine me, and let me understand that we are
    all compassion.
Who maketh to walk about the social people? A birth maketh to walk about
    the social people.
I fly about, and if anywhere I see an animal, I can shoot him.   5
I shoot your heart; I hit your heart, oh animal, your heart, I hit your heart.
I make myself look like fire.
I am able to call water from above, from beneath, and from around.
I cause to look like the dead, a man I did.
I cause to look like the dead, a woman I did.   10
I cause to look like the dead, a child I did.
I am such, I am such, my friends; any animal, any animal, my friends,
    I hit him right, my friends.

Traditional History of the Confederacy

Constitution

Then Dekanahwideh said, Now I and you Lords of the Confederate Nations shall plant a Great Tall and Mighty Tree of the Great Long Leaves.

Now this Tree which we have planted shall shoot forth four great long white roots. These Great Long White Roots shall shoot forth one to the North and one to the South and one to the East and one to the West, and we shall place on the top of it an Eagle which has a great power of long vision, and we shall transact all our business under the shade of the Great Tree. The meaning of planting this Great Tree is the Great Peace, and Good Tidings of Peace and Power, and the Nations of the earth shall see it and shall accept and follow the Root and shall arrive here at this Tree and when they arrive here you shall receive them and shall seat them in the midst of your Confederacy, and the meaning of placing an Eagle on the top of the Great Tall Tree is to watch the Roots which extend to the North and to the South and to the East and to the West, and the Eagle will discover if any evil is approaching your Confederacy, and will scream and give the alarm and all the Nations of the Confederacy at once shall hear the alarm and come to the front.

Then Dekanahwideh said again, We shall now combine our Power into one Great Power which is this Confederacy, and we shall now therefore symbolize the union of these powers by each Nation contributing one arrow each which we shall tie up together in a bundle, which when it is made and completely tied together no-one can bend or break it.

Then Dekanahwideh further said, We have now completed this union in securing one arrow from each Nation, it is not good that one should be lacking or taken from the bundle, for it would weaken our power and it would be still worse if two arrows were taken from the bundle. And if three arrows were taken, then any one could break the remaining arrows in the bundle.

Then Dekanahwideh continued his address and said, We shall now therefore tie this bundle of arrows together with deer's sinew which is strong, durable and lasting and then this Institution will be strong and unchangeable. This bundle of arrows signifies that all Lords and all the Warriors and all the Women of the Confederacy have become united as one person.

Then Dekanahwideh said, We have now completed our power so that we, the Five Nations Confederacy, shall in the future only have one body, one head and one heart.

Then he further said, If any evil should befall us in the future we shall stand or fall unitedly as one man.

Condolence Ceremony

Now hear us our Uncles, we have come to condole with you in your great bereavement.

We have now met in dark sorrow to lament together over the death of our brother Lord. For such has been your loss. We will sit together in our grief and mingle our tears together, and we four brothers will wipe off the tears from your eyes, so that for a day period you might have peace of mind. This we say and do, we four brothers.

Now hear us again, for when a person is in great grief caused by death, his ears are closed up and he cannot hear, and such is your condition now.

We will therefore remove the obstruction from your ears, so that for a day period you may have perfect hearing again. This we say and do, we four brothers.

Continue to bear the expression of us four brothers, for when a person is in great sorrow his throat is stopped with grief and such is your case now. We will therefore remove the obstruction so that for a day period you may enjoy perfect breathing and speech. This we say and do, we four brothers.

The foregoing part of the Condolence Ceremony is to be performed outside of the place of meeting.

HAIL

I come to greet and thank my uncles,
I come again to greet and thank the League;
I come again to greet and thank the Kindred;
I come again to greet and thank the Warriors;
I come again to greet and thank the Women;   5
My forefathers—what they established—
My forefathers—hearken to them.

At the Wood's Edge

Oh, my grandsires! Even now that has become old which you established—the Great League. You have it as a pillow under your heads in the ground where you are lying—this Great League which you established; although you said that far away in the future the Great League would endure.

*　　*　　*

Now listen, ye who established the Great League of Peace. Now it has become old. Now there is nothing but wilderness. Ye are in your graves who established it. Yet have taken it with you and have placed it under you, and there is nothing left but a desert. There ye have taken your intellects with joy. What ye established ye have taken with you. Ye have placed under your heads what ye established—the Great League.

Song for the Burning of the White Dog

Great Master, behold here are all of our people who hold the old faith, and who intend to abide by it.

By means of this dog being burned we hope to please Thee, and that just as we have decked it with ribbons and wampum, Thou wilt grant favours to us Thy own people.

I now place the dog on the fire that its spirit may find its way to Thee who made it, and made everything, and thus we hope to get blessings from Thee in return.

He throws the dog on the fire and proceeds:

Although, Great Master, there are not so many of us who worship Thee in this way as there were in old times, those who are here are as faithful as ever—now, therefore, listen to us—Thou who art far away above us, and who made every living thing.

We ask that the sun will continue to shine on us and make all things grow.

We ask that the moon may always give us light by night.

We ask that the clouds may never cease to give us rain or snow.

We ask that the winds from the east and west and north and south may always blow.

We ask that the trees and everything that springs from the ground may grow.

We ask that these blessings may help us through life, and that we may remain true to our belief in Thee, and we will make Thee another offering like this next year.

Save us from all harm until that time, and make us obedient to our chiefs and others who have power.

Guide them so that they may act wisely for the people and save them from all harm.

Be good, Great Master, to the warriors and to the young men, making them strong and healthy so that they may always be able to do everything they ought to do.

Great Master, we ask also that Thou wouldst be kind to the women until our next feast. Make them strong and healthy so that they may always be able to do everything they ought to do.

Take away all our sickness and all our troubles. Make us happy and healthy and strong to enjoy life.

Great Master, make us all peaceable and kindly that we may live happily and contentedly as we should do.

Cause the plants that cure us when we are ill to grow up strong for our use so that they do what Thou madest them to do.

And, Great Master, may the coming season bring us plenty of sunshine and breezes, and may everything grow well for our use during the summer time.

May all the trees that bear fruit, and may everything that comes out of the ground as our food grow in the best way for us to enjoy.

Great Master, we ask, too, that Thou wouldst send us all sorts of animals, large and small, for food and clothing, and cause the birds to live and increase in number.

May the scent of the tobacco I have thrown on the fire rise till it reaches Thee to let Thee know that we are still good—that we do not forget Thee, and that Thou mayest give us all we have asked.

Traditional Songs

INUIT

Much of the note on traditional orature from the Southern First Nations can be applied here, with the exception that the records are much later. These songs are again taken from a collection by John Robert Colombo, *Poems of the Inuit* (1981). Colombo's primary source was Knud Rasmussen, but all of his sources were from the twentieth century. One might assume that the combination of the greater isolation of the Inuit with developments in scientific ethnography should make for greater accuracy. But by the same token, the Inuit's absence from the white culture that had had centuries to influence other First Nations by the time of the collecting of their traditional material made the Inuit that much more difficult for white explorers to begin to understand. Thus, it once again would be best to assume that accuracy is not to be found, and to see these as samples of a recording process that comments on both cultures involved.

My Breath/Orpingalik

I will sing a song,
A song that is strong.
    Unaya—unaya.
Sick I have lain since autumn,
Helpless I lay, as were I
My own child.

5

Sad, I would that my woman
Were away to another house
To a husband
Who can be her refuge,   10
Safe and secure as winter ice.
    Unaya—unaya.

Sad, I would that my woman
Were gone to a better protector
Now that I lack strength   15
To rise from my couch.
    Unaya—unaya.

Dost thou know thyself?
So little thou knowest of thyself.
Feeble I lie here on my bench   20
And only my memories are strong!
    Unaya—unaya.

Beasts of the hunt! Big game!
Oft the fleeting quarry I chased!
Let me live it again and remember,   25
Forgetting my weakness.
    Unaya—unaya.

Let me recall the great white
Polar bear,
High up its black body,   30
Snout in the snow, it came!
He really believed
He alone was a male
And ran toward me.
    Unaya—unaya.   35

It threw me down
Again and again,
Then breathless departed
And lay down to rest,
Hid by a mound on a floe.   40
Heedless it was, and unknowing
That I was to be its fate.
Deluding itself
That he alone was a male,
And unthinking   45

That I too was a man!
    Unaya—unaya.

I shall ne'er forget that great blubber-beast,
A fjord seal,
I killed from the sea ice   50
Early, long before dawn,
While my companions at home
Still lay like the dead,
Faint from failure and hunger,
Sleeping.   55
With meat and with swelling blubber
I returned so quickly
As if merely running over ice
To view a breathing hole there.
And yet it was   60
An old and cunning male seal.
But before he had even breathed
My harpoon head was fast
Mortally deep in his neck.

That was the manner of me then.   65
Now I lie feeble on my bench
Unable even a little blubber to get
For my wife's stone lamp.
The time, the time will not pass,
While dawn gives place to dawn   70
And spring is upon the village.
    Unaya—unaya.

But how long shall I lie here?
How long?
And how long must she go a-begging   75
For fat for her lamp,
For skins for clothing
And meat for a meal?
A helpless thing—a defenceless woman.
    Unaya—unaya.   80

Knowest thou thyself?
So little thou knowest of thyself!
While dawn gives place to dawn,
And spring is upon the village.
    Unaya—unaya.   85

Magic Words/Aua

To Lighten Heavy Loads

> I speak with the mouth of Qeqertuanaq, and say:
> I will walk with leg muscles strong as the sinews on the shin of a little caribou calf.
> I will walk with leg muscles strong as the sinews on the shin of a little hare.
> I will take care not to walk toward the dark.
> I will walk toward the day.

To Cure Sickness among Neighbours

> I arise from my couch with the grey gull's morning song.
> I arise from my couch with the grey gull's morning song.
> I will take care not to look toward the dark,
> I will turn my glance toward the day.

To Cure a Sick Child

> Little Child! Your mother's breasts are full of milk.
> Go to her and suck, go to her and drink. Go up into the mountain.
From the mountain's top shalt thou find health; from the mountain's top shalt thou win life.

To Stop Bleeding

> This is blood from the little sparrow's mother.
> Dry it up! This is blood that flowed from a piece of wood. Dry it up!

From Calling Game to the Hunter

> Beast of the sea! Come and place yourself before me in the dear early morning!
> Beast of the plain! Come and place yourself before me in the dear early morning!

Magic Words/Nakasuk

To Heal Wounds

You, like a ringed plover,
You, like a wild duck,
The skin's surface here,
Full of wounds,
Full of cuts,   5
Go and patch it!

Song of the Girl Who Was
Turning into Stone/Ivaluardjuk

Men in kayaks,
come hither to me
and be my husbands;
this stone here
has clung fast to me,   5
and lo, my feet
are now turning to stone.

Men in kayaks,
come hither to me
and be my husbands;   10
this stone here
has clung fast to me,
and lo, my legs
are now turning to stone.

Men in kayaks,   15
come hither to me
and be my husbands;
this stone here
has clung fast to me,
and lo, now my thighs   20
are turning to stone.

Men in kayaks,
come hither to me
and be my husbands;

this stone here   25
has clung fast to me,
and lo, from the waist down,
I am turning to stone.

Men in kayaks,
come hither to me   30
and be my husbands;
this stone here
has clung fast to me,
and lo, my entrails
are turning to stone.   35

Men in kayaks,
come hither to me
and be my husbands;
this stone here
has clung fast to me,   40
and lo, my lungs
are now turning to stone.

Dead Man's Song/Netsit

Dreamed by One Who is Alive

I am filled with joy
When the day peacefully dawns
Up over the heavens,
    ayi, yai ya.

I am filled with joy   5
When the sun slowly rises
Up over the heavens,
    ayi, yai ya.

But else I choke with fear
At greedy maggot throngs;   10
They eat their way in
At the hollow of my collarbone
And in my eyes,
    ayi, yai ya.

Here I lie, recollecting   15
How stifled with fear I was
When they buried me
In a snow hut out on the lake,
    ayi, yai ya.

A block of snow was pushed to,   20
Incomprehensible it was
How my soul should make its way
And fly to the game land up there,
    ayi, yai ya.

That door-block worried me,   25
And ever greater grew my fear
When the fresh-water ice split in the cold,
And the frost-crack thunderously grew
Up over the heavens,
    ayi, yai ya.   30

Glorious was life
In winter.
But did winter bring me joy?
No! Ever was I so anxious
For sole-skins and skins for kamiks,   35
Would there be enough for us all?
Yes, I was ever anxious,
    ayi, yai ya.

Glorious was life
In summer.   40
But did summer bring me joy?
No! Ever was I so anxious
For skins and rugs for the platform,
Yes, I was ever anxious,
    ayi, yai ya.   45

Glorious was life
When standing at one's fishing-hole
On the ice.
But did standing at the fishing-hole bring me joy?
No! Ever was I so anxious   50
For my tiny little fish-hook
If it should not get a bite,
    ayi, yai ya.

Glorious was life
When dancing in the dance-house.   55
But did dancing in the dance-house bring me joy?
No! Ever was I so anxious,
That I could not recall
The song I was to sing.
Yes, I was ever anxious,   60
     ayi, yai ya.

Glorious was life. . . .
Now I am filled with joy
For every time a dawn
Makes white the sky of night,   65
For every time the sun goes up
Over the heavens,
     ayi, yai ya.

Joseph Brant *c.* 1742–1807

MOHAWK

Joseph Brant, Thayendanegea, was born in what is now Ohio in either 1742 or 1743. He was with Sir William Johnson as early as his expedition against Fort Niagara in the Seven Years' War (1759) and as Johnson's protegé was sent in 1761 to Moor's Indian Charity School for two years. In the following years he acted as an interpreter for Johnson, for his successor Guy Johnson, and for missionaries.

A Loyalist, after the outbreak of the American Revolution he chose to lead Native forces as a war chief against the Americans. Following the Revolution he worked to create a new confederacy of Native peoples to block American expansion westward.

In 1784 Brant led a group of Mohawk Loyalists to a settlement on the Grand River (named Brant's ford in 1827, now Brantford) in what is now Ontario. The land was a grant given by the British in compensation for loss of land in the United States, and for support to the British cause. Brant's activities have had longstanding repercussions. For example, his

conviction that the Native future must be tied to developing white methods of agriculture and his attempt to lease land to whites in order to gain working capital resulted in extended conflict with both Native people and the government. He died in Burlington, Ontario.

Brant is better known as a figure in literature than as an author. His Christianity, his Loyalism, his statesmanship, and his military reputation have made him a perfect subject for depiction as a 'noble savage'. These portraits range from the nineteenth-century closet drama *Thayendanegea*, by J.B. Mackenzie, to the television miniseries *Divided Loyalties*. Still, Brant, who in his later years worked to translate the Bible into Mohawk, devoted significant energy to his words as a statesman, as is typical of Native politicians, from the oratory of the pre-contact culture to the essays and speeches of Native leaders today. The following examples of his writing embrace sophisticated rhetorical principles, with a forthright commitment to the power of language.

Letter

Sir,   Grand River, Dec. 10, 1798

Our former acquaintance encourages me to take the freedom of writing you; but knowing the multiplicity of business you have on your hands, I would not trouble you with this, did not the particular situation of our affairs seem to require it, thinking it necessary for me candidly to acquaint my friends with the feelings of my mind.

I presume that you are well acquainted with the long difficulties we had concerning the lands on this river—these difficulties we had not the least idea of when we first settled here, looking on them as granted us to be indisputably our own, otherwise we would never have accepted the lands, yet afterwards it seemed a little odd to us that the writings Gov. Haldimand gave us after our settling on the lands, was not so compleat as the strong assurances and promises he had made us at first, but this made no great impression on our minds, still confiding in the goodness of his Majesty's intentions, and in the weight we caputed our former services would have with him—Had it not been for this confidence and affection we bore the Kings we still had opportunities left after the war, in providing for ourselves in the free and independent manner natural to Indians, unhappily for us we have been made acquainted too late with the first real intentions of Ministry; that is, that they never intended us to have it in our power to alienate any part of the lands; and here we have even been prohibited from taking tenants on them, it having been represented as inconsistent for us, being but King's allies, to have King's subjects as tenants, consequently I suppose their real meaning was, we should in a manner be but tenants ourselves, as for me I see no difference in it any farther than that we are as yet rent free—they seemingly intending to forbid us any other use of the lands than that of sitting down or walking on them. It plainly appears by this that their motives can be no other than to tie us down in such a manner, as to have us entirely at their disposal for whatever services they may in future want from us, and that in case we should be worried out, and obliged to move the lands would then fall to them with our improvements of labour.

Sir, I hope I shall not tire your patience, in making a few remarks on what I suppose may naturally be the thoughts of Government on our conduct—With respect to myself they might say he has half pay and yet talks so much on these matters, it is very true I enjoy that bounty of his Majesty, so many worthless fellows like me do, that have never risked their property or any thing else in his causes but am I for this entirely to forsake the interests of my people? that put their dependence on me besides my family which is very numerous cannot be benefitted by my half pay when I am no more; which at my time of life I have reason to look on as a period not so very distant. I think it therefore incumbent on me to secure what they must look to for a future support. With respect to the Nation they may also say, that they have received their losses, for instance our hunting grounds that were very extensive, besides several other tracts of land were never mentioned—The Miller, blacksmith, and School-master, that is allowed us by government may also be spoken of—we are indeed very thankful for it; but we look upon this as all temporary and the continuance of it to be uncertain—it may likewise be said they receive annual presents what do they want more, we gratefully thank his Majesty, for his bounty in this respect; but I am sorry to have to observe that this goes very little ways in clothing the poor and helpless—and the country is so much changed that hunting is of very little account to the young and robust.

I beg have to say a few words more on this subject, the movements of Gov. Simcoe in attempting to curtail our lands to one half of the River, and recollecting our deed from Gov. Haldimand to be unequal to his first promises caused us to make such a large sale at once that the matter might come to a point and we might know whether the land was ours or not—the next reason was, that the lands all round us being given away to different people, some of them, those that had even been engaged in war against us, we found it necessary to sell some land, that we might have an income, the hunting being entirely destroyed.—We now learn that the ministry never intended we should alienate the lands, alleging that by doing so, disaffected people might be introduced into the country that might injure government—the people we have sold the lands to are loyalist & we expect, that as other people settled in the province, they will become subjects to His Majesty, the same as if Gov. Simcoe had himself curtailed the land and given it to them, as he has done with the adjacent lands.

I am sorry for having   Sir
taken up so much of your   I am
time with so tedious a letter   Your most obed^t and
but I assure my present disagree-   Humb. Servt.
able situation, affects my feelings   Jos. Brant
so much, that I cannot avoid expressing
it rather fully especially as I think
this shall be the last time I will trouble
you on the subject.   Capt. Green

Condolence Speech

To Captain Claus on the death of his mother (Ann Johnson Claus) made by Captain Joseph Brant, 24 February 1801 at Fort George.

Brother! We are here now met in the presence of the Spirit above, with the intent to keep up the ancient custom of condolement. We therefore condole with you for your late loss of our well beloved sister, whom now you have interred.

Brother! We hope that this may not damp your heart so much as to make you forget us, who are your brothers, not only ourselves but our wives and children.

Brother! We say now again that by our late loss it seems our fire is somewhat extinguished. But now we have found a few brands remaining and have collected them together and have raised a straight smoke to the clouds.

Brother! We therefore with this string of Wampum wipe away the tears from your eyes and would take away all sorrow from your heart. But that is impossible, still it is the customary way of making the speech. We, therefore, mention it and with the said Wampum we wipe away all stains of whatever should remain on your seat so that you may sit down in comfort.

Brother! We say again with this string of Wampum, as you seem to be all in darkness, we with the same string enlighten the skies about us so that it may appear to us all as it formerly used to do.

Brother! We say again with this string of Wampum as we now have made our speech of condolement, we hope to raise you upon your feet as you formerly used to be for since our late loss it seems you have been confined as one absent.

Brother! We hope you will not forget our calamities; hoping that this shock may not put us out of your memory entirely; and also that you may continue to keep us as you formerly used to do.

Brother! This last string which now I give you is given by the whole Six Nations so as to strengthen your mind and body that you may not be cast down by the occasion of our late loss.

George Copway 1818–1869

OJIBWA

George Copway, Kahgegagahbowh ('He Who Stands Forever'), was born near what is now Trenton, Ontario. His father, a medicine man and one of the chiefs of the Rice Lake Indian Village, was converted by Native Methodist missionaries in 1827, and his mother soon after. George converted in 1830, at the age of twelve, and began work as a teacher in 1834. He was sent to Jacksonville, Illinois, in 1836 to study for two years at the Ebenezer Methodist Seminary. He became an ordained minister and travelled with his English wife as a missionary to Native communities in both the United States and Canada. When two Native bands in Canada accused him of embezzlement, the Methodists expelled him, and in 1846 he returned to the US, where he became a successful lecturer and author.

Copway translated part of the Bible into Ojibwa, but his major literary achievement was his autobiography, *The Life, History, and Travels of Kah-ge-ga-gah-bowh* (1847), from which the following selection is taken. It was the first book in English written by a Canadian Native person. Copway also wrote *The Traditional History and Characteristic Sketches of the Ojibwa Nation* (1850) and *Running Sketches of Men and Places in England, France, Germany, Belgium and Scotland* (1851)—an account of his European travels— and edited the short-lived weekly *Copway's American Indian* (1851).

Copway had prominent supporters in the United States, including James Fenimore Cooper, Washington Irving, Henry Wadsworth Longfellow, Francis Parkman, and Henry Rowe Schoolcraft. His books were popular successes, with his autobiography published in six editions. That book's anti-paganism and passionate faith in conversion seem obsessive today, but Copway's attacks on British and American Native policy and his imaginative proposals on land rights were decidedly progressive.

A Word to the Reader

It would be presumptuous in one, who has but recently been brought out of a wild and savage state; and who has since received but three years' schooling, to undertake, without any assistance, to publish to the world a work of any kind. It is but a few years since I began to speak the English language. An unexpected opportunity occurred of submitting my manuscript to a friend, who has kindly corrected all *serious* grammatical errors, leaving the unimportant ones wholly untouched, that my own style may be exhibited as truly as possible. The public and myself are indebted to him for his kind aid, and he has my most sincere thanks. The language, (except in a few short sentences,) the plan, and the arrangement are all my own; and I am wholly responsible for all the statements, and the remaining defects. My work is now accomplished; and I am too well aware of the many faults which are still to be found therein. Little could I imagine, that I should have to contend with so many obstacles. All along, have I felt my great deficiency; and my inadequacy for such an undertaking. I would fain hope, however, that the kind Reader will throw the mantle of charity over errors of every kind. I am a stranger in a strange land! And often, when the sun is sinking in the western sky, I think of my former home; my heart yearns for the loved of other days, and tears flow like the summer rain. How the heart of the wanderer and pilgrim, after long years of absence, beats, and his eyes fill, as he catches a glance at the hills of his nativity, and reflects upon the time when he pressed the lips of a mother, or sister, now cold in death. Should I live, this painful pleasure will yet be mine. '*Blessed be the Lord, who hath helped me hitherto.*'

KAH-GE-GA-GAH-BOWH,

ALIAS

GEORGE COPWAY

July 1847.

The Life of Kah-Ge-Ga-Gah-Bowh

The Christian will no doubt feel for my poor people, when he hears the story of one brought from that unfortunate race called the Indians. The lover of humanity will be glad to see that that once powerful race can be made to enjoy the blessings of life.

What was once impossible—or rather thought to be—is made possible through my experience. I have made many close observations of men, and things around me; but, I regret to say, that I do not think I have made as good use of my opportunities as I might have done. It will be seen that I know but little—yet O how precious *that little!*—I would rather lose my right hand than be deprived of it.

I loved the woods, and the chase. I had the nature for it, and gloried in nothing else. The mind for letters was in me, *but was asleep*, till the dawn of Christianity arose, and awoke the slumbers of the soul into energy and action.

You will see that I served the imaginary gods of my poor blind father. I was out early and late in quest of the favours of the *Mon-e-doos* (spirits,) who, it was said, were numerous—who filled the air! At early dawn I watched the rising of the *palace* of the Great Spirit—*the sun*—who, it was said, made the world!

Early as I can recollect, I was taught that it was the gift of the many spirits to be a good hunter and warrior; and much of my time I devoted in search of their favours. On the mountain top, or along the valley, or the water brook, I searched for some kind of intimation from the spirits who made their residence in the noise of the waterfalls.

I dreaded to hear the voice of the angry spirit in the gathering clouds. I looked with anxiety to catch a glimpse of the wings of the Great Spirit, who shrouded himself in rolling white and dark clouds—who, with his wings, fanned the earth, and laid low the tall pines and hemlock in his course—who rode in whirlwinds and tornadoes, and plucked the trees from their woven roots—who chased other gods from his course—who drove the Bad Spirit from the surface of the earth, down to the dark caverns of the deep. Yet he was a kind spirit. My father taught me to call that spirit Ke-sha-mon-e-doo—*Benevolent spirit*—for his ancestors taught him no other name to give to that spirit who made the earth, with all its variety and smiling beauty. His benevolence I saw in the running of the streams, for the animals to quench their thirst and the fishes to live; the fruit of the earth teemed wherever I looked. Every thing I saw smilingly said Ke-sha-mon-e-doo nin-ge-oo-she-ig—*the Benevolent spirit made me.*

Where is he? My father pointed to the sun. What is his will concerning me, and the rest of the Indian race? This was a question that I found no one could answer, until a beam from heaven shone on my pathway, which was very dark, when first I saw that there was a true heaven—not in the far-setting sun, where the Indian anticipated a rest, a home for his spirit—but in the bosom of the Highest.

I view my life like the mariner on the wide ocean, without a compass, in the dark night, as he watches the heavens for the north star, which his eye having discovered, he makes his way amidst surging seas, and tossed by angry billows into the very jaws of death, till he arrives safely anchored at port. I have been tossed with hope and fear in this life; no star-light shone on my way, until the men of God pointed me to a Star in the East, as it rose with all its splendour and glory. It was the Star of Bethlehem. I could now say in the language of the poet—

> 'Once on the raging seas I rode,
>   The storm was loud, the night was dark;
> The ocean yawned, and rudely blowed
>   The wind that tossed my foundering bark.'

Yes, I hope to sing some day in the realms of bliss—

> 'It was my guide, my light, my all!
>   It bade my dark foreboding cease;
> And through the storm and danger's thrall,
>   It led me to the port of peace.'

I have not the happiness of being able to refer to written records in narrating the history of my forefathers; but I can reveal to the world what has long been laid up in my memory; so that when 'I go the way of all the earth', the crooked and singular paths which I have made in the world, may not only be a warning to others, but may inspire them with a trust in God. And not only a warning and a trust, but also that the world may learn that there once lived such a man as Kah-ge-ga-gah-bowh, when they read his griefs and his joys.

My parents were of the Ojebwa nation, who lived on the lake back of Cobourg, on the shores of Lake Ontario, Canada West. The lake was called Rice Lake, where there was a quantity of wild rice, and much game of different kinds, before the whites cleared away the woods, where the deer and the bear then resorted.

My father and mother were taught the religion of their nation. My father became a medicine man in the early part of his life, and always had by him the implements of war, which generally distinguish our head men. He was a good hunter as any in the tribe. Very few brought more furs than he did in the spring. Every spring they returned from their hunting grounds. The Ojebwas each claimed, and claim to this day, hunting grounds, rivers, lakes, and whole districts of country. No one hunted on each other's ground. My father had the northern fork of the river Trent, above Bellmont Lake.

My great-grandfather was the first who ventured to settle at Rice Lake, after the Ojebwa nation defeated the Hurons, who once inhabited all the lakes in Western Canada, and who had a large village just on the top of the hill of the Anderson farm (which was afterwards occupied by the Ojebwas), and which furnished a magnificent view of the lakes and surrounding country. He was of the *Crane tribe*, i.e. had a crane for totem—*coat of arms*—which now forms the totem of the villagers, excepting those who have since come amongst us from other villages by intermarriage, for there was a law that no one was to marry one of the same totem, for all considered each other as being related. He must have been a daring adventurer—*a warrior*—for no one would have ventured to go and settle down on the land from which they had just driven the Hurons, whom the Ojebwas conquered and reduced, unless he was a great hero. It is said that he lived about the islands of Rice Lake, secreting himself from the enemy for several years, until some others came and joined him, when they formed a settlement on one of the islands. He must have been a great hunter, for this was one of the principal inducements that made him venture there, for there must have been abundance of game of every kind. The Ojebwas are called, here and all around, Massisuagays, because they came from Me-sey Sah-gieng, at the head of Lake Huron, as you go up to Sault St. Marie falls.

Here he lived in jeopardy—with his life in his hand—enduring the unpleasant idea that he lived in the land of bones—*amidst the gloom*, which shrouded the once happy and populous village of the Hurons; here their bones lay broadcast around his wigwam; where, among these woods once rang the war cry of the Hurons, echoing along the valley of the river Trent, but whose sinewed arms now laid low, with their badges and arms of war, in one common grave, near the residence of Peter Anderson, Esq. Their graves, forming a hillock, are now all that remain of this once powerful nation. Their bones, gun barrels, tomahawks, war spears, large scalping knives, are yet to be found there. This must have taken place soon after the formation of the settlement in Quebec.

The *Crane tribe* became the sole proprietors of this part of the Ojebwa land; the descendants of this tribe will continue to wear the distinguishing sign; except in a few instances, the chiefs are of this tribe.

My grandfather lived here about this time, and held some friendly intercourse with the whites. My father here learned the manners, customs, and worship of the nation. He, and others, became acquainted with the early settlers, and have ever been friendly with the whites. And I know the day when he used to shake the hand of the white man, and, *very friendly*, the white man would say, '*take some whiskey.*' When he saw any hungering for venison, he gave them to eat; and some, in return for his kindness, have repaid him after they became good and great farmers.

My mother was of the *Eagle tribe*; she was a sensible woman; she was as good a hunter as any of the Indians; she could shoot the deer, and the ducks flying, as well as they. Nature had done a great deal for her, for she was active; and she was much more cleanly than the majority of our women in those days. She lived to see the day when most of her children were given up to the Lord in Christian baptism; while she experienced a change of heart, and the fulness of God in man, for she lived daily in the enjoyment of God's favours. I will speak more of her at a proper time, respecting her life and happy death.

My father still lives; he is from sixty-five to seventy years old, and is one of the chiefs of Rice Lake Indian Village. He used to love fire-water before he was converted to God, but now lives in the enjoyment of religion, and he is happy without the devil's spittal—*whiskey*. If Christianity had not come, and the grace of God had not taken possession of his heart, his head would soon have been laid low beneath the fallen leaves of the forest, and I, left, in my youthful days, an orphan. But to God be all the praise for his timely deliverance.

The reader will see that I cannot boast of an exalted parentage, nor trace the past history to some renowned warrior in days of yore; but let the above suffice. My fathers were those who endured much; who first took possession of the conquered lands of the Hurons.

I was born in *nature's wide domain!* The trees were all that sheltered my infant limbs—the blue heavens all that covered me. I am one of Nature's children; I have always admired her; she shall be my glory; her features—her robes, and the wreath about her brow—the seasons—her stately oaks, and the evergreen—her hair—ringlets over the earth, all contribute to my enduring love of her; and wherever I see her, emotions of pleasure roll in my breast, and swell and burst like waves on the shores of the ocean, in prayer and praise to Him who has placed me in her hand. It is thought great to be born in palaces, surrounded with wealth—but to be born in nature's wide domain is greater still!

I was born sometime in the fall of 1818, near the mouth of the river Trent, called in our language, Sah-ge-dah-we-ge-wah-noong, while my father and mother were attending the annual distribution of the presents from the government to the Indians.

I was the third of our family; a brother and sister being older, both of whom died. My brother died without the knowledge of the Saviour, but my sister experienced the power of the loving grace of God. One brother, and two step-brothers, are still alive.

I remember the tall trees, and the dark woods—the swamp just by, where the little wren sang so melodiously after the going down of the sun in the west—the current of the broad river Trent—the skipping of the fish, and the noise of the rapids a little above. It was here I first saw the light; a little fallen down shelter, made of evergreens, and a few dead embers, the remains of the last fire that shed its genial warmth around, were all that marked the spot. When I last visited it, nothing but four poles stuck in the ground, and they were leaning on account of decay. Is this dear spot, made green by the tears of memory, any less enticing and hallowed than the palaces where princes are born? I would much more glory in this birth-place, with the broad canopy of heaven above me, and the giant arms of the forest trees for my shelter, than to be born in palaces of marble, studded with pillars of gold! Nature will be nature still, while palaces shall decay and fall in ruins. Yes, Niagara will be Niagara a thousand years hence! The rainbow, a wreath over her brow, shall continue as long as the sun, and the flowing of the river! While the work of art, however impregnable, shall in atoms fall.

Our wigwam we always carried with us wherever we went. It was made in the following manner: Poles were cut about fifteen feet long; three with crotches at the end, which were stuck in the ground some distance apart, the upper ends meeting, and fastened with bark; and then other poles were cut in circular form and bound round the first, and then covered with plaited reeds, or sewed birch bark, leaving an opening on top for the smoke to escape. The skins of animals formed a covering for a gap, which answered for a door. The family all seated tailor-fashion on mats. In the fall and winter they were generally made more secure, for the purpose of keeping out the rain and cold. The covering of our wigwam was always carried by my mother, whenever we went through the woods. In the summer it was easier and pleasanter to move about from place to place, than in the winter. In the summer we had birch bark canoes, and with these we travelled very rapidly and easily. In the winter everything was carried upon the back. I have known some Indians to carry a whole deer—not a small one, but a buck. If an Indian could lift up his pack off the ground by means of his arms, it was a good load, not too light nor too heavy. I once carried one hundred and ninety-six weight of flour, twelve pounds of shot, five pounds of coffee, and some sugar, about a quarter of a mile, without resting—the flour was in two bags. It felt very heavy. This was since I travelled with the missionaries, in going over one of the portages in the west.

Our summer houses were made like those in gardens among the whites, except that the skeleton is covered with bark.

The hunting grounds of the Indians were secured by right, a law and custom among themselves. No one was allowed to hunt on another's land, without invitation or permission. If any person was found trespassing on the ground of another, all his things were taken from him, except a handful of shot, powder sufficient to serve him in going *straight* home, a gun, a tomahawk, and a knife; all the fur, and other things, were taken from him. If he were found a second time trespassing, all his things were taken away from him, except food sufficient to subsist on while going home. And should he still come a third time to trespass on the same, or another man's hunting grounds, his nation, or tribe, are then informed of it, who take up his case. If still he disobey, he is banished from his tribe.

My father's hunting ground was at the head of Crow River, a branch of the River Trent, north of the Prince Edward District, Canada West. There are two branches to this river—one belongs to George Poudash, one of the principal chiefs of our nation; the other to my father; and the Crow River belongs to another chief by the name of John Crow. During the last war the Indians did not hunt or fish much for nearly six years, and at the end of that time there were large quantities of beaver, otter, minks, lynx, fishes, &c.

These hunting grounds abound with rivers and lakes; the face of the country is swampy and rocky; the deer and the bear abound in these woods; part of the surrendered territory is included in it. In the year 1818, 1,800,000 acres of it were surrendered to the British government. For how much, do you ask? For $2,690 per annum! What a *great sum* for British generosity!

Much of the back country still remains unsold, and I hope the scales will be removed from the eyes of my poor countrymen, that they may see the robberies perpetrated upon them, before they surrender another foot of territory.

From these lakes and rivers come the best furs that are caught in Western Canada. Buyers of fur get large quantities from here. They are then shipped to New York City, or to England. Whenever fruit is plenty, bears are also plenty, and there is much bear hunting. Before the whites came amongst us, the skins of these animals served for clothing; they are now sold from three to eight dollars apiece.

My father generally took one or two families with him when he went to hunt; all were to hunt, and place their gains into one common stock till spring, (for they were often out all winter,) when a division took place.

*   *   *

My beloved Reader—I am now about closing my narrative, and in doing this there are but a few things to say. Throughout the work, I have confined my remarks chiefly to my own nation. But it must not be supposed, on this account, that I am forgetful of my brethren of the other Indian nations. The prayers and benevolent efforts of all Christendom should be directed towards all men everywhere. The gospel should be preached to every creature; and the field is the *wide* WORLD.

The Menomenees in Wisconsin, the Winebagoes and Potawatamies in Iowa, the warlike nations of the Sacs and Foxes, the Osages, Pawnees, Mandans, Kansas, Creeks, Omahas, Otoes, Delawares, Iowas, and a number of others elsewhere, must perish as did their brethren in the Eastern States, unless the white man send them the Gospel, and the blessings of education. There is field enough for all denominations to labour in, without interfering with each other. It is too late in the day to assert that the Indians cannot be raised up out of their degraded state, and educated for God and heaven. None need be discouraged since the Ojebwas in Western Canada have been converted. No language is adequate to portray the misery, wretchedness, and degradation in which we were, when the word of God was first brought and preached to us.

It is not necessary to detail each and every wrong, that my poor people have suffered at the hands of the white man. Enough has already been said in various parts of the work, to prove that they have been most grossly abused, peeled, and wronged. Nor shall I notice the *personal wrongs* that I myself have received; and from those, too, of whom I had good reason to hope better things. I once thought, that there were some things that I could never forgive; but the religion of Jesus, and the law of love, have taught me differently. I *do* forgive them; and may God forgive them and me too.

I have sometimes heard it said, that our forefathers were cruel to the forefathers of the whites. But was not this done through ignorance, or in self-defence? Had your fathers adopted the plan of the great philanthropist, William Penn, neither fields, nor clubs, nor waters, would have been crimsoned with each other's blood. The white men have been like the greedy lion, pouncing upon and devouring its prey. They have driven us from our nation, our homes, and possessions; compelled us to seek a refuge in Missouri, among strangers, and wild beasts; and will, perhaps, soon compel us to scale the Rocky Mountains; and, for aught I can tell, we may yet be driven to the Pacific Ocean, there to find our graves. My only trust is, that there is a just God. Was it to perpetrate such acts that you have been exalted above all other nations? Providence intended you for a *blessing* and not a *curse* to us. You have sent your missionaries to Burmah, China, the Sandwich Islands, and to almost every part of the world; and shall the Indians *perish at your own door?*

Is it not well known that the Indians have a generous and magnanimous heart? I feel proud to mention in this connection, the names of a Pocahontas, Massasoit, Skenandoah, Logan, Kusic, Pushmataha, Philip, Tecumseh, Osceola, Petalesharro, and thousands of others. Such names are an honour to the world! Let a late Governor of Massachusetts* speak for our fathers, when they first beheld the trembling white man:—

'Brothers! when our fathers came over the great waters, they were a small band. The red man stood upon the rock by the seaside, and saw our fathers. He might have pushed them into the water and drowned them. But he stretched out his arms to our fathers and said, "Welcome, white men!" Our fathers were hungry, and the red man gave them corn and venison. Our fathers were cold, and the red man wrapped them up in his blanket. We are now numerous and powerful, but we remember the kindness of the red man to our fathers.'

And what have we received since, in return? Is it for the deeds of a Pocahontas, a Massasoit, and a host of others, that we have been plundered and oppressed, and expelled from the hallowed graves of our ancestors? If help cannot be obtained from England and America, where else can we look? Will you then, lend us a helping hand; and make some amends for past injuries?

It is often said, that the Indians are *revengeful, cruel,* and *ungovernable.* But go to them with nothing but *the* BIBLE *in your hands,* and LOVE *in your hearts,* and you may live with them in perfect safety, share their morsel with them, and, like the celebrated

---

* Edward Everett, Esq.

Bartram, return to your homes UNHARMED. They very soon learn to venerate the Bible; as a proof of this, I will give an instance, that came under my own eye:—While at the Rabbit River Mission, a chief from the west, visited me. After reading to him several chapters from the Bible, he said, with much surprise, 'Is *this* the book, that I hear so much about in *my* country?' I replied, yes; and these are the words of *Ke-sha-mon-e-doo* (the Great Spirit). 'Will you not,' said he, 'give me one? I wish to show it to my people.' I told him, not without you first promise that you will take care of it. He promised me that he would. I handed it to him; he took it, and turned it over and over, and then exclaimed, '*Wonderful, wonderful! This is the book of the Great Spirit!*' He then wrapped it up in a silk handkerchief, and the handkerchief in three or four folds of cloth. I heard, afterwards, from the trader, that the book was still kept sacred. O, if my poor brother could but *read* and *understand* that blessed volume, how soon would his dumb idols be 'cast down to the moles and to the bats'! Will no one go and tell him and his nation, of the boundless, beseeching, bleeding, dying love of a Saviour; and urge upon them the importance of such a preparation of heart, as will enable them 'to give up their account with joy'? The Great Spirit is no respecter of persons; He has made of one blood all the nations of the earth; He loves all his children alike; and his highest attributes are *love, mercy,* and *justice.* If this be so,—and who dare doubt it?—will He not stretch out his hand and help them, and avenge their wrongs? 'If offences *must* come', let it be recollected, that *woe* is denounced against them 'from *whom* they come'.

I again propose that the territories of the Indians, in the British dominions, be annexed to that Government, and those in the American dominions to the Federal Union. And, finally, in the language of that excellent, magnanimous, and benevolent friend of the poor children of the forest, Col. Thomas McKenney, I would say,

'I have already referred, in the commencement of this proposal to annex the Indian territory to our Union, to those good men, who, in the character of missionaries, have kept side by side with the Indians in so many of their afflictions and migrations. I will again refer to them, and implore them by all the lost labour of the past, and by the hopes of the future; by the critical condition of the pacific relations that exist between the Indians and us; and by the sacredness of the cause in which they are engaged, to look well and earnestly into this subject, and learn from the past what *must* attend upon their labours in the future, if the change I propose, or some other change equivalent to it, be not brought about. And, seeing, as they must see, that the plan I propose, or some other, is indispensable to the success they seek to command, I implore them to take up the subject in all its bearings, and by the instrumentalities which they have at command, manufacture, collect, and embody public opinion, in regard to what may be determined to be done; and by memorial, and personal agencies, bring this opinion to bear upon Congress, with whom alone the power is vested, to redeem, disenthrall, and save, and bless, the remnants of this aboriginal race. And I make the same appeal to all the good, of all religious persuasions, both in the Church and out of it, and politicians of all parties, to second this attempt, feeble as I know it to be, to save the Indians, and consolidate, and perpetuate peace between them and us, and, by so doing, ward off the terrible retribution which must sooner or later, unless it be averted, fall upon this nation.'

Catherine Soneegoh Sutton 1822–1865

OJIBWA

Catherine Soneegoh Sutton, whose Ojibwa name was Nah-nee-bah-wee-quay ('Upright Woman'), was born near the Credit River in present-day Ontario. When she was two, her family moved to the Credit Indian village, a Methodist settlement. In 1837 she went to England with her aunt, who was the wife of Peter Jones, the first Native Canadian to be ordained.

After attending school in England for a year, Sutton returned to Canada and in 1839 married an English immigrant, William Sutton. Together they served as Methodist missionaries in various venues, including a model farm near Sault Ste Marie in 1852 and a mission in Michigan two years later. The Nawash band of Owen Sound had ceded them land in 1845, but when they returned to Owen Sound in 1857 the land had been laid out for sale. Sutton was first refused a share of the Nawash band's annuities for having married a white man and for having being absent from the country, and then was not allowed to purchase the land because she was an Indian. By giving a series of lectures in Canada and the United States, Sutton was able to raise money for a journey to England, where she petitioned the Queen. As a result, she was able to return to Canada and buy back some of the land. She continued actively to pursue Native rights until her death in 1865.

The following selection is from an entry in her journal, which is held in the Grey County and Owen Sound Museum. It is taken here from *Native Literature in Canada* (1990), by Penny Petrone, who surmises that it is a copy of a letter written in response to an editorial in the periodical *The Leader*. The entry is dated 8 September 1864.

Letter

On the shores of Goulais Bay Lake Superior and the neighbouring one of Batchawana, one of these publick nusiances—an Indian reserve was laid of a few years ago under Lord Elgin's Government the reserve covered a portage of 30 miles on the Lake with a sufficient depth into the country to make up an area of 300 square miles of land—some of the best land in the country and so situated as to block up the means of access to the entire regions lying in the rear of it and all this for about a dozen of the most wretched, squalid, miserable specimens of human nature that I have ever seen: indeed a close inspection of, and a little acquaintance with, these creatures leads one to doubt whether they are human, but whether they are men or monkeys it matters not now, the present administration have found means to extinguish their title so far, that the country is now surveyed, and will soon be in market.

I suppose the individual who published the above and Mr Charles Linsey, the great Hearo who tried last fall to frighten the Manitoulin Indians out of their sences and their Lands, are, one and the same—if they are not their certanly is a great family likeness between them I have lived for several years with in a few miles of Goulais bay and I have frequently seen those Indians aluded to but I never took them for

Monkyes neither did I ever hear such a thing hinted at by the white people I think they were allways, considered to be human beings, possessing living souls, I did not think monkeys lived so far north I allways understood that they were found in warm climates, when I was in England I went to the zoological garden were I saw a great maney monkeys and of various sises and kinds but I observed their was one trait coman to them all and a close inspection & a litle acquaintance with the Editor of the Leader has led me to the conclusion that the same trait stands out prominently in his natural disposition and character, and when I state what is the nature of that trait so comon to all the monkeys I ever saw I will leave you to guess who is by nature verey closly related to these four leged animals well I will tell you the trait wich I observed so comon to every variety of monkeys was an entire absence of humanity.

I have allso frequently seen the litle trained monkey exibeted in our canadian towns and vilages with pants red coat and cap, but every child could tell that it was a monkey because its tail would stick out and I noticed that after he had played of his money anticks he allways went round with his hat for a colection and as far as I can learn this is just what a certen creature does after he as performed something wich is pleasing to a certen party he expects them in return to throw something handsome into his cap.

The Editor of the Leader apears to think that every indian reservation is a publick nusiance so I conclude that if he could have his will, he would have every band of indians drove on to the baran waste of granite rocks north of Lakes huron and superior but why are indian reservations aney more a publick nusiance then large blocks of land bought and held by speculators I argue that Indians have a right to be paid a fair valuation for aney lands wich they may agree to surrender, I suppose the Leader would not have a word to say if a dozen or two poor hard working white men should get scatered through the Goulais bay teritory, while all the remainder was bought up and held by a few speculators untill those poor men by hard persevering industry had cleared up their lands and made roads and thus by the poor mans hard labour raised the value of the rich land speculators property—the Editor of the Leader states that the present administration have found means to extinguish their title, my english his so poor that I frequently have to consult Webster and I find the word extinguish means to destroy to put an end to; to extinguish a claim or title, a wonderful feat surely for the present administration to perform and for the Editor of the Leader to brag of; this shows another instance of the uter helplessness of the poor indian they apear to be at the mercy of such men as Mr Charles Linsey our present administration can extinguish the red mans title at pleasure, what hope is their for the remnant that are yet left to whom can they go for redress who will help them or are they entirely without helper, I suppose Mr Linsey will answer these questions when the present administration give him a commission to go to manitolin with soldiers to subdue the Indians or monkeys as he calls them.

Ghandl *c. 1851–c. 1920*

HAIDA

Ghandl was born in Qaysun, Haida Gwaay (Queen Charlotte Islands). Blinded early in life, he was christened 'Walter McGregor' by a visiting missionary in 1887.

'In His Father's Village' is an example of *qqaygaang*, a narrative poem set in myth-time. It is one of a collection of stories that were phonetically recorded in 1900 by the linguist John Reed Swanton with the help of another Haida man, Henry Moody. Swanton and Moody then provided an interlinear translation. All that is left today, however, is a prose translation that Swanton produced in 1902.

The translation offered here was made by Robert Bringhurst from Swanton's 1902 document and published in *Nine Visits to the Myth-world* (2000). Bringhurst is a celebrated poet whose translations of and commentary on Haida stories have made a major contribution to public awareness of traditional orature.

In His Father's Village, Someone Was Just About to Go Out Hunting Birds

Translated by Robert Bringhurst

There was a child of good family, they say.
He wore two marten-skin blankets.
After he took up the shooting of birds,
he went inland, uphill from the village, they say.

Going through the pines,   5
just to where the ponds lay,
he heard geese calling.
Then he went in that direction.

There were two women bathing in a lake.
Something lay there on the shore.   10
Two goose skins were thrown over it.
Under their tails were patches of white.

After watching for a while,
he swooped in.
He sat on the two skins.   15
The women asked to have them back.

He asked the better-looking one to marry him.
The other one replied.
'Don't marry my younger sister.
I am smarter. Marry me.'   20

'No. I will marry your younger sister.'

And she said that she accepted him, they say.

'Well then! Marry my younger sister.
You caught us bathing in a lake
that belongs to our father.   25
Now give me my skin.'

He gave it back.
She slipped it on
while she was swimming in the lake.

A goose swam in the lake then,   30
and then she started calling.
And then she flew, they say,
though leaving her younger sister
sickened her heart.

She circled above them.   35
Then she flew off, they say.
She passed through the sky.

He gave the younger woman one of his marten-skin blankets,
and he brought her home, they say.

A two-headed redcedar stood at the edge of the village,   40
and he put his wife's skin between the trunks.
Then he brought her into his father's house.

The headman's son had taken a wife.
So his father invited the people, they say.
They offered her food.   45
She did nothing but smell it.
She would eat no human food.

Later, her husband's mother started steaming silverweed, they say.
Then she paid closer attention.
When her husband's mother was still busy cooking,   50
she asked her husband
to ask her to hurry, they say.

They placed it before her.
It vanished.
And then they began to feed her this only, they say.   55

After a time, as he was sleeping,
his wife lay down beside him, and her skin was cold.
When it happened again,
he decided to watch her, they say.

He lay still in the bed,   60
and he felt her moving away from him slowly, they say.
Then she went out.
He followed behind her.

She walked along the beach in front of the village.
She went where the skin was kept.   65
From there, she flew.
She landed beyond the point at the edge of town.

He started toward her.
She was eating the eelgrass that grew there,
and the breaking waves were lifting her back toward shore.   70
He saw her, they say.
And then she flew back where they kept her skin.

He got back to the house
before she did, they say.
There he lay down,   75
and soon his wife lay down beside him, cold.

A famine began in the village, they say.
One day, without leaving her seat, she said,
'My father is sending things down through the clouds to me.'

Back of the village, geese began landing and honking.   80
She went there.
They followed her.
Food of many kinds was lying there:
silverweed and clover roots.
They carried it home.   85
And her father-in-law invited the people, they say.

When that was entirely gone,
she said it again:
'My father is sending things down through the clouds to me.'
Geese began landing and honking again in back of the village.   90

They went there.
There were piles, again, of many kinds of food.
Again they brought it home.
And her father-in-law again invited the people.

Then, they say, someone in the village said,   95
'She thinks very highly of goose food.'

The woman heard it.
She got up to leave at that moment, they say.
Her husband tried to dissuade her.

No use.   100
She had settled on leaving.

It was the same when he tried to dissuade her in front of the town.
She went where her skin was.
Then she flew.
She flew in circles over the town,   105
and leaving her husband sickened her heart, they say.

And then she passed through the sky.
After that, her husband was constantly weeping, they say.

An old man had a house at the edge of the village.
He went there and asked,   110
'Don't you know the trail that leads to my wife?'

'Headman's son, you married a woman whose mother and father are not of
this world.'

And the old man began to fit him out.
He gave him a bone marlinspike for working with cedar-limb line.
Then he said,   115
'Now, sir, get some oil.
Get two sharp wedges too.
And a comb and a cord and salmon roe and a coho skin and a spearhead.
Get all these.'

After he had gathered what he needed,   120
he came back to him, they say.
'Old one, here are all the things you spoke of.'

'Now, sir, you may go.
Take the narrowest of the trails that lead from my house.'
Then he set off.   125

After walking awhile,
he came upon someone infested with lice.
He was trying to catch the lice by turning around.

After he had stared at him awhile,
the other said,   130
'Sir, don't just tickle me with your eyes.
I've been waiting a long time for you.'

Then he went up close,
and he combed out his hair.
He rubbed him with oil   135
and picked off the lice.
And he gave him the comb and the rest of the oil.

The other one said,
'This is the trail that leads to your wife.'

Again he set off.   140
After walking awhile,
he saw a small mouse in front of him.
There was a cranberry in her mouth.

Then she came to a fallen tree,
and she looked for a way to go over it.   145
He let her step onto his open hand
and put her across.

She laid her tail up between her ears
and ran ahead.

Not far away, she went under some ferns.   150

He rested there,
and something said,
'A headwoman asks if you wish to come in.'
Then he parted the fronds of the ferns.

He was standing in front of a large house.   155
He walked through the door.

There was the headwoman dishing up cranberries.
She spoke with grace.
Her voice had big round eyes.

Once she had offered him something to eat,   160
Mouse Woman said to him,
'When I was bringing a bit of a cranberry back from my berry patch,
you helped me.
I intend to lend you something that I wore
for stalking prey when I was younger.'   165

She brought out a box.
She pulled out four more boxes within boxes.
In the innermost box was the skin of a mouse with small bent claws.
She said to him,
'Put this on.'   170

Small though it was, he got into it.
It was easy.
He went up the wall and into the roof of the house.
And Mouse Woman said to him,
'You know what to do when you wear it.   175
Be on your way.'

He set out again on the trail.
After walking awhile,
he heard someone grunting and straining.
He went there.   180

A woman was hoisting a pile of stones.
The cedar-limb line she was using kept slipping.
He watched her awhile
and then he went up to her.

'Excuse me,' he said,   185
'but what are you doing?'

The woman replied,
'They told me to hold up the mountains of the Islands on the Boundary
    between Worlds.
That is what I am doing.'

Then he remembered his spruce-root cord   190
and he said, 'Let me help you.'

He made splices with the cord.
'Now take the load on your back,' he said,
and she hoisted it up on her back.
It did not slip off.   195

And she said to him,
'Sir, you have helped me.
Here is the trail that leads to your wife.'

Then he went on.

After a time, he came to a hump in the muskeg.   200
Something slender and red grew from the top of it.
He went up close to it.
All around the bottom of the tall, thin thing lay human bones.

He saw no way of going up.
Then he entered the mouse skin.   205
Pushing the salmon roe ahead of him, he climbed.
He went up after it.
When he came to the top,
he pulled himself onto the sky.

The trail stretched ahead of him there too.   210
He walked along.
After travelling awhile,
he began to hear a noise.

After travelling further,
he came to a river.   215
It was running high.

Near it perched an eagle.
A heron perched on the opposite bank.
A kingfisher perched upstream.
A black bear sat on the opposite bank,   220
and he had no claws, they say.

Then, they say, the black bear said to the eagle,
'Lend me something, grandfather.'
Then, they say, the eagle did as he asked.
Then and there the black bear got his claws.   225

When the young man had been sitting there awhile,
half of a person lurched by,
leaning himself on a fishing spear.

He had one leg and one arm,
and his head was half a head.   230
He speared the coho that were swimming there
and put them into his basket.

The man unrolled his coho skin and put it on
and swam in that direction.
When the half man speared him,   235
he was unable to pull him in.

The young man cut the spearhead from the spear, they say.
And the half man said,
'Human beings sometimes do this sort of thing.'

The younger man went up to him then, they say.   240
'Sir, did something take your spearhead?'

'Yes,' he said.

And the young man gave him the one he had.
That was Stickwalking God, they say.

When he went up further,   245
two men, old and fat, came out collecting firewood.
They chopped at the roots of windfall trees,
and they scattered the chips on the water.
The coho were coming from there.

He went back of the fallen tree,   250
pushing stones in from behind,
and their wedges shattered, they say.

And one of them said,
'Ooooow! We'll get a beating!'

Then he went up to them.   255
He gave them the two wedges that he had.
And they stared at him and said,
'This is your wife's house.'

He went up to it, they say.
He stood waiting in front of the house.   260
His wife came out to meet him.

He went in with her.
She was happy to see him.
She was the village headman's daughter, they say.

In that village too, they were man and wife.   265
And everything they gathered,
he gathered as well.

After living there for a time,
he began to dislike the entire country.
Then his wife spoke to her father.   270
And his father-in-law called the villagers in.
There in the house, he asked them, they say,
'Who will carry my son-in-law back?'

And a loon said,
'I will carry your son-in-law back.'   275

'How will you do it?' he asked.

The loon said,
'I will put him under my tail
and dive right in front here.
Then I'll come up again at the edge of his father's town   280
and release him.'

They thought he was too weak to do it, they say.

His father-in-law asked the question again.
A grebe gave the same reply.
They thought she was also too weak.   285

And a raven said he would carry him back.
And they asked him, 'How will you do it?'

'I will put him under my wing
and fly with him from the edge of the village.
When I'm tired,   290
I'll let myself tumble and fall with him.'

They were pleased with his answer, they say,
and they all came down to the edge of the village to watch.

He did as he said.
When he grew tired,   295
he let himself fall down through the clouds with him
and dropped him onto a shoal exposed by the tide.

'Hwuuu! What a load I have carried.'

Becoming a gull, he squawked and went on squawking.

This is where it ends.   300

E. Pauline Johnson 1861–1913

MOHAWK

Pauline Johnson's place in Canadian literature has always been political. Emily Pauline Johnson, Tekahionwake, was born on the Six Nations Reserve at a time when Canadian culture was mainly imperialist. The daughter of a Mohawk chief, George Henry Martin Johnson, and his English wife, Emily Susanna Howells, her family connections established her as both Native aristocracy and Loyalist descendant. Her pro-British proclamations continued the allegiance of her illustrious ancestors, such as her grandfather, John Smoke Johnson, a hero of the War of 1812.

Johnson originally performed only as a means of supporting her poetry, but she became one of Canada's most prominent recitalists. She was an ethereal, enigmatic love figure in her stage persona of the Indian princess, and the oral traditions gave her the status of a bard or orator. And Johnson, usually appearing in buckskin and beads, had the obvious theatrical aid of a good costume.

Johnson's poetry covers a range of subjects but focuses on the patriotic or pastoral 'Indian'. Almost all are short lyrics and narratives. Her short prose narratives often have a moral direction. Her *Legends of Vancouver* (1911) is a collection of mythic narratives as told by Chief Capilano.

Johnson's work combines genre writing, with all of its popular appeal, with substantial comments on the position of Native peoples in her society. This combination causes A. LaVonne Brown Ruoff to consider Johnson a late but typical example of the Victorian woman writer. Johnson's adventure stories, many of which are collected in *The Shagganappi* (1913), demonstrate a clear moral agenda. In their publication in *The Boy's World*, a prominent American example of 'muscular Christianity', they provide a constant recitation of the moral character of Native peoples and, in particular, their civilization, as shown particularly in 'We-hro's Sacrifice'. Johnson's stories for another periodical from the same publisher, *Mother's Magazine*, show that she grasped the didactic potential of her venue and produced material that is, as Ruoff notes, both pro-Native and feminist. Perhaps the best example is 'My Mother', which emphasizes the matriarchal elements of Mohawk society.

Johnson always possessed clear perceptions of her racial position. In his introduction to *The Shagganappi*, Ernest Thompson Seton quotes her: 'There are those who think they pay me a compliment in saying that I am just like a white woman. My aim, my joy, my pride is to sing the glories of my own people.' Another quotation by Seton shows Johnson's romantic histrionics but also her recognition of her symbolic position:

> Oh, why have our people forced on me the name of Pauline Johnson? Was not my Indian name good enough? Do you think you help us by bidding us to forget our blood? by teaching us to cast off all memory of our high ideals and our glorious past? I am an Indian. My pen and my life I devote to the memory of my own people. Forget that I was Pauline Johnson, but remember always that I was Tekahionwake, the Mohawk that humbly aspired to be the saga singer of her people, the bard of the noblest folk the world has ever seen, the sad historian of her own heroic race.

Johnson used the 'noble savage' archetype implied by the words 'saga singer' and 'bard' to argue against the racist assumption of the dying Native society, which 'sad historian' implies, and to create a space in popular literature for Native issues presented from a specifically Native perspective. This achievement has recently begun to be more recognized, as shown by the biography *Paddling Her Own Canoe: The Times and Texts of E. Pauline Johnson (Tekahionwake)* (2000) by Veronica Stong-Boag and Carole Gerson, and by the collection they edited, *E. Pauline Johnson, Tekahionwake: Collected Poems and Selected Prose* (2002).

The Cattle Thief

They were coming across the prairie, they were galloping hard and fast;
For the eyes of those desperate riders had sighted their man at last—
Sighted him off to Eastward, where the Cree encampment lay,
Where the cotton woods fringed the river, miles and miles away.
Mistake him? Never! Mistake him? the famous Eagle Chief!   5
That terror to all the settlers, that desperate Cattle Thief—
That monstrous, fearless Indian, who lorded it over the plain,
Who thieved and raided, and scouted, who rode like a hurricane!
But they've tracked him across the prairie; they've followed him hard and fast;
For those desperate English settlers have sighted their man at last.   10

Up they wheeled to the tepees, all their British blood aflame,
Bent on bullets and bloodshed, bent on bringing down their game;
But they searched in vain for the Cattle Thief: that lion had left his lair,
And they cursed like a troop of demons—for the women alone were there
'The sneaking Indian coward,' they hissed; 'he hides while yet he can;   15
He'll come in the night for cattle, but he's scared to face a *man*.'
'Never!' and up from the cotton woods rang the voice of Eagle Chief;
And right out into the open stepped, unarmed, the Cattle Thief.
Was that the game they had coveted? Scarce fifty years had rolled
Over that fleshless, hungry frame, starved to the bone and old;   20

Over that wrinkled, tawny skin, unfed by the warmth of blood.
Over those hungry, hollow eyes that glared for the sight of food.

He turned, like a hunted lion: 'I know not fear,' said he;
And the words outleapt from his shrunken lips in the language of the Cree.
'I'll fight you, white-skins, one by one, till I kill you *all*,' he said;   25
But the threat was scarcely uttered, ere a dozen balls of lead
Whizzed through the air about him like a shower of metal rain,
And the gaunt old Indian Cattle Thief dropped dead on the open plain.
And that band of cursing settlers gave one triumphant yell,
And rushed like a pack of demons on the body that writhed and fell.   30
'Cut the fiend up into inches, throw his carcass on the plain;
Let the wolves eat the cursed Indian, he'd have treated us the same.'
A dozen hands responded, a dozen knives gleamed high,
But the first stroke was arrested by a woman's strange, wild cry.
And out into the open, with a courage past belief,   35
She dashed, and spread her blanket o'er the corpse of the Cattle Thief;
And the words outleapt from her shrunken lips in the language of the Cree,
'If you mean to touch that body, you must cut your way through *me*.'
And that band of cursing settlers dropped backward one by one,
For they knew that an Indian woman roused, was a woman to let alone.   40
And then she raved in a frenzy that they scarcely understood,
Raved of the wrongs she had suffered since her earliest babyhood:
'Stand back, stand back, you white-skins, touch that dead man to your shame;
You have stolen my father's spirit, but his body I only claim.
You have killed him, but you shall not dare to touch him now he's dead.   45
You have cursed, and called him a Cattle Thief, though you robbed him first
      of bread—
Robbed him and robbed my people—look there, at that shrunken face,
Starved with a hollow hunger, we owe to you and your race.
What have you left to us of land, what have you left of game,
What have you brought but evil, and curses since you came?   50
How have you paid us for our game? how paid us for our land?
By a *book*, to save our souls from the sins *you* brought in your other hand.
Go back with your new religion, we never have understood
Your robbing an Indian's *body*, and mocking his *soul* with food.
Go back with your new religion, and find—if find you can—   55
The *honest* man you have ever made from out a *starving* man.
You say your cattle are not ours, your meat is not our meat;
When *you* pay for the land you live in, *we'll* pay for the meat we eat.
Give back our land and our country, give back our herds of game;
Give back the furs and the forests that were ours before you came;   60
Give back the peace and the plenty. Then come with your new belief,
And blame, if you dare, the hunger that *drove* him to be a thief.'

Shadow River

Muskoka

A stream of tender gladness,
Of filmy sun, and opal tinted skies;
Of warm midsummer air that lightly lies
In mystic rings,
Where softly swings   5
The music of a thousand wings
That almost tones to sadness.

Midway 'twixt earth and heaven,
A bubble in the pearly air, I seem
To float upon the sapphire floor, a dream   10
Of clouds of snow,
Above, below,
Drift with my drifting, dim and slow,
As twilight drifts to even.

The little fern-leaf, bending   15
Upon the brink, its green reflection greets,
And kisses soft the shadow that it meets
With touch so fine,
The border line
The keenest vision can't define;   20
So perfect is the blending.

The far, fir trees that cover
The brownish hills with needles green and gold,
The arching elms o'erhead, vinegrown and old,
Repictured are   25
Beneath me far,
Where not a ripple moves to mar
Shades underneath, or over.

Mine is the undertone;
The beauty, strength, and power of the land   30
Will never stir or bend at my command;
But all the shade
Is marred or made,
If I but dip my paddle blade;
And it is mine alone,   35

O! pathless world of seeming!
O! pathless life of mine whose deep ideal
Is more my own than ever was the real.
For others Fame
And Love's red flame,   40
And yellow gold; I only claim
The shadows and the dreaming.

The Corn Husker

Hard by the Indian lodges, where the bush
    Breaks in a clearing, through ill-fashioned fields,
She comes to labour, when the first still hush
    Of autumn follows large and recent yields.

Age in her fingers, hunger in her face,   5
    Her shoulders stooped with weight of work and years,
But rich in tawny colouring of her race,
    She comes a-field to strip the purple ears.

And all her thoughts are with the days gone by,
    Ere might's injustice banished from their lands   10
Her people, that to-day unheeded lie,
    Like the dead husks that rustle through her hands.

The Song My Paddle Sings

West wind, blow from your prairie nest,
Blow from the mountains, blow from the west.
The sail is idle, the sailor too;
O! wind of the west, we wait for you.
Blow, blow!   5
I have wooed you so,
But never a favour you bestow.
You rock your cradle the hills between,
But scorn to notice my white lateen.

I stow the sail, unship the mast: 10
I wooed you long but my wooing's past;

My paddle will lull you into rest.
O! drowsy wind of the drowsy west,
Sleep, sleep,
By your mountain steep,   15
Or down where the prairie grasses sweep!
Now fold in slumber your laggard wings,
For soft is the song my paddle sings.

August is laughing across the sky,
Laughing while paddle, canoe and I,   20
Drift, drift,
Where the hills uplift
On either side of the current swift.

The river rolls in its rocky bed;
My paddle is plying its way ahead;   25
Dip, dip,
While the waters flip
In foam as over their breast we slip.

And oh, the river runs swifter now;
The eddies circle about my bow.   30
Swirl, swirl!
How the ripples curl
In many a dangerous pool awhirl!

And forward far the rapids roar,
Fretting their margin for evermore.   35
Dash, dash,
With a mighty crash,
They seethe, and boil, and bound, and splash.

Be strong, O paddle! be brave, canoe!
The reckless waves you must plunge into.   40
Reel, reel,
On your trembling keel,
But never a fear my craft will feel.

We've raced the rapid, we're far ahead!
The river slips through its silent bed.   45
Sway, sway,
As the bubbles spray
And fall in tinkling tunes away.

And up on the hills against the sky,
A fir tree rocking its lullaby,   50
Swings, swings,
Its emerald wings,
Swelling the song that my paddle sings.

We-hro's Sacrifice

We-hro was a small Onondaga Indian boy, a good-looking, black-eyed little chap with as pagan a heart as ever beat under a copper-coloured skin. His father and grandfathers were pagans. His ancestors for a thousand years back, and yet a thousand years back of that, had been pagans, and We-hro, with the pride of his religion and his race, would not have turned from the faith of his fathers for all the world. But the world, as he knew it, consisted entirely of the Great Indian Reserve, that lay on the banks of the beautiful Grand River, sixty miles west of the great Canadian city of Toronto.

Now, the boys that read this tale must not confuse a pagan with a heathen. The heathen nations that worship idols are terribly pitied and despised by the pagan Indians, who are worshippers of 'The Great Spirit', a kind and loving God, who, they say, will reward them by giving them happy hunting grounds to live in after they die; that is, if they live good, honest, upright lives in this world.

We-hro would have scowled blackly if anyone had dared to name him a heathen. He thoroughly ignored the little Delaware boys, whose fathers worshipped idols fifty years ago, and on all the feast days and dance days he would accompany his parents to the 'Longhouse' (which was their church), and take his little part in the religious festivities. He could remember well as a tiny child being carried in his mother's blanket 'pick-a-back', while she dropped into the soft swinging movement of the dance, for We-hro's people did not worship their 'Great Spirit' with hymns of praise and lowly prayers, the way the Christian Indians did. We-hro's people worshipped their God by dancing beautiful, soft, dignified steps, with no noisy clicking heels to annoy one, but only the velvety shuffle of the moccasined feet, the weird beat of the Indian drums, the mournful chanting of the old chiefs, keeping time with the throb of their devoted hearts.

Then, when he grew too big to be carried, he was allowed to clasp his mother's hand, and himself learn the pretty steps, following his father, who danced ahead, dressed in full costume of scarlet cloth and buckskin, with gay beads and bear claws about his neck, and wonderful carven silver ornaments, massive and solid, decorating his shirt and leggings. We-hro loved the tawny fringes and the hammered silver quite as much as a white lady loves diamonds and pearls; he loved to see his father's face painted in fierce reds, yellows, and blacks, but most of all he loved the unvarying *chuck-a, chuck-a, chuck-a* of the great mud-turtle rattles that the 'musicians' skilfully beat upon the benches before them. Oh, he was a thorough little pagan, was We-hro! His loves and his hates were as decided as his comical but stately step in the dance of his ancestors' religion. Those were great days for the small Onondaga boy. His father taught him to shape axe-handles, to curve lacrosse sticks, to weave their deer-sinew netting, to tan skins, to plant corn, to model arrows, and—most difficult of all—to 'feather' them, to 'season' bows, to chop trees, to burn, hollow, fashion, and 'man' a dugout canoe, to use the paddle, to gauge the wind and current of that treacherous Grand River, to learn wild cries to decoy bird and beast for food. Oh, little pagan We-hro had his life filled to overflowing with much that the civilized white boy would give all his dimes and dollars to know.

And it was then that the great day came, the marvellous day when We-hro discovered his *second self,* his playmate, his loyal, unselfish, loving friend—his underbred, unwashed, hungry, vagabond dog, born white and spotless, but begrimed by contact with the world, the mud, and the white man's hovel.

It happened this way:

We-hro was cleaning his father's dugout canoe, after a night of fish spearing. The soot, the scales, the fire ashes, the mud—all had to be 'swabbed' out at the river's brink by means of much water and an Indian 'slat' broom. We-hro was up to his little ears in work, when suddenly, above him, on the river road, he heard the coarse voice and thundering whipfalls of a man urging and beating his horse—a white man, for no Indian used such language, no Indian beat an animal that served him. We-hro looked up. Stuck in the mud of the river road was a huge wagon, grain-filled. The driver, purple of face, was whaling the poor team, and shouting to a cringing little drab-white dog, of fox-terrier lineage, to 'Get out of there or I'll—!'

The horses were dragging and tugging. The little dog, terrified, was sneaking off with tail between its hind legs. Then the brutal driver's whip came down, curling its lash about the dog's thin body, forcing from the little speechless brute a howl of agony. Then We-hro spoke—spoke in all the English he knew.

'Bad! Bad! You die some day—you! You hurt that dog. White man's God, he no like you. Indian's Great Spirit, he not let you shoot in happy hunting grounds. You die some day—you *bad!*

'Well, if I *am* bad I'm no pagan Indian Hottentot like you!' yelled the angry driver. 'Take the dog, and begone!'

'Me no Hottentot,' said We-hro, slowly. 'Me Onondaga, all right. Me take dog'; and from that hour the poor little white cur and the copper-coloured little boy were friends for all time.

The Superintendent of Indian Affairs was taking his periodical drive about the Reserve when he chanced to meet old 'Ten-Canoes', We-hro's father.

The superintendent was a very important person. He was a great white gentleman, who lived in the city of Brantford, fifteen miles away. He was a kindly, handsome man, who loved and honoured every Indian on the Grand River Reserve. He had a genial smile, a warm hand-shake, so when he stopped his horse and greeted the old pagan, Ten-Canoes smiled too.

'Ah, Ten-Canoes!' cried the superintendent, 'a great man told me he was coming to see your people—a big man, none less than Great Black-Coat, the bishop of the

Anglican Church. He thinks you are a bad lot, because you are pagans; he wonders why it is that you have never turned Christian. Some of the missionaries have told him you pagans are no good, so the great man wants to come and see for himself. He wants to see some of your religious dances—the "Dance of the White Dog", if you will have him; he wants to see if it is really *bad*.'

Ten-Canoes laughed. 'I welcome him,' he said, earnestly, 'Welcome the "Great Black-Coat". I honour him, though I do not think as he does. He is a good man, a just man; I welcome him, bid him come.'

Thus was his lordship, the Bishop, invited to see the great pagan Onondaga 'Festival of the White Dog'.

But what was *this* that happened?

Never yet had a February moon waned but that the powerful Onondaga tribe had offered the burnt 'Sacrifice of the White Dog', that most devout of all native rites. But now, search as they might, not a single spotlessly white dog could be found. No other animal would do. It was the law of this great Indian tribe that no other burnt sacrifice could possibly be offered than the strangled body of a white dog.

We-hro heard all the great chiefs talking of it all. He listened to plans for searching the entire Reserve for a dog, and the following morning he arose at dawn, took his own pet dog down to the river and washed him as he had seen white men wash their sheep. Then out of the water dashed the gay little animal, yelping and barking in play, rolling in the snow, tearing madly about, and finally rushing off towards the log house which was We-hro's home, and scratching at the door to get in by the warm fire to dry his shaggy coat. Oh! What an ache that coat caused in We-hro's heart. From a dull drab grey, the dog's hair had washed pure white, not a spot or a blemish on it, and in an agony of grief the little pagan boy realized that through his own action he had endangered the life of his dog friend; that should his father and his father's friends see that small white terrier, they would take it away for the nation's sacrifice.

Stumbling and panting and breathless, We-hro hurried after his pet, and seizing the dog in his arms, he wrapped his own shabby coat about the trembling, half-dry creature, and carried him to where the cedars grew thick at the back of the house. Crouched in their shadows he hugged his treasured companion, thinking with horror of the hour when the blow would surely fall.

For days the boy kept his dog in the shelter of the cedars, tied up tightly with an old rope, and sleeping in a warm raccoon skin, which We-hro smuggled away from his own simple bed. The dog contented himself with what little food We-hro managed to carry to him, but the hiding could not keep up forever, and one dark, dreaded day We-hro's father came into the house and sat smoking in silence for many minutes. When at last he spoke, he said:

'We-hro, your dog is known to me. I have seen him, white as the snow that fell last night. It is the law that someone must always suffer for the good of the people. We-hro, would you have the great "Black-Coat", the great white preacher, come to see our beautiful ceremony, and would you have the great Onondaga tribe fail to show the white man how we worship our ancient Great Spirit? Would you have us fail to burn the sacrifice? Or will you give your white dog for the honour of our people?'

The world is full of heroes, but at that moment it held none greater than the little pagan boy, who crushed down his grief and battled back his tears as he answered:

'Father, you are old and honoured and wise. For you and for my people alone would I give the dog.'

At last the wonderful Dance Day arrived. His lordship, the Bishop of the Anglican Church, drove down from the city of Brantford; with him the Superintendent of Indian Affairs, and a man who understood both the English and the Onondaga languages. Long before they reached the 'Longhouse' they could hear the wild beat of the drum, could count the beats of the dance rattles, could distinguish the half-sad chant of the worshippers. The kind face of the great bishop was very grave. It pained his gentle old heart to know that this great tribe of Indians were pagans—savages, as he thought—but when he entered that plain log building that the Onondagas held as their church, he took off his hat with the beautiful reverence all great men pay to other great men's religion, and he stood bareheaded while old Ten-Canoes chanted forth this speech:

'Oh, brothers of mine! We welcome the white man's friend, the great "Black-Coat", to this, our solemn worship. We offer to the red man's God—the Great Spirit—a burnt offering. We do not think that anything save what is pure and faithful and without blemish can go into the sight of the Great Spirit. Therefore do we offer this dog, pure as we hope our spirits are, that the God of the red man may accept it with our devotion, knowing that we, too, would gladly be as spotless as this sacrifice.'

Then was a dog carried in dead, and beautifully decorated with wampum, beads, and porcupine embroidery. Oh! so mercifully dead and out of pain, gently strangled by reverent fingers, for an Indian is never unkind to an animal. And far over in a corner of the room was a little brown figure, twisted with agony, choking back the sobs and tears—for was he not taught that tears were for babies alone, and not for boys that grew up into warriors?

'Oh, my dog! my dog!' he muttered. 'They have taken you away from me, but it was for the honour of my father and of my own people.'

The great Anglican bishop turned at that moment, and, catching the sight of suffering on little We-hro's face, said aloud to the man who spoke both languages:

'That little boy over there seems in torture. Can I do anything for him, do you think?'

'That little boy,' replied the man who spoke both languages, 'is the son of the great Onondaga chief. No white dog could be found for this ceremony but his. This dog was his pet, but for the honour of his father and of his tribe he has given up his pet as a sacrifice.'

For a moment the great Anglican bishop was blinded by his own tears. Then he walked slowly across the wide log building and laid his white hand tenderly on the head of the little Onondaga boy. His kindly old eyes closed, and his lips moved—noiselessly, for a space, then he said aloud:

'Oh, that the white boys of my great city church knew and practised half as much of self-denial as has this little pagan Indian lad, who has given up his heart's dearest because his father and the honour of his people required it.'

John Brant-Sero 1867–1914

MOHAWK

John Brant-Sero, Ojijatekha ('Burning Flower'), was born on the Six Nations Reserve in Ontario, his mother a descendant of Joseph Brant, his father a Bay of Quinte Mohawk, the two great traditions of the Mohawk Loyalist heritage. He went to the reserve school and to the Mohawk Institute, where he studied carpentry, before eventually taking a business course.

Among Brant-Sero's various occupations, he was translator to the curator of the Archaeological Museum in Toronto. His history, however, suggests his vocation was as an actor and recitalist. He toured in North America and Europe, following the path later pursued more notably by Pauline Johnson. A promotional brochure depicts him in a suit, his hair flowing, under the caption: 'The only Canadian Mohawk Indian now before the English public

in a Concert & Lecture Tour'. Most of Brant-Sero's extant material suggests his role as second vice-president of the Ontario Historical Society. Such prominent journals as *Man* and the *Journal of American Folklore* record his comments on specific points of Native history.

The following selection is representative of Brant-Sero, with its apparent 'humility' that still asserts his importance as a cultural figure, the representative Native Loyalist, and, as this piece suggests, the political descendant of Joseph Brant. The imperial tone to his record of his South African experience, as well as the significant absence of concern for either the Boers or the Native peoples of South Africa, seems relevant here. Brant-Sero's comments show concern for inequities in the treatment of Native peoples, but his focus is never far from himself.

Letter

Sir, will you allow me space in your columns, as a humble Canadian Mohawk Indian, hailing from the Six Nations Reserve, Brant county, Ontario? I have just returned from South Africa, disappointed in many respects, but I do not wish these lines to be understood as a grievance. I went to that country from Canada hoping that I might be allowed to enlist in one of the mounted rifles; however, not being a man of European descent, I was refused to do active service in Her Majesty's cause as did my forefathers in Canada.

Reaching South Africa about the middle of August, I attempted to join, as a Canadian, at East London, in Kitchener's Horse, Roberts' Horse, Driscol scouts, and at Queenstown the Cape mounted rifles, the Orange River Colony police, and again Driscol scouts. Here one young Englishman resigned his position to make way for me, but it was hopeless, my credentials were never questioned, I easily satisfied the officer where I came from; that was the trouble. I was too genuine a Canadian. One medical officer who examined me pronounced me unfit; on my questioning him the nature of my unfitness he simply remarked, very good-naturedly, 'There is nothing serious; don't you worry.' After all my failures to handle the rifle, I managed to secure employment at the Queenstown remount depot No. 4. My duties consisted in taking animals up to the front and bossing the Kaffirs. I was on the civilian staff. I have had my share of tent life, army rations, and dodging sand storms during my stay at the seat of war. At various times I visited Springfontein, Bloemfontein, Aliwai North, Colesberg, Stormberg, De Aar, and Bethulie. On one occasion the Boers were considerate enough to let me sneak past Bethulie bridge with 200 entrained mules before they blew up the rails. However, it was not their fault; the circumstance was purely accidental.

At Springfontein, just after the siege of Philippolis, a Boer, a sentry, captured me as I had to get my Kaffirs to identify me. Shortly after that, seeing it was useless remaining in the country, I resigned, and, armed with my honourable discharge, I proceeded to Cape Town, where, upon my arrival, I again made attempts to join a mounted corps, and met the same refusals. . . .

The history of the Mohawk and others of the Six Nations Confederacy residing in Canada is well known in Canada, in fact, a history of Canada cannot be written impartially without recounting the warlike deeds of the Six Nations. We believe we have an interest in the empire, bought by the blood of our ancestors. The name of Captain Joseph Brant (Thayandanegea) is imprinted upon the mind of every student and traveller. It was under his banner the Mohawks left their once beautiful homes in the Mohawk Valley, New York State, trekking northward to Grand River and the Bay of Juriste [Quinte], where they might enjoy a comfortable retreat safe to follow the customs of their forefathers. Here for over a century they have lived, cultivating their farms and their progress is the pride of all true Canadians. They are not degenerating, neither are they decreasing, but upon the other hand, in common with the Indian population of Canada they are rapidly increasing in numbers. There is scarcely a calling, trade, or profession in which these Indians are not represented. In social life, politics, and literature we occupy no small place.

J.O. Brant-Sero
8 Dartmouth Street, Westminster, S.W.
Dec. 30

Mary Augusta Tappage 1888–c. 1978

SHUSWAP

Mary Augusta Tappage, known to her community as Augusta, was born at Soda Creek in British Columbia's Cariboo country, 11 February 1888. Her background was Shuswap and Métis. At the age of four, she was sent to a Catholic mission school near Williams Lake. Her memories of that period are typical of students from residential schools:

> If we were heard speaking Shuswap, we were punished. We were made to write on the board one hundred times, 'I will not speak Indian any more.' . . . And now we are supposed to remember our language and our skills because they are almost lost. Well, they're going to be hard to get back because the new generations are not that interested.

Augusta left school at thirteen and returned to the reservation at Soda Creek. In 1903 she married George Evans, a non-status Shuswap, and so she lost her own Indian status. Augusta's working life was spent homesteading and subsistence farming on Deep Creek, near her birthplace. The education of her sons reflects her non-status position:

> My two boys, Joseph and George, they never went to school. Taxpayers' children couldn't go to the Mission. Well, I didn't care about that. But there was no other school close by, so I taught them myself. Yes, I guess they can read and reckon as good as most folk can. I taught them myself.

After the deaths of her husband and eldest son, Augusta worked cooking and cleaning for various families. She acted as informal foster mother to many young people. Like many other Native people of her generation, Augusta committed great energy to cultural education, to keep Shuswap, which is not a written language, alive.

Tyee—Big Chief

Tyee Lake was called after big chief—it means big chief.
But *Tyee* is not Shuswap.
It's Chinook, I think.
But it's not my language.

Pashish'kwa—that means lake in my language.   5
Shadad'kwa—that means river.

I can't tell you how to spell it.
But that's how we say it.
It's a hard language, Shuswap—real hard.

When I got out of Mission school   10
I had to ask what the Indians were saying.
I couldn't understand them.
We were only allowed to speak English at school.
I almost forgot my own language.
It's Shuswap, my language.   15

The Lillooets

That was a big cloud of dust 'way down
to the south in the spring, yes.
It was the Lillooet Indians coming north,
coming north to the goldfields
up by Barkerville.   5

They go north into that country to work,
to work all the time, hard,
horses and wagons, women and children,
and dogs, hiyu dogs, all going
up by Barkerville.   10

They work from the time they get there
till fall, till the leaves drop, yes,
and the snow comes and it freezes
the lakes and the creeks
up by Barkerville.   15

It was the Lillooets going by in the spring
with packing horses, packing freight, yes,
into the mines somewhere in the mountains
and into the creeks
up by Barkerville.   20

All from Lillooet and I see them passing,
They are passing and passing and, no,
I couldn't ask them where they go—
they speak a different language,
but they go up by Barkerville.   25

We speak Shuswap, all of us Shuswap—
Soda Creek, Sugar Cane, Alkali, Canoe Creek,
Dog Creek, Canim Lake—all speak Shuswap,
except the Lillooets who go
up by Barkerville.   30

They come back in the fall, these Lillooets,
tired, I guess, but lots of money, lots of fish,
not minding snow or mud. They laugh
thinking of summer, yes,
up by Barkerville.   35

Christmas at the Mission

I remember Christmas at the Mission.
Always we used to have midnight mass.

But we didn't know about Christmas and holidays
Until the Sisters came.
The Sisters came from France, you know,   5
And they brought Christmas with them.

They were the Sisters of Infant Jesus,
Those who came.

The teachers who had been teaching us before,
They didn't bother or care   10
Or hold Christmas. When the Sisters came
Was when we first knew Christmas!

The Sisters made us a Christmas concert, taught us
To sing hymns and songs,
Say recitations to everybody, helped us   15
Decorate our first Christmas tree.

I can't tell you how beautiful that first Christmas tree!
Everything was changed!

And our shoe, our right shoe, had to be polished
And put up on a bench   20
On Christmas Eve for holding candies, yes,
And whatever present you were going to get.

And then we all went to chapel through the snow
That first Christmas for midnight mass.

At Birth

I used to help at times of birth, yes,
I used to help all the women around here.
I learned it from my book, my blue doctor's book.
I used to read it all the time.

I made up my mind that if she needs help,   5
I will help her. I'm not scared.
You've got to be awfully quick. There's two lives there.
The baby and the mother.

Yes, two lives, and what you got to do it with
Those days? You've got to be quick   10
To cut the cord, keep the bed clean, take out
The afterbirth, discard it, burn it.

Yes, you've got to be quick, fix the baby,
Tie its navel so it will not bleed
To death—cut it about that long.   15
When it heals there's nothing left, you know.

Then you bandage the mother, pin her up,
Keep her clean, keep her in bed ten days.
The doctor told us this—but if I leave,
I guess she got up.   20

I never had to spank a baby
To make him cry—they always cried.
They were always alive and healthy.
Yes, mother and baby, alive and healthy.

Martin Martin 1889–1976

INUIT

Martin Martin, born at Oka, Labrador, is part of a very specific environment. The Labrador coast has been used by whites as fishing grounds for centuries. A few remained on the shore to become known as 'settlers'. The population has remained small, and devoted to its own traditional ways—trapping and fishing— thus giving rise to the Canadian anomaly of a longstanding, isolated, subsistence-based white population.

As a result, there has been intermarriage and a general intermingling between Inuit, white, and Innu and Naskapi for a long time. Although the identities of the cultures have remained separate, and although there has been significant racial tension at times, there has also been an acceptance of the rights of tenure of all these populations, often stated in opposition to newcomers, and specifically to Newfoundlanders and Québécois.

The following reminiscences are taken from the Labrador magazine *Them Days*, which contains a multitude of personal-experience narratives from all of the cultures. In its accounts of mixed-race lives from this unusual 'melting pot', it provides insights unseen in the records of other Canadian areas. And like various magazines and newspapers that represent other First Nations, it also shows the 'literary' responses from Native cultures at a time when there was no literary culture that included them.

We, the Inuit, Are Changing

Translated by William Kalleo

We, the Inuit here in Labrador, right to this day still have the traditional ways of our forefathers. Right to this day we eat what our forefathers used to eat, food with no price tags on it, food created for us ever since the earth was created. People have different foods according to their land. This I was not aware of in the past. Some eat only what is grown in gardens, others eat whatever food they can get their hands on and we the Inuit people, have a different diet because we are people of a cold land. Because we are people of a cold land, wildlife is our main diet. Our forefathers were strong because nothing was scarce, everything was plentiful in those past years. We, the younger generation, think we are hungry but we are not because there is plenty of the white man's foods available for us to obtain at any time. We only are hungry for wildlife meat because some years are plentiful and some years there is none at all. This I have found.

Our forefathers' ancestors, which we have just heard of but not seen, taught our fathers how to share any kill made amongst their people. So my father taught me to share my kill as it was the traditional way. When I was a young man every time I went hunting and came back successful I invited the poor, the less fortunate, and the old Inuit to share my kill. After they had eaten they would joke around and tell stories of the past. When I heard these happy people I was aware that this was a blessing. I had made my fellow people happy through sharing. Our Creator had blessed me and I had carried on this blessing by sharing because this was meant to be. It is sad how this tradition is being forgotten. Young people now keep their kill to themselves. Some will give a little to those they wish to share with. I have said what I have seen and experienced and I am aware that this tradition is no longer practised. I hope this will be written down so that our children can be made aware of what used to take place in past years.

We have not lost all our traditions and culture yet. We have not lost our ability to hunt wildlife game. We know how to locate and hunt the game. Our young men still try to hunt in the traditional ways but they have difficulties because there is less game now. But our young Inuit have not given up trying their best to hunt for wildlife food. This we will never lose as long as there are Inuit in Labrador.

I am one hundred per cent pure Eskimo. I was never educated in the white society way because when I was a child this was not practised. Our school term lasted only six months and our main subject was studying the word of God. We had to memorize Bible verses and speak them out from memory while our teachers listened. The only time we were given a new verse was when we mastered the one before. Because of this teaching we, the elderly Inuit, can still speak out by heart many verses of the Bible, at least I always could. I don't know of my fellow elders but I'm sure they too can speak out what they memorized as children. In this generation our children have almost a whole year to learn and study but they are learning only the white society way. No wonder they have a better knowledge than we, the elderly. I am not happy that they are only being taught the white society system. I would be happy if they were taught first the word of God, then how to deal with life. I say this because I think our children don't know the true meaning of life because they refuse to hear the word of God, or are encouraged to do so. Our Inuit children are taught, I suppose, how to survive in white communities but not in the Inuit land. When learning the white society way was first introduced, or enforced, as a way of teaching our Inuit children, I strongly objected because I foresaw that in the future they would forget our Inuit language and also the word of God. I have said this because it is what I have wanted to say for ever so long. I was involved when teaching our children in the white society way was forced on us. I was out-voted when I suggested that our children be taught the word of God first and other subjects after. I had no power to alter what was being forced on our children, my objections were not considered important. Now, what I tried to bring to attention, about our children losing their traditions and culture, is beginning to be realized by Inuit in different parts of Canada. All I have said is true. Our young Inuit have a complete new way of living and if it is let to continue, something will happen to show them they are leading a dangerous life.

In such a short time we, the Inuit of Labrador, have changed in many ways. We do not carry on many of our traditions. We are forced into many new ways which we do not even understand. Also in these days we have seen Inuit from other regions, those we had only heard about but we did not know if they had traditions and cultures which were similar to ours. Now, we see them in the flesh and see that our fellow Inuit share our traditions and culture.

Last March, when I reached the age of eighty-seven, I started to think that I had lived too long. Then another thought occurred to me, why am I still living when I am no longer able to live off the land and sea? Why am I still wandering among my fellow Inuit and being observed and told that I am no longer useful to my people? I thought once more, the Lord God has been merciful to me to this day because although I am an old man I still have a mouth which can give guidance to our younger Inuit. The years have taken their toll on me, on my hearing, my sight, and my ability to walk long distances. All are no longer good and I know why this is so. When I was a young man we used to hunt caribou in the different seasons. One spring we were returning from the land when the river trails were starting to get water on the ice. Early one morning, before the sun rose, we slid from the top of the country down to a lake. The river trail had frozen over during the night and so it was usable but as the sun rose the ice melted and we began to break through into the water. When our komatiks fell through we went over knee deep in the icy water to push and pull them out. We carried on all through the day, wading, pushing, and pulling our heavily laden komatiks. My legs became so numb that I could feel nothing. Ever since that time my legs are no longer good.

I wish you peace on earth. We may never see each other on earth but through God's will we will see each other in Heaven when we are removed from the earth. So, let us look forward to meeting each other where there will be no pain or sorrow but happiness and eternal life. I am an old man now. My name is Martin Martin. I wish all a happy and successful life.

Alma Greene 1896–1984

MOHAWK

Alma Greene, Gah-wonh-nos-doh ('Forbidden Voice'), was a Mohawk of the Turtle clan, a clan mother and a medicine woman who championed Longhouse traditions. She lived on the Grand River Lands of the Six Nations all her life.

I dreamed once that I went to the door of a longhouse here on the reserve. It was not, of course, the Mohawk longhouse, thanks to Joseph Brant. But it was one of the others where the Indians hold their own ceremonies.

When I got there the door would not open. I tried again and again, but it seemed as though something was pushing against it, holding it closed.

So I went around to the side, to a window, and looked in. There was the faithkeeper, crouched in horror in a corner. And the rest of the longhouse was filled with a serpent, as big around as a seven-inch pipe, lying from one end of the room to the other.

That's one dream I think has already come true.

From 'A New Clan Mother',
Forbidden Voice

From *Forbidden Voice: Reflections of a Mohawk Indian*

Everything was starting to change.

Both Forbidden Voice's big brothers were married now, and the older one had taken over the farm. The younger one had always preferred his paycheck to the life of a farmer, so his father had settled him in a house on a lot elsewhere on the reservation and the son went off to work every day. Forbidden Voice's big sister had gone to the city. People shook their heads when they talked about her.

Even Sundays were different now. Sunday had always been a special day in their house, Sunday was extra good meals, Sunday was put away all your work, even the doll's clothes you had been sewing. Sunday was visitors, Methodist church in the morning, and the Anglican church in the afternoon, and in the evening the whole family into the parlour for father to read from the Bible that sat on the fall-leaf table with the red cloth.

Her father was a lay reader in the Anglican church, and the first English Forbidden Voice had ever heard was her father reading the Bible on Sundays. For a long time the reading was just a monotone to her. She couldn't make out any of the words and the tiresome noise seemed to go on and on forever. It wasn't at all like the liquid Mohawk tongue, or even the jerky syllables of the Cayugas. Later, when she heard white men speak it, English was always to sound loud and quarrelsome in her ear.

Now her father had left the church and, though she asked him, he wouldn't say why. One day she mentioned this to an old chief who knew about affairs on the reserve, and he said he could tell her why. He took her to his house and there he showed her a document, which was a copy of the Exchequer Court proceedings between the Six Nations and the New England Company.

The New England Company was a curious organization that had been formed in the seventeenth century for the express purpose of 'civilizing' the North American natives and propagating the gospel. The company had sent missionaries to the Grand Valley in the 1820s and they had built a school for the Mohawks that later came to be known as the Mohawk Institute. Now it seemed that these 'Christians' had sold the land they had got from the Indians, which to Forbidden Voice was the same as stealing it.

Forbidden Voice knew that many of her people believed the Christian missionaries had no right to try to make Indians change their own religion and way of worship. Didn't it say in the Bible, at the very beginning of Genesis, 'And God said, "Let us make man in Our own image, after Our likeness, and let them have dominion over the fish of the sea and over the fowl of the air". So God created men in His own image, in the image of God created He him male and female created He them'?

And wasn't it only later, in Chapter Five of Genesis, that God created Adam and Eve to inhabit the Garden of Eden in the old world? Surely this meant that Adam and Eve were created to inhabit a specific place in the old world and that the Indians were the original man-beings created in the new world, with the eternal right to hunt and fish for their food?

Hadn't Christ told his apostles when he sent them to teach and baptize in the old world, 'I have other sheep which are not of this fold; them I will gather in'? Surely this meant the Indians were Christ's special charges, and that all the popes and kings and bishops of the old world had no authority to interfere.

Forbidden Voice had seen with her very own eyes evidence that the Creator kept an eye on his special children. A tornado had swept through one summer causing death and destruction in its path. When it had started to get very dark on the reserve, and they could see the funnel-shaped cloud coming from the west, all the families had been called together. As they watched, the funnel cloud lifted high aloft and passed over their heads. When it had gone past Indian territory, they could see it come to earth again and go on its angry way. Didn't this mean the Creator was not displeased with the red men?

Her mother had taught her a prayer in Mohawk to repeat every night before she went to bed. All it said was 'God the Father, God the Son, God the Holy Ghost; Creator of the sun, the moon, the stars, and the earth. Amen.' Its form was Christian, but she thought about it now and its spirit seemed to her more like a true Mohawk prayer. It was like the six annual festivals held at the other longhouses on the reserve. (The Mohawks were supposed to be Christians so their own longhouse had been destroyed.) The festivals were held according to the moon and their purpose was to thank the Creator for the seasons and for the ripening of each crop as it came on. This was her people's ancient religion, and it began to seem to her the purest way of worship. Wasn't it better than always asking the Creator to do something or to give something more than He already had?

Yet, even though the Indians worshipped the Creator in constant gratitude and remembrance, and were His charges, and practised the stern morality of Handsome Lake, the white men called them heathens.

There was another thing. Forbidden Voice could read very well now, and one day among the Six Nations' records she came across a document. It was a letter containing a list and a speech. It seemed there had been a pledge to the Iroquois just before the American War of Independence that any of the Iroquois who remained loyal to England in her war would at the close of the war receive the protection of Britain. When the war was over, it had been required of her forefathers to prove in any way they could that they had fought for England's cause, and this is what they had sent.

January 3, 1782

May it please your Excellency:

I send herewith to your Excellency under the care of James Boyd, eight pecks of scalps, cured, dried, hooped, and painted with all the Indian triumphal marks of which the following is invoice and explanation.

No. 1—Containing 43 scalps of Congress soldiers killed in different skirmishes. These are stretched on black hoops, four-inch diameter, the inside of the skin painted red with a small black spot to note their being killed with bullets. Also, 62 of farmers, killed in their homes, the hoops red, the skin painted brown and marked with a hoe, a black circle all around to denote their being surprised in the night and a black hatchet in the middle signifying their being killed with that weapon.

No. 2—Containing 98 of farmers, killed in their homes, hoops red, figure of a hoe to mark their profession, great white circle and sun to show they were surprised in the daytime, a little red foot to show they stood upon their defence and died fighting for their lives and families.

No. 3—Containing 97 of farmers, hoops green to show they were killed in their fields, a large white circle with a little round mark on it for the sun to show that it was in the daytime, black bullet marks on some, hatchets on others.

No. 4—Containing 102 of farmers, mixed of the several marks above, only 18 marked with a little yellow flame to denote their being of prisoners burned alive after being scalped, their nails pulled out by the roots and other torments, one of these latter supposed to be of a rebel clergyman, his band being fixed to the hoop of his scalp. Most of the farmers appear by the hair to have been young or middle-aged men, there being but 67 very grey heads among them, which makes the service more essential.

No. 5—Containing 88 scalps of women, hair long, braided in the Indian fashion to show they were mothers, hoops blue, skin yellow ground with little red tadpoles to represent by way of triumph, the tears of grief occasioned to their relations, a black scalping knife or hatchet at the bottom to mark their being killed, with these instruments; 17 others hair very grey, black hoops, plain brown colour, no mark but the short club to show they were knocked down dead or had their brains beat out.

No. 6—Containing 103 boys' scalps of various ages, small green hoops, whitish ground on the skin, red tears in the middle and black bullet mark, knife, hatchet, or club as their deaths happened.

No. 7—211 girls' scalps, big and little, small yellow hoops, white ground, tears, hatchet, club, scalping knife, etc.

No. 8—This package is a mixture of all the varieties above mentioned to the number of 122 with a box of birch-bark containing 29 little infants' scalps of various sizes, small white hoops.

With these packs, the chiefs send to your Excellency the following speech:

Your Excellency's most obedient and humble servant,

Signed James Crawford.

SPEECH

'Father, we send you herewith many scalps that you may see that we are not idle friends.

'Father, we wish to send these scalps over the water to the Great King that he may regard them and be refreshed and that he may see our faithfulness in destroying his enemies and be convinced that his presents have not been made to ungrateful people.

'Father, attend to what I am now going to say, it is a matter of much weight. The Great King's enemies are many and they grow fast in numbers. They were formerly like young panthers, they could neither bite nor scratch. We could play with them safely, we feared nothing they could do to us but now their bodies are become as big as the elk and strong as the buffalo. They also have got great and sharp claws, they have driven us out of our country by taking part in your quarrel. We expect the Great King will give us another country that our children may live after us and be his friends and children as we are. Say this for me to the Great King.

'Father, we have only to say further that your traders exact more than ever for their goods and our hunting is lessened by the war, so that we have fewer skins to give them. This ruins us. Think of some remedy.

'We are poor and you have plenty of everything. We know you will send us powder and guns and knives and hatchets, but we also want shirts and blankets.' I do not doubt that your Excellency will think it proper to give some further encouragement to those honest people. The high prices they complain of are the necessary effect of the war. Whatever presents may be sent for them through my hands shall be distributed with prudence and fidelity.

> I have the honour of being
> Your Excellency's most obedient and most
> humble servant.
> James Crawford'

It was after sending this proof that the Six Nations had been given the lands in the Grand River Valley and had moved there from the United States and had rekindled their Great Council Fire in their new home. But the treaty of pledge, which had been executed on April 7, 1779, had promised the Six Nations not just land to replace what they had lost but the same status as before the war, which meant the right to be an independent nation; to be allies of the English, not British subjects; to be brothers of the sovereign with their own equal sovereignty.

And now what had happened? Their lands had been sold or stolen; the Canadian government treated them as silly children for whom it was quite all right to make laws without consultation; and the white men called them heathens.

Now there were even mutterings among some on the reserve that the Six Nations should abandon the ancient hereditary council of chieftains and have a white man's kind of elected government.

Forbidden Voice wondered what it would have been like for the Mohawks if there had never been a Captain Joseph Brant, though everyone seemed to think of him as an illustrious warrior and remembered him for saying in the English court, 'I bend my knee for no man.' For Brant, who was not even a chief but just a Mohawk warrior, was the one who had got the Six Nations mixed up with the white man and who had helped talk the Six Nations into fighting for England. And he was the one who had been so eager to see the Mohawks become Christians that he had destroyed their longhouse.

Though Forbidden Voice's father no longer went to the Christian church, the rest of the family did, and it was their strong custom at Easter to come back from wherever they might be to go to their own church.

This was why Forbidden Voice's sister came home from Brantford that Easter. She had come with her cousin and when her mother asked her why her husband did not come, she did not answer right away.

But after they had come back from the service and had dinner, the sister told her parents that her husband had been staying out almost every night all winter. She had found out from the place where he worked that he had been seeing a married woman. She had not talked to him about this because he never wanted to talk when he came home.

He had been out all the night before and had come in only as she was getting ready to leave for the trip to her parents' home. She had asked him to come with her to church, but he got very angry and said the devil himself could not make him go to church.

She returned to Brantford the same night. Afterwards Forbidden Voice was told that just as her sister reached home, a policeman stopped her and told her that if she wanted to see her husband alive she must go at once to the hospital. She had no money left to take a cab, so she walked. When she got there, they let her go in at once to see her husband. She hardly recognized him, his face was so disfigured. The doctor said he was dying, but he did not tell her what had happened. No one told her. They just gave her his blood-soaked suit to take home. She walked back all the way from the hospital, carrying the suit, and by the time she reached home she herself was soaked with his blood.

Her husband died that night. Afterwards another policeman told her that while she was gone for Easter, her husband and his brother had got into an argument over a girl. They were both big men and under the influence of liquor, and the older brother had thrown her husband down and jumped on his face and head and that was how he had died.

His body was released to a local undertaker directly from the hospital. But after the funeral the pallbearers, who were friends of his, began to wonder. The husband had been a tall man, while the coffin they had been given to carry was short and light.

Finally the widow and the man's father got an order to have the grave dug up. With some friends they went that night carrying lanterns, spades, and shovels. They started to dig. All was silent but the noise of the shovels. When the coffin was opened the widow and the father moved closer. There was a gasp. The body in the coffin had no shroud to cover it. And it had no head. No one else could identify it, so the widow said her husband had had a birthmark on his chest that she would recognize. They let her look. Hardly above a whisper she said it was the body of her husband.

The white man's world was beginning to intrude on Forbidden Voice's life. Some of it, like what had happened to her sister's husband, made no sense to her at all.

Harry Robinson 1900–1990

OKANAGAN

Harry Robinson was born on 8 October 1900 in Oyama, near Kelowna, in the Okanagan Valley of British Columbia, where his mother's family were seasonal farm workers. They soon moved back to the Similkameen Valley near Keremeos. Robinson's early years were spent primarily with his aged grandmother, one of many elders and storytellers who influenced him. This was his education, as he spent only five months in school, at the age of thirteen, and did not learn to read and write until he became an adult. A ranch hand from the age of seventeen, Robinson was twenty-four when he married a rancher. By the mid-1950s he owned four ranches, but when his wife died in 1971 he sold everything and moved to a small bungalow. He died in 1990.

Wendy Wickwire provides the following information in her introduction to *Write It On Your Heart: The Epic World of an Okanagan Storyteller* (1989), which she compiled from twelve years of interviews with Robinson. She has since produced another collection, *Nature Power: In the Spirit of an Okanagan Storyteller* (1992).

Robinson's purpose as a writer was to create a record: 'I'm going to disappear and there'll be no more telling stories.' For him, this was only part of a general deterioration of his way of life: 'I think way back is better than now. Old days lots of fish.'

As Robinson grew older, he found that even his Native listeners were unable to understand the Okanagan language, so he decided to tell his stories in English. Wickwire chose to present the stories in lines of text rather than in run-on prose: 'I searched for a presentational style to capture the nuance of the oral tradition—the emphasis on certain phrases, intentional repetition, and dramatic rhythms and pauses. I have, therefore, set the stories in lines which mirror as closely as possible Harry's rhythms of speech. Harry's stories are really performed events, rather than fixed objects on a page.' Wickwire made no other changes except to regularize the pronouns.

Wickwire recorded more than a hundred stories, but she acknowledges that the selection was Robinson's and that the choice might have been shaped by his sense of what a young white female would want to, or perhaps should, hear. Still, she tried to present a 'cross-section' in her collections. 'Captive in an English Circus' is not altogether representative of Robinson's writings, as the majority of these writings are in some sense animal stories, many of which folklorists label 'pourquoi tales'—narratives explaining how an element of nature came to have a certain form. Only 'Captive in an English Circus' and three other poems are in the section of the first book that Wickwire titled 'World Unsettled: The Age of the White Man'. This separation is Wickwire's, however, as Robinson, like storytellers of many traditional cultures, distinguished subject matter, not historical veracity. Wickwire comments: 'All the stories are considered true stories. . . . Stories describe either situations experienced personally or they describe situations passed on by others who similarly experienced them, however long ago. In the case of the latter, Harry simply explains, "This is the way I heard the stories so I tell it that way." ' Robinson perceived himself as not an author but a transmitter.

Wickwire notes that 'Captive in an English Circus' is the only story in the first collection that has no displays of ' "power", no transformations, no dying and coming back to life, no spiritual healing by Indian doctors, and no *shoo-MISH* [guardian spirit].' The story shows the maintenance of Okanagan culture, and yet the absence of such power suggests the community can no longer be strong in the face of white control. This perhaps represents Robinson's feeling of loss, which led him to tell these stories.

Captive in an English Circus

*A man from the Similkameen Valley goes to prison in New Westminster for killing
a man. One night he is secretly abducted and taken on a long journey.*

This is about George Jim.
He belongs to Ashnola Band, George Jim.
Those days, I had it written down—1886.
No, I mean 1887.
That's one year I'm out there.   5
That's supposed to be in the 1886
    instead of 1887.
That time, 1886,
    the people, Indians from Penticton,
        all the Okanagan Indians,   10
            they were some from Similkameen,
                and they all move to where Oroville is now
                    in the month of August,
                        about the last week in the month of August.
And they all get together in Oroville.   15
And that's when the salmon coming up.
The salmon comes up, you know, from way down.
They come up on the Columbia River
    and they come up on the Okanogan, some.
And some of them go up, they split up there.   20
Some of them go up the Columbia River.
But some of them, they coming up on the Okanogan River.
They had a good place for catching them there in Oroville.
Kind of shallow.
Only a small river.   25

So the people moved over there.
They stay there.
Put in a camp.
There is no town there yet.
There was some white people,   30
    they got two or three houses there.
Not many.
Then they get the salmon.
They get the salmon for,
    could be about a week or ten days.   35
Then the salmon keep going and go by.

They come to Osoyoos Lake
  and they follow Osoyoos Lake
    and then they come to Okanogan River again
      and they keep going to Okanagan Falls.   40
They can never go any farther than Okanagan Falls.
There's a dam there.
That's as far as the salmon can go.

These Indian, when they run out of salmon,
  they know the salmon, they go by.   45
So they move.
Follow the salmon.
Then they come to Okanagan Falls.
Then the salmon, they can't go no more.
They were there.   50
They can get salmon.
Some of them died in the water
  and get bad, you know, get spoiled.
Then they quit.
When they get together at Falls,   55
  there's a lot of Indians and they put in a camp.
Some of them, they play stickgame.
They kind of celebrate.
But still some of them get the salmon
  at night or the daytime.   60
And some of them get whiskey from someplace,
  from Penticton, I guess, or somewhere.
And they drink.

And this time,
  that Jim,   65
    supposed to be a big man, stout man.
And he's a funny looking man.
He's got short legs,
  but he's pretty wide in the shoulders.
And he's got big hips.   70
Kinda tough-looking man.
And he was.
He's a strong man.

Then there was a white man
  that lived there at Okanagan Falls.   75
And he's got an Indian woman from Penticton.

And they got some children,
    maybe one or two.
And this white man, his name, Shattleworth.

A lot of people drinking, you know.   80
And then George Jim, and Shattleworth, and some others,
    they drinking at night,
        and then they fighting.
But this time, that Shattleworth,
    he got beat badly by George Jim.   85
George Jim, he beat him almost till death.
Then, some of the boys, they stopped him and grab him.
Because he's strong, it takes a few men to hold him.
Then they take the man who's wounded.
They take him to the camp.   90
They laid him in the camp.
He's hurt very bad.
He's got a broken ribs
    and he was hurt in the head, you know.
Quite a few cuts.   95
With a club, you know, he hit him in the head with a club
    and then he cut the skin, you know, by the club.
Not knife, but the club.
Then he kicked him in the ribs
    and his ribs were broken inside.   100
And then some of that bone,
    they must have gone to the lungs.
Could be.

He thought,
    I hurt him badly   105
        and I might as well kill him.

So, who's going to stop him?
He's a strong man.
He went to the teepee.
Bunch of women in there,   110
    maybe two or three old men
        and maybe five women, old women.

So, he come there and he says,
    'How's that Shattleworth?
    I'm going to kill him if he's alive yet.'   115
And these people told him,

'He's dead.
He died.
Already died.'

And they covered him with a white blanket.   120
He lay on the bed
   and they cover him, all his head.
And he looked like he was dead all right
   because he was covered with a white cloth.
They tell him,   125
   'You better stay away.
He died.
He dead already.'

All right, he go away.

But he didn't die, that Shattleworth.   130
After that he was living for about seven or eight months.
But he died just from getting beat
   because the way I see, maybe the ribs they were broken
      and maybe some, they go to the lungs.
But if not go to the lungs,   135
   the ribs they be heal up.
He wouldn't die.
But this one here, it's bad.
Maybe it goes in the lung,
   the bone, the broken rib.   140

But anyway, George got away.
And then they report that to the policeman
   because this Shattleworth, he's a white man
      and he's got an Indian wife.
And it was reported to the police.   145
But the police, they couldn't get him.
Kinda scared of him because Jim,
   he's got a revolver on his hip all the time,
      and yet he's a strong man.
And the policeman, they kinda scared of him.   150
They just let him go.
They look for a chance to sneak to him and then get him.

So Jim, he stay away for quite a while,
   for almost one year.
About eleven months after he did that,   155
   that was next August and somebody, they cheat him.

Then they got him.
And he been around to Ashnola and down to Chopaka.
But he always keep away from the policeman.
They go over there and look for him,   160
    but they're scared of him.
They always around there but nobody get him.
He hide in the daytime in the hillside.
At night he goes to the Indian camp
    and sometimes he didn't.   165

Then, there was one boy, eleven years old.
And he make a lunch,
    a big lunch for Jim.
Then he told that boy,
    he told an old man,   170
        'You take that boy
           and show him the place
               where he can leave that lunch for Jim.
           And tell him what he's going to do.
           And tell him what's he's got to say if somebody met him.'   175
That old man used to take the lunch,
    but he a little afraid
        maybe the policeman or some man
           might think the old man
               must have take a lunch to that wanted man.   180
But if the boy,
    he give him a gun, you know,
        a 22-gun, you know,
           to shoot the grouse.
And he tell him,   185
    'If somebody come and met you,
        if they ask you what you're doing here,
           you tell 'em,
               "I'm hunting, hunting for grouse,
                  willow grouse, or rabbit, or something like that." '   190

Then, he's got bags on his shoulders.
    'When I get a grouse I can put it in there.'
But that's where he had the lunch.
And he showed him where he can take the lunch
    and where he can leave it.   195
There was a big stone
    and there was kind of hollow underneath the stone.
That was kind of a shade.
In the daytime he could put the lunch there.

But this man is up on the hill. 200
He could be watching him.
When it gets dark,
    this man will come down and take the lunch
        and go up the hill again.
That's Jim. 205
So the old man, he show the boy
    and tell all about what to do and what to say.
And he can take the lunch every once in awhile,
    every two days,
        because they make a big lunch at a time. 210

But not long after that,
    that was in the month of August, could be,
        because they say that choke cherries were ripe.
They don't know if it was August or September those days.
Now I can figure myself. 215
When they say it's choke cherries time,
    choke cherries, they ripe,
        choke cherries they ripe in the month of August.
I know that.
That could be August. 220
Then he was there for quite a while.

And the road gang, they building a road.
And they call it McCurdy place.
And after that, they call it,
    I forget the new man that lived there. 225
Anyway, McCurdy place,
    that's the first man that lived there.
McCurdy for about a mile
    and the river it's curved like that.
Kind of bent. 230
And that's where they camp, the road gang,
    they had a camp there.
Those days wherever they can build a road,
    if it's far away from town,
        they can move camp. 235
They got to have a camp there.
But nowadays, the workers,
    they can go from town.
It don't matter how far.
They don't put no camp. 240
But those days they got a camp.

They use horses, you know,
    scraper and plough to make a grade.
And they had a camp there,
    the road gang, the bunch of them.   245
And they had a cookhouse and a cook.
Bunch of men workers.
And there was a trail,
    but they widen out that trail to be a wagon road.
That was in 1887 then.   250
That's a long time ago.
No highway those days.

So the road gang was there.
and one of these boys, like the boss,
    maybe, the foreman, you know,   255
        he has to ride the horse.

No car those days,
    no motorcycle,
        no bicycle,
            no nothing.   260
Only saddle horse.
You know that.

Then these men
    they go to Fairview.
That's a town, you know.   265
Mine town.
Their head boss is there.
Government.

All right.
They went over there to see him   270
    and come back.
So he went over there
    and then in the afternoon, he come back from Fairview.
He went over there in the morning.
In the afternoon he come back from there.   275

And this George Jim,
    he took a horse and ride him around by Nighthawk.
Then he must have gone by Oroville or somewhere.
But he come back
    and he come back where that Osoyoos Road is now.   280

You remember when we come up there?
And I showed you, 'Here is the old road'?
But now the highway is above the old road.

So Jim, he come on that road.
And the other one,   285
   that man who goes to Fairview,
      he takes the trail like from Fairview.
And they met at the top, just above Spotted Lake.

When we were at Spotted Lake
   and you took pictures, I and him?   290
And I told you, the old road, it's higher up there?
Yeah, that's where they meet,
   this man from Fairview.
He go by Spotted Lake.
And Jim was coming on the road   295
   and they met there.
Then, because Jim, he's a 'wanted man',
   it was written in the government office,
      his name and how he look like and all that.
And all the white people knew that   300
   even if they never seen him before.
But as soon as they see him,
   they can tell that was the 'wanted man'.

So this man, one of the government men,
   the one that goes to Fairview,   305
      soon as he met him,
         he knew he was the one.
There was a reward, you know,
   because whoever catch him is going to get paid.
Then he said to George,   310
   they go together and they talk
      and they make a good friend to one another,
         and they are good friend
            and it's getting late in the afternoon.
Finally they rode together   315
   and they're getting close to the camp.
Then, it's just about supper-time then.
And this white man, he tell Jim,
   'You better come with me to the camp.
   Then you can eat there.   320
   Eat supper.

Now, it's just about supper-time.'
He tell him,
   'I am one of the bosses in that camp,
      so you come with me   325
         and you stay there
            and after supper you can go.'
And Jim, he says,
   'No, I better keep going.
   I can stop someplace in some of them Indians.'   330
   'Oh no. You better come.
   You eat here. You'll be all right.'

But you know, he figure,
   when he get there,
      he figure he can tell the other boys right away   335
         and that was their judge to catch him.
So anyway,
   George, he must have been hungry or something
      because he stop there
         and he went with that man.   340
And he tie up his horse.
Then, I think this white man,
   the one that's with him,
      he must have tell the other ones right away.
And then he didn't know.   345

And then,
   one of the working man,
      big man, strong man,
         he take the apron and he put it here.
He's not a waiter.   350
He's not a cook.
He's one of the ploughmen.
But he puts the apron on so he looks like a waiter, cook.
Long table
   and he takes the grub   355
      and he move over there
         and he goes back and gets some more.

And Jim was sitting there
   and he wanted to sit on the other side against the tent wall.
But they tell him   360
   'You can sit here.
   Already the boys are over there.'

He didn't like to sit there because it's open.

So this waiter goes by him
   on his back two, three times.   365
And then I guess these other boys,
   nobody know,
      they might get a club and then they hide it.
When the waiter gets over the other end of the table
   and he give him that club.   370
Then he come back.
That was the fourth time or the fifth time
   when he go by George's back.

Then this time when he go by there,
   and George was watching all the time.   375
He always watching.
But finally he quieted down
   and he eat.
And he's got a revolver on his hip, you know.

And when this waiter go by him,   380
   down it went on the back of his head
      and George just drop!
And he knocked out
   and drop off the chair.
And all the men are just on him, you know.   385
Bunch of men, three or four men,
   they just right on him.
And they get the rope
   and they tie his arms
      and they tie his feet.   390
Before he come to, he's already tied up.
He can't do nothing.
They take his gun away from him.

Then they sent one of the boys to Fairview for the policeman
   after supper, after six o'clock.   395
Then, whoever they went from there to Fairview,
   that's about ten or fifteen miles,
      they get there and tell the police
         and then the policemen come.
When the policemen gets there   400
   and they handcuff him,
      put the handcuffs on him.

Then, nothing he can do after they got the handcuffs.
They take the ropes off his feet
   and then they tell him, 405
      'Get on your horse.'
And these policemen,
   they come on horses,
      the two of them.
Then they lead him 410
   and they tie his feet with a rope under the belly
      so he could never jump off.
They got handcuffs, iron handcuffs.
He can't get away.
So they lead him to Fairview 415
   and then they put him in jail.

Because the one, he beat Shattleworth.
He did.
After the six or seven months after he was beat,
   he died. 420
He's a murderer anyway.

So, they held him in that jail for a while
   and they had a trial there once or twice.
Then they take him to Penticton.
There was another courthouse there. 425
Just small.
They held him there awhile
   and then they took him to Kamloops.
There must have been a little court in Vernon those days.
But Kamloops. 430
Then they had him there for a while
   and then they got a sentence seven years.
Only seven years.
Take him to Westminster.
And the railroad drives into Westminster in 1886. 435
And they already had a railroad right in Vancouver.

And Mr. Jim,
   they sent him from Kamloops on the railroad to Westminster.
And then they had him in that penitentiary.
And he was in there three years. 440
Supposed to be seven years and then he'll come out.
That's his sentence.
Seven years.

He was in jail three years
    and one night towards morning,   445
        about two o'clock in the morning then
           because all the cells, you know,
               whoever's in the cell, maybe one or two,
                  the policeman lock 'em.
Then, in the morning they could open 'em.   450
Unlock 'em.
But Jim was locked.
All alone in one cell.
But towards morning,
    about two o'clock in the morning,   455
        somebody open that.
They got a key,
    open the door,
        and they come in.
There's three of them—policemen.   460
They got the clothes, uniform—guards.
Those days, the policemen,
    they haven't got no uniform.
But the guards, they got some kind of a uniform.

So, the three of them come in.   465
And Jim, he wake up.
Still in bed.
And told him,
    'Jim, you get up and put your clothes on.
    We come and get you.'   470

I'm not sure if it was three.
I think it's only two.
But the driver, that makes three.
They got a driver on the buggy out there.
But these two,   475
    they're both guards,
        go in and tell Jim,
           'You dress up and we come and get you.
           There's a buggy outside with a driver.
           You get on the buggy   480
               and we all get on and we go to Vancouver.
           Early in the morning,
               the train is going to leave Vancouver.
           We got to go on the train.
           We move you.   485

There was one jail a long long way from here.
We move you.
You're going to be over at that jail.
Long ways from here.
You leave this place.'   490

Well what can he say,
    because this is the policeman, guard, you know.
He has to do whatever they tell him.
All right, he dress up and he went out.
There was a buggy there   495
    and he get on the buggy
        and they all get on the buggy
            and they go to Vancouver early in the morning.

At that time they got a different time.
Now, they leave there eight o'clock in the evening from Vancouver.   500
But at that time it might have been in the morning.
Might be four o'clock in the morning
    or something like that.

Anyway,
    early in the morning they get on the train   505
        and they went.
And they going all day and all night
    and all day and all night again.
And Mr. Jim, he thinks,
    By God, that was a long way.   510
    Where did they take me?
    I wonder where they take me.

They take him into where they eat, you know,
    on the train.
And he got a chance to ask the waiter.   515
I guess the policemen who look after him, they went back,
    and just only himself.
And he asked the waiter,
    and the waiter told him,
        'They take you to Halifax.   520
        Then there, you're going to take the boat
            from Halifax to England.'

So he find that out,
    but what has he got to say?
So anyway, they get him to Halifax.   525

Then they told him,
    'We're going to be here for a while.
    We're waiting for the boat.'
Because those days
    it takes the boat a month to go over the sea to England.   530
One month.
But now it's only about four days.
So they wait there about four or five days.
Then the boat came.
Then they put him in the boat,   535
    the whole bunch.
These two, they always along with him,
    the same man.

So, he mention that.
He see one Indian in England   540
    and he told him,
        this Indian from Enderby,
           not Indian altogether,
              he's a half-breed,
                 but he speak in Okanagan.   545
So, he says in his stories that he went on the water.
He could see the mountains, the ground,
    for one week and no more.
Two weeks,
    never see nothing but water.   550
Then he see again a little ridge.
Little ground.
One week and then they landed.
Then from there
    they took him on the buggy   555
        or on the train or something for quite a ways.
Then they leave him there.
But not in jail no more.
They give him a good house,
    a good big house,   560
        big room,
           good bed.
They feed him good
    and then they kept him.
They watch him all the time.   565
But once in awhile they took him
    and put him on the train
        and they went away.

They stay away for two or three months
    and then come back.   570
That was his home place.
In two months or more,
    they come back to England
        and they stay there for two or three weeks,
            maybe one month,   575
                then they took him to another direction.
That's in European somewhere.

They took him everywhere for show.
Whenever they get somewhere
    and there's be a big forum   580
        and table or something.
Then they tell him to get up there
    and walk around there.
Then, the people in the big room,
    big house chock full of people,   585
        and he watching them.
And these people, they pay.
Pay money to see that Indian.
There is no Indian in Europe at that time.
Only him.   590

So the white people, they make money out of him.
And he was there four years.

And this man from Enderby,
    he's a half-breed.
His name, Charlie.   595
Charlie Harvie, his name.
He talks in Okanagan.
He's half-breed.
And he don't say,
    but I think myself he must be in the army,   600
        that Charlie,
            because he went and he get to England.
Then he come back from England
    and he came home to Enderby.
And when he got home,   605
    he said when he was in England,
        he said, there's a big bunch of boys,
            all young boys just like he was,
                just like his age.
Bunch of them and they were there.   610

So one of these boys told him,
   asked him where he come from.
And he said he came from the Okanagan, British Columbia.
Okanagan.
Then, he told him,   615
   'There was a man not far from here,
      he is supposed to come from Okanagan, British Columbia.
   He is supposed to speak in your language.
   Maybe we should take you over there
      and then you can see that man.'   620

Then, he said,
   'No, I don't like to go because',
   (see, he's got a boss, he must be an army man),
   'My boss they may not like it that way.'
So, the other boss says,   625
   'Your boss, he's not going to know that.
   We take you over there.
   We're not going to tell your boss.
   You're going to see that man.'

All right.   630
So they went.
The boys took him over there.
Then they get to that place
   and they go in to where that Jim was.
That's his house.   635
Then the boys told him,
   'This man, he speak in your language.'
Then the both of them started to speak in Okanagan.

Not only one.
He went over there two or three times   640
   to see him and visit him
      for quite a while.

And Jim,
   he told him all about what they have done
      and so on.   645
And then they took him from Westminster
   and they took him on the train a long ways
      and they put him on the boat for one month.
Then they had him there.
   'Then they take me out from here a long ways.   650

I don't know which way,
    but they take me out a long ways.
Whenever I stop, a lot of people get in there.
    Then they make me walk around on the boards.
    High.   655
    Then I walk around and all the people look at me.
    Then I go.
    We go to another place.
    Then we go to another place.
    A lot of places.   660
    In one month or two months
        we come back.
    And this is my home place.'

But he says,
    'Charlie, when you get back to British Columbia,   665
        you can go from Enderby to Ashnola.'
Right in Ashnola he's got aunt and he's got uncle.
And he said to Charlie,
    'You could tell my uncle and my aunt
        to make a business,   670
        to see if they can come and get me.
    They got a lot of money.
    They got a lot of cattle.
    They got enough money.
    They should come and get me.   675
    In another way they can talk to the Indian agent.
    And then the Indian agent can contact to Ottawa,
        to the Indian Affairs.
    Then, whoever they is coming to get me,
        their fare can be paid that way.   680
    But maybe they'll have a little money with them anyway.
    But my people, they're well-off.
    They should do that and come and get me.'

So Charlie, he said,
    'I will when I get home.'   685

And about a year after that,
    Charlie came back.
Come back to Enderby.
He stay there almost one year after that and he come back.
And then he ride on the saddle horse all the way to Ashnola.   690
Then he see that John, his name was,
    and Mary.

They are cousins.
That's Jim's aunt, that Mary,
   and his uncle, John.   695
He told them all about it
   to contact the Indian agent and to Ottawa
      and all that.
And he said,
   'If you want me, I can be with you,'   700
      because he can speak in English, you know.

But these Indians, they couldn't understand.
They don't know.
In another way, they don't like it.

They say,   705
   'He should not pay for our fare
      because that's a lot of money.'
They figure they could pay for their own fare
   but it takes a lot of money
And they could never understand about the contact   710
   so they could get paid their fare from the Indian Affairs.
Charlie told them,
   but they couldn't understand.
Charlie, he was waiting around,
   and he said,   715
      'I go home, but if you need me, I come back and help you,
         or else I can go with you for interpreter over there
            to get that man back.'

But they just dismissed.
No more.   720
They never get him.

But, before they find out he was alive yet
   at the time when they took Jim from Westminster,
      take him away,
         then they rode from the jail to John.   725
He was a chief, you know.
And they told John that
   'Jim was in jail here
      but he died and we bury him.'

But he not die.   730
They lie.
They take him away.

So they think, his people,
   they just got to know he died and that's all.
But they decided they should come and get the body.   735
Take it out and bring him home.
So they did.
They come, that John and Mary and some others.
They got an interpreter, you know,
   who can speak in English.   740
Then they come on horseback with the packhorses to Hope.
Then they talk to the people in Hope
   and they tell them,
      'You can't leave your horses here.
      There's no feed for the horses.   745
      You have to go to Chilliwack
         and then you can put your horses in there with the Indians.
      There's all kinds of feed there for horses.
      And then you can take the boat from Chilliwack to Westminster.'

So, they did.   750
They did get to Westminster
   and then they go to the jail office
      and they tell 'em,
         'We're coming to get George Jim.
         He's already buried here.'   755
So, they said,
         'Yeah, we talk to one another.
         We'll see.
         Just wait awhile, a couple of days.'

Then, they talk to one another   760
   and I guess they find out what to say about him.
Then they say,
   'All right, we know,
   This is the one right there in the graveyard.
   We can dig him.   765
   We dig him out and we clean 'em and we change the coffin.
   Then you guys can take him on the boat as far as Chilliwack
      and then you could put him on the packhorse.'

Well, it's in a box
   because they could pack the horse on each side of something.   770
Then they could put the box crossways
   all the ways from Chilliwack to Ashnola.
Then they did that

and they take him out and clean him
    and put medicine on him 775
        so he wouldn't be smell.
Change the coffin and seal it
    and told them not to open it.
        'Don't open it
            because we give him medicine. 780
        But in the box he's not cold.
        They might be kinda smell,
        by the time you get it over there,
            not to open 'em.'

All right, they bring 'em 785
    and they never open 'em.
But when they get him to Ashnola,
    then, whoever they were there,
        and they tell 'em,
            'We should open 'em. 790
            We should make sure if that was him.'
Well, these other people said,
    'If he's going to be smelly, that don't matter.
    Open 'em.
    We want to see.' 795
So, they break it open and they looked at 'em.
    'That's not Jim. That was a Chinaman.'
Kinda stout Chinaman.
He must have been in jail.

They can't take him back, so they bury him there. 800
They were around there for a while
    and they thought maybe they make a mistake over there.
        'We better go again to get Jim.
        They might mistake.
        Maybe Jim is still there.' 805

They went again
    and they get there
        and they told 'em,
            'This is not Jim you give us.
            This is a Chinaman.' 810
            'By gosh, that's too bad.
        We made a mistake.
        We know that.
        We find that out,

but you fellas are gone.   815
George is there.
Now that you've come back,
        we can take him out and clean him
                and you can take him away.
    Take him home.'   820

They do the same thing.
Dug him out, clean him, put medicine on him
    and changed the box, and tell him not to open it.

So, they bring him,
    and that was the second time.   825
From Westminster to Chilliwack.
Then, they packed him from Chilliwack to Ashnola.
When they got there,
    whoever they were home tell 'em,
        'We got to open 'em, see,   830
            to make sure if it was Jim.
            Maybe another Chinaman.'

Anyhow, they open 'em.
They looked at him
    and he was a negro boy.   835
A small man too.

Well, they bury him there.
But there's no use to go back and get George.

And George is not dead.
They take him away.   840

Then later on, a few years after that,
    and Charlie Harvie come back from England.
Then he ride over there and he tell them about it.

Long time, quite a few years after that,
    and then they find out   845
        George Jim, he's not dead.
He's alive yet, but he's in England.

So, that's the end of that story.

Marion Tuu'luq 1910–2004

INUIT

Marion Tuu'luq, born in Chantrey Inlet, Northwest Territories, lived a traditional nomadic life before she moved to Baker Lake in 1961. She married twice and had sixteen children. Beginning with small scenes sewn on fabric, she became part of the burst of development in Inuit art at Baker Lake in the early seventies.

Tuu'luq's achievements as an artist—a creator of wall hangings, drawings, and prints— were remarkable. She had various two-person shows with her artist husband, Luke Anguhadluq, and participated in group shows of Inuit art in Winnipeg, Ottawa, Vancouver, and New York. Her work was included in the Inuit Masterworks exhibit at the McMichael Canadian Collection in Kleinburg, Ontario, in 1983 and in the show 'Contemporary Indian

and Inuit Art of Canada' at the United Nations in New York in 1983. One of her wallhangings was included in the 1974 World Crafts Council show 'In Praise of Hands'. She was elected a member of the Royal Academy of Arts in 1978, and the University of Alberta awarded her an Honorary Doctorate of Laws in 1990.

'A Story of Starvation', which first appeared in *Inuit Today* in 1977, is a true and not unusual story, notable for its strong sense of pacing and of what might be called a narrator's feel for the order of things. The diction is subtle and appropriate, particularly in the brief dialogue included. Recorded by Susan Tagoona as orature, not literature, it shows the creativity possible in what folklorists call the 'personal-experience narrative'.

A Story of Starvation

As told to Susan Tagoona

I am going to recount a story that I am sure I have told over and over again in the past. It is not a happy story. At the time it took place, it looked as though we weren't going to survive. I will tell you some of those terrible events.

My name is Marion Tuu'luq, and my story goes back to the time when my father couldn't walk. My father was lame for as far back as I can remember into my childhood. We used to carry him on our backs when we travelled during the summer. In the winter, we pulled him on the qamutik.

One time, while we were at Tipyalik, there were no caribou to be found, and we became very hungry. Being just a young girl at the time, it didn't occur to me that the people I was with were very concerned and afraid.

While my brother Angutituaq and Oonark's husband were out searching for game, they came upon several traps, which brought them to some people. But they soon discovered that these people with the traps had been reduced to killing one of their dogs, since there was no game whatsoever in the area.

They skinned the dog, and when it was cooked, they told me to eat some of the meat. But I was so repelled by the meat of the dog that I was unable to eat. I really meant it with my whole heart when I said I didn't want to eat it, and they couldn't make me change my mind. I remember someone saying that the meat tasted just like a wolf.

When everyone was eating the dog meat, I too was given a piece. I tried to smell it, but I couldn't smell anything. Then, I put the piece in my mouth and I took it out again. I did this several times. I remember clearly how much I was repelled that day at the thought of eating a dog.

While the eating was going on, my father was lying down on the bed as usual. He was scarcely breathing. I didn't know then that the following day he would strangle himself with a rope, and we would have to leave him behind. When he was asked to eat, on that final day of his life, he refused. He didn't want to take even a sip of broth.

The next day, my brother Quenungnat and I were directed to go a little distance away from the igloo. We were told to stay there until someone called for us and we were ready to leave our camp. Of course, we wondered at the reason for this command. But we stayed as we were told until Nattaq, Quenungnat's mother, waved at us, signalling that it was now okay for us to return. It was then that I learned that my father had died and that I would not be seeing him again. I cried, for I loved my father very much. His name was Ekinilik.

Innakatsik, who was just a kid, even younger than myself, was asked to lead the way, but he didn't want to. So then, I was asked to lead and was told to follow the tracks on the snow.

While I was walking in the lead, I spotted a rock that was barely showing in the snow ahead of me. It indicated that a sled had passed by that spot only the day before. As I started to approach the rock, I heard the voice of my father say to me, 'It is a cache, it is a cache.' And here he had just died a short while before!

I started kicking at the rock, shouting 'It's a cache! It's food!' And I would not leave the rock.

'There can't be anything around here. You wouldn't know of any caches around here, you are not able to know!' answered my brother Angutituaq in a scolding voice. But I just kept on kicking at the rock and shouting, 'It's food! It's a cache!' For some reason, I just couldn't leave the rock alone.

'It's nothing. It can't be anything!' Angutituaq kept answering back at me.

Then the others started shovelling at the rock, and, true to my words, they uncovered—a cache! As we loaded it on to our sled, it seemed as though we were stealing someone else's cache. But we didn't know of anyone who would have a cache, and we were threatened with starvation. We had sighted some fox traps the previous day, which probably belonged to the Akiliningmiut, and maybe the cache was theirs.

When we had loaded the meat on our sled, my father's voice again spoke to me: 'Daughter, I don't want you to eat the liver and the heart of this caribou.' I told him that I would do as he said.

After the men had made an igloo, I was allowed to feast on the meat which I had discovered. The men told me to eat all that I wanted. They fed me everything—the heart, the liver—everything! They told me that there would have been nothing to eat if it hadn't been for me.

The next day, when I woke up, I was unable to open my eyes.

'What is the matter with her now? Look at her, she can't even open her eyes! Did somebody hurt you?' Nattaq shouted at me. It must have been because I had eaten the meat after my father had told me not to. Again, I heard the voice of my father warning me, 'Daughter, do not eat the heart and the liver of the caribou.'

'I forgot,' I answered. No sooner had I said this than my eyes were opened.

When I try to tell this part of the story, I am not confused about the details. It is something I will never forget.

Later, there were no caribou at all. We didn't even see any caribou tracks. We were forced to live on dog meat. Killing and eating our dogs was the only way we could survive. As we travelled, we came across scraps of dried meat and the bones of caribou left over from the winter before, but they did not satisfy our hunger.

One day, Innakatsik went off on his own to search a nearby igloo for food. When he returned, he said he had discovered that it was full of dried meat. We all went straight to the igloo he had found. When we entered it, the people there just kept looking down and did not raise their heads. We were deeply disappointed, for there was no food there—nothing to eat at all. 'Is there food?' asked my brother Angutituaq. But no one had the heart to answer him.

As we no longer had any dogs, we packed all our belongings on our backs, and we started to walk. Along the way, we caught a rabbit and ate it, and that was all we had to eat.

For a time, we kept on walking, but it was not long before we realized that we weren't going to run into any people. Instead, we decided to search for igloos. We came across two—one large, one small—and we looked for tracks around them, but there were none. It was bitterly cold by now, and there were frequent blizzards and storms, so we decided to return to the shelter of our old igloo. There was just a small group of us together at that time—Angutituaq, Tamalik, and myself. Weak from starvation, we were forced to leave clothes, blankets, and other belongings behind. I took only a blanket with me, and I wrapped it around my shivering body. When we lay down to sleep, I made sure that all my body was covered, and I had no trouble going to sleep.

Each time we awoke, we would force ourselves to start walking again. Angutituaq was close to starvation. We were just beginning to give up ourselves because of him, when we finally reached our old igloo.

Before we could enter the welcome shelter of the igloo, we had to dig a hole through the side to make a door. After our last stay there, we had sealed the door with snow to protect some skins we had left inside. Finally, we succeeded in digging ourselves an entrance way, but it was very narrow. Then, my brother said, 'I think Tuu'luq should be able to squeeze in through.' 'It's too small!' I shouted back at him. But I tried to pass through the narrow hole, and at last I succeeded. Angutituaq followed behind me.

I don't know how many days we had wandered and nights we had slept before we reached our igloo. We had not had anything to eat for a long time, and we were very thin and nearly starved to death.

'I smell hide!' we all shouted out as we reached the inside of the igloo, for we found skins there that were to have been used for whips. We cut the skins in pieces and devoured them hungrily. Then we scraped up and ate some blood that we discovered on a block of snow. White people use plates to eat off—we used snow. There was a lot of blood on the snow plate, so we ate from that, and that was the way we survived.

Whenever Angutituaq came across little pieces of meat, he offered them to me, even though I begged him to eat them himself instead. But he wanted so badly for me to eat.

It was a while before we felt we had gathered enough strength to leave the igloo again. We decided from then on that, if we wanted to eat, we would have to look for left-over caribou stomachs in abandoned caches. So, that is what we did. Sometimes we were lucky enough to come across caribou stomachs in old caches and we would eat their contents. Other times, we would find nothing and would return to our igloo and empty stomachs.

One time, Angutituaq and Oonark's husband decided to go out hunting for game. So Quenungnat and his brother went to look for a cache to provide the hunters with some food to take on their way. But the two men returned after just a short while to say that there were no caches left.

Angutituaq, however, said he knew of a place close by that he wanted to check. So we went to that place and discovered there what appeared to be a cache. Again, I started shouting—as I used to be very outspoken at that time—'It's a cache! It's a cache! It's a whole caribou!' One of the men answered me: 'Your brother and I tried to find food, but we returned empty-handed because it had been moved to a different area. You know that. There couldn't be anything in here.'

Still, we spent the whole day trying to shovel off the snow with a pana (Eskimo snow knife). 'I smell a cache. It is a cache, and I know it hasn't been touched,' I continued to insist. I think, by that time, the others were almost ready to give up. But I never used to think of how I was feeling. And the thing turned out to be a cache, after all.

We each loaded pieces of meat on our backs and prepared to return to the igloo. But we had scarcely moved more than a few feet away when we decided to stop right there and eat our fill. And did we ever eat! We chopped at the meat, pounded it, chipped and cracked it in halves with our snow knife. We had tried to walk with the meat on our backs, but we were so skinny by then, that we had no strength left for walking with such a weight to carry. So we ate the whole caribou, leaving only the neck and the head, which we took back with us.

After we reached our igloo, the men made plans to set out again to search for caribou stomachs on top of a hill. So we did, wandering further and further away. We walked the whole afternoon and didn't find a thing, so we decided to return home. All we had with us were the gun and the pana. We had left everything else we owned behind for we were too weak to carry anything with us. It was very hard for us. Every time I offered to carry the gun, my brother said no. I felt that, since I was the one with the most strength left, I should be the one to carry the gun.

Sometime later, we neared the igloo where we had been making our home. As we approached, we suddenly became aware of a group of people standing there. Oh, how frightened we were! We had finished off all their hides that were to have been used for making whips, and now they had come back for them.

'They've caught some caribou and they're bringing it back here!' Quenungnat was running and shouting at the same time. He was also trying to eat and getting scolded for his behaviour. I was still so afraid of what the men might do!

As it turned out, these hunters had caught some caribou and were returning to their overnight camp. They started to make themselves an igloo and I tried to help by cutting out blocks for them. My brother Angutituaq was still too weak from lack of food.

After the igloo was completed, Oonark's husband started to work on the porch. But the men told him not to bother as they would be on their way again by the next day. Then, one of them said, 'These people are not helping themselves to food. Get them something to eat.'

That night, after all of us had eaten our fill, we started to tell stories. As usual, I found lots to laugh at. In those days, I used to laugh often and was very talkative. Now, everything seemed so funny.

Some of our group told how, each time they approached an igloo, they would yell through the ice window, 'Is there anyone in there? Anyone in there?'

Nattaq said that, upon reaching our old igloo, they had spotted our fresh tracks in the snow, but there had been no one around. And Talluq had started to imagine that our dead bodies were in the porch. They had all looked around, then entered the igloo and found it empty. When they came out of the igloo, they saw us coming towards them, and they were so happy to see that we were all still together.

When Nattaq started to talk again about how she thought I might be dead and how she had searched the igloo looking for me, I started to laugh.

'This girl never runs out of laughs,' Angutituaq said.

Alexander Wolfe *b.* 1927

SAULTEAUX

Alexander Wolfe was born on the Sakimay Reserve in south central Saskatchewan during the Depression. His early education took place at a boarding school operated by the United Church of Canada. In 1950, he moved to the Turtle Mountains of North Dakota, where his family had originated. In 1964, he participated in President Johnson's Great Society Community Action Program and earned his high school diploma and a teacher's aide certificate in preschool education.

Wolfe explains the importance of maintaining the tradition of oral storytelling:

To be responsible for retelling the stories of the grandfathers today, the *Anishnaybay* must renew their commitment to the oral tradition. At the same time, we must turn to a written tradition and use it to support, not destroy, our oral tradition. The structure of our society in the days when the grandfathers were still with us was very different from what we have today. Information and instruction were transmitted to us orally, in story form, by our old people. Listening and absorbing what was told required great lengths of time. The use of the mind and memory were important; this is why the stories were told over and over again. The environment of that time held nothing to distract the listener and storyteller.

Today many things distract the listener and disrupt the storytelling. Radio, television, video, and printed material take precedence in the everyday lives of many children, and even the adults, in our present society. We are ceasing to be story-tellers and listeners, and in so doing we are losing that great virtue called patience, so strongly emphasized by the grandfathers. If we are to preserve the stories that contain our history we must restore the art, practice, and principles of oral story-telling. We must also commit our oral history to written form. That written form, however, must still comply with the wishes and aspirations of the grandfathers, now long gone from our numbers.

The Last Grass Dance

Told by Standing Through the Earth

Grandfather Standing Through the Earth was an elder who was knowledgeable about many things, both social and spiritual, and their application to the traditional and cultural ways of our people. Many times during his life I found him to be strange. Maybe this was because he was of one era and I was of another.

Whenever I would ask Grandfather a question that was of a humorous nature, his response was immediate. Sometimes he would ask Grandmother to provide an answer. Whenever I asked questions that dealt with the facts of life, Grandfather was quick to respond, 'A'how, Medimoya (all right, old lady), our grandson wants to know, tell him what he wants to know.' Usually this amused him and he laughed.

Then there were times I would ask a certain kind of question and receive no immediate response. Instead he would remain motionless, and after a period of silence, he would say, 'There is a period in the life of every person in which there is foolishness. When this period passes some people will grow up, remembering and using what they were told. For this we have a saying, "When you have had enough foolishness, then you become knowledgeable and know your mistakes." There are others who never go beyond this first stage; they remain foolish for the rest of their lives. To those people we say, "Your foolishness will accompany you to your old age."'

When I received this kind of response I was forced to practise patience and wait for a later time to ask my question. Very early in life I learned not to ask questions about spiritual things—particularly those things directly related to Grandfather or any other older person. These things, I was told, were very personal and were to be held in utmost respect. They were only alluded to in story form. Ceremonies and rituals were never described in detail. To ask old people questions about their spiritual attributes was unthinkable.

When I first asked Grandfather about the grass dance I already knew some things about it. From the stories told by Grandfather Earth Elder I knew where it had come from, and how it had come. On occasions when I asked my mother about it she only told me who performed the dance, not how or why the dance was performed. To these questions, she always replied, 'Ask your grandfather, he was part of it.'

Once she made a comment that revealed her recollection of that period, 'The dancer who wore the eagle belts in the grass dance looked beautiful. They were good dancers, very quick and beautiful to watch.'

My desire to know about the grass dance was to be satisfied one day.

It was a day in early summer. In the morning I helped Grandfather hitch his ponies to the wagon. After this was done I was told to help load the wagon with the berry-picking pails, some water containers, and a box of food. I was told that my mother and grandmother were going to pick saskatoon berries and Grandfather was going to chop willow pickets for fence posts. I was to help him. I was to be the pack horse who pulled the pickets out of the bush as they were cut, a job I wasn't really looking forward to. After hours of going from this bush to that bush, and finding only a few pickets, we came upon the Goose Lake from a northerly direction. We were on an abandoned trail along what was once the northwestern shoreline of Goose Lake. Suddenly Grandfather pulled his ponies to a stop and said, '*Medimoyea* (old lady), remember a long time ago when the shoreline was here and there were many kinds of summer fowl on the lake? At times there were so many geese they looked like snow upon the water.'

After the old people reminisced for several minutes about the old days we continued along what used to be the lake shore. A short time later we came upon a small clearing between two fairly large patches of trees and bushes. This was the place where the old log hall had stood by the shores of Goose Lake. The old hall was now gone.

As we approached the site I began to remember something about this place. The winter before I went to boarding school we came here once to watch a dance which I knew was the grass dance. We lived about three quarters of a mile north of here, and the whole family piled into the sleigh to make this trip. That evening and night were very cold. I knew it was very cold because from the time we left our house till we got here I was completely covered in blankets. I could not see anything. All I could hear was the sound of sleigh runners as they slid along the snow, and the sound of harness tugs as the horse pulled the sleigh.

When we arrived and went into the hall, we saw many people with children and many old people. Grandfather was there, so was Grandmother. My mother told me to sit in one place and to be quiet during the entire time we would be there. I cannot remember any of the other children making noise or running about either.

As we waited quietly for what was about to take place, I saw Grandfather dressed in a white traditional costume sitting by the door. To his left, and coming from the far opposite side of the hall, was the sound of bells and the aroma of burning sweet grass. A drum was placed in the centre of the hall. All was quiet. Then one of our grandfathers, whom I knew quite well, said a prayer. His name, the name I always called him, was *Wahpossway* (Old Man Bunnie).

I remembered seeing men seated on the floor around the drum. These were the singers. To one side of the singers stood another of the grandfathers, a brother to Grandfather Standing Through the Earth. His name was North Wind. This grandfather never danced. All he did was stand by the drum throughout the entire dance. The singing began and the dancers began their dance. During parts of the dance they danced slowly and at other times very fast. They let out shouts as they danced round and round the drum. On the ladies' side of the hall some elderly women stood dancing in one place. All at once there was a great shout. The dancers stopped dancing and the singers stopped singing.

There was something going on behind the drum and dancers that I could not see. Then the singing began again. This time some other men danced, just plain men. They carried ladles which they waved as they shouted.

The best part came after the dance was finished. Food was served, along with apples and bags of candy. My mother told me not to eat right away, first we had to listen. I remembered listening to another grandfather speak for a long time. He talked about us children and other children. This grandfather talked for such a long time, I couldn't hold out, I just had to dig into the candy. I'm sure I was not the only child to do this. I didn't remember what happened after that. I do know that a social dance followed—a round dance. I awoke the next morning back at our house. I knew that it had not been a dream because I still had some candy and apples.

As we neared the site where the old log hall had stood, Grandfather pulled his ponies to a turn and made for the edge of the bush.

There in the shade of the trees and bushes Grandfather stopped and said, 'We will stop here and eat.' Pointing to the bush along the lake bed, he said, 'The saskatoons used to be good here.'

We all got off the wagon and I helped Grandfather unhitch his ponies. In a short time a fire was built, the tea made, and we all sat down to eat. As we ate I thought again about the old log hall, about the time we came here during that one winter. In my mind I debated whether I should ask or not.

Finally I turned to my mother, 'Should I ask Grandfather about the old hall and what happened when we came here that one winter?'

Without saying a word she took out her tobacco, placed a pipeful in my hand, and said, 'Here. Ask him.'

As I was about to offer the tobacco to Grandfather my mother spoke to him. 'He wants to ask you about the old hall and about the last time there was a grass dance here.'

With a look on his face that suggested he was deep in thought, Grandfather took the tobacco.

'*Noozis* (grandchild),' he said, 'you have given me much tobacco in the past. I have told you stories. These stories I have told you were stories by the old men (elders) who lived here at Goose Lake since the reserve was here. Some of these stories were told when there was no reserve, no whiteman, so long ago we don't know when.

'This,' he said, pointing to the sky and around him, 'what you see around you is a story. What the *Anishnaybay* does and how he lives is a story. You, in time to come, will tell about me. Your children will tell about you—if you are foolish or not foolish—whatever they say about you will be a story. When your grandchildren come you will look back. You will see and know many things. This will be your story. What you ask I will tell you.

'Long ago when your grandmother and I were young, we came here to Goose Lake. (Grandfather was originally from the Riding Mountain area in central Manitoba and Grandmother came from the Turtle Mountains in Dakota Territory.) The people here at Goose Lake already had the grass dance. The elder *Sanquis*, father of my son-in-law, *Macheeaniquot* (Floating Cloud), had the ceremony. Elder *Sanquis* lived west of here at the other lake and had a big house. Round dances were held there and sometimes at mid-winter the grass dance was held there. I am told he got the dance as a gift from the Assiniboine people. This hall that was here was not the first. There was another across the lake to the east side. It was not really a hall but a big house.

'To have a part in the ceremony of the grass dance is an honour. In this dance there were four dancers, four singers, and four servers. There were speakers, a keeper of the drum, which at that time was *Mechee* (brother) *Keewaytinopeenace* (North Wind), and a keeper of the door. I was the last keeper of the door. When everyone who was to take part in the dance was ready, my part was to shut the door. I didn't let anyone in or out until the dance was over. When the door was shut a pipe was given to a speaker. Before the Elder *Sanquis* passed on, this was his part, as leader and headman of the Grass Dance Society. There had been other speakers in the past, like the father of *Nokeequon* (Soft Feather), Jim Bunnie. The speaker prayed to the Thunder Bird Eagle to bless the men who were holding the eagle belts which they were going to wear. These belts were sacred and used only for this dance. I have never been given the right to wear the eagle belt, only the eagle feather hat that I still have today. He also prayed for the keeper of the drum and the men seated around the drum. Four rainbows were painted on the drum, one for each direction, and at each direction sat a singer. The keeper of the drum stood at the east side of the drum. On the women's side stood four elderly women. They were noted in the community for their generosity and sharing with others. For these women, too, the speaker prayed. And for the children, and for all children yet to come. He prayed that each would be blessed with a head of grey and a long life.

'When this was done the dancers put on their belts. The dance was ready to begin. These belts came from an eagle that had been skinned, removing the head, the legs, the wings, and some of the tail feathers, and leaving only the back. From this section the belt was made and then decorated with ribbons of different colours.

'There were four main songs in this dance. The keeper of the drum kept track of them by passing a certain number of sticks from one hand to the other. The last two songs were sung twice. When the keeper of the drum held up four sticks in each hand we knew that this was the last part of the ceremony. This song was very fast and the dancers had to be very quick. The song ended when the lead dancer, who carried a sharpened stick, pierced a portion of the contents of a kettle, and held it up for all to see. The kettle held a cooked young dog that had been raised and prepared for this purpose. The lead dancer then took an eagle feather and dipped the tip of it into the broth and dropped one drop onto the tongue of each of his fellow dancers. Another song was sung to which the four men danced. They were the servers; their work, then, was to serve the food to the people.

'When this song was ended all the members of the Grass Dance Society were served the contents of the kettle. When the meal was ended the chief of the band, or some other headman, recounted why this ceremony was held—it meant that one half of the winter was now past. The hardships of the second half would soon be over. With the coming of spring it would be as morning after a dark night. We would be glad when the grandfathers*, among whom would be Thunder Bird Eagle,

---

* Grandfathers, as used here, denotes Thunderbirds, the rolling thunder of the early spring, among whom, it was said, was the Eagle Thunder Bird.

would come to give rain and life to all things, and we, too, the *Anishnaybay* would have life.'

When Grandfather had finished his story, he added the comment, 'Because of the changing times and forces outside our community, the Indians of tomorrow will never see, only hear of, the sacred ceremony and ritual called the grass dance.'

Basil H. Johnston *b.* 1929

OJIBWA

Basil Johnston was born on the Parry Island Reserve and received his education at Cape Croker Public School, the Spanish Residential School, Loyola College (Montreal), and the Ontario College of Education. Johnston has spoken on and has taught Ojibwa history, language, and culture in a variety of settings, from university conferences to public schools. His writing includes translations, language primers, satire, autobiography, fiction, essays, poems, reviews, and material for children. His publications include *Ojibway Heritage* (1976),

How the Birds Got Their Colours (1978), *Moose Meat and Wild Rice* (1978), *Indian School Days* (1988), *The Manitous: The Spiritual World of the Ojibway* (1995), and *Crazy Dave* (1999). He has also worked in film and television.

Johnston is now retired from the Department of Ethnology of the Royal Ontario Museum, which published a number of his collections of Ojibwa tales. He is a member of the Order of Ontario and holds an honourary doctorate from the University of Toronto.

The Prophecy

'Tonight I'm going to tell you a very different kind of story. . . . It's not really a story because it has not yet taken place; but it will take place just as the events in the past have occurred.' Daebaudjimoot paused to fill his pipe. 'And even though what I'm about to tell you has not yet come to pass, it is as true as if it has already happened because the auttissookaunuk told me in a dream.'

They, the men, women, and children from the neighbouring lodges who had come, waited for Daebaudjimoot to begin. The adults had long ceased to believe the tribal storyteller. Still they came, as they had done so for years, to relive the delight and faith of childhood which moved some of the old to say, 'he makes me feel like a child again sitting at my grandparents' feet.' But unlike the children present who believed Daebaudjimoot, the adults spoke slightingly of the storyteller but not without affection. 'W'zaumaudjimoh' (he exaggerates), they said of him. But there was not a man, woman, or child in the village who was not enriched in some way, either in mind or happier in spirit, once having heard Daebaudjimoot.

'Tonight I'm going to tell you about white people.' There was a moment of silence, astounded silence, and then an outburst of laughter as the audience perceived the incongruity of the notion. An albino caribou; an albino beaver, yes! but albino people? Who ever heard of White People? Even Daebaudjimoot had to laugh. The laughter gradually subsided.

'Are they like the maemaegawaehnsuk (little people like leprechauns, elves)?' a man asked, inciting another wave of laughter.

'Are they like the Weendigoes?' an old woman enquired, igniting more guffaws. The old laughed at such notions; the young laughed to hear the adults giggle, roar, snigger and to see them twist their mouths and cheeks into a hundred shapes. At the same time the young wondered what beings in addition to the Weendigoes, maemaegawaehnsuk, pauheehnsuk, zauwobeekumook, and Pauguk lurked in the forests and roamed about at night.

'What do these White People look like?' another old lady asked when she dried her eyes.

'The men and women that I speak of are all white, face, bodies, arms, hands, and legs, pale as the rabbits of winter. And . . . they are hairy . . . hair growing on their arms, legs, chests, backs, and arm-pits . . . and some men grow hair upon their faces around their mouths, drooping down from their chins, like moose beards.' Daebaudjimoot had to interrupt his narrative again for the nervous titters and embarrassed cackles that set off another uproar. The children chuckled and chortled as they imagined their playmates, maybe brothers and sisters, goateed like moose. Daebaudjimoot continued, 'different too is the colour of their hair; some yellow as goldenrod; a few red as cranberries, and others black as our hair. In old age the white people's hair turns white; on some men the hair falls off entirely so that their heads are as smooth and shiny as are pumpkins.

'Their eyes too are unlike ours; round . . . quite round . . . like the eyes of racoons . . . and blue like the colour of blueberries.'

There was more laughter but by now the men, women, and children were nursing aching bellies and paining sides.

'And their dress too is as quaint as their appearance. For one thing, they cover their bodies completely, day and night, summer and winter; only their faces being visible. On their heads are head-winders that they wear indoors and out-of-doors, in sunshine and in rain. The men and boys wear a peculiar garment which is a loin cloth and leggings made of one piece to cover their hams but the garment is so tight that the men walk like mud-hens. Each time that they go to toilet even to drain their bladders they must unfurl these rump binders down to their ankles. The women's garments are not much better than those of their men. The women wear a robe that covers them from their wrists and neck down to the very ankles. Underneath these loose bad-hangers the women wear tit flatteners and belly compressors. Their moccasins are made of a very hard substance, almost like wood, and cover their legs up to their very knee caps. It is only at night that the White People remove some of these garments.'

'Are they ashamed of their hair? of their organs?' an old woman quipped, rousing tired laughter.

Daebaudjimoot resumed his narrative. Hours later he predicted, 'When they come, they will come from the east across a great body of salt water; and they will arrive on board great wooden canoes five times the length of one of our own canoes. At either end of these long canoes are tall timbers. From the limbs of these timbers are suspended blankets for catching the wind to drive the canoes without the aid of paddles.'

'Are they ash or maple? Fresh wood or dead? They go against the wind?' voices asked and made remarks ridiculing the idea of an oversized canoe with trees at either end.

'You laugh because you cannot picture men and women with white skins or hair upon their faces; and you think it funny that a canoe would be moved by the wind across great open seas. But it won't be funny to our grandchildren and their great-grandchildren.

'In the beginning the first few to arrive will appear to be weak by virtue of their numbers, and they will look as if they are no more than harmless passers-by on their way to visit another people in another land who need a little rest and direction before resuming their journey. But in reality they will be spies for those in quest for lands. After them will come countless others like flocks of geese in their migratory flights. Flock after flock they will arrive. There will be no turning them back.

'Some of our grandchildren will stand up to these strangers but when they do, it will have been too late and their bows and arrows, war-clubs, and medicines will be as nothing against the weapons of these white people whose warriors will be armed with sticks that burst like thunder-claps. A warrior has to do no more than point a fire stick at another warrior and that man will fall dead the instant the bolt strikes him.

'It is with weapons such as these that the white people will drive our people from their homes and hunting grounds to desolate territories where game can scarce find food for their own needs and where corn can bare take root. The white people will take possession of all the rest and they will build immense villages upon them. Over the years the white people will prosper, and though the Anishinaubaeg may forsake their own traditions to adopt the ways of the white people, it will do them little good. It will not be until our grandchildren and their grandchildren return to the ways of their ancestors that they will regain strength of spirit and heart.

'There! I have told you my dream in its entirety. I have nothing more to say.'

'Daebaudjimoot! Are these white people manitous or are they beings like us?'

'I don't know.'

As the men, women, and children went out, a young man who had lingered behind remarked: 'It's good to listen to you, but I don't believe you.'

One Generation from Extinction

Within the past few years, Gregor Keeshig, Henry Johnston, Resime Akiwenzie, Norman McLeod, and Belva Pitwaniquot died. They all spoke their tribal language, Anishinaubae (Ojibwa). When these elders passed away, so did a portion of the tribal language come to an end as a tree disintegrates by degrees and in stages until it is no more; and, though infants were born to replenish the loss of life, not any of them will learn the language of their grandfathers or grandmothers to keep it alive and to pass it on to their descendants. Thus language dies.

In some communities there are no more Gregor Keeshigs, Henry Johnstons, Resime Akiwenzies, Norman McLeods, Belva Pitwaniquots; those remaining have no more affinity to their ancestral language than they do to Swahili or Sanskrit; in other communities the languages may not survive beyond a generation. Some tribal languages are at the edge of extinction, not expected to survive for more than a few years. There remain but three aboriginal languages out of the original fifty-three found in Canada that may survive several more generations.

There is cause to lament but it is the native peoples who have the most cause to lament the passing of their languages. They lose not only the ability to express the simplest of daily sentiments and needs but they can no longer understand the ideas, concepts, insights, attitudes, rituals, ceremonies, institutions brought into being by their ancestors; and, having lost the power to understand, cannot sustain, enrich, or pass on their heritage. No longer will they think Indian or feel Indian. And though they may wear 'Indian' jewellery and take part in pow-wows, they can never capture that kinship with and reverence for the sun and the moon, the sky and the water, or feel the lifebeat of Mother Earth or sense the change in her moods; no longer are the wolf, the bear, and the caribou elder brothers but beasts, resources to be killed and sold. They will have lost their identity which no amount of reading can ever restore. Only language and literature can restore the 'Indian-ness'.

Now if Canadians of West European or other origin have less cause than 'Indians' to lament the passing of tribal languages and cultures it is because they may not realize that there is more to tribal languages than 'ugh' or 'how' or 'kimo sabi'. At most and at best Euro-Canadians might have read or heard about Raven and Nanabush and Thunderbirds and other 'tricksters'; some may have even studied 'Culture Myths', 'Hero Tales', 'Transformation Tales', or 'Nature Myths and Beast Fables', but these accounts were never regarded as bearing any more sense than 'Little Red Riding Hood' or 'The Three Little Pigs'. Neither language nor literature were ever considered in their natural kinship, which is the only way in which language ought to be considered were its range, depth, force, and beauty to be appreciated.

Perhaps our Canadian compatriots of West European origin have more cause to lament the passing of an Indian language than they realize or care to admit. Scholars mourn that there is no one who can speak the Huron language and thus assist scholars in their pursuit of further knowledge about the tribe; scholars mourn that had the Beothuk language survived, so much more would be known about the Beothuk peoples. In mourning the extinction of the language, scholars are implicitly declaring that the knowledge derived from a study of snowshoes, shards, arrowheads, old pipes, shrunken heads and old bones, hunting, fishing, transportation, food preparation, ornamentation, and sometimes ritual is limited. And so it is; material culture can yield only so much.

Language is crucial. If scholars are to increase their knowledge and if they are to add depth and width to their studies, they must study a native language and literature.

It is not enough to know linguistics or to know a few words or even some phrases or to have access to the Jesuit *Relations*, Chippewa *Exercises*, Ojibwa *Texts*, or a *Dictionary of the Otchipwe Language*. Without a knowledge of the language scholars can never take for granted the accuracy of an interpretation or translation of a passage, let alone a single word; nor can they presume that their articles, tracts, treatises, essays bear the kind of accuracy that scholarship and integrity demand. They would continue to labour under the impression that the word 'manitou' means spirit and that it has no other meaning. Superstitious nonsense, according to the white man. They do not know that the word bears other meanings even more fundamental than 'spirit', such as, and/or pertaining to the deities; of a substance, character, nature, essence, quiddity beyond comprehension and therefore beyond explanation, a mystery; supernatural; potency, potential. What a difference such knowledge might have made in the studies conducted by Ruth Landes or Thomas B. Leekley, and others on the Anishinaubae tribe. Perhaps, instead of regarding 'Indians' as superstitious for positing 'spirits' in trees or in other inanimate or insensate objects, they might have credited them with insight for having perceived a vital substance or essence that imparted life, form, growth, healing, and strength in all things, beings, and places. They might have understood that the expression 'manitouwan' meant that an object possessed or was infused with an element or a feature that was beyond human ken; they might have understood that 'w'manitouwih' meant that he or she was endowed with extraordinary talents, and that it did not mean that he or she was a spirit.

Language is essential. If scholars and writers are to know how 'Indians' perceive and regard certain ideas they must study an 'Indian' language. When an 'Anishinaubae' says that someone is telling the truth, he says 'w'daeb-awae'. But the expression is not just a mere confirmation of a speaker's veracity. It is at the same time a philosophical proposition that, in saying, a speaker casts his words and his voice only as far as his vocabulary and his perception will enable him. In so doing the tribe was denying that there was absolute truth; that the best a speaker could achieve and a listener expect was the highest degree of accuracy. Somehow that one expression 'w'daeb-awae' set the limits of a single statement as well as setting limits on all speech.

There was a special regard almost akin to reverence for speech and for the truth. Perhaps it was because words bear the tone of the speaker and may therefore be regarded as belonging to that person; perhaps it is because words have but a fleeting momentary existence in sound and are gone except in memory; perhaps it is because words have not ceased to exist but survive in echo and continue on in infinity; perhaps it is because words are medicine that can heal or injure; perhaps it is because words possess an element of the manitou that enabled them to conjure images and ideas out of nothing, and are the means by which the autissokanuk (muses) inspired men and women. It was not for nothing that the older generation did not solicit the autissokanuk to assist in the genesis of stories or in the composition of chants in seasons other than winter.

To instil respect for language the old counselled youth, 'Don't talk too much' (Kegon zaum-doongaen), for they saw a kinship between language and truth. The expression is not without its facetious aspect but in its broader application it was intended to convey to youth other notions implicit in the expression 'Don't talk too much', for the injunction also meant 'Don't talk too often . . . Don't talk too long . . . Don't talk about those matters that you know nothing about.' Were a person to restrict his discourse, and measure his speech, and govern his talk by what he knew, he would earn the trust and respect of his (her) listeners. Of that man or woman they would say 'w'daeb-awae'. Better still, people would want to hear the speaker again and by so doing bestow upon the speaker the opportunity to speak, for ultimately it is the people who confer the right of speech by their audience.

Language was a precious heritage; literature was no less precious. So precious did the tribe regard language and speech that it held those who abused language and speech and truth in contempt and ridicule and withheld from them their trust and confidence. To the tribe the man or woman who rambled on and on, or who let his tongue range over every subject or warp the truth was said to talk in circles in a manner no different from that of a mongrel who, not knowing the source of alarm, barks in circles (w'geewi-animoh). Ever since words and sounds were reduced to written symbols and have been stripped of their mystery and magic, the regard and reverence for them have diminished in tribal life.

As rich and full of meaning as may be individual words and expression, they embody only a small portion of the entire stock and potential of tribal knowledge, wisdom, and intellectual attainment; the greater part is deposited in myths, legends, stories, and in the lyrics of chants that make up the tribe's literature. Therein will be found the essence and the substance of tribal ideas, concepts, insights, attitudes, values, beliefs, theories, notions, sentiments, and accounts of their institutions and rituals and ceremonies. Without language scholars, writers, and teachers will have no access to the depth and width of tribal knowledge and understanding, but must continue to labour as they have done these many years under the impression that 'Indian' stories are nothing more than fairy tales or folklore, fit only for juvenile minds. For scholars and academics Nanabush, Raven, Glooscap, Weesaukeechauk, and other mythological figures will ever remain 'tricksters', culture heroes, deities whose misadventures were dreamed into being only for the amusement of children. Primitive and pagan and illiterate to boot, 'Indians' could not possibly address or articulate abstract ideas or themes; neither their minds nor their languages could possibly express any idea more complex than taboos, superstitions, and bodily needs.

But were ethnologists, anthropologists, linguists, teachers of native children and writers of native literature—yes, even archaeologists—to learn a native language, perhaps they might learn that Nanabush and Raven are not simply 'tricksters' but the caricatured representations of human nature and character in their many facets; perhaps they might give thought to the meaning and sense to be found in Weessaukeetchauk, The Bitter Soul. There is no other way except through language for scholars to learn or to validate their studies, their theories, their theses about the values, ideals or institutions or any other aspect of tribal life; there is no other way by which knowledge of native life can find increase. Not good enough is it to say in hushed tones after a reverential description of a totem pole or the lacing of a snowshoe, 'My, weren't they clever.'

Just consider the fate of 'Indian' stories written by those who knew nothing of the language and never did hear any of the stories in their entirety or in their original version but derived everything that they knew of their subject from second, third, and even fourth diluted sources. Is it any wonder then that the stories in *Indian Legends of Canada* by E.E. Clark or in *Manabozho* by T.B. Leekley are so bland and devoid of sense. Had the authors known the stories in their 'Indian' sense and flavour, perhaps they might have infused their versions with more wit and substance. Had the authors known that the creation story as the Anishinaubae understood it to mean was intended to represent in the most dramatic way possible the process of individual development from the smallest portion of talent to be retrieved from the depths of one's being and then given growth by breath of life. Thus a man and woman are to develop themselves, create their own worlds, and shape their being and give meaning to life. Had the authors known this meaning of the Creation Story, perhaps they might have written their accounts in terms more in keeping with the sense and thrust of the story. But not knowing the language nor having heard the story in its original text or state, the authors could not, despite their intentions, impart to their accounts the due weight and perspective the story deserved. The stories were demeaned.

With language dead and literature demeaned, 'Indian' institutions are beyond understanding and restoration. Let us turn back the calendar two and a half centuries, to that period when the 'Indian' languages were spoken in every home, when native literature inspired thought, and when native 'Indian' institutions governed native 'Indian' life. It was then that a native institution caught the imagination of the newcomers to this continent. The men and women who founded a new nation to be known as the United States of America took as their model for their constitution and government the principles of government and administration embodied in The Great Tree of Peace of the Five Nations Confederacy. The institution of The Great Tree of Peace was not then too primitive nor too alien for study or emulation to the founders of the United States. In more recent years even the architects of the United Nations regarded the 'Indian' institution of The Great Tree of Peace not as a primitive organization beneath their dignity and intellect, but rather as an institution of merit. There exist still 'Indian' institutions that may well serve and benefit this society and this nation, not as dramatically as did The Great Tree of Peace the United States of America, but bestow some good as yet undreamed or unimagined. Just how much good such institutions may confer upon this or some future generation will not be known unless the 'Indian' languages survive.

And what is it that had undermined the vitality of some of the 'Indian' languages and deprived this generation and this society the promise and the benefit of the wisdom and knowledge embodied in tribal literature?

In the case of the Beothuk and their language, the means used were simple and direct: it was the blade, the bludgeon, and the bullet that were plied in the destruction of the Beothuk in their sleep, at their table, and in their quiet passage from home to place of work, until the tribe was no more. The speakers were annihilated; no more was the Beothuk language spoken; whatever their wisdom or whatever their institutions, the whole of the Beothuk heritage was destroyed.

In other instances, instead of bullets, bludgeons, and bayonets, other means were used to put an end to the speaking of an 'Indian' language. A kick with a police riding boot administered by a 175-pound man upon the person of an eight-year-old boy for uttering the language of a savage left its pain for days and its bruise upon the spirit for life. A boy once kicked was not likely to risk a second or a third. A slap in the face or a punch to the back of the head delivered even by a small man upon the person of a small boy left its sting and a humiliation not soon forgotten. And if a boot or a fist were not administered, then a lash or a yardstick was plied until the 'Indian' language was beaten out. To boot and fist and lash was added ridicule. Both speaker and his language were assailed. 'What's the use of that language? It isn't polite to speak another language in the presence of other people. Learn English! That's the only way you're going to get ahead. How can you learn two languages at the same time? No wonder kids can't learn anything else. It's a primitive language; hasn't the vocabulary to express abstract ideas, poor. Say "ugh". Say something in your language! . . . How can you get your tongue around those sounds?' On and on the comments were made, disparaging, until in too many the language was shamed into silence and disuse.

And how may the federal government assist in the restoration of the native languages to their former vigour and vitality and enable them to fulfil their promise?

The Government of Canada must finance the establishment of either provincial or regional language institutes to be affiliated with a museum or a university or a provincial native educational organization. The function of the 'institute', to be headed by a native person who speaks, reads, and writes a native language, will be to foster research into language and to encourage the publication of lexicons, dictionaries, grammars, courses, guides, outlines, myths, stories, legends, genealogies, histories, religion, rituals, ceremonies, chants, prayers, and general articles; to tape stories, myths, legends, grammars, teaching guides and outlines and to build a collection of written and oral literature to make same accessible to scholars, teachers, and native institutions; and to duplicate and distribute written and oral literature to the native communities and learning institutions. The native languages deserve to be enshrined in this country's heritage as much as do snowshoes, shards, and arrowheads. Nay! More.

But unless the writings, the essays, stories, plays, the papers of scholars, academics, lexicographers, grammarians, etymologists, playwrights, poets, novelists, composers, philosophers are published and distributed, they can never nurture growth in language or literature. Taking into account the market represented by each tribe, no commercial publisher would risk publication of an 'Indian' book. Hence, only the federal government has the means to sponsor publication of an 'Indian text', either through a commercial publisher or through the Queen's Printer. The publication of an 'Indian' book may not be a commercially profitable enterprise, but it would add to the nation's intellectual and literary heritage.

Is That All There Is? Tribal Literature

In the early sixties Kahn-Tineta Horn, a young Mohawk model, got the attention of the Canadian press (media) not only by her beauty but by her articulation of Indian grievances and her demands for justice. Soon after Red Power was organized threatening to use force. Academics and scholars, anxious and curious to know what provoked the Indians, organized a series of conferences and teach-ins to explore the issues. Even children wanted to know. So for their enlightenment experts wrote dozens of books. Universities and colleges began native studies courses. Ministries of Education, advised by a battery of consultants, adjusted their Curriculum Guidelines to allow units of study on the native peoples of this continent. And school projects were conducted for the benefit of children between ten and thirteen years of age.

One such project at the Churchill Avenue Public School in North York, Ontario lasted six weeks and the staff and students who had taken part mounted a display as a grand finale to their studies. And a fine display it was in the school's library.

In front of a canvas tent that looked like a teepee stood a grim chief, face painted in war-like colours and arms folded. On his head he wore a headdress made of construction paper. A label pinned to his vest bore the name, Blackfoot. I made straight for the chief.

'How!' I greeted the chief, holding up my hand at the same time as a gesture of friendship.

Instead of returning the greeting, the chief looked at me quizzically.

'How come you look so unhappy?' I asked him.

'Sir! I'm bored,' the chief replied.

'How so, chief?'

'Sir, don't tell anybody, but I'm bored. I'm tired of Indians. That's all we've studied for six weeks. I thought they'd be interesting when we started, because I always thought that Indians were neat. At the start of the course we had to choose to do a special project from food preparation, transportation, dwellings, social organization, clothing, and hunting and fishing. I chose dwellings' and here the chief exhaled in exasperation '. . . and that's all me and my team studied for six weeks: teepees, wigwams, longhouses, igloos. We read books, encyclopedias, went to the library to do research, looked at pictures, drew pictures. Then we had to make one. Sir, I'm bored.'

'Didn't you learn anything else about Indians, chief?'

'No sir, there was nothing else . . . Sir? . . . Is that all there is to Indians?'

Little has changed since that evening in 1973. Books still present native people in terms of their physical existence as if Indians were incapable of meditating upon or grasping the abstract. Courses of study in the public school system, without other sources of information, had to adhere to the format, pattern, and content set down in books. Students studied Kaw-lijas, wooden Indians, who were incapable of love or laughter; or Tontos, if you will, whose sole skill was to make fires and to perform other servile duties for the Lone Ranger; an inarticulate Tonto, his speech limited to 'Ugh!' 'Kimo Sabi', and 'How'.

Despite all the research and the field work conducted by anthropologists, ethnologists, and linguists, Indians remain 'The Unknown Peoples' as Professor George E. Tait of the University of Toronto so aptly titled his book written in 1973.

Not even Indian Affairs of Canada, with its more than two centuries of experience with natives, with its array of experts and consultants, with its unlimited funds, seems to have learned anything about its constituents, if we are to assess their latest publication titled 'The Canadian Indian'. One would think that the Honourable William McKnight, then Minister of Indian and Northern Affairs, under whose authority the book was published in 1986 should know by now the Indians who often come to Ottawa, do not arrive on horseback, do not slay one of the RCMP mounts and cook it on the steps of the Parliament Buildings. Moreover, most Indians he has seen and met were not dressed in loincloths, nor did they sleep in teepees. Yet he authorized the publication of a book bereft of any originality or imagination, a book that perpetuated the notion and the image that the Indians had not advanced one step since contact, but are still living as they had one hundred and fifty, even three hundred years ago. There was not a word about native thought, literature, institutions, contributions in music, art, theatre. But that's to be expected of Indian Affairs; to know next to nothing of their constituents.

Where did the author or authors of this latest publication by Indian Affairs get their information? The selected readings listed at the back of the book provide a clue; Frances Densmore, Harold Driver, Philip Drucker, Frederick W. Hodge, Diamond Jenness, Reginald and Gladys Laubin, Frank G. Speck, Bruce G. Trigger, George Woodcock, Harold Innes, Calvin Martin, E. Palmer Patterson, eminent scholars, none of whom spoke or attempted to learn the language of any of the Indian nations about whom they were writing. Modern scholars because they are not required by their universities to learn, are no more proficient in a native language than were their predecessors.

Herein, I submit, is the nub and the rub. Without the benefit of knowing the language of the Indian nation that they are investigating, scholars can never get into their mind, the heart and soul and the spirit and still understand the native's perceptions and interpretations. The scholar must confine his research and studies to the material, physical culture, subsistence patterns, and family relationships.

Without knowing the spiritual and the intellectual, aesthetic side of Indian culture, the scholar cannot furnish what that little grade five youngster and others like him wanted to know about Indians.

Admitting his boredom was that grade five youngster's way of expressing his disappointment with the substance of the course that he and his colleagues had been made to endure. In another sense, it was a plea for other knowledge that would quench his curiosity and challenge his intellect.

Students such as he, as well as adults, are interested in the character, intellect, soul, spirit, heart of people of other races and cultures. They want to know what other people believe in, what they understand, what they expect and hope for in this life and in the next, how they keep law and order and harmony within the family and community, how and why they celebrated ceremonies, what made them proud, ashamed, what made them happy, what sad. Whether the young understand what they want to know and learn does not matter much, they still want to know in order to enrich their own insights and broaden their outlooks.

But unless scholars and writers know the literature of the peoples that they are studying or writing about they cannot provide what their students and readers are seeking and deserving of.

There is, fortunately, enough literature, both oral and written, available for scholarly study, but it has for the most part been neglected. Myths, legends, and songs have not been regenerated and set in modern terms to earn immortalization in poetry, dramatization in plays, or romanticization in novels.

What has prevented the acceptance of Indian literature as a serious and legitimate expression of native thought and experience has been indifferent and inferior translation, a lack of understanding and interest in the culture, and a notion that it has little of importance to offer to the larger white culture.

In offering you a brief sketch, no more than a glimpse, as it were, of my tribe's culture, I am doing no more than what anyone of you would do were you to be asked 'What is your culture? Would you explain it?' I would expect you to reply, 'Read my literature, and you will get to know something of my thoughts, my convictions, my aspirations, my feelings, sentiments, expectations, whatever I cherish or abominate.'

First, let me offer you an observation about my language for the simple reason that language and literature are inseparable, though they are too often taught as separate entities. They belong together.

In my tribal language, all words have three levels of meaning; there is the surface meaning that everyone instantly understands. Beneath this meaning is a more fundamental meaning derived from the prefixes and their combinations with other terms. Underlying both is the philosophical meaning.

Take the word 'Anishinaubae'. That is what the members of the nation, now known as Chippewa in the United States or Ojibway in Canada, called themselves. It referred to a member of the tribe. It was given to the question 'What are you?' But it was more than just a term of identification. It meant, 'I am a person of good intent, a person of worth' and it reflected what the people thought of themselves, and of human nature; that all humans are essentially, fundamentally good. Let's separate that one word into its two terms. The first, 'Onishishih' meaning good, fine, beautiful, excellent; and the second 'naubae' meaning being, human being, male, human species. Even together they do not yield the meaning 'good intention'. It is only by examining the stories of Nanabush, the tribes' central and principal mythical figure who represents all men and all women, that the term Anishinaubae begins to make sense. Nanabush was always full of good intentions, ergo the people of the tribe, the Anishinaubae perceive themselves as people who intended good and therefore of merit and worth. From this perception they drew a strong sense of pride as well as a firm sense of place in the community. This influenced their notion of independence.

Let's take another word, the word for truth. When we say 'w'daeb-awae' we mean he or she is telling the truth, is correct, is right. But the expression is not merely an affirmation of a speaker's veracity. It is as well a philosophical proposition that in saying a speaker casts his words and his voice as far as his perception and his vocabulary will enable him or her, it is a denial that there is such a thing as absolute truth; that the best and most the speaker can achieve and a listener expect is the highest degree of accuracy. Somehow that one expression, 'w'daeb-awae', sets the limits to a single statement as well as setting limits to truth and the scope and exercise of speech.

One other word 'to know'. We say 'w'kikaendaun' to convey the idea that he or she 'knows'. Without going into the etymological derivations, suffice it to say that when the speaker assures someone that he knows it, that person is saying that the notion, image, idea, fact that that person has in mind corresponds and is similar to what he or she has already seen, heard, touched, tasted, or smelled. That person's knowledge may not be exact, but similar to that which has been instilled and impressed in his or her mind and recalled from memory.

The stories that make up our tribal literature are no different from the words in our language. Both have many meanings and applications, as well as bearing tribal perceptions, values, and outlooks.

Let us begin at the beginning with the tribe's story of creation which precedes all other stories in the natural order. Creation stories provide insights into what races and nations understand of human nature; ours is no different in this respect.

This is our creation story. Kitchi-manitou beheld a vision. From this vision The Great Mystery, for that is the essential and fundamental meaning of Kitchi-manitou and not spirit as is often understood, created the sun and the stars, the land and the waters, and all the creatures and beings, seen and unseen, that inhabit the earth, the seas, and the skies. The creation was desolated by a flood. Only the manitous, creatures and beings who dwelt in the waters were spared. All others perished.

In the heavens dwelt a manitou, Geezhigo-quae (Sky-woman). During the cataclysm upon the earth, Geezhigo-quae became pregnant. The creatures adrift upon the seas prevailed upon the giant turtle to offer his back as a haven for Geezhigo-quae. They then invited her to come down.

Resting on the giant turtle's back Geezhigo-quae asked for soil.

One after another water creatures dove into the depths to retrieve a morsel of soil. Not one returned with a particle of soil. They all offered an excuse; too deep, too dark, too cold, there are evil manitous keeping watch. Last to descend was the muskrat. He returned with a small knot of earth.

With the particle of mud retrieved by the muskrat Geezhigo-quae re-created an island and the world as we know it. On the island she created over the giant turtle's shell, Geezhigo-quae gave birth to twins who begot the tribe called the Anishinaubaeg.

Millennia later the tribe dreamed Nanabush into being. Nanabush represented themselves and what they understood of human nature. One day his world too was flooded. Like Geezhigo-quae, Nanabush recreated his world from a morsel of soil retrieved from the depths of the sea.

As a factual account of the origin of the world and of being, the story has no more basis than the biblical story of creation and the flood. But the story represents a belief in God, the creator, a Kitchi-manitou, the Great Mystery. It also represents a belief that Kitchi-manitou sought within himself, his own being, a vision. Or perhaps it came from within his being and that Kitchi-manitou created what was beheld and set it into motion. Even the lesser manitous, such as Geezhigo-quae and Nanabush, must seek a morsel of soil with which to create and recreate their world, their spheres. So men and women must seek within themselves the talent or the potential and afterward create their own worlds and their own spheres and a purpose to give meaning to their lives.

The people begotten by Geezhigo-quae on that mythological island called themselves Anishinaubaeg, the good beings who meant well and were human beings, therefore fundamentally good. But they also knew that men and women were often deflected from fulfilling their good intentions and prevented from living up to their dreams and visions, not out of any inherent evil, but rather from something outside of themselves. Nanabush also represented this aspect of human nature. Many times Nanabush or the Anishinaubaeg fail to carry out a noble purpose. Despite this, he is not rendered evil or wicked but remains fundamentally and essentially good.

Men and women intend what is good, but they forget. The story called 'The Man, The Snake, and The Fox' exemplifies this aspect of human nature.

In its abbreviated form the story is as follows. The hunter leaves his lodge and his family at daybreak to go in search of game to feed his wife and his children. As he proceeds through the forest, the hunter sees deer, but each time they are out of range of his weapon.

Late in the afternoon, discouraged and weary, he hears faint cries in the distance. Forgetting his low spirits and fatigue he sets out with renewed optimism and vigour in the direction of the cries. Yet the nearer he draws to the source of the cries, the more daunted is the hunter by the dreadful screams. Only the thought of his family's needs drove him forward, otherwise he might have turned away.

At last he came to a glade. The screams came from a thicket on the opposite side. The hunter, bow and arrow drawn and ready, made his way forward cautiously.

To his horror, the hunter saw an immense serpent tangled fast in a thicket as a fish is caught in the webbing of a net. The monster writhed and roared and twisted. He struggled to break free.

The man recoiled in horror. Before he could back away, the snake saw him.

'Friend!' the snake addressed the man.

The man fell in a heap on the ground the moment that the snake spoke. When he came to much later the snake pleaded with the man to set him free. For some time the man refused but eventually he relented. He was persuaded by the monster's plea that he too, though a serpent, had no less right to life than did the man. And the serpent promised not to injure the man on his release. The hunter was convinced.

The snake sprang on his deliverer the moment the last vine was cut away.

It was like thunder as the man and the snake struggled. Nearby a little fox heard the uproar. Never having seen such a spectacle the fox settled down to watch. Immediately he realized that the man was about to be killed.

Why were the snake and the man locked in mortal struggle? The little fox shouted for an explanation. The man and the snake stopped.

The hunter gasped out his story, then the snake gave his version. Pretending not to understand the snake's explanation the fox beguiled the aggressor into returning to the thicket to act out his side of the story.

The snake entangled himself once more.

Realizing that he had been delivered from the edge of death by the fox, the man was greatly moved. He felt bound to show his gratitude in some tangible way. The fox assured him that no requital was required. Nevertheless the hunter persisted. How might he, the hunter, perform some favour on behalf of the fox?

Not only was there no need, the fox explained, there was nothing that the man could do for the fox; there was not a thing that the fox needed or desired of human beings. However, if it would make the man happier, the fox suggested that the man might feed him should he ever have need.

Nothing would please the man more than to perform some good for his deliverer; it was the least that he could do for a friend who had done so much.

Some years later the hunter shot a little fox who had been helping himself to the family storage. As the man drew his knife to finish off the thief, the little fox gasped, 'Don't you remember?'

That no snakes as monstrous as the one in the story are to be found on this continent makes no difference to the youngsters' sense of outrage over the treachery of the snake and the forgetfulness of the man; nor does the exercise of speech which enables the snake and the fox to communicate with the hunter and each other prevent the young from being moved to compassion for the fox. Their sense of justice and fairness bears them over the anomalies in the story.

Before the last words 'Don't you remember?' have echoed away, the young begin to ask questions. 'Why? Why did the man not recognize the fox? Why did he forget? How did the man feel afterwards? Why did the snake attack the man? Why did the snake break his promise? Why didn't the man leave the snake where he was? Do animals really have as much right to live as human beings do?'

Indians cared, loved as passionately as other people.

The story called 'The Weeping Pine' raises the same questions about love and marriage and the span of either that have been asked by philosophers, poets, and lovers of every race and generation. It does not pretend to give answers to these age old questions beyond suggesting that love may bloom even in circumstances where it is least expected to flower and endure. But owing to shoddy translation, the story has been presented as an explanation for the origin of pine trees.

According to the story, the elders of a village came to a certain young woman's home where she lived with her parents, brothers, and sisters. They had come to let her family know that they had chosen her to be the new wife to an old man. This particular man had been without a friend since the death of his first wife some years before. The old man was described as good-natured and kind. As one who had done much to benefit the tribe in his youth, the old man deserved something in return from his neighbours. In the opinion of the elders the most fitting reward the old man could have was a wife. In their judgement the young woman they had chosen would be a suitable companion for the old man.

They assured her that the tribe would see to it that they never had need.

Because this sort of marriage was a matter that the young woman had not considered, it was unexpected. The delegation understood this. They did not demand an immediate answer but allowed the woman a few days in which to make up her mind.

The young woman cried when the delegation left. She didn't want to marry that man. That old man whose days were all but over and who could never look after her. She had, like every young girl her age, hoped to marry someone young, full of promise, someone she would love and who would love her in return. Besides, it was too soon. How could she, not yet eighteen, be a companion to an old man of seventy or more? The disparity was too great.

At first her parents too were aggrieved. But soon after they prevailed upon her to defer to the wishes of the elders, and her father delivered word of their daughter's consent to the elders.

But neither the disparity in age nor the disposition of the young girl to enter into a loveless marriage were too great; in the years that followed she came to love this old man. And they had many children.

Thirty years later the old man died.

On the final day of the four day watch, the mourners went home but the widow made no move to rise. She continued to keen and rock back and forth in great sorrow.

'Come mother, let us go home,' her children urged, offering to assist her to her feet and to support her on their way home.

'No! No! Leave me. Go,' she said.

'Mother! Please. Come home with us,' her children pleaded. Nothing they said could persuade their mother to leave.

'No. You go home. This is where I belong. Leave me.'

Her children prayed she would relent; give in to the cold and hunger. They went home, but they did not leave their mother alone. During the next few days a son or daughter was always at her side, watching with her and entreating her to come home. They tried to comfort her with their own love and care, assuring her that her wound would pass and heal. They even brought her food and drink to sustain her. She refused everything.

As their mother grew weaker with each passing day, the children besought the elders to intercede on their behalf. Perhaps the elders could prevail on their mother.

But the elders shook their heads and said, 'If that is what she wants, there is nothing that you can do to change her mind. Leave her be. She wants to be with him. Leave her. It's better that way.'

And so the family ceased to press their mother to come home, though they still kept watch with her. They watched until she too died by the graveside of her husband, their father.

Using the term 'grandchild' that all elders used in referring to the young, the elder who presided over the woman's wake said, 'Our granddaughter's love did not cease with death, but continues into the next life.'

The next spring a small plant grew out of the grave of the woman. Many years later, as the sons, daughters, and grandchildren gathered at the graveside of their parents, they felt a mist fall upon their faces and their arms. 'It is mother shedding tears of love for dad,' cried her daughter.

And it is so. On certain days, spruces and pines shed a mist of tears of love.

By remaining at her husband's graveside until she too died, the woman fulfilled the implied promise, 'whither thou goest, there too will I go' contained in the term 'weedjeewaugun', companion in life, our word for spouse.

As she wept for her love she must have wept for the love of her children. Their love threatened to break that bond that held her to her husband. No! She would not sever that bond; she would not let even death part her from the man to whom she had given her heart, her soul, her spirit forever.

It is unlikely that the woman ever uttered more than 'K'zaugin' (I love you) during her marriage. In this respect she was no different from most other women, or men for that matter, who are not endowed with the poetic gift, though they feel and love with equal passion and depth. K'zaugin said everything. I love you, today, tomorrow, forever. It expressed everything that the finest poets ever wrote and everything that the unpoetic ever thought and felt but could not put into rhyme or rhythm.

In sentiment the story compares to Elizabeth Barrett Browning's immortal poem, 'How do I love thee' which ends with the words 'and if God grant, I shall love thee better after death.'

Rita Joe *b.* 1932

MI'KMAQ

Born on 15 March 1932 in Whycocomogh, Cape Breton, Nova Scotia, Rita Joe spent her childhood with foster families. At the age of twelve, she recalls, 'I put myself into the Indian Residential School in Shubenacadie. That school plays an important part in my life, along with Native upbringing by many mothers.' After completing high school, she pursued a business educational program in typing and completed a twelve-week course on reading and writing Mi'kmaq at the University College of Cape Breton.

Joe now lives on the Eskasoni Reserve in Cape Breton. The widowed mother of ten children—two adopted—and now a grandmother as well, she is active in the education of Native children, both within her family and throughout the country. She is also involved in the education of the world at large on the subject of Native culture. She talks to a broad range of groups, from university students to Brownies and Boy Scouts: 'My education is my people— I have a front seat to see and feel their needs, the major one being that we, too, live with ideal productiveness.'

In 1974, Joe entered and won a competition held by the Nova Scotia Writers Federation: 'The surprise had even more meaning to it; I remember thinking at the time, now my people will think, "If she can do it, so can I."' Thus, for Joe, to be a Native writer is a significant responsibility: 'The label is deep-rooted and the stroke of a Native pen does wonders, especially for the coming generation.'

Joe's first book, *Poems of Rita Joe* (1978), consists of twenty-six untitled poems, for the most part brief, some with Mi'kmaq translations. Her second book, *Song of Eskasoni:*

More Poems of Rita Joe (1988), has no full translations but features Micmac lines and phrases. The book's editor, Lee Maracle, sees an inner force to this combination of cultures: 'Her Micmac spirit—her love of the land—peers through her strong sense of Christendom and dominates her sense of spirituality.' Since 1988 Joe has published another poetry collection, *Lnu and Indians We're Called* (1991) and, with the assistance of Lynn Henry, *Song of Rita Joe: Autobiography of a Mi'kmaq Poet* (1996). She was awarded the Order of Canada in 1990.

The hallmark of Joe's poetry, in form and content, is simplicity: 'The attitude I have in writing is a positive outlook on life. Sure, we all have a hard time sometime or other, but we cannot dwell on the negativeness forever; at times I get discouraged but do not let it get to me.' The politics of Joe's poems, while subtle, is always an important element. In response to the Oka crisis, for example, she declared, ' "This is my country!" yet my country was doing things I never for a moment thought they would do to my people. I know there are two sides to any story, but I have to side with my people here.' Lee Maracle has stated, 'Rita Joe's poems pen for the reader that most important love of all—the love of people in their quest for a just society.' Joe's statement on the appropriation of voice is typical in its rejection of confrontation and its assertion of the positive over the negative: 'If we consider our Native culture important, we the Native people must put it down on paper our way. . . . If I get too sentimental in my choice of words, excuse me. I have to call attention to the gentle people of Canada. My song is gentle, bear with me.'

Today's Learning Child

I see the bronze hue of skin
The dark eyes flashing.
The arrogant hold of that stare
Into the dream of that softness of life
Just out of reach.   5

The angry hold onto the reality
Into determination.
To see the life of improvement
Someday soon.

The head is bent, the shoulders round   10
That force upon learning, commanding,
Until dignity nods.

We are different to this age
We rely so much.

Please understand;   15
The chisel must continue to carve an image
Because all our life has already been labelled.

I Lost My Talk

I lost my talk
The talk you took away.
When I was a little girl
At Shubenacadie school.

You snatched it away: 5
I speak like you
I think like you
I create like you
The scrambled ballad, about my word.
Two ways I talk   10
Both ways I say,
Your way is more powerful.

So gently I offer my hand and ask,
Let me find my talk
. So I can teach you about me.   15

Micmac Hieroglyphics

'I noticed children
Making marks with charcoal on ground,'
Said LeClerq.
'This made me see
That in form would create a memory   5
Of learning more quickly
The prayers I teach.

'I was not mistaken,
The characters produced
The effect I needed.   10
For on birchbark they saw
These familiar figures
Signifying a word,
Sometimes two together.
The understanding came quickly   15
On leaflets
They called kekin a'matin kewe'l
Tools for learning.

'The preservation of written word
Was in so much care.   20
They kept them neatly in little cases
Of birchbark
Beautified with wampum
Of beadwork and quills.
These were the Micmac hieroglyphics   25
The written word of the Indian
That the world chooses to deny.'

Shanawdithit

(Pronounced Shaw-now-dih-diht)

She was born in Ktaqamkuk
Shanawdithit her name
To a family life like yours or mine
Of caring people
The Beothuks of Newfoundland.   5
And then her people passed away one by one
Endurance no meaning anymore because of strife
By the newcomers who must own all land
No matter the price.
But survival became her way, even venturing close   10
To these strange people who can hurt so much
But there were women who cared enough to feed her
Allowing her to earn her keep as a servant.

And then six winters passed
A strange man with kindness in the eyes approached her.   15
The wounded heart replaced by warmth
Of a father image, a caring brother,
She tried to please him, learning the language
The strange ways these people questioned her.
She drew pictures   20
Trying to remember the implements of life.
Always working, repaying the life spared her.
Until she became easily tired
Needing the land of her people, to be close
To walk where they walked. Feeling the spirits   25
In dreamland, their nearness, so close but handshake away.

Finally she joined them, in the everland of red ochre
Shanawdithit, the flower of the Beothuks
The last martyr of Taqmkuk.

The Lament of Donald Marshall Jr.

Everybody knows the story about Donald Marshall Jr.—how he served eleven years in prison for a crime he did not commit. The sad irony of the whole story is that they were both minorities, the one gone and the one accused. In 1971 these two young people got together that night as easily as any young people would. It ended in tragedy.

The hurt of rejection is sometimes there in our society, the failure of some people who take part in it are the ones to be pitied. They are the ones who are blind to love, humanity, kindness, and compassion. I speak for the Indian, or any minority. The pain of rejection will always be there as long as people fail to educate themselves that we are all the same. We are all one.

How do we remove injustice? Try moving hearts.

Song
I have served prison term, with locks on the door
My pain it is known, it is known the world over.
On my heart's aching core, I didn't do, I was told
He was my friend
We are the same, we are the same, we are the same.   5

My hurt is not gone, the key is beyond
The pain that is known, it is known the world over.
On my heart's aching core, I didn't do, I didn't do
He was my friend
We are the same, we are the same, we are the same.   10

The pain will be there, as long as men fail
My hurt it is known, it is known the world over.
On my heart's aching core, I didn't do I was told
He was my friend
We are the same, we are the same, we are the same.   15

Anthony Apakark Thrasher 1937–1989

INUIT

Anthony Thrasher began life as a nomadic Inuk in the small community of Paulatuk. At the age of six, he was sent to Aklavik, to a residential school, as what he later called 'a Grade 1 captive' of a Roman Catholic mission. He recalled the joys of his summers when he felt a full participant in hunting, fishing, and all aspects of traditional life, and then the severe shock of each fall when the nuns would harshly reintroduce him to the rules of school.

When Thrasher was twelve his father had a stroke, and Thrasher was discharged from the school to help the family. He worked at first in traditional pursuits but at seventeen went to Tuktoyaktuk to work on the construction of military stations for the Distant Early Warning Line. He realized this was part of a general change in the North and at nineteen went south to take a course in driving machines. 'Half of the population of Aklavik was relying on government hand-outs. It was either that, or join the white construction gangs, or starve.'

In Edmonton, Thrasher was amazed by everything from traffic lights to prostitution. Alcohol became a major problem for Thrasher and for the other Inuit new to the South. When he got back to the North he was able to get work in the creation of the new town of Inuvik.

The early entries in Thrasher's criminal record suggest a series of petty misunderstandings. Many, if not all, of the convictions were alcohol-related. At twenty-seven he was sent to an alcoholic rehabilitation centre. This helped only for a time. He soon returned to alcohol. He described himself during this period as 'anybody's riverbank pal'. Now sniffing glue and

nailpolish remover, he returned to the rehabilitation centre, but it had no long-term effect. In jail, he tried unsuccessfully to hang himself. Then he was charged with murder, for the death of a man he couldn't remember even meeting.

Given seven years for manslaughter, Thrasher was sent to the Prince Albert Penitentiary, where he felt, from both the other inmates and the guards, 'the ever-present danger'. The worst thing, he recalled, was trying to deal with the racism—of whites, 'niggers', and 'Indians': 'As an Eskimo, I was in the middle.'

Thrasher records other terrors of prison life, from drugs through suicides. He tried to set down his own experiences but found it impossible. Instead, he turned to education, as both student and lecturer, and began to speak about his culture to southern Native groups. A transfer to a minimum-security camp on Vancouver Island followed, but drugs and alcohol led to a fight and he was sent next to the BC Penitentiary. He was soon transferred to a hospital for the criminally insane. Although eventually released, Thrasher never succeeded in regaining control of his life. He died in 1989.

Thrasher's autobiography, *Thrasher: Skid Row Eskimo* (1976), was written at various times. At the urging of his lawyer Thrasher's 'collaborators', Gerry Deagle and Alan Mettrick, collated 'what was essentially a loose-leafed diary into narrative form'. The result is a combination of two stories common to Native biographies: the nostalgic recall of traditional life, most common in Inuit narratives, and the decay through alcohol and institutional racism, more often seen in the stories of southern Native peoples.

Playing with Girls is a Sin

All told, there must have been around eight hundred people living in Aklavik at that time. The rich families—they mostly worked for the Federal Government which had its Western Arctic headquarters there—lived in one- or two-room houses built of lumber and heated with wood or oil. They were over near the hospital, and the Anglican school and cathedral, on the other end of town. A wooden sidewalk ran along in front of them, a wide ditch separating the sidewalk from the snow-packed road. Out back of the houses were the RCMP barracks, the police dog kennels, and the radio tower. Closer to our school was the Hudson's Bay Company store, the biggest of the stores in town, where the Indians and Eskimos who huddled in little huts and tents would sell their furs. Some Indians lived across the river and every day I'd see them crossing the ice on their way to jobs in town. The trappers all had happy expressions on their faces because the flat delta land on which Aklavik was located was rich with muskrat. In those days their pelts were worth as much as two dollars apiece.

The nuns in charge of us were Sister Bessant, Sister Soka, Sister Gilbert, and Sister Alice Rae, who I loved as much as my real mother. Sister Bessant was nice, too, but Sister Soka used a ruler on our hands and Sister Gilbert was hell-on-wheels for pulling ears, brushing our mouths with lye soap, and whipping us with a watch chain. I could never understand how she could be so mean, and yet be very kind at the same time.

Sister Soka was my teacher. I couldn't catch on to the ABCs, and Sister Soka got a girl called Lena to show me. I was just a little guy, much smaller than Lena, but I wondered if she knew I thought she was pretty.

In the seat ahead of me was a boy named Danny Norris. Behind me was Freddie Carmichael. Whenever I wasn't eating my pencil, I was poking them with it. We had elastic slingshots, too, and every time the teacher turned her back, she was the target.

I was eating cooked food for the first time. I didn't like it and, like the other boys, I would sneak into the kitchen whenever I could and slip away with some frozen meat. We tossed our bones into the school yard and that's how it came to look more like a bone yard than a playground.

When anyone complained about the food, the nuns would make the complainer drink a whole can of cod liver oil, to do penance for committing something they called a venial sin. That was smaller than a mortal sin, and something else called a sacrilege was an even bigger sin than a mortal sin.

You never went to Hell on venials.

There were as many girls as boys at the school. The girls' dormitory was on the top floor at one end of the main building, the boys' at the other end. We even ate in separate rooms.

We were told not to play with the girls, because that would also be a sin. I thought that was strange, because I had played with girls before I came to school. Now they were telling me I shouldn't touch them. I was taught not to look at girls, and not to look at dogs mating. But I had seen these things long before I went to school. I had seen people in the sex act when I was as young as three years of age. I knew exactly what it was, and how to do it, by the time I was six.

I was forever being scolded for eating with my hands. I didn't like using knives and forks and spoons. I'd drink my soup and rip the meat apart with my teeth. Then I'd wipe my mouth on my sleeves and wipe my hands on my clean knee-length pants. Sister Gilbert put a stop to that.

My grades were somewhere between one and zero. But I was a good wood hauler. About five or six of us would drag loads of wood for the furnaces—four in the school and hospital, one in the parish house, one in the laundry, and one in the kitchen. They all used kindling.

When Hallowe'en came, we got to see our first movie—a silent one with Charlie Chaplin. It was scary, and a lot of us hid under the benches and cried. Brother Jack made things worse by coming in with a pumpkin with a candle glowing inside and holes carved to make the pumpkin look like an evil spirit. At that point I escaped into the arms of dear Sister Alice Rae.

When Sister Gilbert was in a good mood, she used to tell us stories from the newspapers she got sent up from the South. She told us about Adolf Hitler and Mussolini, Joseph Stalin and Churchill, and she said that the German war was going on strong and that Hitler was raising Cain all over Europe and Africa. We prayed a lot that it would end soon.

There was a half hour of prayers in the morning, before and after breakfast. Dinner was at eleven o'clock, and there were prayers before and after that, too.

That fall we went on a picnic, camping overnight in the school shack about two miles into the snow-covered bush out back. I set a trap and caught a whisky-jack. I made a little fire, and burned the feathers off the big blue bird, then let it freeze, and ate it when it was frozen hard. It tasted like caribou liver.

That night someone told the legend of another Eskimo boy, Iliapaluk, an orphan who lived with his grandmother Ananaa, in the bush country. They had a little house, Kutuk, of the kind that is dug into the earth with the roof at ground level. Iliapaluk was just a small boy. He used to snare rabbits with sinews, while the old woman fished with a bone hook. No one knew that this old woman possessed the magic power we call Angatkolik.

They had only the snares to count on for meat. One day, the boy came home and told his grandmother that someone had stolen them. They went to the nearby village to try and get them back, but whoever took the snares would not come forward. The old woman warned the village people not to make fun of a poor orphan boy. She told them she would give whoever took Iliapaluk's snares a chance to return them to him.

Still no one came forward, so they went back home, and the old woman told her grandson to go and hook a fish with roe in it. The boy did this, and the old woman cut the fish open, and took out the eggs. She told her grandson not to watch her for a moment. When the boy turned around, he saw she was covered with fish eggs from head to toe. She told him they were returning to the village, to get the snares.

When they arrived, she told the boy to call everyone out of their houses. When he had done this, the old woman began talking to them.

'I will touch all of you, one by one,' she said. 'If you are good people, do not be afraid. Only the liar will get hurt.'

She then touched everyone, until she got to a man who suddenly dropped dead. He was the thief. He had the snares.

Then the grandmother told the people, 'Whatever you do, do not ever steal from an orphan who has no mother, and who fights hard to live. He only has those little strings to live on, and when you take them away, he can starve and die.'

Storytelling was a part of life in the North. My brothers and I were always competing to tell the best story. But we were no match for our grandfather. He was the greatest of them all. As he talked, he would light his pipe, and smoke 'Old Chum' tobacco. Then he would pick up his drum, and sing. He would sing of Herschel Island in the Arctic Ocean, and tell of times that were good. He would sing of happiness after a successful whale hunt, about the big dances people used to have, of his young days, and his women, and of the medicine man of old.

One of my jobs at the school, with a boy called Douglas Dillon, was emptying the toilet pails. One day, we toppled down a twenty-foot bank on our way to the river to dump the slop. We came out looking like a couple of O'Henry chocolate bars. The outhouse at the end of the playground had sixteen seats, for over two hundred boys. Some of the seats were too big for the little boys, and they used to fall through them. I had the honour of being one of the lucky ones.

Christmas week, we spent four days at the camp shack in the bush. We trapped muskrat, caught one cross fox, snared rabbits, climbed trees, and chewed spruce gum. We also got a chance to see inside the girls' camp.

The toys we got for Christmas were great. I ran away from my first one, a rolling clown. It scared the Christmas spirit right out of me.

On New Year's Day there was a concert, and the RCMP were called in to take some drunks out of the school. They were trappers, and some people from town.

Duke Redbird *b.* 1939

CHIPPEWA

Duke Redbird was born 18 March 1939 on the Saugeen Reserve on the Bruce Peninsula, near Owen Sound, Ontario. A former president of the Ontario Métis and Non-Status Indian Association, former director of Land Claims Research, and former vice-president of the Native Council of Canada, he has worked with all levels of government and with the private sector to meet the needs of Native people in the fields of education, alcohol and drug abuse, economic development, housing, tourism, culture, the arts, and healthcare.

A respected poet and scholar, Redbird's work has been widely published and recognized. In the 1970s, Redbird performed his poetry to audiences throughout Canada and the United States. In 1977, a multimedia musi-

cal based on his poetry was performed in the presence of Queen Elizabeth and the Duke of Edinburgh during Silver Jubilee celebrations in Ottawa. In 1985, he represented Canada at the Valmiki World Poetry Festival in Delhi, India, and that same year he was recognized by the Native Council of Canada for his contributions to Aboriginal people. In 1989, he composed a commissioned work to be read at the opening of the Canadian Museum of Civilization in Hull, Quebec.

Each event of Redbird's life is a stage in the development of his own Native consciousness and in his efforts to develop the Native awareness of all Canadians. *We Are Métis* represents yet another step. Written as an interdisciplinary thesis at York University, where he received his

Master's degree in 1978, it is part of the recent renaissance of the Métis, asserting themselves as a nation within Native cultures in Canada.

Redbird continues to write poetry and paint canvasses and original works of art on pine carvings that reflect his love of the wilderness. In addition to writing, Redbird has worked as an arts and entertainment reporter for CityPulse News in Toronto.

I am a Canadian

I'm a lobster fisherman in Newfoundland
I'm a clambake in PEI
I'm a picnic, I'm a banquet
I'm mother's homemade pie
I'm a few drafts in a Legion hall in Fredericton   5
I'm a kite-flyer in a field in Moncton
I'm a nap on the porch after a hard day's work is done.
I'm a snowball fight in Truro, Nova Scotia
I'm small kids playing jacks and skipping rope
I'm a mother who lost a son in the last great war   10
And I'm a bride with a brand new ring
And a chest of hope
I'm an Easterner
I'm a Westerner
I'm from the North   15
And I'm from the South
I've swam in two big oceans
And I've loved them both
I'm a clown in Quebec during carnival
I'm a mass in the Cathedral of St. Paul   20
I'm a hockey game in the Forum
I'm Rocket Richard and Jean Beliveau
I'm a coach for little league Expos
I'm a baby-sitter for sleep-defying rascals
I'm a canoe trip down the Ottawa   25
I'm a holiday on the Trent
I'm a mortgage, I'm a loan
I'm last week's unpaid rent
I'm Yorkville after dark
I'm a walk in the park   30
I'm a Winnipeg gold-eye
I'm a hand-made trout fly
I'm a wheat-field and a sunset
Under a prairie-sky
I'm Sir John A. Macdonald   35

I'm Alexander Graham Bell
I'm a pow-wow dancer
And I'm Louis Riel
I'm the Calgary Stampede
I'm a feathered Sarcee   40
I'm Edmonton at night
I'm a bar-room fight
I'm a rigger, I'm a cat
I'm a ten-gallon hat
And an unnamed mountain in the interior of BC   45
I'm a maple tree and a totem pole
I'm sunshine showers
And fresh-cut flowers
I'm a ferry boat ride to the Island
I'm the Yukon   50
I'm the North-West Territories
I'm the Arctic Ocean and the Beaufort Sea
I'm the prairies, I'm the Great Lakes,
I'm the Rockies, I'm the Laurentians,
I am French   55
I am English
And I am Métis
But more than this
Above all this
I am a Canadian and proud to be free.   60

From *We Are Métis*

MODERN MÉTIS CONSCIOUSNESS

The Cultural Initiative

Modern Métis leadership has been plagued by an official division between political activism and cultural or artistic expression. The problem was put succinctly at the fifth annual convention of the Native Council of Canada. The spokesman for the British Columbia delegation, disturbed by the inclusion of cultural activities at a convention whose theme was unity and aboriginal rights, stated: 'Our homes are going to be torn up by pipelines, hydro developments, and various other things, and we're fiddle-farting around with jigging contests. I just don't understand.' Another delegate from Alberta responded immediately: 'As for jigging and contests—I'm for that. I'm a jigger, I'm a fiddler, and I don't want any sucker to tell me that I can't do that any time, any place. That's part of my culture and I'll fight anybody that says it's not part of my culture.'

The two extremes that were expressed by these two delegates is the dilemma facing much of the present Métis leadership in Canada. There are those who believe that active political posturing can only make things difficult.

'If you take on the establishment head-on, you are just indicating to them ways of making better chains for you. To meet them head-on is just suicide. What you have to do is approach the whole thing obliquely. You have to change people's ideas, and the only way you can do that is through the media. You have to attack on a cultural, rather than a political level.'

The modern Métis, especially in the eastern provinces, need to realize a solid cultural base before significant political gains may be achieved. The Métis activists who reject the need for cultural renaissance, such as Howard Adams, fear a 'cultural colonialism' imposed somehow by contact with white society. The fear is as unfounded and paranoid as the establishment fear of 'red nationalism'. The executive of the Native Council of Canada have, from time to time, used both techniques for penetrating the consciousness of the larger society. The Indians, for example, who ride in full regalia in a parade are as harmless to the image of the 'real Indian' as the rhinestone cowboys in the same parade are to the 'real cowboy'.

Howard Adams states that 'the Métis has internalized the myths of inferiority', then claims it is wrong for the Métis to try and change these myths. 'It is useless for us to become involved in a struggle to improve our image, because native people did not create these images.'

The modern Métis are rapidly adopting, in a modern context, as many symbols of the traditional Métis lifestyle as possible. The Native Council of Canada, in 1976, reintroduced the flag of Louis Riel and made it the official flag of the Métis people. At a provincial board meeting of the Ontario Métis Non-Status Indian Association in January of 1978, the Métis sash was adopted as an official badge of office of the association. There is, of course, the danger of imitating traditional ways as a kind of cultural eccentricity, but that is the 'kindergarten' of the modern Métis cultural renaissance. As the Métis become more aware of themselves as a unique cultural entity, they will evolve broader social, artistic, and eventually political expressions that accurately reflect the role of Métis consciousness in Canadian life. The key is not imitation, or even revival of traditional ways, but rather evolution of self-actualization by the Métis individual. Through increased awareness of his heritage, an understanding of his role in modern Canada will emerge.

The problem facing the Métis community today is how to begin the process of cultural education. Certain conditions have to exist in the environment of those who are to learn. Maslow stated that an individual requires food, shelter, a sense of love, of belonging, of self-esteem, and the opportunity to self-actualize before he will develop the desire, or need, for education. The task of the Métis community is extremely difficult, and the Métis have to develop their own solutions and establish these conditions for themselves and their children. The need for creative thinking by all sectors of the Métis community is essential to the process.

Cultural development as a political strategy is a viable vehicle for change, simply because it is a non-threatening activity to most sectors of the establishment. In fact, multicultural policies of the sixties and seventies make funding available for culture-related activities that can have a powerful effect on those who take part. The pitfalls of cultural colonialism and ethnic eccentricity can be avoided by careful development in terms of local organization and participation. But this development must be backed by an increased emphasis on cultural priorities by local, provincial, and national Métis organizations.

Media and the Role Model

Although Howard Adams has decried image improvement and belittles attempts by active leadership to penetrate the CRTC and the CBC, he contradictorily admits the effects of media images on his own life. 'Native people cannot avoid seeing the cultural images and symbols of white supremacy because they are everywhere in society, especially in movies, television, comic books, and textbooks. As these native children grow up, these white supremacist images become more alive, but natives are powerless to do anything about them. Consequently, the children internalize inferior images as part of their true selves, often with strong feelings of shame. As a result, I attempted to disassociate myself from everything and everyone that appeared halfbreed. I wanted to be a successful white man in mainstream society.'

It would be hard to find a better description of the need to develop strong positive Métis models for the Métis people to identify with, and for the proliferation of those models through media of mainstream society. Although many people in the white society take 'image' for granted, or regard it as superficial, that luxury is only available to those who have established their image in the mainstream society. Certainly the emphasis that the Black movement in the United States placed on their 'Black is Beautiful' campaign can hardly be called insignificant or superficial in terms of its penetration into white culture. Métis models do exist, but they are rarely identified specifically as Métis, or emerge only in the traditional or historic sense.

There has been an increasingly wider use of the media by Métis during the past ten years. More and more books, magazines, newspapers, and newsletters are being published by the Métis themselves. In the beginning this material reached only a small number of people and mostly in native communities. Now, however, this is changing. The media generated by natives is penetrating into the majority culture, even into the academic world of the universities. The Métis are becoming aware of the need to develop their understanding of the function of media to produce in whatever medium they choose, rather than be limited by the majority society's prerogatives. Gains are rapidly being made in this regard by various provincial communications groups, such as Alberta Native Communications Society, who have access to North American satellite broadcasting. The most important steps to be taken now are: to achieve access to production in broadcasting; to maintain a unique point of view rather than adopt the white-oriented historical frame of reference; to penetrate professional show business on the entertainment level as well as creating documentary or information-oriented productions. These are all essential elements in the development of Métis consciousness and its role in Canadian society.

Raising Métis Consciousness

There is an extant, strong, identity base that the Métis can build upon—the legacy of Louis Riel. However, the western Métis image and cultural characteristics that now serve as a bridge to connect the halfbreed on a national scale, must not rely solely on the historic context. It must now develop an awareness of values in a modern context, and of the Métis' contribution—not only in Canadian history—but also in present-day Canadian life. There have been significant gains over the past ten years, but this is only the beginning in terms of what is needed.

An example of a successful consciousness-raising event was the 'Back to Batoche' festivals held in Saskatchewan for the past several years. Federal and provincial governments agreed to fund the event providing it was not used as a political rally. Based on local and provincial co-operation, the 'Back to Batoche' movement had a national impact. Thousands of Métis from all across Canada travelled to Saskatchewan to participate in an event designed mainly to bring Métis people together to enjoy their new-found identity and sense of national purpose. The cynics in the movement dismissed the event as 'cultural imperialism', but only because they neglected to see the importance of the human quality of the experience, and the personal value it had to the individual Métis. The experience had a pronounced effect in the Métis world with implications far beyond the control of any group or government.

The 'Back to Batoche' movement and other events like it could very well be the basis of a more coherent program of cultural awareness and development.

The significance of this kind of event may well escape the understanding of those who, in contrast, think marches, sit-ins, and demonstrations are still effective when dealing with the majority society.

In the early sixties a research study was conducted in the Lesser Slave Lake area to determine the self-image evaluation of native children. In that area at least, Métis children rated themselves eight on a scale of twenty-one. Indians, in fact, rated Métis higher than the Métis rated themselves, but not as low as they were rated by whites—seventeenth. The revival of native awareness would probably change that scale if the test were done today.

However, much still remains to be done. A native, John Cuthand, echoes the thoughts of most leaders today. 'The real issues Riel and Dumont fought for are the issues Métis people are fighting for today.' It is on that basis that the new awareness must develop.

The social status of today's Métis is summed up in a single word—'marginal'. Whether in the bush of Northern Ontario or on road allowances in the prairies, on marginal farmland in BC, or on the fringes of industrialized areas, the one feature common to all Métis is their 'marginality'. There is a certain irony in the fact that their very marginality or 'forgotten people' status gives them more in common than most other Canadians have with each other.

The Native Council of Canada put it even more bluntly in a paper in 1973. 'We are not speaking of low-income people, we are talking about no-income people.' Métis are likely to be found at the bottom of every social ladder one might name. In terms of schooling, housing, and employment, the Métis are at the bottom. The only lists Métis head are those for infant mortality, school dropouts, occupants of jails, and suicide. Of course there are success stories and exceptions to all of these conditions. But as a people—ethnic or racial—the Métis do not have a proportionate share of the fruits of the so-called just society. Nevertheless the Métis are, in terms of political and self-actualization, in the best condition since the days of Louis Riel. The role of native organizations has proven their value on several levels, creating a sense of racial or ethnic cohesion.

Although the political status of today's Métis has improved considerably, the ethnic status of today's Métis is largely mythical in both the best and worst sense of the word. At its worst, it becomes a catch-all for people with no identity to hang on to and is 'created primarily by common threat from without' and it becomes a kind of 'non-culture' for the Métis themselves. In the best sense it becomes 'non-nation' or 'psychological nation' in David Bell's context and is identifiable in terms of its own communication network, parallel to, but independent of, those of the Inuit, Indian, or White. Since the function of myth-making is to bolster the confidence to act and create a belief that things can be done, myth-making in the Métis context becomes necessary for independent actions.

Base for Tomorrow

The Canadian public is beginning to realize that there is an important distinction between assimilation and integration, and the supposition that native people are, or ever will be, assimilated into Canadian life is totally unrealistic. The government is beginning to discard assimilation features of their native policies in the light of a new awareness of the native reality in Canada. Today there are more persons of native ancestry than ever before. The native population is the fastest-growing racial group, per capita, in Canada in spite of the high infant mortality rate. The fact is that all of the races and ethnic groups in Canada are being integrated into the psychological and geophysical reality that is North America and that THE MÉTIS ARE THE ONLY ETHNIC GROUP INDIGENOUS TO THE CONTINENT. All other races, including Indian and Inuit, came from elsewhere at some other time. Integration is a two-way street and the white majority society is reflecting the native reality more and more specifically as the years go by.

The reality of North America is the architect of the consciousness of its people and, to extend the Jungian concept of mind and earth, let me quote my own thinking in *Red on White*. The pre-Columbian European created a physical and social super-structure for himself that might be described as a labyrinth. When a European child was born, he was introduced to this maze and spent his lifetime searching through the many passages. Within that structure, with rare exceptions, persons were born, lived, and died without ever knowing a sense of freedom, peace, or enlightenment. When the European came to North America, he brought with him his closed super-structure in the name of civilization. Fortunately, it did not fit the gestalt of the North American continent. Here, closed systems do not work, and the European was forced to create both an entrance and an exit to his super-structure.

The North American continent, in its own way, shapes the type of super-structure that it will accept. It has the quality of a self-correctional process almost cybernetic in its function. This is the natural process that is North America, and a process that is natural to its indigenous people, the Métis.

In order for the Métis to assume their proper role in modern Canadian society, a number of factors must be developed simultaneously. First, the aboriginal rights of the Métis must become a reality so that the minimal conditions for learning may be met. Secondly, the Métis must be allowed to be educated and developed in terms of their own inherent cultural characteristics, and finally, once that process becomes a reality, the context must be communicated to the majority society. This means, by and large, access to modern print and electronic media and other means of communication. Then and only then will the full impact of the consciousness of the Métis people be evident in the mosaic of Canadian society. In political terms, the role of the Métis as a founding partner in the Canadian confederacy must be recognized and guaranteed in a new British North America Act, along with the French and English.

Again, to quote briefly from *Red on White*: 'What I have to say is that the modern world of technology, the electronic, tribal total-systems cybernetic society, is the real manifestation of the potential Métis personality. We no longer have to live on the road allowances and margins of North American society. What we have to do is go out into the world and become the manifestation of what the real North American is going to become—the ideal, whole man. We, as Métis, can represent the best possible example of what everyone in North America can eventually become.'

CONCLUSIONS

Summary of Métis Perspective

This book demonstrates that, from the Métis point of view, current conceptions of Métis history are totally—albeit inadvertently—misrepresented by most academic historians. Contrary to the implications and assumptions of most writing on the Métis, the Métis see themselves through their oral traditions and myths as:

(1) A race apart from both white and Indians and the only race indigenous to Canada;

(2) Having established a viable—if conceptually invisible to white perception—civilization at least a century before Confederation;

(3) A founding nation equal to the French and the English in the development and growth of Confederation;

(4) A people shamelessly exploited, initially by a minority of political and land-grabbing carpetbaggers, and presently by the majority of Canadians through their indifference to the very real plight of the Métis people;

(5) An ethnic and racial component with great potential for future development and contribution to Canadian life—if the opportunity to unfold that potential is returned to them via aboriginal rights and land claims;

(6) A people capable of building and designing their own future on their own terms within the context of the recognition of their reality so long denied them and as presently focused in the northwest and far north of Canada.

The Reality of the Métis Myth

The role of so-called myth in oral and/or linear culture, such as that of the Métis, is of much greater significance in terms of self-identification and self-realization than can be conceived by most western European linear minds. What the Métis think of themselves, in terms of their past, present, and future, is far more real to them than the dictates of conventional history, law, and government policy in a majority society that barely even recognizes the existence of a great, proud, and significant people.

The prophecies of Louis Riel are the song of the Métis soul and they will be sung, if necessary, in the face of the cacophony of international corporations, but preferably in the synchronistic harmony of a pluralistic and truly Canadian reality. The song of the Métis is already being heard by thousands of non-status Indians who are united with the traditional Métis in a participation mystique that is launching a whole new movement in Canada. But before the majority of Canadians can hear the Métis song, much must be done.

The young and old alike must be prepared for education and then educated to the almost forgotten realities of their people. Organizations like ONTARIO MÉTIS AND NON-STATUS INDIAN ASSOCIATION must communicate the reality of the 'myth' in forms more conducive to that communication than history books, or even theses and dissertations. Through poetry, song, film, and drama communicated through all of the media that have such a powerful effect on the quality of awareness we have about our reality, the song of the Métis must be sung.

This is how myth, echoing in the memory of the soul, regenerates the mangled spirit of a nearly defeated people. This is how the consciousness of a people, dominated for a time by the insanity of an invader, comes to resurrection. This is how the Métis myth will become a reality.

The Reality of Métis Reality

A balance must be achieved. It is evident that the most exotic rhetoric is meaningless in the face of horrible poverty and alienation. There are many, many hard, cold, and only too real problems of housing, education, and land claims to be solved. The recognition of injustice has been accomplished in the last decade. The compensation for that injustice is slowly coming to fruition in this decade. The greatest care and thought must be taken by the Métis, by government, and by the Canadian people to avoid a repetition of the tragedies of 1869 and 1885—and they could easily be repeated in the closing decades of this century. Above all, the Métis must be recognized as a people who—in the greatness of their race—have the seeds of the solutions to their own problems. They need only the space and light to grow.

This book is dedicated to the day when all Canadians can join the Métis as they say to each other:

'SING YOUR SONG—YOUR CHILDREN ARE STRONG'
'WE ARE MÉTIS'

Maria Campbell *b.* 1940

MÉTIS

Maria Campbell describes herself as a story-teller, which is the role she plays in *Stories of the Road Allowance People* (1995), her versions of traditional Métis tales. *Halfbreed* (1973), her first publication, is an autobiography that describes the situation of the contemporary Métis. *Little Badger and the Fire Spirit* (1977), *Riel's People* (1978), and *People of the Buffalo* (1976) were written in response to needs expressed by her grandchildren. *The Book of Jessica* (1989), which includes the play she co-authored with Linda Griffiths, documents the difficulties of such cross-cultural projects.

Campbell has been writer-in-residence at the Banff School of Fine Arts and at the universities of Alberta and Regina. She also works extensively in film and video and helps run the Gabriel Crossings Foundation, a Native arts school dedicated to the preservation of traditional culture and the arts. She was awarded the Molson Prize in 2004, arguably the highest award in the arts in Canada. Campbell is currently on the faculty of the University of Saskatchewan.

In the following passage, Campbell describes the indissoluble link between story and storyteller, and the particular importance of storytelling to the Métis:

> The storyteller was not only a skilled entertainer, but he/she was also an historian, a teacher and healer as well. Stories could not be told just any old time—each group had their specific time, i.e., some were winter stories, others were only told in the summer or spring. . . . Stories are precious to all Aboriginal people, but to the Métis they are the greatest inheritance of all. Land you can't give away because it doesn't belong to you. And it is not 'it' anyway, 'she' is your Mother. . . . No one ever told a story that was not his/her own, and if they did, it was only if the story had been given to them or if the story was purchased by way of trade. Even then, the storyteller would begin the story by telling how he/she came by it, and the name of the original creator would be given. The storyteller who had been given the story could not pass it on to anyone else without permission or prior consent.

Jacob

Mistupuch he was my granmudder.
He come from Muskeg
dat was before he was a reservation.
My granmudder he was about twenty-eight when he
marry my granfawder.   5
Dat was real ole for a woman to marry in dem days
But he was an Indian doctor
I guess dats why he wait so long.

Ooh he was a good doctor too
All the peoples dey say dat about him.   10

He doctor everybody dat come to him
an he birt all dah babies too.
Jus about everybody my age
my granmudder he birt dem.

He marry my granfawder around 1890.   15
Dat old man he come to him for doctoring
an when he get better
he never leave him again.

Dey get married dah Indian way
an after dat my granfawder   20
he help him with all hees doctoring.
Dats dah way he use to be a long time ago.
If dah woman he work
den dah man he help him an if dah man he work
dah woman he help.   25
You never heerd peoples fighting over whose job he was
dey all know what dey got to do to stay alive.

My granfawder his name he was Kannap
but dah whitemans dey call him Jim Boy
so hees Indian name he gets los.   30
Dats why we don know who his peoples dey are.
We los lots of our relations like dat.
Dey get dah whitemans name
den no body
he knows who his peoples dey are anymore.   35

Sometimes me
I tink dats dah reason why we have such a hard time
us peoples.
Our roots dey gets broken so many times.
Hees hard to be strong you know   40
when you don got far to look back for help.

Dah whitemans
he can look back tousands of years
cause him
he write everything down.   45
But us peoples
we use dah membering
an we pass it on by telling stories an singing songs.
Sometimes we even dance dah membering.

But all dis trouble you know   50
he start after we get dah new names
cause wit dah new names
he come a new language an a new way of living.
Once a long time ago
I could 'ave told you dah story of my granfawder Kannap   55
an all his peoples but no more.
All I can tell you now
is about Jim Boy
an hees story hees not very ole.

Well my granmudder Mistupuch   60
he never gets a whitemans name an him
he knowed lots of stories.
Dat ole lady
he even knowed dah songs.
He always use to tell me   65
one about an ole man call Jacob.

Dat old man you know
he don live to far from here.
Well hees gone now
but dis story he was about him when he was alive.   70

Jacob him
he gets one of dem new names when dey put him in dah
residential school.
He was a jus small boy when he go
an he don come home for twelve years.   75

Twelve years!
Dats a long time to be gone from your peoples.
He can come home you know
cause dah school he was damn near two hundred miles
away.   80
His Mommy and Daddy dey can go and see him
cause deres no roads in dem days
an dah Indians dey don gots many horses
'specially to travel dat far.

Dats true you know   85
not many peoples in dem days dey have horses.
Its only in dah comic books an dah picture shows dey
gots lots of horses.
He was never like dat in dah real life.

Well Jacob him 90
he stay in dat school all dem years an when he come
home he was a man.
While he was gone
his Mommy and Daddy dey die so he gots nobody.
An on top of dat 95
nobody he knowed him cause he gots a new name.
My granmudder
he say dat ole man he have a hell of time.
No body he can understand dat
unless he happen to him. 100

Dem peoples dat go away to dem schools
an come back you know dey really suffer.
No matter how many stories we tell
we'll never be able to tell
what dem schools dey done to dah peoples 105
an all dere relations.

Well anyways
Jacob he was jus plain pitiful
He can talk his own language
he don know how to live in dah bush. 110
Its a good ting da peoples dey was kine
cause dey help him dah very bes dey can.
Well a couple of summers later
he meet dis girl
an dey gets married. 115

Dat girl he was kine
an real smart too.
He teach Jacob how to make an Indian living.
Dey have a good life togedder an after a few years
dey have a boy. 120
Not long after dat
dey raise two little girls dat was orphans.

Jacob and his wife dey was good peoples
Boat of dem dey was hard working
an all dah peoples 125
dey respec dem an dey come to Jacob for advice.

But dah good times dey was too good to las
cause one day

dah Preeses
dey comes to dah village with dah policemans.   130
Dey come to take dah kids to dah school.

When dey get to Jacob hees house
he tell dem dey can take his kids.
Dah Prees he tell him
he have to lets dem go cause dats the law.   135
Well dah Prees
he have a big book
an dat book he gots dah names
of all dah kids
an who dey belongs to.   140

He open dat book an ask Jacob for his name
an den he look it up.
'Jacob' he say
'you know better you went to dah school an you know
dah edjication hees important.'   145

My granmudder Mistupuch
he say Jacob he tell that Prees
'Yes I go to dah school
an dats why I don wan my kids to go.
All dere is in dat place is suffering.'   150

Dah Prees he wasn happy about dat
an he say to Jacob
'But the peoples dey have to suffer Jacob
cause dah Jesus he suffer.'

'But dah Jesus he never lose his language an   155
hees peoples' Jacob tell him.
'He stay home in hees own land an he do hees
suffering.'

Well da Prees him
he gets mad   160
an he tell him its a sin to tink like dat
an hees gonna end up in purgatory for dem kind of words.

But Jacob he don care
cause far as hees concern
purgatory   165

he can be worse den the hell he live with trying to
learn hees language an hees Indian ways.

He tell dat Prees
he don even know who his people dey are.
'Dah Jesus he knowed his Mommy and Daddy'   170
Jacob he tell him
'and he always knowed who his people dey are.'

Well
dah Prees he tell him
if he wans to know who hees peoples dey are   175
he can tell him dat
an he open in dah book again.

'Your Dad hees Indian name he was Awchak'
dah Prees he say
'I tink dat means Star in your language.   180
He never gets a new name cause he never become a
Christian.'

Jacob he tell my granmudder
dat when da Prees he say hees Dad hees name
his wife he start to cry real hard.   185

'Jacob someday you'll tank the God we done dis.'
dah Prees he tell him
an dey start loading up dah kids on dah big wagons.
All dah kids dey was crying an screaming
An dah mudders   190
dey was chasing dah wagons.

Dah ole womans
dey was all singing dah det song
an none of the mans
dey can do anyting.   195
Dey can
cause the policemans dey gots guns.

When dah wagons dey was all gone
Jacob he look for hees wife but he can find him no
place.   200
An ole woman he see him an he call to him
'Pay api noosim'

'Come an sit down my granchild I mus talk to you.
Hees hard for me to tell you dis but dat Prees
hees book he bring us bad news today.   205
He tell you dat Awchak he was your Daddy.
My granchild
Awchak he was your wife's Daddy too.'

Jacob he tell my granmudder
he can cry when he hear dat.   210
He can even hurt inside.
Dat night he go looking
an he fine hees wife in dah bush
Dat woman he kill hisself.

Jacob he say   215
dah ole womans
dey stay wit him for a long time
an dey sing healing songs an dey try to help him
But he say he can feel nutting.
Maybe if he did   220
he would have done dah same ting.

For many years Jacob he was like dat
just dead inside.
Dah peoples dey try to talk wit him
but it was no use.   225
Hees kids dey growed up
an dey come home an live wit him.
'I made dem suffer' he tell my granmudder.
'Dem kids dey try so hard to help me.'

Den one day   230
his daughter he get married an he have a baby.
He bring it to Jacob to see.
Jacob he say
he look at dat lil baby
an he start to cry and he can stop.   235
He say he cry for himself an his wife
an den he cry for his Mommy and Daddy.
When he was done
he sing dah healing songs dah ole womans
dey sing to him a long time ago.   240

Well you know
Jacob he die when he was an ole ole man.
An all hees life
he write in a big book
dah Indian names of all dah Mommies an Daddies.   245
An beside dem
he write dah old names and
dah new names of all dere kids.

An for dah res of hees life
he fight dah government to build schools on the   250
reservation.
'The good God he wouldn of make babies come
from Mommies and Daddies'
he use to say
'if he didn want dem to stay home   255
an learn dere language
an dere Indian ways.'

You know
dat ole man was right.
No body he can do dat.   260
Take all dah babies away. Hees jus not right.
Long time ago
dah old peoples dey use to do dah naming
an dey do dah teaching too.

If dah parents dey have troubles   265
den dah aunties and dah uncles
or somebody in dah family
he help out till dah parents dey gets dere life work
out.
But no one   270
no one
he ever take dah babies away from dere peoples.

You know my ole granmudder
Mistupuch
he have lots of stories about people like Jacob.   275
Good ole peoples
dat work hard so tings will be better for us.
We should never forget dem ole peoples.

Joseph's Justice

You know dah big fight at Batoche?
Dah one where we fight dah Anglais?
Well dat one.
Dis story he happen den
an dah name of dah man is Joseph.   5
He was a Halfbreed guy
An he don take part in dat war.

Dere was lots of mans like dat in dem days.
Dey wasen't scare of dah Anglais
or dah government.   10
Oh no!
Dey jus wasen interest in fighting for land
or edjication
cause dey don believe dat Anglais government
hees gonna give dem anyting.   15
So
dey jus mine dere own business.

Deres lots of peoples like dat
even today.
Dey jus like to stick to demselves dats all.   20

Well shore
some of dem dey was cowards
an udder ones dey was jus plain lazy.
But most of dem
dey jus got no believing dats all.   25
Dis Joseph
he was one of dem dat don believe.
He was jus minding hees own business
trapping an working for hees ownself
while dah udder mans dey was fighting dah war.   30
An den dah war he was over
an our peoples dey lose.

Dah Anglais General he take Louis
an dah udder mans to Regina
where hees gonna put dem in dah jail so dey can go to   35
dah court.
Of course he never got all of dem
jus Louis

cause Louis him
he give hees self up. 40
Dah udder ones
dey was capture but not Gabriel dough.
Oh no!
Him an Michel Dumas
dey run away to dah States an hide. 45
Ooh Gabe him
he die before he give hisself up.
Dats dah kine of man he was.

Louis him
he was differen. 50
Differen from Gabe an all dah udders.
I guess you can say he was a spirit man.
He give hisself to dah peoples
an he do dat when he was a small boy.
Hees Daddy you know 55
he was dat kine of man too.
He put dah peoples before hees family even.
Dere's not many mans you know
dere born like dat.

Yeah dat Louis 60
he give us anudder kine of membering.
But not Gabe.
Hoo
he was a wile tough man him.
He was dah kine of man he can make you believe you 65
can do anyting on dis eart
long as you was tough enough to stay on your feet.

But you know dis Joseph
dah one I'm telling dah story about?
He was jus ordinary. 70
Ordinary Halfbreed like us.
Not dah kine of mans anyone he tell stories about.

Well dere he was him
minding hees own business
when dah General he win dah war an he comes riding by 75
wit hees Halfbreed prisoners.

Joseph he say he was walking home wit hees gun an
hees beaver pelts
when dah soldiers dey see him.
He say dey was making a hell of a racket.   80
Celebrating I guess
cause dey win dah war.
Dey damn near scare him to det he say.
Well dem soldiers
soon as dey see him   85
dey grab him an dey haul him to dah General

Well my ole uncle
hees name he was Alcid
hees dah one who tell me dis story.
He say dat Anglais General   90
he was riding a big white horse dat dance all dah time.
An dat horse
he was dancing all over when dah soldiers dey bring
Joseph to him.
An dem soldiers   95
dey trowed Joseph right in front of dat dancing
horse.
Well Joseph he tell my Uncle
he jump up as fas as he can.
He don wan to get step on.   100

An den
dat horse he start bucking an he buck dat General
right off.
I guess dat Anglais horse
he never smell a Halfbreed trapper before.   105

When dat General he finely get dat horse to settle
down
he tell Joseph
'Batoche he fall an your leader
Louis Riel he surrender.   110
Him an all dese mans dere under arres. An you my good
man, your under arres too.'

'If I'm a good man' Joseph he say to him
'den what for you arres me?'
Dah General he don like dat very much an he say   115
'Dah charge hees high treason.'

Joseph him
he don know what dat word treason he mean
But he say
it sound awful dangerous   120
so he talk real careful
jus in case hees got someting to do wit shooting.
Dem soldiers you know
dey got guns an he say
dey look like dey wan to use dem.   125
Joseph you know
him he don trus dah Anglais.
He never trus dem in hees whole life.

Well dah General he yell at dah soldiers to put
Joseph in dah wagon wit dah udders mans.   130
So dah soldiers dey put chains on him
an dey trowed him in dah wagon.
Joseph he say
dah Halfbreeds an dah Indians dey was all chained togedder.
Some of dem   135
dey was on dah wagons an some of dem dey was walking.
He say he look for Louis
but he can see him no wheres.

Maybe he was in a cover wagon
cause he was dah leader   140
an dey don wan nobody to see him or talk to him.
But Joseph
he say he knowed dah udder mans.
Dere was ole Parenteau
he was wearing chains like an outlaw.   145
Dat ole man he can hurt nobody hees over eighty
years ole.
An dere was dah Vandal boys
an one of dah Arcands.
Even hees brudder-ing-law Moise Touronde he was   150
dere.

Boy he say
dey look rough.
He was raining and real cole and all dey was wearing
was raggy ole clothes.   155
Some of dem dey don even got no shoes.
An lots of dem dey was wounded

an all of dem
dey was real hungry.

Well Joseph him   160
he tink he better try an say someting
cause dis whole damn ting
hees starting to look pretty damn scary.
An him
he wan dem to know he wasen mix up in it.   165

Well he try talking to dem soldiers but dey don even
listen to him.
So he start hollering an yelling
but hees brudder-ing-law Moise
he tell him to shut up   170
cause nobody he gives a damn if hees guilty or not
anyways.

Well
it took dem a long time to get to Regina
an when dey get dere   175
dey was trowed in dah jail.
Joseph him
he was dere for six monts before he come up for trial.
An when he do
he tell dah Judge what he happen to him   180
an dat Judge he believe on him an he let him go.

But Joseph him
he want hees gun an hees furs back
So he ask for dem.
He say dah Judge an all dah government peoples   185
dey jus laugh at him
an dey tell him
he should be grateful he don get hanged or go to
Stony Mountain Jail.

Well he leave dere   190
an he go to dah policemans.
Dey tell him he should jus forget about it an get
dah hell home as fas as he can
But dat Joseph you know
he was a real hard headed mans   195
not dah kine dat give up jus like dat.

He tell dem policemans
dat if it was him dat steal from dah General
he would of got charge.
An him   200
he never even done nutting
an hees dah one dat gets treated like a crimnal.

Finely
my ole Uncle he say
one of dah policemans he gets tired of him   205
an he say
'Okey Joseph. You can press charges. But me I
shore hope you know what your doing cause dis is
gonna be one hell of a mess before hees over.'

Well   210
it took a long time before dey go to dah court.
An when he gets dere
Joseph he meet dis lawyer
an dis lawyer
he ask him what hees doing dere.   215
When Joseph he tell him
dat lawyer he laugh like hell an he tell Joseph
he'll help him.
Dat lawyer he was an Irishman
an dem Irish you know   220
dey don like dah Anglais eeder.

My ole Uncle Alcid
he say
dem Irish
dey was dah only ones dat really try to help us in dem days.   225
I guess dats because dah Anglais dey take all dere lan to.

Well
Joseph he lose in dah court in Regina but he knowed
he wouldn win dere
cause Regina   230
he was an Anglais town.
So him an dat lawyer
dey take it to dah high court.
Again he took a long time
but finely he heered.   235
Dat General
he was foun guilty for stealing.

You know dey say everybody he steal in dah war time.
But hees agains dah law you know.
Dats true.   240
Dah soldiers dere suppose to honor cause dey belongs
to dah Queen
Well at Batoche
dem soldiers
dey eeder don know dat or dey gots no respec for dere Queen   245
cause all of dem dey steal.
Not jus from Joseph eeder
dey steal from all dah peoples.

Dah Halfbreeds
dey wasen rich you know   250
dey jus gots a few little nice tings.
When dem soldiers come
dey chase dah peoples away
an dey go into dah howses
an dey clean dem out.   255
Dey even burn some of dah howses to dah groun.
Dey do dat to Gabe hees house you know.
Burn it to dah groun.
To damn bad nobody else he press charges agains dem.

Well Joseph him   260
he won hees case an dah General he don look so good.
But Joseph
he don get no compansation from no one.
He never even get hees gun back.
Well he really get mad den.   265
Whats dah damn use of winning if you don get your
stuff back?
He don care if dah General he look good or bad
all he want
is hees gun an hees furs back.   270

Well he don know what hees gonna do now
cause dat General he leave our country not long after
dah court.
He go back to hees own country in Angleterre.
Dere dah Queen he make him a gentlemans   275
You know dah kine dat wear dah armor.
An dah Queen he even put him in charge of all hees
jools.

Dat General
he become a hell of a hero for putting down dah   280
Breeds at Batoche.
Fars I'm concern
he don have much to brag about.
Five tousan of dem an less den a hundred of us.

Oh I know dah history books dey say we was two   285
hundred an fifty.
But you gotta member
dey write dah history books.
My ole Uncle Alcid
he was dere   290
an he say dere was less den a hundred at Batoche.
An mos of dem
dey was ole mans.

Well never mine about dat
cause Joseph him   295
he don care anyways.
All he want is hees gun an hees furs.
He go to dah court again
Dis time hees dah high court in Angleterre
an over dere he gets in dah newspaper an dem Anglais   300
dey write all about it.
Dat really help him you know.
But dats shore funny how he is.
Dey like dah Breeds over dere
but dey hate dem here.   305
Me I jus never can figure out dem Anglais.

Well dat Irish lawyer he win dah case for Joseph.
An in dah court
he make a hell of a fool out of dah General
at lees   310
dats what all dah ole mans dey say.

Jimmy Isbister
he use to say dat too
cause he read dah newspapers dat come from over
dere.   315
Dat Jimmy you know
he was well edjicated.
He was one of dah mans dat go wit Gabe to Montana to

get Louis.
He was a smart man dat Jimmy   320
he understan dah Anglais.
He was a Scotch Halfbreed
an hees Daddy
he sen him to Angleterre to get hees edjication.

Me I always like dah story about Joseph.   325
Cause you know
maybe we lose dah war
but one man he win
Cause him he believe on hisself
an he don give up.   330
Dat kine of man hees real important.
Jus as important as Louis an Gabe
cause hees story
he tell you a little bit about how our peoples dey
was like in dem days.   335

Tanks for listening to me.

Richard G. Green *b.* 1940

MOHAWK

Richard Green was born in Grand River Territory—'commonly known', he says, 'as the Six Nations Indian Reserve'—in Ontario. He attended school in that province and in New York State. Since 1972, his stories, articles, and cartoons about North American Native people have appeared in periodicals and literary anthologies devoted to Aboriginal life in both the United States and Canada.

'I write just about anything except poetry, lyrics, and three-act plays,' he explains. 'This includes legislation, legal and commercial writing, and writing for all media, including entertainment media. . . . I think Onkwehonwe people have much to contribute and teach.

While we have not been invited to this table until recently, we are now able to share some of our knowledge as caretakers of North America. This information is needed not only to fortify our own people, but also to teach those who are not indigenous to our homeland. It is up to us writers to communicate the natural law that governs Turtle Island.'

Green's publications include *The Last Raven: and Other Stories* (1991) and *Sing, like a Hermit Thrush* (1995), a novel for young adults. In addition to his career as a writer, Green is also a publisher in his community and a teacher of Native studies at Mohawk College in Brantford, Ontario.

The Last Raven

Looking at Dan and Nola Goupil, you'd never guess they're married. Not that they're unworthy but she's at least two heads taller which makes you wonder how they make out physically. They subtly administer the word of God each week, while we sit in a circle trying to overcome hardness from the high-backed wooden chairs. This circle is part of a continuing plot to get us closer to God, nature, and each other by moulding us into a team of young-adult Christians. Truth is, Sunday school attendance is mandatory to play on the hockey team, which is why I'm here.

When I adjust my tie clasp, my elbow presses against the flesh of a bare-armed girl sitting beside me. She brushes at the spot as if removing bacteria, folds her hands with kindergarten precision, and places them in her lap. She knows I'm Mohawk and I know that's why she brushed off her arm. Girls outnumber boys two-to-one in this class, and none of them drives you mad with desire.

'Well, Mr Silverheels,' Nola says, her voice one octave above a whisper in true Christian fashion. 'What do you think the meaning of Christ's action toward the penitent woman at the home of Simon the Pharisee was?' Hanging *Mr* and *Miss* to surnames is supposed to elevate us to adult status, though we're expected to call Dan and Nola by their given names. When the Goupils first arrived, I labelled this a get-acquainted trick, but I accept their eccentricities, though it's weird not being called Jim.

'What?' I say. 'I . . . I don't think I heard the question.' I glance toward Bill Shostrom, as he flashes a devilish smile. He slouches in his chair, the lapels of his blue suit flex into a diamond shape exposing the too short length of his polka-dotted tie. His punk hair is greasy with hair-goo, and a glimmer from the ceiling lamp reflects off his forehead. If you believe opposites attract, then you know why we're chums.

Tracking down the direction of my eyes, Nola says: 'Now don't you tell him the answer, Mr Shostrom.' The class laughs. She turns to the fat girl beside me, who's impatiently waving an arm.

'Yes, Miss Breen.'

Miss Breen leaps to her feet. 'I think it's a story to remind us that even though we're constantly submerged in sin,' she says, confidence rampant in her tone, 'Christ loves those who love.' Satisfied with her brief moment of superiority, she directs a smirk toward me as she plops her oversized buttocks back into the chair.

'I disagree,' I say. I'm not sure why this blurted out, but now I'm committed to explanation. I feel tension in the wily shifting of everybody's eyes.

Dan Goupil glares at me, and a nervous hush settles over the room. He never enters class discussion, but I can see he's interpreted my remark as an attack on his wife. He removes a handkerchief, holds his plastic-rimmed glasses toward the ceiling light, and huffs on the lenses. Wiping them with a fluid motion he says quietly, 'Exactly what do you disagree with, Mr Silverheels?' A smile curls his thin lips as he scans the class. 'Surely you don't challenge the love of Jesus, eh?'

'No, sir,' I say.

'Well I'm glad to hear that.' The class translates his actions, and, suddenly, I'm in a sea of snickering faces. 'Well then, Mr Silverheels.' He puts on his glasses. '*What* do you disagree with?'

'It's just that . . . well, I, uh, I don't think the love of Jesus is in question here. That's the constant theme of the New Testament and is indicated in many previous occasions. I think that, by forgiving this woman of all her sins, Christ is directing a lesson of humility toward Simon.'

'Humility?'

'Yes. He's raised Mary Magdalen to a level of respectability above that of His host. He's used her to show Simon that her example of love makes her superior.'

'You think Christ would *use* somebody for His own gain?'

'In this case, yes.'

All eyes rest upon Dan. It's plain that emphasis has shifted from correct and incorrect and is now a question of vanity. To these people, Christ is their saviour; to me, He's a prophet. I realize Dan's next statement decides the outcome. He glances at his wristwatch, and I'm reminded that it's almost time for dismissal. Perhaps I'll be saved by the bell.

Nola raises her eyes above an opened Bible. 'Mr Silverheels?' she asks. 'What do you think Christ means when He says, "Therefore I tell you her sins, which are many, are forgiven for she loved much; but he who is forgiven little, loves little."'

Dan brushes dandruff specks from his lapel. Simultaneously, shuffling feet and voices penetrate from the corridor outside. Looking at me, Dan says, 'I think you've misconstrued the point of today's lesson . . .'

'Dan,' Nola smiles. 'I think you're *both* right.' Everybody closes their Bible, with a thump. 'Now, class,' Nola continues. 'Before you all run off, don't forget our house-party this afternoon. We expect to have a lot of fun, and I pray none of you will miss it.'

I stand and file toward the door, a feeling of betrayal welling up inside me. If the objective of this class is participation, why haven't I been shown any mercy? Passing Dan in the doorway, I smile meekly. He squeezes my shoulder and says, 'See you this afternoon.' But I'm unable to answer.

On our way home, Bill and me and a skinny kid named Hartmann always stop at Gimpy's Diner. Our arrangement is we keep Gimpy's shovelled in winter and he lets us in on Sundays to play a pinball machine everybody calls 'The Chief'. Light the 975,000 point-feather, and with Gimpy's verification you get a dollar from the 'Picnic Fund' jar. In three years of play, I've won twice.

'Are you going to the Goupils' this afternoon, Jim?' Hartmann stares at my reflection in the machine's glass panel.

'Not in a million years.'

'What about you, Bill?'

'I dunno. I've got a lot of homework to do.'

Hartmann looks back at me. 'What are you going to do?'

'I don't know,' I say, tearing open my collection envelope.

'Hey,' Bill says, 'Your parents are supposed to take mine to a lacrosse game, eh? You're not going with them, are you?'

'No,' I say. 'The Warriors are in last place, and they'll probably lose again. I'll probably stay home and terrorize my sister.'

'Get out of the way, amateurs.' Bill squeezes between Hartmann and me. 'Make way for the pro.'

'Speaking of girls,' Hartmann says, 'maybe I'll go to the Goupils' party. Linda'll probably be there.'

'Nola's kid sister?'

'Yeah.'

Inserting a quarter into the slot, Bill says, 'Don't tell me you're in love with Linda Switzer?' He pushes the coin-return button with the heel of his hand and takes out a jackknife. 'Hey Gimpy,' he works the blade into the slot. 'This damn thing's jammed again!'

'I wouldn't say I was in *love* with her,' Hartmann says.

Gimpy walks over, scratches his belly, and pounds on the machine. To Bill, he says, 'I don't know why you're the one who always screws up this machine.'

'Because he's just a big *screw*-up,' I say, overcome with cleverness.

'When they get older, you gotta prime 'em a bit.' Gimpy kicks the machine and the coin clinks inside. Lights flash. Bells clang. The caricature of an Indian in Sioux headdress swings his tomahawk and dances backward into starting position. 'There. What did I tell ya, eh?' Gimpy winks and limps back to his cleaning chores.

'I wouldn't say I was in love with her,' Hartmann repeats. 'But if you guys aren't going to be doing anything,' he cracks a knuckle, 'then I'm going to the Goupils' party.'

Bill launches his first ball. 'Who says we're not going to be doing anything?' He pushes a flipper button, and a wave of satisfaction sweeps his face. 'We're going to be shooting drunken crows this afternoon.'

According to Bill's latest plan, after our parents leave for the lacrosse game, we're going to take our fathers' shotguns on a hunting trip. Bill says the radio reported that a flock of crows has been gathering on the edge of town menacing people for several days. Because of something called jurisdictional ingress and egress over the woods they're in, nobody can do anything about removing them.

'We're going to be big heroes, eh?' Bill says, as we leave Gimpy's. 'We're going to do our duty and eliminate those hazardous crows. Meet you at the bridge at two o'clock.'

When my parents leave the house, my older sister curls up on the sofa and flashes her beady eyes. '*Sehksatiyohake Senta: whah*,' she says in Mohawk. She does this to aggravate me. We left the reserve when I was three, and my family seldom speaks Mohawk here in Brantford. Sometimes, when the house is full of visitors, she gets everybody going and there's always a point where they all look at me and laugh. But she can't fool me. She wants me out of the house this afternoon, so she can cuddle with her boyfriend. She's hovering around me like a fruit fly on a puckered apple, and it's impossible to get the shotgun from my parents' closet. To avoid suspicion, I put on my new maroon windbreaker and depart for the woods in street shoes.

I'm first to arrive. I sit on my favourite girder at the railroad bridge listening to creek water gurgle far below. To the west, a band of nimbus gathers on the horizon, promising rain. Bill and Hartmann laugh while they goose-step the railroad ties, gleaming shotgun barrels propped between body and forearm. Bill wears a red plaid jacket and a ludicrous straw hat, whose front brim is folded flat; 'BILL' is inscribed there in red paint. Two ragged pheasant feathers jut from a hatband, denoting hunting prowess. Hartmann's olive jacket has 'SMITH' in stencil letters above his left breast pocket. They both notice I don't have a shotgun, but say nothing.

I step atop a gleaming rail and gingerly keep their pace, my shoes making a tap-dancer sound. We hike down the straight tracks, grateful that railroads always take the shortest, most private routes. I've never seen more than two crows in the same place at one time and believe Bill's story to be false. We turn and cross a field, their heavy boots clearing a path for me through chest-high thistles.

We march toward a stand of hemlock when Bill signals a halt. From an opening beyond us, I hear a confused hum of shufflings and scattered caws. Perched amid saplings and clusters of lobe-leafed bushes, crows occupy the centre of a U-shaped clearing. Bill and me are going to circle, leaving Hartmann stationed at the opening to block any escape attempts. To the northwest, the woods thicken, and, when we reach our position, the crows are between us and a barrier of trees.

Bill hands me a yellow box of shells and we begin. Each squawk, each shriek intensifies, and it's plain we've been detected. It's so noisy I'm forced to cover an ear.

A sea of bobbing heads covers the ground like a rippling stadium tarpaulin. Branches bend in smooth arcs to accommodate squawking occupants. The crows compete for tiny red berries; they rape the bushes and peck each other in rages of greed. One bird leaps from his branch, frantically beats his wings, and flutters to the ground. These birds aren't drunk as Bill reported; most are too bloated to fly. Smaller crows retreat to the woods beyond, but the majority continue their indulgence in spite of our presence.

Bill inserts two shells into his double-barrelled shotgun and closes it with a snap. Signalling Hartmann, he drops to one knee, cocks the hammer, and aims into a crowded sapling. I've been instructed to pass two shells into his palm and stand clear when spent casings are rejected. One hundred metres away, Hartmann slams the breech of his gun closed and raises its barrel in readiness. It's clear we've entered a world not intended for humans.

Bill's first blast shatters the air; my eardrums ring in response. Again he cocks, sights, and squeezes the trigger. *Boom!* He breaks the gun, and two casings spiral to the ground; a stench of sulphur bites my nostrils. 'Shells!' he yells. I slap two cylinders into his open palm, like an intern assisting at surgery. An unexpected blast from Hartmann's direction makes me flinch. Bill smiles.

Fluttering and squawking, the crows are in chaos. Their numbers work against them; wings become entangled, foiling attempts to fly. Where Bill has fired into loaded branches, twin holes poke through the blackness. Leaning forward, he aims at the base of a crowded bush. *Boom!* His body jerks up with the recoil of the gun. In its panic, one crow hovers above us. It flaps its wings to escape, but Bill blows it into an inkblot of swirling feathers. 'Shells!' Bill shouts, waving away down-fluff. I barely hear him through the liquid hum in my ears.

Some of the crows fall to the ground, others scurry through the grass toward Hartmann. Some flap their wings, crane their necks, and scold, but remain imprisoned in their branches. Hartmann concentrates his blasts on those who manage flight, his left arm pumping with mechanical precision. Bill can hit three crows with one barrage. It's evident from his cursing that he considers it a miss if only one falls. Hartmann lowers his weapon at the black army advancing toward him. His first explosion pours through their ranks like a splash of soapy water on a ship-deck, lifting and transporting those in its wake.

Drops of rain hiss against Bill's hot gun barrel, but he continues his shooting oblivious of weather conditions. 'Shells!' he yells, blowing at smoke billowing from the breech.

A thunderclap booms across the terrain. The OPP must be on their way. 'It's starting to rain!' I shout, relieved at the possibility of leaving.

'Good,' Bill says. 'It'll muffle our shots.' I hear the clink of shell casings dropping into a pile at my feet. 'Come on, we've got to chase them toward Hartmann!' We advance, Bill firing once every three strides. It's like walking through a ploughed field, clods of black bodies occasionally squishing under our feet, the sensation plastic and awkward.

A crow deliriously wanders about the ground, dragging a broken wing. I stoop, hypnotized by its misery. It trips and falls forward on its side, desperately clawing at the earth for traction. I reach to help, but it pops its smooth head between twisted wing feathers into a contorted position of defence. Eyes shrivelling with betrayal, it arches its neck to peck my hand. Instead, its eyelids squeeze shut, muscles relax, and it rolls over on its back. An eyelid pops open and an empty black sphere gazes at me. I scoop up cartridges from the shell box. I drop them into my pocket, and tear the cardboard into a sheet. Covering the crow's body, I marvel at its design, reminded that things intended for a simpler function can be separated so easily from it.

When we rendezvous with Hartmann, a squadron of crows approaches head-on as if in attack formation. They are flying at eye level, their silhouettes barely visible against the backdrop of trees. In his haste to reload, Bill grabs a jammed shell casing and burns his fingertips. 'Damn it,' he winces. 'Quick, Jim, gimmie two more shells!' He loads, waits for Hartmann, and takes aim.

Their first volley flashes with the ferocity of a howitzer; two crows erased in the blink of an eye. Bill's second shot hits its target, too, but the bird's inertia carries it into his chest. Bill pushes it to the ground and squashes it with his boot. Hartmann's second burst is true, and the largest crow, bomber-sized in comparison to the others, dives to the ground. Watching the crows falling like black snowflakes, I'm amazed at Bill's and Hartmann's skill at killing. Two crows peel off in an escape manoeuvre, but Hartmann's capable pump gun sweeps them to obscurity.

'We got 'em, Hartmann! We got every one of them!' Bill pushes his hat back. 'Did you see how beautiful that big one rolled off and dove to the ground? Just like a Snowbird.'

'Guess what, Bill?' Hartmann inspects his remaining ammo. 'I hit that big one with my deer slug. You remember that deer slug I showed you?'

Bill nods. He blows at blue smoke rising from his barrels. 'Hey, Jim.' He slides a shell into the left chamber. 'I want you to hit that crow in the tree over there.' He closes the gun with a snap of authority and offers it to me.

I had hoped that Bill, consumed in his frenzy, would forget about my participation. Yet, like a substitute player sitting on the bench, I've been rehearsing all afternoon. 'I'm not a very good shot,' I say, not really wanting to be heard.

'Take it,' Bill thrusts the weapon into my hands. 'And don't miss.'

I plant my feet, pull back the hammer, and raise the barrel. Raindrops poke at the shoulders of my jacket; one ricochets off the stock and splashes into my eye. I squeeze my eyelid, accept the brief sting, and shake my head. Bill sighs impatiently. Raising the front sight into the crotch of the V, I fix it on the silhouette beyond. My target twists its neck in puppet fashion against the pink colouring of the uncertain sky. I hunch my shoulder, tighten my grip, close my eyes, and pull the trigger. *Boom!*

'You missed!' Bill grabs the gun, breaks it open, blows at the chamber, and inserts one shell. 'You don't sight a shotgun, stupid. You aim it with both eyes open. And don't pull the trigger, squeeze it.' Bill hands me the gun. 'Don't miss this time—this is the last one.'

I wipe my brow, seat the gun butt against my shoulder, and pull the hammer back. I take a deep breath, raise the barrels, and sight according to Bill's advice. Suddenly, the crow kicks away, flaps its wings, and climbs toward the horizon. I follow it and calculate its path. Hatred in the dying crow's eyes nags my mind, but it's erased by my passion for success. Squeezing the trigger, I can almost see the pellet pattern sink into the feathers. 'I got him,' I say, exhaling. Wings spread like sagging semaphores, the crow glides down breast first, bouncing in slow motion as it hits the ground. I feel a surge of triumph. I try to push my face into a smile.

Bill slaps my shoulders. 'Nice shooting,' he says, taking the gun.

Sheets of rain force us into the woods seeking shelter, but sunbeams isolate the clouds and begin melting them. Each imprisoned with our own thoughts, we view black specks dotting the landscape. Blotches of blood coating tree branches, bushes, and grass begin washing away. Divots in the ground smooth their sores. Severed branches remain, permanent scars to today's memory.

When sunlight finally blasts through, we cross the open peninsula toward the tracks, the ground sucking at our feet. Bill ransacks the largest black feathers and adds them to his hatband, his singed fingertips provoking an occasional grimace. In a show of humanity, Hartmann plods across the field, finishing off dying survivors with his gun butt. I pick up a shell casing and blow on its open end, the lonely whistle recalling the dead crow's eye and its echo of emptiness.

Beneath the bridge, I wash mud from my shoes with a gnarled twig. I notice a brown splatter of blood on my pant leg. It's partially dry, and I splash cold creek water on it to prevent a stain. Gusts of wind, already frigid, push at bushes along the bank sending messages of winter to those who are listening. I gaze at Bill and his Medusa-like headdress. A feeling of sardonic ridicule blossoms inside me, but humility pacifies the notion.

Beth Brant *b.* 1941

MOHAWK

Beth Brant, Degonwadonti, is a Bay of Quinte Mohawk from Tyendinaga Mohawk Territory in Ontario. She considers storytelling a part of her family heritage:

I come from a long line of storytellers and I feel that my written words are just another form of translating the language of the oral.

I started writing when I turned forty. It was a gift brought to me by Eagle. In these ten years I have been writing, I am always conscious that I am writing for my own People. That is my audience. That is who the stories are about and for. And if non-Natives pick up a book of mine and learn about the effects of racism and colonialism on Native Peoples and then take

that within themselves to make change, that is a good thing.

Brant has a firm sense of the integration of her life and work. Her biography describes her as 'born May 6, 1941—a Taurus with Scorpio rising', 'a mother and grandmother' who 'lives with her partner of twenty years, Denise Dorsz'. Brant states, 'All of my writing identifies as Native, lesbian, and working class.' She is the author of two books of short stories—*Mohawk Trail* (1985) and *Food & Spirits* (1991)—and of *Writing as Witness: Essay and Talk* (1994). She is the editor of *A Gathering of Spirit* (1984), an anthology of writing and art by Native women. Her most recent publication is *I'll Sing Till the Day I Die: Conversations with Tyendinaga Elders* (1995). Brant is also known as a generous teacher of creative writing.

A Long Story

Dedicated to my Great-Grandmothers Eliza Powless and Catherine Brant

'About 40 Indian children took the train at this depot for the Philadelphia Indian School last Friday. They were accompanied by the government agent, and seemed a bright looking lot.'

The Northern Observer
(Massena, New York, July 20, 1892)

'I am only beginning to understand what it means for a mother to lose a child.'

Anna Demeter, *Legal Kidnapping*
(Beacon Press, Boston, 1977)

1890
It has been two days since they came and took the children away. My body is greatly chilled. All our blankets have been used to bring me warmth. The women keep the fire blazing. The men sit. They talk among themselves. We are frightened by this sudden child-stealing. We signed papers, the agent said. This gave them rights to take our

babies. It is good for them, the agent said. It will make them civilized, the agent said. I do not know *civilized*.

I hold myself tight in fear of flying apart in the air. The others try to feed me. Can they feed a dead woman? I have stopped talking. When my mouth opens, only air escapes. I have used up my sound screaming their names—She Sees Deer! He Catches The Leaves! My eyes stare at the room, the walls of scrubbed wood, the floor of dirt. I know there are people here, but I cannot see them. I see a darkness, like the lake at New Moon. Black, unmoving. In the centre, a picture of my son and daughter being lifted onto the train. My daughter wearing the dark blue, heavy dress. All of the girls dress alike. Never have I seen such eyes! They burn into my head even now. My son. His hair cut. Dressed as the white men, his arms and legs covered by cloth that made him sweat. His face, streaked with tears. So many children crying, screaming. The sun on our bodies, our heads. The train screeching like a crow, sounding like laughter. Smoke and dirt pumping out of the insides of the train. So many people. So many children. The women, standing as if in prayer, our hands lifted, reaching. The dust sifting down on our palms. Our palms making motions at the sky. Our fingers closing like the claws of the bear.

I see this now. The hair of my son held in my hands. I rub the strands, the heavy braids coming alive as the fire flares and casts a bright light on the black hair. They slip from my fingers and lie coiled on the ground. I see this. My husband picks up the braids, wraps them in cloth; he takes the pieces of our son away. He walks outside, the eyes of the people on him. I see this. He will find a bottle and drink with the men. Some of the women will join him. They will end the night by singing or crying. It is all the same. I see this. No sounds of children playing games and laughing. Even the dogs have ceased their noise. They lay outside each doorway, waiting. I hear this. The voices of children. They cry. They pray. They call me. *Nisten ha.* I hear this. *Nisten ha.**

1978
I am wakened by the dream. In the dream my daughter is dead. Her father is returning her body to me in pieces. He keeps her heart. I thought I screamed . . . *Patricia!* I sit up in bed, swallowing air as if for nourishment. The dream remains in the air. I rise to go to her room. Ellen tries to lead me back to bed, but I have to see once again. I open her door. She is gone. The room empty, lonely. They said it was in her best interests. How can that be? She is only six, a baby who needs her mothers. She loves us. This has not happened. I will not believe this. Oh god, I think I have died.

Night after night, Ellen holds me as I shake. Our sobs stifling the air in our room. We lie in our bed and try to give comfort. My mind can't think beyond last week when she left. I would have killed him if I'd had the chance! He took her hand and pulled her to the car. The look in his eyes of triumph. It was a contest to him, Patricia the prize. He will teach her to hate us. He will! I see her dear face. That face looking out the back window of his car. Her mouth forming the words *Mommy, Mama.* Her dark braids tied with red yarn. Her front teeth missing. Her overalls with the yellow flower

* Mother

on the pocket, embroidered by Ellen's hands. So lovingly she sewed the yellow wool. Patricia waiting quietly until she was finished. Ellen promised to teach her designs— chain stitch, french knot, split stitch. How Patricia told everyone that Ellen made the flower just for her. So proud of her overalls.

I open the closet door. Almost everything is gone. A few things hang there limp, abandoned. I pull a blue dress from the hanger and take it back to my room. Ellen tries to take it from me, but I hold on, the soft blue cotton smelling of my daughter. How is it possible to feel such pain and live? 'Ellen?!' She croons my name. 'Mary, Mary, I love you.' She sings me to sleep.

1890

The agent was here to deliver a letter. I screamed at him and sent curses his way. I threw dirt in his face as he mounted his horse. He thinks I'm a crazy woman and warns me, 'You better settle down, Annie.' What can they do to me? I am a crazy woman. This letter hurts my hand. It is written in their hateful language. It is evil, but there is a message for me.

I start the walk up the road to my brother. He works for the whites and understands their meanings. I think about my brother as I pull the shawl closer to my body. It is cold now. Soon there will be snow. The corn has been dried and hangs from our cabin, waiting to be used. The corn never changes. My brother is changed. He says that *I* have changed and bring shame to our clan. He says I should accept the fate. But I do not believe in the fate of child-stealing. There is evil here. There is much wrong in our village. My brother says I am a crazy woman because I howl at the sky every evening. He is a fool. I am calling the children. He says the people are becoming afraid of me because I talk to the air and laugh like the raven overhead. But I am talking to the children. They need to hear the sound of me. I laugh to cheer them. They cry for us.

This letter burns my hands. I hurry to my brother. He has taken the sign of the wolf from over the doorway. He pretends to be like those who hate us. He gets more and more like the child-stealers. His eyes move away from mine. He takes the letter from me and begins the reading of it. I am confused. This letter is from two strangers with the names Martha and Daniel. They say they are learning civilized ways. Daniel works in the fields, growing food for the school. Martha cooks and is being taught to sew aprons. She will be going to live with the schoolmaster's wife. She will be a live-in girl. What is a *live-in girl*? I shake my head. The words sound the same to me. I am afraid of Martha and Daniel, these strangers who know my name. My hands and arms are becoming numb.

I tear the letter from my brother's fingers. He stares at me, his eyes traitors in his face. He calls after me, 'Annie! Annie!' That is not my name! I run to the road. That is not my name! There is no Martha! There is no Daniel! This is witch work. The paper burns and burns. At my cabin, I quickly dig a hole in the field. The earth is hard and cold, but I dig with my nails. I dig, my hands feeling weaker. I tear the paper and bury the scraps. As the earth drifts and settles, the names Martha and Daniel are covered. I look to the sky and find nothing but endless blue. My eyes are blinded by the colour. I begin the howling.

1978

When I get home from work, there is a letter from Patricia. I make coffee and wait for Ellen, pacing the rooms of our apartment. My back is sore from the line, bending over and down, screwing the handles on the doors of the flashing cars moving by. My work protects me from questions, the guys making jokes at my expense. But some of them touch my shoulder lightly and briefly as a sign of understanding. The few women, eyes averted or smiling in sympathy. No one talks. There is no time to talk. No room to talk, the noise taking up all space and breath.

I carry the letter with me as I move from room to room. Finally I sit at the kitchen table, turning the paper around in my hands. Patricia's printing is large and uneven. The stamp has been glued on halfheartedly and is coming loose. Each time a letter arrives, I dread it, even as I long to hear from my child. I hear Ellen's key in the door. She walks into the kitchen, bringing the smell of the hospital with her. She comes toward me, her face set in new lines, her uniform crumpled and stained, her brown hair pulled back in an imitation of a french twist. She knows there is a letter. I kiss her and bring mugs of coffee to the table. We look at each other. She reaches for my hand, bringing it to her lips. Her hazel eyes are steady in her round face.

I open the letter. *Dear Mommy. I am fine. Daddy got me a new bike. My big teeth are coming in. We are going to see Grandma for my birthday. Daddy got me new shoes. Love Patricia.* She doesn't ask about Ellen. I imagine her father standing over her, coaxing her, coaching her. The letter becomes ugly. I tear it in bits and scatter them out the window. The wind scoops the pieces into a tight fist before strewing them in the street. A car drives over the paper, shredding it to garbage and mud.

Ellen makes a garbled sound. 'I'll leave. If it will make it better, I'll leave.' I quickly hold her as the dusk moves into the room and covers us. 'Don't leave. Don't leave.' I feel her sturdy back shiver against my hands. She kisses my throat, and her arms tighten as we move closer. 'Ah, Mary, I love you so much.' As the tears threaten our eyes, the taste of salt is on our lips and tongues. We stare into ourselves, touching the place of pain, reaching past the fear, the guilt, the anger, the loneliness.

We go to our room. It is beautiful again. I am seeing it new. The sun is barely there. The colours of cream, brown, green mixing with the wood floor. The rug with its design of wild birds. The black ash basket glowing on the dresser, holding a bouquet of dried flowers bought at a vendor's stand. I remember the old woman, laughing and speaking rapidly in Polish as she wrapped the blossoms in newspaper. Ellen undresses me as I cry. My desire for her breaking through the heartbreak we share. She pulls the covers back, smoothing the white sheets, her hands repeating the gestures done at work. She guides me onto the cool material. I watch her remove the uniform of work. An aide to nurses. A healer of spirit.

She comes to me full in flesh. My hands are taken with the curves and soft roundness of her. She covers me with the beating of her heart. The rhythm steadies me. Heat is centring me. I am grounded by the peace between us. I smile at her face above me, round like a moon, her long hair loose and touching my breasts. I take her breast in my hand, bring it to my mouth, suck her as a woman—in desire, in faith. Our bodies join. Our hair braids together on the pillow. Brown, black, silver, catching the last light of the sun. We kiss, touch, move to our place of power. Her mouth, moving over my body, stopping at curves and swells of skin, kissing, removing pain. Closer, close, together, woven, my legs are heat, the centre of my soul is speaking to her, I am sliding into her, her mouth is medicine, her heart is the earth, we are dancing with flying arms, I shout, I sing, I weep salty liquid, sweet and warm it coats her throat. This is my life. I love you Ellen, I love you Mary, I love, we love.

1891
The moon is full. The air is cold. This cold strikes at my flesh as I remove my clothes and set them on fire in the withered corn field. I cut my hair, the knife sawing through the heavy mass. I bring the sharp blade to my arms, legs, and breasts. The blood trickles like small red rivers down my body. I feel nothing. I throw the tangled webs of my hair into the flames. The smell, like a burning animal, fills my nostrils. As the fire stretches to touch the stars, the people come out to watch me—the crazy woman. The ice in the air touches me.

They caught me as I tried to board the train and search for my babies. The white men tell my husband to watch me. I am dangerous. I laugh and laugh. My husband is good only for tipping bottles and swallowing anger. He looks at me, opening his mouth and making no sound. His eyes are dead. He wanders from the cabin and looks out on the corn. He whispers our names. He calls after the children. He is a dead man.

Where have they taken the children? I ask the question of each one who travels the road past our door. The women come and we talk. We ask and ask. They say there is nothing we can do. The white man is like a ghost. He slips in and out where we cannot see. Even in our dreams he comes to take away our questions. He works magic that resists our medicine. This magic has made us weak. What is the secret about them? Why do they want our children? They sent the Blackrobes many years ago to teach us new magic. It was evil! They lied and tricked us. They spoke of gods who would forgive us if we believed as they do. They brought the rum with the cross. This god is ugly! He killed our masks. He killed our men. He sends the women screaming at the moon in terror. They want our power. They take our children to remove the inside of them. Our power. They steal our food, our sacred rattle, the stories, our names. What is left?

I am a crazy woman. I look to the fire that consumes my hair and see their faces. My daughter. My son. They still cry for me, though the sound grows fainter. The wind picks up their keening and brings it to me. The sound has bored into my brain. I begin howling. At night I dare not sleep. I fear the dreams. It is too terrible, the things that happen there. In my dream there is wind and blood moving as a stream. Red, dark blood in my dream. Rushing for our village. The blood moves faster. There are screams of wounded people. Animals are dead, thrown in the blood stream. There is nothing left. Only the air echoing nothing. Only the earth soaking up blood, spreading it in the four directions, becoming a thing there is no name for. I stand in the field watching the fire. The People watching me. We are waiting, but the answer is not clear yet. A crazy woman. That is what they call me.

1979

After taking a morning off work to see my lawyer, I come home, not caring if I call in. Not caring, for once, at the loss in pay. Not caring. My lawyer says there is nothing more we can do. I must wait. As if there has been something other than waiting. He has custody and calls the shots. We must wait and see how long it takes for him to get tired of being a mommy and a daddy. So, I wait.

I open the door to Patricia's room. Ellen and I keep it dusted and cleaned in case my baby will be allowed to visit us. The yellow and blue walls feel like a mockery. I walk to the windows, begin to systematically tear down the curtains. I slowly start to rip the cloth apart. I enjoy hearing the sounds of destruction. Faster, I tear the material into strips. What won't come apart with my hands, I pull at with my teeth. Looking for more to destroy, I gather the sheets and bedspread in my arms and wildly shred them to pieces. Grunting and sweating, I am pushed by rage and the searing wound in my soul. Like a wolf, caught in a trap, gnawing at her own leg to set herself free, I begin to beat my breasts to deaden the pain inside. A noise gathers in my throat and finds the way out. I begin a scream that turns to howling, then becomes hoarse choking. I want to take my fists, my strong fists, my brown fists, and smash the world until it bleeds. Bleeds! And all the judges in their flapping robes, and the fathers who look for revenge, are ground, ground into dust and disappear with the wind.

The word *lesbian*. Lesbian. The word that makes them panic, makes them afraid, makes them destroy children. The word that dares them. Lesbian. *I am one.* Even for Patricia, even for her, *I will not cease to be!* As I kneel amidst the colourful scraps, Raggedy Anns smiling up at me, my chest gives a sigh. My heart slows to its normal speech. I feel the blood pumping outward to my veins, carrying nourishment and life. I strip the room naked. I close the door.

Thanks so much to Chrystos for the title. Thanks to Gloria Anzaldúa for encouraging the writing of this story.

Swimming Upstream

Anna May spent the first night in a motel off Highway 8. She arrived about ten, exhausted from her long drive—through farmland, bright autumn leaves, the glimpse of blue lake. She saw none of this, only the grey highway stretching out before her. She stopped when the motel sign appeared, feeling the need for rest, it didn't matter where.

She took a shower, lay in bed, and fell asleep, the dream beginning again almost immediately. Her son—drowning in the water, his skinny arms flailing the waves, his mouth opening to scream with no sound coming forth. She, Anna May, moving in slow motion into the waves, her hands grabbing for the boy but feeling only water run through her fingers. She grabbed frantically, but nothing held to her hands. She dove and opened her eyes under water and saw nothing. He was gone. Her hands connected with sand, with seaweed, but not her son. He was gone. Simon was gone.

Anna May woke. The dream was not a nightmare anymore. It had become a companion to her, a friend, almost a lover—reaching for her as she slept, making pictures of her son, keeping him alive while recording his death. In the first days after Simon left her, the dream made her wake screaming, sobbing, arms hitting at the air, legs kicking the sheets, becoming tangled in the material. Her bed was a straitjacket, pinning her down, holding her until the dream ended. She would fight the dream then. Now, she welcomed it.

During the day she had other memories of Simon. His birth, his first pair of shoes, his first steps, his first word—*Mama*—his first book, his first day of school. His firsts were also his lasts, so she invented a future for him during her waking hours: his first skating lessons, his first hockey game, his first reading aloud from a book, his first. . . . But she couldn't invent beyond that. His six-year-old face and body wouldn't change in her mind. She couldn't invent what she couldn't imagine.

She hadn't been there when Simon drowned. Simon had been given to her ex-husband by the courts. She was judged unfit. Because she lived with a woman. Because a woman, Catherine, slept beside her. Because she had a history of alcoholism. The history was old. Anna May had stopped drinking when she became pregnant with Simon, and she had stayed dry all those years. She couldn't imagine what alcohol tasted like after Simon was born. He was so lovely, so new. Her desire for a drink evaporated every time Simon took hold of her finger, or nursed from her breast, or opened his mouth in a toothless smile. She had marvelled at his being—this gift that had emerged from her own body. This beautiful being who had formed himself inside her, had come with speed through the birth canal to welcome life outside her. His face red with anticipation, his black hair sticking straight up as if electric with hope, his little fists, grabbing, his pink mouth finding her nipple and holding on for dear life. She had no need for alcohol. There was Simon.

Simon was taken away from them. But they saw him on weekends, Tony delivering him on a Friday night, Catherine discreetly finding someplace else to be when Tony's car drove up. They still saw Simon, grateful for the two days out of the week they could play with him, they could delight in him, they could pretend with him. They still saw Simon, until the call that changed all that. The call from Tony saying that Simon had drowned when he fell out of the boat as they were fishing. Tony sobbing, 'I'm sorry. I didn't mean for this to happen. I tried to save him. I'm sorry. Please, Anna, please forgive me. Oh God, Anna. I'm sorry. I'm sorry.'

So Anna May dreamed of those final moments of a six-year-old life. And it stunned her that she wasn't there to see him die when she had been there to see him come into life.

Anna May stayed dry, but she found herself glancing into the cupboards at odd times. Looking for something. Looking for something to drink. She thought of ways to buy wine and hide it so she could take a drink when she needed it. But there was Catherine. Catherine would know, and Catherine's face, already so lined and tired and old, would become more so. Anna May saw her own face in the mirror. Her black hair had streaks of grey and white she hadn't noticed before. Her forehead had deep lines carved into the flesh, and her eyes, her eyes that had cried so many tears, were a faded and washed-out blue. Her mouth was wrinkled, the lips parched and chapped. She and Catherine, aged and ghostlike figures walking through a dead house.

Anna May thought about the bottle of wine. It took on large proportions in her mind. A bottle of wine, just one, that she could drink from and never empty. A bottle of wine, the sweet, red kind that would take away the dryness, the withered insides of her. She went to meetings but never spoke, only saying her name and 'I'll pass tonight'. Catherine wanted to talk, but Anna May had nothing to say to this woman she loved. She thought about the bottle of wine: the bottle, the red liquid inside, the sweet taste gathering in her mouth, moving down her throat, hitting her bloodstream, warming her inside, killing the deadness.

She arranged time off work and told Catherine she was going away for a few days. She needed to think, to be alone. Catherine watched her face, the framing of the words out of her mouth, her exhausted eyes. Catherine said, 'I understand.'

'Will you be alright?' Anna May asked her.

'Yes, I'll be fine. I'll see friends. We haven't spent time with them in so long, they are concerned about us. I'll be waiting for you. I love you so much.'

Anna May got in the car and drove up 401, up 19, over to 8 and the motel, the shower, the dream.

Anna May smoked her cigarettes and drank coffee until daylight. She made her plans to buy the bottle of wine. After that, she had no plans, other than the first drink and how it would taste and feel.

She found a meeting in Goderich and sat there, ashamed and angered with her-self to sit in a meeting and listen to the stories and plan her backslide. She thought of speaking, of talking about Simon, about the bottle of wine, but she knew someone would stop her or say something that would make her stop. Anna May did not want to be stopped. She wanted to drink and drink and drink until it was all over. *My name is Anna May and I'll just pass.*

Later, she hung around for coffee, feeling like an infiltrator, a spy. A woman took hold of her arm and said, 'Let's go out and talk. I know what you're planning. Don't do it. Let's talk.'

Anna May shrugged off the woman's hand and left. She drove to a liquor outlet. Vins et Spiritueux. *Don't do it.* She found the wine, one bottle, that was all she'd buy. *Don't do it.* One bottle, that was all. She paid and left the store, the familiar curve of the bottle wrapped in brown paper. *Don't do it.* Only one bottle. It wouldn't hurt. She laughed at the excuses bubbling up in her mouth like wine. Just one. She smoked a cigarette in the parking lot, wondering where to go, where to stop and turn the cap that would release the red, sweet smell before the taste would overpower her and she wouldn't have to wonder anymore.

She drove north on 21, heading for the Bruce Peninsula, Lake Huron on her left, passing the little resort towns, the cottages by the lake. She stopped for a hamburger and, without thinking, got her thermos filled with coffee. This made her laugh, the bottle sitting next to her, almost a living thing. She drank the coffee driving north, with her father—not Simon, not Catherine—drifting in her thoughts. Charles, her mother had called him. Everyone else called him Charley. Good old Charley. Good-time Charley. Injun Charley. Charles was a hard worker, working at almost anything. He worked hard, he drank hard. He tried to be a father, a husband, but the work and the drink turned his attempts to nothing. Anna May's mother never complained, never left him. She cooked and kept house and raised the children and always called him Charles. When Anna May grew up, she taunted her mother with the fact that *her Charles* was a drunk. Why didn't she care more about her kids than her drunken husband? Didn't her mother know how ashamed they were to have such a father, to hear people talk about him, to laugh at him, to laugh at them—the half-breeds of good-old-good-time-Injun Charley?

Anna May laughed again, the sound ugly inside the car. Her father was long dead and, she supposed, forgiven by her. He had been a handsome man back then, her mother a skinny, pale girl, an orphan girl, something unheard of by her father. How that must have appealed to the romantic that he was. Anna May didn't know how her mother felt about the life she'd had with Charles. Her mother never talked about those things. Her mother, who sobbed and moaned at Simon's death as she never had at her husband's. Anna May couldn't remember her father ever being mean. He just went away when he drank. Not like his daughter who'd fight anything in her way when she was drunk. The bottle bounced beside her as she drove.

Anna May drove and her eyes began to see the colours of the trees. They looked like they were on fire, the reds and oranges competing with the yellows and golds. She smoked her cigarettes, drank from the thermos, and remembered this was her favourite season. She and Catherine would be cleaning the garden, harvesting the beets, turnips, and cabbage. They would be digging up the gladioli and letting them dry before packing the bulbs away. They would be planting more tulips. Catherine could never get enough tulips. It was because they had met in the spring, Catherine always said. 'We met in the spring, and the tulips were blooming in that little park. You looked so beautiful against the tulips, Simon on your lap. I knew I loved you.' Last autumn Simon had been five and had raked leaves and dug holes for the tulip bulbs. Catherine had made cocoa and cinnamon toast, and Simon had declared that he liked cinnamon toast better than pie.

Anna May tasted the tears on her lips. She licked the wet salt, imagining it was sweet wine on her tongue. 'It's my fault,' she said out loud. She thought of all the things she should have done to prevent Simon's leaving. She should have placated Tony; she should have lived alone; she should have pretended to be straight; she should have never become an alcoholic; she should have never loved; she should have never been born. Let go! she cried somewhere inside her. 'Let go!' she cried aloud. Isn't that what she learned? But how could she let go of Simon and the hate she held for Tony and herself? How could she let go of that? If she let go, she'd have to forgive—the forgiveness Tony begged of her now that Simon was gone.

Even Catherine, even the woman she loved, asked her to forgive Tony. 'It could have happened when he was with us,' Catherine cried at her. 'Forgive him, then you can forgive yourself.' But Catherine didn't know what it was to feel the baby inside her, to feel him pushing his way out of her, to feel his mouth on her breast, to feel the sharp pain in her womb every time his name was spoken. Forgiveness was for people who could afford it. Anna May was poverty-struck.

The highway turned into a road, the trees crowding in on both sides of her, the flames of the trees almost blinding her. She was entering the Bruce Peninsula a sign informed her. She pulled off the road, consulting her map. Yes, she would drive to the very tip of the peninsula and it would be there she'd open the bottle and drink her way to whatever she imagined was waiting for her. The bottle rested beside her, and she touched the brown paper, feeling soothed, feeling a hunger in her stomach.

She saw another sign: Sauble Falls. Anna May thought this would be a good place to stop, to drink the last of her coffee, to smoke another cigarette. She pulled over onto the gravel lot. There was a small path leading down to the rocks. Another sign: Absolutely No Fishing. Watch Your Step. Rocks Are Slippery. She could hear the water before she saw it.

She stepped out of the covering of trees and onto the rock shelf. The falls were narrow, spilling out in various layers of rock. She could see the beginnings of Lake Huron below her. She could see movement in the water coming away from the lake and moving towards the rocks and the falls. Fish tails flashing and catching light from the sun. Hundreds of fish tails moving upstream. She walked across a flat slab of rock and there, beneath her in the shallow water, saw salmon slowly moving their bodies, their gills expanding and closing as they rested. She looked up to another rock slab and saw a dozen fish congregating at the bottom of a water spill—waiting. Her mind barely grasped the fact that the fish were migrating, swimming upstream, when a salmon leapt and hurled itself over the rushing water above. Anna May stepped up to a different ledge and watched the salmon's companions waiting their turn to jump the flowing water and reach the next plateau.

She looked down toward the mouth of the lake. There were others, like her, standing and silently watching the struggle of the fish. No one spoke, as if to speak would be blasphemous in the presence of this. She looked again into the water, the fish crowding each resting place before resuming the leaps and the jumps. Here and there on the rocks, dead fish, a testimony to the long and desperate struggle that had taken place. They lay, eyes glazed, sides open and bleeding, food for the gulls that hovered over Anna May's head.

Another salmon jumped, its flesh torn and gaping, its body spinning until it made it over the fall. Another one, the dorsal fin torn, leapt and was washed back by the power of the water. Anna May watched the fish rest, its open mouth like another wound. The fish was large, the dark body undulating in the water. She saw it begin a movement of tail. Churning the water, it shot into the air, twisting its body, shaking and spinning. She saw the underbelly, pale yellow and bleeding from the battering against the rocks, the water. He made it! Anna May wanted to clap, to shout with elation at the sheer power of such a thing happening before her.

She looked around again. The other people were gone. She was alone with the fish, the only sound besides the water was her breath against the air. She walked further upstream, her sneakers getting wet from the splashing of the salmon. She didn't feel the wet, she only waited and watched for the salmon to move. She had no idea of time, of how long she stood waiting for the movement, waiting for the jumps, the leaps, the flight. Anna May watched for Torn Fin, wanting to see him move against the current in his phenomenal swim of faith.

Anna May reached a small dam, the last barrier before the calm water and blessed rest. She sat on a rock, her heart beating fast, the adrenalin pouring through her at each leap and twist of the salmon. There he was, Torn Fin, his final jump before him. She watched, then closed her eyes, almost ashamed to be a spectator at this act, this primal movement to the place of all beginning. He had to get there, to push his bleeding body forward, believing in his magic to get him there. Believing, believing he would get there. No thoughts of death, of food, of rest. No thoughts but the great urging and wanting to get there, get *there*.

Anna May opened her eyes and saw him, another jump before being pushed back. She held her hands together, her body willing Torn Fin to move, to push, to jump, to fly! Her body rocked forward and back, her heart madly beating inside her chest. She rocked, she shouted, 'Make it, damn it, make it!' Torn Fin waited at the dam. Anna May rocked and held her hands tight, her fingers twisting together, nails scratching her palms. She rocked. She whispered, 'Simon, Simon.' She rocked and whispered the name of her son into the water, 'Simon, Simon.' Like a chant. *Simon. Simon. Simon.* Into the water, as if the very name of her son was magic and could move the salmon to his final place. She rocked. She chanted. *Simon. Simon.* Anna May rocked and put her hands in the water, wanting to lift the fish over the dam and to life. As the thought flickered through her brain, Torn Fin slapped his tail against the water and jumped. He battled with the current. He twisted and arced into the air, his great mouth gaping and gasping, his wounds standing out in relief against his body, his fin discoloured and shredded. With a push, a great push, he turned a complete circle and made it over the dam.

'*Simon!* Torn Fin slapped his tail one last time and was gone, the dark body swimming home. She thought . . . she thought she saw her son's face, his black hair streaming behind him, a look of joy transfixed on his little face before the image disappeared.

Anna May stood on the rock shelf, hands limp at her sides, watching the water, watching the salmon, watching. She watched as the sun fell behind the lake and night came closer to her. Then she walked up the path and back to her car. She looked at the bottle sitting next to her, the brown paper rustling as she put the car in gear. She drove south, stopping at a telephone booth.

She could still hear the water in her ears.

Grandmothers of a New World

Pocahontas and Nancy Ward hold a special fascination for me because of the legends that have arisen around their names and lives. They are presented, by white historians, as good friends of the white man, helping colonialists gain a foot-hold in Indian Country. At the same time, some Natives have used the word 'traitor' to describe them.

Defiled and vilified. Somewhere outside their legends the truth lies. As a poet, rather than a historian, I feel I have a freedom of sorts to explore and imagine what those truths are.

According to 'history', Pocahontas was a favoured daughter of Wahunsonacock ('Powhatan'), chief of the Algonquian Confederacy in what is now called Virginia. In 1607 or 1608 she saw her first white man, John Smith, on a ship sailing into the harbour. She immediately became enamoured of his colour and promptly fell in love with him. Wahunsonacock, being the 'savage' he was, hated John Smith and for no apparent reason gave the order to have him executed. Right before he was to be tomahawked, Pocahontas threw herself on Smith, telling her father that he'd have to kill her too. Since Pocahontas was willing to die for this particular white man, there must be something wonderful about all white men, so Wahunsonacock spared not only Smith's life but the lives of his crew as well.

Smith eventually returned to England, leaving Pocahontas to pine away until she met John Rolfe. Pocahontas must have thought that all white men looked alike, or maybe she liked the name John, because she enthusiastically fell in love with Rolfe and became a good Christian. She also became a good capitalist since she helped her husband grow rich in the tobacco trade, and took up wearing white women's clothing, had a son, went to England where she was a celebrity, and finally died happily there—her soul eternally saved.

Quite a story. Even Hollywood couldn't improve this tale.

But I can.

Wahunsonacock had twenty children, ten of them daughters. Pocahontas was a favoured daughter, but more than that, was a child in her father's confidence. She understood only too well what the invasion of Europeans meant for her people. I also must tell you at the time she met John Smith, she was twelve or thirteen—a woman by Native standards of the day. Pocahontas was not just a good listener, she was listened to. When she spoke, the Pamunkey people heard her and respected her voice. While not a true matriarchy like the Mohawk of Molly Brant or the Cherokee of Nanye'hi (Nancy Ward), Pamunkey women held sway in the disposition of enemy warriors and matters pertaining to war. John Smith's so-called rescue was, in fact, a mock execution—a traditional ritual often held after the capture of enemies. This ritual, in the eyes of John Smith, must have held all the trappings of a play with Smith in the starring role. Pocahontas also played her part. She chose to adopt Smith as her brother since this was her right as a Pamunkey woman. Smith began writing letters home of how his life was saved by a genuine Indian princess, and of how he held the Algonquian Confederacy in the palm of his hand. Of course, this was nonsense.

Wahunsonacock and his daughter/confidante were not fools. They had a sophisticated view of the English and the other European nations who were clamouring to capture the 'new' continent and claim it for their own. The continuation of their people was uppermost in the daughter's and father's minds. They thought to establish their Nation by making alliances with the British. Then, as now, survival was the most important thought on Native agendas. The art and practice of diplomacy was not a new concept to North American Native peoples. If we were as savage and warlike as the history books would like us to believe, there would not have been any of us left when the first white man staggered onto our lands. Pocahontas was probably the first ambassador to the British, just as La Malinche was to the Spanish. Not an easy task for anyone, let alone a thirteen-year-old woman who could not read, write, or speak the language of the intruders, and who most likely figured out early on that the British held little esteem for women—especially if they weren't white. Pocahontas saw as the alternative to genocide, adopting Smith as her brother.

History books speculate on whether Smith and Pocahontas were lovers. I doubt this is important, but 'history', intent on romanticizing Pocahontas and Smith, seems to linger on this attachment. I think that 'history' is a lie—written down to bolster the ego of the white man, and to promulgate their status as macho and clever warriors, *and* the ludicrous idea that white men are irresistible to Native women. Boastful and self-involved, John Smith eventually left the Jamestown Colony and went home to England. He hadn't made his fortune, but he was to make a mark in books to come through his lies and distortion of Aboriginal peoples.

There are reports that Pocahontas and her father were greatly angered at Smith's leave-taking. Why? Did they see it as a withdrawal of agreement made between Great Britain and the Algonquian Confederacy? Through Smith's adoption, they had woven a tenuous connection between the Nations. The Algonquian Confederacy had lost few people to these British invaders. The Confederacy was still strong in the eyes of other First Nations. They were not weakened by their relationship with the British, due to the diplomatic skills of Wahunsonacock and Pocahontas. The British had done fairly well in the Colony. Natives taught them what to eat, how to eat, how to plant what they ate. It amazes me how Thanksgiving in the States is portrayed as whites and Natives happily sharing food in a gesture of friendship. The pilgrims had nothing to share. Suspicious and ignorant of new kinds of food, as well as Native peoples, it is a wonder to me that any of them survived at all. But we were generous—a generosity that became the beginning of the end of our cultures as we knew them. My eldest grandsons are righteously appalled when Thanksgiving is celebrated in their schools.'Teacher, the pilgrims were bad guys. They killed Indians!' Of course, 'teacher' continues to perpetuate this mythical holiday as a story where the white man is the good guy, feeding the starving Natives! When *will* they get it right?

In Aboriginal languages, there are no words for stingy or selfish, except to describe aberrant behaviour requiring a shaman's intervention. Our generosity comes from the complex and sophisticated worldview of thousands of years of belief and practice. The concept of family is a wide and far-reaching part of our worldview. By adopting John Smith as her brother, Pocahontas was opening her home and family to him. Smith violated this honour and the meaning of family by leaving Jamestown without a proper goodbye and thank you. This violation brought humiliation to the family, clan and Nation. As a result of Smith's behaviour, Wahunsonacock and Pocahontas left the Jamestown settlement and went home, enjoining other Natives to follow them. Jamestown suffered heavy losses of life. They literally starved. Pocahontas was sent on various missions to other Nations by her father. Serving as a spokesperson for the Algonquian Confederacy, she arranged new trade agreements, cemented old friendships, built new ones. There is no doubt that Pocahontas was a skilled orator and politician. It sickens me that the story we learn in school is the racist and untrue depiction of her romance with John Smith, and her willingness to die for him.

During her travels, Pocahontas took a Native husband. Of him, we can find no trace. She must not have had children, or they would have remained with their mother on her sojourns and her eventual return to her home and family. When Wahunsonacock and Pocahontas were ready to visit Jamestown again (to see what the white man was up to), they were taken prisoner. I imagine the settlers wanted to vent their anger on them for being deserted. It would never have occurred to the pilgrims that their own racism and stupidity had led to this 'desertion' and ultimate loss of lives. Pocahontas and her father were not free to leave the colony, but could wander among the people and houses. They found a man who must have intrigued them to no end. He was a missionary and was teaching people to read and write. Reading was something the white man did, and because of it, he held a certain kind of power. Bargaining with the British, Pocahontas arranged for her father to be sent home and she would stay to learn more about the Christian way. 'History' says Pocahontas was an eager convert. I submit that her conversion to Christianity was only half-hearted, but her conversion to literacy was carried out with powerful zeal.

I feel in my heart that Pocahontas was guided by divine power. Not a god in Christian terms, but a communion with Creator. 'Living with the spirits', as my father used to say. Pocahontas lived with and listened to these spirits. There is a term and philosophy that has been used for centuries—Manifest Destiny. It is a white man's term and logic implying that whites are superior and therefore, it is Nature's law that the white race hold dominion over all natural things. In other words, the white man is king and emperor over all—Indigenous peoples, animals, plants, the very air. I propose that Pocahontas had her own destiny to fulfil—that of keeping her people alive. Would Wahunsonacock and his people have listened and learned so readily from Pocahontas if she had not already given evidence of being a person who 'lived with the spirits'? Was Pocahontas a shaman, a seer, a holy woman? In some English translations of her name, it appears to come up as 'getting joy from spirits'. Name-giving in Native cultures is a serious event. Many signs and omens are consulted before giving a name and getting a name. In many Nations, it was the role of the berdache, or Two-Spirit, to bestow this honour. History will not tell us that Pocahontas was a holy woman, but there is a feeling inside me that tells me this is so. I know my feeling cannot be substantiated by academic literature; but I am not a member of the academy, nor am I a scholar of institutions—I am a Mohawk woman storyteller who knows there were and are prophets among my people. Pocahontas was such a prophet who lived her prophecy.

Linda Hogan, Chickasaw poet, has written letters to me about the 'New People'. These are people like her and me—the mixed-bloods. Did Pocahontas envision Nations of New People? Did she vision a New World? A world where people would say, 'I am a human being of many races and Nations.' Is this the real destiny? Vine Deloria once said, 'Blood quantums are not important; what really matters is who your grandparents were.' These women I am writing about were our grandparents. They are our Grandmothers in spirit, if not actual blood. This does not mean that I think every person who dwells on this continent is a spiritual Indian. That would be a dishonour to my ancestors. I emphatically believe that our culture and ritual belong to us—First Nations. A person does not become an Indian by participating in a sweat, or observing a Sun Dance, or even working on political issues that affect our Nations. One cannot choose to be Indigenous like one chooses new clothes or chooses a brand of toothpaste. One is not Indigenous because they believe in our values. But the prophecy of New People *can* mean the beginning of a different kind of discourse between Nations and races.

While learning to read and write, Pocahontas met John Rolfe. The accounts come down through time that he greatly admired her. He may indeed have admired her. She was a powerful voice in the territory; she held great wealth of land; she knew the many secrets of growing tobacco which Rolfe had come to realize could make him a rich man. Rolfe came from gentry stock, but was fairly poor compared to others of his class. Why else would he have come to the continent, except in search of untold wealth, just waiting for him to take? 'History' tells us that Rolfe was taken with Pocahontas because of her 'regal bearing, her Christian demeanor, her wisdom'. All this may be true and perhaps even love entered into it. Did Pocahontas love John Rolfe? Maybe. Did the spirits tell her that Rolfe was a good choice to begin the prophecy? There were other white men waiting in the wings to know the favours of Pocahontas and her father, for one was not possible without the other. John Rolfe was a man easily handled by those who had more charisma and political savvy than he. And he was not ugly. The courtship began, but not without obstacles. The court of King James was very adamant in discouraging contact between the races (although I doubt there was discouragement against rape and pillage). The issue of class was a barrier to the marriage. This is why we end up with the ridiculous legends of Pocahontas being a princess. John Smith had started the flame of this particular bonfire when he wrote home about having his life saved by a princess of the realm. John Rolfe added more fuel to the legend in his desire to be married. Thus Wahunsonacock is made a king and Pocahontas a princess. In reality, kings and princesses—royalty—do not exist and never have existed in our cultures.

Of a dowry there is no mention, but it would be fair to speculate that Rolfe received a parcel of land on which to experiment with tobacco. The smoking of tobacco was a great hit in England among the royals. King James was said to disapprove of the habit, but it doesn't appear that too many people paid attention to what he had to say. Queen Anne was addicted to the stuff and she and her ladies-in-waiting spent hours smoking tobacco and requesting more.

The myth of Pocahontas wants us to believe that after marrying Rolfe, she quickly became a lady of leisure, even acquiring the name of Rebecca. I find this choice of names intriguing and prophetic. In Pocahontas' quest for literacy, the Bible was the only tool she had at that time. Did she read the story of another ancient legend, Rebecca, who was told 'Be thou the mother of thousands of millions, and let thy seed possess the gate of those which hate them'? When Pocahontas found herself pregnant did she feel the joy of having a child of her prophecy? A child of mixed-blood who would learn to read and write as a matter of course, while inheriting the wisdom, political skills and rich culture of his mother?

To ensure that this child would come into the best of all worlds, Pocahontas surrounded herself with female relatives and her father. John Rolfe may have been alarmed that Lady Rebecca was choosing to have her child in what he considered a primitive and heathen manner, but, then again, maybe he wasn't. We do know that in 1615, Pocahontas gave birth to a son amidst the chanting and singing of her people. So much for Pocahontas' Christian submissiveness. After the birth, the relatives stayed on. Unlike John Smith, Rolfe seemed to recognize the honour of being part of Pocahontas' family. When a non-Native becomes part of a Native household or family group, whether through marriage or companionship, the Native family takes over. This is assimilation of a kind that is never discussed or written about. The non-Native often has to put up small battles to hang on to a separate personality rather than the personality of the Native group.

I have seen this happen in my own family with my non-Native uncles, mother, and my lover. Soon they are talking like Natives, joking like Natives; the prevailing Native culture and worldview is assimilated by the non-Native. I suspect this process is not discussed because the dominant culture does not want to admit that another way of *seeing* may be a more integrated way of being in the world, as opposed to Manifest Destiny. Again, this process of assimilation is *not* becoming Indigenous. It is a recognition that every part of what constitutes life, *makes life*.

This integrity of life can be explained through the example of the Sun Dance of the Plains Indians. Each person entering the circle to dance has an objective. Whether he or she is dancing for strength, for healing the body and/or mind, that purpose will be reflected on the community, for the good of community. In Oklahoma a few years ago, a Vietnam veteran asked to participate in the Sun Dance while using his wheelchair. This had never been done, but a way was worked out where a guide would maneuver him through the rigorous ceremony. This was not an easy task for veteran or guide. The Sun Dance can last for hours; it has been known to last for days until communion with Creator has taken place. Later, when the Dance was done, the vet told a friend of mine that he was dancing to be forgiven for the 'sins' (his word) he had committed in Vietnam. As he was dancing, he began to relive his experiences in Vietnam; he began dancing for his buddies, dancing for the Vietnamese people, he began dancing for peace and the end to racism, he began dancing for the spiritual health that would bring him home to his own people again. This story has everything to do with Pocahontas and her prophecy. While not belonging to the Plains worldview that produces a Sun Dance, Pocahontas was doing her own dance for the good of the community. Her community, because of the child she bore, was an enlarged one. And I am wondering if John Rolfe's idea of family and community was also enlarged.

Pocahontas and Rolfe were invited to England to be presented to the king and queen. The tobacco industry was a profitable one to the monarchy. They wanted to meet Pocahontas, the 'princess' of the Indians. Natives were becoming the rage in England. Natives were 'in'. To this day, Natives remain an object of fascination to European people. Perhaps they are fascinated by the fact that we still exist after five hundred years of persistent genocide. North Americans are not much better—to them we are invisible, extinct, or relics of a past ('primitive') way of life.

The England of the 1600s was a primitive, filthy place and must have been a terrifying sight to Pocahontas and her relatives. For she did not travel to London with just her husband and son, she took many female relatives and her uncle, Uttamatamakin, a medicine man to her people. It has been recorded that while in London, Pocahontas and her Native relatives swam daily in the waters of the Thames. This was seen as a heathen aberration by the British who were accustomed to taking baths perhaps once or twice a year. Some of Pocahontas' relatives became ill from the polluted waters and had to stop their 'savage' habit of bathing daily.

Pocahontas met the king and queen. It is reported that they were impressed. We have no account that Pocahontas reciprocated the feeling. And this leads to another question—where are Pocahontas' writings? We know she could read and write in English; does it not seem likely that she kept a diary or journal of the events in which she was participating? Illness made inroads into the health of the Native people. John Rolfe got permission to take the family to the country where the air and waters were cleaner. Thomas, the son, could play and Pocahontas and her relatives could relax away from the rude stares and comments that followed them everywhere. Pocahontas also met up with her old acquaintance/brother, John Smith. He wrote in his diary that the princess seemed angry with him. He was probably quite angry himself. The reception accorded Pocahontas and Rolfe must have rankled him. The 'princess' of his making was truly being treated as royalty.

Pocahontas fell ill. She had already lost some of her people to England's diseases and had spent her time in the country in mourning. Thomas was also ill, which must have sent his mother into a frenzy of trying to get him away from a country that did nothing but kill her people. Rolfe and Pocahontas prepared to take their leave and go home. They set sail; but in Gravesend, in the county of Kent, the ship had to stop and Pocahontas was removed to receive medical care. Perhaps she had tuberculosis or smallpox. Uttamatamakin performed healing rituals for her. This may have been enough to ease her mind and spirit, but British doctors came, and over the protestations of her relatives, applied leeches and gave her purges. This weakened her further. Pocahontas died and her last reported words were, 'It is enough that the child liveth.' John Rolfe, a weak man without Pocahontas' intervention, failed her in death, since he had her buried Christian-style. Uttamatamakin was furious and the anti-white feelings that were held at bay during Wahunsonacock's tenure began stirring and set the scene for hard times to come in Virginia.

Why did Rolfe fail Pocahontas? It may be due to the fact that his son was still very sick and he wanted to leave for Virginia as soon as possible. Rolfe may have chosen the most politically expedient way to placate his British hosts. Pocahontas was no longer there to strengthen him. Or perhaps John Rolfe was always a fool, believing that the Brit was the only way. Pocahontas' relatives were token Christians as she was, and probably would have gone along with a Christian burial *if* they also could send her to the Spirit World through Pamunkey ministrations. But Pocahontas was interred at Gravesend in full English dress and tradition; her body remains there to this day.

Wahunsonacock died within a short time after receiving news of his daughter's death. He longed to stay alive to take his grandson to live with him. He must have mourned and longed himself to death. His beloved daughter would never come home again. Her bones would nourish British land instead of her own. And the precious child Thomas, so important to Pocahontas' vision of a new world? He stayed in England and was reared by his father's uncle. John Rolfe went back to Virginia and died shortly after the Native uprising. This foolish, weak man who failed his wife's dream, failed all of us. As a teen, Thomas did return to Virginia and experienced the desire to see his mother's land and the place he first drew breath. He journeyed to the Pamunkey, which was considered enemy territory by the British. What happened to Thomas as he journeyed to the land and language of his birth? A few years later, he was commissioned as a lieutenant in the colonial militia and took up duty as a colonist against the Native people. The so-called Peace of Pocahontas was at an end. Had his mother lived, would the outcome have been different? It is hard to speculate. La Malinche lived to see her son by Cortez take up arms against her people and his. The Pamunkey people and those of many other Nations were on a path to extinction through the Europeans' greatest weapon—disease. It is estimated by Native historians that two-thirds of Indigenous North Americans were wiped out by measles, chicken pox, tuberculosis, smallpox, and the common cold. Did Pocahontas see this in her vision?

It is ironic and horrible that Pocahontas became grandmother to an estimated two million people who lay claim to being her descendants. Ironic, because a Virginian who would recoil in horror at having a Black ancestor, points with pride to the Native blood in his body. Horrible, because the British did their job well—anointing Pocahontas a princess, while excising her Native blood. We are left with the legend of a woman made into an 'incidental' Indian. There was nothing incidental about Pocahontas. She fought for her people and for the future of her people. She spoke in her own language even at the end. She brought her son into the world through Native womb and hands. Even her final words—'It is enough the child liveth,' speak volumes of her plan. The false European legend must end. Pocahontas' honour demands it.

Nancy Ward was also a woman committed to vision. Her name Nanye'hi, 'Spirit People' or 'Spirit Path', describes communion with a dream that gave direction to her life and that of her people, the Cherokee Nation.

Nanye'hi became the wife of Kingfisher in 1750 and the stories about her begin at that time. While a mother of two young children, she went into battle with her husband to fight the Creek, traditional enemies of the Cherokee. The Cherokee Nation was a true matriarchy, meaning the blood lines flowed through the mother. Clans of the mother became the clans of the children. Women influenced all political and family matters. Accompanying her mate into battle was not a new phenomenon to the Cherokee. While in what is now called Georgia, Nanye'hi took up the arms of her husband who lay dying, and continued to fight and rally the people around her. This inspiration led her people into ultimate victory over the Creek Nation. Stories began to circulate among the Cherokee about Nanye'hi's heroism. She soon was chosen to become a Beloved Woman of the Cherokee. Beloved Woman means just that; she was beloved by the people, but even more, was beloved by the Creator and was a conduit through which Creator spoke.

It seems that only Indigenous people could come up with this particular way of being and seeing. Most of us know some stories of Christian saints who supposedly were in communication with a god, but Native peoples so cherish and personalize Creator and the spirits who make the mysteries that this Great Mystery chooses to speak through women's voices. This is not unique only to the Cherokee. Across North America one will hear the voices of women speaking from the spirits. Again, I think of Christian women saints who had to be martyred and *die* before achieving the state of grace their religion told them they didn't have in life. How much more sensible to be in a state of grace as a living human.

When Nanye'hi became a Beloved Woman, the Cherokee were literally caught in the middle between France and England. Each European nation was panting and scheming for Cherokee land and it fell on Nanye'hi to negotiate with each nation while retaining and preserving the integrity and strength of her own Nation. Like Pocahontas, she was a diplomat of skillful means. She worked in close connection with her uncle, Attakullakulla, maintaining a balance of power. Imagine it—young woman, aging man, holding war at bay, gathering strength to withstand the onslaught they knew would eventually come. Because she maintained this balance and peace, Nanye'hi has been seen by some of her descendants as a traitor and lackey to the British. But this story is old and familiar. Take strong Nationalist women and turn them into pale myth. Make *our own people* believe the lies. This is what oppression is—the enforcement of amnesia—to make us forget the glory and story of our own history. These women called traitors, what was their treachery? Neither Pocahontas nor Nanye'hi handed over lands or people to the white man. For one thing, it would not have been in the Native consciousness to do so. Land was given by Creator. Neither woman gave up secrets or culture. These women knew what was in their vision. These women lived with spirits.

In 1757, Nanye'hi married a white trader, Bryant Ward. She had a daughter, Elizabeth. Bryant Ward did not live with Nanye'hi and the Cherokee. Why? My own guess is that Nanye'hi didn't want him to. She sent him away after her child was born. The words of Pocahontas come back to me—'It is enough the child liveth.' Were these Nanye'hi's words also? Did she have a vision of a New People also?

In 1775, the Watauga Purchase took place. Twenty million acres of Cherokee land were 'sold' to the British for two thousand pounds. There is no record of Nanye'hi's voice, but a woman who always counselled 'never sell the land,' must have been frightened and appalled at what she saw as a break in Cherokee tradition and culture. But already, whether because of her arrangement with Bryant Ward, or the adoption of white values by some of her people, Nanye'hi was losing her influence.

In 1776, a Cherokee faction led by Dragging Canoe and Old Abram set siege to the Watauga fort. They captured a white woman, Lydia Bean, and were going to burn her alive. It is said that Nanye'hi stepped to the fire and shouted, 'No woman shall be burned at the stake while I am still Beloved Woman.' This story has a familiar ring to it, but it is true. Cherokee men, after years of staving off the white man, were nevertheless learning from him. The very notion of murdering a woman, regardless of her being non-Cherokee, reflects how Native beliefs were being swept away by colonialism. In all the horror stories that have been told since we first laid eyes on the white man, I find this one the most telling—how Native attitudes towards women changed and became more and more like the oppressors'. This change was not everywhere, and not in everyone, but enough change to freeze the blood and enrage the heart. Nanye'hi must have felt similar horror. For if attitudes towards women could go against Creator's wishes, what other terrors would follow? This is not to say that we Native peoples brought this destruction upon ourselves. Such a statement would be untrue. But this change in a religious worldview surely helped to lay us open to the self-doubt and self-loathing imposed by the 'Manifest Destiny' that tore the material of our Nations.

After saving Lydia's life, Nanye'hi took this woman to live at Chote, Nanye'hi's ancestral home. History does not tell us how long they lived together, or what they talked of together. Did they talk of politics and raising children? Did they become lovers? One thing is known—Nanye'hi learned to make butter and cheese from the milk of the 'white man's buffalo'. She later used this knowledge to introduce dairying into the Cherokee Nation. But what of Lydia Bean? Did she learn of the spirits? Did she learn that women's voices were the means to the Creator? Did she become assimilated into a Native way of seeing and being? I want to know the answers to these questions because it is essential to the tenuous discussion that is taking place between Native and non-Native women. I am reminded of a time when Denise and I went to Tyendinaga for a visit. We stayed with one of my many great-aunts and cousins living there. One night we sat at the kitchen table, shelling beans. We sat for a few hours, five of us, doing women's work—making food for the family. There was a magic to that evening, probably because we were performing a simple and primal act of love. Denise, always aware she is a white woman among the Mohawk, felt loved and filled to be part of this act. We Mohawk women felt the same. I think of that evening, especially when I am asked to speak or read in unfamiliar places. Lydia and Nanye'hi made food together—physically and spiritually. Surely this is a possibility for us. Pocahontas saw a new world, filled with new people. Can we be less visionary than she?

War intensified between the Cherokee and the emerging American nation. The Cherokee found themselves defeated at every turn, while Nanye'hi stood her ground and shouted for peace. In 1781, trying to negotiate a peace treaty, she cried, 'Peace . . . let it continue. This peace must last forever. Let your children be ours. Our children will be yours. Let your women hear our words.' The idea that differing races could belong to each other in family and love is the most radical of ideas. Did the white women hear Nanye'hi's words? It is doubtful. How could they have heard unless their men chose to tell them?

The year 1785 found Nanye'hi living at Chote with her children and grandchildren. Elizabeth had married an Indian agent. Her two children by Kingfisher had married and produced children. She had also opened her home to orphans, of which there were many. Deep changes were occurring within the Cherokee Nation. In 1817, the last Cherokee Council meeting was held, and Nanye'hi was expected to speak and bring counsel. Old and ill, she sent her son Fivekiller to represent her and to read her written message. And here I have another question. Nanye'hi was a literate woman, *where are her words?* As a Native woman it makes me weep to know that 'history' has not deemed it worthwhile to note that Nanye'hi and Pocahontas could write and think and feel, and therefore must have put ideas and thoughts onto paper. Nanye'hi and Lydia must have corresponded. Where are these precious documents I long to see? Were they lost? Were they thrown away like *we* have been thrown away? Were they burned—like the truth of their lives was burned out of history and memory? Fivekiller read his mother's message to the people, words that have survived history:

Your mothers, your sisters, ask you not to part with any more of our land. We say you are our descendants and must listen to our request. Keep the land for our growing children for it was the good will of Creator to place us here. Keep your hands off of paper for it is our own country. If it was not, they (the white man) would not ask you to put your hands on paper. It would be impossible to remove us all for as soon as one child is raised, we have others in our arms. Therefore children, don't part with any more of our land but continue on it and enlarge your farms and cultivate and raise corn so we may never go hungry. Listen to the talks of your sisters. I have a great many grandchildren and I wish them to do well on the land.

Nanye'hi's words were a prophecy, especially about the impossibility of removing all the people from the land. Even during the forced removal of southeastern Nations to Oklahoma, known as the Trail of Tears, many Cherokee escaped and blended into other families and races. Nanye'hi died in 1818. She had lived a long life as compared to Pocahontas. When she died, there were no last words reported, but her great-grandson said that a light rose from her body and fluttered like a bird around her body and her family in attendance; then flew in the direction of ancestral land. If Nanye'hi had spoken last words, I imagine they would have been Cherokee words she had spoken all her life—Don't sell our land. Let the women hear my words. Our cry is for peace.

My friend Awiakta, Cherokee writer and champion of Nanye'hi, has told me of the historic reunion of the Cherokee Eastern and Western Councils in 1984 at the Red Clay Historical area in East Tennessee. 'These are the same council grounds,' Awiakta said, 'where the last council met before the Removal and also where Nanye'hi came during her lifetime. (Her homesite and grave are in the vicinity.) The Cherokee had carried the Sacred Fire with them on the Trail of Tears. At the Reunion they brought brands of it back. On a hill, in a receptacle made of native stone, they relit the Sacred Fire which will burn eternally.' Awiakta also said that 20,000 people were there, the descendants of Nanye'hi's vision of a new world. Red and white, Red and Black, Red, white and Black. All these glorious mixtures come together as family. 'Let your children be ours. Our children will be yours.' How prophetic those words!

What is history? Does it still lie in the domain of the white man who churns it out according to *his* politic? What is women's history? Is it still the history of white women who were privileged by their birth? Will history become something new—a story of all Nations—instead of the story of European conquest? I am a grandmother and I feel it is imperative that I tell the truthful story of the Americas. My grandsons will need this story to help them grow into good men—the kind of men our Nations deserve. My grandsons—so many kinds of blood flow in their veins. Among the four of them flows the blood of Mohawk, Irish, Scots, Polish, Cree, French, Norwegian, Cherokee—the blood of the future.

Buffy Sainte-Marie *b.* 1941

CREE

Buffy Sainte-Marie was born on the Pay-e-pot reserve in the Qu'Appelle Valley of Saskatchewan. She was raised by foster parents in Maine and Massachusetts. Her foster mother was part Mi'kmaq, but Sainte-Marie recalls all her childhood environments as being 'very white'. She was adopted by the Cree at a powwow when she was eighteen.

Sainte-Marie has had significant successes as a singer and songwriter from her early twenties. One of her best-known songs, 'Until It's Time For You To Go', has been recorded in seven languages by more than a hundred artists, from Elvis Presley to the Boston Pops. Sainte-Marie has published hundreds of other songs, which have been recorded in sixteen languages. One early song, 'The Universal Soldier', written in a Toronto folk club, became one of the anthems of the peace movement, and it continues to be sung in that context. But in spite of her successes, Sainte-Marie found it difficult to book performances in the United States in the 1970s and 1980s, apparently because of her political activities. Thus, at a time when she was drawing an audience of 90,000 in Paris, she appeared in the US only on reserves.

Many of Sainte-Marie's songs, such as 'Now That the Buffalo's Gone' and 'My Country 'Tis of Thy People You're Dying', focus directly on Native causes. She recorded an album for the American Indian Movement and has donated much of her royalties to a foundation she created for Native education, the Nihewan Foundation. For five-and-a-half years she was a regular performer on the children's television program *Sesame Street*, where her main activity was to increase awareness of Native cultures. She saw this as part of a general transition in her public persona from despair to pride. In 1978 she commented: 'I began to have this feeling that a lot of people were coming to see me just to watch this Indian cry, and I didn't accept that for a minute. I looked around at my culture and said, what do Indian people need? We need a sense of our own joy, our own beauty, our own dignity, our own life and laughter.'

Today, Sainte-Marie lives in Hawaii, but she continues to compose and perform throughout North America and has become a leader in the use of computer and Internet technology in both music and design. Many of her songs have been composed for films; for example, 'Up Where We Belong', which won an Academy Award for best song in 1982, was recorded for the Hollywood movie *An Officer and a Gentleman*.

Sainte-Marie was awarded the Order of Canada in 1997.

Universal Soldier

He's five foot two and he's six feet four
He fights with missiles and with spears
He's all of thirty-one and he's only seventeen
He's been a soldier for a thousand years.

He's a Catholic a Hindu an Atheist a Jain
A Buddhist and a Baptist and a Jew
And he knows he shouldn't kill and he knows he always will
Kill you for me my friend and me for you.

5

And he's fighting for Canada and he's fighting for France
He's fighting for the USA   10
And he's fighting for the Russians and he's fighting for Japan
And he thinks we'll put an end to war this way.

And he's fighting for democracy, he's fighting for the reds
He says it's for the peace of all
He's the one who must decide who's to live and who's to die   15
And he never sees the writing on the wall.

But without him how would Hitler have condemned them at Dachau
Without him Caesar would've stood alone
He's the one who gives his body as a weapon of the war
And without him all this killing can't go on.   20

He's the Universal Soldier and he really is to blame
His orders come from far away no more
They come from here and there and you and me
And brothers can't you see
This is not the way we put an end to war.   25

My Country 'Tis of Thy People You're Dying

Now that your big eyes are finally opened
Now that you're wond'ring, 'How must they feel?'
Meaning them that you've chased 'cross America's movie screens.
Now that you're wond'ring, 'How can it be real?'
That the ones you've called colourful, noble, and proud in your   5
    school propaganda,
They starve in their splendour!
You've asked for my comment,
I simply will render,
My country, 'tis of thy people you're dying.

Now that our longhouses breed superstition   10
You force us to send our toddlers away
To your schools where they're taught to despise their traditions;
Forbid them their languages, then further say
That American history really began when Columbus set sail out of
    Europe!
And stress that the Nation of leeches that's conquered this land   15
Are the biggest and bravest and boldest and best!

And yet, where in the history books is the tale of the genocide basic
    to this country's birth?
Of the preachers who lied? How the Bill of Rights failed?
And where will it tell of the Liberty Bell as it rang with a thud over
    Kinzua mud?
And of brave Uncle Sam in Alaska this year?   20
My country, 'tis of thy people you're dying.

Hear how the bargain was made for the west,
With her shivering children, in zero degrees;
'Blankets for your land'; so the treaties attest
Now blankets for land is a bargain, indeed,   25
But the blankets were those Uncle Sam had collected
From small pox-diseased dying soldiers that day,
And the tribes were wiped out, and the history books censored!
One hundred years of your statesmen have felt it's better this way;
Yet a few of the conquered have somehow survived—   30
Their blood runs the redder, though genes have been paled;
From the Grand Canyon's caverns to Craven's sad hills
The wounded, the losers, the robbed sing their tale,
From Los Angeles County, to up-state New York, the white nation
    fattens while others grown lean.
Oh, the tricked and evicted, only know what I mean;   35
My country, 'tis of thy people you're dying.

The past, it just crumbled; the future just threatens,
Our life-blood's shut up in your chemical tanks,
And now here you come, bill of sale in your hand.
And surprise in your eyes that we're lacking in thanks   40
    for the blessings of civilization you've brought us.
The lessons you've taught us, the ruins you've wrought us!
Oh, see what our trust in America's bought us!
My country, 'tis of thy people you're dying!
Now that the pride of the sires receive charity,
    now that we're harmless and safe behind laws,
Now that my life's to be known as your heritage,   45
    now that even the graves have been robbed.

Now that our own chosen way is a novelty
Hands on your hearts, we salute you your victory,
Choke on your blue-white-and-scarlet hypocrisy,
Pitying your blindness, that you've never seen
That the eagles of war whose wings lent your glory   50

Were never no more than carrion crows;
Pushed the wrens from their nest, stole their eggs,
changed their story,
The mocking-bird sings it—it's all that she knows,
'Oh, what can I do?' say a powerless few, with a lump in your throat   55
    and a tear in your eye,
Can't you see that their poverty's profiting you?
My country, 'tis of thy people you're dying!

Now That the Buffalo's Gone

Can you remember the times
That you have held your head high
And told all your friends of your Indian claims
Proud good lady, and proud good man.
Your great, great grand-father from Indian blood sprang,   5
And you feel in your heart for these ones.

Oh it's written in books and in songs
That we've been mistreated and wronged
Well, over and over I hear the same words
From you, good lady, from you good man.   10
Well listen to me if you care where we stand,
And you feel you're a part of these ones.

When a war between nations is lost
The loser we know pays the cost
But even when Germany fell to your hands   15
Consider, dear lady, consider dear man.
You left them their pride and you left them their land,
And what have you done to these ones.

Has a change come about Uncle Sam
Or are you still taking our land   20
A treaty for ever George Washington signed
He did, dear lady, he did, dear man.
And the treaty's being broken by Kinzua Dam,
And what will you do for these ones?

Oh it's all in the past you can say   25
But it's still going on till today
The government now want the Iroquois land
That of the Seneca and the Cheyenne.
It's here and it's now you must help us, dear man,
Now that the buffalo's gone.   30

Emma Lee Warrior *b.* 1941

PEIGAN

Emma Lee Warrior grew up on the Peigan Reserve in southern Alberta, close to the American border, a member of the North Peigan (Blackfoot) band. She attended a boarding school there, but she remarks that though the school was not far from home, 'with all the rules and restrictions, it might as well not have been anywhere near home.' Warrior says she writes to overcome the effects of that early repression: 'I find great freedom in writing. I find myself.'

Warrior's stories and poems have appeared in *Wicazo Sa*, *A Gathering of Spirit*, *Harper's Anthology of Twentieth Century Native American Poetry*, and *Canadian Fiction Magazine*. She acquired a Master of Arts degree from the University of Washington, and she continues to live in the state of Washington, where she is writing and training to be a counsellor. She remains, however, tied to her home community: 'That landscape is within me.'

Compatriots

Lucy heard the car's motor wind down before it turned off the gravel road a quarter of a mile west of the house. Maybe it was Bunky. She hurried and left the outhouse. She couldn't run if she wanted to. It would be such a relief to have this pregnancy over with. She couldn't see the colour of the vehicle, for the slab fence was between the house and the road. That was just as well. She'd been caught in the outhouse a few times, and it still embarrassed her to have a car approach while she was in there.

She got inside the house just as the car came into view. It was her aunt, Flora. Lucy looked at the clock. It was seven-thirty. She wondered what was going on so early in the morning. Flora and a young white woman approached the house. Bob barked furiously at them. Lucy opened the door and yelled at him. 'I don't know what's wrong with Bob; he never barks at me,' said Flora.

'He's probably barking at her,' explained Lucy. 'Not many whites come here.'

'Oh, this is Hilda Afflerbach. She's from Germany,' began Flora. 'Remember? I told you I met her at the Calgary Stampede? Well, she got off the seven o'clock bus, and I don't have time to drive her all the way down to my house. I took her over to my mother's, but she's getting ready to go to Lethbridge. Can she stay with you till I get off work?'

Lucy smiled. She knew she was boxed in. 'Yeah, but I've got no running water in the house. You have to go outside to use the toilet,' she said, looking at Hilda.

'Oh, that's okay,' her aunt answered. 'She's studying about Indians, anyway. Might as well get the true picture, right? Oh, Hilda, this is my niece, Lucy.' Flora lowered her voice and asked, 'Where's Bunky?'

'He never came home last night. I was hoping it was him coming home. He's not supposed to miss any more work. I've got his lunch fixed in case he shows up.' Lucy poured some water from a blue plastic water jug into a white enamel basin and washed her hands and face. 'I haven't even had time to make coffee. I couldn't sleep waiting for him to come home.' She poured water into a coffeemaker and measured out the coffee into the paper filter.

'I'd have some coffee if it was ready, but I think I'd better get to work. We have to punch in now; it's a new rule. Can't travel on Indian time anymore,' said Flora. She opened the door and stepped out, then turned to say, 'I think the lost has returned,' and continued down the steps.

The squeak of the dusty truck's brakes signalled Bunky's arrival. He strode toward the door, barely acknowledging Flora's presence. He came in and took the lunch pail Lucy had. 'I stayed at Herbie's,' was all he said before he turned and went out. He started the truck and beeped the horn.

'I'll go see what he wants.' She motioned to Flora to wait.

When Bunky left, she went to Flora: 'Maybe it's a good thing you came here. Bunky didn't want to go to work 'cause he had a hangover. When he found out Hilda was going to be here all day, he decided he'd rather go to work.'

'If I don't have to leave the office this afternoon. I'll bring the car over and you can drive Hilda around to look at the reserve, okay?'

'Sure, that'll be good. I can go and do my laundry in Spitzee.' She surveyed the distant horizon. The Rockies were spectacular, blue and distinct. It would be a nice day for a drive. She hoped it would be a repeat of yesterday, not too hot, but, as she stood there, she noticed tiny heat waves over the wheat field. Well, maybe it won't be a repeat, she thought. Her baby kicked inside of her and she said, 'Okay, I'd better go tend to the guest.' She didn't relish having a white visitor, but Flora had done her a lot of favours and Hilda seemed nice.

And she was. Hilda made friends with the kids, Jason and Melissa, answering their many questions about Germany as Lucy cooked. She ate heartily, complimenting Lucy on her cooking even though it was only the usual scrambled eggs and fried potatoes with toast and coffee. After payday, there'd be sausages or ham, but payday was Friday and today was only Tuesday.

'Have you heard of Helmut Walking Eagle?' Hilda wanted to know.

'Yeah, well, I really don't know him to talk to him, but I know what he looks like. He's from Germany, too. I always see him at Indian dances. He dresses up like an Indian.' She had an urge to tell her that most of the Indians wished Helmut would disappear.

'I want to see him,' Hilda said. 'I heard about him and I read a book he wrote. He seems to know a lot about the Indians, and he's been accepted into their religious society. I hope he can tell me things I can take home. People in Germany are really interested in Indians. They even have clubs.'

Lucy's baby kicked, and she held her hand over the spot. 'My baby kicks if I sit too long. I guess he wants to do the dishes.'

Hilda got up quickly and said, 'Let me do the dishes. You can take care of the laundry.'

'No, you're a visitor. I can do them,' Lucy countered. But Hilda was persistent, and Lucy gave in.

Flora showed up just after twelve with the information that there was a sun-dance going on on the north side of the reserve. 'They're already camping. Let's go there after work. Pick me up around four.'

'I can't wait to go to the sun-dance! Do you go to them often?' Hilda asked Lucy.

'No, I never have. I don't know much about them,' Lucy said.

'But why? Don't you believe in it? It's your culture!' Hilda's face showed concern.

'Well, they never had sun-dances here—in my whole life there's never been a sun-dance here.'

'Really, is that true? But I thought you have them every year here.'

'Not here. Over on the Blood Reserve they do and some places in the States, but not here.'

'But don't you want to go to a sun-dance? I think it's so exciting!' Hilda moved forward in her seat and looked hopefully at Lucy.

Lucy smiled at her eagerness. 'No, I don't care to go. It's mostly those mixed-up people who are in it. You see, Indian religion just came back here on the reserve a little while ago, and there are different groups who all quarrel over which way to practise it. Some use Sioux ways, and others use Cree. It's just a big mess,' she said, shaking her head.

Hilda looked at Lucy, and Lucy got the feeling she was telling her things she didn't want to hear.

Lucy had chosen this time of day to do her wash. The Happy Suds Laundromat would be empty. As a rule, the Indians didn't show up till after lunch with their endless garbage bags of laundry.

After they had deposited their laundry in the machines, Lucy, Hilda, and the kids sauntered down the main street to a café for lunch. An unkempt Indian man dogged them, talking in Blackfoot.

'Do you know what he's saying?' asked Hilda.

'He wants money. He's related to my husband. Don't pay any attention to him. He always does this,' said Lucy. 'I used to give him money, but he just drinks it up.'

The café was a cool respite from the heat outside, and the cushioned seats in the booth felt good. They sat by the window and ordered hamburgers, fries, and lemonade. The waitress brought tall, frosted glasses, and beads of water dripped from them.

'Hello, Lucy,' a man's shaky voice said, just when they were really enjoying their lunch. They turned to look at the Indian standing behind Hilda. He was definitely ill. His eyes held pain, and he looked as though he might collapse from whatever ailed him. His hands shook, perspiration covered his face, and his eyes roamed the room constantly.

Lucy moved over to make room for him, but he kept standing and asked her, 'Could you give me a ride down to Badger? The cops said I have to leave town. I don't want to stay 'cause they might beat me up.'

'Yeah, we're doing laundry. I've got Flora's car. This is her friend, Hilda. She's from Germany.'

The sick man barely nodded at her, then, turning back to Lucy, he asked her, 'Do you have enough to get me some soup? I'm really hungry.'

Lucy nodded and the man said, 'I'll just sit in the next booth.'

'He's my uncle,' Lucy explained to Hilda as she motioned to the waitress. 'His name is Sonny.'

'Order some clear soup or you'll get sick,' Lucy suggested to her uncle.

He nodded, as he pulled some paper napkins out of a chrome container on the table and wiped his face.

The women and children left Sonny with his broth and returned to the laundromat. As they were folding the clothes, he came in. 'Here, I'll take these,' he said, taking the bags from Lucy. His hands shook, and the effort of lifting the bags was clearly too much for him. 'That's okay,' protested Lucy, attempting to take them from him, 'they're not that heavy. Clothes are always lighter after they've been washed.'

'Hey, Lucy, I can manage. You're not supposed to be carrying big things around in your condition.' Lucy let him take the plastic bags, which he dropped several times before he got to the car. The cops had probably tired of putting him in jail and sending him out each morning. She believed the cops did beat up Indians, although none was ever brought to court over it. She'd take Sonny home, and he'd straighten out for a few weeks till he got thirsty again, and he'd disappear as soon as he got money. It was no use to hope he'd stop drinking. Sonny wouldn't quit drinking till he quit living.

As they were pulling out of town, Lucy remembered she had to get some Kool-Aid and turned the car into the Shop-n-Go Mart. Hilda got out with her and noticed the man who had followed them through the street sitting in the shade of a stack of old tires.

'Hey, tamohpomaat sikaohki,' he told Lucy on her way into the store.

'What did he say? Sikaohki?' queried Hilda.

The Kool-Aid was next to the cash register and she picked up a few packages, and laid them on the counter with the money. When the cashier turned to the register, Lucy poked Hilda with her elbow and nodded her head toward the sign behind the counter. Scrawled unevenly in big, black letters, it said, 'Ask for Lysol, vanilla, and shaving lotion at the counter.'

They ignored the man on the way to the car. 'That's what he wants: he's not allowed to go into the stores 'cause he steals it. He wanted vanilla. The Indians call it "sikaohki"; it means "black water".'

Although the car didn't have air-conditioning, Lucy hurried toward it to escape the blistering heat. When she got on the highway, she asked her uncle, 'Did you hear anything about a sun-dance?'

At first he grunted a negative 'Huh-uh', then, 'Oh yeah, it's across the river, but I don't know where. George Many Robes is camping there. Saw him this morning. Are you going there?'

'Flora and Hilda are. Hilda wants to meet that German guy, Helmut Walking Eagle. You know, that guy who turned Indian?'

'Oh yeah, is he here?' he said indifferently, closing his eyes.

'Probably. He's always in the middle of Indian doings,' said Lucy.

'Shit, that guy's just a phony. How could anybody turn into something else? Huh? I don't think I could turn into a white man if I tried all my life. They wouldn't let me, so how does that German think he can be an Indian. White people think they can do anything—turn into Chinese or Indian—they're crazy!'

Sonny laid his head back on the seat and didn't say another word. Lucy felt embarrassed, but she had to agree with him; it seemed that Indians had come into focus lately. She'd read in the papers how some white woman in Hollywood became a medicine woman. She was selling her book on her life as a medicine woman. Maybe some white person or other person who wasn't Indian would get fooled by that book, but not an Indian. She herself didn't practise Indian religion, but she knew enough about it to know that one didn't just join an Indian religious group if one were not raised with it. That was a lot of the conflict going on among those people who were involved in it. They used sacred practices from other tribes, Navajo and Sioux, or whatever pleased them.

The heat of the day had reached its peak, and trails of dust hung suspended in the air wherever cars or trucks travelled the gravel roads on the reserve. Sonny fashioned a shade behind the house underneath the clothesline in the deep grass, spread a blanket, and filled a gallon jar from the pump. He covered the water with some old coats, lay down, and began to sweat the booze out.

The heat waves from this morning's forecast were accurate. It was just too hot. 'Lordy, it's hot,' exclaimed Lucy to Hilda as they brought the laundry in. 'It must be close to ninety-five or one hundred. Let's go up to Badger to my other aunt's house. She's got a tap by her house and the kids can cool off in her sprinkler. Come on, you kids. Do you want to go run in the sprinkler?'

The women covered the windows on the west side where the sun would shine. 'I'm going to leave all the windows open to let the air in,' said Lucy, as she walked around the house pushing them up.

Lucy's aunt's house sat amongst a clutter of junk. 'Excuse the mess,' she smiled at Hilda, waving her arm over her yard. 'Don't wanna throw it away, it might come in handy.' There were thick grass and weeds crisscrossed with paths to and from the clothesline, the outhouse, the woodstove. Lucy's aunt led them to an arbour shaded with huge spruce branches.

'This is nice,' cooed Hilda, admiring the branches. Lucy's aunt beamed, 'Yes, I told my old man, "Henry, you get me some branches that's not gonna dry up and blow away," and he did. He knows what's good for him. You sit down right here, and I'll get us some drinks.' She disappeared and soon returned with a large thermos and some plastic tumblers.

They spent the afternoon hearing about Henry, as they watched the kids run through the sprinkler that sprayed the water back and forth. Once in a while, a suggestion of a breeze would touch the women, but it was more as if they imagined it.

Before four, they left to pick Flora up and headed back to Lucy's. 'It's so hot after being in that cool cement building all day!' exclaimed Flora, as she settled herself into the car's stifling interior. 'One thing for sure, I'm not going home to cook anything. Lucy, do you think Bunky would mind if you came with us? I'll get us some Kentucky Fried Chicken and stuff in town so you don't have to cook. It's too hot to cook, anyway.' She rolled up a newspaper and fanned her face, which was already beginning to flush.

'No, he won't care. He'll probably want to sleep. We picked Sonny up in town. Both of them can lie around and get better. The kids would bother them if we were there.'

It was a long ride across the Napi River toward the Porcupine Hills. A few miles from the Hills, they veered off until they were almost by the river. 'Let's get off,' said Flora.

Hilda gasped at what she saw before her. There was a circle of teepees and tents with a large open area in the middle. Exactly in the centre of the opening was a circular structure covered with branches around the sides. Next to this was a solitary unpainted teepee. Some of the teepees were painted with lines around the bottom; others had orbs bordering them, and yet others had animal figures painted on them. Smoke rose from stoves outside the teepees as people prepared their evening meals. Groups of horses stood languidly in the waning heat of the day, their heads resting on one another's backs and their tails occasionally flicking insects away. The sound of bantering children and yapping dogs carried to where they stood.

'Let's eat here,' the kids said, poking their heads to look in the bags of food. Flora and Lucy spread a blanket on the ground, while Hilda continued to stand where she was, surveying the encampment. Flora pointed out the central leafy structure as the sacred area of prayer and dance.

'The teepee next to it is the sacred teepee. That's where the holy woman who is putting up the sun-dance stays the entire time. That's where they have the ceremonies.'

'How many sun-dances have you been to?' asked Hilda.

'This is my first time, but I know all about this from books,' said Flora. 'Helmut Walking Eagle wrote a book about it, too. I could try to get you one. He sells them cheaper to Indians.'

Hilda didn't eat much and kept looking down at the camp. 'It's really beautiful,' she said, as if to herself.

'Well, you better eat something before you get left out,' advised Lucy. 'These kids don't know when to stop eating chicken.'

'Yeah,' agreed Flora. 'Then we can go down and see who's all there.' Hilda had something to eat, and then they got back into the car and headed down toward the encampment. They drove around the edge of the camp and stopped by Flora's cousin's tent. 'Hi, Delphine,' said Flora, 'I didn't know you were camping here.'

Lucy knew Flora and Delphine were not especially close. Their fathers were half-brothers, which made them half-cousins. Delphine had grown up Mormon and had recently turned to Indian religion, just as Flora had grown up Catholic and was now exploring traditional beliefs. The same could be said about many of the people here.

To top things off, there was some bad feeling between the cousins about a man, some guy they both had been involved with in the past.

'Can anybody camp here? I've got a teepee. How about if I camp next to you?'

Delphine bridled. 'You're supposed to camp with your own clan.'

Flora looked around the camp. 'I wondered who's my clan. Say, there's George Many Robes, he's my relation on my dad's side. Maybe I'll ask him if I can camp next to him.'

Delphine didn't say anything but busied herself with splitting kindling from a box of sawn wood she kept hidden underneath a piece of tarp. Jason spied a thermos under the tarp and asked for a drink of water.

'I have to haul water, and nobody pays for my gas,' grumbled Delphine, as she filled a cup halfway with water.

'Oh say,' inquired Flora, 'do you know if Helmut Walking Eagle is coming here? This girl is from Germany, and she wants to see him.'

'Over there, that big teepee with a Winnebago beside it. That's his camp,' Delphine answered, without looking at them.

'Is she mad at you?' Jason asked Flora.

'Yeah, it must be the heat,' Flora told him with a little laugh.

Elsie Walking Eagle was cooking the evening meal on a camp stove outside the teepee. She had some folding chairs that Lucy would've liked to sit down in, but Elsie didn't ask any of them to sit down though she was friendly enough.

'Is your husband here?' asked Flora.

'No, he's over in the sacred teepee,' answered Elsie.

'How long is he going to take?'

'Oh, he should be home pretty soon,' Elsie said, tending her cooking.

'Do you mind if we just wait? I brought this girl to see him. She's from Germany, too,' Flora said.

Lucy had never seen Helmut in anything other than Indian regalia. He was a smallish man with blond hair, a broad face, and a large thin nose. He wore his hair in braids and always wore round, pink shell earrings. Whenever Lucy saw him, she was reminded of the Plains Indian Museum across the line.

Helmut didn't even glance at the company but went directly inside the teepee. Flora asked Elsie, 'Would you tell him we'd like to see him?'

'Just wait here. I'll go talk to him,' Elsie said, and followed her husband inside. Finally, she came out and invited them in. 'He doesn't have much time to talk with you, so . . .' Her voice trailed off.

The inside of the teepee was stunning. It was roomy, and the floor was covered with buffalo hides. Backrests, wall hangings, parfleche bags, and numerous artifacts were magnificently displayed. Helmut Walking Eagle sat resplendent amidst his wealth. The women were dazzled. Lucy felt herself gaping and had to shush her children from asking any questions.

Helmut looked at them intently and rested his gaze on Hilda. Hilda walked toward him, her hand extended in greeting, but Helmut ignored it. Helmut turned to his wife and asked in Blackfoot, 'Who is this?'

'She says she's from Germany,' was all Elsie said, before making a quick move toward the door.

'Wait!' he barked in Blackfoot, and Elsie stopped where she was.

'I only wanted to know if you're familiar with my home town Weisbaden?' said Hilda.

'Do you know what she's talking about?' Helmut asked Elsie in Blackfoot. Elsie shook her head in a shamed manner.

'Why don't you ask *her* questions about Germany?' he hurled the words at Hilda, then, looking meanly at his wife, he added, 'She's been there.' Elsie flinched, and, forcing a smile, waved weakly at the intruders and asked them in a kind voice to come outside. As Lucy waited to leave, she looked at Helmut whose jaw twitched with resentment. His anger seemed to be tangibly reaching out to them.

'Wow!' whispered Hilda in Lucy's ear.

Outside, Flora touched a book on the fold-out table. Its title read *Indian Medicine* and in smaller letters, *A Revival of Ancient Cures and Ceremonies*. There was a picture of Helmut and Elsie on the cover. Flora asked, 'Is this for sale?'

'No, that one's for someone here at camp, but you can get them in the bookstores.'

'How much are they?' Flora asked, turning the book over.

'They're twenty-seven dollars. A lot of work went into it.' Elsie replied.

Helmut, in Blackfoot, called out his wife's name, and Elsie said to her unwelcome callers, 'I don't have time to visit. We have a lot of things to do.' She left them and went in to her husband.

'He's the brains, she's the source,' Flora said. 'Let's go. My kids are probably wondering what happened to me.'

'I'm sorry I upset her husband. I didn't mean to,' said Hilda. 'I thought he would be willing to teach me something, because we're both German.'

'Maybe you could buy his book,' suggested Lucy.

'Look,' said Flora, 'if you're going to be around for a while, I'm going to a sundance this next weekend. I'm taking a few days off work. I have a friend up north who can teach you about Indian religion. She's a medicine woman. She's been to Germany. Maybe she even went to your home town.'

'Oh, really!' gushed Hilda. 'Of course, I'll be around. I'd love to go with you and meet your friends.'

'You can come into the sweat with us. First, you'll need to buy four square yards of cotton . . .' began Flora.

But Hilda wasn't really listening to her. She looked as if she were already miles and miles away in the north country. Now, a sweat, she thought, would be real Indian.

Annharte *b.* 1942

ANISHNAABE

Born in 1942 to an Anishnaabe mother and an Irish father, Marie Annharte Baker was raised in Winnipeg, where she could see the hard life of the streets. She describes herself as a cultural worker who wants to produce 'films, plays, and books that celebrate cultural survival after five hundred years of resistance to settler lit(ter) (not literature).'

Baker's publications include three books of poetry—*Being on the Moon* (1990), *Coyote Columbus Café* (1994), and *Exercises in Lip Pointing* (2003)—and a play, *ALTERNATIVE: The Only Native Alternative* (1994). Her writing shows her concern with 'the smallest stories; stories in our everyday conversations (wrongfully dismissed as gossip), stories of how we survived and resisted (cheeky stories), and, of course, the "lost stories" (stories of men, women, and children who are lost or outcast to their own people, the ones who have "no voice" but speak to us in dreams or haunt our every waking moment with their shocking statistics).'

Baker was a co-founder of the Regina Aboriginal Writers group. Her broader interests include the writings of Women of Colour and the forms of street poetry, dub poetry, and rap. She has a son who is also a writer.

Coyote Trail

warm this trail
      my nose picks you to follow

your tracks quiver my whisker
      my nostrils fill

you are a chunky one   5
      your tail dragged a leaf
        overturned bark

you too are hungry
      fat
        depressed   10
      I know all this news

I see your weight in microns of earth pressed
          down
      you won't be an easy meal

like last week I sssll unk into town   15

I mean slunk not what I usually do

QUICK PAWS QUICK PAWS GOTCHA

YOU DON'T HEAR MY CLAWS UNLESS YOU PAUSE

that was something dead and delicious in that town

growing more foul each day   20

I call it fast food
though it don't move much
until I touch my paw to it
I drool again over that thought

the last time we met One Gulp   25
you kicked against my canines
eager to become me
why are you making me exercise
to get a bite or two?

I was a writer once   30
know how to keep track of things
how interdependence works for me

Penumbra

for Betty

Temporary the shade my straw hat weaves
across my basket face of Caribe pleasure.
The bright sun makes me want to run and jump,
I had been told if I were smart, I'd stay hidden.
On my island, I keep to myself & lie around.   5
Turtles crawl past me to dig their nests.
Tortuga oil is outlawed and so am I.

Odd, this exposure of my not too recent killing.
Seventeen years it took getting to court
those who mashed my face because of dark skin.   10
Hating the contrast of each pinky penis
I left The Pas to be a turista and relax

They understand I stayed away to make sure
I'm not the only witness to their sorry act.
Not even good at it, I might add as insult.   15
The reserve is a huge donut around the town,
no place to go unless you're an Indian like me.
Laughing at the other end of the beach
gets me wondering how it's my turn.

Raced Out to Write This Up

I often race to write   I write about race   who do I write
about race   I must erase all trace of my race   I am an
eraser abrasive bracing myself embracing

it is classic to want to write about class   not low class but
up the nose class   I know I am classy   brassy   crass ass   5
of a clash comes when I move up a rung

we are different skins   different bins for brown rice and
white rice   not even a container of wild rice   you know
what they do when you are white and not rich   poverty
counts big when you count the cost of a caste a colourful   10
past

drunk as a skunk he danced at the Lebret Hotel   what for
no   not really   says he's not writing because they won't
publish his books   he does a number for a book   he
hugged me like I was his old Tibetan guru out on the   15
dance floor teleporting again

white racists notice colour when they don't have   you
might be off-white   a bone white   a cream white
alabaster white   dingy white if you don't wash often
enough   nevermind a non-bleached white   white with   20
pinkish undertone   peaches and cream   white with
freckles   who is colour blind   I write my black ink on
white paper   I white out write out my colour lighten up
full of self I saw old whitey again but he wanted to be a
part of a pure religion not like ours   not that he was a   25
white racist but a pure racist in his heart which had no
colour but our colour   red   red   mind you a few white
corpuscles but compared to the red they were a minority
not invisible

so few of me yet I still write not for the white audience but   30
the colour of their response to my underclassy class   the
flash of their fit to kill me why race away to the finish
when I cross the finish line will it be white   will I be red
from running   hot and cold touch me not less I am to be
divided against my self who is both red and white but not a   35
shade of pink maybe a beige pink blushed flushed off
white right I colour my winning everytime   I am still in the
red not the black   blackened red   reddened black   but
what about black n' blue   green at the gills   yellow belly
but what about the whitish frightish part I put it behind   40
behind me when I need to say my piece about togetherness
that we must breed not by ourselves but with everyone
out in the world who will listen   hey   I'm a half a half
breed   a mixed bag breed bread and butter bred my
whole grain bannock will taste as good to me even if I   45
smear on red jam sink my white teeth down into it down
the red hatch to the black hole   that is behind it all   the
whole black of me   the whore backing up behind me
the sore holy part of me which is the blackest darkest most
coloured most non-Indian, non-white slice of me bred to   50
wonder

One Way to Keep Track of Who Is Talking

If I change one word, I change history. What did I
say today? Do I even remember one word? Writing is
oral tradition. You have to practise the words on
someone before writing it down.

I do not intend to become the world's greatest Indian   5
orator. Maybe I might by accident. I might speak my
mind even when running off my mouth like I'm doing.
Language finds a tongue. Maybe it will be an Indian
accent.

Counting hostile Indians is made easier because they   10
don't talk much or very little. They look the part
—the part in the middle with braids. You never do
know if you are talking to an Indian.

Frozen Indians and frozen conversations predominate.
We mourn the ones at Wounded Knee. Our traditions   15
buried in one grave. Our frozen circles of silence
do no honour to them. We talk to keep our
conversations from getting too dead.

Coyote Columbus Cafe

1. once more it's Indian time

always good to be
born the midnight star
500 night years ago
quincentennial dawn
time worth waiting for   5
never a dull moment
time circles
how a weasel pops
in & out of old tunes

at closing time   10
I always spot a guy
other end of the bar
time for one more cruise
& conquest sneak up time
dare I ask Sh Sh   15
be still my boogit

I know the proper approach

Boozho Dude. Hey, I'm talking
to you, Bozo Dude. My name is
Conquista. Come on adore me.   20

my optimism looks good on me
in my territory my favourite bar
& grill I bar none grill some
bungee little bit twobitz
too bitzy for you?   25

why beat around the bush?

suppose my moccasin looms
over your border, mistah,
& you put a teensy toe
on my medicine line.   30

no problem lucky for me
I put my 'c' mark
that's coyote country 'cc'
not 'ccc' for cheap colonial crap

I have an attitude how to frequent   35
with colonizers (dey got me surrounded)
the right time is now
to get discovered again
& again very frequently
on a repetitive basis   40

2. what does a poor coyote girl do?

I act choosy about what abuse
my clientele gets
I am the first one got Coyotisma
(dey all say dey ever met one)
if they don't like dis talk   45
I do tease'em up to the climax
of my act but I am too damn direct
for the colonized coyote
poor oppressed critter

hey, you on the Columbus trip   50

even when I yell at them
I get the usual ho hum complaint
as Coyotrix I lie and trick
what does the poor coyote girl do?

sure I pose baffling questions   55
administer random coyote IQ tests

what is paler than stranger?

I warn you multiple answers possible
circle (a) the landlord comes around
first of the month to collect rent   60
wrong answer but don't pick that one
please follow directions & circle choice
what about (c) a landlord of colour?
right answer is (d) I got my rights
(b) I am the landlord around here   65

how about solving the mystery
did I discover Columbus first?

it could happen in a Woody Allen movie
Columbus gives a squirmy spiel

I don't know anybody on this
boat. Strong chance we won't
make it to land.   70

The map I made shows the Indies
beyond the curve in the earth.
Most of the crew are already
around the bend.

Columbus did lack   75
   cultural awareness
   equity
   affirmative action
   political correctness

3. Discovery is a hard act to follow

Colon would get comforted   80
by a kindly Native who'd say

Don't feel bad bro.
You're lost like the rest of us.

if Columbus was looking for turkey
he came to right place   85

he'd get the deserved treatment
join our healing process

Do you feel like a wounded
buffalo raging within?

mine's ready & raring to stampede   90
right over a cliff

ever wonder if Colon confessed
to a priest? what did he say
to turn on church officials
start a catholic Rambo trend   95

now they stalk our organizations
get on the board of directors
become an Indian expert and
discover more Indians
meet up with famous ones   100

take a class Native Studies
begin with Precolumbian Era

receive an embossed buckskin
certificate or a stone with
your name in petroglyph   105

if the class is full
because too many Indians
are just learning about
their culture & identity
then simply select a popular   110
bestseller HOW TO OUTINDIAN ANYONE

don't read any works
by First Nations writers
that's an advanced course
& you must crawl before you   115
creep up to rich Indians
playing casino bingo warriors
subscribe to Aboriginal news
& pretend Indian sympathy

                              lo, the po'Indian   120

                              Indian Act

                              Tell Old Indian joke
                              like Indian Affairs

                              Act Indian
                              had an Indian affair lately?   125
learn how to approach an elder
& what to do if a fakey one comes up
do you talk his or her talk?

I said sweat lodge   *I shed shwatch ludge*
makes body clean inside.   *meks buddy kleen insaid.*   130
Keep it up. Dance pow wow.   *Kip it up. Danz pahwah.*
After this, boy. You me   *Hafter, dis, bah. You me,*
go off big West German First   *go hoff big wes churman Furz*
International Wannabe Annual   *Hinter Natchinel Wanbee Annal*
Celebration. Take first; don't   *cel brayshun. Tek furz; don*   135
need to take plastic money   *need tek plashtik monhee*
visacard. You me same team.   *vissacad. You me sam tim*
Same team. Like hockey team.   *Sam tim. Lak hocky tim.*
Zjoonias, my boy. Think of it.   *Sch—oo—nash, my bah. Tinkobit*
Swiss bank account, hey boy!   *Swish bank a cunt, hey bah!*   140

discover an authentic Indian colonizer
slaver inside you & check your tongue
if still forked continue to discover
Other Indians do it to other Indians
first who do it to them first   145

former Columbus clones I implore you
you still got a chance, discover a first
nation friend lover first nation first
for keeps person

4. culture vulture voyeur trips

check coyote channel check   channel   150
check coyote check just thought I'd
check out my cheque what happened to
my cheque do you have my cheque
just came to pick up my cheque I
hope nobody cashed my cheque check   155
coyote channel check

the other day I got welfare
I had a big zit on my face
with a bandaid to cover up
I practised with my tough look   160
in the mirror
                          give me my cheque
I always forget to mention
we were too good way back when
to be real people before discovery   165

when I'm having an Indian taco day
I discover it's just about too late
not to educate the oppressor
but am I ever good at doing it

my tiny whiny coyote heart   170
thump de thump thump thump
kicking on the inside
to get outside to howl

how does a coyote girl get
a tale outta her mouth?   175

I Want to Dance Wild Indian Black Face

I want to dance with the five tribes of wild Indians. Them
Wild Magnolias, Golden Eagles, Golden Stars, Black Eagles and
Young Sons of Geronimo dance wild Indian black face.

I want to hear the crowd say 'Ooh, them Indians are pretty today.'

I want to see a tribal official ready to lead his gang into battle   5
like Council Chief, Second Chief, Trail Chief and Wild Man.

I want to shout back wild calls and big boasts of Big Chiefs in
uptown New Orleans. I want to shout in my own city rez way.

I want to play in an inner circle of raggedy rhythm with beat-up
drums, cowbells, tambourines, whistles, wine bottles and sticks.   10

I want to carry on in a parade to sing Two Way Pak E Way. In
   Cajun,
Tuez bas qu'ou est means *Kill anyone who gets in the way.* I could
   be a mean Indian some days.

I want to honour the spirits of Black Indians and Choctows,
Cherokees, Natchez and Seminoles who resisted the slave masters.

I want to wear a turkey feather in my hair and join the tribe of   15
the Creole Wild West. I don't want to be authentic all the time.

I want to be a Tribal 'Hawk' sing some jazz gospel ratty chanting.
Shout my spirit. Claim black and blues brothers same as sisters.

I want to mask Indian, adopt the Indian spirit figure once a year
dance in public with my big black face and talk back to chiefs.   20

I want to dance wild Indian blackface. I want to be that big bad
black Indian in a carnival parade. I want an Indian day off.

Got Something In the Eye

Morbid finding a body in a ditch edge of town. Mirrored disco ball lodged in eye socket. Glamour eyeball throws dots of light horn ceiling to floor. Swirl around in shadows. Dance round with shut eyes.

Typical tumbleweed guy. That dazzle eye looks impressive on a police cruiser. Hypnotize. Arrest. Interrogate. Chill out. Warriors on the street looking for political party. War party. Join any party since the last one wasn't greatest ever party. Keep in mind life doesn't have to be a party.

Last I saw him he was practicing dealer phone stance. His claim to fame was writer working on the next novel. Drunk and disgusting came later with offer of special discount price Only five hog skins. Boozer breath too much.

Speculative fiction not the I files. If he survives celebrity status, then long live Daddy Cyclops.

Learn to become victim and statistic after one Saturday night performance. Advantage author. Disadvantage audience. Hold on. He never looked up to his own kind. Publisher cranked out Indian books. Portrait on cover made so easy to hitch a ride.

The ball had to land on his face. Asked him was he alright. He assumed I wanted fisticuffs. Right left right out of it. Interfere with tough ex-con act. Eye eye eye amigo. Better approach horn our blind spot.

The Mandan Hidatsa held two creators responsible for the mess of the world. The perfectionist located the wolf carcass full of maggots. Then he confronted the other creator about the botch job. Maybe this way someone much better at defects gets reminded of truest creation.

Exercises in Lip Pointing

Okay today
let's have the lips speak for themselves
shall we let them say what they must
say if asked
if ever asked   5
as if anyone ever asks
just the lips to speak
                    because the totality
                    of a person counts more

dominates   10
          what the lips want
                    koochy koo lips
                    lips pursed
          lips pointed full forward tilt
          top lip extended   15

signals

          watch ahead to the side
          either side
          take a peek

but don't say anything out loud   20
to Mr Mrs Ms Authority Person In Charge

                    don't say   aw fuck off either
                    you bug me   aw come off it
                    enough enough
                    that bullshit   25

ever hear the one
about what the one lip said to the other

                              ridiculous if
                              ever heard
                              one lip talk   30

point out impossible wish
if one had one wish

                    rapid lip movements as if talking
                    lips walking
                    to the convenience store   35

back alley lips
holding a cigarette
unable to scream
get that damn paper toxic
tobacco product out of me   40

exception none
    a language probes   prods
    asks all the right questions right
    meets its match in lips
    that won't respond in kind   45
                sorry lips droop and sag
command
        lips move
                quick march
                single up   50
    form a circle around the wagons

    hey lips over there doing nothing
    lips don't pout
    grab those arrows

start firing   55
                lips on the other side of face
                light a few guided missiles

                to Hell with Tomahawks
                let's Scud doo

what a range   60
lips lips lips
hold formation

                lips keep still
                mike's on
                quiet on set   65

somebody might hear
somebody already knows
what lips to listen for
what lips to look out for

snarl Elvis lip   70
lip shake lips

lips don't betray
stop that quiver
stop that whimper

    blubbering   75
    how many times have you
    lips been told to say

    now just how many of you
    at attention
    just a couple last count   80
            surrounded in ambush lips

       lots of lips surrendered

lips lips hold back tighten
tighten up your ranks
files empty   85
yet not one word gets through

remember the cowboy Indian movie
          especially starring in it

    don't get lines
    just come out trilling   90
    give us lots of tongue
    pow wow lips
    contest time
    ceremonial lips action

    like how do you do that poise   95
    make more noise make me notice you
                  biting too much
                  ouch sado-macho

stop stoic lips
stop bleeding heart   100
winding down whine lips
if there's one thing else

try to keep shut

How to Write About White People

From a distance & keep them outside
even if it seems cruel to do that.
They will sit on the prairie horizon
left to silhouette as grain elevator
once you rode up on a spotted stallion.   5

The inner Trojan fears kept them
talking too much about the country they took.
Look how rats took over the greedy stores.
Grain sprouts grew outside walls of wooden wars.

Pony charger nibbles on blades brushed by hooves.   10
Bannocks were white seeds kept in towers.
We never climbed up to the top but rats did.

The white chief told me he ran from the city.
He was made lumpy and grumpy.
Innoculations were frequent.   15
They tried every day to kill him.
Psychology was what they called the war.

Laboratory used to be his first name.
He changed his address after the millennium.

Saskatchewan Indians Were Dancing

60s pulled us from starvation into government jobs
antiquated Indians in Saskatchewans danced for rain
Manitoba Indian doings were hidden for a jealous me
all I had was a 50s rock'n'roll step to copy from
not shy you danced for strangers from deep defiance   5
full regalia hid other dangerous rope dancing kicks
Crees got out of line on the scaffold teaching Cree
readiness to enter the earth at the exact spot left
following a song trail maybe even a we want a chant
chant after teasing hey boy you first boy first one   10
dancing in the air show them how to teach us lesson
a public display of rationed revenge serves nothing
show example to culture clashed passive politicians

Crees hit them notes higher boys cover up ear drums
let other drums beat out natural powwow exhibitions   15
boys in the pen idle for a time listen up flag song
Cree hit parade will release some traditional lives
dancing not allowed behind bars then songs bring us
back to good times Saskatchewan Indians danced free

I Shoulda Said Something Political

you spoke to me Emilia   I chiquita
tiny bit lick paste on label   you compañera
green tinge pretty banana   wait for ripe
yellow chiquita skin moment   takes more
than Spanish descent I mean   to be decent   5
descend   even the imported banana gets mushy

hey, hey, celtic conquistadora   my ancestry
a search for potatoes   why have a famine
in the first place I say   I ask how about you
where you come from   we have it in common   10
so far away do you happen on a feast often
grab a clean plate   sit down next to
talk to someone like me   talk turkey

I'm so serious   cute tomato   how you gave
them yourself   had to had to   so did I   15
me too, I shared so I did   I share more
did you forget the gold   did you did you
give it away   the gold chain
my friend gave me to wear   gets in the way
when I eat   my fingers catch it   put it   20
in my mouth   so you passed the ketchup
to them   too bad it happens   squashed tomatoes

we are just delicious   they put us on
french fries I gave up   potatoes to make poutine
now that's strange   does it have much blood   25
any barter   taste enough gravy

you sprawl next to me   long legs   logjam
look you harvested timber   you fall

your arms reach across miles   how do you
do that trick   for agricultural sake   30
you fondle the cornsilk   kiss up pumpkin vine

your anatomy & mine   separate from what belongs
to the Mohawk tobacco trader   asks for a light
gets up to smoke outside the lodge   we see him
give offering of tobacco   pray   we watch him   35
without him to watch us play   entangle
human sculpture   should he take notice be bold
scold after doing righteous act   gotta brace
for trouble   entwine legs arms minds
if he comes back without smokes   let's behave   40
give thanks for lights   surprise spirit sparks

how queer for you, for me to lay back   wonder
the rest of the summer   I lazy ass down
druggy park kept vigil unlike   outhouse poet
behind the treatment center   kept folks   45
occupied, safe   he loved laughs and war alike
it occupied my mind   no fierce risky business
stopped my preoccupations   gross everyone out
arouse oppositions   shoulda been the poet
at Oka, sneak up in monk habit   fire words   50
take the straight forward approach   fire at
choppers   write poetry on walls waste less
paper, words   maybe Emilia, I apologize

should go to Peru   accompany each other
be safe escorts   for us mixed up together   55
just us tourists   in blond California wigs
dark Barbie twins   shining our hair
right shampoo   the Shining Path   economy
we set up a stall to sell   big words
to fatten the skull   trepinate paths   60
poem trouble again   I instead

made myself comfy   lying on railway track
to blockade national trains   gave support
warriors need more uplift   hard curve balls
pitched   at their athletic supporters   65
makes me wince groan ow   my fast lips came
in handy where it should be   the groin
talking   such Indian woman heterophobia

that summer   I just missed it   had to be
there to catch a great conference   needed   70
the proper lesbian lovemaking   establish
Indian men higher awareness   now
that's revolution   maybe it will happen

in Peru the altitude does it   guaranteed
an identity   that doesn't split sexes up   75
first time dropped   nothing breaks out
sags, or leaks   the victim in you refuses
everything that happened before   doesn't

want explanations   make it right for others
be a non-statistic   be understood   80
in the marketplace   let's for once
inside you let that jaguar purr   asleep
she shifts leg but inside growl   deep
I hear it compañera   growl dark like me

Me Tonto Along

My old man was a good screw they say
all the ladies who chanced his waylay
he took my money time any hour he pleased
cost me to see how his manhood freezed
kicked him out he kicked down the door   5
punched my face through the apartment floor
no way to stop him but once he caught zzz's
had my chance to plot his murder with ease
I pretend I let him move on to a next wife
Me Tonto along what I got left—my life   10

Dad's Zipper

My father's fingernails got more brittle
and curved under. I trim them back
when he asked. Twist his thumb back
and make sure to use the pointy scissors.

He was proud of the black hightop runners   5
he wore without laces. Cost him six bits.
Gave him slippers but he wears them to please
me and his grandson when we visit.

He tied a shoelace to the zipper tab
in case he had trouble opening his fly.   10

Thomas King *b.* 1943

CHEROKEE

Thomas King's mother is Greek and his father Cherokee, and he was born in California, but his practice as a Native writer is much more complicated than this heritage suggests. In 1980, he arrived at the University of Lethbridge in Alberta to teach Native studies. There he combined his extensive knowledge of Native American literary traditions, as shown in his doctoral dissertation from the University of Utah, with various explorations of Native life in Alberta. One of his comments about his writing is especially revealing: 'I write about Natives because it's the subject matter I know and enjoy. I know it has something to do with who I am, but I can't quantify it in any way.'

King, who now teaches Native literature and creative writing at the University of Guelph, produced his first book as an academic editor— *The Native in Literature: Canadian and Comparative Perspectives* (1987). His second book was *All My Relations: An Anthology of Contemporary Canadian Native Fiction* (1990). Since then he has published a children's book, *A Coyote Columbus Story* (1992), and a collection of short fiction, *One Good Story, That One* (1993). However, he has made his greatest mark through his novels.

Medicine River (1990) shows his flair for humorous anecdote and his unusual combination of irony and sensitivity in his portrayal of the Native cultures he encountered in Alberta. In the 1993 film produced from the novel, King

maintained this sensibility in his screenplay and enhanced it by his own appearance in the movie, playing a slow-moving, sardonic basketball player. His second novel, *Green Grass, Running Water* (1993), features a postmodern structure constantly informed by Native oral tradition and theology. The comic fun is still there, but within a portrait of politics and cosmology that is near overwhelming. *Green Grass, Running Water* sets a standard seldom equalled by novelists of any culture. With its publication, King received attention given to few Canadian writers, with notices in a variety of mainstream American periodicals.

Since the publication of *Green Grass, Running Water* King has gone on to develop his talents in yet other directions, writing scripts for the television show *North of Sixty* as well as a series of film treatments and radio dramas. His radio series *The Dead Dog Cafe Comedy Hour* exemplifies his ability to recognize the potential of a creative medium. The miniature scale of the setting of Dead Dog, a small reserve café with a one-man radio station visited by a writer (King as himself), seems almost the antithesis of the epic comedy in *Green Grass, Running Water*.

While it has not achieved the same degree of commercial success as its predecessor, King's third novel, *Truth and Bright Water* (2001), is certainly a success for the way King manages to blend history and contemporary Native culture, from the narrator with the telling name of

Tecumseh, to the satirically tawdry Indian Days Tribal festival. Probably more important as a statement of King's achievement are the 2003 Massey Lectures, a series of radio broadcasts now collected as *The Truth About Stories*. In a chatty, easy discourse, King explores many complexities of Native storytelling. The result is a book that is essential to anyone interested in the value of narrative.

The One About Coyote Going West

This one is about Coyote. She was going west. Visiting her relations. That's what she said. You got to watch that one. Tricky one. Full of bad business. No, no, no, no, that one says. I'm just visiting.

Going to see Raven.

Boy, I says. That's another tricky one.

Coyote comes by my place. She wag her tail. Make them happy noises. Sit on my porch. Look around. With them teeth. With that smile. Coyote put her nose in my tea. My good tea. Get that nose out of my tea, I says.

I'm going to see my friends, she says. Tell those stories. Fix this world. Straighten it up.

Oh boy, pretty scary that, Coyote fix the world, again.

Sit down, I says. Eat some food. Hard work that fix up the world. Maybe you have a song. Maybe you have a good joke.

Sure, says Coyote. That one wink her ears. Lick her whiskers.

I tuck my feet under that chair. Got to hide my toes. Sometimes that tricky one leave her skin sit in that chair. Coyote skin. No Coyote. Sneak around. Bite them toes. Make you jump.

I been reading those books, she says.

You must be one smart Coyote, I says.

You bet, she says.

Maybe you got a good story for me, I says.

I been reading about that history, says Coyote. She tricks that nose back in my tea. All about who found us Indians.

Ho, I says. I like those old ones. Them ones are the best. You tell me your story, I says. Maybe some biscuits will visit us. Maybe some moose-meat stew come along, listen to your story.

Okay, she says and she sings her story song.

> Snow's on the ground the snakes are asleep.
> Snow's on the ground my voice is strong.
> Snow's on the ground the snakes are asleep.
> Snow's on the ground my voice is strong.

She sings like that. With that tail, wagging. With that smile. Sitting there.

Maybe I tell you the one about Eric the Lucky and the Vikings play hockey for the Old-timers, find us Indians in Newfoundland, she says.

Maybe I tell you the one about Christopher Cartier looking for something good to eat. Find us Indians in a restaurant in Montreal.

Maybe I tell you the one about Jacques Columbus come along that river, Indians waiting for him. We all wave and say, here we are, here we are.

Everyone knows those stories, I says. White man stories. Baby stories you got in your mouth.

No, no, no, no, says Coyote. I read these ones in that old book.

Ho, I says. You are trying to bite my toes. Everyone knows who found us Indians. Eric the Lucky and that Christopher Cartier and that Jacques Columbus come along later. Those ones get lost. Float about. Walk around. Get mixed up. Ho, ho, ho, ho, those ones cry, we are lost. So we got to find them. Help them out. Feed them. Show them around.

Boy, I says. Bad mistake that one.

You are very wise, grandmother, says Coyote, bring her eyes down. Like she is sleepy. Maybe you know who discovered Indians.

Sure, I says. Everyone knows that. It was Coyote. She was the one.

Oh, grandfather, that Coyote says. Tell me that story. I love those stories about that sneaky one. I don't think I know that story, she says.

All right, I says. Pay attention.

Coyote was heading west. That's how I always start this story. There was nothing else in this world. Just Coyote. She could see all the way, too. No mountains then. No rivers then. No forests then. Pretty flat then. So she starts to make things. So she starts to fix this world.

This is exciting, says Coyote, and she takes her nose out of my tea.

Yes, I says. Just the beginning, too. Coyote got a lot of things to make.

Tell me, grandmother, says Coyote. What does the clever one make first?

Well, I says. Maybe she makes that tree grows by the river. Maybe she makes that buffalo. Maybe she makes that mountain. Maybe she makes them clouds.

Maybe she makes that beautiful rainbow, says Coyote.

No, I says. She don't make that thing. Mink makes that.

Maybe she makes that beautiful moon, says Coyote.

No, I says. She don't do that either. Otter finds that moon in a pond later on.

Maybe she makes the oceans with that blue water, says Coyote.

No, I says. Oceans are already here. She don't do any of that. The first thing Coyote makes, I tell Coyote, is a mistake.

Boy, Coyote sit up straight. Them eyes pop open. That tail stop wagging. That one swallow that smile.

Big one, too, I says. Coyote is going west thinking of things to make. That one is trying to think of everything to make at once. So she don't see that hole. So she falls in that hole. Then those thoughts bump around. They run into each other. Those ones fall out of Coyote's ears. In that hole. Ho, that Coyote cries. I have fallen into a hole. I must have made a mistake. And she did.

So, there is that hole. And there is that Coyote in that hole. And there is that big mistake in that hole with Coyote. Ho, says that mistake. You must be Coyote.

That mistake is real big and that hole is small. Not much room. I don't want to tell you what that mistake looks like. First mistake in the world. Pretty scary. Boy, I can't look. I got to close my eyes. You better close your eyes, too, I tell Coyote.

Okay, I'll do that, she says, and she puts her hands over her eyes. But she don't fool me. I can see she's peeking.

Don't peek, I says.

Okay, she says. I won't do that.

Well, you know, that Coyote thinks about the hole. And she thinks about how she's going to get out of that hole. She thinks how she's going to get that big mistake back in her head.

Say, says that mistake. What is that you're thinking about?

I'm thinking of a song, says Coyote. I'm thinking of a song to make this hole bigger.

That's a good idea, says that mistake. Let me hear your hole song.

But that's not what Coyote sings. She sings a song to make the mistake smaller. But that mistake hears her. And that mistake grabs Coyote's nose. And that one pulls off her mouth so she can't sing. And that one jumps up and down on Coyote until she is flat. Then that one leaps out of that hole, wanders around looking for things to do.

Well, Coyote is feeling pretty bad, all flat her nice fur coat full of stomp holes. So she thinks hard, and she thinks about a healing song. And she tries to sing a healing song, but her mouth is in other places. So she thinks harder and tries to sing that song through her nose. But that nose don't make any sound, just drip a lot. She tries to sing that song out her ears, but those ears don't hear anything.

So, that silly one thinks real hard and tries to sing out her butt-hole. Pssst! Pssst! That is what that butt-hole says, and right away things don't smell so good in that hole. Pssst.

Boy, Coyote thinks. Something smells.

That Coyote lies there flat and practise and practise. Pretty soon, maybe two days, maybe one year, she teach that butt-hole to sing. That song. That healing song. So that butt-hole sings that song. And Coyote begins to feel better. And Coyote don't feel so flat anymore. Pssst! Pssst! Things still smell pretty bad, but Coyote is okay.

That one look around in that hole. Find her mouth. Put that mouth back. So, she says to that butt-hole. Okay, you can stop singing now. You can stop making them smells now. But, you know, that butt-hole is liking all that singing, and so that butt-hole keeps on singing.

Stop that, says Coyote. You going to stink up the whole world. But it don't. So Coyote jumps out of that hole and runs across the prairies real fast. But that butt-hole follows her. Pssst. Pssst. Coyote jumps into a lake, but that butt-hole don't drown. It just keeps on singing.

Hey, who is doing all that singing, someone says.

Yes, and who is making that bad smell, says another voice.

It must be Coyote, says a third voice.

Yes, says a fourth voice. I believe it is Coyote.

That Coyote sit in my chair, put her nose in my tea, say, I know who that voice is. It is that big mistake playing a trick. Nothing else is made yet.

No, I says. That mistake is doing other things.

Then those voices are spirits, says Coyote.

No, I says. Them voices belong to them ducks.

Coyote stand up on my chair. Hey, she says, where did them ducks come from?

Calm down, I says. This story is going to be okay. This story is doing just fine. This story knows where it is going. Sit down. Keep your skin on.

So.

Coyote look around, and she see them four ducks. In that lake. Ho, she says. Where did you ducks come from? I didn't make you yet.

Yes, says them ducks. We were waiting around, but you didn't come. So we got tired of waiting. So we did it ourselves.

I was in a hole, says Coyote.

Pssst. Pssst.

What's that noise, says them ducks. What's that bad smell?

Never mind, says Coyote. Maybe you've seen something go by. Maybe you can help me find something I lost. Maybe you can help me get it back.

Those ducks swim around and talk to themselves. Was it something awful to look at? Yes, says Coyote, it certainly was. Was it something with ugly fur? Yes, says Coyote, I think it had that, too. Was it something that made a lot of noise? ask them ducks. Yes, it was pretty noisy, says Coyote. Did it smell bad, them ducks want to know. Yes, says Coyote. I guess you ducks have seen my something.

Yes, says them ducks. It is right behind you.

So that Coyote turn around, and there is nothing there.

It's still behind you, says those ducks.

So Coyote turn around again but she don't see anything.

Pssst! Pssst!

Boy, says those ducks. What a noise! What a smell! They say that, too. What an ugly thing with all that fur!

Never mind, says that Coyote, again. That is not what I'm looking for. I'm looking for something else.

Maybe you're looking for Indians, says those ducks.

Well, that Coyote is real surprised because she hasn't created Indians, either. Boy, says that one, mischief is everywhere. This world is getting bent.

All right.

So Coyote and those ducks are talking, and pretty soon they hear a noise. And pretty soon there is something coming. And those ducks says, oh, oh, oh, oh. They say that like they see trouble, but it is not trouble. What comes along is a river.

Hello, says that river. Nice day. Maybe you want to take a swim. But Coyote don't want to swim, and she looks at that river and she looks at that river again. Something's not right here, she says. Where are those rocks? Where are those rapids? What did you do with them waterfalls? How come you're so straight?

And Coyote is right. That river is nice and straight and smooth without any bumps or twists. It runs both ways, too, not like a modern river.

We got to fix this, says Coyote, and she does. She pours some rocks in that river, and she fixes it so it only runs one way. She puts a couple of waterfalls in and makes a bunch of rapids where things get shallow fast.

Coyote is tired with all this work, and those ducks are tired just watching. So that Coyote sits down. So she closes her eyes. So she puts her nose in her tail. So those ducks shout, wake up, wake up! Something big is heading this way! And they are right.

Mountain comes sliding along, whistling. Real happy mountain. Nice and round. This mountain is full of grapes and other good things to eat. Apples, peaches, cherries. Howdy-do, says that polite mountain, nice day for whistling.

Coyote looks at that mountain, and that one shakes her head. Oh, no, she says, this mountain is all wrong. How come you're so nice and round? Where are those craggy peaks? Where are all them cliffs? What happened to all that snow? Boy, we got to fix this thing, too. So she does.

Grandfather, grandfather, says that Coyote, sit in my chair, put her nose in my tea. Why is that Coyote changing all those good things?

That is a real sly one, ask me that question. I look at those eyes. Grab them ears. Squeeze that nose. Hey, let go my nose, that Coyote says.

Okay, I says. Coyote still in Coyote skin. I bet you know why Coyote change that happy river. Why she change that mountain sliding along whistling.

No, says that Coyote, look around my house, lick her lips, make them baby noises.

Maybe it's because she is mean, I says.

Oh, no, says Coyote. That one is sweet and kind.

Maybe it's because that one is not too smart.

Oh, no, says Coyote. That Coyote is very wise.

Maybe it's because she made a mistake.

Oh, no, says Coyote. She made one of those already.

All right, I says. Then Coyote must be doing the right thing. She must be fixing up the world so it is perfect.

Yes, says Coyote. That must be it. What does that brilliant one do next?

Everyone knows what Coyote does next, I says. Little babies know what Coyote does next.

Oh no, says Coyote. I have never heard this story. You are a wonderful storyteller. You tell me your good Coyote story.

Boy, you got to watch that one all the time. Hide them toes.

Well, I says. Coyote thinks about that river. And she thinks about that mountain. And she thinks somebody is fooling around. So she goes looking around. She goes looking for that one who is messing up the world.

She goes to the north, and there is nothing. She goes to the south, and there is nothing there, either. She goes to the east, and there is still nothing there. She goes to the west, and there is a pile of snow tires.

And there is some televisions. And there is some vacuum cleaners. And there is a bunch of pastel sheets. And there is an air humidifier. And there is a big mistake sitting on a portable gas barbecue reading a book. Big book. Department store catalogue.

Hello, says that mistake. Maybe you want a hydraulic jack.

No, says that Coyote. I don't want one of them. But she don't tell that mistake what she wants because she don't want to miss her mouth again. But when she thinks about being flat and full of stomp holes, that butt-hole wakes up and begins to sing. Pssst. Pssst.

What's that noise? says that big mistake.

I'm looking for Indians, says that Coyote, real quick. Have you seen any?

What's that bad smell?

Never mind, says Coyote. Maybe you have some Indians around here.

I got some toaster ovens, says that mistake.

We don't need that stuff, says Coyote. You got to stop making all those things. You're going to fill up this world.

Maybe you want a computer with a colour monitor. That mistake keeps looking through that book and those things keep landing in piles all around Coyote.

Stop, stop, cries Coyote. Golf cart lands on her foot. Golf balls bounce off her head. You got to give me that book before the world gets lopsided.

These are good things, says that mistake. We need these things to make up the world. Indians are going to need this stuff.

We don't have any Indians, says Coyote.

And that mistake can see that that's right. Maybe we better make some Indians, says that mistake. So that one looks in that catalogue, but it don't have any Indians. And Coyote don't know how to do that, either. She has already made four things.

I've made four things already, she says. I got to have help.

We can help, says some voices and it is those ducks come swimming along. We can help you make Indians, says the white duck. Yes, we can do that, says the green duck. We have been thinking about this, says that blue duck. We have a plan, says the red duck.

Well, that Coyote don't know what to do. So she tells them ducks to go ahead because this story is pretty long and it's getting late and everyone wants to go home.

You still awake, I says to Coyote. You still here?

Oh yes, grandmother, says Coyote. What do those clever ducks do?

So I tell Coyote that those ducks lay some eggs. Ducks do that, you know. That white duck lay an egg, and it is blue. That red duck lay an egg, and it is green. That blue duck lay an egg, and it is red. That green duck lay an egg, and it is white.

Come on, says those ducks. We got to sing a song. We got to do a dance. So they do. Coyote and that big mistake and those four ducks dance around the eggs. So they dance and sing for a long time, and pretty soon Coyote gets hungry.

I know this dance, she says, but you got to close your eyes when you do it or nothing will happen. You got to close your eyes tight. Okay, says those ducks. We can do that. And they do. And that big mistake closes its eyes, too.

But Coyote, she don't close her eyes, and all of them start dancing again, and Coyote dances up close to that white duck, and she grabs that white duck by her neck.

When Coyote grabs that duck, that duck flaps her wings, and that big mistake hears the noise and opens them eyes. Say, says that big mistake, that's not the way the dance goes.

By golly, you're right, says Coyote, and she lets that duck go. I am getting it mixed up with another dance.

So they start to dance again. And Coyote is very hungry, and she grabs that blue duck, and she grabs his wings, too. But Coyote's stomach starts to make hungry noises, and that mistake opens them eyes and sees Coyote with the blue duck. Hey, says that mistake, you got yourself mixed up again.

That's right, says Coyote, and she drops the duck and straightens out that neck. It sure is good you're around to help me with this dance.

They all start that dance again, and, this time, coyote grabs the green duck real quick and tries to stuff it down that greedy throat, and there is nothing hanging out but them yellow duck feet. But those feet are flapping in Coyote's eyes, and she can't see where she is going, and she bumps into the big mistake and the mistake turns around to see what has happened.

Ho, says that big mistake, you can't see where you're going with them yellow duck feet flapping in your eyes, and that mistake pulls that green duck out of Coyote's throat. You could hurt yourself dancing like that.

You are one good friend, look after me like that, says Coyote.

Those ducks start to dance again, and Coyote dances with them, but that red duck says, we better dance with one eye open, so we can help Coyote with this dance. So they dance some more, and, then, those eggs begin to move around, and those eggs crack open. And if you look hard, you can see something inside those eggs.

I know, I know, says that Coyote, jump up and down on my chair, shake up my good tea. Indians come out of those eggs. I remember this story, now. Inside those eggs are the Indians Coyote's been looking for.

No, I says. You are one crazy Coyote. What comes out of those duck eggs are baby ducks. You better sit down, I says. You may fall and hurt yourself. You may spill my tea. You may fall on top of this story and make it flat.

Where are the Indians? says that Coyote. This story was about how Coyote found the Indians. Maybe the Indians are in the eggs with the baby ducks.

No, I says, nothing in those eggs but little ducks. Indians will be along in a while. Don't lose your skin.

So.

When those ducks see what has come out of the eggs, they says, boy, we didn't get that quite right. We better try that again. So they do. They lay them eggs. They dance that dance. They sing that song. Those eggs crack open and out comes some more baby ducks. They do this seven times and each time, they get more ducks.

By golly, says those four ducks. We got more ducks than we need. I guess we got to be the Indians. And so they do that. Before Coyote or that big mistake can mess things up, those four ducks turn into Indians, two women and two men. Good-looking Indians, too. They don't look at all like ducks any more.

But those duck-Indians aren't too happy. They look at each other and they begin to cry. This is pretty disgusting, they says. All this ugly skin. All these bumpy bones. All this awful black hair. Where are our nice soft feathers? Where are our beautiful feet? What happened to our wonderful wings? It's probably all that Coyote's fault because she didn't do the dance right, and those four duck-Indians come over and stomp all over Coyote until she is flat like before. Then they leave. That big mistake leave, too. And that Coyote, she starts to think about a healing song.

Pssst. Pssst.

That's it, I says. It is done.

But what happens to Coyote, says Coyote. That wonderful one is still flat.

Some of these stories are flat, I says. That's what happens when you try to fix this world. This world is pretty good all by itself. Best to leave it alone. Stop messing around with it.

I better get going, says Coyote. I will tell Raven your good story. We going to fix this world for sure. We know how to do it now. We know how to do it right.

So, Coyote drinks my tea and that one leave. And I can't talk any more because I got to watch the sky. Got to watch out for falling things that land in piles. When that Coyote's wandering around looking to fix things, nobody in this world is safe.

Harold Cardinal *b.* 1945

CREE

Harold Cardinal was born in High Prairie, Alberta. In the late 1960s, when the social activism of youth became a major force in North America, Cardinal was one of a number of young Native people who introduced their own agenda. In 1966, with Duke Redbird and Tony Mandamin, Cardinal set up the Canadian Indian Youth Council, which was intended to be, among other things, a Native arm of the Company of Young Canadians (a voluntary government agency focused on social, economic, and community development).

In 1968, Cardinal became the youngest elected president of the Indian Association of Alberta. During his time in office, from 1968 until 1977, he became a national spokesperson on a variety of Native issues and was probably the best-known Native to appear in the media throughout Canada in this period. His comments on preserving Aboriginal culture and religions, and on issues of special status, received wide attention.

Cardinal titled his first book, *The Unjust Society* (1969), in response to one of Prime Minister Pierre Trudeau's most famous catch-phrases, 'the just society'. Although at times attacked for the level of its polemic, *The Unjust Society* became the most significant book produced on Native rights in Canada. Its influence on other Native people and on government might be questioned, but its impact on the Canadian public cannot be.

Cardinal later participated in drafting a reply by Alberta Natives to a government white paper. This 'Red Paper', *Citizens Plus*, was part of a broader exploration of Native possibilities in Canada. Cardinal served as regional director of the Alberta department of Indian Affairs, becoming the first Native to be appointed to the position. He has also served as a consultant to band councils, as chief of his home reserve (the Sucker Creek band), and in 1983 as vice-chief for the prairie region under the Assembly of First Nations.

The selection here is taken from Cardinal's second book, *The Rebirth of Canada's Indians* (1977). Considered together, Cardinal's books can be seen as the best of Native writing before 1980.

A Canadian *What the Hell It's All About*

Over the past century, the Indian people, and many white people as well, have become increasingly aware of the aura of conflict surrounding the relations between white man and red man in Canada. The struggle now has become so intense and so emotional for so many of our people, especially our young people; and has led to equally intense but opposite emotional response from elements of white society, that I think the time has come for us to sit back and try to determine in our minds just what the hell this struggle really is all about.

We have been fighting for so long now that the original misunderstandings and differences that created this conflict have been forgotten. Various tactics have been tried by one side and countered by the other; emotions have taken over from reason; and the passions born of hatred have grown until neither fighter any longer knows, or cares, what the fight is about. The fight has become an end in itself.

In the long run such an attitude can only be disastrous, not just for our people, but for our country. To reverse this unfortunate trend of confrontation, we must examine some of the myths that have contributed to the situation currently faced by the Indian people in this country. We must re-examine the basic philosophies inherent in any discussion with white society, or with white individuals.

The past and the present are important, but basically we have to look to the future. In that context, many people concerned about the current economic conditions in Canada are closely examining just what kind of future, what kind of country they really want to build; not for a minority but for all Canadians; not for their generation but for all future generations. It must be with this in mind that we begin re-examining the relationship between Indians and members of the larger Canadian society. This is true whether we are talking about individuals in that larger society, or whether we are talking in collective terms about the Indian entity, the Indian nation, or about the white entity, the white nation.

One problem that has largely contributed to the misunderstanding between us is the terminology we use in efforts to relate to each other. Not only are the languages of the opposing sides drastically different, but the societies using those languages are in so many respects so very strange to one another that communication becomes almost impossible. A perfect example of this type of problem was the confrontation between Nikita Khrushchev and John Kennedy in Vienna. To a person not overly familiar with the opposing ideologies it would be difficult to understand, from the translation of what was said, why the two leaders disagreed so violently when to all appearances what they said differed so little. Only with a thorough knowledge of the background and opposing ideologies of each side could one hope to understand what the shouting was all about.

The situation faced in Canada between Indian and white races is much the same.

There has always been one question that a white man asks an Indian. It is asked by the average Joe on the street of an Indian just off the reserve; professional people of both sides ask it of each other. It is, to the Indians, a Have-you-stopped-beating-your-wife? sort of question. It may be posed in many ways, not only by the individual white person, but by the government as well. It is being posed more frequently and even more demandingly these days by the unelected government—the civil servants, provincial or federal. It is being posed with perhaps more integrity by political leaders; from MLAs to premiers, from MPs to the Prime Minister. The question, simplistically put, is: 'Why do you not want to be Canadian?'

Today, an Indian person has great difficulty responding to that question rationally, because the term *Canadian* means so many different things to the people of Canada, be they white or red.

Whatever we may think about the differences between Canada and the United States of America, at least people in the United States learn one lesson early and well. They are taught, virtually from the cradle on, what being an American is all about. Such teaching may seem to many of us to be chauvinism—distasteful and propagandistic—but from the time they are able to reason, children go through an indoctrination process that gives them a sense of patriotism, a sense of pride in being American. They may not always articulate this clearly, but a sureness of their identity as Americans is instilled in them. While Americans still may not fully understand the meaning of cultural plurality, at least they are not asking each other who they are.

In Canada there is no such universally accepted definition of the concept of Canadianism. There is no easy, sure national identity for Canada or for Canadians. When the question, 'You do want to be a Canadian, you don't want to be something else?' is asked it's always immensely difficult for an individual or a group to answer, because so much depends upon the questioner's concept of Canadianism. Unless we reach a common agreement on the meaning of that term, we must always define the concept as we understand it, so that others will know what we mean when we discuss Canadianism.

For too long, both the white and the Indian political leaders have been involved in a Quixotic battle. Our imaginary windmills have been our varying concepts and definitions of what being Canadian is all about. Our feelings, our emotions, our passions have almost reached their climax. It is even more necessary for Indian people to really look at what they are talking about; to understand the full meaning of their terms when they are defining themselves to each other or to members of the larger society. Only then can we understand what we are fighting about, what we are trying to work out together, what it really is that we are after.

One of the most personally rewarding, and, paradoxically, the most frustrating experiences of my life has stemmed from my attempts to decipher the meaning our people attach to the term, *Canada*, and to being *Canadian*. It is rewarding to catch a glimpse of what our old people who speak no English mean when they tell us of their concept of Canada and of Canadianism.

Canada is a word taken from the Cree language. Other tribes may claim it also, but from the Cree point of view, the word *Canada* stems from the Cree word *Ka-Kanata*, a word that translated literally means 'that which is clean'. The full Cree term to describe the country is *Ka-Kanata-Aski*—'the land that is clean'. Thus, when we speak of our country in Cree, at the same time we define it as 'the clean land'. We describe our country as the clean land because it belongs to our Creator, who is a clean being.

If we, as Cree-speaking people, use the term *Ka-Kanata* or *Canada* then, we know precisely what we are talking about. But when a white man calls this country *Canada*, I don't know what he means; I don't know what the meaning is from the white point of view. I don't have any precise definition to go by.

For the Cree-speaking person, the term *Nee-yow* is used when that person is affirming his or her Canadianism. When a white person says, 'I am a Canadian', a Cree-speaking person says, 'I am a *Nee-yow*'. Typically, it is a descriptive term. A Cree-speaking person, describing himself in his own language, does not say, 'I am Cree', because *Cree* is merely a word used by whites to describe one group of Indians. When those Indians known as Cree to the white world, describe themselves as *Nee-yow* they are saying, 'We are members of that nation of people who are part of the four seasons of Mother Earth.' They are saying, 'We are part of this land, and because we are part of this land we are also part of our Father's creation and hence His children.'

This is where the problem of definition crops up. It is difficult for a white man, not understanding Indian culture, to know what someone means when he says, 'I am a member of a nation of people who are part of Mother Earth.'

When a white person describes him or herself as Canadian, it is difficult for me to know what his or her definition of that term is. When a Cree-speaking person says that he or she is *Nee-yow*, that person is also describing precisely what being a Canadian is all about to him or her. I do not know if the white man's understanding and definition of the word is as precise as ours when he identifies himself as a Canadian.

Another way to explain the Cree use of such a term is to use an analogy of the Roman Catholic Church. Other religions in other parts of the world may provide similar analogies, but whenever a person is baptized into the Catholic Church, that person is given a special name. Usually the name is that of a saint who will give guidance and protection to the child as he or she goes along the path of life; a patron saint who in fact will be the spiritual guardian of the child. The same process applies to Indian name-giving, but it also applies to tribes. The tribes have a patron saint who will look after them. Thus when a Cree-speaking person says *Nee-yow* he is saying, 'I am born into that tribe which will look to this land as its patron, or as its guardian and guide through life.' It's a religious-cultural definition of being a Canadian.

Therefore, I believe that a part of our communal problem is that there have never been any precise translations between the Indian and white languages.

Other tribes, such as the Chipewyan, the Slavey, the Dogrib, the Navajo, call themselves *Dene*, giving their definition of themselves as a people in their language. In fact, all tribes across the continent have their own particular definitions of themselves as they relate to their environment, whether that environment is Mother Earth, as it is on the prairies, or the water, as it may be for the Indians living on the coasts. I think it is that thinking that distinguishes the traditional element right across the country.

For a long time much of the heritage of our culture has been lost even to Indians and is only now beginning to be understood again. When an Indian person describes this land as *Ka-Kanata*, 'the clean land', he is implicitly defining his responsibility to that land. If it is a clean land, then he has a responsibility to keep himself clean. Not just clean in the sense of television's White Tornado, but clean in the sense of maintaining a balanced relationship with the land. This means that whatever an Indian takes from the land, he will replace somehow. At the very least he will return the proper respect to the land for the gifts the land has given to him.

It goes even further than that. If one talks about a clean person, in a very broad sense one is talking in a philosophical way about a person who is honest with himself, with his family, with his neighbours, with all people; a person who is clean in the sense that purity is cleanliness. To the white man, some of these responsibilities are religious, and some are the responsibilities of citizenship. More simply they describe the way people *should* relate to one another, the way they should help one another.

When a person speaking from the traditional point of view says, in Cree, that he is a clean person, he relates himself to the clean land. This signifies recognition of the fact that this land belongs to, and was created by a clean being; a being known as God to some people, Jehovah to some, perhaps Manitou to others. Whatever the name used, the Creator's existence is recognized, and because people believe that He is clean and pure, and that all things He has created are clean, then one has to be pure in order to relate to Him.

Unfortunately there are many Indians today who do not understand this. While this may be the case for perhaps even the majority of Indians, I suspect that almost universally the white man has no awareness of our people's perception of their land and of themselves. Few white men have even an inkling of what Indians mean when they describe themselves and their relationship to the land, and to Canada. Consequently, there is a mistaken belief that our people's concept of Canada and of being Canadian is necessarily in conflict with the concept that white people have.

When the Prime Minister talks about the kind of country he would like Canada to be, and the type of Canadians he would like to see develop within such a country, and when an elder from any of Canada's tribes explains his vision of what this country and its people should be, the concepts are not that dissimilar. Two more disparate people, speaking in different tongues, speaking from different worlds, would be hard to find anywhere, and yet their dreams, their visions, their hopes, and their aspirations could not find any greater fusion.

But all too often, both sides: Indians and their political leaders, whites and their political leaders: unable to see except through the tunnel-vision of their respective cultures, fail entirely to look beyond the surface differences which loom so large, and go on determinedly believing that there has to be an inherent conflict between the dreams of a Prime Minister and the dreams of a tribal elder.

It is the absurdity of the Khrushchev-Kennedy dialogue all over again. Of course the white Prime Minister and the Indian elder have different personal perceptions, but must the white man believe that because an old Indian, giving a definition of nationhood and its responsibilities, expresses his beliefs in a language that is different, that draws its images from a different culture, therefore he does not merit consideration? Must the Indian, because the white man dresses differently, behaves differently, and uses words that sound strange, be convinced that there can be no common meeting ground? Must each then, based on his own narrow perceptions, reject the other, perhaps even launch wars to make certain the other side comes around to the 'proper' point of view?

I think the difference in definition and the lack of understanding has created what I call a *mirage gap* between people in this country. What appears to be a divergence on the meanings of *Canada* and *Canadian* as used by people on both sides is more mirage than reality. Close examination of the definitions clearly shows that there isn't really that much of a gap between them. But the practical point of this is, and it's a major point based on that mirage gap in understanding, we have a government that has developed policies aimed at assimilating Indians to make them into what the larger, white society perceives to be Canadians. Thus one finds all programs emanating from the federal or the provincial governments, whether concerned with economic development, education, or anything else, having as their central purpose the assimilation, or, at the very least, the integration of Indians into the Canadian mainstream.

Assimilation, integration—the two favourite terms used by the white society over a century of relationships between Indians and whites. Over a hundred years of relationships have been based on a complete misunderstanding. What it amounts to is simply that the larger society has never understood, and still doesn't understand the Indian concept of the terms *Canada* and *Canadian*.

As an illustration of how completely overwhelming such a misunderstanding can be: when an Indian suggests that he simply wants to remain an Indian, that declaration is perceived as both un-Canadian and a wholly undesirable goal. Naturally it follows that no effort must be left untried to prevent that poor, benighted Indian from pursuing such a goal.

To a large degree it was on this basis that the Trudeau Government came up with their white paper in 1969 which proposed nothing less than total assimilation of the Indian people. In spite of the quick and fiercely emotional rejection of that proposal, the government to this day does not know why the Indians reacted so violently, and cannot understand why they wouldn't accept such a reasonable philosophy. For the most part the government remains convinced that if only the Indians understood what that white paper was talking about they would accept it as being the best path for them to follow.

Because of such a major, fundamental misunderstanding a lot of wrong assumptions are being made by people both in the larger society and within the Indian community. We have what seems to be a Mexican stand-off between two sides, each passionately believing that what they stand for is right, and that if only those other fellows would understand there would be no problem. In maintaining such a stand-off, incidences of emotional confrontation between Indians and whites are escalating across the land. Many individuals who mean well now find themselves in a fight that they did not start and worse yet don't know how to get out of. Consequently, and quite understandably, they are committed to winning that fight—however they can.

Because so few people on either the Indian or the white side really understand the basis of the relationship between the two societies, or the differences in cultural definitions and perspectives, we face another danger. This is the intrusion into the battleground of people who mistakenly identify and confuse their own ideological beliefs with Indian problems and grievances. This can be a dangerous intrusion. A left-wing element in this country, not really understanding what the Indian nations are all about, nevertheless has seized upon the opportunity of the present unsettled Indian situation as ripe for promotion of their kind of thinking and action. Their doctrinaire-oriented operation is in opposition to the values put forward by the establishment. Over the next few years as this left-wing element strives to assert itself, such action undoubtedly will spawn a counter-balancing right-wrong faction. Then there arises a real danger that Indian people in this country will polarize around different ideologies with which perhaps they have no legitimate reason to be involved. I very much fear that Indians, as did the whites before them, will get sucked unwittingly into a purely political battle of ideologies which can do them no good and more likely will harm them and their cause.

This, it seems to me, is one of the oncoming dangers that we face, especially in the type of economic climate that this country is moving toward. As individuals search for ways to meet the threat posed to their society by world and national economic ailments, members of both the larger society and the minorities will tend to look for pat answers. Perhaps the easiest of such answers are precisely those backed by differing ideological movements.

Already there are definite signs that this is happening. Not long ago a caravan of young Indians marched from western Canada to Ottawa, only to wind up getting their heads smashed by police on Parliament Hill. Individuals who were involved have identified a very strong influence, indeed almost a take-over of that caravan, by Maoists and other leftist groups.

Even more seriously there seems to be emerging from the Northwest Territories' Dene Declaration (a statement of Indian nationhood issued by the tribes of the Northwest Territories), an intrusion of left-wing thinking that is perhaps much closer to the academic community in Toronto than it is to the Dene. With that tainted declaration as a guide, I fear that the Indian people of the Northwest Territories may well find themselves locked in a needless battle with the federal government; a futile battle fought for purposes foreign to their own, a battle that can only serve to divert their attention and energies away from their true goals. They may also find themselves dragged willy-nilly into the conflict with little, if any, control over why such a fight must be waged.

Careful study of the varying definitions of what Canada and being Canadian mean makes it obvious that concepts proposed by the Prime Minister are not that much different from ideas suggested by tribal elders. With that mutual recognition perhaps we can at least begin to create the environment that will allow a start at tackling the real problems without getting bogged down in a cold-war mentality between whites and Indians. By wiping out the misunderstandings that have existed for so long we can create an opportunity for members of both societies to attack the very real problems that do exist and work toward mutually-identified goals.

Essentially then, when we talk about Canada or Canadianism it is even more vital now than ever before that Indians across the country define their terms more precisely.

One of the reasons for the apparent misunderstanding between Indian people and the larger society, particularly in recent times, may have been a tendency by Indians to rely too greatly upon white consultants hired, paradoxically, to improve communications between the two societies. Such consultants usually are quite expert in one field—they satisfactorily provide Indians with the badly needed expertise in defining English terminology. The problem is that they seldom know anything about Indian people or the Indian nations, let alone the definitions Indians apply to themselves. Consequently what emerges is the white academic's imperfect understanding or interpretation of what Indians are all about, rather than the facts in Indian terms. The hired experts may, and often do, make valiant efforts to explain, but they end up creating more confusion because all they are explaining is their own confusion. Another vital area in which this sort of error is surfacing is the problem of defining the term *aboriginal rights* as it relates to Indian claims right across Canada.

In essence then, part of the difficulty in communication has been the barrier, linguistic and cultural, between Indian tribes, Indian nations, and members of the white society.

The basic task that remains after three or four centuries of contact between Indians and whites is still the construction of a bridge of understanding between two worlds that exist as separate realities.

Wayne Keon *b.* 1946

OJIBWA

Born on 12 December 1946 in the Ottawa Valley, Wayne Keon grew up with a strong sense of Native heritage in an extended-family setting about forty miles west of Pembroke: 'Everyone was about two generations away from the reserve but still involved in hunting, fishing, and trapping.'

Keon attended high school in Elliot Lake, where his father, Orville, worked for Denison Mines. Wayne also worked in the mines during summer holidays, and a developing interest in the financial side of mining led him to take business administration courses at the Northern Institute of Technology in Kirkland Lake. Keon now lives in Toronto, where he is an internal auditor for the mining conglomerate Rio Algom.

Keon's writing career began when his father gave him some poetry to submit to a school newspaper. Thinking it unlikely that a father's work would be published in a school paper, Wayne presented the poems under his own name. When he admitted the hoax, he was forced to come up with his own material to

prove himself one result was *Sweetgrass* (1972), a collection of poetry by Wayne, his father, and his brother Ronald, which also featured some of Wayne's sketches. Wayne and Orville then published a novel, *Thunderbirds of the Ottawa* (1977), and Wayne went on to publish poetry in various periodicals, including *NeWest Review, Canadian Forum, Queen's Quarterly, Exile*, and *The Malahat Review*. He published three collections of poetry in the 1990s: *Sweetgrass II* (1990), *Storm dancer* (1993), and *My Sweet Maize* (1997).

Describing his view of traditional storytelling, Keon says, 'We, my father and my brother and myself, have never taken the traditional Native storytelling as fact, the way some storytellers see it as living history. I take as background all that I know of the traditional values and spiritual heritage of all Native peoples.' Keon feels such connections are treated differently in a Native context: 'It's a funny thing to grow up in a Native home because there's so much that is different from a regular Canadian home. I don't ever recall having an argument with any member of my family about a case of ownership. I used to get really confused when a non-Native friend would shout, "This is mine!" I guess that all came because in the past the subsistence of a Native group required interdependency.'

Keon is a careful reader of contemporary poetry in general, and notes his particular appreciation of bill bissett in one of his poems: 'bill bissett is a writer that I've read a lot of, perhaps because bill has quite an interest in Native peoples' culture and spiritual values.' Keon does not automatically reject a white writer's use of such material:

> It depends on how you do it. I belong to the Pan American Indian Association. You don't have to be a Native to join, you just aspire to the same spiritual creed. I guess it's a bit like how I relate to my ancestry. I don't have any aspiration to live the life my mother did on the traplines. That was a hard life, too hard. Yet I still have the values my mother and my aunts and uncles held.'

heritage

AlgonkinAssiniboineAthapaskanB
eaverBellaCoolaBeothukBlackfoo
tCarrierCaughnawayaCayuyaChilk
atChilcotinChipewyanCreeCrowDe
lewareDogribEskimoFlatheadFoxG   5
rosVentreHaidaHareHuronIllinoi
sIroquoisKickapooKitwancoolKoo
tneyKoskimoKutchinKwakiutlLake
LilloetMaleciteMalouinMenomine
eMetisMiamiMicmacMississaugaMo   10
hawkMohicanMontagnaisMuskogeeN
ahaniNaskapiNeutralNicolaNipis
singNootkaOjibwayOkanaganOneid
aOnondagaOttawaPequotPetunPieg
anPotawatomieSalishSarceeSaukS   15
aulteauxSekaniSenecaShawneeSho
shoniShuswapSiouxSlaveStoneySu
squehannaTagishTalhltanThompson
TlinkitTsetsautTsimshianTuscar
oraWinnebagoWyandotYellowknife   20

howlin at the moon

take the moon
nd take a star
when you don't
know who you are

paint the picture in your hand   5
nd roll on home
take my fear
nd take the hunger
take my body
when i'm younger   10

paint the picture in your hand
nd roll on home

take my ghost
nd make the claim
stake it out   15
to feel the pain

paint the picture in your hand
nd roll on home

take the moon
nd make it talk   20
take your soul out
make it walk

paint the picture in your hand
nd roll on home

take my anguish   25
take the air
make it into
my despair

paint the picture in your hand
nd roll on home   30

take my anger
nd the greed
make it into
what you need

paint the picture in your hand   35
nd roll on home

take my pride
nd all my joy
take my woman
nd my boy   40

paint the picture in your hand
nd roll on home

paint the picture once again
i'm rollin home

for donald marshall

i've no secret old
time answer in
my hand

i've no majik justice in my sand

to challenge all   5
the inmate
time

to pray beside the sacred pine
i've no blazin fire trail
to sear the   10
wounds

nd close the ruptured aura burns

but seek her now nd
make it
end   15

seek her now nd see my friend

o great bear of the southern wheel
o great bear of the southern wheel
o great bear of the southern wheel
o great bear of the southern wheel 20

take the power
nd the
earth

take this breath to heal the hurt
take the power   25
nd your
healing

take the breath nd take this feeling

travel now in
breath nd   30
wind

travel now nd take the wind

travel now in
earth nd
land   35

travel now nd take the land

clothe him in
a yellow
gold

touch the pain nd make it old   40

i'm not in charge of this ritual

i'm not in charge of this
sun dance anymore
i'm hanging here
completely out of it
the lawyers nd therapists   5
have taken over
my breasts are pierced
nd writhin in the blood
nd pain
i'm not that brave you know   10
that's why my children
nd woman were
taken from me

that's why i'm takin it on alone again
i never did any of those purification rituals   15
that's probably why this isn't working
nd hallucinations start sneakin
into my work, i can't say home
because i don't have a home
i live in a room   20
making medicine bags nd
wonderin if the silver strands
nd gems i'm putting in them will do the trick
i escape temporarily at nite catching
my breath at donut & pizza shops   25
where nobody talks nd everyone just eats
munchin nd chewin nd swallowin down
hunger in the nite
hah! despair wouldn't have the nerve to come
waltzin through the door here   30
it would be devoured whole
in one fat gulp
they're all lookin at me wonderin why
i'm so skinny nd still losing weight
they know i'm not one of them   35
but i'm there every nite
shakin over another cup of coffee
tired nd numb from another day of torture
i'm glad when the sun goes down
nd the crazy cool of dark comes   40
b'cos there's hardly anywhere left to hide
nd they'll find me in the mornin
nd drag me back to the dance
in front of the sun
i wish i knew how long this was gonna take   45
but there's always tonite
nd ah! there's always linda
always linda waitin in the nite
with smoky topaz eyes
with smokin lips nd thighs   50
pressed like a gem
from the earth
into mine
but even she's started lockin
her door at nite   55

if i ever heard

if i ever heard
your love had gone pale
i would come out of this wilderness
with ojibiway majik
    for you   5

if i ever heard
your love had gone without rain

i would come out of this wilderness
with my ojibiway river
    for you   10

if i ever heard
your love had gone in the sea

i would come out of this wilderness
with ojibiway earth
    for you   15

if i ever heard
your love had gone in the nite

i would come out of this wilderness
with my ojibiway stars
    for you   20

my sweet maize

corn
goddesses
and maidens
prancing around in the moonlight
direct the planting with some kind   5
of wild and crazy incantations
everywhere you look
boy, those were the good old days
coming all the way

from tehuacan valley   10
i guess it was about 7000 b.c., they said
spreading north around 3000 b.c.
this was all proven of course
poking around in bat caves
down around new mexico   15
finding the grinding stones
and all that old pod corn
each kernel enclosed in a husk of its own
scientifically carbon dated
approximately 5605 to 5931 b.c.   20
by carbon 14
yeah, all the way from the gulf of mexico
to the gulf of st lawrence
coming from yucatan and quintana roo
this is the stuff that built nations   25
cherokee
fed on corn
developed an alphabet
in a lifetime what other cultures
took generations to do   30
and
yeah! we had free trade way back then
mayans
took it
600 miles up the coast   35
by sea-going canoe pushed by 25 paddlers
and aztecs
exacted
it as tribute
from just about everyone in the valley   40
in the pueblos
men grew it
and women ground it
yeah! those were the good old days
when men were men and women were women   45
none of this 'uh, i guess i'll go out and find myself' routine.

1493
sent over there to europe
with tomatoes, white potatoes, tobacco
quinine and chocolate   50
but let's get back to the exciting stuff

stolen on a daring raid
by pawnee soldiers
who added insult to injury
made the vanquished   55
and conquered lug the bags
loaded and full on their backs
into the village
before becoming
slaves   60
yeah! those were the good old days all right
but now it's a lot simpler
sold at supermarkets
everywhere
at loebs, iga   65
you know the kind
packed, canned, creamed, popped and frozen
by mccains, libbys, green giant, and aylmer, canada fancy
white corn, mexicorn, cream-style corn
whole kernel, valley crisp they say   70
delmonte summer, frozen
peaches and cream
and the super sweet variety
you name it, they done it
as if it were found   75
just last month
at the comer
store
my
honourable culture   80
has come down to this
a lousy deal, you might say
but that's the way things go
and that's the way things change
i guess   85
and maybe i should too
main stream it they told me
whatever the hell
that means

i guess the trouble   90
is i'm one of the few
left remembering these
things about the people

and about the good old days
and about   95
my
sweet
sweet
maize

the apocalypse will begin

and
we'll convene
again all right
and it'll be nothing
like you could ever imagine   5
and there won't be any petitions
seeking permission from anyone
there'll just be medicine wheels and dream catcher rings
everywhere and blow-outs that'll start to make Oklahoma
look like   10
a saturday afternoon tea and nostalgia to get back
to something less onerous like maybe the little
big horn lyin' there naked and
frozen in the
dust   15

but
the claws
of these melodious birds
will be at your throat caressing
the chords and veins to choke out that   20
warbler sound and have you trill as sweet
as any song bird ever could
because this ain't gonna
be no picnic bein'
force fed   25
like

this
so get
ready for
that elixir so wild   30

and free and sweet that
you'll never go back, never again,
to the way you used to be
and the way you used
to see and the way   35
you used to
never
be

and
hear anything at all   40
except lightning and pounding
and all the people telling you loud enough
to hear enough to hear and scare
the livin' jesus out of you
with the announcement   45
coming directly
directly

from magicians
and sorcerers
and wizards   50
and the shaman
and raven
himself out
in front
of the   55
mob

dancing
a spooky kind
of ghost
dance   60

and
voices
everywhere
i repeat 'They will be everywhere!'
so you won't go mad at all at the big   65
finale you never ever ever thought
could ever happen at any time
of history or any place
you ever thought
you might   70

get to
be

the past
the future
and the present   75
grinding together all
at once you try to forget
and all the times you wished
for and all the times you couldn't be there
for all the times i needed you for the times   80
i longed for you and the times you
forgot who i was and the times
i wanted you close to me
wrapped up in some kind
of divine circle you   85
never understood
what happened
if i explain
it all
to you   90

again
and again
and again

it won't be the end of the world
but it sure as hell's gonna be   95
the end of something so don't
get this one confused with
the way you'll be able to
tell the difference
in the voices   100
and believe
me they
will
be

different   105
all different
all right

there'll be so many voices
you'll gag on so many words from the likes of

alootook and jordan, thomas and duke and buffy   110
and annharte, simon and joseph and sarain
and skyros and rita and harold
lee and tomson and daniel
and ruby and wayne
and jeannette   115
and jack
and jim
drew and pauline
and beth and george and fred and marty
basil and margo and lenore and emma lee   120
you'll start to shake and shudder
when they come swarming
out of those stormy
clouds right out of the sky
with their last   125
breath lasting
just about
for ever
and ever
and ever   130

so
get ready
cos i don't wanna
have to say this all again
because things   135
aren't
ever
ever

gonna
be   140

quite
the same

ever

the same
again   145

replanting the heritage tree

<pre>
                          A
                       Igonkin
                     Assiniboine
                  AthapaskanBeaver
                  BellaCoolaBeothuk   5
               BlackfootCarrierCaughnawaga
                 CayugaChilkatChilcotin
            ChipewyanCreeCrowDelewareDogrib
            EskimoFlatheadFoxGrosVentreHaida
            HareHuronIllinoisIroquoisKickapoo   10
         KitwancoolKootneyKoskimoKutchinKwakiutl
          LakeLilloetMaleciteMalouinMenomineeMetis
      MiamiMicmacMississaugaMohawkMohicanMontagnais
    MuskogeeNahaniNaskapiNeutralNicolaNipissingNootka
            OjibwayOkanaganOneidaOnondaga   15
              OttawaPequotPetunPiegan
             PotawatomieSalishSarceeSauk
            SaulteauxSekaniSenecaShawnee
           ShoshoniShuswapSiouxSlaveStoney
                 SusquehannaTagis   20
                      HTah
                      Itan
                      Thom
                      Pson
   TlinkitTsetsautTsimshianTuscorora Winnebago WyandotYellowkn   25
                     ifeZuni
</pre>

back in therapy

<pre>
for
one
long
night

again   5

and
the misery
is nothing
</pre>

like

it ever   10
was

before

i don't
know
if   15
i

can
keep
this up

is this   20
a
test

or
something

i mean   25
and
now
being
sentenced
back   30

again
to this
bondsman's
barge

to sail   35
and sail
seven
times
to sail

around the world   40
in one single
savory

night

on this
sweating   45
galley ship
called

love

isn't
exactly   50
my idea

of
getting
cured

on studying ojibway (the people)

Ba (barium)
Bi (bismuth)
by
bay
bow   5
boy
jab
jaw
jay
jib   10
job
Job
joy
obi
way   15
yaw
iowa
Ojibwa
Ojibway

meegwich   20

on studying ojibway (earth mother)

am
an
Mn (magnetic north)
mo (month)
Na (sodium)   5
No
on
awn
man
ma   10
mow
now
own
won
moan   15
mown
woman

meegwich

on studying ojibway (great mystery)

my
met
set
sty
try   5
yes
rest
stem
term
trey   10
tyre
stymy
treys
tyres
mystery   15

meegwich

Jeanette C. Armstrong *b.* 1948

OKANAGAN

Born on the Penticton Indian Reserve in British Columbia, Jeannette Christine Armstrong is a fluent speaker of the Okanagan language and a student of her community's traditional teachings. 'The Native people of this land developed a lifestyle through a unique worldview,' she explains. 'I believe its underlying values and structures are important contributions to the pool of knowledge and critical factors in reversing and reshaping a worldview whose values foster an attitude of self-destruction.'

Armstrong holds a Bachelor of Fine Arts degree from the University of Victoria and is recognized as a visual artist as well as an activist and author. Her publications include two children's books, the groundbreaking novel *Slash* (1987), the collection of poems *Breath Tracks* (1991), and her latest novel, *Whispering in Shadows* (2000). She has also edited a collection of essays, *Looking at the Words of Our People: First Nations Analysis of Literature* (1993). She says that she writes 'because it is a way to contribute to the vast dialogue of the human spirit in its course through time. It is a way to reach others I may never meet in person now and in the future. I appreciate voices from the past like Pauline Johnson and my own great aunt, Mourning Dove. They are windows into a time and place I can never experience directly myself. I write because oral literature is now extremely vulnerable.'

Armstrong is the director of the En'owkin International School of Writing in Penticton, British Columbia, which offers Canada's only creative writing program designed for Native people. She has also served on her community's traditional council, and she consults with international councils and working groups on the wide variety of issues of concern to indigenous cultures. She received the Buffet Award for Indigenous Leadership in 2003 and has an honourary doctorate from St Thomas University.

History Lesson

Out of the belly of Christopher's ship
a mob bursts
Running in all directions
Pulling furs off animals
Shooting buffalo   5
Shooting each other
left and right

Father mean well
waves his makeshift wand
forgives saucer-eyed Indians   10

Red coated knights
gallop across the prairie
to get their men
and to build a new world

Pioneers and traders   15
bring gifts
Smallpox, Seagrams
and Rice Krispies

Civilization has reached
the promised land.   20

Between the snap crackle pop
of smoke stacks
and multi-coloured rivers
swelling with flower powered zee
are farmers sowing skulls and bones   25
and miners
pulling from gaping holes
green paper faces
of smiling English lady

The colossi   30
in which they trust
while burying
breathing forests and fields
beneath concrete and steel
stand shaking fists   35
waiting to mutilate
whole civilizations
ten generations at a blow.

Somewhere among the remains
of skinless animals   40
is the termination
to a long journey
and unholy search
for the power
glimpsed in a garden   45
forever closed
forever lost.

For Tony

Words were always
easy for you
You played with them
in long chains
or little piles   5
People laughed at your stories
and were happy
for a few moments
you would be too

Then you would return   10
to that cold and wordless place
where the only sounds
were those of an always new beast
waiting just in the shadows
where emptied bottles   15
spoke of the battles
now lost

All we have of you now
are echoes of words
to make us laugh   20
and we are poorer
but the war you fought alone
is ours now too
Already our people gather
to choose their weapons   25

We all walk in the shadow
of the beast
but we will step lightly
and all the stories
you used to make laughter   30
will be told
around the tables of your people
and we will be rich with weapons.

Sketches

```
                        a man's
            pure sperm
            got stuff
            in it        most
people                               couldn't              5
believe                              the
                        ordered      world
in                      pieces
            that        are          more or less
                        big                               10
            death
            rattles     cock
carriers                                       presumers
            hard                               on
dancers                                                   15
drainers                             let me feel  your
                        ass          smooth        cunt
                                     gentle
                        blood        hairy
tribes                                                    20
```

Indian Woman

I am a squaw
a heathen
a savage
basically a mammal

I am a female   5
only in the ability
to breed
and bear papooses
to be carried
quaintly   10
on a board
or lost
to welfare

I have no feelings

The sinuous planes   15
of my brown body
carry no hint
of the need
to be caressed
desired   20
loved
Its only use
to be raped
beaten and bludgeoned
in some   25
B-grade western

I have no beauty

The lines
cut deep
into my aged face   30
are not from bitterness
or despair
at seeing my clan destroyed
one by one
they are here   35
to be painted or photographed
sold
and hung on lawyers walls

I have no emotions

The husky laughter   40
a brush of wings
behind eyes
soft and searching
lightly touching others
is not from caring   45
but from the ravaged
beat of black wings
rattling against the bars
of an insanity
that tells me   50
something is wrong here.

Some one is lying.

I am an Indian Woman

Where I walk
beauty surrounds me   55
grasses bend and blossom
over valleys and hills
vast and multicoloured
in starquilt glory

I am the keeper   60
of generations

I caress the lover gently
croon as I wrap the baby
with quietness I talk
to the old ones   65
and carefully lay to rest
loved ones

I am the strength
of nations

I sing to the whispering   70
autumn winds
in the snow
I dance
slowly
filling my body   75
with power
feeling it
knowing it

I am the giver of life
to whole tribes   80

I carry the seeds
carefully   through   dangerous
wastelands
give them life
scattered   85
among   cold   and   towering
concrete
watch them grow

battered and crippled
under all the lies   90
I teach them the songs
I help them to hear
I give them truth

I am a sacred trust
I am Indian woman.   95

Threads of Old Memory

Speaking to newcomers in their language is dangerous
for when I speak
history is a dreamer
empowering thought
from which I awaken the imaginings of the past   5
bringing the sweep and surge of meaning
coming from a place
rooted in the memory of loss
experienced in ceremonies
wrenched from the minds of a people   10
whose language spoke only harmony
through a language
meant to overpower
to overtake
in skillfully crafted words   15
moving towards surrender
leaving in its swirling wake
only those songs
hidden
cherished   20
protected
the secret singing of which
I glimpse through bewildered eyes
an old lost world
of astounding beauty   25

When I speak
I attempt to bring together
with my hands
gossamer thin threads of old memory

thoughts from the underpinnings of understanding 30
words steeped in age
slim
barely visible strands of harmony
stretching across the chaos brought into this world
through words 35
shaped as sounds in air
meaning made physical
changers of the world
carriers into this place of things
from a place of magic 40
the underside of knowing
the origination place
a pure place
silent
wordless 45
from where thoughts I choose
silently transform into words
I speak and
powerfully become actions
become memory in someone 50
I become different memories to different people
different stories in the retelling of my place
I am the dreamer
the choice maker
the word speaker 55
I speak in a language of words
formed of the actions of the past
words that become the sharing
the collective knowing
the links that become a people 60
the dreaming that becomes a history
the calling forth of voices
the sending forward of memory
I am the weaver of memory thread
twining past to future 65
I am the artist
the storyteller
the singer
from the known and familiar
pushing out into darkness 70
dreaming splinters together
the coming to knowing

When I speak
I sing a song called up through ages
of carefully crafted rhythm   75
of a purpose close to the wordless
in a coming to this world
from the cold and hungry spaces in the heart
through the desolate and lost places of the mind
to this stark and windswept mountain top   80
I search for the sacred words
spoken serenely in the gaps between memory
the lost places of history
pieces mislaid
forgotten or stolen   85
muffled by violence
splintered by evil
when languages collide in mid air
when past and present explode in chaos
and the imaginings of the past   90
rip into the dreams of the future

When I speak
I choose the words gently
asking the whys
dangerous words   95
in the language of the newcomers
words releasing unspeakable grief
for all that is lost
dispelling lies in the retelling
I choose threads of truth   100
that in its telling cannot be hidden
and brings forward
old words that heal
moving to a place
where a new song begins   105
a new ceremony
through medicine eyes I glimpse a world
that cannot be stolen or lost
only shared
shaped by new words   110
joining precisely to form old patterns
a song of stars
glittering against an endless silence

Fire Madness

god   bellied
you danced
around my pyre
and spoke in a language
that was mine alone   5

with bluejay eyes
you watched
as they piled broken branches
high over me

the flame of my blood   10
is red
the leap of it
greets you
firewalker

come   15
before the spider
draws her web
across the sky
walk quietly
on these embers   20
to me

lift me
bluejay dancer
and we will laugh
from a high green branch   25
at the mourners gathered to watch
this death
that we defy

Wind Woman

Maggie at night sometimes I hear you laugh

when I was ten we rode to huckleberry mountain
carrying ragged quilts and pots and pans
packed on an old roan mare called jeep
given to Maggie to help fill her baskets   5
I followed her
picking berries her failing eyes had missed
I listened as she talked in our language
half singing sometimes
for all the pickers to hear   10
her voice high and clear in the crisp mountain air
telling about coyote

I know how the trees talk
I said to Maggie
I heard their moaning in the night   15
while we lie so tiny in our tents
with all those tall black pines swaying over us

she told me a story then
of how the woman of the wind
banished by coyote   20
carried her eternally howling child
tied to her back
as they moved forever through the tree tops
mother crooning to the child
how sometimes she would swoop down in anger   25
scattering berries off bushes

Maggie told me I had heard
the wind woman sing
she told me that I would remember that song always
because the trees were my teacher   30

I remember the song clearly
but it is always Maggie's voice singing
her songs
filling my world
with the moan of old dark pines   35
as the wind woman

that sings to me
follows
with her hungry child
wherever I go   40

Keepers Words

Makers are mockers
so said the grandmother
Her tribal conscience
rode at her elbow
as inherited as her brown skin   5
Her words   smooth   carved as bone
and so old no one remembered
were placed side by side
in a pattern
fashioned in the beginning   10
of her kind

There will be no new words
in man-designs
to break up what is sacred
and leave forget in its place   15
We are keepers   we must not change
On this earth
lives a cannibal monster
who devours himself
because he changes so much   20
as he grows
that he forgets
what his tail looks like

I'll be around   she said
soon after death lunges forward   25
out of the rabble
I will stand on a hilltop
a black dot against blazing red
and my shadow will stretch
long and narrow over the earth curve   30
to seep into the little shadows
even now
skipping behind you

All your sound songs
will be no more than food for the monster   35
but the sacred words
will still be whispered
in shadows
You will hear and understand
nothing is new   only changed   40
there are no men who are makers
just changers

Blue Against White

Lena walked up the steep hill toward her mother's house. She could see the bright blue door. It stood out against the stark white of the house. It was the only house with a door like that on the hill. All the houses on that part of the reserve looked a lot alike, the colours ranging from mostly white to off-white to grey, and a few with light pastel colours. All the doors matched the houses.

Thinking of it now, Lena realized that it was funny how she had always thought of it as her mother's house rather than her father's house, though it had been his idea to paint the door a bright blue. He had said that the houses up there on the hill all looked too much alike. He had said that their home would be easy to see because of the door. He was right, but there was a question that had always been silent: 'Who would have a problem?' She had known that all the Indians in a thousand-mile radius knew each other and that they didn't find their way to each other by the description of their houses.

As she walked toward the house she realized that she had kept that door in her mind all the years she had been away. It has been there as always, a bright blue against the white. A blue barrier against the cold north wind. A cool blue shield against the summer heat. She remembered having hated the door and having wished it would just be white like the rest of the house. But while she was away, it had been the part of the house that had been a constant clear image. Behind that door, warm smells and laughter mixed into a distinct impression of the way it was back home. Her mother, long braids tied together in the back, smiled at her from behind that door.

Now, she walked up the hill toward the house carrying the one bag that held her things. She felt light, weightless and somehow insubstantial like the last fluffseeds still clinging shakily to the milkweeds that lined the narrow dirt road gutted with deep, dry ruts. In this country the summer rains left cracked mud tracks which froze in the fall and stayed hidden under the snow and ice in winter.

At this moment she felt she could easily be lifted to float up and away from those deep earth gashes, to move across the land with the dry fall drifting of seeds and leaves. She had hated this dirt road and the mud in the spring and the dust in the summer, the ruts in the fall and the ungraded snow in the winter. She had mostly hated the dry milkweeds crowding together everywhere. As always, on this road the lumps of soil were uneven and slow to travel over. She felt like turning and bolting back to the bus to catch it before it could leave her here, but running was hard on this broken ground.

The door seemed to loom ahead of her, though the house was no taller than the rest. She hated the way all the cheap government houses on the row facing the road were so close together and had paint peeling and dry weedy yards with several mangy dogs. She turned to look back at the road winding steeply down to the crossroad where the bus stopped momentarily to drop off or pick up people from the reserve. The freeway stretched away into a hazy purple distance where night was beginning to shadow the land. Only the white line dividing those coming from those going was visible after a certain point. The red lights of the bus were fading straight into that shadow line between sky, asphalt and the darkened earth.

Turning, she faced the rest of the climb. A single black crow cawed at her from its perch on the steeple cross of the village church, raising a ruckus in the quiet. It screeched and flapped its wings, dove over her mother's house and then flew lazily overhead, looking down at her as it passed, flying over the dirt road toward the crossroad in the direction of the twilight.

She watched the crow disappear into dark blue. She knew his name from the old stories. She wanted to laugh and say it. She knew he hung around only in the summer months and then flew away when the shadows in the fall grew long and the days short. She wanted to say, 'You, old pretender, you don't fool me. You're not going to preach to me, too, are you? You're no smarter than me!' Instead she found tears wetting her cheeks.

Her tears brought the memory of a dream from the week before she had started the long bus ride home. In her dream she had been in a large building with many bright lights and shiny reflections. Although there was a lot of noise, she couldn't see anyone. She felt totally alone as she walked down a long white hallway. She remembered looking, one by one, at the doors she passed, feeling like the only thing behind each one was a patch of sky. In the dream she remembered feeling something like dizziness as she saw how many doors there were and how they seemed to stretch into darkness on and on without end. She recalled running and stumbling past the doors and calling out. When she awoke she had been crying.

She was almost at the top of the hill now. She stopped and put down her bag. A couple of reserve dogs barked at her and then wagged their tails, trotting toward her, making greeting noises in their throats. She looked down at the one that was obviously a lady dog with her sagging dry milk sacs and she stroked her ear. She thought of the city she had left and said, 'Mamma dogs don't just walk around free there, you know. You're pretty lucky to be here.' The lady dog sat down and thumped her tail against some of the weeds, sending puffs of seed floating with each excited wave.

Behind the houses farther up into the dark hills, she heard the high, far-away yipping of a coyote. She saw the dogs' ears perk up. She saw the way their eyes glowed a deeper orange as they forgot her and pointed their noses toward the hills above them, a low, crooning echo rumbling deep in their throats. She, too, looked up there and whispered, 'How are you, brothers?' in the language. She knew them, too.

She thought of that one coyote in the papers, in some city, that had got trapped in a hallway after coming in from an alley door. How somebody mistaking it for a dog had opened an elevator for it and how it had ridden to the roof of an apartment building and ran around crazily, and then jumped to its death rather than run back through the elevator door and ride back down into the hallway and out the alley door. She had known that it hadn't been a matter of animal stupidity, because a coyote always remembered where it had come from. She had secretly known that it had more to do with the quick elevator door and the long lonely ride up to the top. She thought of the coyotes hanging around in the cities these days. Nobody wanted them there, so nobody made friends with them, but once in a while they made the papers when they did something wrong or showed up, trotting along Broadway, cool as could be.

Lena thought about all the time she had spent away from this place of hard, cracked earth, seedpods and clean coyote prints in the new snow up in the hills. She looked up at the bright blue surface directly in front of her, waiting to open, and felt the bone-aching, deep tiredness of long journeys over the hard even surface of freeways into alleys and white hallways. As she reached for the door knob she looked down and realized that the freeway's white line and the mud ruts ended here, right at her mother's door. The door that her dad had painted bright blue so that it stood out clearly against the white.

The Disempowerment of First North American Native Peoples and Empowerment Through Their Writing

Paper prepared for Saskatchewan Writers Guild 1990 Annual Conference

PANEL DISCUSSION: EMPOWERING ABORIGINAL WRITERS

In order to address the specifics of Native people's writing and empowerment, I must first present my view on the disempowerment of first North American Nations.

Without recounting various historical versions of *how* it happened, I would like to refer only to *what* happened here.

Indigenous peoples in North America were rendered powerless and subjugated to totalitarian domination by foreign peoples, after they were welcomed as guests and their numbers were allowed to grow to the point of domination through aggression.

Once total subjective control was achieved over my peoples through various coercive measures and the direct removal of political, social, and religious freedoms accomplished, the colonization process began.

In North America this has been to systemically enforce manifest destiny or the so-called 'White Man's burden' to civilize. In the 498 years of contact in The Americas, the thrust of this bloody sword has been to hack out the spirit of all the beautiful cultures encountered, leaving in its wake a death toll unrivalled in recorded history. This is what happened and what continues to happen.

There is no word other than totalitarianism which adequately describes the methods used to achieve the condition of my people today. Our people were not given choices. Our children, for generations, were seized from our communities and homes and placed in indoctrination camps until our language, our religion, our customs, our values, and our societal structures almost disappeared. This was the residential school experience.

Arising out of the siege conditions of this nightmare time, what is commonly referred to as the 'social problems' of Native peoples emerged. Homes and communities, without children, had nothing to work for, or live for. Children returned to communities and families as adults, without the necessary skills for parenting, for Native life style, or self-sufficiency on their land base, deteriorated into despair. With the loss of cohesive cultural relevance with their own peoples and a distorted view of the non-Native culture from the clergy who ran the residential schools, an almost total disorientation and loss of identity occurred. The disintegration of family and community and nation was inevitable, originating with the individual's internalized pain. Increasing death statistics from suicide, violence, alcohol and drug abuse, and other poverty-centred physical diseases, can leave no doubt about the question of totalitarianism and genocide.

You writers from the dominating culture have the freedom of imagination. You keep reminding us of this. Is there anyone here who dares to imagine what those children suffered at the hands of their so-called 'guardians' in those schools. You are writers, imagine it on yourselves and your children. Imagine you and your children and imagine how they would be treated by those who abhorred and detested you, all, as savages without any rights.

Imagine at what cost to you psychologically, to acquiesce and attempt to speak, dress, eat, and worship, like your oppressors, simply out of a need to be treated humanly. Imagine attempting to assimilate so that your children will not suffer what you have, and imagine finding that assimilationist measures are not meant to include you but to destroy all remnants of your culture. Imagine finding that even when you emulate every cultural process from customs to values you are still excluded, despised, and ridiculed because you are Native.

Imagine finding out that the dominating culture will not tolerate any real cultural participation and that cultural supremacy forms the basis of the government process and that systemic racism is a tool to maintain their kind of totalitarianism. And all the while, imagine that this is presented under the guise of 'equal rights' and under the banner of banishing bigotry on an individual basis through law.

Imagine yourselves in this condition and imagine the writers of that dominating culture berating you for speaking out about appropriation of cultural voice and using the words 'freedom of speech' to condone further systemic violence, in the form of entertainment literature about *your* culture and *your* values and all the while, yourself being disempowered and rendered voiceless through such 'freedoms'.

Imagine how you as writers from the dominant society might turn over some of the rocks in your own garden for examination. Imagine in your literature courageously questioning and examining the values that allow the dehumanizing of peoples through domination and the dispassionate nature of the racism inherent in perpetuating such practices. Imagine writing in honesty, free of the romantic bias about the courageous 'pioneering spirit' of colonialist practice and imperialist process. Imagine interpreting for us *your own people's* thinking toward us, instead of interpreting for us, our thinking, our lives, and our stories. We wish to know, and you need to understand, why it is that you want to own our stories, our art, our beautiful crafts, our ceremonies, but you do not appreciate or wish to recognize that these things of beauty arise out of the beauty of our people.

Imagine these realities on yourselves in honesty and let me know how you imagine that you might approach empowerment of yourselves in such a situation. Better yet, do not dare speak to me of 'Freedom of Voice', 'Equal Rights', 'Democracy', or 'Human Rights' until this totalitarianistic approach has been changed by yourselves as writers and shapers of philosophical direction. Imagine a world where domination is not possible because all cultures are valued.

To the Native writers here, my words are meant as empowerment to you. In my quest for empowerment of my people through writing, there are two things of which I must steadfastly remind myself.

The first is that the reality I see is the reality for the majority of Native people and that although severe and sometimes irreparable damage has been wrought, healing can take place through cultural affirmation. I have found immense strength and beauty in my people.

The dispelling of lies and the telling of what really happened until *everyone*, including our own people understands that this condition did not happen through choice or some cultural defect on our part, is important. Equally important is the affirmation of the true beauty of our people whose fundamental co-operative values resonated pacifism and predisposed our cultures as vulnerable to the reprehensible value systems which promote domination and aggression.

The second thing I must remind myself of is that the dominating culture's reality is that it seeks to affirm itself continuously and must be taught that *numbers* are not the basis of democracy, *people* are, *each one* being important. It must be pushed, in Canada, to understand and accept that this country is multiracial and multicultural now, and the meaning of that. I must remind myself constantly of the complacency that makes these conditions possible, and that if I am to bridge into that complacency that I will be met with hostility from the majority, but, that those whose thoughts I have provoked may become our greatest allies in speaking to their own. It is this promotion of an ideal which will produce the courage to shake off centuries of imperialist thought and make possible the relearning of co-operation and sharing, in place of domination.

Our task as Native writers is twofold. To examine the past and culturally affirm toward a new vision for all our people in the future, arising out of the powerful and positive support structures that are inherent in the principles of co-operation.

We, as Native people, through continuously resisting cultural imperialism and seeking means toward teaching co-operative relationships, provide an integral mechanism for solutions currently needed in this country.

We must see ourselves as undefeatably pro-active in a positive sense and realize that negative activism actually serves the purpose of the cultural imperialism practised on our people. Lies need clarification, truth needs to be stated, and resistance to oppression needs to be stated, without furthering division and participation in the same racist measures. This is the challenge that we rise to. Do not make the commonly made error that it is a people that we abhor, be clear that it is systems and processors which we must attack. Be clear that change to those systems will be promoted by people who can perceive intelligent and non-threatening alternatives. Understand that these alternatives will be presented only through discourse and dialogue flowing outward from us, for now, because we are the stakeholders. We need the system to change. Those in the system can and will remain complacent until moved to think, and to understand how critical change is needed at this time for us all. Many already know and are willing to listen.

The responsibility of the Native writer is tremendous in light of these times in which world over, solutions are being sought to address the failed assimilationist measures originating out of conquest, oppression, and exploitation, whether under the socialist or capitalist banner. We as writers can show how support for Lithuanian independence and support for South African Black equality became farcical in the glare of the Constitutional position to First Nations here in Canada, who seek nothing more than co-operative sovereign relationships guaranteed in the principles of treaty making. No one will desire or choose to hear these truths unless they are voiced clearly to people who have no way to know that there are good alternatives and that instead of losing control we can all grow powerful together.

Finally, I believe in the basic goodness of the majority of people. I *rely* on the common human desire to be guilt free and fulfilled, to triumph, towards attainment of our full potential as wonderful, thinking beings at the forward edge of the Creator's expression of beauty.

I believe in the strength and rightness in the values of my people and know that those principles of peace and co-operation, in practice, are natural and survival-driven mechanisms which transcend violence and aggression. I see the destructive paths that have led us to this time in history, when all life on this planet is in peril, and know that there *must* be change. I believe that the principles of co-operation are a sacred trust and the plan and the intent of the Creator and therefore shall endure.

Beth Cuthand *b.* 1949

CREE

Beth Cuthand was born in La Ronge, Saskatchewan, and grew up there and in Alberta. She attended the University of Regina and the University of Saskatchewan, where she received a Bachelor of Arts degree in sociology; she then earned a Master of Fine Arts degree in creative writing from the University of Arizona. She has been a teacher at a variety of Native institutions, including the Gabriel Dumont Institute, the Saskatchewan Indian Institute of Technology, the Saskatchewan Indian Federated College, and the En'owkin International School of Writing in Penticton, British Columbia. Her columns and stories have appeared in *UBCIC News*, *Indian World*, *Saskatchewan Indian*, *From the Pipe*, and *Tomorrow File*. She has also worked for *Saskatchewan Indian Magazine* as an editor and for the Institute for the Development of Indian Government.

Cuthand has edited a number of books, including Maria Campbell's *Stories of the Road Allowance People*, Ruby Slipperjack's *Silent Words*, and the anthologies *Gatherings V*, with William George, and *Reinventing the Enemy's Language*, with Joy Harjo and others. She wrote and produced twenty-five scripts for CBC Radio's *Our Native Land*, as well as scripts for various television programs, including *The Story of George* and the documentaries *Indians and the Constitution* and *Indian Government Today*. In addition, she co-wrote a made-for-television movie, *The New Kid*. She has published poetry and short stories in a number of periodicals and anthologies, as well as in her own books, *Horse Dance to Emerald Mountain* (1987) and *Voices in the Waterfall* (1989; second expanded edition, 1992).

Shake 'N Bake

He wore the uniform of the lowly
like a cop wears a gun and a badge;
worn blue jeans neatly patched
by his woman of the moment,
and a humble shirt of plaid flannel   5
muted and discreet
Oh so discreet.

And when he went to advise the lowly
he played his sombre medicine man voice;
turned up the bass, lowered the treble   10
and cleared his throat.
Yes, always cleared his throat.

He talked as though he were barely literate
and he had just learned English last week.
He didn't like to read   15

and would sometimes take two whole days
to finish *Black Elk Speaks* or
Selected Studies in Native American Shamanism

He would talk ever so discreetly
about 'the others'   20
the shake 'n bake medicine men
who didn't know what they were doing
and didn't deserve to do it anyway.
Yes, they were wrong and they
would be sorry.   25

'There is so much to teach people'
he would say. 'So much has been lost.
You've got to watch the old guys, even
the old people have forgotten. It's sad,'
he would say, clearing his throat   30
'the way those young people go to them.'
But he knew the score. He was real.
He had *earned* the right to do what he did.
Every summer he took great pains
to fast at someone else's expense   35
and performed the requisite ceremonies
diligently and correctly.
So correctly.

There was no one whom he trusted
and no one whom he loved.   40
He rarely really laughed. He would
tell crude jokes to the boys
but always made sure
he was pure before
he performed a   45
ceremony.
For this
was the way
he understood
it to be:
   Step 1   50
   Step 2
   Step 3

Zen Indian

Zen Indian tiptoes into Taos
watches coyote disguised
as an ice-cream vendor
sell dollar popsicles
to thirsty tourists.   5

Fishes down the Fraser
for dried salmon
thinking a No. 10 hook
will catch those freeze-dried suckers.

Careens into Calgary in time   10
for Stampede; bells polished
feathers fluffed
to dance three times a day
for a free pass to the rodeo.

Makes it to Winnipeg   15
just after Bismark and right before
wild rice time
to get folk-sey at the Indian Pavilion

Then it's on to pick wild rice
for Uncle Ben;   20
drop a few rocks in the sacks,
shoot at the crows and reminisce
about how it used to be
before the harvest became
the domain of Bros in hydro   25
planes and enough money for gas.

Oh oh, cold's coming.
Time to find a fine filly
with a job, not too many kids
and a warm place to lay up for   30
the winter.

Put cities in a hat:
    Minneapolis, LA
         Boulder, Santa Fe
Calgary, Seattle, Salt Lake.   35

Yee-ha! Watch out Boulder!
Here he comes.
Zen Indian on the road to enlightenment!

He Told Me

He told me
    when his father died
    he felt him heave
    his last breath
       and though   5
    he was miles away
    he heard his father say

Louis David, to you
    I transfer my bundle.
    It is small and humble   10
    wrapping little things,
    a bone
    from the last buffalo,
    a stone
    from the Assiniboine,   15
    a small pipe and
    tobacco pouch
and,
    a feather
    from the broken wing   20
    of one
    who flew too low.

He told me
that
    he couldn't bear   25
    the burden
    of that bundle.
And when
    his father died
    he was alone   30
    and darkness
    and voices
    and phantom

winds
  blew   35
    his soul
      away.

'Evelene,'   40
  he would say,
'Evelene—I have been
  chasing my shadow
  ever since.'

Four Songs for the Fifth Generation

Drums, chants, and rattles
pounded earth and
   heartbeats
   heartbeats.

'They were our life the life   5
   of the prairies
We loved them
    and they loved us.
Sometimes they were so many
they flowed like a river   10
over the hills into the valleys.
I saw them. I knew them.
I helped my mother
   cut away their skin
   chop their bones   15
and dry their meat
   Many times
   many times.

Aye, but now they are gone
  ghosts all ghosts.   20

The sickness came
   we were hungry
I saw my children die
one by one
one by one.   25

There was no freedom   then my girl
        They were stronger
        They thought they knew
what it was   their God wanted

Aye, but now   they are gone   30
        ghosts   just ghosts.

Sometimes   I think I hear
their thunder   smell their dust
at night my girl
        at night I dream   35
dream of their warm blood
        their hides covering
Aye, covering   all my children
        in their sleep.'

Drums, chants, and rattles   40
pounded earth and
        heartbeats
        heartbeats.

'That's the old Simmons homestead.
        He's dead now   45
I don't know what happened
        to his wife   and children.

Back in the thirties
        we cut posts for him
10 cents a post   that was good money   50
        back then.
Clarence Simmons was his name
        came from England
        with his skinny little wife
and a bunch of pale scrawny little kids.   55

Poor Simmons   we felt sorry for him
        so we helped him
        as much as we could.

Back in the thirties,
things weren't so bad for us   60
        as it was for the homesteaders
We hadn't cut our trees

or tore up the land.
    We still had deer
        and fish   65
           rabbits
and gophers and fat dogs
           heh heh

But the settlers really suffered.
        It was pitiful.   70
My dad would tell us
    "take this meat over to the Simmons
    place. Drop it at the door."

So I'd ride over   real quiet
and hang it by the house   75

Poor Simmons
        one day he hung himself
          from a tree
            in his yard.
Couldn't take it no more.   80
        Dad found him,
          cut him down
and laid him   real gentle
        on the ground
          under the tree.   85

That was one of the few times
        I ever saw him cry.

I don't know what makes
        some men
          go on living   90
while other men
        give up.'

Drums, chants, and rattles
pounded earth and
        heartbeats   95
        heartbeats.

'It was 1960
        when dad and mom
        got the vote.

All us kids got copies of Canada's   100
     "Declaration of Human Rights"
and took them home
      and put them up
      all over the walls.
Yeah, that was a great day   105
for Canada
     "Oh Canada
     Our true north strong and free."

We moved south when I was ten
      to a town with sidewalks   110
      and running water
and a playground with a pool
      not a lake
"Hey Injuns!   Yer not allowed
      in the pool.   115
You'll get it dirty,
      dirty."

We closed ranks after that
      spent a lot of time
      exploring the creek.   120
My brother found an arrowhead
     Some white kid said
     it didn't belong to us,
so my brother beat him up.

My brother was always   125
      fighting
     It seemed
    he had a rage
     that wouldn't go out.
Me,   I just retreated   130
   and retreated
     until I couldn't
     find myself.

There was a boy down the street
     who had it in   135
      for my brother
      called him dirty Indian.
He'd sick his dog on him
     every time

we'd walk to school.   140
We took to walking the long way,
        everyone   except my brother.

One time my brother hit that dog
        smack between the eyes
                with a rock   145
The old dog tucked his tail
        between his legs and
        went howling off
                behind the house.

The boy came to our place   150
        with a baseball bat
We were all going to go out
        and kick that kid around,
but dad said "No
        let your brother   155
        fight it out."

They were pretty evenly matched
        the kid with his bat,
        my brother with his stones
                they fought   160
                for an hour
kicking
hitting
scratching
punching   165
thwacking
ripping

Mom wanted to stop them
        but Dad said no.
        "He's got to take a stand."   170

Finally it was over
                nobody won.

That kid never sicked
        his dog on my brother again.
                but   175
my brother's rage
never did go away.'

Drums, chants, and rattles
pounded earth and
> heartbeats   180
> heartbeats.

'I don't want to go
> to a white high school
> Mama.
My spirit would die   185
> in a place like that
I love our little school
> us Indians
> we help each other.
> We care.   190
We share smokes Mom

When I grow up
will my kids
have to fight
for a place in the neighbourhood   195
too?'

Drums, chants, and rattles
pounded earth and
> heartbeats
> heartbeats.   200

Post-Oka Kinda Woman

Here she comes strutting down your street.
This Post-Oka woman don't take no shit.

She's done with victimization, reparation,
degradation, assimilation,
devolution, coddled collusion,   5
the 'plight of the Native Peoples.'

Post-Oka woman, she's o.k.
She shashay into your suburbia.
MacKenzie Way, Riel Crescent belong to her
like software, microwave ovens,   10
plastic Christmas trees and lawn chairs.

Her daughter wears Reeboks and works out.
Her sons cook and wash up.
Her grandkids don't sass their Kohkom!
No way.   15

She drives a Toyota, reads bestsellers,
sweats on weekends, colors her hair,
sings old songs, gathers herbs.
Two steps Tuesdays,
Round dances Wednesdays,   20
Twelve steps when she needs it.

Post-Oka woman she's struttin' her stuff
not walkin' one step behind her man.
She don't take that shit
Don't need it!   Don't want it.   25
You want her   then treat her right.

Talk to her of post-modern deconstructivism
She'll say: 'What took you so long?'

You wanna discuss Land Claims?
She'll tell ya she'd rather leave   30
her kids with a struggle than a bad settlement.

Indian Government?
            Show her cold hard cash.

Tell her you've never talked to a real live 'Indian'
    She'll say: 'Isn't that special.'   35

Post-Oka woman, she's cheeky.
    She's bold.   She's cold.

And she don't take no shit!
No shit.

Lenore Keeshig-Tobias *b.* 1949

ANISHNAABE

Lenore Keeshig-Tobias is a member of the Chippewas of the Nawash First Nation, situated on the Bruce Peninsula on land that is commonly known as the Cape Croker Reserve, which she describes as 'unceded territory surrounded by the province of Ontario'. She received her Bachelor of Fine Arts degree from York University.

Keeshig-Tobias is a storyteller, culture worker, mother, and grandmother. She has served as the founding chair of the Racial Minority Writers Committee of The Writers Union of Canada and has worked as editor of *The Ontario Indian, Sweetgrass,* and *The Magazine to Re-establish the Trickster.*

> I write for the enjoyment of language, and, when necessary, out of a sense of responsibility to 'speak up' or 'speak out'. I write mostly about the experiences of Anishnaabe children, and poetry. My writing (whatever genre) is always related to my identity as a Native person, whether or not it is marked by themes or with

language specifically identifying Anishnaabe culture and heritage.

> Storytelling has always been part of our family life, not just as a heritage in the traditional stories, but as a necessary function in our individual life circle. Some of these stories are not flattering, but nevertheless will be told time and again—reflections of the Trickster–Teacher, and of what not to do.

Keeshing-Tobias's publications include *Bird Talk* (1991) and *Emma and the Tree* (1996), bilingual children's books in Anishnaabemowin (Ojibwa) and English, both illustrated by her daughter Polly. *Bird Talk* won the 1993 Living the Dream Book Award (an award that commemorates the life and work of Dr Martin Luther King, Jr).

Keeshing-Tobias is part-time professor at George Brown College in Toronto and a naturalist and oral history researcher at the Fathom Five National Marine Park on the Bruce Peninsula.

After Oka—How Has Canada Changed?

O Canada, we have always walked on the edge
of your dreams, stalked
you as you made wild your way
through this great land

And O Canada, you have always been   5
afraid of us, scared because you know
you can never live without us.

The summer for First Nations peoples has been a review of history, a history we know so well, and a reality we have lived through generation after generation.

My people are the Saugeen Ojibway. Our earliest claim against the Crown dates back to the Treaty of 1836 when our people were forced to cede '1.5 million acres of the richest land in Upper Canada'. The Government refused to protect our land from encroachment by white settlers. This is only one of our treaties. What did we receive for this land—the indifference, the impatience, the ignorance, and the scorn of Canadians, not the 'proper housing' nor the assistance promised to help us 'become civilized' unless you consider subsistence on social welfare and other government programs to be pillars of civilization.

The Saugeen Ojibway have been patient for over 150 years. The Mohawks of Kanesatake have been patient for 200 years. Quebec and Canada lost patience after only 48 days. And think, your Prime Minister praises the army for its patience?! What about the patience of the Mohawks in the treatment centre after so many days and nights of harassment?

I have been asked how has Canada changed after Oka? I would sincerely like to say Canada has changed. Since childhood, I remember wanting Canada to change, wanting to see the land claims my gramma talked about resolved.

And I am sure you, after having witnessed the horrid reality of Canadian justice and democracy at work this summer, would like to hear that Canada has changed. But the sad truth is that Canada has not changed. And Canada will not change until Canadians are truly ready to turn around and confront their own psyche and history. Canada will not change until Canadians make of this Turtle Island what our prophets, long before the appearance of the white man, foretold it would be. These prophesies tell of the four colours of people, distinct societies, coming together as sovereign nations within a nation to work for a better society, a better way of life for all of us.

Why is Canada and why are Canadians so afraid to deal with us as equals? And yet, the very same Canadians continue to shout out with pride our names, the names of their provinces and cities—Quebec, Ontario, Manitoba, Saskatchewan—Toronto, Winnipeg, Saskatoon, and Ottawa to name a few. And, of course, we must not forget Ken-a-tah, or as Canadians so proudly say Canada.

This has not been an 'Indian Summer' to remember as so many of you want to romanticize it to be. 'Indian' is a figment of your imagination. 'Warrior' is a figment of your imagination. And the Mohawk called your bluff. No, this has not been an 'Indian Summer' to remember. It's been a 'Canadian Summer', a 'Canadian Summer' to be reckoned with.

From *Trickster Beyond 1992: Our Relationship*

If you have not learned from your foolishness, you will remain foolish
all your life.   —Alexander Wolfe, *Earth Elder Stories*

When men no longer believe in us we are dead.   —Maori myth

He is like me, a Trickster, a liar . . . a new kind of man is coming,
a White Man.   —Iktomi

I

          and with the altitude scream

from the north
he approaches,
coming in from
'the other side'   5

he nods
and seats himself
as people gather

we sit with dry
prairie grass atop   10
a rocky hill

LET'S BE OUR
TRICKSTERS say i

into animals
change we, in all   15
directions, race
over the earth

me, northwest over the
prairie, running like
a wolf/coyote and rabbit   20

you coming up behind
me to over take

then momentum i change

and soar upward through
layers of clouds, i can   25
not see, not see,
and with the altitude
scream,
turn flight horizontal
i and scream again   30
i through clouds

what is this, why is
this screaming?

is it raven? no?

it is eagle   35
it is me

        · · ·

3

      what happened to you?
i figured you
got scared
i figured you
ran off   5

i figured you
left us to face
those white men
all by ourselves

that made me mad   10
'cause every
where i looked

there was more
heart break
than happiness   15

i thought THAT
GODDAMN NANABUSH
WHERE IS HE WHEN
WE NEED HIM

you were always   20
around back then,
the stories say so

and Coyote and Hare
and Raven finished
their work, but   25

you, what ever
happened to you,
TRICKSTER

you left us dangling
in mid-air   30
with those missionaries,
politicians and other
Christians snapping
at our heels

well, i never saw   35
Santa Claus either
goodness knows i tried

to be a good child

then i found Christmas
goodies stacked in my   40
parents' bedroom cupboard

there was Jesus Christ too
and his blessed mother
these people were good as gold
but didn't know a thing   45

about INDIANS
nor really cared to

anyway, Nanabush
i figured you
turned coward   50

        .   .   .

11

THE WHITE MAN'S BURDEN

I
burden—something
carried, a load, heavy
responsibility or anxiety

the white man's burden
(as he sees it)   5
to spread culture
among the primitive
(indigenous)
peoples of the world

the white man's burden   10
(as we know it)
a heavy load
that he does not
have to carry

II

the white man's solution   15
to the white man's burden
            No. 1
(as he sees it)

WHITE OUT[1]

to lose visibility   20
because of snow or fog;
to create
or leave white
white   spaces in
the white man's solution   25
to the white man's burden
            No. 2
(as he sees it)

WHITE OUT

1 *Collins English Dictionary.*

an atmospheric con-   30
condition con-
consisting of
lack of visibility
visibility and sense
sense (less   35
less humour sense
less humour)
h a h a h a
lack of sense
sense of dis-   40
tance, sense of
distance and
distance and di-
direct
direction   45
direction direction
take or give
lack of visibility and
sense of distance and
direction due to doo doo   50
dog doo doo
it's everywhere
due to due north south
east west due to
uni-   55
universal glo
bal village
(we all bleed red blood)
uni-
form uniform   60
uniform white
white nest
(How would you feel
if suddenly,
out of the blue,   65
a little brown
baby bird
got plopped down
in your white
feathered nest?)[2]   70
white nest

2 Daniel David Moses, a radioscript.

whiteness
of a heavy cloud (head
in the clouds) cover and
snow-covered ground (zero),   75
which reflects
reflects reflects
reflects almost all
almost all light
it receives.   80

the white man's solution
to the white man's burden
        No. 3
(as he sees it)

WHITE WASH   85

dye
die
die hard
di
direct direct cur   90
rent
(pay the rent or get out)
die out
dying race
run Indian run   95
dye die di
direct cur
(oh you dog you)
direct cur current
direct current   100
DC AC/DC
dece
ease
(easy)
dis   105
ease
dece
eve

deceptive
specious   110
(capricious)

words or act
(Indian)
actions
intended to con   115
ceal defects, gloss
(loss)
over over
(t) fee
lings   120

the white man's solution
to the white man's burden
        No. 4
(as he sees it)

WHITE WASH   125

to white(n)
with white(wash)

—a little soap,
a little water and a
good scrubbing will make   130
things clear, whiter
My poor cousin Betsy became
a ward
(award?)
of the Children's Aid.   135
Her foster mother insisted
on bathing her every day and
scrubbed her with a brush.

Hallelujah!
Praise the Lord!   140
Clorox bleach gets whites whiter.
Amen.   Amen.
Aye men.

How would you feel if
a little brown baby bird   145
plopped down in your nest?

How about a whole
nest of brown baby birds?

Know what happens
when you throw shit   150
on little brown baby birds?
They GROW UP . . . AND
COULD SCARE YOU!

the white man's solution
to the white man's burden   155
            No. 5
(as he sees it)

WHITE PAPER[3]

document outlining
government policy   160
and possible
action, including
legislation. White
Papers can be less
embarrassing   165
than legislation

                        9
                      6 9
                    9 6 9
                  1 9 6 9   170
        W H I T E   P A P E R
                  1 9 6 9
                    9 6 9
                      6 9
                        9   175

W H I T E
    W H I T E M A N
            W H I T E M A N-I Z E
        F A N T A S I Z E
        D R E A M O N   180
D R E A M

the white man's solution
to the white man's burden

---

3 Hurtig's *The Canadian Encyclopedia.*

No. 6
(as we know it)   185

PUT DOWN THE LOAD, STUPID

.   .   .

12

HOW TO CATCH A WHITE MAN
(OOPS) I MEAN TRICKSTER.

First, find yourself a forest. Any stand of ancient trees will do; in fact, the older the better. Stand in the middle of it and tell your stories. Soon the white man! (I mean Trickster) will come by, carrying a big pack on his back. In that pack he carries the voices of his women and the voices of other people he has walked over with his long legs. 'I'm going to tell those stories for you,' he'll say. 'You're far too primitive to tell them yourself. I am going to let the world know what you think. I am going to tell the world how you think when you think. And I'm going to build a golf course here, too. These trees are so old, and besides you're not using them trees.'

Tell him you heard some people talking about better stories and a better place for a golf course, perhaps even a h-y-d-r-o e-l-e-c-t-r-i-c dam, or two. Say, you could even push for a super fantasyland golf course. Anyhow, tell him he could make the stories into TV movies, docudramas, feature films. He could write novels using the stories. He could receive all kinds of literary awards for his great imagination, with these stories. He could even achieve world acclaim for telling others how it is with the 'Native Indian'. (God, how I hate that word 'Indian'.)

Okay, then tell him to wait there while you'll go find out more about those stories and that other place. He'll say, 'Okay, but come right back.' Only don't go back.

Find another forest and dig a big big hole in the middle of it, beside a pine tree. Then climb up and sit in the branches of that tree and call out saying, 'Hey, white man! (I mean Trickster. You could call him a trickster, you know. He's like that, clever. But he's not smart.) These stories are not for you, and you can't build your golf course here either.'

It won't be long and he'll come by with that great big pack and this time with his guns and tanks, too—ready to take those stories—ready to build his golf course.

Then you tell him from that tree you can see, hear everything all over the world, and know exactly what's going on, too. He'll say, 'That's new to me.' Ask him if he would like to see these things, too. Of course, he'll say, 'Yes.' Tell him to leave his heavy pack at the bottom of the tree. He won't. He'll climb up into that tree with his weapons, too. Ask him if he's comfortable. He'll say, 'I'm comfortable anywhere.' Be careful now because he'll want to sit right on top of you.

Now, tell him to close his eyes. He has to close his eyes if he is to know and see all the things you do. He has to listen to the trees and grass. Tell him it takes a while for the vision to come clear, and he should sit quietly and wait and listen. As soon as his eyes are closed, run away and watch. Get other people to watch, too. And the children. Don't forget about the children.

Of course, that man won't see anything. Never did. And he certainly won't hear anything. Never has. And after a bit he'll become uncomfortable, restless, impatient and he'll cock his gun and open his eyes. When he sees you are gone he'll get mad as heck and fall out of the tree, shooting himself in the foot, dropping his great pack and tumbling into the hole, his foot in his mouth.

That's when you run over and grab his great pack, open it up and set free the voices of the people he has walked over and the voices of his women.

Now that white man (I mean Trickster) will scramble. And he'll fight, digging himself deeper into the hole, but he won't ever get out this time. His women will see to that. Then tell the children. Teach them. Teach them the history of this land, the real history, before 1492 and since. Those stories will guide them into the next 500 years. Tell them not to do as the Trickster (I mean white man) has done. And tell them to listen to the trees and grass. The trees and the grass hold on to heaven for us.

· · ·

16

TRICKSTERS

A WORN ROCKY HILL
JUST AFTER SUNRISE.

FOCUS ON

a cluster of ancient rock amid clumps of   5
dry prairie grass.

WIDER ANGLE

now includes an assemblage of larger
rocks (cairns), a medicine wheel spoke,
and reveals that we are at the centre of a   10
hillock.

OFF CENTRE to the right, a ghostly
FIGURE approaches from the north,
coming in from 'The Other Side' and
becoming more visible—wearing a single   15
braid, the man is dressed in a country-
plaid shirt, denim jeans and cowboy
boots. He nods and seats himself.

Over this, we HEAR

the rustling approach of others, men and   20
women. They gather closely, not speak-
ing, sit and remain unseen.

NEW ANGLE

shows the complete assembly within the
medicine wheel and the LEADER, a   25
woman, sitting in the centre, faces north.

We HEAR only the whisper of wind
through the grass, then

> LEADER
> Let's be our Tricksters.   30

There is a CLAMOUR of consent, an
awareness of metamorphosis as human
utterances warp into animal intonations.

> CUT TO:

LEADER'S POINT OF VIEW (POV)   35

the peripheral landscape springs down
the hillock into distortion as the prairie
plunges into high-speed visual images,
while the northwest horizon floats in the
distance.   40

We hear PANTING.

CUT TO:

AERIAL VIEW

of assembly, all animal tricksters, some
still part human, all bounding out from   45
the hub of the medicine wheel and radi-
ating out over the prairie.

CUT TO:

Leader, in incomplete transfiguration,
racing northwest like a wolf, a coyote, a   50
rabbit.

CLOSE IN TO

OVER THE SHOULDER SHOT

of Leader in lower left foreground of
frame. Directly behind and gaining, a   55
larger wolf threatens to overtake.

DISSOLVE TO:

LEADER'S POV

a view of the prairie rim and skyline. The
horizon BLURS and crests skyward pene-   60
trating cloud strata.

Over this, we HEAR the Leader shriek as if
in horror and pain.

There is a sense of flight becoming hori-
zontal into cloud strata followed by   65
waves of myopic blurring.

As the clouds give way to the blinding
shimmer of sunlight, we HEAR the Leader
shriek again.

There is another bank of clouds; another   70
shriek, intonation uncertain and more like
the RAUCOUS CRY of a raven/eagle.

                    CUT TO:

CLOSE SHOT

SCREAMING EAGLE   75

                    CUT TO:

EAGLE'S POV

the medicine wheel, now a delicate
pattern etched on an expansive prairie.
Some animal tricksters are still visible,   80
still running.

A PANORAMIC VIEW closing in on the
medicine wheel.

REVERSE ANGLE

in a now-clear sky, barely visible, is the   85
Eagle riding the currents of air, circling
slowly northwest—

We HEAR her exalted cry.

John McLeod 1949–?

MISSISSAUGA

John McLeod was born in Oakville, Ontario, but lived most of his life, as he explained, in 'what is now known as The City of Mississauga (correctly pronounced Miss-is-aw-gee). I am a Mississauga Tribesman by birth, a Treaty Indian and a member of the Alderville Band by law.'

McLeod wrote stories and cartoons that began to appear in Native journals such as the *Ontario Indian* and the *Toronto Native Times* in the early 1970s. He describes his first work, 'The Shivering Tree', as 'a quasi-traditional work, a working together of old traditional tales and a few small products of my own imagination. That, I believe, is what storytelling (I told the story before I wrote it) is all about.' McLeod also produced a play, *Diary of a Crazy Boy*, which was produced by Native Earth and enjoyed a strong run in Toronto; it was published by Theatrum.

McLeod once described himself as 'a cranky, bookish bachelor whose hobbies include Canadian military history (there's a strong military streak in my family. I'm a son, nephew, and grandson of war veterans), studies of espionage, and paleontology. I'm also a collector of Yardbird recordings. (Make that re-recordings in view of my financial situation.)' He went on to add: 'I don't own a working typewriter.'

The Shivering Tree

Nanabush was walking; he'd been walking a long time. He'd been walking a long time and he was feeling very tired and thirsty.

'My, my, my,' Nanabush said to himself, 'I've been walking a long time and boy oh boy am I tired and thirsty. It's a good thing I'm such a smart fellow and decided to follow this river. This way, if I get lost, I'll still know where I am even though I won't.'

And he liked what he said to himself.

'Goodness me but I'm a bright fellow,' Nanabush said to himself. And he had to stop in his tracks and smile and just shake his head, he was just so proud of himself for what he'd just said just before telling himself how bright he was.

'Well, Nanabush, you bright fellow, let's go down to the river and have a drink and rest our old bones for a year or two . . . heh, heh,' Nanabush said to himself. And he agreed.

Feeling very proud of himself, Nanabush strutted down to the river. It wasn't far at all and when he got there Nanabush took a good long drink, threw some water in his face, and lay back on the sandy bank.

'It certainly is a big world,' he thought. 'Somewhere to the west of here are the Tall Mountains that mark the approach of the Home of the West Wind. Someday I'll go there, for I've a score to settle with that Old Fellow.'

That's when his quick ears caught another sound above the voice of the river. It was another voice, a man's voice.

Nanabush sat up, fast.

'A man?' Nanabush thought. 'That just can't be. No human being has come this far.'

But it was a man. At least it looked like one. But that meant nothing back in those times; after all, Nanabush looked like a man—most of the time. But Nanabush was far from being human. But just who or what was this fellow anyway?

Like I said, the stranger looked human at least. He was tall and thin, clad in buckskins with long fringe that fluttered and shivered in the breeze. He wore warm leggings and moccasins as it was autumn and the weather getting colder.

The stranger was juggling something. Now that was interesting.

He was juggling with his eyes closed. And that was mighty interesting.

Nanabush stood up, slowly, never taking his eyes off the juggling stranger.

'Hello, Nanabush,' The Juggler said, still juggling, his eyes still shut firmly. 'It is Nanabush, isn't it?'

Nanabush felt insulted.

'Of course I'm Nanabush,' Nanabush said. 'Who else could I be?'

The Juggler, eyes still firmly shut, still juggling what now appeared to be a pair of small crystals, just smiled.

'Well, let me see now,' The Juggler said, still juggling, his eyes still shut firmly. 'You could be Me, seeing as I'm the only person in these parts, but as you are you and not me and I'm here to see it, I guess I'm me and you're you and you must be Nanabush, because I've heard you've been spotted in these parts and I'm the only person here who would have heard about you besides you.'

Nanabush glared at The Juggler.

'It's a fortunate thing for you that I'm such a clever fellow,' Nanabush said, 'because if I wasn't I might've been confused by what you just said and I'd've become very angry.'

The Juggler just kept on juggling, eyes closed and all.

Nanabush felt himself getting impatient.

'Well?' Nanabush said. 'Are you going to tell me who you are?'

With a big, wide grin, The Juggler stopped what he was doing, opened his eyes, and turned to Nanabush.

'Very well,' The Juggler said, 'I'm a juggler and conjuror and I am known as Restless As The Wind; but most people just call me The Juggler.'

'I have never heard of you,' Nanabush said. He didn't like this fellow at all. No sir, Nanabush didn't like him at all.

'I was just playing around with a couple of pieces of crystal,' The Juggler said. 'That was nothing at all. That was just ordinary juggling that a child can do, eyes closed or not. Just watch. I'll show you some real conjuring . . . Look, Nanabush, look.'

Quick as lightning, The Juggler plucked out his own eyes and started to juggle them, rapidly from hand to hand. He started to dance, leaping into the air, all the while juggling his eyes hand to hand, back and forth, back and forth, hand to hand.

Nanabush was stunned, couldn't move.

Now that in itself was something. It takes a great deal to shake up someone like Nanabush, and everyone knows that there just isn't anyone to compare with The Great Nanabush.

The Juggler kept it up. Juggling, hand to hand, back and forth, back and forth, hand to hand, dancing, leaping, juggling. Juggling his eyes.

'Stop,' Nanabush said, shouting. 'Stop, you're making me dizzy . . . *stop it.*'

And, just as quickly as he had started, The Juggler stopped, came to a halt just like that, arms out wide, head back, just in time for his eyes to fall right straight into their sockets.

Nanabush's own eyes almost fell out, he stared so hard.

The Juggler grinned: boy did he grin.

Nanabush still couldn't stop staring.

I don't blame The Great Nanabush one bit, my friends. A sight like that would be enough to jar anyone's preserves.

'Now that is most certainly conjuring at its best,' Nanabush said, 'and you may take that as the word of the very one who invented conjuring.'

The Juggler grinned.

'Well, Great Nanabush, Father of Conjuring. Perhaps I can show my gratitude, indeed the gratitude of all of us Conjurors,' The Juggler said, smiling. 'Allow me to show you how it's done. Allow me to show you how to juggle one's own eyes in one's own hands.'

Now that got to Nanabush. For great and powerful as he can be, Nanabush can make the odd blunder now and then, and when he does, it's usually a bad one. This was going to be one of the worst.

'I'm flattered,' Nanabush said, smiling like a proud father. 'And I'm never too old to learn.'

How true that was. Nanabush was about to learn a lesson that he and we are never going to forget.

'Will you allow me, then, to show you how it is done?' The Juggler said, smiling.

'The honour will be mine,' Nanabush said, stepping forward. 'Show me how it's done, Nephew.'

'Removing the eyes is the really dangerous part,' The Juggler said. 'You have to apply some pressure just below each eye, like this.'

The Juggler demonstrated how it was supposed to be done. Using his thumbs, he applied some pressure underneath his eye-sockets, and . . . POP . . . out came the eyes. Very quickly, but carefully, he caught the eyes and, quickly and just as carefully, placed them back in his sockets.

'Did you see that?' The Juggler said. 'Now, very carefully, 'cause it's just the first time, try it yourself and on yourself. Not too fast. This is only the First Lesson.'

Nanabush placed his thumbs under his eye-sockets, carefully applied some pressure.

'Good, good . . . that's good,' The Juggler said, directing and urging Nanabush. 'Careful now . . . be very careful.'

Then . . . POP . . . out came Nanabush's eyes . . . Then . . . WHOOSH out shot The Juggler's right hand and grabbed Nanabush's eyes in mid-air.

'I've got them . . . HA HA. I've got them,' The Juggler cried, leaping into the air and spinning like a top. 'I've got the most powerful charms of any conjuror in The North. I have the very eyes of Nanabush . . . HA HA I have them.'

Then, as quick as lightning, The Juggler turned and ran, ran faster than he'd ever run in his life, for Nanabush is still Nanabush, blind or not.

But Nanabush was blind. Even before The Juggler turned and ran, Nanabush had made a lunge forward, instinctively knowing that something had gone wrong.

As The Juggler ran off, laughing and whooping, Nanabush landed, face down in the river. Almost immediately, he was on his feet. Almost immediately he was the real Nanabush. He stood still, turned his fear into caution.

'I've been a fool, a vain, yes . . . even a blind fool. With both my eyes in my head, I was blind,' he said to himself. He stood still, silent. He listened. He began to take his bearings.

The river was in front of him. He turned his back to it.

'Until I regain my sight . . . and I will regain my sight, I must feel my way about. I also need a weapon which I can use easily and quickly should one of my old enemies come upon me,' Nanabush said to himself. 'A staff, that's it. A big heavy staff, sharpened at one end; it'll act as a cane and a weapon. I must find my way to the bush.'

So, stumbling over bits of driftwood and rocks, falling painfully but always getting right back up on his feet, Nanabush made his way towards the bush, feeling his way with his hands, carefully keeping his ears open for every sound.

'If a friend finds me, may he truly be a friend,' Nanabush said. 'If an enemy should come upon me, may he act with honour. If my enemy should save me, I will gladly be in his debt. If my enemy finds me and chooses to kill me, then fine, I will still owe him something, if only a good fight.'

All around him was darkness. But he knew that to be a false darkness. The birds still sang and the warmth of the sun made itself felt on his body and he knew it to be daylight and he knew himself to be in full view of friend, foe, and stranger alike. But he stumbled on, into the bush. He knew he was in the bush, for he smelt pine needles and the odour of fallen leaves. He bent over and felt a pine cone beneath his hand.

'I must find a stout pole to carve into a pointed staff,' he said, feeling about, moving more cautiously than before.

The forest was thick, for he continually bumped into trees and stumps.

'Trees, stumps, but no limbs of any good size,' he thought. 'At least one old enemy of mine has been at work here, Old Man Beaver and his clan.'

Then his left hand touched on something, a young fallen tree. This was it. He ran his hands up and down the narrow trunk. This was exactly what he wanted. He pulled out his knife after using his great strength to break off an appropriate length of trunk. Carefully, he sat down and carefully, very carefully, he began to carve.

A staff alone won't be enough. Nanabush knew that. He'd have to find help from someone who knew the country, someone he could trust, someone who could be trusted as a guide.

But Nanabush had to concentrate on his carving. He had to be really, really careful or, in his blindness, he might cut a finger or two off.

So far, he hadn't given a thought to The Juggler.

He kept on carving, clumsily but carefully.

Then, suddenly, he stopped. Stopped everything. He had a strong feeling that he was being watched. He tightened his grip on the knife.

Though he had no eyes with which to see, he still instinctively moved his head back and forth as if scanning the area around him. He was certain that he was being watched. The feeling was even stronger.

Then he heard the voice, a deep clear voice, from somewhere above him.

'Well?' The Voice said, 'Why have you stopped? You were doing well.'

Knife in hand, Nanabush leaped to his feet.

'Who is there?' he snapped. 'If you're an enemy, come out and fight.'

'Fight?' The Voice said. 'I thought you were busy working with that piece of wood.'

Nanabush recognized the voice. It was indeed the voice of an enemy; a very old enemy, too.

'Owl, so it's you,' Nanabush said, more on his guard than ever. 'Well. What are you waiting for? Come and fight.'

'I'm an old warrior, not an old fool,' Owl said. 'There's a thousand eyes in these woods. If I fought you and if I slew you in the condition which you are in the whole of Creation would hear of it. You'd be honoured. I'd be disgraced.

'No, Nanabush. I'm no coward. I may be your enemy, but I would like to think that I'm a worthy enemy.

'Lower your weapon. There is no danger from me, you have my word as a Warrior and as the head of my clan.'

Nanabush, on hearing this solemn oath, placed his knife back into its sheath.

'I know that you're blind,' said the Owl. 'So will others and soon, Nanabush. Others who may not be so generous. Something must be done to restore your vision to you.'

'I'll find a way myself,' said Nanabush. 'I'm already far too much in debt to you, Owl.'

'Not if we decide to be friends,' Owl said. 'I am willing, for I wish there to be peace for my children. If you agree, then it's done.'

'Then it's done,' Nanabush said.

Their friendship sealed, the two began to talk of Nanabush's trouble.

'There is a way to restore your vision,' Owl said. 'I will give you a pair of eyes. I will give you my eyes.'

'But Owl, my friend. That will leave you with no eyes. You will be as blind as I now am,' Nanabush said.

The Owl shook his head. If he could have smiled, he would have.

'Oh no, not me,' Owl said. 'You see, Nanabush, I have two sets of eyes. One set for daytime and another set for night. As most of my enemies are daylight hunters like the hawk, I'll do my hunting at night from now on. During the day, I'll rest and stay safely with my family. I'll need only one set of eyes then. The other set I give to you.'

Owl told Nanabush to hold out his hands. Nanabush did so, and a pair of eyes dropped into Nanabush's hands. Then . . . POP . . . Nanabush dropped the eyes into his own sockets.

'They are perfect, Owl,' Nanabush said, joyously but seriously, as befits a Warrior.

'From this day, Owl, the night is yours,' Nanabush declared. 'From this day and for all time, you will be the Bird of The Night. You will be my eyes at night. At night your vision will be sure and your flight safe and clear. You will be to night as the Eagle and the Falcon are to the daylight. You'll rule the night skies. And out of respect for the great favour you have done for me, all who hear you call at night shall show their respect. They must not mimic your call if they hear you; that is to say, they will not answer your call. For them to do so would be to mock you. Your call will be my message in the night that I, Nanabush, never sleep but with my ears open, that even at night I watch those whom I protect, and that I keep a watch out for those who would do harm to The Creation. So call out at night, Owl, my friend and my Emissary.'

Their friendship sealed for all time, Owl and Nanabush bade each other good hunting and a long life. And so they parted, Owl with his new honours, Nanabush with his new eyes.

Springtime.

Springtime, and Nanabush was home. New eyes and everything. 'The World is very beautiful this day,' Nanabush said to himself as he walked along. 'All is green and fragrant with new life and the birds are back. Yes, this is truly a beautiful day.'

'Can't wait till the butterflies come out,' Nanabush said. 'My, but it's a wonderful day. Good thing that I have my eyes to see it all.'

Then came that little voice that is sometimes to be heard in the back of Nanabush's mind. 'Ah, Nanabush, but they weren't always your eyes, were they?' Nanabush remembered, of course. He remembered where his new eyes had come from and he remembered also what had happened to his old eyes. For the first time in months he thought of The Juggler. That ruined his day.

'The Juggler,' Nanabush thought. 'If I ever again meet up with that thieving rascal, he will regret the day his parents met. He will need more than an extra pair of eyes when I get through with him.'

His day was ruined, he sat down and sulked. He couldn't help but think of The Juggler, couldn't think of anything else.

In the days which followed, Nanabush was obsessed with his strange enemy. He talked of little else. He began to worry his friends and his family.

His Grandmother advised him to stop thinking about The Juggler.

'You still have a great deal of work to do in this world,' Grandmother said. 'You've much to do. You are the teacher, the helper of all living things. Go about your work, Grandson. Don't seek out enemies. They will find you soon enough if they are not cowards.'

So Nanabush carried on as always. Sometimes sure of himself, sometimes blundering, but always leaving his mark somewhere, somehow, on the world around him, making it more and more like the world we know today.

Then, one afternoon in late summer, he felt in need of a drink of water. He was deep in the woods at this time, but he knew where there was a clear, cold pool of water not far from where he stood. Picking up his kit, he made his way through the bush. He'd just about reached the pool when he saw, through the bushes around him, that another was at the pool.

A man.

A tall, thin man.

A tall thin man who was juggling a pair of crystals hand to hand, back and forth, hand to hand, back and forth.

Nanabush's eyes narrowed; he clenched his teeth.

'I must think this out,' Nanabush said to himself. 'I must think quickly, though. I may not get another chance at this rascal; besides, in addition to being my enemy, he's a Sorcerer and a dangerous one. Who is to tell how much damage he has done to others besides me? This fellow is very dangerous and I must do something about him.'

Quickly and quietly, as only he can do it, Nanabush changed his appearance. He took on the appearance of an old man. Then he stepped out into the open.

The Juggler gave him a quick glance but kept right on juggling.

'Good day, Old One,' The Juggler said. 'I'd wish you long life but it seems a good number have already done so.'

'So they have, Nephew,' Nanabush said. 'And they did so out of respect.'

'Forgive me if I sound disrespectful,' The Juggler said, continuing to juggle, 'but I'm a very happy fellow these days and I sometimes don't give thought to what I'm saying. It could be that you've heard of me. I'm The Juggler. My name is Restless As The Wind.'

'So,' Nanabush said. 'You are the fellow Nanabush is looking for, the one who stole Nanabush's eyes.'

'That's me all right, Old One,' The Juggler said. 'Tell Nanabush if you like to. Maybe I'll take his ears this time.'

'He'll find you without my telling him,' Nanabush said, trying to hold back a smile. 'He is no longer blind, by the way. A friend gave him a new pair of eyes.'

The Juggler stopped his juggling.

Nanabush, still looking like an Old Man, stepped over to the pool and took a drink of water.

'So, he's got new eyes, has he?' The Juggler said, trying not to sound as scared as he was beginning to feel. 'Well, good for him. If he comes to me, I just might take his new eyes, too. I did it before and I can do it again.'

Nanabush stood up.

'So you're a mighty, powerful fellow?' Nanabush said. 'You think that you can beat Nanabush?'

'I am a Great Sorcerer,' The Juggler said. 'I can defeat anything or anyone.'

'Can you beat me?' Nanabush said.

'Anyone or anything,' The Juggler said, trying very hard to sound brave.

'I've heard that you can juggle with your eyes out of your head. That you don't need eyes to see,' Nanabush said.

The Juggler grinned, popped out his own eyes, and juggled them, hand to hand, back and forth, hand to hand, back and forth. Then he stopped, threw his head back. Then he tossed his eyes into the air. Up went his eyes, down they came and . . . plunk . . . landed safely in their sockets.

'Is that good enough for you, Old One?' The Juggler said, grinning at Nanabush.

But it wasn't Nanabush as an old man standing there. It was Nanabush as The Juggler remembered him.

'Well. If it isn't The Great Nanabush himself,' The Juggler said, grinning and try-ing to sound (and feel) braver than he really was.

'I've already seen that trick,' Nanabush said. And he was grinning too.

'So, Nanabush, are you tired of your new pair of eyes already?' The Juggler said. 'If you want to save us both time and work, you can just hand your eyes over to me right now.'

'If you really want my eyes, you're going to have to work for them, Nephew,' Nanabush said.

'Fine by me. Just tell me how,' The Juggler said.

'Very good, Nephew. Nothing fancy—I'll toss my eyes to you and you catch them,' Nanabush said. 'If you catch them, you get to keep them. If you miss you won't owe me a thing. All or nothing. Fair enough.'

'Too easy,' The Juggler said. 'No real challenge. Tell you what, Nanabush. I'll seal my eyes shut. How does that sound?'

'Fine by me, Nephew,' Nanabush said. 'But I warn you. I'm going to be throwing from quite a distance, from the very rim of the world itself.'

'Ha. Go to the rim of the world. Even that wouldn't be far enough. I'd know when it's coming. I'll just stand here and wait. You're the one who'll have all the work to do. If you want to walk all the way to the edge of Creation just to toss a couple of eyes, that's fine by me, I'll catch them. I never miss,' The Juggler said proudly.

With a shrug of his shoulders, The Juggler obtained some sap from a nearby tree. This sap he used to seal his eyes shut. Then he stood calmly and with very great confidence.

'Well, Nanabush. I'm ready if you are. Be on your way. It's a long walk, but I'll wait. When victory is a sure thing, I can wait,' The Juggler said. Then he folded his arms in front of his chest and said no more.

Nanabush walked away.

Nanabush walked away, but not to the rim of the world. He just plain walked away and didn't look back.

Nanabush went about his work of making the world what it was meant to be. He never gave The Juggler another thought. Why?

Because Nanabush knew that The Juggler, like all Sorcerers, was a vain fellow more than eager to show off his power no matter how long it took. The Juggler said he'd wait and so he did.

He's still waiting. And he will wait for all time, until The End of Time. Oh, it's not at all difficult to find him. He's very well known. He's easily recognizable.

His name, you recall, is Restless As The Wind. It's a very descriptive name. He's still to be seen standing, day in, day out, standing, rooted to the spot, his fringes and hair swaying and shivering constantly in the wind, at the slightest breeze or draught. Even when the air is perfectly still.

To pass the long hours away, you see, The Juggler, Restless As The Wind, has taken the form of a tree. A tree that never rests, whose leaves and branches still shake and shiver even when the air is still and quiet.

He's become the Shivering Tree.

The Poplar Tree.

And that's the way it is to this good day.

Beatrice Mosionier *b.* 1949

MÉTIS

Born in St Boniface, Manitoba, Beatrice Mosionier (formerly Culleton) was the youngest of four children of Louis and Mary Clara Mosionier. At the age of three, she was taken by the Children's Aid Society of Winnipeg to grow up in foster homes, away from her family and her people, with the exception of several years when she lived in one foster home with one of her older sisters. Two of her sisters committed suicide.

Her first novel, *In Search of April Raintree* (1983), based largely on her life experience, was welcomed by the Native community as part of its healing process and was reissued in 1984 as *April Raintree*. Mosionier has also worked in Native publishing; has written books for children, *Spirit of the White Bison* (1985) and *Christopher's Folly* (1996); and has scripted *Walker* (1991), a short film for the National Film Board. Her most recent publication, *In the Shadow of Evil* (2001), is a mystery that continues to explore her concerns with race and gender.

From *April Raintree*

Our free, idle days with our family came to an abrupt end one summer afternoon. We came home and there were some cars in front of our house. One had flashing red lights on it and I knew it was a police car. When we entered the house, Mom was sitting at the table, openly weeping right in front of all the strangers. There were empty medicine bottles on the small counter and the table. I couldn't figure out why the four people were there. A nice-smelling woman knelt down to talk to me.

'My name is Mrs Grey. I bet you're April, aren't you? And this little girl must be Cheryl.' She put her hand on Cheryl's head in a friendly gesture, but I didn't trust her.

I nodded that we were April and Cheryl but I kept my eyes on my mother. Finally, I asked, 'Why is Mom crying? Did you hurt her?'

'No, dear, your mother is ill and she won't be able to take care of you any more. Would you like to go for a car ride?' the woman asked.

My eyes lit up with interest. We'd been in a taxi a few times, and it had been a lot of fun. But then I thought of Baby Anna. I looked around for her. 'Where's Anna?'

'Anna's sick,' the woman answered. 'She's gone to the hospital. Don't worry, we'll take you for a ride to a nice clean place. You and Cheryl, okay?'

That was not okay. I wanted to stay here. 'We can stay with Daddy. He will take care of us. You can go away now,' I said. It was all settled.

But Mrs Grey said in a gentle voice, 'I'm afraid not, honey. We have to take you and Cheryl with us. Maybe if your Mommy and Daddy get well enough, you can come to live with them again.'

The man who was with Mrs Grey had gone to our bedroom to get all our things. When he came back, I became more uneasy. I looked from the woman to the man, then over to one policeman who was writing in a notepad, then to the other one who was looking around. I finally looked back at my Mom for reassurance. She didn't look at me but I said in a very definite manner, 'No, we'd better stay here.'

I was hoping Dad would walk in and he would make them all go away. He would make everything right.

The man with our belongings leaned over and whispered to my mother. She forced herself to stop sobbing, slowly got up and came over to us. I could see that she was struggling to maintain control.

'April, I want you and Cheryl to go with these people. It will only be for a little while. Right now, Daddy and me, well, we can't take care of you. You'll be all right. You be good girls for me. I'm sorry . . .'

She couldn't say any more because she started crying again. She hugged us and that's when I started crying too. I kind of knew that she was really saying goodbye to us. But I was determined that we were not going to be taken away. I clung to my Mom as tight as I could. They wouldn't be able to pull me away from her and then they would leave. I expected Mom to do the same. But she didn't. She pushed me away. Into their grasping hands. I couldn't believe it.

Frantically, I screamed, 'Mommy, please don't make us go. Please, Mommy? We want to stay with you. Please don't make us go.'

I tried hard to put everything into my voice, sure that they would all come to their senses and leave us be. There were a lot of grown-up things I didn't understand that day. My mother should have fought with her life to keep us with her. Instead, she simply handed us over. It didn't make any sense to me.

The car door slammed shut on us.

'Please don't make us go,' I said in a subdued, quiet voice, more to myself. I gripped Cheryl's hand and we set off into the unknown. We were both crying and ignored the soothing voices from the strangers in front.

How could Mom do this to us? What was going to happen to us? Well, at least, I still had Cheryl. I thought this to myself over and over again. Cheryl kept crying, although I'm not sure she really knew why. She loved car rides but if I was crying, I'm sure she felt she ought to be crying too.

We were taken to an orphanage. When we got there, Cheryl and I were hungry and exhausted. Inside the large building, all the walls were painted a dismal green. The sounds we made echoed down the long, high-ceilinged corridors. Then this person came out of a room to greet us. She was dressed in black, from head to foot, except for some stiff white cardboard around her neck and face. She had chains dangling around her waist and she said her name was Mother Superior and she had been expecting us. My eyes widened in fear. It was even worse than I had imagined. We were being handed over to the boogeyman for sure!

When Mrs Grey and the man said goodbye and turned to leave, I wanted to go with them but I was too scared to ask. Mother Superior took us into another room at the far end of the corridor. Here, another woman in the same outfit undressed us and bathed us. She looked through our hair for bugs, she told us. I thought that was pretty silly because I knew that bugs lived in trees and grass, not in people's hair. Of course, I didn't say anything, not even when she started cutting off my long hair.

I was thinking that this was like the hen my mother had gotten once. She plucked it clean and, later, we ate it. I sat there, wondering if that was now to be our fate, wondering how I could put a stop to this. Then the woman told me she was finished and I was relieved to find that I still had some hair left. I watched her cut Cheryl's hair and reasoned that if she was taking the trouble to cut straight then we had nothing to fear. Between yawns, Cheryl complained that she was hungry so, afterward, we were taken to a large kitchen and fed some dry tasteless food. When we finished eating, we were taken to the infirmary and put to bed.

We were finally left alone to ourselves and it really did feel like we were completely abandoned in that pitch black space. Cheryl groped her way to my bed and crawled in with me. She spoke for the first time since we got here, 'Apple, them was boogeywomen?'

I smiled in the darkness for two reasons. I hadn't thought to call them that and she had been thinking the same thing I had. 'No, I don't think so. They didn't eat us,' I said to reassure her.

For a minute, she was silent. 'They didn't like us?'

'I don't know.'

After more silence, she asked, 'Apple, we will go home in the morning time?'

'I don't think so, Cheryl.'

'But I want to.'

'So do I,' I said. By now, Cheryl had laid her head down and I could hear the breathing she used for sleeping. I lay there for a while, thinking, wondering.

*　　*　　*

I wasn't really thinking about anything when I noticed my arms and hands. They were tanned a deep, golden brown. A lot of pure white people tanned just like this. Poor Cheryl. She would never be able to disguise her brown skin as just a tan. People would always know that she was part Indian. It seemed to me that what I'd read and what I'd heard indicated that Métis and Indians were inclined to be alcoholics. I guess that was because they were a weak people. Oh, they were put down more than anyone else, but then, didn't they deserve it? Anyways, I could pass for a pure white person. I could say I was part French and part Irish. If I had to, I could even change the spelling of my name. Raintree looked like one of those Indian names but if I changed the spelling to Raintry, that could pass for Irish. And when I grew up, I wouldn't be poor; I'd be rich. Being a half-breed meant being poor and dirty. It meant being weak and having to drink. It meant being ugly and stupid. It meant living off white people. And giving your children to white people to look after. It meant that kids like me had to take what kids like the DeRosiers gave, and none of that was good. Well, I wasn't going to live like a half-breed. When I got free of this place, when I got free from being a foster child, then I would live just like a real white person.

Then a question came to mind. What about Cheryl? How was I going to pass for a white person when I had a Métis sister? Especially when she was so proud of what she was? I loved her. I could never cut myself off from her completely. And she wouldn't go along with what I planned. I would never even be able to tell her what I planned. I sat there thinking but the problem wouldn't be resolved. Well, I had a long time to figure that one out. For sure, she would never turn out to be like the rest of the Métis people. She and maybe Mrs MacAdams were special people. Cheryl was already a whole lot smarter than all the rest of the kids in her class and that counted for a lot. I sighed, stood up, and stretched. Now I felt ready to face whatever the DeRosiers had in store for me. One day I would be free of them. One day . . .

*   *   *

I entered the house which now seemed so empty, so cold. I decided I would pack all of Cheryl's things away in a big trunk, even her clothes. That way I'd always have a part of her. And being able to touch her belongings would strengthen that feeling.

I opened the door to Cheryl's room and the first thing I noticed was an empty whiskey bottle. I hadn't really noticed it before when I had gone into her room, to look for addresses or names. But there it stood on Cheryl's dresser, mocking me. Suddenly, I was filled with a deep hatred of what it had once contained. I grabbed it by the neck, raised it high, and brought it down, smashing it against the edge of the dresser. Again and again, I brought it down, until it was smashed into a million pieces. I was screaming, 'I hate you! I hate you! I hate you!'

My tears came flooding out and I continued screaming, 'I hate you for what you've done to my sister! I hate you for what you've done to my parents! I hate you for what you've done to my people! Our people!'

I threw myself on Cheryl's bed, letting all my pent-up tears pour out. I pounded my fists into the bed, allowing my emotions to tumble out. I felt a frenzied rage at how alcohol had torn our lives apart, had torn apart the lives of our people. I felt angry for having done so many wrong things at so many wrong times. And I felt self-pity because I would no longer have Cheryl with me.

'Oh, Cheryl, why did you have to go and kill yourself? All those people at the funeral, they loved you so much. Didn't they count? I loved you so much. Didn't that count? Didn't it matter to you? You had so much going for you. You didn't have to kill yourself, Cheryl! Why? Why?'

I writhed on the bed as if I were in physical pain. At times I would become still, but not for long. Stronger emotions would come crashing down on me and I would toss and turn again, trying to exorcise the painful anguish from within. I pounded my fists into the bed, again and again, in frustration. 'If only . . .' Those words repeated themselves over and over in my head. But it was too late. Cheryl's death was final.

When I had spent the last of my tears, I sat on the edge of the bed and surveyed the mess I had made in the room. The floor had scattered fragments of the whiskey bottle all over it. Cheryl's pillow was soaked with my tears. I looked again at the floor. If only I could smash the problem of alcoholism as easily as I had that bottle.

Temporarily void of all emotion, I systematically began to clean the room. I put the Kleenex tissues into the garbage container. I began picking up the larger pieces of glass. I grabbed one piece a little too savagely and it cut my hand. I looked at the blood oozing out in a thin red line.

'Still after more blood, are you? Well, you cut down my sister, my parents, my people. But no more. I'll see to it. Somehow. Some way.'

When I had finished cleaning Cheryl's room, I sat down again on Cheryl's bed. I wondered where to start, not wanting to start. Then I remembered all of Cheryl's papers, the journals she had kept. There were two boxes under her bed and I began going through them. The first was full of newspaper clippings, but I wanted her journals. They were in the other box.

I began looking through them. The last entry she had made was in January 1972. That was the month I had been raped. I looked for a 1970 journal. It was this one that I was most interested in, because that was when I had first lost touch with Cheryl.

The entries for January indicated she had started the search for our parents. February had occasional references to her continued search. There was more in March.

I see more and more of what April sees, broken people with broken houses and broken furniture. The ones I see on Main Street, the ones who give us our public image, the ones I see puking all over public sidewalks, battling it out with each other, their blood smearing up city-owned property, women selling what's left of themselves for a cheap bottle of wine. No wonder April ran. She was horrified that this was her legacy. She disowned it and now she's trapped in that life of glitter and tinsel, still going nowhere. Charitable organizations! What a load of crap. Surrounded by a lot of people, business-wise but empty. Just like the Main Street bums.

The more I see of these streets, the more I wonder if April isn't right. Just maybe. Better to live that empty life than live out on the streets. What if I do find our parents? Sometimes I can't help it, I feel like April does, I despise these people, these gutter-creatures. They are losers. But there is a reason why they are the way they are. Everything they once had has been taken from them. And the white bureaucracy has helped create the image of parasitic natives. But sometimes I do wonder if these people don't accept defeat too easily, like a dog with his tail between his legs, on his back, his throat forever exposed.

April, 1970—Happy Birthday, April. What do you give the person who has everything? I can give peace of mind with a few lies.

May, 1970—Struck paydirt with a new address on Austin. The place is rented by a woman named Josie Pohequitas. I knock on the door and it is opened by this little, bent, old woman who is stoned out of her mind. But happy as hell. I have figured out by now, it's better to see these people at certain times of the day. You have to be late enough, so they can start getting over last night's drunk and early enough, so they're not whacked out of it yet. I ask if she knows Henry or Alice Raintree.

'Henri, Henri Raintree?' She says in a French-type accent.

'Yes, I'm his daughter and I've been looking for him,' I say in a pleasant, polite voice.

'Ah, yes, mais oui, we're good friends, you know. Come in. Here, sit down, here. He comes to our place when the snows are gone. He goes north for winters. He is welcome here. He stays. Sometimes, we have big party. Sometimes, we have big fight. Then he goes. But he always come back, Henri does. He will come back. You come back in a couple of weeks. You will see. He will be here then.'

I'm tickled a deeper shade of brown, you might say. I tell the toothless woman with her toothless smile that I will be back.

June, 1970—*I knock at this door again, having been here a few times with no luck and expecting none this time.*

'Ah, Cheryl, it's you again. Come in, come in,' her face lights up into a big grin, still toothless.

'Henri, Henri, come out here and see the surprise that is here for you. Hurry up, Henri,' her voice is high-pitched and squeaky. She never pronounces the 'h's.

An old, grey-haired man comes walking out of the kitchen. He is trying to keep his balance, curiosity is piercing through his drunken haze. I assume that Josie has told him about me but still it's a few minutes before he realizes it's me.

My smile disappears but a smile slowly appears on that leathery, unshaven face.

'No, no, it can't be. Not my little daughter, Cheryl. My little baby. You're all grown up now.'

He chuckles and staggers a little closer to me. He makes a visible effort to draw himself up, but he has drunk too much already and the feat is beyond him. His clothes are worn, dirty, and dishevelled. Tears of happiness and perhaps awakened guilt pour from his watery eyes.

The woman, Josie, is beaming with pride as if this 'joyful' reunion were all her doing.

'It's like a miracle. It's like a miracle,' she cackles over and over again, watching father and daughter facing each other. I am rooted to the very spot, absorbing the true picture of my father. I make no effort to move towards him. This goes unnoticed and the old man approaches me.

'I cannot believe that we are standing here, face to face, at long last. At long, long last,' the decrepit, old man says.

I stand quietly, hiding the horror which is boiling inside of me. I hadn't known what to expect. But it wasn't this, this bent, wasted human form in front of me. My father! I am horrified and repulsed; by him; by the cackling, prune-faced woman; by the others who have crawled out of the kitchen to watch all this 'happiness', all of them with stupid grins on their faces; by the surrounding decay; by the hopelessness. The cancer from the houses I've been to has spread into this house, too. To destroy.

All my dreams to rebuild the spirit of a once proud nation are destroyed in this instant. I study the pitiful creature in front of me. My father! A gutter-creature!

The imagination of my childhood has played a horrible, rotten trick on me. All these years, until this very moment, I envisioned him as a tall, straight, handsome man. In the olden days he would have been a warrior if he had been all Indian. I had made something out of him that he wasn't, never was. Now I just want to turn and run away, pretend this isn't happening, that I have never laid eyes on him. Pretend I was an orphan. I should have listened to April.

Awkwardly, he hugs me. I smell the foul stink of liquor on him. Hell, he probably sweats liquor out of his pores. I close my eyes so no one will see what's in them. I hold my breath against the gutter smell. Seems like ages before he releases me. When he does, he turns to the others and says, 'Don't just stand there, bring her a drink. Now we have something to celebrate. I found my little girl after all these years. Tell me, Cheryl, where is your sister? Where is April? I missed you both so much. Ah, here we are.'

He hands me a beer and wipes his tears and runny nose on the sleeve of his shirt. I don't answer. I just think, 'April is far away from you and she'll never know what you are, you, you gutter-creature!'

Gratefully, I swallow some beer. Disgust, hatred, shame . . . yes, for the first time in my life, I feel shame. How do I describe the feeling? I swallow more beer.

I stay for the rest of the day in spite of my desire to flee. I stay because I want to know about Mom. But I want Dad sober when I ask him about Mom. Funny, I can still refer to him as Dad. I drink away the hours and pass the dizzy, nauseous sensations, laughing stupidly with them. Josie puts me to bed, just in time, on a battered couch in the living room.

Next morning. I wait patiently for Dad to get up. It is almost noon. He comes into the kitchen. He looked in rough shape last night but now he looks worse, with his weak, flabby arms showing because he's in a torn, greyish undershirt. His dark-coloured baggy pants are held up by suspenders that are frayed to the breaking point and all twisted. I get coffee for Dad. Josie is busy puttering around the kitchen. No one talks, the only noises come from Dad slurping his coffee.

Finally, I ask him, 'Dad, could we talk?' Sounds like I'm shouting. I lower my voice. 'I want to talk about Mom. How is she? Do you see her?'

Dad makes a gesture as if he doesn't want to talk about her right now but I persist. 'Please, Dad. Tell me about Mom. Where is she?'

Tears come to his eyes again. He says simply, 'She died last July.'

'Died? Mom died?' I ask, not believing. I then figure out that Mom was in poor health when we were kids and that's why she died. I wish I could have seen her. Poor, dear mother. Maybe that's why Dad turned to booze. He misses her so much he can't live without her. I can forgive that, retract all the bad thoughts about him.

But Dad speaks again. 'I may as well tell you everything.' He sighs and lapses into another long silence.

I try to make it shorter by urging him to continue. 'Tell me what, Dad?'

'Your mother took her own life. She killed herself,' he says at last. 'She left a letter for me but I had gone up north early that year. I have a nephew in Dauphin. I stop in there sometimes. They sent the letter there. She jumped off the Louise Bridge last July. I took the letter to the RCMP and they checked with the Winnipeg police. They had found a body and everything matched your Mama. She was not happy with her life. Once she lost you girls and Anna died, she knew she would never get you girls back again. Those visits were too hard on her. So she stopped going. She tried to kill herself before, once, a long time ago.'

I digest what he says. '. . . too hard on her?' What about April and me? In those foster homes? Okay, only one was real bad and April suffered most of that one. But I suffered for April. And the other ones? Those people weren't our flesh and blood. They weren't even our race. I remember now, those promises you made us, promises we believed, all the waiting for you to take us back home, all the loyalty we gave you—all for nothing.

'Who's Anna?' I'm angry but I don't want to fight. I want information.

Dad looks at me, surprised. 'You don't know about Anna? Oh, of course not. You were just a baby yourself when she died. April must remember her. Maybe not. She was just little too, and Anna wasn't with us very long. She was your baby sister. But she was a sick baby. They should have kept her in the hospital longer, but, no, they sent her home too early and she died. They blamed your Mama and me. That was their excuse for taking you girls away from us. No, my girl, your Mama was not a happy woman.'

'Why didn't you come to see us when we were kids?' I ask in a soft voice, afraid of an honest answer.

There is another long pause. 'I went up north for a long time. I was never here to visit you again,' he says as if that's a good enough reason. 'No, your Mama did not want you girls to see the way she was. She was too ashamed. She couldn't face you again. They shouldn't have taken you away from us. The baby was just sick, that's all.' Dad drifts off into silence again.

Dad asks me to come back and see him tomorrow. I say I will. I do. Josie says Dad left that morning to see some friends of his for a few days. Here I thought he would be impatiently waiting for me. Ha! What a joke!

I sat on the bed with the journal clutched to me. This was the second mention of Anna. I'd been thinking of Anna after Cheryl had told me about her. Baby Anna. I remembered that's what I had called her. Recollections of my mother rocking a baby had come back, much clearer. I'd always had vague pictures in mind but I'd never realized the baby was our own sister. Baby Anna. She'd been with us for just a fraction of our lives. But she was sick and had to go to the hospital. And now, here, in Cheryl's journal were Dad's words saying the same thing. Baby Anna. Such a small part of our lives. Yet she had changed our lives the most.

This was exactly how Cheryl felt when she found Dad. After all that he told her, she still went back to see him the next day. She was still loyal to him. How was it she had the natural family instinct? I had instincts only for self-preservation, pushing anyone away from me who might hurt me. I was a loner. Only recently, had I let Roger in. Then Nancy and her mother, hugging me that night, giving me all that they had felt for Cheryl. Before Roger, who else besides Cheryl had hugged me and meant it? Well, maybe Mrs Dion. I remembered wishing many times that I could be as affectionate as Cheryl. That meeting with Dad, maybe it destroyed her self-image. Strange, though, since she had seen that side of native life before. I wondered what sort of image she had built up about our parents? Was it that image of long ago that had sustained her, given her hope?

February 18, 1971—So. A son is born to me. It should have been a very special day for him. A day when his aunt and grandparents and all his relatives rejoiced. Instead, it's just him and me. What's that joke I read? If he had known what was going to be in store for him, he would have cried a whole lot louder?

February 22, 1971—Having pondered over what to call you, my dear son, I've decided on Henry Liberty Raintree. May you grow up to be all that your grandfather is not.

A son? Cheryl had a son? I felt anger and bewilderment. Not at Cheryl or anyone else. The anger was for me. For being the way I was. Because it had caused Cheryl to feel so alienated from me that she couldn't share the most important event in her life with me. Henry Liberty Raintree. Then I smiled. A part of Cheryl still lived. After a while, I continued reading.

March 10, 1971—Nancy is babysitting and I'm free for a while. Feels great to be let out. Henry Lee's been so cranky lately. On top of that, we've got to move cause kids aren't allowed. Landlord's just a bigot, always looking down his nose at me when I pay the rent. I thought Henry Lee would change my life for the better but I can see I thought wrong. Must say I do feel good about this watering hole. Don't think Nancy will mind my coming home late. She'll understand.

April 8, 1971—Sure am glad Nancy's Mom is letting Henry Lee stay at her place. I'm not so tied down anymore. She sure gives him some good mothering. I don't think motherhood was meant for me. I'd rather be out partying than sitting at home changing dirty diapers.

June, 1971—Nancy's Mom is keeping Henry Lee for me for good now. Do I feel guilty? Only when I'm sober. And I try very hard to see that doesn't happen. I give her money all the time, so I'm sure she doesn't mind. Wish I had a mother like that.

October, 1971—Today Dad says he doesn't know where he is going to stay because he can't pay his rent. I know what he wants so I give him forty bucks. His eyes bulge. Usually I only give him ten or twenty.

At Decarlos with Nancy. The gang is all here, too. Already we got suckers to pay for our drinks. It's cheap coming here. I give my money to Dad so he can go get tanked and I come here and get mine free. I have to laugh at dumb jokes, let these guys run their hands up my legs. They think they're going to get more later, but I can avoid that.

Mark DeSoto. Now if all these guys were like Mark . . . but they're not. Nancy says Mark's ol' lady, Sylvia, is going to have it in for me if I hang around with Mark. He's over there at another table. He comes to say hello. I ignore him. He was supposed to call during the week and didn't. The suckers at my table are really playing up to me tonight. Got to go say hi to Marie.

I'm walking back to my table and I hear this shrill voice. 'Hey, squaw, I don't share my man with no one. You hear me? Especially no squaw.'

Sylvia comes into my path and stops. I stop. I look her in the eye. 'What's your problem, sweetheart? Can't hang on to your guy? And I ain't no squaw, I'm a half-breed.' I feel ridiculous and powerful at the same time. I know what I'm capable of. I give her my coldest stare. I know I've won this round. She can't match my gaze. The 'blond bomb-shell' jabs a finger into my shoulder, telling me what she's going to do to me. I twist around slightly and bring my fist into the side of her face, not real hard but hard enough to back her off. The dumb broad trips over a chair and sprawls on the floor. Everyone laughs, hoping for a fight. I step over her and continue on my way.

'You're going to pay for this, Cheryl.'

'Yeah? Well you'd better give it your best shot, Sylvia.'

Mark struts over to my table. My precious companions scatter. He sits down and grins. 'So you're my prize,' I say to him sarcastically. But the evening ends with Mark in my bed.

Mark moves in. Nancy moves out. Landlord requests that we remove ourselves after the first party. I find a cheap place on Elgin.

November, 1971—*I'm working. Mark is working the streets. We're always broke. I sell all the furniture, except the typewriter. I wonder why April gave it to me? She's the one with the writing talent. I give it to Nancy for safekeeping, so Mark won't sell it.*

We're stone broke. Mark owes everyone so we can't hit anyone up for a loan. Mark says to me, 'You know that guy who comes to Neptune's and he always looks the chicks over. Well he's loaded and sometimes I sit and talk to him.'

'I know who you mean. What about him? You're going to borrow some money from him?'

'He never lends money. But sometimes he sees a chick he likes and asks me if I can arrange a meeting. So, I go to her and if she's interested we share the money he pays, see?'

'You mean you're some kind of pimp?'

'Not a pimp, Cheryl. I just do two people a favour and I get some money out of it. We need money now, bad, and I know he's got the hots for you. I just thought you might consider it, just this once.'

'You're asking me to go to bed with another man?'

'Well, it's not like there's any feelings between you. Just think of it as a business transaction. I told him you were a very special girl and he's willing to pay more for you. Come on, Cheryl, one hour's work and you could make fifty bucks. I'll try to get more.'

'Forget it.' I'm bloody mad.

'I ain't no prostitute.' I storm out of the house. A week later. We're still broke. I'm drinking at Neptune's. I'm almost drunk. Mark comes over. This sucker who's been buying me drinks leaves quickly. Funny the power Mark has. 'Cheryl, please, we gotta get some money. The landlord today said he'd give us another twenty-four hours and no more.'

'Is he kinky?' I'm just dirt. Who cares if he's kinky.

Later, I'm back at Neptune's. We have our rent money now, plus some. I have a drink. Another one. Another one. My parents deserted me, April has left me, Mark . . . is a good for nothing woman user. Make that last word, abuser. I have another drink. And another one. Let Mark use me. I don't care. Let April sit in her fancy white palace. I just don't care any more.

January, 1972—*I'm an old pro now. I'm working the streets full time. I avoid the pigs by picking johns that are obviously not pigs. Well, they're pigs, too, but in another way. Mark arranges a lot of meetings, too. I've gotten into other things I bet Mrs Semple never heard of in her old 'syndrome speech'. I'm still broke. First thing Dad says when I see him is, 'Cheryl, I need twenty for groceries.'*

'I don't have any.'

He goes into a rage. 'What do ya mean, you don't have any? You got enough to go drinking but you can't spare your poor Pa any? Did that bum you're shacked up with tell you not to give me any more? You're just as bad as your ol' lady was, you know that? A lazy no good for nothing. Running around all the time, living with bums. I need some money. I need groceries and I got to pay the rent. Now I got nothing, just cause you couldn't hang onto a simple job.'

I tell him he's worse. I swear at him. I tell him what I think of him, that he's a parasite, a gutter-creature. I tell him it's his fault Mom killed herself. The tears spring to his eyes. I leave him. Let him stew in his guilt. I sure as hell stew in mine.

At home, Mark comes in. I'm angry and still brooding. Mark is angry. I'm supposed to be at Neptune's. We need money real bad. He yells. I yell. He beats me. I'm used to it. He avoids hitting my face. He has learned it's not good business. He leaves.

I walk along Main Street. This is where I belong. With the other gutter-creatures. I enter a hotel. I don't know which one. The word 'Beverage' is all I see. I need a drink. A couple of drinks. The depression is bitterly deep. The booze doesn't help this time. I'm back on the street. I'm drunk. I want to run in front of a car. The guy who was buying my drinks comes with me. What a creep. We head to my place on Elgin. We take a short-cut down a back lane. The creep wants to fondle me and kiss me. He can't wait. 'Back off, you ugly old man. I'm no whore, you know?' I don't know why I say that, but I repeat it. I can scarcely keep my balance. It's like there are two of me, one watching, one doing. 'I wanna kiss you. You know what you are. So don't pretend with me, I paid for you.'

'You stink. Leave me alone, you filthy pig!' I slur the words. He gives me a push. I slam into the wall and fall into a sitting position. My legs have given out. They're sprawled out in front of me, like they don't want to go on, any more. I close my eyes. I like the sensation of everything spinning around at full speed. I half open my eyes. I watch the man. He's looking real scared. He turns and runs, clumsily, boozily. I smile and shut my eyes again.

I come to. I'm still lying around with my legs out there in front of me, still going nowhere. I notice the garbage cans and garbage bags on either side of me. 'Hello there!' I says to them. 'I've come home. At long, long last.' I chuckle to myself. I hiccup. I chuckle some more. I think in the morning the garbage men will take us all away, me and my friends. I giggle. I try to get up. I can't. So I stay put. Every once in a while I chuckle to myself. And hum a tuneless song.

I wake up. April holding my hand. I can't see her but it's April. I squeeze her hand.

For a long time, I sat very still, thinking. Then I looked at my watch. And sighed. It was three a.m. I knew what I had to do. I knew now, why it had been so important for me to return to Nancy's place. I'd have to wait until morning. I paced around the room and finally returned to the journals. I put them back in the box and set them on the floor. Then I laid on Cheryl's bed, on top of the covers, still clothed. With my hands under my head, I stared up at the ceiling. The clock downstairs was abnormally loud and so, so slow. A few hours more and I could be on my way to Nancy's place to Henry Lee.

For the moment, I thought of Cheryl. Memories came back, memories of her voice, the memory of her reciting her powerful message at the Pow Wow. Why, oh why didn't she talk to me? Why couldn't we have talked to each other? And would it have helped? At times I was overwhelmed with her memories and tears would trickle down the sides of my face.

The next morning I woke up, dismayed that I had fallen asleep. Then I was dismayed to find it was still too early to go to Nancy's place. The sun was just beginning to rise, spreading orange yellowish hues across the skies. I went downstairs to make coffee and freshen up. My eyes felt swollen. Again the house seemed so empty, cold, lifeless. With my cup of coffee in hand, I opened the front door and stood looking out at the still empty street. The birds were just beginning to sing their morning praises to their Creator. It had rained during the night. Everything was wet. The smell of wet earth was invigorating, so clean. I stood there breathing deeply when I noticed there was a letter in the mailbox. I thought of leaving it for the moment, but didn't. The moment I saw it was Cheryl's handwriting, my heart started to pound. I tore it open and sat down, heedless of the damp step.

Dear April,
By the time you get this, I will have done what I had to do. I have said goodbye to my son, Henry Liberty. I couldn't bring myself to tell you about him before. Now I know you will do what is right where he is concerned. I also know that Mary and Nancy will do as you wish. They're taking care of Henry Lee. All my life, I wanted us to be a real family, together, normal. I couldn't even mother my own baby!
Do not feel sorrow or guilt over my death. Man thinks he can control Nature. Man is wrong. The Great Spirit has made Nature stronger than man by putting into each of us a part of Nature. We all have the instinct to survive. If that instinct is gone, then we die.
April, there should be at least a little joy in living and when there is no joy, then we become the living dead. And I can't live this living death any longer. To drink myself to sleep, day in and day out.
April, you have strength. Dream my dreams for me. Make them come true for me. Be proud of what you are, of what you and Henry Lee are. I belong with our Mother.
Love to you and Henry Lee,
Cheryl

An hour later, I was at Nancy's place once again. She opened the door for me, as if she had been expecting me right at that precise moment. I followed her down the hall to the kitchen. Sitting at the table, was a small boy eating some cereal. He looked up at me as I walked into the room. He smiled, the same kind of smile I had seen a long time ago, on his mother's face when she was that age, the age of innocence.

Nancy began explaining, but I stopped her. I told her I understood everything. As I stared at Henry Liberty, I remembered that during the night, I had used the words, 'my people, our people', and meant them. The denial had been lifted from my spirit. It was tragic that it had taken Cheryl's death to bring me to accept my identity.

But no. Cheryl had once said, 'All life dies to give new life.'

Cheryl had died. But for Henry Liberty and me, there would be a tomorrow. And it would be better. I would strive for it. For my sister and her son. For my parents. For my people.

Lee Maracle *b.* 1950

MÉTIS/SALISH

Lee Maracle was born in North Vancouver, the daughter of a Salish father and a Métis mother. Despite not finishing high school, she has become a prolific essayist, poet, and writer of both short and long prose fiction. 'The difficulty for me has been mastering a language different from my own, without having my own. Most of us learned English from parents who spoke English in translation. Many of our parents had been to residential school and thus did not speak the old language any better than the average five-year-old speaks English.'

Maracle has read widely in history—that of her own people in particular—and has studied sociology and creative writing at Simon Fraser University in British Columbia. She has taught at the University of Toronto, the University of Waterloo, and the University of Western Washington.

With her first publication, *I Am Woman* (1988), Maracle defined her way of writing as 'oratory'. 'As orators, we are not short on vocabulary. . . . Our best orators, in English or their own language, are those who have struggled with the language unencumbered by the tedious commas and colons of the English language.' Maracle's other publications include *Bobbi Lee: Indian Rebel* (1990), *Sojourner's Truth and Other Stories* (1990), *Oratory: Coming to Theory* (1990), *Sun Dogs* (1991), *Ravensong* (1993), *Bent Box* (2000), and *Daughters are Forever* (2001). She is also a co-editor of and a contributor to *Telling It: Women and Language Across Cultures* (1990).

Yin Chin

For Sharon Lee, whose real name is Sky, and Jim Wong Chu

she is tough,
she is verbose,
she has lived a thousand lives

she is sweet,
she is not,   5
she is blossoming
and dying every moment

a flower
unsweetened by rain
untarnished by simpering   10
uncuckolded by men
not coquettish enough
for say the gals
who make a career of shopping
at the Pacific Centre Mall   15

PACIFIC CENTRE, my gawd
do North Americans never tire
of claiming the centre
of the universe, the pacific and
everywhere else . . .   20

I am weary
of North Americans
so I listen to SKY.

Standing in the crowded dining hall, coffee in hand, my face is drawn to a noisy group of Chinese youth; I mentally cancel them out. No place to sit—no place meaning there aren't any Indians in the room. It is a reflexive action on my part to assume that any company that isn't Indian company is generally unacceptable, but there it was, the absence of Indians not chairs determined the absence of a space for me. The soft of heart, guilt-ridden liberals might argue defensively that that sweeping judgement is not different from any other generalization made about us. So be it; after all it is not their humanity I am calling to question. It is mine. Along with that thought dances another. I have lived in this city in the same neighbourhood as Chinese people for twenty-two years now and don't know a single Chinese person.

It scares me just a little. It wasn't always that way. The memory of a skinny little waif drops into the frame of moving pictures rolling across my mind. Unabashed she stands next to the door of Mad Sam's market across from Powell Street grounds surveying 'chinamen' with accusatory eyes. Once a month on Saturday the process repeated itself; the little girl of noble heart studied the old men. Not once in all her childhood years had she ever seen an old man steal a little kid. She gave up, not because she became convinced that the accusation was unfounded, but because she got too big to worry about it.

'Cun-a-muck-ah-you-da-puppy-shaw, that's Chinee for how are you,' and the old pa'pa-y-ah would laugh. 'Don't wander around town or the old Chinamen will get you, steal you' . . . 'Chinkee, chinkee chinamen went down town, turned around the corner and his pants fell down' and other such truck had been buried somewhere in the caverns of the useless information file tucked in the basement of her mind, but the shape of her social life was frighteningly influenced by those absurd sounds. The movie was just starting to lag and the literary theme of the pictures was coming into focus when a small breath of air, a gentle touch of a small woman's hand invited me to sit. How embarrassing. I'd been gaping and gawking at a table-load of Hans long enough for my coffee to cool.

It didn't take long. Invariably, when people of colour get together they discuss white people. They are the butt of our jokes, the fountain of our bitterness and pain, and the infinite well-spring of every dilemma life ever presented to us. The humour eases the pain, but always whites figure front and centre of our joint communication. If I had a dollar for every word ever said about them instead of to them I'd be the richest welfare bum in the country. No wonder they suffer from inflated egoism.

I sat at the table-load of Chinese people and toward the end of the hour I wanted to tell them about Mad Sam's, Powell Street, and old men. I didn't. Wisely, I think now. Our sense of humour was different then. In the face of a crass white world we had erased so much of ourselves and sketched so many cartoon characters of white people over-top the emptiness inside, that it would have been too much for us to face that we really did feel just like them. I sat at that table more than a dozen times but not once did it occur to any of us that we were friends. Eventually, the usual march of a relentless clock, my hasty departure from college the following semester, and my failure to return for fifteen years took its toll—now even their names escape me.

Last Saturday (seems like a hundred years later) was different. The table-load of people was Asian/Native. We laughed at ourselves and spoke very seriously about our writing. We really believe we are writers, someone had said, and the room shook with the hysteria of it all. We ran on and on about our growth and development and not once did the white man ever enter the room. It just seemed all too incredible that a dozen Hans and Natives could sit and discuss all things under heaven, including racism, and not talk about white people. It only took a half-dozen revolutions in the Third World, seventeen riots in America, one hundred demonstrations against racism in Canada, and thirty-seven dead Native youth in my life to become. (For grammar fanatics I am aware that the preceding is not 'gutt Inklish'.) I could have told them about the waif but it didn't seem relevant. We had crossed a millennium of bridges the rivers of which were swollen with the floodwaters of dark humanity's tenacious struggle to extricate themselves from oppression and we knew it.

We were born during the first sword wound that the Third World swung at imperialism. We were children of that wound, invincible, conscious, and movin' on up. We could laugh because we were no longer a joke. But somewhere along the line we forgot to tell the others, the thousands of our folks that still tell their kids about old chinamen.

It's Tuesday and I'm circling the block at Gore and Powell trying to find a parking space, windows open, driving like I belong here. A sharp 'Don't come near me, why you bother me?' jars me loose. An old Chinese woman swings a ratty old umbrella at a Native man who is pushing her, cursing her, and otherwise giving her a hard time. I lean toward the passenger side and shout at him from the safety of my car: 'Leave her alone, asshole.'

'Shut-up you f'ck'n' rag-head.' I jump out of the car, without bothering to park it—no one honks, they just stare at me. He sees my face and my cowichan, bends deeply and says very sarcastically that he didn't know I was a squaw. Well, I am no pacifist; I admit, I belted him, gave him what for and the coward left. I helped the old woman across the street, then returned to park my car. She was still there where I left her, shaking, so I stopped to try and quell her fear.

She wasn't afraid. She was ashamed of her own people, men who had passed her by, walking around her or crossing the street to avoid trying to rescue her from the taunts of one of my people. The world raged around inside me while she copiously described every Chinese man who had seen her and kept walking. I listened to her in silence and thought of me and old Sam again.

Mad Sam was a pioneer of discount foods. Slightly over-ripe bananas (great for peanut butter bannock sandwiches), bruised apples, and day-old bread were always available at half the cost of Safeway and we shopped there regularly for years. I am not sure if he sold meat, in any case we never bought meat; we were fish-eaters then. I doubt very much that Sam knew we called him 'Mad' but I know now the mad was intended for the low prices and the crowds in his little store, not him. In the fifties, there were store owners that concerned themselves with their customers, established relationships with them, exchanged gossip, and shared a few laughs. Sam was good to us.

If you press your nose up against the window to the left of the door you can still see me standing there, ghostlike skinny brown body with huge eyes riveted on the street and Powell Street grounds. Sometimes my eyes take a slow shift from left to right, right to left. I'm watchin' ol' chinamen, makin' sure they don't grab little kids. Once a month for several years I assume my post and keep my private vigil. No one in the street seems to know what I'm doing or why, but it doesn't matter. The object of my vigil is not appreciation but catchin' the old chinamen in the act.

My nose is pressed up against the window pane, the cold circles the end of my flattened nose; it feels good. Outside, the window pane was freckled with crystal water drops; inside, it was smooth and dry, but for a little wisp of fog from my breath. Round 'o's of water splotched onto the clear glass. Not perfectly round, but just the right amount of roundness that allows you to call them 'o's. Each 'o' was different as on the page at school when you first print 'o's for the teacher. On the paper are lots of them. They are all kind of wobbly and different, but still 'o's.

I could see the rain-distorted street scene at the park through the round 'o's of water. There are no flowers or grass in this park. No elaborate floral themes or landscape designs, just a dozen or so benches around a wasteland of gravel, sand, and comfrey root—weeds—and a softball backstop at one end. What a bloody long time ago that was, mama.

Blat. A raindrop hit the window, scrunching up the park bench I was looking at. The round 'o' of rain made the park bench wiggle toward my corner of the store. I giggled.

'Mad Sam's . . . Mad Sam's . . . Mad Sam's?' What began as a senseless repetition of a household phrase ended as a question. She knew that Mad Sam was a chinaman . . . Chinee, the old people called them . . . but, then, the old people can't speak 'goot Inklish'—know what I mean? But what in the world made him mad? I breathed at the window. It fogged up. The only kind of mad I know is when everyone runs aroun' hollering and kicking up dust.

I rocked back and forth while my finger traced out a large circle which my hand had cleared. Two old men on the bench across the street broke my thoughts of Sam's madness. One of them rose. He was wearing one of those grey tweed wool hats that people think of as English and associate with sports cars. He had a cane, a light beige cane. He half bent at the waist before he left the bench, turned and, with his arms stretched out from his shoulders and flailing back and forth a few times, accentuated his words to the other man seated there.

It would have looked funny if pa'pa-y-ah had done it, or ol' Mike, but I was acutely aware that this was a chinaman. Ol' chinamen are not funny. They are serious and the words of the world echoed violently in my ears . . . 'don't wander off or the ol' chinamen will get you and eat you.' I pouted about the fact that mama had never warned me about them. 'She doesn't care.'

A woman with a black car coat and a white pill-box hat disturbed the scene. Screek, the door of her old Buick opened. Squeak, slam, it banged shut. There is something humorously inelegant about a white lady with spiked heels, tight skirt, and a pill-box hat cranking up a '39 Buick. Thanx, mama, for having me soon enough to have seen it.

Gawd, I am so glad I remember this: there she be, blonde as all get out, slightly hippy, heaving her bare leg, that is partially constrained by her skirt, onto the bumper of her car, and cranking at the whatever had to be cranked to make the damn thing go. All of this wonderfulness came squiggling through a little puddle of clear rain. The Buick finally took off and from the tail end of its departure I could see the little old man still shuffling his way across the street. Funny, all the cars stopped for him. Odd, the little Chinese boy talked to him, unafraid.

Shuffle, shuffle, plunk of his cane, shuffle, shuffle, plunk; on he trudged. The breath from the corner near my window came out in shorter and louder gasps. It punctuated the window with an on-again, off-again choo-choo rhythm of clarity. Breath and fog, shuffle, shuffle, plunk, breath and fog. BOOM! And the old man's face was right on mine. My scream was indelicate. Mad Sam and mama came running.

'Whatsa matter?'

'Whah iss it,' from Sam and mama respectively.

Half hesitating I pointed out the window. 'The chinaman was looking at me.' I could see that that was not the right answer. Mama's eyes yelled 'for pete's sake' and her cheeks shone red with shame, not embarrassment, shame. Sam's face was clear. Definably hurt. Not the kind of hurt that shows when adults burn themselves or something but the kind of hurt you can sometimes see in the eyes of people who have been cheated. The total picture spelled something I could not define.

Grandmothers you said if I was ever caught doing nothing you would take me away for all eternity. . . . The silence was thick, cloying, and paralyzing. It stopped my rain and stilled my emotion. It deafened my ears to the rain. I could not look out to see if the old man was still there. No grannies came to spare me.

My eyes fell unseeing on a parsnip just exactly in front of my face. They rested there not to stray until everyone stopped looking at my treacherous little body and resumed talking about whatever they were talking about before I had brought the world to a momentary halt with my astounding stupidity. What surprises me now is that they did eventually carry on as though nothing was wrong.

The floor swayed beneath me, while I tried hard to make it swallow me and carry out my wish, but I didn't quite make it. A hand loaded with a pear in front of my face jarred my eyes loose from the parsnip.

'Here,' the small, pained smile on Sam's face stilled the floor but the memory remained a moving moment in my life.

The old woman was holding my hands saying she felt better now. All that time, I did not speak or think about what she said. I just nodded my head back and forth and relived my memory of Mad Sam's.

'How unkind of the world to school us in ignorance' was all I said, and I made my way back to the car.

Sojourner's Truth

From inside my box, an ugly thought occurs to me. I know what hell is—actually, I knew it all along, but in my haste to barrel along and live, I had not thought about it until just now. Hell just might be seeing all the ugly shit people put each other through from the clean and honest perspective of the spirit that no longer knows how to lie and twist the truth.

Can you imagine, there you are watching some maniac jerk his wife or kids around, pulling arms out of their rightful places in sockets and you walk on minding your own business, only this time you don't feel like just shuffling along and ignoring it. Your spirit cries out for humanity, but all you get to do is weep and remember that you didn't care when your soul was housed in living meat. You could have struck a blow at violence against women and children, but the little whisper from your living soul was drowned by the reality of all that flesh.

In its final resting pose your soul knows that all the maxims that guided your hypocrisy are just so much balderdash. 'Spare the rod and spoil the child.' 'Don't let her get away with it.' Whoever heard of such a ridiculous proposition! 'Don't drop the apples, they bruise easily' is more like it. Pictures of all the lickings I laid on Emma and the kids file through my mind. In my newly dead state I try to rationalize one more time: if you don't subject the kid to a certain amount of brain rot, the kid is apt to object to even a minimum of authoritarian discipline. Hell is seeing the lie in all your excuses.

My thoughts come to an abrupt halt. I know that I am in the box and must get out. How convenient: the very moment you realize you must get out, there you are outside, watching everyone from the most advantageous viewpoint. They are all gathered around the box. Those that talk are whispering as though they might interrupt the soul of me; others are in tears. The kids are playing. Why everyone gathers around the boxes housing the bodies of the dead is beyond me, though. The truth of me has long left the box.

The truth of me is a little unnerved by the realization that there are not as many living bodies gathered around my box as I expected. I face it, though. What the hell did I expect? I didn't do anything to inspire anyone to show up and grieve my departure, permanent though it is. (At least there aren't any Chinamen.)

Oh God, there are a hundred thousand Chinamen living in this city and I cannot count even one of them as a human being who will miss me. I weep. No tears, just the kind of pain of the inner self that goes with the action; the sort of hot, wracking emptiness, but without the tears to cool it off. There aren't any Indians or Blacks. *Oh God, there aren't even many white people here.* I lived for seventy years moving around in a sea of almost a million people and only fifty show up to bury my body and bid my spirit adieu.

'It's a crying shame, he wasn't that old.' Thanks, Mike, but it really isn't a shame. Death is natural, but then we are inclined to add shame to all that is natural. The naked body and spirit is a deep source of shame to the mortal beings crawling about the earth. Life does look a little different from the vantage point of death.

A ripple of pleasure overtakes me as Emma speaks. 'You know he didn't take care of himself.' It is the worst she could come up with and still wear a mask of polite mourning. Hate jumps out at me and for a moment the essence of me is seared by it. A storm of hidden knowledge, secret pain, leaps at my soul, accusing, huge in its condemnation of my treatment of her as wife. I can see where it all comes from: the mind-bending brutality, the intimidation, the violence, the erasure of her soul—the screaming soul she denied. *Oh God, the living body of me scarred and twisted the very soul of Emma.*

In a corner, my brother and sister are secretly plotting for the spoils of my bodily being. Jerks. My spirit rolls back to my own plotting for the spoils of my parents before they were properly laid to rest. The twisting begins again, the terrible, unbearable heat of deceit in life burns my soul in death.

Oh God, I cry, *Don't do this to yourselves.* No one hears me. It is a little confusing being dead. You feel more alive than ever, except no one knows you are there. No soul present actually misses me, most particularly not Emma. She is relieved.

Shit. And mountains of it appear from nowhere. Shit loads tumbling down from above me. A wall of crap. *I don't believe this.* The spirit of me is swept up in this sheet of rank-smelling human feces. *What's going on here?* We hit the water together, the shit and the truth of me. The water is filthy without the help of the crap. Rushing along, spreading itself out, and running for the vast bankless river of salt, the crud holds my truth in a vice-grip of gut-wrenching stink. *What the hell is this all about?* The water ejects me at the exit of the river just next to an old man sitting on a park bench reading a newspaper.

I remember it now. Three million metric tonnes of untreated sewage dumped into the Fraser River, protested, of course, by a few crazies—college rejects, calling themselves eco-something or others. *Oh God. I wish I had been one of them.*

Hey, you oughta be reading that with a little more soul, old man. The polluting happened before I died so my words are wasted, but the truth is, it still goes on.

On the wings of a snow white dove, my truth sails across the vast expanse of weeping earth and choking fauna and my soul mutters helplessly to the wreckage below: *Jesus, I didn't know.*

'Oh yes, but you didn't seek.' From out of the blue, he appears on the tip of the dove's other wing, looking just as normal as can be. He can't be normal, though—he must be just as dead as me. The dove dips and drops us both in a mountainous wasteland—earth brutalized by a flurry of murderous chainsaws that massacred her treasured children. Not satisfied, man consigned the weak, the unusable seedlings and brush to a widow's pyre.

Didn't seek? I repeat dumbly.

'Yes, you know, seek and ye shall find,' and he fades away.

WAIT.

No presence, just a soft chuckle and a clean voice: 'You silly fellow, you cannot command another man's soul here.'

Oh Lord.

'That's another thing, the whole business of lords has no roots in heavenly reality.' At first I think he is kidding. But after I listen to it, I realize the whole notion of lords in heaven is ridiculous. It could not have been contrived by ethereal souls.

From inside the stone walls of Parliament, the House of Lords drivels nonsense while their lying souls convince their mouths that the bullshit they are peddling is true. I can't believe that I ever had faith in these fools. It's embarrassing. 'Apartheid is not a question for us to address,' some wigged lord with South African investments is saying. *I'll bet not. After all, you're the white guys.* I would laugh, but the truth stops me and there in the kitchen of my own neighbourhood is Mike, being disgusted by all the uppity Blacks 'who had a lotta nerve shooting us', and the body of me is agreeing. The blood of Soweto runs thick in the kitchen. The screaming pain of children being shot fills me. It muffles the stupid words uttered by pompous arrogance, and soils forever my truth.

A child, heartsick and ashamed, appears in the school yard with my grandson, who leads the others in cruel taunts against the solitary child.

Oh don't. Jesus don't.

'I never did. I always maintained that all children are a great offering to life.' There he is again and the truth of his African heritage is written on his soul.

Actually, I was talking to my grandson.

'His name is not Jesus,' and he disappears.

Is this all there is? Endless pictures of the whole suffering world? The wind carries my longings to the mouth of a poet whose words are secretly laughed at. *Oh God,* and a vast sense of nothingness sweeps over me. The nothingness is unmoving, cloying in its inertia. It suspends my soul in a terrifying void. It ends like it began, suddenly and of its own will. Nothingness is scary, but still it offers temporary relief from the tearless weeping. Since I came to this God-forsaken place, I have laughed but once.

In the meadow where the void jerks to a halt, children are playing, chasing illusive butterflies. Peace rests within me. Laughter delights their little bodies, captures the heart of the grasses, and the trees chatter, echoing the sensuous happiness of childhood. The sun whispers gently and its light plays about on the skin of the earth's young. Grass, trees, and little children are swollen with peace and joy. It is the first moment of rest for my soul.

'Growth is joyous. The knife that inhibits growth is the sword of death,' the grasses breathe in blessed refrain.

The children disappear and a plane carrying defoliants flies overhead spraying the meadow below in preparation for clear-cutting the forest at the edge of the meadow. The horror of the whir from the airplane's engine slaps the peace from my soul.

Jesus, when does it all end?

'Be clear. When does what all end?' (*Jesus, I am getting tired of this guy. Every rhetorical or philosophical remark prefaced by his name calls him forth.*)

'You won't be so tired when your novitiate is over. I don't have to answer forever, you know.' I did not know that there are no private thoughts in heaven. Jesus smiles.

Well, the butchery?

'Ah,' and he leaves. The earth sighs to the sun, 'It ends when the body of people stop hiding from the truth of the spirit.' It seems too simple.

'It is simple. Why are you, of all people, doubting that?' she asks. And suddenly, I need the comfort of Emma's long suffering presence . . .

*   *   *

'Hallo-oo, how are you?' and the lilt in Mike's voice veils his discomfort at seeing Emma again. He doesn't want to know how Emma is. His deception is an ugly sight. Deception has got to be hell's inner face. A deluge of scenes of deception bombards my truth: verbal garbage, physical garbage, and most criminal of all, food garbage—all deceptively rationalized as respectable by the bodies of humanity that race across my view. The soul of people takes the shape of their deception, and the eyes of my essence ache with the unbearability of the sight.

Jesus. What is going on?

'Well, this is heaven and here you are, dead, looking at life through the honest eyes of your soul.'

Well, if this is heaven, what is hell?

'You already know the answer to that one. Perhaps you want to know more about how it all works. You see, heaven is simply the sky. At the point of mortal departure, your spirit gets to walk the wing tips of the wind witnessing the reality of your life. The soul is not blind, however. In death the truth is not dressed in the deceptive clothes of mortal flesh. The soul is incapable of rationalization.'

You mean I have to watch over and over, everything I have just seen?

'That is about it, but for a minor exception.'

What do you get to see—the same thing?

And he laughs. The sound comes from deep within the earth, rich and resonant. It spreads out thick and joyous. The winds catch the laughter and layer the seas and grasses with it. Embarrassed, I try digging around inside for guilt to hide my shame. Only shame blossoms, relentless in its flowering. I yearn for the agony of guilt to absolve me. I fall over in a foolish, prostrate position of remorse, but guilt does not come.

Oh Jesus, can't I even enjoy the comfort of guilt?

'Oh no. Heaven is not like that. Here, there is but pleasure and pain. You see, if pain were experienced with the absolving comfort of guilt, it would be impure. Guilt is an intellectual contrivance that reduces the pain the spirit needs to experience if it is to alter the actions of the body. In that sense, guilt is the ultimate deception—hell. The spirit resides in heaven; it knows not hell.'

Holy mother of Jesus. I can't go through this for all eternity.

'Yes you can. People do it all the time.' She said it without sympathy—just a matter of fact, eternal reality.

'Hello mom,' Jesus purrs.

'Jesus, how nice for our paths to cross.'

Christ, this is insane. I balk at the bizarre meeting between mother and son, two thousand years dead. In my mortal life the idea of Mary as Jesus' mother ended with his birth.

'You called?' Jesus interrupts my thoughts.

I meant God, really.

His voice swells with magnificent urgency: 'Man in his opportunist desire to ease life and deceive himself that the torment of others is no concern of his distorts the natural world of the spirit. Man creates a vision of heaven and hell for himself that he might justify his selfishness and appease his conscience while outraging human and natural life. God, good, all began as the 'great offering' of one's life to the world. But now, it is a catch-all word for every kind of desperate anguish living mortals wish to hide from. The offering is disempowered, destroyed, and its meaning lost to humanity by the distortion of godliness. God has become the mantle for the greatest human atrocity—war.'

Horseshit, I snap, and it begins again, the crap, the children, the hunger of humanity. *Oh Jesus. I want to go back to my box and rest.*

'You can't. It has been buried. Heaven is the sky and you cannot return to the earth. How long did you think eternity was?' Jesus leaves and the terror of having to walk the winds witnessing my life's trials without the comfort of his company follows his departure. The memory of my mortal life, cold nights warmed by Emma's yielding flesh, fill me with desire. *Emma, help me.* Below my shameless begging stands Emma, staring hard at the window of her quiet living room. She hears nor sees a thing. She is busy making a decision.

'He seems like a nice fellow. Not like the last,' she whispers silently to herself, not even according me my name or the title of husband. 'Ah courtship, if only love could grow from the sweet seed of courtship to the lovely flower marriage was intended to be.' The inside of her new love lays itself bare to me. While the man's body anxiously occupies my chair and waits for her reply, his damaged soul shouts his truth at mine. I try to warn her but know she hears not a word. Alone at fifty-six, afraid, desperate for affection, Emma says 'yes.'

In the beginning he is sweet, as though he has not fully awakened to the realization that the courtship is over. For a while there is laughter in Emma's little house. But, as men are wont to do from time to time, he screws up at work. The boss gives him 'what for' and he comes home, full to the brim with another man's anger and his own humiliation.

Like a replay of my own mortality, the beer follows, then drunken, impotent raging about the boss, and wild, unreasonable demands on Emma. She is slow to move on his drunken commands. (Sabotage, I had surmised as a living person, and quite correctly. What woman jumps happily to a drunken husband's command?)

Then the fists fly. The thud of human meat battered by the hammer that can be a man's hand. The tears, the screams, the agony of his perverse triumph over the lively body that he alone has reduced to limp life. And my wasted soul stretches itself over her body in a futile attempt to protect my Emma from this other man's fists.

Inside the body of Emma a black emotion rises and spirals to the centre of her being. The soul of me catches in the madness of her emotion, captivated by her bleakly intense struggle to convert her outrage to despair. A crazy cacophony of raw passion carries me to that magical place where all feelings begin. A single crystal teardrop, alone in a fit of rage, rests peacefully. In shocked disbelief, my truth stares at the perfect droplet.

Jesus . . .

'But it is beautiful, isn't it?' His voice brings momentary relief from the desperation that lingers in the clarity of the tear.

Is this all there is left, just one tear, one tear to account for her entire life?

'Imagine, if you will, that she can hear the mutterings of her innermost self and rise up. Imagine the great flood that this little tear could become in the tide of her resistance. Bear witness, my friend.'

Jesus fades and compassion rises in the soul of me. My soul envelops the tear. I plead for its life, praying for it to swell and to multiply. Softly murmuring, I cajole the tear to grow. *Not twice, Emma. I am dead. Surely you must know that I should never have lived thus, comfortable with your suffering. Emma, hear the words whispered to thee by thy self, thy perfect self. Abide by thy perfect right to be.*

I stretch my truth throughout her body, grow small around the tear, my soul rhythmically undulating with my fervent desire for her salvation. My love reaches its purest moment. Spent, my passion drapes itself in a perfect circle around the lonely tear. I feel her body rise. I hear the resounding 'no' from every cell of her flesh. In my death watch, there is great rejoicing. The knife in her hand drives through the sleeping man's heart. The blood mesmerizes her and then the wall of tears drives me outside herself.

But more my spirit knows. Police and courts are next. Emma sits in wordless teary repose, my own madness her defence. 'Not twice.' The very words of my soul she repeats to her counsellor. From my sky perch I am compelled to watch. Jesus came first among the throng that gather. Curious, I ask why his presence.

'This is the very thing to which I am called, the judging of the meek and courageous by the lords of violence.'

Nine Black boys gather next to us, giggling and shuffling and watching by turns.

Who are they?

'The Scottsboro boys. You must remember them.'

How could I forget. The boys hung for a rape they were much too innocent to commit. The madness of racism runs sour and acrid in my soul. I, coward that I was, sanctioned the dirty deed. Sympathy, simpering and jelly soft, obscures my outrage.

It must have been terrible for them to come here.

'Not at all. They have enjoyed themselves immensely since being freed from the prison of racial violence. Why, they have participated in every glorious riot, in every movement of Black resistance from Birmingham in 1948 to Soweto, just a short time ago. They have had their vengeance.'

Is there then only freedom in death?

'Quite the contrary. When the slave is no longer a slave, what you have left is an ex-master. If the master insists on protecting his position with weapons, the slaves will have to covet the gun.'

The congregation includes the strangest people.

Who is the funny-looking little fellow who speaks a strange language?

'Why that's Vladimir Ilyich Ulyanov, you probably know him as Lenin.'

But he is an atheist.

'Heaven is the one place that does not discriminate.'

The congregation swells its ranks with the champions of the meek and poor: those who so loved the world that they sacrificed their selves that justice to earth and people might prevail. Marx, Fred Hampton, Jackson, Krupskaya, Gwarth-Es-La and his standard bearer . . .

These people are all rebels.

'Yes, they are all in their own way like myself.'

I am no rebel.

'Ah, but you unlocked the door to Emma's rebellion.'

The court case drags on in its usual ceremony of arrogant rigidity and stupid exactitude of language without sentiment. My life with her is dragged forward couched carefully in legal mumbo-jumbo. Her character is attested to by women who assure the world that Emma was a kind and devoted wife to a brutal first husband. Even our children testify that they and their mother had been abused. Emma rises to her own defence. She refuses to deny that her hand held the knife that stabbed her second husband, but she confesses no guilt.

'I am a Christian woman. This is supposed to be a Christian country. Jesus himself forbade the abuse of the meek, but he did not deny our sacred right to resist abuse. "Where ye shall have no justice, ye shall have no peace." The man that would batter his wife is less than a serpent. I was born three months ago; until that day, I wandered the world a slave . . .'

'Oh, ain't she a woman? . . . Ain't she a woman?' and the tall reedy body of an old Black woman waltzes and sways to the music of her own words.

Who are you?

'Why, I'm Sojourner Truth. An' Emma an' me was born on the same day. I was delivered from slavery at fifty-six years ol' and so was she.'

'I should have killed that first brute,' Emma says, 'but he died on me. And this lawyer sitting here doesn't know what he is about. Didn't know what I was doing? No one who feels the plunge of a blade through the human heart can ever testify that they did not know what they were doing. I knew I stabbed him. I knew it would send him to his maker. But I am guilty of no crime. I did not kill a man; I stabbed a snake.'

The judge looks aghast. She feels her own emotion rising, contemplates quitting herself of the case, but a voice whispers from within that the jury, not she, would be pronouncing the verdict on Emma. She remains riveted to her throne. She counsels the jury that she must resolve some legal questions before they can retire to decide Emma's fate, and she buys time for her own troubled soul.

In the week that follows, the congregation remains vigilant. There is a hubbub of discussion about the possibilities that lay ahead for woman and earth should Emma win. Joy hangs in the air, visible as Thoreau's lily. Even the old woman next to me, grim-faced most of the time, chuckles now and then.

What is your name?

'Emily.'

Carr, the artist?

'Hmph.'

I am honoured, I pule.

'I would rather you be enjoyed.'

The week draws to a close and the judge counsels the jury. 'The defendant takes precedence over her own counsel. Indeed, according to Benjamin Franklin, Thomas Jefferson, and the "defender of the constitution", Daniel Webster, the founding fathers of this United States of America intended the values of this country to reflect those of the New Testament. The jury is to decide the fate of Emma in accordance with the book of Revelations and the word of Jesus. There is no doubt that Emma slew her second husband, but the law governing America, and finally Emma, is the law of Christ.'

The jury retires, armed with twelve New Testaments. And the heavenly congregation replies in blessed song:

Praise her soul, she saw the light
The truth of this sojourner,
has been seen at last.
Praise her soul, she saw the light.

Tomson Highway *b.* 1951

CREE

Tomson Highway was born on his father's trap-line, in a tent on an island in Maria Lake, a hundred miles north of his home reserve at Brochet in the far northwest of Manitoba. The eleventh of twelve children, his early years were spent there, travelling by sled and canoe, hunting and fishing, speaking only Cree.

At six years of age, he was sent to a Roman Catholic boarding school in The Pas, Manitoba, where he learned English and started playing the piano. At that time he was able to visit with his family only two months each summer. At fifteen, he moved again, to Winnipeg, to attend high school.

After studying piano for two years at the University of Manitoba's Faculty of Music, he spent a year studying to be a concert pianist with William Aide in London, England. He returned to Canada to complete his Honours Bachelor of Music degree (1975) at the University of Western Ontario and to spend another year completing English courses necessary for a Bachelor of Arts degree (1976). During this time he met and worked with James Reaney and saw his first Michel Tremblay play. The works of these artists, who find their subject matter in their own communities, became touchstones for Highway.

Highway spent the next seven years working in his own community on culture and recreation programs for Native people in friendship centres, prisons, bars, on reserves and on the streets, familiarizing himself with the networkings of Native lives and politics in Canada. At the age of thirty, he began writing plays and working with the Native theatre community with De-Ba-Jeh-Mu-Jig Theatre on Manitoulin Island, Northern Delights in Sioux Lookout, and Native Earth Performing Arts in Toronto. With these companies he wrote words and/or music for and produced and/or performed in theatre works such as *The Rez Sisters* (1986), *Aria* (1987), *New Song . . . New Dance* (1988), *The Sage, the Dancer, and the Fool* (1989), and *Dry Lips Oughta Move to Kapuskasing* (1989). *The Sage, the Dancer, and the Fool*, in its second production, and *Aria* were both nominated for Dora Mavor Moore Awards, and both *The Rez Sisters* and *Dry Lips* won Dora awards for best new play (*The Rez Sisters* also garnered a Chalmers Award) and have been published by Fifth House (1989 and 1990, respectively). Highway's plays emphasize the Trickster figure derived from the Native storytelling traditions, who is emblematic of indigenous humour and spirit in the face of both historical and existential dilemmas.

Most recently, Highway has been focusing on prose works: a novel, *The Kiss of the Fur Queen* (1998); two bilingual books (English and Cree) for children, *Caribou Song (Aithko Nikamon)* (2001) and *Fox on Ice: Mahkesis Miskwamihk E-Cipatapit* (2002); and a lecture, *Comparing Mythologies* (2004). His most recently published play is the musical *Rose* (2003), and his most recently produced play, *Ernestine Shushwap Gets Her Trout* (2004). Highway has also directed, composed, and written for film, and works to encourage literacy and the development of literature in all the languages Native people use. He is concerned that Canada's culture may lose the unique contributions of the living Cree, Ojibwa, and Inuit languages. He hopes his work in English can teach his audience 'something new and something terribly relevant and beautiful about the particular landscape that they too have become inhabitants of'. His ambition in life is to 'make the "rez" cool and to show and celebrate what funky folk Canada's Indian people really are'.

The Lover Snake

The magazine photograph is of a Sikh. A male Sikh. Male Sikhs wear turbans. It's a tradition that goes back many, many generations, so it is said. You can always tell a Sikh when you see one by the turban he wears. Most, as I recall, also wear beards like this one in the photograph does. Fine beards. A fine-boned people. This particular Sikh, the man in the photograph, has, pictured with him, the uppermost portion of a large snake slithering down over the front and centre of the bright orange turban he wears, the reptile's diamond-shaped head, with its distended eyes, hovering just centimetres over the man's forehead, its flickering tongue slicing air between his eyes. This is the photograph in the magazine.

Dahljeet has always worn a turban, as I remember. In fact, he has an entire closet full of them at his home in Vancouver. Dahljeet is a Sikh.

Now Dahljeet and I have been friends for many years. An unusual alliance, people would observe from time to time. And between us, Dahljeet and me, we would agree that the friendship was an unusual friendship. I mean, there he was, very much an Indian and here I was, also very much an Indian. Only, we were such totally different kinds of Indian. Worlds apart. So different, it was laughable. And we'd laugh.

North Cree hunter ambles down the slope of Robson Street beside north Indian maharajah. An odd pair. To be sure.

And yet, we became close, Dahljeet and I. More than friends, more than brothers, more than lovers, even. It was almost as if, in the midst of certain totally unexpected moments in time we spent together, there would arrive from somewhere a certain buzzing half-sound, a certain inner ringing as perfect in pitch and purity as the tone from a tuning fork. It was beautiful. We met when we were both just short of twenty years of age.

Dahljeet would talk of elephant parades at magnificent royal weddings in the heat and dust of not-so-long-ago north India and of dark women in rainbow-coloured saris, draped in silver and gold and diamonds at summer places in the mountains and at winter places away from mountains. He had stories, too, of cobras that I remember particularly well.

And me? Well, I would talk to him of pure white snow and of rivers that never run dry and of ice-cold lakes from which you could drink by simply dipping your hand through crystal surfaces and cupping and lifting water to your mouth. I talked—not to be outdone by his stories of elephant parades and gold-sprinkled saris—of vast herds of caribou in spring-time, a sea of rolling, shifting, swaying antlers before my hunter father's keen, watchful eye. And of moccasins and belts covered with the most fanciful patterns and designs in glass beads. My sister, Marie-Adele, in particular, I'd confide to Dahljeet, is an artist at the art of applying beadwork to the smoked hide of young caribou. He owned twenty-seven turbans, my friend said in reply, and, later that afternoon, he showed me these twenty-seven turbans in his closet at his home in Vancouver: the colours were fantastic!

There are no snakes where I was born, so Weesageechak, that half-crazed little Cree Indian clown whom no one's ever seen, though he's lived ten thousand years and more among us, I told Dahljeet, this particular Weesageechak, well, he's never seen a snake or done anything with one or ridden one or cooked one and eaten one. He would have danced with one if he'd met one, I laughed. No. No snakes in far north Saskatchewan . . . which made his stories of maharajahs and cobras, yes, cobras in particular, that much more fascinating. I was electrified!

They say, in north India, according to my friend, Dahljeet—he of the twenty-seven multi-coloured turbans and the fine, dark beard—that cobras mate at a certain time in their lives, the male with the female, and that they then sustain this relationship for the rest of their lives, as a couple—unlike sled dogs and caribou and men and women. And there comes a time when the occasional cobra will get killed by some over-zealous hunter, some nervous little man. And when this happens, the surviving cobra, the mate of the snake just killed, will find that man, the killer of his mate, will hunt him down even if it should take him thirty years and more, even if he should have to travel from the pale yellow dust of Punjab province to the border of Nepal or even to North America somewhere, perhaps Vancouver—he will travel there, this other cobra, somehow, even in the realm of the dream world, and he will find that man and he will kill that man, that over-zealous hunter, that nervous little man. Then, and only then, will that cobra, the lover snake, lie down and die.

Many, many years later, Dahljeet and I ceased to be friends. Something happened. Something died inside of me. I haven't seen him in many years; he and I, we've lost touch. I understand that he lives still in Vancouver and has become even more the academic, the scholar, the thinker he so much was back then, that he teaches at one of the universities, so I've learned only recently, lecturing on the teachings of some obscure Eastern philosopher whose work relies to a great degree on the inner workings of myth and legend. I, on the other hand, now make my home in northwestern Ontario, working in the field of radio broadcasting and helping as much as I can—as poet, writer, thinker after my own fashion—to revive the breathing, the singing, and the shrieking of that half-crazed little Cree clown, Weesageechak, that essential spirit many had thought was on his way to dying, to leaving forever these snow-white landscapes so precious to us all. Now that we're over thirty years of age, we've lost touch, Dahljeet and I. This is the way of things, they say, the natural course of events in the lives of friendships, of love.

But I refuse that explanation. For me, it is a pale, flimsy story, of no consequence, no fantastic substance. I hold, instead, this magazine photograph in front of me and I gaze into it and I wonder if that isn't Dahljeet there in his brilliant orange turban and his fine, dark beard. And the snake? The cobra, the lover snake, come to lay claim to his over-zealous hunter, his nervous little man. And kill him . . . kill . . . kill . . .

Dahljeet and I, we are no longer friends.

Aria
A One-Woman Play in One Act

CHARACTERS
All played by one woman:

THE KO-KUM	THE SECRETARY
THE MOTHER	THE EXECUTIVE SECRETARY
THE LITTLE GIRL	THE EXECUTIVE
THE LOVER OF MEN	THE DIVA
THE LOVER OF WOMEN	THE WOMAN OF THE ROLLING HEAD
THE BRIDE	MARILYN
THE WIFE	THE PROSTITUTE
THE INDIAN WOMAN	THE EARTH
THE WHITE WOMAN	

THE KO-KUM

There was a time I could make my way through these stands of trees, endless forever stands of green trees . . . white spruce and pale green tamarack . . . green needles quiver in these many, many northern summers of my life. Time was, yes, when my feet were sure and certain in their grip upon this reindeer moss, this grey rock. And yet I flew, like a spray of twelve fluttering songbirds . . . my spirit . . .

like a mist . . . floating through tall trees and the bark, the veins of the trunk, nursing like a babe on the very sap. The taste was sweeter than anything this old life or mine has ever known.

I taught these twelve children of mine . . . to walk through this muskeg . . . to spring quick and light. Taught these seven daughters to tell the many moods of wind, rain of tomorrow, my five sons to hold conversation with fire and the northern lights. I spent a hundred years and more in the teaching of these things. Yes, time was when I could swim through this sea of green with the ease and toughness of young trout.

I sit here now in this ramshackle house. . . .The colour TV sits four feet in front of me. There's the smell of unclean babies; small children run crazy in this house-they're all mine, they say, these swarms . . . little boys . . . little girls-and they stink. This thing they call a telephone is a living thing. There's the smell of liquor and . . .

I sit here waiting to die. I sit here all my dark nights, looking into myself and seeing the spirit of other times and better times . . . I'll never, never see again.

I'm blind. I'm deaf now and my feet are motionless. Sitting here, I wrap my hand around the curve of this cane and search deep into myself, all the nights of my long life, and gaze at boughs of spruce and tamarack . . . even the singing of the bird I can see now . . . my spirit . . . like a mist . . . .

THE MOTHER

There was a gift came down to me. The seed was planted deep. And deep in me began a breathing, taking shape of little arms, little legs, the spine, little liver.

I drink the water and the water seeps into the belly of the child. My liquid is electric . . . I breathe the breath of self.

—THE BIRTH—

Blood sprays out like sunlight.
Gurgle, my folding flesh, a whisper all in one.
The salty liquid from my eyes is hers.

Hey! The child. My child.
Her veins held up against the light
Are filigree and webs of wonder to behold.
I was mother
I am mother now.

My child flies out the window of my dream and climbs aboard the Earth, straddles it and makes its loamy texture part of her. Her arm, her little shoulder blade, her pumping heart covers the surface of my breast . . . ihhhh . . .

There was a gift came down to me.

THE LITTLE GIRL
Mother, Mama, Mom, *ni-mama!*
(sings) Kees-pin ki-sa-gee-hin
See-mak ka-wee-chee-win.
(speaks) Hello.
Wonderful fun kind
Of wonderful wonderful sunbeam
Fancy in the air there
And down upon the ground there
And here
And around and through the sun—
Beam and poked by magic stick.
Choing!
Oh-oh . . . *(sunbeam out)*
Ma! *(sunbeam back on)*
The wall by my bed
Is the wave on the lake
On top of the wave there's me and my mom
The wave is big
Inside the wave there's me and my mom
The wave is ten, weeny, weeny, weeny
I'm half-way into sleep
The wave.
Sparkle spray
Sunbeam and songbird
Fancy that . . . .
(sings) Sitting in the tall grass
Wave in the white breeze.
(speaks) My magic stick legs like 'Y'
Ohhhh, I feel good . . . .
The magic stick prickle and poke
Skin
Nice. . . . Nice. . . . *(touches 'herself')*
Oh-oh . . .
Mother, mama, mom where are you?
You, *ni-mama,* gave me
These bones and skin
Hair, teeth, lips and eyes that see
See fancy fly among sunbeam and
My magic stick . . .

I was playing
Lovely games with sun—

Beam and the little stick . . .
Lovely.

THE LOVER OF MEN
    (sings) Hail Mary Mary Mary
    Full of grace grace
    Full of grace
    The Lord is with thee
    Hail Mary Mary
    Blessed art, blessed art thou amongst women women
    (speaks) And blessed is the fruit of thy womb, Jesus.
    Pssst!
    I'm alive.
    I'm for real.
    I tell you, I ain't a statue
    But the real thing for sure.
    You've all seen me before.
    Remember me?
    On picture postcards.
    Standing still as death in church corners
    Beside those crucifixes . . . *(pose)*
    Crucifixes plentiful as Coca-Cola.

I was pretending to be Virgin Mary. It's the costume Saladia Big Bush is wearing for the Christmas concert, Sister. Sister Mary Joseph only asked me to be the cow in the manger . . . beside the manger. Saladia Big Bush is too fat to play the Virgin Mary, Sister, she should be the cow and I should be the Virgin Mary. Because she was beautiful and holy and . . . the mother of Jesus. Because if I think of her more often and pray more to her, I can forget Cree faster and not have to be punished for speaking it in this residential school. Because she will help us become more like you, Sister. That's why. I wasn't laughing at her, I was laughing with her. Cuz where I come from, Sister, we're allowed to laugh and I think this poor woman, mother of us all, including you, Sister Mary Alexander, should be allowed to have fun just once in a while. I mean, even the Blessed Virgin Mary herself had to take a shit at least once a day, didn't she? *N'pug-wa-teen oo-ta, ni-mama.*

Holy Mary, mother of God
Pray for us sinners
Now and at the hour of our . . .

There's this fascination with my body, the sudden appearance of hair in certain corners. Strange and mysterious goings-on. All of a sudden: *je suis la femme d'amour!* I'm aware of the bodies of boys and young men, the way their asses look in skin-tight faded blue jeans, the way the muscles of their arms flex under those

T-shirts, the way their . . . thighs . . . move . . . the sweat! I like standing close to them, the way they smell, the way they run, sway, swagger. . . . So many boys! To be held . . . held fast . . . by the arms of my men . . . on hot musky nights . . . on nights when the mist has risen . . .

THE LOVER OF WOMEN
(Lying on floor, she groans with pain)
I sound like a moose . . .

The rising and the falling
Of a sea . . .
The moon is silent but not still
My body in her time of fullness
. . . we have a centre here
And here . . .
And here is the flame
And pain becomes power, beauty . . .

There the moon,
Time
Of my moon;
Moon
Lover
Of
Woman.

THE BRIDE
Here is the aisle before me now
The pews lined row on row
Flowers all in place, organ
Music colours air and I in white
The veil behind me falls in folds
Brushing stone floor with pale whisper.

This man,
He of the long stem and the brazen,
brazen flower I clasp in
Hand as my bouquet
Forever
To the day we die, one or the other.

Given to this man as gem
Cherished and admired for the year.
As food
To be eaten and digested

As receptacle
To children.
Or am I given to this man
As pleasure trove
To be indulged in.

How do I hold his limbs as he makes love
to me.

By my heart he is present
His body close to mine
His hand, his skin that touches mine
The hair . . .

My white dress is like the dove
That flutters, hovers and descends
The last breath of airborne freedom, I feel.
Pinned by male fuse to the soil
Will I be forever bound
to house
and bound
to giving of my body night and day
and evening time . . . and teeming
life should sprout out from my flesh?
WHO IS THIS MAN?!

Here is the aisle before me now
And the pews lined row on row
The man in priestly vestments beckons
with his sacred smile
The blood-red carpet awash with holy water
This is the river down which I float
to join him.
He shall fashion from my body, my soul,
the complete being, the complete . . .

Here is the aisle . . .

Oh, my God . . .

> THE WIFE stands on the porch landing of her house on the reserve. A rickety old
> washing machine is before her; she is doing laundry. She 'talks' a lot with her hands.

THE WIFE

My husband's socks, my husband's pants, my husband's shirt, my husband's underwear. My shirt, my socks, my pants, my underpants. Hey, the way this life of mine

has gone, loving him and him loving me and me and him go fishing in the lake. You throw the net. And the water sticks in the *(hand motions making the shape of the webbing in the net)* catching the sun. Handfuls of light come 'phht-phht' in your face. '*Hera Keechigeesik,* don't rock the boat too much. Scare the fish away,' he say to me. Me and him. Hey, *ta-p'wee-sa pee-sim*[1] . . .

The years me and Zachary were fishing and trapping up north, summertime we live in tents. The lake is there, the island, the island hanging from the sky. Our men were all gone hunting. So it was just us women. And the children. Alone.

All of a sudden 'haw-woomp'. This 'phhhrrroommm'. Very black. First I thought it was a moose. But no. 'Haw-woomp, haw-woomp,' the water went, 'haw-woomp, haw-woomp, haw-woomp.' It was terrible. There was this . . . *pee-s'tew*[2] . . . this . . . foam . . . foaming in the water. It reached the shore. It was huge. Bigger than any man. Covered with hair. No lips. Eyes flames of ice. It was. The Weetigo! Ohhh, the breath of the Weetigo can freeze you till you're stiff as a statue. Then the Weetigo enters you. Right into your soul. And you become. The Weetigo! And you eat people. Brrrr.

So anyway. There. The Weetigo. On the shore. Right before our very eyes. So us women. We grab our children and take to the hills. And we waited. And I watched.

The Weetigo went into my tent! Rowwwowwwooorrrr! *(roars and bangs the sides of the washing machine)* It roared and raged. The tents were in shreds. The dogs? All dead. He was so big he tripped on the stove and burned our camp to the ground. Everything was in flames.

Then. And only then. 'Haw-woomp, haw-woomp, haw-woomp, haw-woomp, haw-woomp,' it swam back to the island. Brrrr! The Weetigo is a terrible, terrible thing to see.

(Abruptly, she begins to sing, happy as a lark.) La-la-la-la-la-la-la the mouth of high July, hey! *(speaks)* The life of wives sings in the summer the furniture needs dusting, hey! *Ta-p'wee-sa pee-sim nee-ta-cha-ga-soo.* '*Hera Keechigeesik,* that yellow sunshine sure looking good on that brown belly of yours,' he say to me. Zachary. My Zachary.

My husband's socks, my husband's pants, my husband's shirt, my husband's under. . . . The time that Nataways woman brought his underwear home to me. In a box, all nice washed and folded.

She stands there. Curlers. Blouse wrinkled and dirty tits stink of ashtrays and men. One step down on my rickety porch, paint is gone long ago, wood rotten sand

1 This phrase is used at various times in this monologue, in various permutations. Its approximate meaning, in Cree, is 'Hey this sunshine sure feels good. . . .'
2 'Pee-s'tew' means 'foam' in Cree.

blow through the cracks. Jacket, Zachary's pup, the ugly one, dropped his shit by the step again.

That Giselle Nataways. She took a shit on Liza Jane Manitowabi's lawn. She opened her legs to seventeen-year-old Dickie Bird Halked right in front of Black Lady Halked's face. She made two babies by Raggedy Annie Cook's husband without missing one single goddamn bingo game. But no woman come near Zachary Keechigeesik.

I, Zachary Keechigeesik's wife, never let her children go hungry, never missed a payment at Andy Manitowabi's store. I, Zachary Keechigeesik's wife, walked 40 miles to the Anchor Inn in January through that blizzard to sober up Rosie Kakapetum the medicine woman to save this woman's own mother from the blood from that accident, the gun in that drunken brawl this woman's own father was the one that pulled the trigger and just about shot her foot off I walked that 40 miles.

She stands there. Her lips smile. But her eyes? *Ee-pa-pee-it a-wa k's'ka-na-goos. Ku-nu-wa-pa-ta oos-kee-si-g'wa.*[3] I freeze. I hear rushing water in my head. *(screams uncontrollably)* I kick with my knee. I kick and I kick and I kick and I kick and I kick. *(Pause. Calm again, she whimpers.)* Blood got allover my hands. Blood and clumps of sticky bloody hair. I kicked her in her pregnant belly. Her shitty brown bum spread naked in the dirt by my broken steps, squeaking like a sick mink.

I was ever alone. Three days. I sit in my living room. Curtains shut. Don't eat. Don't wash. Nothing. Three days. Stare straight ahead. Three days.

He come home, shy as a puppy dog, this . . . suitcase full of dream visions under his arm—the very first TV on the reserve. So. So now me and him and him and me. We lie on this couch at midnight. *(pause)* Can't see the TV too good cuz his knobby old knee's in the way, hey. *Ta-p'wee-sa ma-na a-wa pee-sim.*

THE INDIAN WOMAN
Oo-oo n'si see-tuk
Hey, ta-p'wee sa mi-thoo ki-noh-s'koo-si-wuk
Oom-see-si ka-ga-noh-pi-ma-g'wow ma-na see-tuk
Hey, tas-kootch ma-na oo-tee pee-cha-eek
Ee-moo-see-thi-muk a-wi-nuk
U-wi-nuk ee-nee-pa-wit
U-wi-nuk ee-pa-gi-ta-ta-moot
U-wi-nuk ee-p'mat-sit
Oo-oo n'si see-tuk
Hey, ta-p'wee sa mi-thoo us-ki-tu-goo-si-wuk

---

3 Cree: 'She's laughing at me, this female dog. Look at her eyes.'

I-thi-gook ma-na een-tay-thee-ta-man Ta-na-ta-g'wow; ta-na-ta-g'wow
I-goo-see-si nee-s'ta tay-si-pa-gi-ta-ta-moo-yan
Tay-si-moo-see-ta-an pee-cha-eek
Oo-oo n'si see-tuk these trees . . .[4]

THE WHITE WOMAN
    The taxis.
    The taxis are yellow this afternoon
    And seem to float just centimeters
    Above the grey cement, the two
    the taxis and cement—
    Are separate and apart.

    The traffic.
    The traffic is heavy, this afternoon
    And seems to float just centimeters
    Above the grey cement, the two
    The traffic and cement—
    Are separate and apart . . .
    makes horrible racket,
    This traffic.

    The stores.
    The stores are numerous this afternoon
    So are the windows in these stores
    You can see your own reflection in them
    As you pass. There are also many
    Restaurants in which to have lunch
    And talk business and sometimes
    Of things that touch the heart.

---

4 (Translation for production personnel only, not for audiences.)
   These trees
  So tall, straight
  I look at trees like this
     Inside of me—here—
     I feel someone, a being
     Someone standing there
     Someone breathing there
     Spirit alive and living
     These trees
     Green so rich
     I want
     To talk to them
     Walk in them
     Breathe in them
     Live inside their breathing
     These trees.

The spirits.
I see no spirits whatsoever
On this cement, I don't know
What this other woman is talking about.
I walk on this cement, and the two
This cement and I—
Are distinctly separate and apart.

THE SECRETARY
What the well-dressed girl will wear:

Wash'n'wear polyester chalk-stripe wrap-around in slimming come-again
navy blue. Sixteen ridiculous dollars. Designed to please the man who calls
her 'secretary girl'.

Cute little navy blue pumps with heels high enough to entice, low enough
to run. *Armé de Salvation.* $4. But only her best friend needs to know.

This snappy ensemble is completed by a fin-blue cotton T-shirt with
slit-neck and droopy loopy sleeves by Alfred Sung. $125. She was depressed
and she . . . simply had to go shopping.

Nevertheless.
She stands.
A veritable soldierette.
On the brink of pay equity.
Success will be hers before you can say:
'Phew-phew!'

THE EXECUTIVE SECRETARY
(in the rhythm of a slow samba)
Today:
I live in closer proximity
To the man in the pin-striped suit
My vocabulary has increased
The first time I heard the word
'Proximity' I thought it was some new
Disease or at least some obscure Brazilian
Dance not unlike the bossa nova, the cha-cha
Or the samba. Hey!
Living in closer proximity
To the man in the pin-striped suit
I'm aware of the greater power
I've acquired over my own fate

My destiny; my life
My will and I appreciate
That power I embrace that power
And that power looks attractive
And beguiling on my sleeve
On the shank of the old left leg.
I'm no longer some lowly minion
A servant girl, a lackey
A gofer or an ornamental exercise
I'm Executive Secretary now and
I live in more intense proximity
To the man, the man in the pin-striped suit
More intense proximity to
The man in the pin-striped suit
Is a state of being I much
Appreciate I get to stand
Behind the man and place my
Hands upon his back so that
He doesn't fall when he finds
He doesn't have the time or
Finds he is incapable or
Finds he doesn't have the answer
Like right now, he'll ask me and
I'll go: 'Yes, this is the way'
Or 'No, that's not the way'
Or 'Yes, I'd do it this way'
Or 'No, the prices are extravagant'
                    horses are an asset'
        begonias will not do'
Or 'It's more than once I've
Climbed into your shoes and
Steered you through the darkness
Of your pin-striped mind, my man
That's my job'
Living in such intimate proximity
To the man in the pin-striped suit
I began to feel that the pin-striped
Suit is sticking to my skin.
In little bits and pieces this morning
I got up and there before me
In the glass two pins and a stripe
Were sunk into the
Outer layer of my forehead not an inch
From my brain at noon I'm

Eating lunch with my soup spoon
Raised with three pins and two stripes
Announce themselves on the palm
Of my right hand so it seems
That if I choose persistence
In this close proximity to the man
In the pin-striped suit! Oh . . . but . . .
Well, it's like a tool, a hammer
Or a sickle or a sword that I
Wield and I flash and I order
Secretaries hither and secretaries thither
Flocks, gangs, hordes of secretaries
At my bidding and they part
Like the deep Red Sea before
My gliding, whispering
Sleek and sinuous Executive
Secretary form young girls
Sprouting shards of fire-painted
Fingernails in love within electrified
By their IBM Selectrics and I
Glide past them like an elegant fish
To the side of the man
The man in the pin-striped suit.

My vocabulary has expanded
'Proximity' is a concept
That I appreciate
So
Much.

THE EXECUTIVE
Good morning, gentlemen.

Gentlemen, in October of 1986, the Executive Committee of the Ontario League
of Native Brotherhood Centres hired me as Executive Director to operate and
monitor the costs of programmes province-wide. It must have become evident to
the Executive Committee and every member of the Board that the status of the
organization is tenuous and unstable at best.

With reference to the Ontario Native Courtworker programme, first put into
place in 1961 to reduce the percentage of Natives incarcerated in the Canadian
penal system, the success quotient has stabilized at 40 per cent. It was your goal to
train and equitably distribute Native courtworkers to Brotherhood Centres across
this fair province. It was to be incumbent upon the Courtworkers to interpret

legalese to Native offenders, access lawyers and interpret to the courts the cultural perspective of Natives standing trial.

Time and money for the implementation of this essential service has been eaten away by the bickering, by the jockeying for position and by the ridiculous political posturings within the Executive Committee itself. It is my contention that in becoming abscessed with the might of its own power, this Executive Committee has forgotten what it was first put in place to do.

As a result of mismanagement, misdirection, and what amounts to near criminal negligence, our Courtworkers are facing impossible working conditions and are inadequately paid for responsibilities too numerous for them to negotiate.

I can walk into the Premier's office tomorrow and get that additional $200,000. You've tried. You've failed. I'm telling you, I can do it. I have the interest, the personality, the speaking ability, the power, the vision, the determination, and the drive.

We could put that $200,000 into a comprehensive training package and put at least eight more Courtworkers into the system. However, in the interest of maximum efficiency with respect to the delivery of programmes to our Native community, I can offer each member of the Executive Committee: $100 a week for in-town travel; a Tilden rent-a-car credit card; dental, medical, optical, family, and other benefits. And a darned good business lunch. In return for which, the Executive Committee will grant me tenure. And complete unlimited . . . control.

So this is what it's like. This is what I came to do. To change this fabulous masculine world. Succeed? Of course. I'm a success. I sit on top of the world, men scattered at my feet like roses at a shrine. And here I thought I would move these incredible motionless men, waken them to the voices of these many thousand women in their blood . . . make them understand this energy, my spirit . . . that clings to the pores of my skin like the mouths of a million frightened children. So . . .

Thank you, gentlemen.

THE DIVA
  Woman . . . alone . . . forest
  Hunter
  Marry . . . her lodge
  Two sons . . . good wife
  Grown careless . . . work
  He spies on her
  Naked
  Hissing snakes
  Penetrating . . . every orifice
  Hunter kills . . . snakes

Soup . . . blood . . .
Feeding . . . wife.
'You have eaten blood of your lovers.'
She runs . . . see . . . dead lovers
Sons . . . flee
Hunter gives . . . medicine . . . for protection.
'If sky red tonight,' he tells sons, 'I have died.'
Wife returns
Hunter axes . . . her head
Slashes her body
Throws it to the sky
Woman's skull attacks . . . devours
Fleeing sons see red sky . . . know . . .
Coldness . . .
Mother's rolling skull cries
'Come to mother.'
Sons throw medicine . . .
Thorn patch . . . entangles skull
Boys escape
Beaver helps her
Chase
Mother's skull again cries
'Come to mother.'
Sons throw second medicine
Huge cliff stops skull
Boys escape
May-may-quay-sik helps her
Chase
Skull cries
'Come to mother.'
Sons throw third medicine
Flames surround skull.
But still . . . skull chases
Boys throw fourth medicine
Poplar stumps entangle skull
Skull frees itself
Chase . . .
'Come to mother.'
Boys throw last medicine.
Water gushes
Water bird helps skull
But falls in water
'My sons. Save me.'

Boys throw rocks.
Split skull
Skull sinks
Boys free . . .

THE DIVA/THE WOMAN OF THE ROLLING HEAD
I loved my husband once.

Then in my soul one night
Crept the dark spirit silently
And in the forest I made love
To ten thousand snakes
Night after night.

Crying, writhing,
Singing at the moon,
One night he saw me there
My husband saw me then
And cut my head off with an axe.

My body falls
But I refuse.
I will not die.
I will not die.

My head leaps.
My mouth leaps.
I tear his throat.
Feast on his flesh.

My sons
I tear their throats.
Feast on their flesh.
And my sons, sons
And on and on and on

'Babies. My babies. Come to your loving mother.'
I am the Woman of the Rolling Head
I loved ten thousand snakes
I loved ten thousand snakes
I loved ten thousand snakes
'Children. Come. Come to me. Your mother . . .'

(speaks) I can't. I can't. This is wrong. This is all wrong. The wrong way.
Wrong way. Wrong way to tell the stories. We've forgotten how to tell the
old stories. They're fading. Fading. No. No. They can't. Can't. What am
I doing here. What am I doing here.

MARILYN
Ooooh!
How long
Are you going to
Love me
For?

THE PROSTITUTE
Hey, mister. Gotta cigarette?

Hey, mister. Got the time?

Hey, mister . . .

Hey . . .

Starlight, starry night, bright light and I'm alright . . .

Hey, mister. Wanna buy me a drink?

Hey, mister . . .

He sits there in his brand-new sky-blue/chrome Chevrolet Impala. Drives
by in the starry night and doesn't even see the goddamn stars . . .

Chevrolet Impala, eh? Hey, where's that guy in the great big BMW who
came to me last week, whimpering between my legs like a puppy dog in
need of a home?

Hey, mister. Wanna give me a ride?

Street life gets to one sometimes and after a while . . . what the hell and
damn it all anyway, a girl's gotta make a living and a girl's gotta be able to
buy a drink.

Starlight, moonlight, I'm alright . . .

Car lights glide past me. Glide past. These men, these anonymous men,
these lonely men, they cast their hungry eyes at me and peer real deep into
this little old red heart of mine. What the fuck do they wanna see? The
reflection of themselves and their lolling tongues?

Hey, mister. Wanna see me? The real me?

Wanna see the me beneath all this lipstick, rouge, eye-liner shit I've slapped
on my face to make myself look just a little more white?

Hey, mister. I promise you, mister, it'll make you feel so good you'll come for days. And it'll cost you only sixty bucks. Sixty bucks. That's all. . . . What do you expect, pork chops at the IGA down the street is going for $3.95 a kilo this week and they don't even come anywhere near . . .

Hey, mister. Hey, wait a minute. I was just. . . . Oh shit.

Gettin, a little chilly. Gotta buy me more pantyhose tomorrow. My ass is gettin, a little loose around the edges gotta do something about it, maybe take up judo or Tae-kwon-do or something . . . that way maybe I can protect myself against any man who may come along and abuse me with his . . . his fists, like beat me up, like pulverize me, like beat the shit out of me. This way I could just give him a judo chop right across the neck like this, 'ha!' and he'd fall dead right on top of my two tits . . .

Yes, pantyhose . . .

Well, now, there's starlight and car light and there's nightlight and city light, neon light and street light and starlight and I'm alright and starlight and shit car light's glaring at me like they've never seen a woman before, what's a matter, your wife won't give ya . . .

Hey.

THE EARTH
And the songbird paused.
My spirit . . . like a mist.
There was a gift came down to me.
(sings) Kees-pin ki-sa-gee-hin.
(speaks) Strange and mysterious goings-on.
And pain becomes power.
Here is the aisle.
Me and him and him and me.
U-wi-nuk ee-pa-gi-ta-ia-moot.
Are separate and apart.
Like ahmmm . . . so, anyway.
I touch you and you speak.
Closer proximity to.
I can offer each member.
Ten thousand snakes.
Oooh, how long?
Starlight, moonlight and I'm alright! Hey!

I knew she was alive.
I know Earth is alive.

I can feel through the soles of
My moving feet . . .
Earth.
Nuna.
Us-ki!
> *Blackout.*
> *The end.*

Alootook Ipellie *b.* 1951

INUIT

Alootook Ipellie was born in a camp on the north shore of Frobisher Bay in the Northwest Territories (present-day Nunavut) on 11 August 1951: 'I grew up in the Arctic as a semi-nomad with my family. And then we were forced to settle in a community of other Inuit families. So I spent most of my adolescence in Iqaluit during a period of Inuit cultural upheaval. . . . It was a trying period because most families were struggling to adjust to community living that festered with new social problems mainly associated with alcohol abuse and the generation gap. . . . I went through school wanting to write about what I had seen and what I could do to help my people cope with their problems.'

Ipellie was educated in Iqaluit, Yellowknife, and Ottawa, where he still lives. He has worked for the CBC as an announcer/producer and for the magazines *Inuit Today, Inuit, the Magazine of the Inuit Circumpolar Conference,* and *Nunatsiaq News* as a writer, artist, and editor. From 1989 to 1993 he was the project co-ordinator of the Baffin Writers' Project. Ipellie now works as a freelance editor and edits *KIV-IOQ, Inuit Fiction Magazine.*

'I've always thought writing and storytelling were means of exploring some parts of truth about human nature,' Ipellie says, 'and that stories need to be told or written in order to understand ourselves better. They are essentially tools we use to help express our 'silent voice' within our conscious or unconscious minds. . . . Writing and storytelling allow us to escape our own predicaments in this physical world and free our minds to go beyond it. . . . [They] should sometimes educate but always, always entertain.'

Ipellie's art is featured in the Inuit anthology *Paper Stays Put* (1981), and his writing and art are collected in *Arctic Dreams and Nightmares* (1993). He has completed a number of works as yet unpublished, including a novel, *Akavik, the Manchurian David Bowie.* He is also preparing a collection of his cartoons.

Summit with Sedna, the Mother of Sea Beasts

As a shaman, I had many occasions to visit Sedna, the Mother of Sea Beasts. Making spirit journeys to her home at the bottom of the sea was often perilous. But these journeys were done out of great sense of duty to my people when hard times beset them.

One winter, a great famine was affecting a number of camps in our region of the Arctic. I was curious to know if other regions were having the same problem. So I made a spirit journey in order to contact all my fellow shamans. Indeed, the great famine was not restricted to our area.

A decision was immediately made what we, as a collective of shamans, could do to reverse our bad fortune. This was before I found out that our respective shamanic powers had greatly diminished in recent months. Sedna, in her moodiness, was directing her vengeance toward all shamans by not granting their pleas to release the sea beasts. I began to question my fellow shamans about the type of encounters they recently had with the Goddess of the Sea.

Unbelievably, what I found out from my peers could well go down in history as a 'sexual misconduct' that had the potential to wipe out the Inuit nation from the face of the earth. It was the kind of news I could not have fathomed in my lifetime.

From the beginning of winter, Sedna had apparently been making sexual advances to the visiting spirits of the shamans. Although she was well-acquainted with certain sea animals she controlled, she had never been able to have an orgasm no matter how hard she tried. In her last act of desperation, she had begun to solicit for sexual favours before she could release the sea beasts to the Inuit living in the natural world.

My peers didn't really have any choice but to feel obliged to fulfil her requests fearing that their failure to convince Sedna to release the sea beasts might brand them incapable in the eyes of their people. Being seen as a weak shaman would not only diminish their economic well-being, but most certainly wipe out their prestige among their fellow Inuit. As hard as they tried to use their sexual experience to their advantage, they had all failed the ultimate test.

Sedna, feeling miserable and sexually bankrupt, had decided to withhold all the sea beasts until a shaman, any old shaman, succeeded in releasing her sexual tensions.

After having heard this unbelievable story, I spent some time trying to figure out a way to break the impasse. Our people's predicament became a desperate situation calling for once-in-a-lifetime encounter with the Goddess of the Sea. Being one of the most powerful shamans living in the Arctic, I was selected by my peers to prepare a summit with Sedna.

It took me a week to go back and study all of my shamanic rituals and taboos that had worked before. Then I had to come up with a new technique which might change the course of our misfortune.

My plan called for all shamans of the Arctic Kingdom to get together for a combined spirit journey to the bottom of the sea. Each shaman was asked to invite their respective spirit helpers which would be collectively molded to create a giant malevolent creature, a hundred times larger than a normal human being. This new creature would also possess spiritual powers equivalent to a hundred spirit souls.

From the very beginning, I knew it was quite unusual planning to confront Sedna in such an unorthodox manner. We had never before gone out of our way to try to make her submit to our demands. Our fool-proof method was always to plead with her to release the animals. So it was with some apprehension that we proceeded to try our luck.

Moments after darkness descended over our camp, the ecstatic journey began. I started with a song which I had constructed for this particular journey in order to

evoke my spirit helpers as well as those of my peers. It was one of the most complicated seances I had yet tried.

Finally, after having expended a vast amount of emotional energy through my
songs and chants, I was successful in summoning all the spirit helpers to one spot. The
next step was to make the earth move open so that we could enter it and proceed to
find our way to Sedna's abode. Before we ever got close to its vicinity, we had to pass
through abysses, fire, and ice, and then face Sedna's Sea Dogs which always guard the
entrance to her home.

Moments after successfully passing the Sea Dogs, we got a glimpse of Sedna swimming into her huge bedroom. I motioned my helpers to wait behind as planned so that
I could confront Sedna one on one and try to find my bearings with her.

She lay there on her bed, which was well covered with seaweed. Her long,
unkempt hair had become quite dirty. By the look of her distraught eyes and down-
turned mouth, I had the inkling she was still sexually frustrated.

As was always the case in my past encounters with her, I immediately started to
comb and braid her hair while pleading with her to release the sea beasts. She was perfectly willing to—under one condition. I wanted to know what it was. What I then
heard was a long, drawn-out preamble to her life-long sexual history, or lack of it.

It had all started when she was still a little girl living in the natural world a few
years before she became a Goddess of the Sea. Her father had sexually abused her many
times, and when they occurred, they lasted for hours on end. It was because of this
prolonged abuse that she became emotionally, mentally, and physically doomed to sexual impotency—unable to ever again have an orgasm no matter how hard or what
method she tried.

In a last-ditch effort to turn her misfortune around, she had begun to relegate her
best hopes to the visiting spirits of the shamans from the entire Arctic Kingdom. When
an attempted bribe failed with each spirit, she would try again with another. This sor-
did affair continued for the whole winter. And now, she was asking me to do the
unthinkable. I was perverted by her desperate words.

It was at this moment that I turned and left the bedroom as if I had given up and
was returning to the natural world. Sedna started to sob like a little, trembling child.
I understood that nothing would make her more sad than another opportunity lost for
sexual fulfilment.

My only alternative was to release our version of 'Frankenstein' to confront Sedna.
Frankenstein crawled into Sedna's bedroom. Sensing the presence of unusual energy
around her, Sedna sat up, moving like a cobra, and turned her head to look over
her shoulder.

What she saw in front of her was a giant of a monster, more fearsome than any
creature she had ever encountered at the bottom of the sea. Frankenstein stood up and
towered over the tiny body of Sedna. Sedna shrieked the hell out of her lungs. She
begged the monster to stand back, extending her webbed hands toward the monster's
eyes which were streaked with crimson and glowing like gold.

Frankenstein started a special chant I had composed for him. It was designed to put
Sedna under a trance. This would allow her to have an ecstatic dream—a sensual trip she

had never taken in her lifetime. After all, Sedna had become, over the passing of many years, an almost senseless soul, unable to express intimacy in light of her impotency.

During her forced-sensual dream, Sedna finally met her match. It was her male equivalent, Andes, a God of the Sea, who presided over all the sea beasts on the other side of the universe. In her dream of dreams, Sedna finally had a sexual encounter measurable in ecstatic terms only attainable in the world of Gods and Goddesses.

In her state of heightened sexual ecstasy, Sedna released a perpetual explosion of orgasmic juices. In the same instance, during her virgin joy, she released all the sea beasts who immediately proceeded to travel with impunity to the hungry Arctic world.

It was beautiful to see the lovely beasts, swimming torpedo-like, toward the breathing holes on the sea ice. It was wonderful to experience the same excitement as the unleashing of bottled tension Sedna was going through for the first time in her long vocation.

It was also the first time in the history of the Arctic Kingdom that all of its shamans had worked together to avert an almost certain threat of extinction of its people from the face of the earth. From this day on, the Inuit were assured survival as a vibrant force in what was oftentimes an inhospitable Arctic world.

And, perhaps more importantly for me, in the eyes of my people, my reputation as a powerful shaman remained perfectly intact.

Waking Up

Waking up
Just as I have
In the last one hundred years
Barely ahead of the trickling-in of dawn

But this time there was a difference   5

A rude wakening
Had to blink a few times
To make sure the image stayed the same
After each opening of my lids

Then pinched both my cheeks   10
Slapped them slightly
To neutralize the tinge of pain
Spreading it around more evenly
So they would survive the ordeal

Stood up and looked down at my naked feet   15
Wanting to be re-assured
That they were indeed firmly planted
On the earth-bound moss

Affirmation was there for the taking
If only I could find it   20
Within this misty soul

Turned around in despair
Hoping to see familiar faces
Afraid of what I might see
In the pre-dawn shadows   25
I became terrified of whatever
I had just turned away from
Scared of the unknown

Premature arrival of Armageddon
Just like being trapped in a nightmare   30
Running slightly ahead of certain death
The passage of time lasting forever

Who said waking up
Each morning was a blessing from god
For having survived another night   35
And again face the un-doing
Of your consciousness

Life is like night and day
Painted in black and white
Graphic as ever   40
Does it mean we are headed for paradise
Or doomed to oblivion

That's the beauty of our lives
It is what keeps us going forward
Wondering   45
Wondering what is next to come
Around the next bend
Beyond the next horizon
By experiencing the unravelling of events
Within the edge of our vision   50
And in the universe of our minds

Waking up
From what was literally
A nomadic life the night before
To a lifestyle where Inuit hunters   55
Spend all their precious time

Sitting in front of a computer
Pushing predetermined buttons and keys
That allow them to launch
Rocket-powered harpoon missiles   60
Arrows and fish-spears

These are the days of return to innocence
Since the fish birds and animals
Never get to encounter
Their predatory enemies anymore   65

The Arctic has become a class-less society
Since the tools of the twenty-first century
Have finally arrived

No pride nor dignity in that
And I am saddened   70
Since I cannot show off my skills any more
To my loved ones
As well as to those who are accustomed
To being impressed
By my prowess as a great hunter   75

Waking up
Not needing to go outdoors to meet nature
As I was able to only yesterday

Damn

I had to work hard for my living   80
And I could also reward myself
With a triumphant kill
After having witnessed
The frightened eyes of

The bountiful bull caribou   85
The majestic polar bear
The sleek-backed ringed seal
The lumbering girth of a walrus
The feathered friend of a waterfowl
The slippery skin of an arctic char   90
And the welcome sight of a beluga whale

Waking up
Sitting in front of a damn computer
Breathing only used oxygen
Remembering my glory days   95
As a powerful shaman

Lament my friends and enemies
Lament for the enlightened days of yesterday
Lament for the husky who is forced to retire
Lament for the beautiful Arctic landscape   100
Which will never again be seen with naked eyes
Lament for the salty sea
For it will no more hug me and my kayak
Lament for the sun and the moon
For they will no more show off their shine   105
Lament for the northern lights
For they will no more find human heads
To play ball with
Lament for the great spirit
Which takes care of the natural world   110
For its time has come to an end

Waking up
With a slap in the face
My preference is to go back to yesterday
And begin all over again   115

Tonight
I will think twice about going to sleep
I will be afraid of
Waking up

Journey Toward Possibilities

Nothing should be left to an invaded
people except their eyes for weeping.[1]

Like Mary
My mother and father created
An Immaculate Conception   5

---

1 Prussian chancellor Prince Otto Von Bismarck, late nineteenth century.

Well almost
Who in his right mind would think
He was immaculate
There are plenty of souls out there
Who will make such a confession   10
Woebegone to this vulnerable world
Nothing immaculate in what I
See hear feel taste or smell
But I have always expected immaculateness
Ever since being able to comprehend   15
My fellow man's outpourings
But as these years pass by
My great disappointment is still endless
Man's penchant for immaculate discovery
In human beings will always fail miserably   20
Simply because he is doomed to a
Finite failure
Civilization in its very nature is violent
And we are but a small portion
Of its victims   25
Although it can be said that
Because of man's violent nature
We as a distinct entity
Have survived obliteration
For now   30

Manipulation has played a central role
Within our side of the world
The circumpolar world

But to manipulate men,
to propel them towards goals   35
which you—the social reformers—
see, but they may not, is to
deny their human essence,
to treat them as objects without
will of their own, and therefore   40
to degrade them.[2]

Our homelands have been stamped
With these very words
For as long as dominators

2 Sir Isaiah Berlin, Fellow of All Souls, Oxford University.

Of dominant societies   45
Have dominated us
Unfortunately for the foreseeable future
These very words will remain
Comfortably cemented

Unless a new era dawns   50
In our circumpolar world
A yearning not quite like any
Other hunger is growing
Along with a desire
To break away from the grasp   55
Of colonialism
So we may once again squire dignity
Within our hearts and minds
And replenish our souls with pride
Until we are given back our   60
Lost pride and dignity
We shall drape indignation
On all those who
Enjoy our friendliness
And the splendour of our homelands   65
Until these chains tied
Around our will are removed forever
We as a collective
Will continue to be denied
Our freedom   70

Allow us to imagine that
Wonderful state of mind
When ecstasy runneth over
Our goose pimples
In the final realization   75
Of our greatest desire
To be freed from
Our dominators' cage
The hand that may well
Secure our sacred freedom   80
Is contained in the
Embodiment of a new
Arctic Policy
For our circumpolar world
Our greatest hopes   85
Have found a perfect

Gilded foundation
On which to build a protective structure
For our people's continued existence
As a distinct entity   90
In this global cultural mosaic
Since many of our cherished dreams
Still fade unfulfilled
We are as determined as ever
To embark on a journey   95
Toward possibilities
For our people
And our homelands

Godspeed

Walking Both Sides of an Invisible Border

It is never easy
Walking with an invisible border
Separating my left and right foot

I feel like an illegitimate child
Forsaken by my parents   5
At least I can claim innocence
Since I did not ask to come
Into this world

Walking on both sides of this
Invisible border   10
Each and every day
And for the rest of my life
Is like having been
Sentenced to a torture chamber
Without having committed a crime   15

Understanding the history of humanity
I am not the least surprised
This is happening to me
A non-entity
During this population explosion   20
In a minuscule world

I did not ask to be born an Inuk
Nor did I ask to be forced
To learn an alien culture
With an alien language   25
But I lucked out on fate
Which I am able to undo

I have resorted to fancy dancing
In order to survive each day
No wonder I have earned   30
The dubious reputation of being
The world's premier choreographer
Of distinctive dance steps
That allow me to avoid
Potential personal paranoia   35
On both sides of this invisible border

Sometimes this border becomes so wide
That I am unable to take another step
My feet being too far apart

When my crotch begins to tear apart   40
I am forced to invent
A brand new dance step
The premier choreographer
Saving the day once more

Destiny acted itself out   45
Deciding for me where I would come from
And what I would become

So I am left to fend for myself
Walking in two different worlds
Trying my best to make sense   50
Of two opposing cultures
Which are unable to integrate
Lest they swallow one another whole

Each and every day
Is a fighting day   55
A war of raw nerves
And to show for my efforts
I have a fair share of wins and losses

When will all this end
This senseless battle   60
Between my left and right foot

When will the invisible border
Cease to be

Margo Kane *b.* 1951

SAULTEAUX/CREE

Margo Kane is an interdisciplinary artist who has worked as a storyteller, actor, singer, dancer, choreographer, director, video and installation artist, producer, and teacher. 'I write only because I felt it necessary to develop and perform work that meant something to me,' she explains.

> Waiting and hoping for scripts in the seventies, I finally began to work towards my own script development process. I wanted to perform scripts that spoke to my humanity both as a Native contemporary woman and as an artist.
>
> I began experimenting with style and technique using storytelling methods learned from formal Western theatre and drawing on my experiences of storytelling in the Native community, formal and

informal events, from stories around the campfire to witnessing various ceremonial 'performances' in the West Coast Bighouses.

Kane's best-known piece, *Moonlodge* (1990), was first produced by Native Earth Performing Arts. Other performances include her first one-woman show, *Reflections in the Medicine Wheel*, which was created for Expo 86 in Vancouver; *O Elijah, We've Always Been Here*, *Childhood Burial*, *Memories Springing/ Waters Singing*, *I Walk, I Remember*, and *Confessions of An Indian/Cowboy*. Kane performs in both rural and urban Native communities across Canada, where she carries out her commitment to producing work that is not just socially relevant but empowering as well.

Moonlodge

[NOTE: All characters are played by one woman. As audience enters there is the warm, inviting, playful sound of women's voices in Cree and English around a fire. Agnes enters with a suitcase.]

AGNES: Millie? Are you in there? *[Peeks in door.]* Oh, excuse me—I'm looking for—you are here. Am I late? Thank goodness. Where should I sit? *[Makes her way inside the lodge.]* Ooops, sorry! *[Sits.]* There . . . O.K.

It was Millie who invited me to the lodge. Her round face, sparkle in her eye—her smile, always teasing. And long, thick black braids—tight, neat braids. I trust her like a sister or my mother. Her hands, always busy, darting here—and fluttering like a bird—*[Struggling with a sudden memory.]* the bird that got caught in my house when I was a child.

[She stands and relives memory.] The bird . . . in my house . . . the screen door snaps shut . . . there's a whirr and a flutter. It's a bird! Mom!

MOM: Something's gonna happen! Agnes! Open the door! I'll get the broom! *[Mom swipes at the bird and hits Agnes accidentally.]* Oops, sorry! *[She laughs.]* And the bird crashes into the kitchen window where it bangs and flutters. *[Her hands fly up either side of her face to show the bird crashing into the kitchen window.]* The tea towel! *[Still laughing, she swipes at the ceiling, opens the door.]* And the bird flies out into the yard.

AGNES: *[Hugs mother.]* She was laughing . . . and I hung onto her skirt, my head against her belly.

[Piecing more memory together.] I was making frybread, standing on a stool in front of the stove . . . *[Tends frybread with spatula.]* . . . for a big dinner!

How will we feed everyone? We barely have enough food to last till the next cheque. Auntie Edna always says, 'The Creator will provide.'

[Draws cross in the air with a spatula while intoning . . .] My father can beat your father at domino-o-o-s.

Auntie Edna! Tansi! *[Opens door, takes large bowl.]* Macaroni salad. *[Wrinkles nose distastefully.]* My favourite! Would you like some tea? *[Brings her a cup.]*

Auntie Edna always smelled like powder and lipstick. Her hair was . . . curly and whirly . . .

[Remembers.] Uncle Alvin! *[Moves to hanging drum.]* Before dinner, Uncle Alvin sang . . . in Indian . . . I didn't know what he was singing. We were sitting on the floor . . . the food was on . . . cardboard? . . . on the floor . . . it was full . . . the room was full of people and food! Meat and berries and macaroni salad and . . . frybread. I made the frybread. Uncle Alvin was singing.

I poured the tea for the grownups after dinner. Their voices got louder and louder and my father's was right along with them. He was tall, headscarf . . . *[Imitating.]* They been takin from us for a long time and now we're takin their welfare cheques.

FATHER: I'm not gonna take this lyin down!

AGNES: Us kids, we beat it outta there! *[Runs out of the house.]*

We played down by the creek until it was too dark to play any more. We played . . . One bannock, two bannock, etc. . . . *[Peeking.]* 100 bannock! *[Sneaks directly to Annie's hiding spot.]* I see you Annie!

ANNIE: *[Whining.]* No you don't.

AGNES: Last one home's a mud guppie! *[Agnes races for home.]* Home free! Annie's a mud guppie!

[Laughing, she collapses on ground and looks up at the sky.] It was late. The moon took her light behind the clouds. Some dogs were yappin in the distance. Us kids, ssshhh! *[Signals kids to follow her.]* We crept onto the porch and peeked in through the screen door. Few people sittin. My father. He's still talkin! His head

snaps to attention. Us kids freeze. He comes towards the door and stops. He sniffs. *[She sniffs the air like an animal.]* Eiyiyiy!! We tackled his legs and tried to pull him over. He dragged us around the room!

FATHER: *[Collapsing on the ground.]* Ahhh. My little army. They can take me but they'll never take us all.

AGNES: *[Realizing.]* My father was taken away soon after by some men. And then the welfare came to take us.

Mom, there's two cars pulling up. The priest—and some white people. Mom! *[Runs in house and hides behind Mom.]*

MOM: They're my kids! No you don't!

AGNES: *[Fighting.]* No! Mom! Let me go! No! *[She falls to floor.]*

MOM: They're my kids! *[Trying to grab kids.]* Eddie! You take care of your brother. Robbie, don't cry. Don't hurt her! Sarah stay close to your sister. Annie it'll be okay. Agnes I'll come for you soon.

AGNES: My fists are bruised as they crash against the car window, where I bang and flutter. *[Agnes beats the car window with her fists and open hands alternately as she silently screams* Momma! *She freezes with hands still on window either side of her face in the same motif as the bird against the kitchen window.]*

AGNES: The last time I saw my mother, she was runnin down the road after the car.

[She steels herself against the pain of abandonment.] They moved us from foster home to foster home. They took brothers from sisters and sisters from sisters, until I sat all alone in the car just looking out the window.

I remember moving and moving until I didn't know where I was or where I was going or where I came from.

I had to share beds with all kinds of children. And dinner tables filled with strangers. *[Sits on suitcase and folds hands.]* I had to say grace all by myself.

God is good . . . *[Corrects herself.]* . . . great. God is good. Let us thank him for our food.

[Sing-songie without feeling.] Come Lord Jesus be our guest. And let this food to us be blessed. Amen.

[Sarcastic.] For what we are about to receive. May the Lord make us truly thankful. *[She is slapped.]*

[Retreats with suitcase.] I remember moving and moving.

Finally I came to live with a woman named Aunt Sophie.

[Opens suitcase and dresses in Sophie's scarf, sweater, and shopping satchel.]

Now Aunt Sophie was a very large woman with a very large voice. She was a very practical and sensible woman.

SOPHIE: Now Agnes, if you're going shopping with me today button up your coat. I won't have you catching your death. And get that hair out of your eyes or I'll scalp you. Now stand up straight. Put your shoulders back. Come along.

AGNES: And off we'd go for our weekly shopping. Aunt Sophie knew everybody.

SOPHIE: Well, hello Mrs Rosenberg. How are you feeling today dear? You're still looking a little peaked. Really. I think I maybe should give you my doctor's number because I don't know if yours is doing the best for you dear. Trust me. Ohhh! I've been busier than a one-armed paperhanger. Agnes and I are going shopping today for her first brassiere. You know she's at that age!

AGNES: I hated everyone knowing our business!

SOPHIE: Well, hello Mr Weitzel and how are you today dear? Oh, I hope these aren't the same cabbages you sold me last week. I think you owe me this one. You know the last ones you sold me, when I opened them up to make cabbage rolls I found them crawling with maggots. Believe me! *[Weitzel makes a pass at her.]* Oh, Mr Weitzel!

AGNES: Mr Weitzel had a son named Solomon and I loved to watch him work. I felt kinda sorry for Solomon. He had spectacles and really scrawny arms. When he lifted the banana boxes I just wanted to run and help him!

[Agnes moons over Solomon.] Aunt Sophie! *[Searches the store.]* Oh my God! Aunt Sophie's heading towards the Moonies selling flowers on the street corner. Oh my God!

SOPHIE: Children, now listen to me. I'll give you a quarter to call your parents. They're probably worried sick about you. Look at you. Standing on street corners, givin up your education and job and everything. And for what? You think that Reverend Sun-in-the-Moon would be standing on the street corner for you? Hmmm?

AGNES: And the Moonies just stood there smiling and lovebombing everyone that went by.

[Takes off Sophie's clothes and packs for Brownie camp.] Aunt Sophie knew a lot about a lot of things but she didn't know a thing about Brownies. When my girlfriend Lynnette asked me to join Brownies I had to explain to Aunt Sophie.

Well, there is all kinds of Brownies. There's elves and fairies and gnomes and pixies and sprites and imps and kelpies . . . and they help people. And if you're a Brownie you get badges for making your bed and cleaning your room and helping your mom. And Brownies live in the woods so we get to go to camp and take nature walks and learn about trees and flowers and birds and . . . and . . . things and sing campfire songs.

SOPHIE: I think it's very important that you get in touch with your tribal heritage!

AGNES: Tribal heritage? I just want to go to Brownies! *[Takes suitcase to Brownies, dresses in headband and feather from inside it, sits on it in cartoon Indian pose—arms and legs crossed.]*

It was at Brownies that I learned my first Indian song. *[Gets hanging drum.]* And I got to lead the campfire songs because I had a very strong voice. *[Earnestly drums in Hollywood tom-tom tradition.]*

My Paddle

My paddle keen and bright
flashing with silver
follow the wild goose flight
dip, dip and swing
dip, dip and swing

And the Brown Owl, Mrs Corscadden smiles at me and then signals all the girls to join in.

> dip, dip and swing her back
> flashing with silver
> swift as the wild goose flight
> dip, dip and swing
> dip, dip and swing
> dip, dip and swing

[Stands and grins at audience.]

The next song I'm going to sing is Land Of The Silver Birch.

> Land of the silver birch
> home of the beaver
> where still the mighty moose
> wanders at will
> blue lake and rocky shore
> I will return once more
> boom diddy boom boom
> boom diddy boom boom
> boom diddy boom boom

I loved camp.

There were no Indians in my neighbourhood. The only Indians I saw were on television. I remember the Walt Disney Injuns. They were big, fat redmen with flat noses. 'Ugh! Me wantum smokum peacepipe.' And pretty little princesses named Princess Minni-Haha. And cartoon Injuns that danced the rain dance. *[She whoops and dances.]*

And I remember some of the popular songs on the radio. *[She becomes a country singer.]* Okay all you Injuns out there. This one's for you. Whoo! Whoo! Whoo! *[Starts tom-tom beat.]*

Kawliga

> Kawliga was a wooden Indian
> Standing by the door
> He fell in love with an Indian maid
> over in the antique store

> Kawliga
> Just stood there and never let it show
> so she could never answer yes or no

> He always wore his Sunday feathers
> and held a tommyhawk

The maiden wore her beads and braids
and hoped some day he'd talk

Kawliga
too stubborn to ever show a sign
because his heart was made of knotty pine

CHORUS:
Poor ol' Kawliga
he never got a kiss
Poor ol' Kawliga
he don't know what he missed
Is it any wonder
that his face is red
Kawliga that poor ol' wooden head

Another song that struck a chord in my red soul was the story of Running Bear and Little White Dove who couldn't be together because their tribes were at war. *[Music up/Running Bear. She imitates a cartoon Running Bear doing a war dance.]*

Running Bear

On the banks of the river
stood Running Bear, young Indian brave
on the other side of the river
stood his lovely Indian maid

[She poses on standing suitcase as Little White Dove.]

Little White Dove was her name
such a lovely sight to see

All the women were either subservient or sexy. I preferred sexy! *[Is dancing seductively flaunting and pouting.]* And the women always followed their men ten paces behind.

But their tribes fought with each other
so their love could never be

Hollywood version. Lots of leg. *[Chorus line kicks.]*

Running Bear loved Little White Dove
with a love as big as the sky

Fringed mini-skirts. Lots of skin. *[More chorus line kicks.]*

Running Bear loved Little White Dove
with a love that couldn't die

Savage tragedy! *[Melodramatic pose. Dives onto floor and does frog stroke.]*

> He couldn't swim the raging river
> 'Cause the river was too wide

[Continues swimming various strokes.] Because his name was Running Bear and not Swimming Bear!

> He couldn't reach Little White Dove
> waiting on the other side

[She shades her eyes.] And Indians always looked like this because if they looked like this *[Covers them]* they couldn't see anything.

> In the moonlight he could see her
> blowing kisses across the waves
> her heart was beating faster
> waiting there for her brave

[Much shimmy with breasts and shoulders.] Primitive, primal, savage, supernatural love. *[Music is fading.]*
[Music out.] Indian!

I was one of the few brown faces in school and then Indians were bussed in. Real Indians! Marvin was tall and handsome. His hair was long and wild. All us girls would hang near him waiting to catch his eye. Then he'd turn and flash his famous smile and we'd all melt. I had a crush on him. Even some of the white girls had crushes on him. But I never talked to him. He scared me. I knew he could see the Indian in me. He looked right in and touched it with his eyes. He knew me but I didn't know him. He came from a remote reserve that I knew nothing about. I didn't belong to his world. He didn't fit into the system and eventually he quit school. *[Hangs up drums.]*

Somehow I managed to graduate from high school and everyone was talking about California and San Francisco and Haight-Ashbury and love-ins. It sounded so . . . groovy! And they were all taking their backpacks and hitchhiking . . . all over. There was a bigger world outside of my Aunt Sophie's. *[Packs up feather and headband, takes out flower and psychedelic scarf and ties scarf around waist.]*

Aunt Sophie . . . she'd never let me go. Well I'm old enough. I've saved up my money. I'll leave her a note. I'll send her a postcard from somewhere. I'll phone her from a telephone booth on the highway.

[Placing call.] Hello Aunt Sophie? Yes it's me. No, I'm not going shopping with you today. No, I'm going on a trip. I'm hitchhiking. Aunt Sophie. Aunt Sophie, please don't cry. Please, Aunt Sophie. I'm not running away. I'll call you. I'll phone collect. Aunt Sophie, listen. I love you very much. *[She hangs up and begins to sing.]*

Big Yellow Taxi

> Don't it always seem to go
> That you don't know what you've got
> til it's gone

You pave Paradise
put up a parking lot
doooo doo doo doo doo
doooo doo doo doo doo

[While singing she has put flower in her hair and picked up suitcase.]
Bye Aunt Sophie!
[She begins to hitchhike still singing and dancing 'The Jerk' and then 'The Hitchhiker'.]
Thanks!
My first ride was—well . . . the ashtray was overflowing with butts and ashes and there was a film on the window and he had nicotine stains all over his fingers and teeth. And he kept staring at me. But he bought me lunch.

Well, it was really groovy that you gave me a ride. Thanks for the lunch. But you know I just remembered that my Aunt Delores lives down this way! And it would be really awful if I didn't stop to visit her. These people over here said they would give me a ride. Can you believe it? Miracles! Take care of yourself. Peace. *[Gives him the peace sign and walks away, suitcase in hand.]*

He was playing footsie with me under the table and when he looked at me he wasn't looking at my face if you know what I mean!

There's a gas station down the way. For sure I'll get a ride somewhere.

Oh my God! Harley Davidsons! A whole herd of Harley Davidsons! So much chrome . . . chrome mirrors, chrome pipes, musta cost a mint! Chrome everywhere! Electric colours—fluorescent orange and yellow flames! *[Lowers herself slowly onto the bike suitcase.]* Baby blue metallic! California plates! It's the most incredible, fabulous, outta sight, outta m-i-n-d . . . *[Sees Marlon in front of bike.]*

Hi! Is this your bike? Oh. It's the most incredible bike I've ever seen. I've never been on a bike before. I just had to . . . I just couldn't help myself! *[Gets off the bike.]*

There was this guy and he had a white t-shirt stretched over his tight muscles, cigarette pack under the sleeve and tight jeans and big biker boots. Over his shoulder he carried a black leather jacket and he shifted from hip to hip. He looked like Marlon Brando.

BIKER: 'Charlie, Charlie!'

AGNES: He even sounded like Marlon Brando.

BIKER: 'You were my brother. You shouldda taken care of me!'

AGNES: Are you from California? I see you have California plates. Do you live there? Oh, you're so lucky! Oh God! You know I would do anything to ride on a bike.
I'm just hanging on his every word. He's very cool. Where are you going?

BIKER: 'Charlie! Charlie! I couldda been a contender!'

AGNES: Wow! Santa Fe. Is that on the way to California? I've heard it's really beautiful. It would be great to go there. Then he says . . .

BIKER: Uhhh. You . . . *[Thumb points to her.]* Me . . . *[Points to himself.]* Uhh . . . *[He waves hand between them.]* Eh? *[Points with thumb over shoulder to bike.]*

AGNES: Then he asks me to go along!

[Music up—'Born To Be Wild'. She leaps onto bike, tries to jumpstart it. It rumbles on the second try. She lipsyncs to first verse.]

Born To Be Wild

Get your motor runnin
head out on the highway
lookin for adventure
in whatever comes our way

And here I am riding down the highway on a Harley Davidson. I can just hear Aunt Sophie!

SOPHIE: Hooligans! Riff-raff! No self-respecting girl would be caught dead tearing around the countryside with such . . . neanderthals!

AGNES: Oh Aunt Sophie! You don't know how to live!

[Music up high and she rides away, her skirt flying. She sits backwards, her skirt always billowing and she is smiling and laughing. She sits side saddle the wind blowing her hair all over. She picks up her scarf end and it flies full against her face as she rides. She continues on under the music alternating the billowing from side to side.

She gets off bike and joins a party. She drinks from a bottle, takes a joint, and chokes on the toke. Finishes beer and heaves the empty bottle away. Music fades out. She is high and intoxicated.]

That first night we rumbled into the campground at dusk. I look across the fire to see Marlon beckoning to me. I'm alone with Marlon under the starry sky.

[She rises shyly and moves slowing to biker. She begins to sing 'On The Street Where You Live' in a high soprano. She puts her hand out and he kisses it and sweeps her into a waltz.]

On The Street Where You Live

I have often walked down these streets before
but the pavement always stayed beneath my feet before
All at once am I several stories high
knowing I'm on the street where you live

[She extends her hand and he grabs her and drags her around the stage and pushes her onto the ground. She is startled and grabs the scarf/shawl to keep herself covered. They struggle for the scarf pulling it back and forth.]

And ohhhh, the towering feeling
just to know somehow you are near
that overpowering feeling
that any second you might suddenly appear

[In one strong movement he pulls the scarf off and throws it away. In another he pushes her back on the ground and abruptly separates her legs.]

People stop and stare
They don't bother me

Wait a minute, you're crushing me! *[She struggles.]*

for there's nowhere else on earth
that I would rather be

No!

Let the world go by

Noooooo!
[She freezes. Her head and shoulders just off the floor, her arms tense and stretched out in the air. She sings with the last of her strength at her highest pitch.]

I don't care if I
can be found
on the street
where
you
live!

[She collapses and reaches for the discarded scarf. Very frightened she slowly and painfully moves away from him.]
Somehow I made it all the way to Sante Fe.
[Throws flower away, picks up suitcase, and leaves.]

Sante Fe is the oldest place I've ever seen. I get to the centre of town and there's this little park—plaza they call it. And there's Indians everywhere. They're sitting in doorways and on sidewalks and on blankets full of silver jewellery and weavings and other knick knacks. As Aunt Sophie would say, *[Sophie's voice]* 'You know, peddling their wares. It's good they're getting something for their handicrafts. Lord knows they need jobs!' And the art galleries are full of Indian paintings.

SOPHIE: And they're being sold in the hotels, no less. Is this art or something?

AGNES: And this one woman catches my eye and she's surrounded by the most gorgeous pottery in oranges and browns—very traditional I'm told. And this one piece is at least a foot high. It's this pueblo woman with all these babies hanging off her.

Oh, it's so beautiful! Did you make it? The Storyteller? The Storyteller.

And there's these blue cowboy boots in front of me and these long legs. And there's this Indian man standing under a huge cowboy hat. He's got long braids and a big silver and turquoise belt buckle. And then he turns and strolls away.

Do you know him?

There was something about him. *[She begins to follow him.]* Every time he turned around I pretended I was looking in a store window. I didn't know what to say. Oh my God. He's getting into his truck. I'm going to lose him. I'll head him off at the pass. *[She hitchhikes. The truck stops and she climbs in.]*

Thank you very much. My name is Turtle Dove. Well, my real name is Agnes. So what's your name? Lance.

He had this beautiful brown face with high cheekbones, deep brown pools for eyes, and this big pearly, Colgate smile.

You know, I've never seen blue cowboy boots before. You look like you just got off a horse. *[Pause.]* I'm from Canada. So, where are you from? South Dakota. Oh, I know where that is. It's north of here isn't it? *[Pause.]* Which tribe are you from? I know all about the Sioux. Television. *[Pause.]* What was Custer's famous last words at the Little Battle of Bighorn? These Siouxs are killing me! *[She kills herself laughing. He doesn't enjoy the joke.]*

I see this feather hanging from the rearview mirror.

What kind of feather is this? Eagle! Where did you get it?

Then Lance tells me it was given to him. You can't buy eagle feathers. They have to be given to you. The eagle is a very sacred bird, a messenger. You can't go out and shoot an eagle for its feathers. The eagle will leave them for you.

[Pause.] I'd sure like to have one some day.

So I ask Lance where he's driving to and he says he's meeting some of his brothers down the road.

LANCE: The revolution has already begun—always been there smouldering, waiting for the spark. That spark could be you! I see Alcatraz and Wounded Knee wherever our red brothers and sisters take a stand. When are you gonna get up on your hind legs and fight? I'm not going to take this lying down. They've been takin from us for a long time now you're takin their welfare cheques! Hmmmm?

AGNES: He says that a lot of his brothers will be at the Powwow. Powwow.

What's a Powwow? *[Powwow drum up.]*

It was like a scene out of the movies. Tall teepees standing in the dusk surrounded by a huge encampment of tents and campers, trucks and jeeps and old station wagons loaded with kids. I've never seen so many Indians in one place! Some are covered in feathers and furs with sleigh bells around their ankles that jingle as they walk. Old men walk by in coloured shirts hung with ribbons and grannies in kerchiefs and flower-print dresses. Some men look like cowboys . . . boots and stetsons. They lean against vans and half-tons joking and teasing each other—in a language I don't understand. I notice the people moving towards the sound of the drumming and I don't remember Lance after that. *[Powwow music up higher.]*

I am standing in a huge dance arbour surrounded by bleachers full of Indians. Around the dance floor sit at least a dozen big drums surrounded by singers and their families and friends. The announcer's banter rises above the drumming.

ANNOUNCER: Hooo-yah! Powwow time! Intertribal! Heeeeeyah! Everybody dance! Hokah! Hokah! Hokah! Hey!

AGNES: *[Begins to dance.]* The dancers move around and around in a slow circle. The whole arbour is a sea of rippling fringes and feathers and beads. *[She continues her attempt to dance watching those around her.]*

The old people are so dignified. The women carry shawls over their arms. Feather fans salute the sky. *[She dances on the spot saluting the sky.]*

Children imitate little birds, strutting and hopping. Some are so serious! *[She dances as the little boys and then the little girls.]*

Grass dancers! Long fringes sway like meadow grasses in the wind. *[She dances.]*

Painted traditional men parade in their bustles of eagle feathers. They carry staffs and eagle wings. *[She dances.]*

Acrobatic young men show off feather bustles like huge prairie chickens, strutting and twirling! *[She dances.]*

Young women, fancy dancers! Their braids hung with otter and weasel fur. Their beaded moccasins are a blur as they prance and kick and twirl. Their shawls fly around their shoulders. *[She dances and ends with powwow music.]*

I could have danced all night!

Lance finds me later that night in a crowd around the Black Lodge Singers. Sleep? Do you have a tent? Oh. Are there snakes around here? The back of the truck would be perfect.

[She lies down.] Is that a coyote?

[Lights fade. She sings closing song dreamily, sitting up and looking around. Then lies down and sleeps.]

[Waking up, yawning and stretching.] Mmmm! Coffee! Lance. Lance!

[She sees Millie.] At the camp next to us a woman pours steaming coffee into mugs and hands them around. Her long braids swing, a child clings to her skirt.

[She is caught staring.] Good morning! Coffee? Oh yes, thank you.

MILLIE: Help yourself to some cream and sugar.

[Noticing mess.] Damn dogs! Rooting around in the garbage!

What do you call a dog with no legs? What's the use of calling him. He won't come anyway!

My name is Millie. Agnes. So what are you Agnes? Stoney? Cree? You don't know!? Your first powwow? Ohhhh. You better watch out for them singers. My husband is a singer.

Hey! Remember that song you used to sing when you were first courting me. Aaah!

Okay, then I'll sing it! *[She finds drum.]* Back then he had all his teeth. He could still see his belt buckle. *[She sings and drums.]*

> Oh, yes I love you honey dear
> I don't care if you're married sixteen times
> I'll get you yeah!
> ah yeah hah yeah
> yeah hah hah yeah

Oh I have a very good memory. *[Hangs up drum.]* Would you like some frybread?

It used to be my job to make frybread for the big dinners. I had a stool in front of the stove at—home. . . . *[Retreating.]* I've gotta go. Excuse me. I'll be back later. *[As memory floods in.]*

[She leaves, eating frybread thoughtfully as she goes. As she finishes eating she looks around at craft tables in front of her. Spies a bracelet and picks it up.]

Jewellery! Oooh!

How much is this? *[Replaces it quickly.]* It's very beautiful.

There's this guy at one of the tables dressed like an Indian, sort of. He's got all kinds of beads and claws and stuff hanging off him and his hair is in scrawny braids—but it's blond! Well, Aunt Sophie always says, 'Never judge a man until you've walked a mile in his moccasins!'

Indian Tarot cards? Sacred dog? Sacred eagle? Sacred bat! Your card? *[Reading.]* Peter Many Painted Ponies. Shaman for any occasion. Ceremonies, Sundances, Vision Questing, Rebirthing, and Past Life Regression. Thanks. See ya.

Lance! There's this white guy sellin Medicine things and he's dressed like an Indian! Lance is preening in the truck mirror and doesn't even look at me.

LANCE: Probably a member of the famous Wannabee tribe.

AGNES: Wannabee?

LANCE: Cherokee, Pawnee, Comanche, Wannabee.

AGNES: Wannabee? I met a red-haired woman who said she was Cherokee but she looked like Edna Feinstein who lived down the street. Wannabee. *[Understanding.]* And this blonde woman who called herself Yellow Moon Rising.

And when they found out I was Indian, I had more friends than you could shake a stick at.

WOMEN: Ohhh, so you're an Injun? You don't look Injun. What tribe are you? Well, where're you from? Canada? Ohhhh, so you must be Eskimo.

If you're an Indian what's the colour of North on the Sacred Medicine Wheel? What's your Indian name? You're sure you're an Indian?

Do you have a totem animal? You should go to the sweat lodge to get one! My totem animal is a black panther.

I don't tell everyone this but I'm a pipe-carrier as well and I'm training to be a Medicine-Woman.

AGNES: *[Backs away.]* Medicine? I got to talk to Millie.

MILLIE: Hmmm? Medicine. There's all kinds of medicine for all kinds of people. Could you hand me that box please? *[Packing.]* We're packin up now, so we can get an early start on the trail. *[Gently.]* You look confused. Your medicine will come from your own people.

AGNES: My own people? *[Under her breath.]* But I don't remember who they are.

MILLIE: *[Still packing.]* Where are you headed next? Do you know where you're going? I don't think so. What are you looking for?

AGNES: I didn't know I was looking for anything.

MILLIE: Have you ever looked for your family? Maybe that's what you should be looking for. *[Handing present to her.]* Here, I want you to have this.

This is a special little feather. We call it an eagle plume. You see I've attached it to a beaded rosette. Just tie it into your hair when you're dancing.

AGNES: *[She is overwhelmed.]* A feather. An eagle feather. Thank you Millie! *[Puts feather in hair.]*

MILLIE: You know the eagles watch over all things. They can soar high above the earth close to the Creator Spirit. They bless our ceremonies when they soar overhead. They keep watch for us—keep us on the right road.

Well, you know where to find me. When you're in my neck of the woods just ask around. I'm the only Millie there. Come and stay awhile. I'll be expecting you.

AGNES: *[Quietly.]* Bye Millie. *[Sound of wind is heard.]*

It is miles outside of Santa Fe that I stand in the desert mountains. I stare, transfixed, at ancient cave dwellings carved out of a huge mesa. I crawl through stone chambers and climb stone stairways to the mesa top. The ruins of an old village surround a grassy plaza. I stand all alone breathing in the warm desert wind. I am high above the plains and valleys that stretch for miles and miles. I can see what those ancient people must have seen—the mauve and rose-coloured landscape as the sun begins to hug the horizon. And I am running across that open plaza, climbing through stone buildings, tracing pathways into deep stone wells to sit quiet and hushed on stone benches, feeling the cool earth inside the hot stone village. And I wonder what became of these people. Where did they move to? And why did they leave?

I climb down into a nearby canyon. The moon offers her light to brighten my way. The wind whips the dust into tiny tornadoes. A tumbleweed whirls across my path. No water runs in the dry creek bed. Nothing green grows. Only twisted bushes cling to canyon walls. It feels like something has died here and been blown away and I want to go home.

[She picks up drum and sits on the floor in front of a fire. Sound of women's Cree and English voices.]

It was Millie who pointed me in the right direction.

Outside the wind rustles in the tree leaves. The smell of fresh pine boughs under me. The sparks and ashes from the fire drift up and out the smoke-hole of the teepee of the Moonlodge. I see my grandmothers and sisters and daughters all around me. Millie finishes her preparations and looks at me across the fire.

MILLIE: *[Offers her drum.]* Welcome, my girl. Welcome to the circle. We are grateful and thank the Higher Power that you are here.

AGNES: *[Begins to drum softly.]* I have this dream. A woman gives me a cage with a white bird in it. I don't trust her but I say, 'Thank you very much.' And I back away. I am moving so I get into my car full of my possessions and place the cage on the front seat between me and my big Indian friend. As I drive down the road the bird keeps escaping and my friend shoves it back into the cage but it keeps squeezing out between the bars and both of us are trying to keep it in. And it's growing and its wings are flapping in my face and around my head. I can't see where I'm driving! And my window is open a few inches and it grabs the window with its claws and it's the size of an albatross and its beak is out the window gasping for air. If it doesn't get enough air it's gonna die. And I freak out and stop the car. I wrap the bird in my jacket and hold it very close. Ssshhh.

[She sings same song that she fell asleep to after Powwow dancing, as lullaby which soars as lights fade to black.]

Duncan Mercredi *b.* 1951

INNINEW/CREE

Duncan Mercredi was born in Grand Rapids, Manitoba, and moved at the age of sixteen to Cranberry Portage to finish high school. After graduation he worked for twenty years in construction, much of the time as a surveyor, throughout Manitoba. He recalls the many instances of overt and covert racism he encountered during that time, including the simple surprise of some that a Native man might be employed with a white survey crew. On one occasion his foreman related a comment by a farmer who had been observing Mercredi working: 'That little Japanese guy sure has good eyesight.'

Mercredi is now a researcher with the federal government, but he is also a prolific and committed writer. He recalls the influence of the stories told by his *kookum* [grandmother]: 'I always thought how incredible she was that she could take me places and experience events that she had stored away in her mind and heart.' Although his grandmother gave Mercredi the desire to write, he did not pursue writing until his late thirties: 'After meeting Maria Campbell, Jordan Wheeler, Lee Maracle, and other writers of First Nation ancestry, I began writing with a passion as I felt the need for others, meaning "white society"—or is it mainstream society?—to experience what I have and in my words.'

Mercredi has published four collections of poems: *Spirit of the wolf: raise your voice* (1990), *Dreams of the wolf in the city* (1992), *Wolf and shadows*, and *The Duke of Windsor—Wolf Sings the Blues* (1997).

could be anyone but i call him syd

syd smokes dope most any night he can
he'll visit acquaintances on sundays
taking the back alleys for emphasis
trying to look suspicious
no use wasting the neighborhood watch   5
syd used to roll drunks for a living
course most of the drunks he knew were friends
syd would feel guilty and treat them the next day
with their money
syd smokes dope most any night he can   10
says it don't affect him none
just can't remember what year it is
and if he's a hyphenated canadian
syd he tried going traditional once
but he thought the four day grace period   15
was cruel and unusual punishment
so syd went back to being catholic
only cost a few our fathers and hail marys
the rosary some one had left at some church
downtown it was syd who had gone in to warm up   20

was a cold bitchin' day remember last
syd he'd forget sometimes but he never forgot
‚where i lived
or he'd phone
then he'd stroll up the walk and i'd watch 25
houses around ours would suddenly wake
windows would have eyes
and syd smokes dope most any night he can
he'd turn and face the street and bow
then lift his arms to show he was unarmed 30
nothing had been lifted
syd didn't like being hyphenated
didn't like smoking dope
he was sorry he rolled friends
he hoped god wasn't too upset 35
that he asked the creator not to judge him
syd smokes dope most any night he can
doesn't anymore
he wanders the back alleys he used to live
seeking the memories he left bleeding 40
as they begged for mercy
crying as syd lifted the little money they had left
watching it stagger away with syd
knowing where to find tomorrow's release from demons
that appeared the same time syd did 45
syd smokes dope most every night he can
now he doesn't sleep
haunted by past losers crying for spare change
wondering if he knew them
syd doesn't smoke most nights now
he doesn't need to   his visions are his own now 50

statue

oh bent naked mis-shapen spokesman of god
with nothing to cover your shame
but half built circles to hide you from the cold
faced away from the river that gave your kookum life
now discarded by your descendants 5
with some ill-conceived notion of greatness
oh bastard child of the prairies

whipped and beaten by time and myth
placed on a pedestal made of leather and bones
bleached white by the prairie wind and sun   10
gaunt body holding grotesque head
writhing in pain
forever and ever
in mind's eye we see lies that were told
revealed now in your anguish   15
staring in vain at the doors in front of you
they remain closed
but one of you sits in the queen's house
shoulder to shoulder
with one like them that draped the noose around your neck   20
a brother of the wind
rejecting the past
as though you were pre-ordained to serve your enemies
oh discarded child of the prairies
the wind carries your message   25
but no one hears the agony of defeat
the weight of years lost standing naked
ridicule heavy on your twisted shoulders
insane he spoke to spirits
but we understood   30
oh abused man of god
the tears have not stopped
your sons have discarded the leather and tobacco
trading them for a bible and collar
that binds you to a vengeful god   35
leaving your children to wander for a century
still seeking their place
while hiding a part of themselves
savages
you too lived inside leather houses   40
you slept on buffalo robes
now the pain of rejection by two nations
is etched in your body
mis-shapen man of the prairies
you hold your head high   45
on a false pedestal
your circle is incomplete
what was your dream

god shrugged and turned his back

famine begets hunger distended bellies beget tears
children dance the devil's tune
blood spills and another butterfly dies
silenced rivers criss-cross by humming wires
fish float belly up   5
and i feel the poison in my blood
burning forests clear cuts scar the land
blue waters turn red then black
suicidal whales hit the beaches
awash in oil a bird dies   10
broken treaties broken bodies
money pays for guns not food
people shoot at people who could be brothers
pieces of cloth stitched together
another star's light fades from the sky   15
a sister lives in fear of the night
children selling bodies
for a bit of pain killer
other men decide our futures
as we stand outside the gate   20
watching brothers pocket their seven pieces of silver
riots death dreams rising into the sky on smoke
jesus came down to listen to the wolf sing
and found him dying
smeared on his body a message   25
thou shalt not kill
jesus raised his arms to the sky
and cried why hast thou forsaken me
the priest smiled his smile
as god shrugged and turned his back   30

big bear

i walked where big bear danced
i feel his joy in the wind
that carries his messages
from the past
i danced where big bear danced   5
his dance steps an imprint on the land

his face a shadow that calls to me
the wind whispering his name
i sleep where big bear sleeps
a prisoner with no walls to hold him   10
he remained a prisoner
so he danced in his mind
when he heard the steel doors slam
he journeyed on the breeze
that caressed him in his cell   15
he sang his songs in silence
i walk where big bear danced
i heard his prayer
i felt his pain
i am his anger   20
big bear still dances
on the ground where i walk

kiskisin (i remember)

images
like photographs
of a river
still
silent   5
flashing from time to time
in my mind
and just before sleep you would appear
woman
shoulders slumped in weariness   10
hands immersed in water
coal oil lamp
with feeble light
casting shadows
hiding tears   15
images
woman
silently rocking in a chair
body buried in a shawl
kookum   20
when no one was around
did you speak to spirits

images sounds
when ni-mama laughed
she was dancing   25
but those photographs are rare
images
i recall wandering into the house
my father in the kitchen
stopping me   30
shut out from women things
secrets
but i wanted to see
only to make me wait
till the cry   35
then they would pout
at the snare wire hanging on the ceiling
images
these powerful women
saying   40
the rabbit got away
but we caught the baby
see a girl
then they'd laugh
at my confusion   45
even ni-mama weakly
from the bed
covered in sweat
shoulders slumped in weariness
images   50
kookum
gently blowing on the baby's face
i asked why
she would say
this way she will always remember me   55
images
watching the land receding
ni-papa
at the rear of the boat
steering   60
into the waves
getting larger
i would shake
and he'd say
do not fear the lake   65
images

kookum gently blowing on my face
ni-mama
looking north
towards her home   70
she was the stranger
but i remember her gently blowing
on my daughter's face

Daniel David Moses *b.* 1952

DELAWARE

Daniel David Moses recalls his childhood on a farm on the Six Nations lands along the Grand River, near Brantford, in southern Ontario: 'I grew up nominally Anglican in a community of various Christian sects and of the Longhouse, the Iroquoian traditional religious and political system. These form the largely unarticulated base of my understanding of the world.'

Moses often asserts the importance of his Delaware heritage, in opposition to various assumptions that he belongs to other tribal groups more common in southern Ontario. Part of this is pride in heritage, but it also reflects a concern for precision, something clear in all of his work, but most obvious in his poetry.

This devotion to craft is related to Moses's education. After receiving an Honours Bachelor of Fine Arts degree from York University he earned a Master of Fine Arts degree from the University of British Columbia, where he won the creative writing department's prize for play-writing in 1977. Moses also studied Native literatures, and spent three summers during his undergraduate years working on an annotated bibliography of books by or about Native peoples for the Department of Indian Affairs.

Moses returned to Toronto in 1979, where he worked part-time in various occupations, including a stint as an assistant immigration officer at Pearson Airport. After 1986 he devoted all of his time to writing. The results were periodical and anthology publications; his plays *Coyote City* (produced in 1988), *The*

Dreaming Beauty (produced in 1990), *Big Buck City* (produced in 1991), *Almighty Voice and His Wife* (produced in 1991), *The Indian Medicine Shows* (produced in 1996), and *Brébuf's Ghost: A Tale of Horror in Three Acts* (produced in 1996); and two collections of poems, *The White Line* (1990) and *Sixteen Jesuses* (2000). He has read and participated in theatre projects in Canada, the United States, Australia, and Europe, and has had extensive experience as writer-in-residence across Canada. He is presently an assistant professor and Queen's National Scholar in the department of drama at Queen's University.

Moses's first book was *Delicate Bodies* (1980), a collection of poems. He recalls that writing poetry was a purposeful choice, to reflect his perception of his stage of development: 'I felt (and now believe I was wise to feel) that lyric poetry was the only form in which I could combine the techniques of writing with the only thing I could claim to know as truth, my own experience. I told myself in poetry I would perfect my technique while I gave myself time to grow up.' Moses now sees this 'growing up' as also a return to certain perceptions traditional to his culture. He recalls his early years as 'being educated to have—let's call it—a western mind, to balance being a good Judaeo-Christian with being scientific.'

When he came to write *Coyote City* Moses blended these facets with what he terms a 'ghost story'. He recalls that Native actors found it much easier to accept the reality of such spirits than others. Moses associates this with their unconscious understanding of the Trickster and his ambivalent nature. Questions of Native mythology are often central to Moses's prose and drama. His poetry represents a comparable rejection of easy answers, as in his analysis of letters in the poem 'Paper':

It's too bad if anyone imagines
words have ever bled when the clean
    blackness
of letters on this paper should imply
that it's easy to live. You can't deny
the truth of salutation or address—
there is nothing but white between
    the lines.

The Sunbather's Fear of the Moon

Now that I'm out walking alone, old Bone
face looks jealous of the blood ruddiness
of my skin. Just let her try to scrape it
away and she will see it takes more than
petty metal to get to me, she'll see   5

how useless a good cool staring-down is
against skin this tough and crusty. And she
should identify with that. What the pale
fool won't understand quite as easily
is that my shine's not a reflected light   10

because it's always noon inside my chest
where day has a home the size of a fist.
I'm flushed with the heat of its love and of
the pleasures it brings through its bright
probing fingers and tongues. It's made me so   15

young I can go it alone. I don't need
that shine she gives to the land so wanly
old Boneface must know it can't cut the dark,
can't make it bleed anymore than I did
by day. The bit of bright blood I shed soaked,   20

as her light does, into the mud. Might be
red rain subterraneously. Or stars
for the troglodytes to see. It doesn't
matter. I refuse to shatter and set.
Let Boneface put on her idiot gape.   25

Inukshuk

You were built from the stones,
they say, positioned
alone against the sky
here so they might take
you for something human   5

checking the migrations.
That's how you manage this,
standing upright despite
the blue wind that snow is,
this close to Polaris.   10

Still, the wind worries
you some. It's your niches
which ought to be empty.
Nothing but lichen grows
there usually. Now   15

they're home to dreams. Most come
from the south, a few from
further north—but what flows
out of their mouths comes from
no direction you know.   20

They keep singing about
the Great Blue Whale the world
is; how it swims through space
having nightmares about
hunters who only hunt   25

their brothers—each after
the other's snow-white face.
How beautiful frozen
flesh is! Like ivory,
like carved bone, like the light   30

of Polaris in hand.
So it goes on and on,
the hunting refrain. Dead
silence would be better,
the Pole star overhead.   35

The wind agrees, at least
wants to stop up each niche.
How long can you stand it
—that song, the cold, the stones
that no longer hold you   40

up now that they hold you
down? Soon the migrations
recommence. How steady
are you? Dreams, so they say,
also sing on the wing.   45

The Persistence of Songs

The people feed from the river and conceive songs.
But the strangers with the dead heads march towards the long
edges of their own blades. They see a thundering
fog along the horned horizon and turn around
to stalk the rising sun. They find four lanterns made   5
of skin arrayed along the river, the people
still feasting within. The strangers feed off their own
anger, flooding the river with blood. The four songs,
who are the children, go dumb and their white dogs mad
before the people have the strangers rounded up.   10

They bind them with skin from the fog and throw them in;
then, they wait for the river to heal. They try
to feast again. They pray to the children. By noon
the river grows an old skin and the children fade.
In the cold mud the strangers congeal. A fog   15
bleeds from the river, drowns the lanterns and stops up
the ears of the people with a dull, three-note song.
The strangers are praising honed edges and the white
meat of their own bodies. They curse the sun and vow
the moon turns so perfectly round they will square it.   20

They lurch up through the river's dull skin and begin
the marching again. The people search in the skin
for reflected light, the sunset or a lantern,
then assume the skin as mourning. The procession
the people enter tracks the moon through fog, cuts it   25
into quarters. And black dogs track the procession.

They feed off their own hunger and conceive a song
in praise of a perfect horizon made of meat.
That song fades; but, the four songs, who are the children,
return with horned heads. They feed from ears and edges.   30

The Line

This is not the poem, this line
I'm feeding you. And the thought
that this line is not the poem
is not it either. Instead
the thought of what this line is   5
not is the weight that sinks it
in. And though this image of
that thought as a weight is quite
a neat figure of speech, you
know what it's not—though it did   10
this time let the line smoothly
arc to this spot, and now lets
it reach down to one other,
one further rhyme—the music
of which almost does measure   15
up, the way it keeps the line
stirring through the dampening
air. Oh, you know you can hear
the lure in that. As you know
you've known from the start the self   20
referring this line's doing
was a hook—a sharp, twisted
bit of wit that made you look
and see how clear it is no
part of this line or its gear   25
could be the poem. Still it cast
and kept the line reeling out
till now at last the hook's on
to itself and about to
tie this line I'm feeding you   30
up with a knot. Referring
to itself has got the line
and us nowhere. So clever's
not what the poem is about
either. We're left hanging there   35

while something like a snout starts
nudging at your ear, nibbling
near my mouth—and it's likely
it's the poem about to take
the bait. From the inside ought   40
to be a great way to learn
what the poem is. And we'll use
this line when the poem's drawn it
taut and fine as breath to tell
what we know, where we are and   45
where we'll go—unless the line
breaks. How would it feel, knowing,
at last, what the poem really
is, to lack the line to speak?

Hotel Centrale, Rotterdam

I am awake between stiff
sheets tonight in room thirty
four, listening to the heat
tick through the radiator,
seeing a television   5

pour out news of the war,
the war in the air, the war
in the Gulf. The walls vibrate
with video light. This is
no room for sleep anymore.   10

There is no room for dreams.
The shooting stars on the screen
are as real as a rain
of fire can be, falling
on some other city. And   15

here I have a star's eye view
—the glide toward the intended
target, the blink of a bridge
into nothing. Do I want
to see that again? I do.   20

Who am I now? Where? I want
to be in that blue leather

armchair down in the lobby,
talking with the people there
about the stories we're in   25

this city to tell. But now
they're using their several
tongues to question the news and
I want none of that, want not
to fall for it again. I   30

am trying to fall asleep.
Those people keep on asking
all night through. *Where are the wives?*
How much is lost? Just what is
the story? In that, a small   35

glory—like that glow, say, down
below, as my overnight
flight ended, a greenhouse bright
as day, a dream suspended
in the blue and frost of dawn.   40

Report on Anna Mae's Remains

The Micmac woman's body has been disinterred and her severed
hands are being transported by air for identification in Washington.

In a refrigerated drawer in South Dakota a thirty eight
calibre bullet floats, an icy glimmer within her skull.

A similar glimmer comes off her fingernails. In the box passing   5
above the Mississippi her hands are rustling, the nails growing,

the fingers unfolding, refolding, pale wings migrating toward the Atlantic.
      Her body sleeps the sleep of the abandoned. Its marrow

refuses to condense. Her blood searches for the pine ridge
under which the shallow grave is. It finds only turquoise   10

leftover from the last wind and leather so softly cured
it welcomes starlight through. The leather's stained with sweat and

semen, but even these relics fade.
      Her hands remember only
the last jet of breath, the warm gun butt, and   15

the dream of power. They try to dream it again,
the dream of black soil flooding and drowning the prairie,

of the sky clearing with light like the shine of
warm blood, of the woman perching in the palm of

a flying stone. But that dream imploded when the woman   20
died. Through their own glimmer her hands dream the remnants,

dream of men with no faces swimming a storm of
hot powder—their heads oiled and hands sharp as shovels,

they dig up and burn the Dead to ash in
the steely air.   25
    Through the sinking light her body feels

a sound. Her hands have escaped the box and her bones
the wrappings of skin. They swing on their tendons, chiming.

Some Grand River Blues

Look. The land ends up
in stubble every
October. The sky
today may feel as

empty. But just be   5
like the river—bend
and reflect it. Those
blues already show

through the skin inside
your elbow—and flow   10
back to the heart. Why
let a few passing

Canada geese up
set you? Just remind
yourself how the land   15
also renews. Don't

despair just because
they're already too
high to hear. Your heart
started beating with   20

their wings the moment
you got sight of them
—but that's no reason
to fear it will still

when they disappear.   25
Look away now. Let
loose. See? The river's
bending like a bruise.

Party Favour

When you bared your china
coloured shoulder, telling

the whole room how a steel
pin had been popped in, how

thin a feel the air had   5
then, the naked scar blushed

deep enough to kiss. It
seemed the only part of

you in the smoky mix
of your party to keep   10

up modesty, a mouth
shaped spot holding shut while

the rest of your flesh spoke
out, dancing loudly and

alone in the middle   15
of the room. Only at

the end of the night were
you quiet, did that spot

seem to speak through the kiss
on the cheek and embrace   20

each of the last few to
take leave of you received.

Descending to the slick
street where flooded gutters

and darkness chilled my feet   25
and music and an orange

glow seeped out of your bay
window—I thought it had

a magic lantern sort
of look—I felt how close   30

in those inebriate
hours comradery

came to love. As close as
healing did to your wound.

The Witch of Niagara

> *This world was already complete*
> *even without white people.*
> *There was everything*
>
> *Ceremony*
> Leslie Marmon Silko

THE WITCH OF NIAGARA was premiered at the Robert Gill Theatre from
9–12 December 1998, produced by the Centre for Indigenous Theatre with the
following cast:

GIRL	Natalie Bomberry
MOTHER	Veronica Sandy
GRANDMOTHER	Lori New Breast
AUNT	Athena McGregor Pheasant
BOY	Jason Soule
FATHER	Narsiesse Paul

UNCLE   Jeremy Proulx
OLD MAN   Wihse Green
THE CHORUS Tanya Lukin
           Billie-Jo Reynolds
           Harmony Rice
           Kira Thompson

Directed by Carole Greyeyes
Stage Management by Jacquie Carpenter
Lighting by Glenn Davidson
Costumes by M.J. Helmer

CHARACTERS
The GIRL
The BOY, the Girl's cousin through her Father
The Chief, the Girl's FATHER
The Girl's UNCLE through her Mother, a War Chief
The OLD MAN
The Girl's GRANDmother through her Mother, a Clan Mother
The Girl's MOTHER
The Girl's AUNT through her Father
The Thunderer, the God of Rain
The God's Helper
The Snake

SETTING
The action occurs
in a village, in the fields, and on the paths through the forest
along the river and gorge in the vicinity of Niagara Falls,
the residence of the Thunderer, the Iroquois god of Rain.

SCENE I

*The new moon looms over Niagara Falls. The
GIRL lies in her grandmother's lodge in the
village. She opens her eyes.*

GIRL: In the story—. The story? In the dream! In the dream, I'm alone. Alone in the village. Alone in the long house. Alone in my bed. In the dream, everything's quiet. No kids. No dogs. No birds. No wind. I can't even hear the falls. The sun's shining.

Then this shadow's there standing in the doorway. It's a man, a stranger, but in the dream I'm not afraid because he's so beautiful. I can't see his face but I know he's beautiful. He speaks to me. His voice is soft, whispering. He sounds far away, even though he's right here beside me. I don't know the words he uses, it's another language, but I understand him all right. I want to ask him who he is, what's going on, where everyone is, but he puts a finger to my lips, puts a finger to my lips—and then kisses me. In the dream he kisses me. No man has ever ever kissed me before.

Then he's gone and I'm awake. And my belly is big and tight as a drum. And Mama and Grandma, they're standing over me, mumbling and shaking their heads. Shaking their heads. And then this pain like a blade down there makes me look, this tickling and trickling between my legs. We all look under my dress. There's this flood, this flood of little baby baby snakes squirming out of me. I can't breathe, I can't breathe, my Mama, my Grandma, they're the ones, they're the ones in the dream who scream. And this flood, this flood of little baby snakes, it crawls back—back inside me.

[She closes her eyes. Thunder. The moon sets.]

SCENE 2

> *Dawn. The hunting camp. The BOY tends the fire, the Girl's FATHER and UNCLE sleep in the lean-to. The OLD MAN enters from the path from the woods.*

OLD MAN: Hello? Hello! Anybody there?

BOY: Uncle, cousin, wake up.

FATHER: What is it?

OLD MAN: How are you this morning?

UNCLE: Who's that?

FATHER: I recognise him. Long time, no see, Grey Hair!

UNCLE: Oh no. The Trader.

BOY: That's him?

OLD MAN: Long time, no see, Chief. Can I bother you for some tea?

FATHER: Sure. Sit, sit.

BOY: Here you go.

OLD MAN: You've been hunting?

FATHER: Down river, far as the lake.

OLD MAN: No luck?

FATHER: As you see, empty hands.

OLD MAN: Hard times, hard times everywhere.

FATHER: We'll be fine.

OLD MAN: Going home now? I'll walk with you then.

UNCLE: You haven't visited us since when?

OLD MAN: The spring. It's so sad for me, coming home now.

UNCLE: You've been where?

OLD MAN: East and west. The salt lake and the dirty river. I've got shells and copper and seed corn.

FATHER: The women will be glad to see you.

OLD MAN: I'll be glad to see them. I've got herbs for them, some medicines.

BOY: You travel alone?

OLD MAN: Who would go with me?

BOY: Don't you get lonely?

FATHER: Don't be rude. I'm sorry, Grey Hair. He's not used to strangers.

OLD MAN: Your sister's boy? Just out of the house, is he?

FATHER: I'm afraid so.

OLD MAN: He'll learn how to treat his elders someday.

BOY: What's he mean by that?

UNCLE: Sh! Let your uncle do the talking.

FATHER: And you?

OLD MAN: Could be worse. I do get lonely sometimes. I'm thinking about getting me a wife.

BOY: Who would marry him?

UNCLE: Sh!

OLD MAN: Someone will marry me, little boy. I'm a catch!

FATHER: I'm sorry, Grey Hair. Boy, pack up! Go on! Get your stuff and go.

BOY: What? Why?

UNCLE: Go! We'll catch up at the midday camp. Go on. You remember where? Then light a fire. We'll cook some meat for a change.

[The BOY grabs his bed roll, his bow and another pack and walks off.]

FATHER: I'm sorry about my nephew. He's a child with a big mouth.

OLD MAN: Too big for his own good! No, no, I like him.

FATHER: Forgive him.

OLD MAN: Don't worry, Chief. What do I care about children? There are more important things in the world.

UNCLE: I'll start packing too.

OLD MAN: Fresh meat for lunch! You're so generous.

UNCLE: You're our guest.

OLD MAN: Still, I won't let my wife have children. She'll have enough to carry.

FATHER: More tea before I dump it?

OLD MAN: So Chief. These times we're living in. Stories of war, of cannibals.

UNCLE: Cannibals?

FATHER: Where do you hear this?

OLD MAN: Upriver. At the west end of the lake. So tell me. How are things at home?

FATHER: What do you mean?

OLD MAN: I could cry, thinking about it. Every time I come home. The same old story.

FATHER: Can't this wait? The day's half over.

OLD MAN: I'm sorry. Help me. I don't want to hurt anyone's feelings by mentioning names I shouldn't. I know how I felt when, I suppose, my own mother was the first . . .

UNCLE: Since the spring?

FATHER: We shouldn't have to talk about this.
UNCLE: Since the spring my wife, my child have died.
FATHER: My father too.
OLD MAN: That's all?
UNCLE: It's enough.
OLD MAN: It's too much.
FATHER: Come on. It's a long day to get home.
UNCLE: Can I carry something for you?
OLD MAN: Would you? I hope I can keep up.

[*Exeunt.*]

SCENE 3

Mid morning. The GIRL *meets her*
GRAND*mother, carrying a load of sticks along a*
path through the woods.

GIRL: Grandma!
GRAND: Sleepy head!
GIRL: Let me help you.
GRAND: Careful. It's heavy.
GIRL: You didn't wake me up?
GRAND: You need your rest.
GIRL: I'm tired *of* resting!
GRAND: I'm tired *of* working. Time for a breather. You should rest while you can. You
    were awake in the middle of the night.
GIRL: I had a dream.
GRAND: Everyone's having a hard time sleeping.
GIRL: The dream woke me up.
GRAND: Even Mother Earth. There was an earthquake.
GIRL: An earthquake?
GRAND: Like the beat of a heart. You woke right up. Squeaked like a little bird! I was
    awake anyway.
GIRL: I was scared.
GRAND: Scared?
GIRL: When I woke up. This morning. There was nobody around.
GRAND: We all have work to do.
GIRL: Mama usually wakes me up.
GRAND: I made her let you sleep.
GIRL: They in the corn field?
GRAND: Don't tire yourself out now. We don't want to have to lug you home again.
    Your father's still out in the woods.
GIRL: I'll be careful.

GRAND: I'll be back out there soon as I stack this.

GIRL: Grandma, why don't they live together, Mama and my father?

GRAND: He wouldn't do what he was told, so I sent him back to his sister.

GIRL: Because of me?

GRAND: What?

GIRL: Because I'm sick all the time?

GRAND: Yes, that must be the reason. And why he always helps us out when he can.

GIRL: But it doesn't make sense.

GRAND: It doesn't. Come here.

[*The Girl's GRANDmother hugs her.*]

GRAND: Now go on. There's work to do.

[*Exeunt separately.*]

SCENE 4

    The midday camp. The OLD MAN is snoring.
    The BOY and the Girl's FATHER and UNCLE
    wait.

UNCLE: What a noise!

BOY: Sounds like someone dying.

FATHER: Be quiet.

BOY: It'll be dark by the time we get home. I'm going.

FATHER: We'll all go soon as he wakes up.

BOY: Let's wake him.

FATHER: He's an old man. Don't offend him.

BOY: He offends me.

UNCLE: You're downwind.

FATHER: Go ahead then. I'll wait for him.

UNCLE: You sure?

BOY: We'll be upwind!

FATHER: I'll say you saw game or something, maybe there'll be really fresh meat for him when we get home.

BOY: The way he chews!

UNCLE: Three teeth maybe. Come on.

BOY: Why don't we just leave?

FATHER: He's an old man.

UNCLE: He's our guest. Here. You carry his pack. We'll go fishing. We can get fish for sure.

BOY: Not fish!

    [*The BOY and the Girl's UNCLE exit. The Girl's FATHER pours himself more tea. The OLD MAN sits up.*]

OLD MAN: I need to talk with you, Chief.

FATHER: You're awake!

OLD MAN: They think old ears are deaf!

FATHER: That boy, I'm sorry about—

OLD MAN: Never mind. He's a child. They both are. I don't mind either of them. I need to talk to a grown up alone. This is so embarrassing.

FATHER: Tea?

OLD MAN: It's—The sickness in the village.

FATHER: What about it?

OLD MAN: I know what to do about it. That's why I'm coming home now.

FATHER: You have a cure?

OLD MAN: I have a cure. I wasn't sure before.

FATHER: How do you know this?

OLD MAN: Do you really want me to say? Whisper the story in your ear? Something like this happened out west. It seems there was this witch around—

FATHER: I won't listen to gossip. Some things shouldn't be said out loud.

OLD MAN: But you believe me?

FATHER: We'll try anything once.

OLD MAN: Good. But then there's this embarrassing part.

FATHER: What?

OLD MAN: Embarrassing for you. I want to make a trade.

FATHER: A trade.

OLD MAN: We're the same age, but I'm an old man. Remember when we were that boy's age?

FATHER: What do you want?

OLD MAN: I need a wife. Who would marry me? I'll tell you. I'll cure the village, but you, you'll give me your daughter.

FATHER: You're crazy.

OLD MAN: I know she's sickly. No loss to you, giving her to me. And I might make her better too. I'll find the medicine for it. Good for her.

FATHER: She's not mine to give. My daughter's mother, her grandmother—.

OLD MAN: Even to save the village?

FATHER: I don't know.

OLD MAN: How embarrassing for you, Chief.

SCENE 5

Dusk. A bucket under a tree at the edge of the corn field. The GIRL and her GRANDmother enter.

GRAND: It's thirsty work, pulling weeds. Hand me that ladle. Oh that's good.

GIRL: That's the last. Should I go get more?

GRAND: No. Sit back. We're almost done. See?

[The Girl's MOTHER enters.]

MOTHER: You look like a couple of old women.
GRAND: We're tired enough for maybe four.
MOTHER: The water?
GRAND: I just drank it up.
MOTHER: Gone! I give you one job to do all day and you can't even—
GIRL: I'll go to the spring now.
GRAND: No, wait. We're done for the day. What's the point now?
GIRL: I'm sorry, Mama.
MOTHER: Don't whine.
GRAND: I told her she could wait.
MOTHER: Stop covering up for her.
GRAND: I'm not covering up—
MOTHER: Stop it. I know how useless she is.

[The GIRL exits with the bucket.]

GRAND: What's the matter with you?
MOTHER: Nothing. A girl who's good for nothing.
GRAND: Look at me. I said look at me.
MOTHER: I'm tired.
GRAND: Did I teach you to act like this? Did I ever treat you like that? No wonder her
father left you.

[The Girl's AUNT enters.]

AUNT: Water! I'm dying here.
GRAND: The girl's gone to the spring.
MOTHER: I didn't sleep last night.
AUNT: I'll go help her.
MOTHER: No, wait.
AUNT: What's wrong?
MOTHER: Someone saw lights travelling along the creek last night. To the spring.
GRAND: Lights?
AUNT: Witch lights?
GRAND: Who? Who saw them?
MOTHER: I did.
GRAND: Up wandering around in the middle of the night! Serves you right.
AUNT: You all right?
GRAND: Why did you say 'someone'?
AUNT: Something bad going on?
GRAND: You really saw lights?
MOTHER: She really saw lights.
GRAND: Can you make sure the girl gets back before dark?
AUNT: Don't worry.

[The Girl's AUNT exits in the direction the Girl went.]

GRAND: Come on. Let's go home.

[Exeunt toward the village.]

SCENE 6

The Girl's UNCLE, bow at the ready on the creek bank, watching for fish. The BOY enters.

BOY: Let's go.
UNCLE: Not yet.
BOY: I'm hungry.
UNCLE: Eat it raw.
BOY: I'm tired of fish.
UNCLE: Be quiet.
BOY: They'll be home before us at this rate.
UNCLE: Fine with me.
BOY: You don't like that old man any more than I do.
UNCLE: I saw him looking you over. Did he pinch your bum?
BOY: Shut up. Why you treat him so good?
UNCLE: You going to be quiet?
BOY: He's not from here.
UNCLE: He used to be. We treat our elders with respect.
BOY: But he doesn't live here now.
UNCLE: He just lives over on the island.
BOY: Above the falls? But that island's haunted.
UNCLE: Ah!
BOY: What? You see one?
UNCLE: You scared it off.
BOY: Sorry.
UNCLE: The women, they say he has medicine.
BOY: You said he's a trader.
UNCLE: Maybe that's how he gets his medicine.
BOY: Medicine. I'd kill him if . . .
UNCLE: Maybe he's just an ugly old man.
BOY: My father's with him.
UNCLE: He's safe. Doesn't have a big mouth.
BOY: Don't laugh at me.
UNCLE: I'm not laughing at you. Sometimes you almost make sense. You should speak up in council. Be quiet now.

[A moment of silence. Then the GIRL, with bucket, enters from the woods.]

GIRL: Uncle! Welcome back.
UNCLE: I give up!
BOY: Hello, cousin.

GIRL: Cousin. Water?

BOY: Sure.

UNCLE: How's your mother?

GIRL: Working hard.

BOY: It tastes fishy.

GIRL: It's from the spring. Uncle, it's going to be dark soon.

UNCLE: I'm going back the long way.

GIRL: All right.

UNCLE: Your father should be home by now.

    [The Girl's UNCLE exits.]

BOY: Come on.

GIRL: My father went straight home?

BOY: We met this old trader.

GIRL: A trader!

BOY: The Grey Hair.

    [The Girl's AUNT enters.]

AUNT: Pumpkin!

BOY: Ma!

AUNT: I'm just glad to see you. I'm your mother. How'd you do? You'll do better next time. Was that your uncle?

BOY: No, hers.

AUNT: Where's he off to?

GIRL: That path.

AUNT: Past the platforms. Oh, the poor guy.

GIRL: He'll want to be alone anyway.

BOY: Can we go? I'm hungry.

GIRL: My father's got some trader with him.

AUNT: He might have fresh herbs?

BOY: He said he had medicines.

    [Exeunt.]

SCENE 7

    The Girl's GRANDmother and MOTHER are in
    their lodge.

MOTHER: It's late, isn't it?

GRAND: Just sunset.

MOTHER: Where are they?

GRAND: Sit down, rest.

MOTHER: She's the one who rests. What good is she to us?

GRAND: Sit down. What were you doing, wandering around in the dark?

MOTHER: You were awake too.

GRAND: Who sleeps these days?

MOTHER: Who will take care of them if I die? You're too old.

[The Girl's FATHER and the OLD MAN enter.]

FATHER: Can we talk with you? I've brought the trader with me.

OLD MAN: Long time, no see, grandmother.

GRAND: You're welcome. Both of you. Have a seat, Grey Hair.

MOTHER: What do you want here?

GRAND: Forgive her. She's tired.

OLD MAN: Hard times, hard times everywhere.

MOTHER: You want to help me?

OLD MAN: I want to help you, child.

FATHER: He wants to help all of us.

GRAND: What is it?

FATHER: It's hard to say this.

MOTHER: You know what's going on here, don't you?

OLD MAN: I know enough of the story.

MOTHER: What do you know?

GRAND: Be patient.

FATHER: He knows what to do now. Against the sickness.

GRAND: What do you know?

FATHER: He says it's witchery.

MOTHER: Witches!

GRAND: Is this true?

OLD MAN: It's hard to explain it. They're watching us.

MOTHER: I knew it. I knew it.

GRAND: Nobody's seen strangers.

OLD MAN: They've been watching all along. They're all around the village.

GRAND: What do you want? What's he want?

OLD MAN: To make a trade.

GRAND: A trade?

FATHER: We're here to ask your permission for my daughter to marry Grey Hair.

OLD MAN: Your daughter's so lovely.

MOTHER: Who would want a wife so sickly?

OLD MAN: I do. I'll take her.

GRAND: You're old. And you're no hunter. Why would she want to marry you?

OLD MAN: If she marries me, I'll put a stop to the dying.

MOTHER: You'll stop the dying! How?

FATHER: You said it yourself, clan mother. His medicine's powerful.

OLD MAN: Convince her. You'll all be saved. If only I'd known how before my own mother died.

FATHER: My daughter will save us all.

OLD MAN: So lovely, that girl.

MOTHER: Let him have her.

OLD MAN: Oh thank you, thank you.

GRAND: You can't fight witches you can't see.

OLD MAN: I will fight them. For her, I will fight them.

GIRL [with bucket, entering]: Grandma, my uncle and cousin, at the creek said my
    father—

FATHER: Here I am, Girl. Come here.

GRAND: No. Over here.

GIRL: What is it, Grandma?

GRAND: Come. Sit by me.

FATHER: Sit with your Grandma.

GIRL: What's wrong? You guys fighting again?

MOTHER: Be quiet.

FATHER: This is the trader.

OLD MAN: Hello, Girl.

FATHER: Listen to your Grandma. She has something to ask.

GIRL: What is it, Mama?

MOTHER: Listen to her.

GRAND: This man?

GIRL: Why's he looking at me?

GRAND: He's brought us some medicines.

FATHER: He might make you better.

OLD MAN: I'll try.

FATHER: He says he's going to stop the dying.

GIRL: Stop the dying?

GRAND: He needs help. Will you help him?

GIRL: Me? How?

GRAND: Will you marry him?—

FATHER: Marry him.—

MOTHER: Marry him!

GRAND: Will you be his wife?—

MOTHER: His wife.—

FATHER: His wife!

GRAND: Look at me. What's the matter?

GIRL: A pain. Like a blade.

MOTHER: Good for nothing.

UNCLE [off]: Mother? Mother, are you there?

> [The Girl's uncle, a scrap of blanket in hand, enters, followed by her aunt and
> the boy.]

GRAND: What is it, son?

UNCLE: Look at this. Look.

MOTHER: What's wrong, brother?

UNCLE: This is the blanket. This is all that's left.

BOY: It reeks!

UNCLE: The platform's a mess.

GRAND: What are you talking about? This is what blanket?

UNCLE: Where we put my wife and child. It's gone.

FATHER: The platform's gone?

UNCLE: Their bodies are gone.

OLD MAN: This is witchcraft.

UNCLE: Witchcraft?

OLD MAN: This is the witch craft for sure. Witches use dead bodies in their tricks.

GRAND: What's going on . . . ?

OLD MAN: What else could it be? I hate to think what those witches will do to that poor little baby's body.

UNCLE: I'll kill them! Show me how!

MOTHER: Don't cry, brother.

UNCLE: I'll kill them.

OLD MAN: Will you give her to me now? I promise I'll kill them. I'll stop the dying.

MOTHER: We can fix things now.

GRAND: I feel like crying.

MOTHER: Grey Hair knows how.

OLD MAN: Give her to me!

GRAND: Go on. Go to him.

GIRL: Mama? Papa?

GRAND: Go to Grey Hair. Take his hand.

GIRL: Grandma, no.

FATHER: You'll do as you're told.—

MOTHER: Do as you're told!

GRAND: You'll marry him in the morning.

OLD MAN: I'll treat you good. I'll make you better.

GIRL: No!

[The GIRL exits at a run.]

SCENE 8

*The new moon hangs over Niagara Falls. The
BOY sits in his mother's lodge in the village. The
moon grows full during the BOY's monologue
and dawn comes at the monologue's end.*

BOY: Who knew she could run like that? But that old man, hey, you'd run away from him too.

They chased her—we chased her, out of the village. Down the street, through the gate, into the dark. Mostly it was her father, her uncle and me chasing, us and the dogs. Everybody looked at us like we were crazy. Maybe we were. The dogs barking, thinking it was all a game.

Out the gate into the dark and once around the fields, like she used to playing tag. I could have caught her, I saw what she was up to then, circling back, back. Later on my mom says, You know, pumpkin—ya, like I'm still her pumpkin—You know, I used to think maybe you and her would get together someday. I mean I'd never thought of it before that but I think I probably thought so too, ya, otherwise why'd I let her get away like that? I thought about it later a lot, because I thought I'd let her go die.

Ya, she runs out along the path, along the creek past the springs and gets to the river and gets cornered there out on the point. I don't think she's ever been that far from the village before.

I catch up to the men in time to see her climbing into a canoe. What it's doing there, who knows, but it's white like the moon, like the birch bark ones the Ojibwa use, so afterwards her mother says that proves it was just more witchery. It's strange to see, the way it moves out over the river, over the rapids, like a bit of light on the surface, and her not needing to paddle it at all. We call after her to come back. Her grandmother and the other women are there too by now, calling her, saying she don't have to marry the trader after all. He's standing there, just standing there grinning all three teeth, watching it all.

All too late. The canoe rides out to the brink of the falls, out toward the thunderhead of mist, rides out and goes, just like that. No one else sees it. ask. There's a rainbow, ya, the ghost of a rainbow there in the dark, just where she's disappeared.

We can't find her, or the canoe. Or the old man—he just isn't there the next morning. We keep on looking for her though, her grandmother's so sad, right until freeze up. Her grandmother starts to get old. Her uncle too. Her father and mother can't even look at each other any more on the street. My ma and me, we try to help—.

And then one day, in the spring, walking back in through the gate and up the street, there she is, big as life—Big with life, mutters my ma—dogs and kids following her, following her past her grandmother's house, her father's house straight into the meeting, the meeting of the council.

SCENE 9

> *Day. The Girl's MOTHER, GRANDmother and AUNT sit on one side of the council house, her FATHER, UNCLE and the BOY sit on the other, the GIRL stands the space in the centre near the fire. They stare at her.*

BOY: She looked around.
GIRL: They were just staring!
BOY: Then her grandmother—

GRAND: Are you alive?

GIRL: I'm alive, Grandma!

BOY: Then the rest of us, we got brave enough to touch her too. Her story was—

GIRL: —I've been in the caves. The caves under the falls? With the God of Cloud and Rain. The Thunderer. His helpers saved me. When that witch canoe—

MOTHER: It was a witch!

GIRL: When it carried me away over the falls—

GRAND: I wanted to cry!

GIRL: —the God's Helper caught me in a rainbow blanket. He took me into their lodge and gave me rain water and made me well.

[Sunset. Moonrise.]

GRAND: We were so sad.

AUNT: We missed you, didn't we, son?

MOTHER: What about the witch?

GIRL: The God's Helper, he told me the witch is still there. On the island in the river.

FATHER: The Grey Hair!

GIRL: Watching for his chance at the rest of us.

GIRL: The Grey Hair's been trading with a giant snake, it lives underground, dreaming of the meat from dead bodies. The Grey Hair's been trading our dead for power.

UNCLE: A snake that big must get hungry—

GIRL: So that old man's been poisoning our springs.

GRAND: So we die before our time. It isn't fair.

[Moonset. Sunrise.]

BOY: So the very next day—

FATHER: —we moved the village across the river, away from the snake and the poison.

AUNT: We weren't there four days before there's this rumbling coming louder than the falls.

BOY: Worse than the ice at break up.

UNCLE: That snake must have been hungry!

AUNT: It crawled out right in broad daylight.

MOTHER: It's following us! If it gets across the river—

AUNT: Nobody could miss it. The earth was shaking and quaking!

UNCLE: Look at the size of that thing!

BOY: Thick as an oak.

AUNT: Where's it going?

MOTHER: It's heading for the river!

UNCLE: Look at that thunderhead!

GRAND: It's walking off the river.

BOY: The Thunderer! It's the Thunderer!

MOTHER: He's chasing that snake.

FATHER: He's throwing rocks at it.

AUNT: They're turning into bolts of lightning.

UNCLE: Lightning bolts!

BOY: The snake's trying to bite at them but they're too bright!

FATHER: Too loud!

UNCLE: Too many forks!

GIRL: And sharper than it's own tongue. The snake's dead.

[Sunset.]

BOY: The body falls into the river and floats down stream.

MOTHER: That body floated by—

FATHER: —and by—

UNCLE: —and by . . .

AUNT: Lullaby?

[Moonrise.]

BOY: Then the body gets stuck—

FATHER: —stuck on the rocks—

UNCLE: —at the brink of the Falls.

MOTHER: Under all that weight—

GRAND: —the rocks there finally give way.

AUNT: Crash!

FATHER: Boom!

BOY: Bang!

AUNT: What a mess!

BOY: Which is why those Falls don't go straight across today.

GIRL: That crash wrecks the God's cave, so he and his Helper pick up and move out west somewhere. I never saw him again.

AUNT: Typical!

[The sun and moon both rise over Niagara Falls.]

MOTHER: Later, she whispers to her mother about the God's Helper.

GIRL: I'm not afraid because he's so beautiful. I can't see his face but I know he's beautiful. He speaks to me. His voice is soft, like falling rain far away on leaves, even though he's right here beside me. The words he uses, it's strange, but I understand him all right. He puts a finger to my lips and kisses me.

MOTHER: Later, she makes her mother a grandmother.

BOY: Later, we—we have other children, but when her oldest child grows to be a man, he almost kills me with a lightning ball.

GIRL: So I send him west.

BOY: —to live in his father's new house.

GRAND: She lives to be as old as her grandmother.

BOY: The witch disappears from the island and is also never seen again.

GRAND: For which we give thanks.

GIRL: We give thanks to our Mother, the Earth, for sustaining us.

BOY: We thank the rivers and streams for giving us water.

MOTHER: We give thanks to all herbs who furnish medicines for the cure of our sicknesses.

GRAND: We thank the Corn, and her sisters, the Beans and Squashes, who give us life.

UNCLE: We give thanks to the bushes and trees for their fruit.

AUNT: We thank the wind who banishes sicknesses.

FATHER: We give thanks to the moon and stars who give us their light when the sun is gone.

GIRL: We thank our grandfather, The Thunderer, for protecting his grandchildren from witches and serpents, and for giving us his rain.

BOY: We give thanks to the sun for looking upon the earth with a beneficent eye.

GRAND: Finally, we thank the Giver of Life, who embodies all goodness and who directs all things for the good of his children.

[The sun and moon both set over Niagara Falls.]

THE END

◆ *The author thanks the Centre for Indigenous Theatre and the Laidlaw Foundation for their support of the development of this play. He is grateful to Carole Greyeyes for her patience, enthusiasm, and skill.*

Ruby Slipperjack *b.* 1952

OJIBWA

A member of the Eabametoong First Nation, Ruby Slipperjack was born on a trapline near White Water Lake, north of Armstrong, Ontario. She received her education in Collins, Ontario, in Sault Ste Marie at the Shingwauk Residential School, and in Thunder Bay. She received her Bachelor of Arts, Bachelor of Education, and Master of Education degrees from Lakehead University.

Slipperjack's novels *Honour the Sun* (1987) and *Silent Words* (1992) depict Ojibwa life in transition, through the eyes of child narrators:

I write . . . to offer my children an insight into life as it was in my own childhood. I was born and raised in the lands of my ancestors and grew up in a traditional and cultural upbringing with its teachings and discipline as had been passed down for generations past. I cannot teach my children these things in the city. . . . The traditional oral storytelling sessions were very much a part of my life and I have attempted to extend this knowledge and the wisdom of the teachings into the content of my novels.

Slipperjack's most recent novel, *Weesquachak and The Lost Ones* (2000), tells a contemporary story of obsessive love between characters manoeuvring between ancient traditions and modern poverty. An assistant professor at Lakehead University, Slipperjack coordinates the Faculty of Education's Native Teacher Education Program.

Blueberry Days

SUMMER 1962

I stretch out with a big yawn and wriggle my toes. Tony shoves an elbow in my face. Jane throws a leg over me and I lay still while I unclasp a safety pin off my sweater. Slowly, I press the pin against Jane's skin above her knee until she pulls her leg away and turns over. Maggie's snoring softly on the other side of Tony.

I lift my head. We're laying like driftwood on a colourful rocky shore, our blankets have been long since kicked off. I smell wood smoke and fresh air comes through the open door. Dogs are barking somewhere and flies are buzzing around inside the house. Everyone's still asleep. I shall be the first one up again this morning. Mom is very happy in the mornings when everything is quiet. I like it best when there are just the two of us by the fire. Sometimes, Mom leaves in the canoe to check our fishnet and comes back before anyone is up. She likes to sneak off by herself in the early morning.

I'm hungry. I can't smell what's sizzling out there but it sure sounds good. Slowly, I climb over Jane and onto the floor. From the half dozen pairs of socks on the floor I pull on a pair and slip into a pair of running shoes. I run out the door; three steps and off the open porch, barely making it over the dog's head, and off to the outhouse. The outhouse stands about fifty yards in the bushes behind the cabin. What's that noise? Scratching. I peer around the corner of the outhouse. There's a dog digging behind the toilet. I grab a stick and throw it at him. 'Get out of here. Go away!' I watch him slink off into the bushes.

Coming out at a run, I pause to listen to a bird chirping in the bushes beside me, 'Cee-oh-dee, cee-oh-dee.'

I ask, 'C.O.D.? What did you order in the catalogue, silly bird?' I run back behind the cabin, past Mom who kneels beside the cooking fire. I grab a towel and soap from the block of wood and skip over the stepping stones to my special rock to wash my face by the lake. My rock shifts to one side but I know it well. Maggie tried to get my rock one morning. She went off balance when it moved and then, splash, into the water. I laughed for days.

I breathe in the fresh air and hold my face to the warm sun. Oh, it smells so good. The water glistens and sparkles in the sunlight. Today is going to be a nice day again. I hop back onto the grass and drop the towel and soap back on the wood for the next person. I flop down beside Mom. She breaks off a piece of hot soft bannock, puts in a couple of pieces of salt pork she has fried, and hands it to me. Then she hands me another piece of bannock with butter and jam on it.

The flies are driving Mom crazy. She swats them and covers up the food. She also keeps a long stick beside her to keep the dogs away. They wiggle and crawl close to her, hoping for a taste of the morning meal. Jumbo, the black pup, had a long, long tail, until we decided he'd go crazy in the head if it were left that long. So we chopped off about six inches. It's stubby at the end now, but decent in length. The beige female by the door is very gentle. She used to be my father's favourite lead sled dog. She's Jumbo's mother. Her name is Rosiak. They're loose because the flies would get at them if we left them tied up and they're also a lot cleaner now. They can roll in the grass and swim and splash in the water with us. Like us, they get a dose of mosquito repellent around their ears.

Raised voices break out in the house. Mom sighs. Annie and Vera are up and at it again. I wonder if they fight like that when they're not home? Seems like a long time ago since we got out of school for the summer. I miss school. I miss the smell of crayons, paper, plasticine. Mom pokes me, 'Gee, you're always daydreaming! Go get the pan of water I asked you to get.'

In the cabin I watch Annie while I grab the pan from under the water pail shelf by the door. I fill it up from the lake and put it over the dying fire. It will be warm by the time everyone's finished eating. By now, the others are coming out of the house, racing for the outhouse. I smile. I won't be waiting in line this morning.

I sit again with my back comfortably against the tree, knees up. Jumbo comes over and licks my face. Eesh. His tail practically throws his whole back end from side to side. He's going to lose another couple of inches if he's not careful. 'Hey Mom, I heard a bird this morning saying, "C.O.D., C.O.D." He thinks he ordered a C.O.D. from the catalogue,' I giggle.

Mom says, 'Well, I hope he realizes he has to pay for it before he can take it home.'

I laugh again. Annie comes running from the outhouse and asks, 'What are you laughing at?'

Mom answers, 'Oh, about a bird that ordered a C.O.D.'

Annie gives me a look that says I'm strange, shakes her head as she picks up the towel and soap.

Mom and Barbara are cleaning up inside the cabin and the quilts and blankets are already hung on the hanging pole behind the cabin for airing. I jump up and run inside. Mom is packing our lunch in a cardboard box while Barbara fills another box with cups, mugs, and cans. We're going to the portage about three miles away to go blueberry picking. I carry things to the lake where Barbara and Vera have already turned the canoe over and lowered it into the water. Boy, that canoe looks great. A fresh coat of green paint. Mom worked on that last week. I wish I could ride in that canoe, but I usually walk on the railway tracks with the others every time we go to the big portage.

Finally, everyone's ready. The door's locked and I watch them get in the canoe. Barbara gets in, then Cora, Brian, Tony, and Annie. Vera smiles at me, 'All right, get in. I'll walk this time.'

I glance at Mom. She nods. I step into the canoe and sit down beside Annie. She is absorbed in folding her soft, delicate turquoise scarf on her knee. I reach over and touch the material before she tucks the scarf into her pocket. This is my first canoe ride this summer.

Mom gets in and pushes the canoe away. We wave to the others on shore. I know exactly what Mom will say next because she always says the same thing: don't run on the railway tracks and watch out for the trains. Then we paddle away. The water is sparkling and dancing in the sun.

With me paddling in the middle, Mom at the front, and Barbara at the back, we glide across the water pretty fast. I love the feel of water against my paddle and get into the rhythm of pushing the whirlpools created by Mom's paddle. I daydream while I paddle. The pains in my arms come and go in waves but I know if I slack off, I would get a poke from behind. Seagulls circle gracefully above; they screech occasionally. It is so quiet on the lake that we can still hear noises from the village we're leaving behind.

Cora, who's about three years old, sleeps at Barbara's feet behind me. Brian sits in front of Annie and drags a triangular-shaped board for a boat. Tony sits behind Mom. Mom has that thick scarf over her head again. I don't know how she can stand the heat with that thing on. Once in a while Mom remarks on the beaver-chewed poplar sticks that drift along the shoreline or points out a dry tree that would be good firewood in the fall.

We have left the third island behind us now so we should be there soon. There's the point now. A breeze is coming up too. I hope the waves aren't too high by the time we come back. Well I'll be walking home with Jane and Maggie anyway.

Finally, we slow down at the channel going into the portage. We're going to check our fishnet first. I rest my arms while they manoeuvre the canoe for Mom to fish the net cord up with her paddle. Mom pulls us along the net, lifting it to view the width. There's a good sized pike, some suckers, and two pickerel. Mom is good at taking the fish out of the tangled net. She drops the end of the net back into the water and I watch it sink down in a straight line.

We start paddling again, softly this time, into the marshy bay where the portage is. The water lilies are so beautiful. As we pass by, the yellow and white flowers among the lily pads bob in the slight waves. I can smell perfume.

Silently, we check out each hidden bay and dark shadow. This is a moose-feeding area and there are always lots of moose tracks here.

Finally, we come to the end of the long bay to the portage and there's Jumbo, in a whirl of tail and excitement, prancing about.

Vera and Jane emerge from the bush to pull our canoe in. I step out of the canoe and hold it for Annie to step out. We run up the pathway to join Maggie in the shade on the soft moss. Mom calls us for tea and to hand out our containers for the blueberries.

After much shoving and pushing and squeals of laughter, we amble toward the railway tracks where the berries hang in thick clumps. The heat shimmers off the steel tracks. It is very hot here. I can feel the sweat on my neck already.

I step carefully around the bushes and rocks. On blueberry picking days at least two snakes will get their heads bashed in. The paddle for that job is brought up with the bucket for the berries. Sure enough, a yell and commotion on the other side of the tracks, 'There. There it goes!' Maggie is yelling as everyone runs to help. Barbara has the paddle. I sink behind the bush, hoping no one will notice I'm not around. I don't understand why the sight of a snake could be such a bad omen that it has to be killed immediately to ward off the bad luck. I continue picking. Last summer, I'd made the mistake of saying that I had almost stepped on a snake at the corner of the cabin. Everyone stared at me, then dashed out the door. Later, I heard them yell. I felt awful. I saw them carry the dead snake at the end of a stick and throw it into the camp fire. Afterwards, every time I went near the fire, I kept thinking that I might see the bones of the snake, or, perhaps, the head with eyes if it didn't burn. I shudder. It's not that I love snakes but killing them like that because they're messengers of the devil is scary.

It's so hot and that sun just beats down on my head. I've been daydreaming again and my cup is only half full. The other girls are already dumping theirs into the large bucket that Mom and Barbara keep in the shade. Vera drops a handful of berries into my cup as she passes. I like Vera. Her shiny, curly, brown hair is so beautiful in the sun. I didn't comb my long, straight, black hair this morning.

I kick at an anthill to see how fast the ants will scatter. I remember the day Barbara, Vera, and Annie came home laughing after they had gone blueberry picking along the tracks. Railroad section men in a motor car had stopped to chat and Annie stepped on an anthill while they were talking. Next thing she knew, she had ants up her pants. 'What's the matter?' one of the men asked. Then, trying to be helpful, he advised, 'Take your pants off and give it a shake!' Yeah, right.

I'm hungry. It seems like hours and my neck is stiff. I've filled my cup so many times, I've lost count. Mom is very pleased and Barbara hasn't even said anything. I can see smoke and hear pots banging. They're making lunch by the lake on the other side of the railway tracks. That's the camping end of the portage. It's too swampy on this side. I hope we can swim before we eat. I see the others drift towards the fire. I'm done.

Mom smiles at me when I empty my cup and head for the lake. I'm thirsty more than anything else. A train's coming, the third one since we've been here. The men in the caboose always wave at us when they go by. Must be nice to ride in a train all day.

The girls are jumping off the boulder to my left. I drop my cup, kick off my runners, and flop into the water. Clothes and all, of course. We never bother taking off our clothes when we go swimming on blueberry-picking days. We take off our under-things and wash them and the clothes on us at the same time, while we're in the water. Also, we scrub our hair. That, I don't like. When my long hair gets wet, I have a big clump of pulled-out hair by the time Mom combs out the tangles. In a little while, the clothes we're not wearing are hung up to dry. The rest dries on us, keeping us cool until the sun has us dry and hot again.

The girls are still in the water, swimming with bloated tops on the back of their necks. Jane looks like a humpbacked muskrat. I'm always afraid a bloodsucker might get into my blouse. Barbara comes down to the lake, yelling, 'Tony, Brian, come out now!' The boys scramble up the sloping rock, one brown body, one white. Their pants are piled on a rock with their shoes and shirts. They're not allowed to get their jeans wet, they take too long to dry. I pull myself out of the water. Lunch is ready and we all troop to the fire, dripping wet and splashing each other.

Hot bannock, fried slices of bologna, and a cup of tea. And, of course, blueberry jam for bannock dunking. After a while we are smiling with blue teeth, black mouths, and sparkling eyes, laughing at each other. We head back up the trail with our containers. We have already wandered half a mile to get the best berries. Jumbo follows me. He moves from shade to shade at each place I stop, but then he wanders off. I've been here for quite a while. I'll look for a different spot. It's quite rocky here, so I think I'll go across the tracks to where Mom is. More shade there.

As I come around a clump of bush, Jane looks up with a smile. 'You going across?' she asks.

'Yep,' I answer and hop onto the rock where she had her foot. Her other foot is on a small boulder a couple of feet away. She squats with her dress tucked under each knee, picking the berries with one hand and holding her cup with the other. Does she even notice the huge mound of anthill directly behind her? Each time she rocks back on her heels to look up at me, her behind gets closer to it. I point to the anthill. 'You're trying not to step on that?'

She glances behind and says, 'That's an anthill. Some ants are black and some are small. Some can be quite big too.'

I nod, not quite sure about the conversation, and jump onto another rock, going around her.

Jumbo's tail sticks out wagging from behind a rock. Sure enough, a chipmunk chatters and scampers onto the rock above Jane. It turns to give Jumbo a parting shot before it plunges into the thick weeds and grass in front of Jane.

Well, nothing could have saved that girl! Jumbo comes sailing over that rock with large, flopping ears, looking like a giant, black, ugly bird. He pounces on the ground in front of Jane. Jane gasps, waves her arms to get her balance. She looks like she's trying to fly. Then she grabs a branch and thinks she's safe. Jumbo's back end whips around and smacks her across the face with what's left of his tail. Almost in slow motion, Jane sinks down right in the middle of that anthill. Then she comes to life! She shoots out of that anthill. Some of the ants probably land on the nearby trees, as she flails away at her dress. Bounding and panting, Jumbo passes me and heads down the hill. I can't remember if Jane has made any noise the whole time. I disappear behind a boulder and stumble to the tracks with my chest and throat bursting. There, I finally clamp my mouth with both hands and let my laughter out of my chest like a deflating balloon.

I had learned how to keep from laughing when I had been caught in situations where I couldn't laugh. Like the time our storekeeper served each customer with a smile, despite the fact that one eye was almost swollen shut from a mosquito bite. For me, that was torture. Mom's expression never changed. Or there was the time our minister gave a sermon from his open Bible, held upside down for quite a long time before he noticed it. Again, for me, that was murder. Mom's expression never changed. Then there was the time at church and that John, one of the elder men, was a little tipsy and he toppled over backwards, chair and all, and went down with a mighty crash. All we could see were his feet sticking up. Oh, I would have died then, if I hadn't noticed that Mom was silently shaking with laughter, too.

I'm getting tired. I seem to be by myself, too. I don't see anyone anywhere. I don't like to be alone . . . I start thinking about bears. I've filled my cup. I'd better go. I see a snake and jump so fast I stagger and slip down the slope. My feet finally come to rest on the gravel beside the railway tracks. My cup tumbles down the slope. I almost cry when I see the empty cup at my feet. Mom is standing on top of the ridge about ten yards from where I was.

'What's the matter? Are you okay?' she asks.

I nod my head. She has been there all this time. I stand there blinking away my tears.

'Once,' she says, looking at me, 'Wess could fill his cup every two minutes, 'til one day, he tripped in front of me and out rolled a wad of moss he had been using to stuff his cup over halfway full.'

I started to laugh, and she turns away to continue with her picking.

The rest of the afternoon goes quickly. Toward evening, we drift back to the fire. Supper smells delicious—fried fish with onions, mashed potatoes, canned corn, and, of course, the hot bannock and blueberry jam washed down with camp-fire tea. We talk and laugh with our backs against the trees. Mom is telling a story again. The horse-flies bite and drive us crazy because they fly around and around and around our heads. Too bad they don't get dizzy and crash into trees and things. I smile at the thought and then see Barbara glaring at me. Whatever Mom had been saying wasn't supposed to be funny. I put my head down and concentrate on finishing my supper.

After supper, Vera and I wash the dishes by the lake, while Jane and Maggie dry them. It's nice to be with Vera. She is always laughing. We begin carrying our things back to the other side of the tracks, down the portage path to the canoe. Rosiak has just emerged from the shade beside the canoe, yawning and stretching, licking her chops. The bay is absolutely calm. With the birds twirping and flies buzzing, it is so peaceful. 'Get out of the way, will you?' Barbara marches by me with her arms stretched down by buckets full of berries.

I'm so tired after my full meal, I hate the thought of walking the three miles back home. But at least my arms won't feel like they're falling off; only my legs will.

Finally, we push the canoe away from the shore. Jane, Maggie, and I, with Jumbo and Rosiak, straggle back up the path. Then, Jane pipes up, 'Hey, let's see if we can get there before they do! It's not so hot now.'

So, we walk and run for the first mile through two rock cuts. One more to go. Then just around the bend, we'll be at the edge of the village.

It seems like ages that we've been walking. Another train's coming. The dogs won't waste any time getting off the tracks. I hope it's not a cattle train . . . they stink. We wait by the shade of a large pine tree. A small path runs through here. This is called the 'little portage' but it's a miserable looking place at each end.

The train whistle is loud. We turn our faces to the wind as the train rattles by. Again, we wave to the man in the caboose.

After the last half mile, we take the path that leads to our cabin by the lake. The dogs are already gone, probably fast asleep by the doorstep by now. We run all the way to the cabin. There, the dogs are lying in the shade of the tree. Jumbo is cleaning his paws; good idea, he's got tar on them. He'll get clobbered for sure if he puts one dirty paw on our wood floor.

There's the canoe, with paddles flashing in the evening sun. The lake is very still and smooth, like a huge mirror. We splash water on our faces while we sit by the lake. I lean back onto the cool grass to catch my breath.

We'll all have a good sleep tonight. Tomorrow, we'll be going to the general store to trade in our berries. I hope Mom buys bananas and tomorrow is Wednesday, the day the way-freight comes to unload groceries for the general store. I lay on the grass with my eyes closed, smelling the earth and wild flowers beside me.

Joan Crate *b.* 1953

CREE

Joan Crate was born in Yellowknife, Northwest Territories, and grew up moving around British Columbia, Alberta, and Saskatchewan. Although she dropped out of high school, she has since received an MA in creative writing from the University of Calgary. In 1988, she won the Bliss Carman Award for poetry at the Banff Centre for the Arts. She now lives in Red Deer, Alberta, where she teaches English and First Nations Literature at Red Deer College. In addition to her academic work, she has written a novel, *Breathing Water* (1989), and two volumes of poetry, *Pale as Real Ladies: Poems for Pauline Johnson* (1989) and *Foreign Homes* (2001).

The Poetry Reading

Tonight let me tell you of
a world swallowed in one quick gulp
with only crumbs remaining,
while in one stale memory-corner
a small girl shivers on the steps   5
of a tar-paper shack.
Her daydreams are bruises behind her eyes,
oozing songs of suicide
children mouth in her unfinished womb.

Can you hear me?   10

Powdered woman in the first row
your plucked eyebrows creased with concern,
look at me, diseased,
scarred with smallpox,
seeping gonorrhea, lungs smothered with T.B.,   15
drunk,
pushed into a sewer, a reserve,
the weed-choked backyard
you never walk through,
listen.   20

I speak of a history
pieced from a jigsaw of flesh
torn from dumb tongues.
Under my skin
blood beats along roadways   25
barred with DO NOT ENTER signs,

walls of small scars.
I will not return to silence.
Do you hear me?

Hands twitter.   30
You rise to your feet.

   Lovely Miss Johnson
And will you have tea now?
   One lump or two?

You dust biscuit from the corner   35
of your mouth, and I remain
onstage in front of you.
I stare at the pelts
hanging from my shoulder,
and sip from fine bone china.   40

Story teller

Your voice
scrapes the bones of time.

At night by the fire, it is only you,
Chief Joe, who feels
a lost spring flood thirsty cells.   5
In the dark heat you find legends
once buried, now
damp on your dry lips.
Whisper to me and I will write you down.

I will run ink through your long wounds,   10
make your past flash like fish scales
under a sharp knife.
I will give names to the tricks of seasons,
tie your stories of beginnings to weighted ends
with my careful fisher's fingers,   15
lock your chants, spirits,
dances, your paint, your potlatches
into a language you can't speak.
I will frame your history
on a white page.   20

Encounter While Fishing

Joined at the mouth, my reflection
and I ponder the cloudy river,
the wrinkled sky.
I cast a baited hook into my breast,
watch it sink through circles of light,   5
golden strings entwining the line.
Lips kiss lips in a watery smile,
eyes set lazily on my eyes.

Earth-wash layers of river and sky
flood my nostrils, my mouth.   10
I am upside drowning,
no distinction between blue and blue.
Hook lances whites of eyes,
leaps through open mouth
with a silver squirm of fish scales.   15

I paddle for land, dart through the forest,
flee your depths, gills, your taste
for raw meat and salmon roe.
I leave you Emily Pauline.
You leave me Tekahionwake.   20
A long gray cord of shore uncoils between us.

Wife of Son of the Sea

Young woman cleaning salmon on a rock
counts her silvery selves multiplied on scales.
She probes a knife into flesh,
looks into water and glimpses liquid
eyes lapping her knees.   5

Waves pummel her mouth, her ears,
her deep earth eyes. She is a network
of channels, screaming—the gurgle
of a hooked fish—
and the Son of the Sea   10
drops fathoms deep inside her
drowning.

Possessed by tides, her heart
breaks along the salt line.
Between liquid and solid she's pulled   20
with nowhere to fall but in.

Landbound father, she grapples
with fingers and drifting memory
for your deliberate walk, your sweat, your skin
windbruised bark rough under her cheek,   25
and sinks like stone.
In beating fingers she holds the sea body,
hair rising in kelp ribbons
to the corrugated edge of dawn.
Wife,   30
sea daughter, we beat drums,
wave drenched limbs, try to touch
you, undefined as our belief.

The Year of the Coyote

    Oh their terrible stealth!
Babes have been snatched from campgrounds
while parents gathered firewood,
cooked dinner, slept on either side
wild roses bordering carpets of dream.   5
These days wherever you look, coyotes
lope a lullaby across the horizon,
teeth clipping clean as needles through cloth.
    Oh, their red velvet thirst!

We don't allow our kids out the door   10
without a dog anymore, keep a .22 handy.
Even mid-day, I take the truck to Hilda's.
Her husband stares out the window
at wheat spilling over the prairie,
wishes to hell it were legal to kill   15
coyotes, shoot them mid-stride.
    How their howls snarl up the combines!
Grain, never priced lower since 1917, overflows
bins, wails through rust holes.

Post Office closed down, we straggle   20
at Gray's Hardware, talk about bankruptcies,
auctions, dogs killed by coyotes.
A few mate with them, steal home
on a leash of moonlight and treason,
                                        wait.   25

Sometimes I still dream of you,
of you no longer knowing your own children
playing at the edge of twilight. I try
to call them, try and try, but their names
stick to my tongue, consonants, vowels stillborn   30
in the gorge of distant hills.
I wake up to coyotes ripping open the dark.
You gone.
The howl remains.

Driving home, Hilda talks   35
faster and faster down the stuttering gravel road,
says she wants another child
but her husband avoids her. All night long
she hears the pad of his feet down the hallway.
At dawn he slinks to the barn to sleep with the chickens.   40
                                                    I nod,
in the rear view mirror, catch a shape
skirting the truck.

Heirlooms

How the glass came to them—imported from England
in great oak and canvas chests—how it held
the English sun, soft as a worn cotton rag
rubbed into the eye. She dusted each piece,
placed them in the kitchen cupboard.   5

The spring water changed
in those jugs and goblets, tasted
as if drawn from a pond of dead things.
Fruit flies twitched, tadpoles drowned.
Centuries of decay were transported   10
to her mouth, jeers and pronouncements—
whores, witches, niggers, injuns.

Shawnandithit cupped her hands
under the pump after that,
would not drink from cut glass   15
that reflected her misery
and shoved it down her throat.

Sentences: at the Culls'

After working five years at the Peytons'
I have learned their ways, their words,
understand sentences.

What shall we *do with her?*

When I weakened, they moved me to the Culls'   5
where I sit and sketch my lives for them.
I choose graphite, refuse colours—
yellow, blue, the flowing flowing red.

I draw twelve ghosts on the page—the ones
my sister, mother, and I   10
left in camp
    starving.
        All around them
        animals ravaged, land devoured
        sickness passed from mouth to mouth   15
        the new sustenance—a hole
        in the gut, torn tongue—
Let me tell you
about our hunting fences
constructed with just one exit,   20
killers awaiting their prey,
an ocean of assailants chasing behind.
Their only choice was between slayers.
Our only choice was
                nothing   25
              left
                for me to reveal
        on these vast white sheets. So
        let them find
            my people beneath snow   30
            my Beothuk husband never-to-be

babies I will not have
the winter I become

quieter, colder
than their disdain   35

blank pages at the back of the book
they dream in frustrated inks—
New-found-land the title,
a joke, a riddle, and
What shall we *do with*—   40
me: a suspended sentence

Loose Feathers on Stone

White handkerchief to your mouth, Shawnandithit,
white as your mother's fingertips,
that expanding spot on your sister's cheek
the day they came and took you
as you wandered hungry   5
ribs hooking ice.
White as death.

Who could have imagined you'd be taken
to a house in town with a fire and embroidered linen
to spit into. Who would have thought death was warm   10
and plump with meat and men who smile
too much, who ask questions with pencils, wanting
you to draw the canoes, the tents, the chasms
dug for winter houses. They ask you to speak
your language so they can study its sound.   15
How full of holes it is, subterranean tunnels
echo through your failing lungs
(can they hear?)
Blood in your mouth tastes ripe
as a lover, everything   20
gone.

And so Shawnandithit, with mother and sister dead,
and none of your people left beating against winter,
it is your turn, the last Beothuk—
loose feathers on stone.   25
In the whitemen's steaming kitchen, you falter, look
to the wall, the calendar you can't read, sketch

them stories of marriage ceremonies, hunting
parties, bullets, disease, and your lingering
death.   30

Coughing blood,
you fly, you plunge
            alone
                    Shawnandithit,
staining the white, white pages.   35

The Fly and I

Winter—slouched against my window,
biting off heart beat and sap, sucking
light from the sky to pour over
your glistening skin—I'm fed up
with your greed and beauty.   5

A fly left over from summer
buzzes through my room, flight
groggy with its own endurance.

Outside degrees slide into negativity.
Nothing left but my empty sleep   10
and the out-dated fly. Nothing
but evicted seasons. Remember

last summer? Explosions of sun, beds of flowers,
the haemorrhaging moon? Remember heat
as persistent as snow, the buzzing fly,   15
every beat of my galled heart.

And still it snows. And winter grows fatter,
sleeker. The fly thumps against black-eyed
glass. Words of the LAWD GOD ALMIGHTY shatter
through the clock radio. A jack-rabbit   20
dodges street-light, miraculously
escapes into the invisible world DEAR GOD
I long for

dream, the snug universe of a moment,
the molecule a galaxy forms, its climate   25
ripe as forbidden fruit. Fly
us into its slippery arms.

Thank-you Card

To children, man sleeping under blankets
as dawn thumps grey wings—a warning,
a promise, thank-you

air, food, blood, accident of planets
for these luxuries, midnight deep in me.   5
For friends snoring softly in folds
of once, hope of again, again radiating
through wrinkling time, the threads
drawn between us, their discreet
patterns of need. Thank-you   10

for the wild flowers I gathered
on prairie carpets yellow summer long,
for the imprint of a hitch-hiker
with rising-moon smile and knife-blade poems
cut into the blur of hot afternoon,   15
her bright yearning for destination
and a smoke. What to give

in return for mundane miracles?
A kiss, tobacco, prayer to the cycle
of roots, seed, water to the perennial thirst   20
of soil and soul? Reverence?
                    Blessed be the great Mother

Earth—and we your children, inconsequential
as ants marching, as locusts
devouring fields of grain.   25

Louise Halfe *b.* 1953

CREE

Louise Bernice Halfe, whose Cree name in English is Sky Dancer, was born in the town of Two Hills in northern Alberta. She grew up a member of the Saddle Lake Reserve ('My parents were nomads who worked for the Ukrainian farmers and in the sugar beet fields when I was a youngster . . .'), and she attended the Blue Quills Residential School. She has a degree in social work from the University of Regina, as well as training in drug and addiction counselling. In the following passage she describes how she began to write:

I was living in a tepee with my lover in the mountains when Grandfather came in a dream. He was the one who lifted these fingers and said 'Read, write,' lips moving quietly across the syllabics. . . . How could I write when I could barely articulate and identify the pain that controlled my fears? . . . In order to accept the gift of writing, to earn it, to honour it, I turned to my community, ceremony, and ritual. . . . My war party doesn't differ from my ancestors'. Living a nomadic life with lance, bow and arrow, gathering bundles, takes the same precision, thoughtfulness, determination, and discipline. The issues are the same: adversity and joy, unity and harmony, life and death.'

Halfe's first collection of poetry, *Bear Bones & Feathers* (1994), 'focuses on prayer, song, stories of my Grandparents, life on the reserve, residential school, and mixed relationships.' The book was nominated for the Saskatchewan Writers Guild's First Book Award, and it won the 1996 Milton Acorn People's Poetry Award. Her long poem *Blue Marrow* (1998) was shortlisted for the Governor General's Award for poetry. Both books are soon to be republished, *Blue Marrow* in a new edition. Halfe is presently writing a novel tentatively titled *The Crooked Good*.

'I write because I love,' she says. 'I write for the survival of self, my children, my family, my community, and for the Earth. I write to help keep our stories, our truths, our language alive.'

Pāhkahkos

Flying Skeleton
I used to wonder where
You kept yourself.
I'd hear you rattle about
Scraping your bones   5

I opened a door
You grinned at me
Your hollow mouth
Stared through my heart
With empty eyes.   10

You lifted your boney hands
To greet me and I
Ran without a tongue.

You jumped on my back
Clinging to my neck you hugged   15
My mound of flesh.

For a thousand years you were
The heavy bones
The companions who would not leave.

You knocked your skull   20
On my head
I felt your boney feet.
I dragged and dragged
I couldn't carry
Your burden more.   25
I pried you loose
Bone after bone.

We stood, skull to face
Pāhkahkos, your many bones
Exposed   30
I, lighter than I could stand.

I fed you the drink of healing
You ran skeleton fingers
Down your face and onto mine.

I gave you a prayer cloth   35
I wove a blanket of forgiveness
You covered us both, skeleton and flesh.

I gave you the smoke of truth
You lit your Pipe to life
You lifted it to your ghostly mouth,   40
To mine.

My Pāhkahkos companion,
My dancing Skeleton
My dancing friend.

We carry our bundles   45
Side by side
Bones and flesh.

She Told Me

She always told me
to take a willow branch
and gently whip the spirits
out of the house
calling, calling   5

Āstam we are leaving
āstam do not stay.
She always told me
to put the food away at night
to cover the dishes   10
or the spirits
would crackle and dance
whistle in our ears
and drive us mad.

I obeyed.   15

She always told me
never to eat the guts of
animals while I was pregnant
or the baby would be born
with a rope around the neck.   20

I yearned for the guts.

She always told me
never to walk over men
while I was in my moon
or they would die from my power.   25
I thought that was the idea.
She always told me
that *Nōhkom*, the medicine bag
had given her three cigarettes.
That's why the lizards   30
walked around inside her head.
I watched the flicker of her tongue.

Body Politics

Mama said,

Real woman
don't steal
from the sky and wear clouds
on their eyelids.   5

Real woman
eat rabbit well-done
not left half-raw
on their mouth.

Real woman   10
have lots of meat
on their bones.
They're not starving,
hobbled horses
with bony, grinding hips.   15

Real woman caress
with featherstone hands
not with falcon fingernails
that have never worked.

When she was finished talking   20
she clicked her teeth
lifted her arse
and farted
at the passing
city women.   25

Fog Inside Mama

I'm going to take you home, Mama.
Yes, to that log shack where Papa skinned beaver
on the dirt floor.

The grass is tall. There'll be lots of mosquitoes.

Yes, Mama, the old fridge is still there and no, there's no   5
lightning going through to make it breathe.

The windows are broken and the barn swallows have built
their nest where the stovepipe used to smoke.

Oh Mama don't, Papa hasn't walked on that land, not for
years. Not since the last time he crushed your ribs on that   10
fridge.

He's on skid row somewhere.

It's safe. All we have are the old ghosts drifting
through the clouds of our heads.

Yes, Mama. I remember the tadpoles from the slough swishing   15
inside my red fireman's boots. They were my favorite boots.
I slept in them, I never took them off till those little
swimming snakes squished inside.

Your bones are tired and I can't find the road. I've got a
fly in my eye and it's making the rain fall from my nose.   20

Yes, I remember the lard pail hanging from my stomach
with a belt of twine. I'd pick so fast trying to beat Papa,
the berries drummed. Only
I never won. Papa, he picked twigs and bugs and insisted that
he had won the race.   25

What was that Mama?

Oh yeah, for school I had your bannock and fried rabbit.
I'd eat it *kīmōc* in the bathroom so the white kids
wouldn't laugh at me. Oh, it was good. So good.

You want some tea and a cigarette?   30

Yes, we're almost there.

I can see the old shack, the outhouse, the chicken coop,
the jalopy.

Yes, Mama we're going home. No more hiding.

Stones

Men
day hang dere balls
all over da place.

what I didn't no
is day   5
whack dem
fundle dem
squeeze dem
dalk to dem
whisper to dem   10
scream at dem
beg dem
pray to dem
g ah sh
even   15
swear at dem

I no dese
cuz I followed dem
at dat place
where day use ghost berries   20
nd buff alow sticks
nd play in da
buff a low mud
nd day use dat
stick   25
nd whack dem
berries
into
dem
gopher holes   30

dere all ways drying
to put dem
dere balls everywhere
why
I evin saw dem   35
at dem dere
dinner dables
coloured balls
wit a big long broom

boking,   40
rolling,
nd smacking dem
all together
into
six holes   45
in dat dable.

g ah sh
wit all dat whacking
day shoold of come
a long dime ago   50
nd be satisfied.

but no
dere still
jiggling dem
between dere legs   55
drying to find
different hole
to put dem in.

dem balls by now
should be so heavee   60
day make dere walk
hard
liddle bit
like dem
African elephants   65
I saw on
DV

Idylwyld Crow

Rushing home
into the dark
I drive by
a moving scarecrow.

Red cap   5
perched on
grey corn husk hair

toothless mouth
jutting jaw.

Can't help but stop   10
and offer her a ride.
In broken English
she tells me she lives in
Kilburn.

Pulls out her blue   15
hospital card with
her address
explaining all the while

She's been out
buying the cheapest   20
stale bread in town
somewhere in Idylwyld.

A Saulteaux,
a dark crow,
feeding her children   25
crumbs in the city light.

My Ledders

dear pope
i no, i no, you dired of my ledders
i couldn't let dis one go
i dought you could do somedin 'bout it.
years ago you stopped *nōhkom* and *nimosōm*   5
from prayin in da sweatlodge and sundance,
drummin, singin and dancin.
you even stopped dem from Indian speakin
and storydellin.
well you must have some kind of bower   10
cuz da govment sure listen.

well, pope
last night on DV
i watched some whitemen
sweat in da lodge, and at   15

dinner dime on da radio
i heard dat man dell us
dat some darafist was havin a retreat
and to register.
what dat mean, i not sure   20
anyway he is buildin' a sweatlodge.
i never hear anybody before on da radio
dell da whole world dat.
i sure suprise and kinda made me mad.

i wonder if you could dell da govment   25
to make dem laws dat stop dat
whiteman from dakin our *isistāwina*
cuz i dell you pope
i don't dink you like it
if i dook you   30
gold cup and wine
pass it 'round our circles
cuz i don't have you drainin
from doze schools.
i haven't married you jeesuz   35
and i don't kneel to him,
cuz he ain't my god.

dese men, pope, don't know what
tobacco mean, what suffer mean,
alls dey no is you jeesuz die for dem   40
dey don't no what fastin' mean
dey jist dake and gobble our *mātotsān*
as if dey own it.
dey don't no what it mean to dake
from da earth and give somedin' back   45
i so dired of all dis *kimoti*, pope
deach your children.
eat your jeezuz body.
drink his blood.
dell dem to go back to dere own deachings,   50
pope.

for Omeasoo

I lift my wrist
suck out marrow
blow into my daughter.
I spoon the spill
into her lips.   5

I lift my mother's finger,
add *Nōhkom*'s ashes,
and stir.

My daughter dances
a leaf twirling   10
on the wind.

She blows the baritone
a gosling calling,
Kīwētinohk.
She delivers   15
dried meat and croissants
to *Nōhkomāk.*

She is a rainbow,
the give-away feast
of our blood.   20
She bleeds.

The Heat of My Grandmothers

The old man calls my *Nōhkomāk*
a bunch of bitches, *pisikwātisiw.*

Yes, I took painted warriors:
molded their sinew thighs,
into my flesh.   5
Our spirits moaned, laughing between
teepee poles reaching the heavens,
stars leaping against the breathing hide.

I was fourteen winters when I was told
my first husband was the elder's choice.   10

That winter in our teepee
the smoke couldn't hide
the fragrance
of muskeg tea
and juniper   15
we mixed between our bodies.
The second winter two calves
dropped to the earth.

My first husband's bones
I found beneath the autumn buffalo,   20
his arrows in the meat. My moccasins heavy,
I swayed the roundness of my body
wailed till the buffalo sweat
melted his skin into
the prairie grass.   25

My second husband of three winters
I received at a give-away between
the Blackfoot and Cree. He kissed
the valleys of my buttocks, licked
the paths of my swollen breast. He,   30
antelope of clouds. I,
wider than his open mouth.

I found him after a skirmish with
the white meat, a bullet between his eyes.
I was winter in my spring. My braids   35
greyer than the passing snow. I called
magpie, crow, and raven to clean
his body cradled in the trees.

My third husband took my calves and
gave them to the black robes. His   40
eyes bluer than mountain rivers, hands
took half the hide I made for travois. He'd
flicker his eyelashes; Monarchs in my sleep,
while I dreamt of babies hungry and
frightened behind cold fences.   45

Ten babies. Six of prairie blood, four
of meeting rivers. A beaded rainbow,
each child suckled by my wind-bitten nipples
their fathers loved.

Sharron Proulx-Turner *b.* 1953

MÉTIS

Sharron Proulx-Turner, a member of the Métis Nation of Alberta, comes from Mohawk, Algonquin, Huron, Anishnaabe, Mi'kmaq, French, and Irish ancestry. A mother and *nokomis* (grandmother), Sharron is also a writer, educator, and activist. As she explains, she believes in the power of writing to restore Native traditions:

> Louis Riel, a Métis leader and prophet, is known to have said the artists—the writers and sculptors and painters and builders and weavers—will be the ones who bring our people back to their centres after seven generations. I take this sentiment to heart.
>
> I would say that the land gives my work its central focus. As women, we are the land, and our Mother Earth and her blood, the waters, are in danger. Non-natives need to know this in a much more real sense, and I hope this comes across in my writing. In my communities, writing is considered a sacred gift. For me, writing creates a knowing that comes from inside the beauty of the land and her waters. The beauty is felt from the words for the reader. For the writer, the beauty is between the spirit world and the word. The reader sense and feels the beauty because the spirit world exists inside, within what's being told, and the spirit world comes alive through voice.

Proulx-Turner's work has appeared in anthologies and literary journals, including *Gatherings: The En'owkin Journal of First North American Peoples, Prairie Fire, tessera*, and *absinthe*. Her memoir, *Where the Rivers Join* (1995), published under a pseudonym, was shortlisted for the Edna Staebler Award for creative non-fiction. *what the auntys say* (2002), her first collection of poetry, was shortlisted for the League of Canadian Poets' Gerald Lampert Award.

a horse's nest egg is very large

at school they said her face must be erased from the crowd
this is grade four and just after she wins the national poetry contest
cameras camquarters and her just an earshot away
cold on the outside quiet warm calm inside
holding back the sadness   5
to herself

                                        eyes
                                        that teacher

you must not say these things
you must consider your audience   10
you must never under any circumstance
disempower the powerful

please censor your story
and remember we are having this conversation in strictest
confidence   15
the smell of hair spray at the nose

                that's when her mouth goes all thin and tinny
                sour air and shame inside her whole
                heart mommys daddys grannys grampas
                auntys uncles cousins thighs hips arms   20
                maintains remains her silence anger grows
                over and over

                                                her heart bursts out to river
                                                smooths a clearing on the page

the written word does not have to be wrapped in the thoughts of the   25
colonizer
a note the old lady finds frozen in hail the size of connie fife
sweat hoboing with that giant butterfly

and there's that teacher from her school
who speaks from over to the left and all in rows   30
on that new tv all black and white and smiles and white white teeth
embrace and welcome to whitetown
yes she's brilliant for a young sauvage
her favourite food is french fries and there's something about her
writing   35
lazy and arrogant
like a rich french dessert

                the auntys watch that on tv
                laugh and laugh and eat popcorn with extra butter
                clinging to their salt   40
                them folks can't read worth beans
                is what the auntys say

they got it right there on the kitchen wall
all framed with the old lady smiling tight
her false teeth right there beside her in a cup   45
she makes that cup at the senior high
paints words on it too
uses the extra paint left over from her car
big red hen red
words are jewels is what she writes on that cup   50

words are jewels

    grains of rice to kneel on depending on the view

they say that fear runs deep
says the old lady
how deep says the auntys   55
deep deep says the old lady
so says the auntys
just so we know

        wind and water and very few people
        recurring dream in a dentist chair   60
        and there she is that old lady
        sitting in front of her computer
        putting the finishing touches off the line
        and there they are
        the grandmothers   65
        all talking all at once

well blow me over with a feather
says that big red hen warm wise
woman of few words that one
loves to eat with the grandmothers   70
just like that horse says those auntys
comes for dinner and then moves out of reach
cracks a good joke every time though
doesn't have to look for an audience
words herself around pretty good   75
non-verbal too

those teachers down in whitetown

what is essay poem story   any deviation is a

sin

can't see can't read   80
outside their writing on the wall
floors doors windows
all squared and mirrored in

which is what that old lady learns at school
learns how to swear learns how to lie   85
around the same time that halfbreed girl from whitetown says
I'm a two-spirit I thought you were a two-spirit too
and that old lady says no
these are just my eyes   held
the other day though   90
such power of body   lifted
breath gone heart   oh
such wonder   my my my
says the old lady

I'm in love   95

my my my

says
that big red hen warm wise

it's a miracle
but first let me get this kraft dinner out from   100
underneath my false teeth
the ones on the bottom are all mine got none at the back but
the front ones they look fine

one minute I'm burping over there at the library
downtown whitetown and some guy says pick it up   105

        my my my

                so good so close

close so close   touching
warm soft smells so good
nuzzle necks shoulders   melting   110
aroused and lifted   my my my

oh my and there's that giant butterfly
laughs talking through the moon
her yellow shining very yellow for the sun
and all the men in whitetown little boys   115
playing hockey on the road
a very wonderful evening
safe quiet sexy happy day
the sameness of being with a woman

supportive though surprised is what the auntys say   120
getting the words out one by one
you flow like water waves onto the air
my my my says the old lady I am many things
but I am no horsefly
I can score with the best of them   125

                                going home

        where even the smallest egg

smells loving red between the leaves

                        powerful and soft

click click click   130
says that old lady's tongue
click click click

we tell our girl cook a little for a feast
go to sweat lodge purify yourself
rebirth your body   135
mind heart spirit
then go on with our story even though the pain

we tell her prepare share this recipe les boulettes
for those who love ground meat
two pounds lean ground meat   140
medium onion chopped nice and fine
pinch of salt and we like lots of pepper
one half cup of flour mixed into the meat to hold and mix well
then roll into two or three inch balls and roll in flour again then
place in about four cups of boiling lightly salted water and   145
simmer gently for an hour

smells good hey
takes your mind to a good place when you cook my girl
put all your love
into what you prepare   150
thank the plants the animals who give up their lives
remember your ancestors who gave up theirs
put out a plate for them
feed them

we tell her one day when quebec wakes up   155
there'll be seven million more metis
many metis grandmothers didn't know their metis grandmothers
for generations already and still today you'll hear their
daughters
say I am proud to be metis   160
a beautiful long and roaming song a slogan
joining of two cultures a distinct nation of people
forever

generation after generation story after story
in the public and separate schools   165
and you tell us the same stories your daughters tell too
some still in foster care
town after town

little girls having the wisdom of an old woman just to stay alive

all the stories sound the same now but back then   170
there was nowhere to go for help
not that there's so much help out there today our kids still
pushed past childhoods
same old lines
lies on the walls in the halls   175
in the little children's history books
about savages and tipis scalps and great spiritual leaders
of the olden times
like we and our languages all died off
with the royal proclamation   180
and now it's still just a matter of time

that meatball soup and just about anything
tastes great with bannock my girl
four cups flour
one half cup melted shortening   185
four teaspoons baking powder
pinch of salt
one and a half cups cool water
mix the dry well and mix the water and shortening then mix
everything together until you are able to knead about five times   190
then press into a nice circle nine ten inches around and bake at
three hundred seventy-five degrees for about half hour

Monique Mojica *b.* 1954

KUNA/RAPPAHANNOCK

Monique Mojica was born and raised in New York City, the daughter of a theatrical family; both her mother and an aunt are long-time members of the illustrious Spiderwoman Theatre. Mojica migrated to Toronto, Ontario, as a founding member of Native Earth Performing Arts. She has worked in the Toronto theatre and film community as an actor, director, and writer, particularly with Native Earth, The Centre for Indigenous Theatre, and Nightwood Theatre.

In collaboration with Native Earth Performing Arts, Mojica produced *Double Take A Second Look* (1983) and *Give Them A Carrot (For As Long As The Sun Is Green)* (1985). She also collaborated with the Inuit actor Makka Kleist to produce *Sea Cows* (1985–7). Her acting roles have included the title character in the play *Jessica*, Ariel in *The Tempest*, and Marie-Adele in *The Rez Sisters*.

It is as an actor that Mojica found her way to writing. Her play *Princess Pocahontas and the*

Blue Spots (1991) resulted from a recognition that stories important enough to tell as performance also need to be written down, documented, saved. The ephemeral quality of performance, particularly of texts developed in the collective process, threatens truths that need to be told. She still sees herself working as part of a community, 'not as an isolated writer'.

Mojica's other dramatic work includes the radio drama *Birdwoman and the Suffragettes: A Story of Sacajawea* (1991) and *A Fast Growing* *Mould Bitter as Shame* (1994). In addition, she is the co-editor, with Richard Knowles, of *Staging Coyote's Dream: An Anthology of First Nations Drama in English* (2003). In 1999 she joined with Jani Lauzon and Michelle St John to form the drama company Turtle Gals 'to bring Native Women's Stories to the Stage'. Their first production was *The Scrubbing Project* (2002), 'a courageous exploration of racism, tradition, and memory using vaudeville as a madcap metaphor for navigating identity.'

From *Princess Pocahontas and the Blue Spots*

[Alejandra enters as beauty pageant host.]

HOST: Good evening, ladies and gentlemen, and children of all ages, and welcome to the 498th annual—count them, that's nearly 500 years of the North American Indian Beauty Pageant. This is George Pepe Flaco Columbus Cartier da Gama Smith, but you can call me Bob, coming to you live from the Indian Princess Hall of Fame. *[Crosses centre.]* Our first contestant in the Miss North American Indian Beauty Pageant, from her home in the deep green forest on the other side of the mountain, by the shores of the silver sea—Princess Buttered-on-Both-Sides!!

[Host begins to 'oooo' the first line from the 'Indian Love Call' which is echoed by Princess Buttered-on-Both-Sides as she enters dressed in a white 'buckskin' dress and carrying an oversized ear of corn.]

[As she weaves through the audience she offers them handfuls of Cornnuts (from the plastic bag she bought them in).]

PRINCESS B: Corn . . . Corn . . . Corn . . . Corn . . . *[The music is a mixture of Hollywood 'tom-toms', the 'Indian Love Call', 'The good, the bad and the ugly', and the 'Mazola' commercial.]*

PRINCESS B: *[To audience.]* Excuse me, which way is east? *[After a member of the audience answers.]* Many, many thanks.

[Princess Buttered-on-Both-Sides tosses Cornnuts to the four directions and places her ear to the earth, then rises, arms and face lifted to the heavens.]

PRINCESS B: *[Pointing to the ear of corn.]* Corn. *[Pointing to herself.]* Maiden. For the talent segment of the Miss North American Indian Beauty Pageant, I shall dance for you in savage splendour the dance of the sacrificial corn maiden, and proceed to hurl myself over the precipice all for the loss of my one true love, CAPTAIN JOHN WHITEMAN. *[Swoons.]*

[Music starts up—the corn celebration production number from the movie Rose Marie played on pan pipes with vocalized cartoon sound effects. Princess Buttered-on-Both-Sides performs a Hollywood 'Injun dance'.]

PRINCESS B: *[Teetering on the edge of the 'precipice' or stage.]* OH, that's Niagara Falls down there, but I just can't live without him! *[Teeters but is saved by the music beginning again. Princess Buttered-on-Both-Sides dances again, removes the buckskin dress and runs to the edge of the precipice once more. She jumps.]* GERONIMOOOOOOOOO!!!!!

*　　*　　*

PRINCESS B: Live from Tee Pee Town, it's Princess Pocahontas and the Blue Spots!
ALEJANDRA: *[As the 'Blue Spots'.]* Shoo bee, doo bee, wa!
MONIQUE: *[À la Marilyn Monroe.]* Way ya hiya! *[Princess descends pyramid and they sing.]*
MONIQUE: *[Singing with a drawling Country and Western feel.]*

Captain Whiteman, I would pledge my life to you
Captain Whiteman, I would defy my father too.
I pledge to aid and to save,
I'll protect you to my grave.
Oh Captain Whiteman, you're the cheese in my fondue.

Captain Whiteman, for you I will convert,
Captain Whiteman, all my pagan gods are dirt.
If I'm savage don't despise me,
'Cause I'll let you civilize me.
Oh Captain Whiteman, I'm your buckskin-clad dessert.

Although you may be hairy,
I love you so-oo,
You're the cutest guy I'll ever see.
You smell a little funny,
But don't you worry, honey,
Come live with me in my tee pee.

Captain Whiteman, I'm a little Indian maid,
Captain Whiteman, with long ebony braids.
Please don't let my dark complexion
Inhibit your affection.
Be my muffin, I'll be your marmalade.
Be my muffin, I'll be your marmalade.
Be my muffin, I'll be your marmalade.
Way ya hey yo.

ALEJANDRA: *[Before song ends, Alejandra, as the 'Blue Spots', runs up centre aisle, screaming]* ¡Capitán! ¡Capitán! ¡No te vayas, Capitán! Don't leave me!

PRINCESS B: May you always walk in beauty, my dear sister.

Now, was that not spiritual? Many, many thanks, you have made my heart soar like the noble rabbit. My heart, your heart bunny heart, one heart. Um hmm. I would like us to be friends, real good friends, you know what I mean? I mean like blood brothers, and blood sisters.

Um hm.

I have many names. My first name was Matoaka. Some people call me Lady Rebecca, but everyone knows the little Indian Princess Pocahontas, who saved the life of Captain John Smith. *[Four gestures, once with no words, once with sounds]:* (1) NO! *[Hands over head, on knees.]* He's so brave his eyes are so blue, his hair is so blond and I like the way he walks. (2) DON'T! mash his brain out. I don't want to see his brains all running down the side of this stone. (3) STOP! I think I love him. (4) Oooh he's so cute. *[Removes Princess dress, stands downstage right.]*

MONIQUE: Where was her mother?

ALEJANDRA: *[As Troubadour, complete with Robin Hood hat, singing.]*

> In 1607 the English came sailing across the ocean—
> In the name of their virgin queen, they called this land Virginia-O.

[Monique joins.]

> In the gloom and silence of the dark and imprenetrable forest—
> They might all have died if it had not been for the Indian Princess
>   Pocahontas-O.

> Her father was a stern, old chief, Powhatan was his name-O
> Sweet and pretty was Pocahontas
> As he was ugly and cruel-O.

> Then into her village strode a man with steps so brave and sure
> Said he in a deep voice like a God's
> 'My name is Captain John Smith-O'.

[Chorus.]

> Heigh-ho wiggle-waggle wigwam wampum,
>   roly-poly papoose tom-tom,
>   tomahawk squaw.

MONIQUE: *[As Lady Rebecca.]* How cam'st I here? I know how to walk, I know how to stand, I know how to incline my head, how to bow. My heart is on the ground!

MONIQUE AND TROUBADOUR:

> The fiendish red men they did deem that John Smith
>   he must die-O

> They placed his head upon a stone,
>> and raised their tomahawks high-O.

> Then from the crowd there rushed a girl, the
>> maiden Pocahontas
>> Shielding his head with her own,
>>> crying save him, save the Paleface-O.

[Chorus.]

> Heigh-ho wiggle-waggle wigwam wampum,
>> roly-poly papoose tom-tom,
>>> tomahawk squaw.

LADY REBECCA: *[Crosses to wall right, swings out larger-than-life gilded portrait frame which contains Lady Rebecca's Elizabethan ruff and cuffs and her velvet hat with ostrich plume.]* How cam'st I to be caught, stuck, girdled? I'll tell you—Captain John Smith:

'You did promise Powhatan that what was yours should be his, and be the like to you; you called him father. And fear you here I should call you father? I tell you then, I will, and you shall call me child, and so I will be forever and ever your countryman. They did tell us always (that) you were dead, and I knew no other until I came to Plymouth. Yet Powhatan did seek to know the truth, because your countrymen will lie much.'

TROUBADOUR: *[Singing.]*

> When Pocahontas went to see her friend John Smith in
>> Jamestown—
>> She'd run and cartwheel with the boys,
>>> though she be naked underneath it-O.

> John Smith said of the Indian girls 'I could have done
>> what I listed'-O
>> 'All these nymphs more tormented me,
>>> crying "love you not me? Love you not me?"'

[During these verses Lady Rebecca caresses clothing in frame.]

LADY REBECCA: Now see you here I wear the clothes of an Englishwoman and will disturb you less when I walk. Here, I am Princess and Non Pareil of Virginia. I am Lady Rebecca. For me the Queen holds audience. Treachery, Captain, I was kidnapped!

TROUBADOUR:

> There chanced to be in Jamestown a planter named
>> John Rolfe-O
>> His heart was touched by Pocahontas
>>> he claimed her for his bride-y-O.

LADY REBECCA: John, my husband, is a businessman, a merchant, and a tobacco planter. I know how to grow tobacco, it is our sacred tobacco plant.

TROUBADOUR: *[Singing.]* Yo sangro por ti . . . *[Continues under Apostle's Creed; live voice and drum layered over taped voices.]*

LADY REBECCA: *[Fitting neck and wrists into collar and cuffs; fanning herself with ostrich plume fan.]* I believe in God the Father Almighty, maker of Heaven and Earth, and in Jesus Christ his own son our Lord, who was conceived of the Holy Ghost, born of the Virgin Mary, suffered under Pontius Pilate, was crucified, died, and was buried. He descended into hell. I believe in the Holy Ghost, the holy Catholic Church, the communion of saints, the forgiveness of sins, the resurrection of the body and the life everlasting. Amen.

I provided John Rolfe with the seeds to create his hybrid tobacco plants and I provided him with a son, and created a hybrid people. I have such a nice fan to hide my face and fan myself in these hot, heavy clothes.

What owe I to my father? Waited I not one year in Jamestown, a prisoner? One year before sent he my brothers to seek me. 'If my father had loved me, he would not value me less than old swords, guns, or axes: therefore I shall still dwell with the Englishmen who love me.'

Can I still remember how to plant corn? I'll stay. Never, never go back where anyone might know Matoaka. My name is Lady Rebecca forever and always. I am a Christian Englishwoman!

TROUBADOUR:
> Alas for our dear lady, English climate did not suit
> > her—
> > She never saw Virginia again,
> > > she met her end at Gravesend.

LADY REBECCA: Says John, my husband: For the good of God, for the good of the country, for the good of the plantation, it is righteous and it is good. No mark, no trail, no footprint, no way home. It is enough that the child liveth!

TROUBADOUR: *[Joined by Monique.]*
> And so here ends the legend of the Princess
> > Pocahontas—
> > Fa la la la lay, fa la la la la LELF—
> > > if you want any more, make it up yourself.

[Chorus.]

> Heigh-ho wiggle-waggle wigwam wampum,
> > roly-poly papoose tom-tom
> > > tomahawk squaw.

*   *   *

ALEJANDRA: *[Singing with guitar while Monique sheds shawl, kerchief, and calico dress and hangs them on the tree. The buckskin yoke remains on.]* In the middle of my dream I came face to face and the copper hand reached to touch my back. I awakened sad, cold, confused, for the journey had been long and far . . . avec Marie, Margaret, et Madelaine . . . avec Marie, Margaret, et Madelaine . . . avec Marie, Margaret, et Madelaine, Madelaine . . . avec Marie, Margaret, et Madelaine.

ALEJANDRA: Princess, Princess!

MONIQUE: Princess, Princess!

[Princess Buttered-on-Both-Sides as the Cigar Store Squaw crosses centre with an oversized bunch of cigars.]

PRINCESS B: *[Offering cigars.]* UGH! I used to have this job, standing out in front of the tobacco store, but I didn't like the crowd. Besides, do you think anyone would talk to me? Not even chit chat. Do you think anyone would bring me a dozen roses, or an orchid corsage? No. Do you know what they gave me? Cigars. Do you know, the other day, somebody actually lit a match on me. Do you want to know where? So humiliating.

But I want it all! I want to be free to express myself! *[Sets cigars down at tree.]* I wanna be the girl next door! *[Removes buckskin yoke in exasperation.]* I wanna have lots and lots of blonde hair—great big blonde hair. I wanna be—Doris Day, Farrah Fawcett, Darryl Hannah—Oh, you know the one—Christie Brinkley! *[Hums 'Uptown Girl' while putting on white buckskin mini-dress.]* I wanna be a cover girl, a beauty queen, Miss America, Miss North American Indian! That's it!

According to the 'Walk In Beauty Seminar' it's very, very important to have the right look. *[Notices dress; screams.]* O.K. for the talent segment, but for the evening gown competition? The Finals? It's a rag! A rag! *[Pulls out pouch of buckskin dress to reveal a shimmering evening gown of the tackiest sort, and velcros it onto dress.]* Ahhh! Isn't this a devastating gown? I designed it myself. So, here I am a finalist in the Miss North American Indian Beauty Pageant! Think of it! Little me from in front of the tobacco store, fighting for DEMOCRACY!

HELLO WORLD!!

ALEJANDRA: *[Enters up left as beauty pageant host.]* And now, the moment you've all been waiting for . . . the winner of the 498th annual Miss North American Indian Beauty Pageant, from her woodland paradise . . . Miss Congeniality . . .

PRINCESS BUTTERED-ON-BOTH-SIDES!!!!

PRINCESS B: *[Screaming; jumps up and down flat footed as Host presents her with her over-sized corn 'bouquet' and 'crowns' her with a tablita style headdress covered with small ears of corn which light up. She begins her triumphant walk down the runway, weeping and blowing kisses, while Host throws popcorn at her feet and sings Debbie Boone's 'You Light Up My Life'. When Princess reaches upstage centre, she strikes the pose of the Statue of Liberty, and the ears of corn on her headdress are illuminated in full.]* Thank you, thank you . . . Oh! I can't believe it! I love you all . . . You have made my heart soar like a rabbit . . . I'll never forget this moment! *[She unplugs herself; corn lights go out. Exits upstage left.]*

*   *   *

[Lights snap to bright—sudden transition to mundane, urban environment.]

MONIQUE: *[Ramp left.]* It's International Women's Day—No, I didn't go to the march. *[Cross to centre; footprints in sand.]* So many years of trying to fit into feminist shoes. O.K., I'm trying on the shoes; but they're not the same as the shoes in the display case. The shoes I'm trying on must be crafted to fit these wide, square, brown feet. I must be able to feel the earth through their soles.

So, it's International Women's Day, and here I am. Now, I'd like you to take a good look—*[Turns.]* I don't want to be mistaken for a crowd of Native women. I am one. And I do not represent all Native women. I am one. *[Crosses to tree upstage right; brings basin and pitcher centre.]* And since it can get kinda lonely here, I've brought some friends, sisters, guerrilleras—the women word-warriors, to help. *[Pours water; Alejandra approaches, kneels by basin, they wet each other's faces, hair, and arms, purifying. With a cupped handful of water each, they sprinkle stage in opposite circles.]*

MONIQUE: *[Upstage left.]* Gloria Andalzua!

ALEJANDRA: *[Singing softly, under.]*
Una nación no sera conquistada . . .
hasta que los corazónes de sus mujeres
caigan a la tierra.

MONIQUE: 'What I want is the freedom to carve and chisel my own face, to staunch the bleeding with ashes, to fashion my own gods out of my entrails.' *[Dips hand in basin again, sprinkles water to stage right.]*

Diane Burns describes that to hold a brown-skinned lover means: *[Face to face, they wash each other's chests over heart.]* '. . . we embrace and rub the wounds together.' She also says: 'This ain't no stoic look, this is my face.' *[Dips hand in basin again, sprinkles half circle.]*

The Kayapo woman, of the Rain Forest, who stands *[up centre]* painted, bare to the waist, holding a baby by the hand, and confronts the riot squad in the capital of Brazil *[Walks downstage right.]* and says: *[Gesturing with arm; punctuating.]* I am here to speak for my brother and my brother-in-law. Where are your sisters to cry out for you? I am enraged with you! You steal our land! I am calling upon you! I throw my words in your faces!!!! *[Drum kicks in loudly, a 'call to arms'; song begins in Spanish to an Andean rhythm and evolves into a round dance—a '49' (contemporary native song with English words).]*

ALEJANDRA: Una nación no sera conquistada hasta que los corazónes de sus mujeres caigan a la tierra.

BOTH: Una nación no sera conquistada hasta que los corazónes de sus mujeres caigan a la tierra.

ALEJANDRA: No importa que los guerreros sean valientes o que sus armas sean poderosas.

MONIQUE: A nation is not conquered until the hearts of its women are on the ground.

BOTH: Then, it is done, no matter how brave its warriors, nor how strong its weapons.

[Blind faith leaps in the dark.]

BLACKOUT

Marilyn Dumont *b.* 1955

CREE/MÉTIS

Marilyn Dumont was born in Olds, Alberta. As a descendant of Gabriel Dumont, she is clear about the delicate balance between the traditions of the Métis people and those of the various First Nations. In one of her poems she encounters a 'full-blood' who responds to her as if 'he's leather and I'm naugahyde'. Dumont uses a variety of forms in her writing to detail the tensions she feels in her positions within and between cultures; as she observes, '*Cree Language Structures* and *Common Errors in English* book-end my life.'

Dumont earned a Master of Fine Arts degree from the University of British Columbia and has a diverse background in film and video production, as well as in education. Her first book of poetry, *A Really Good Brown Girl* (1996), received wide acclaim. *Globe and Mail* writer Judith Fitzgerald said the collection 'immediately turns readers into willing captives witnessing a preternaturally gifted artist in possession of a world-class bag of poetic tricks.' Her second book, *green girl dreams Mountains*, won both the Alberta Book Award for poetry (2001) and the Writers Guide of Alberta Stephan G. Stephansson Award for poetry (2002). In addition to writing, Dumont has taught creative writing at Simon Fraser University and Kwantlen University College and has been writer in residence at the University of Alberta and writer in electronic residence at the University of Windsor.

Squaw Poems

peyak

'hey squaw!'

    Her ears stung and she shook, fearful of the other words
like fists that would follow. For a moment, her spirit drained like
water from a basin. But she breathed and drew inside her fierce   5
face and screamed till his image disappeared like vapour.

niso

    Indian women know all too well the power of the word *squaw*.
I first heard it from my mother, who used it in anger against
another Indian woman. 'That black squaw,' she rasped. As a young   10
girl, I held the image of that woman in my mind and she became
the measure of what I should never be.

nisto

    I learned I should never be seen drunk in public, nor should I
dress provocatively, because these would be irrefutable signs. So   15

as a teenager I avoided red lipstick, never wore my skirts too
short or too tight, never chose shoes that looked the least
'hooker-like.' I never moved in ways that might be interpreted as
loose. Instead, I became what Jean Rhys phrased, 'aggressively
respectable.' I'd be so god-damned respectable that white people   20
would feel slovenly in my presence.

newo

> squaw is to whore
> as
> Indian maiden is to virgin   25
>
> squaw is to whore
> as
> Indian princess is to lady

niyanan

I would become the Indian princess, not the squaw dragging   30
her soul after laundry, meals, needy kids and abusive husbands.
These were my choices. I could react naturally, spontaneously to
my puberty, my newly discovered sexuality or I could be mindful
of the squaw whose presence hounded my every choice.

nikotwasik   35

squawman:

a man who is seen with lives with laughs with   a squaw.

'squawman'

a man is a man is a whiteman until

he is a squaw he is a squaw he is a squawman   40

Let the Ponies Out

oh papa, to have you drift up, some part of you drift up through
     water through
fresh water into the teal plate of sky soaking foothills, papa,
to have your breath leave, escape you, escape the

weight of bone, muscle and organ, escape you, to rise up, to loft,   5
till you are all breath filling the room, rising, escaping the white,
    the white
sheets, airborne, taken in a gust of wind and unbridled ponies,
    let the ponies
out, I would open that gate if I could find it, if there was one   10
to let you go, to drift up into, out, out
of this experiment into the dome of all breath and wind and
reappear in the sound of the first year's thunder with
Chigayow cutting the clouds over your eyes expanding, wafting,
    wings   15
of a bird over fields, fat ponies, spruce, birch and poplar, circling
wider than that tight square sanitized whiteness
you breathe in, if you could just stop breathing you could
escape, go anywhere, blow, tumble in the prairie grass,
bloom in the face of crocuses   20
appear in the smell of cedar dust off a saw
in the smell of thick leather
in the whistling sounds of the trees
in the far off sound of a chainsaw or someone chopping wood
in the smooth curve of a felt hat, in unbridled ponies   25

Horse-Fly Blue

'. . . d'you believe in god?,' I ask

          he says, he 'doesn't
          know,
          care'
'But,' I say,   5
'can't you see that this sky
is the colour of the Greek Mediterranean,
and won't last?'

          although I've never seen the Mediterranean
          I have faith   10
'Can't you see that this light,'
              'what light?' he says

is the same as all those other afternoons when
the light was receding like
our hairlines, when it shone through   15
our winter skin and we

awoke from a long nap and
it was light all the time we were sleeping?

'Doesn't this light remind you of all those other times
you looked up from your reading   20
and weren't expecting to see
change and nothing
did change except the way
you looked, the way you met the light,
greeted it at the door as a friend 25
or smiled at it from a distance as your lover?

Can't you see that the sky is
horse-fly blue?
I swear I've seen this light before;
before I was born,   30
I knew the colour of the sky.
When I was five
the yard I played in
had a sky this colour,' I say   'what colour?' he says.   35

Circle the Wagons

There it is again, the circle, that goddamned circle, as if we thought
in circles, judged things on the merit of their circularity, as if all we
ate was bologna and bannock, drank Tetley tea, so many times 'we
are' the circle, the medicine wheel, the moon, the womb, and
sacred hoops, you'd think we were one big tribe, is there nothing   5
more than the circle in the deep structure of native literature? Are
my eyes circles yet? Yet I feel compelled to incorporate something
circular into the text, plot, or narrative structure because if it's linear then that proves that I'm a ghost and that native culture really
has vanished and what is all this fuss about appropriation anyway?   10
Are my eyes round yet? There are times when I feel that if I don't
have a circle or the number four or legend in my poetry, I am lost,
just a fading urban Indian caught in all the trappings of Doc Mar-
tens, cappuccinos and foreign films but there it is again orbiting,
lunar, hoops encompassing your thoughts and canonizing mine,   15
there it is again, circle the wagons. . . .

monuments, cowboys & indians, tin cans, and red wagons

We lived at the end of a road
that dissolved into a field
flat as a table and the color of deer;
although I saw no deer there
that field rolled out for miles to a deep cliff   5
that fell to a river
and that Red Deer River
was our source of water
hauled home by our black dog Chinnie

and our old school house   10
jut out of that flatness
like a misplaced monument
to the wanderings home and away
of an extended family of halt-breeds
kids scattering to cowboys and indians, tin cans, red wagons   15
teenagers jiving to Del Shannon
migrating Settlement relatives searching for work
their wives or "old ladies" in tow
and on Saturday nights with two weeks pay
the Silk Tassle, Pilsner, and fiddle tunes would flow   20
weave through auntie's rank laughter, mom's stepdancing and
my brother's yodelling
Cree would occupy the house like a new code, the partying would
heat up the walls and spill out windows and doors like light
through cracks   25

And that old school house had long divided windows and
the same paint the school board issued
when my father bought it
the sun's rays a potato peeler
that curled the paint away from the boards   30
where that field spread out and away from the schoolhouse
like an epic film shot
until the sun sank into the wet field
between the house and river
ending our days like forged steel dipped in water   35

the dimness of mothers and daughters

I.
This is a story shaped by you
as big as your words or
as long as your sentences
This is your story
even though you haven't told it   5
all or don't know how to tell
parts of it yet. By starting the story
the story tells you, tells you how
to go on and how to look back

II.
And   10
you can look back not
to find a way out
or a way around
but a way through
the dimness of mothers & daughters   15

III.
Look back over your life like
looking back over a beaded design, accepting
the misplaced, or the misshapen
even misrepresented
Some beads fell   20
never got stitched in
place, but there was a pattern
there was a plan

jig dream

and the dancers kept streaming past   a long line of dancers
kept passing, kept dancing   children dressed in red and white
and metis sashes, black shoes like a phalanx of soldiers,   red
soldiers   and they were many   as far as the eye could see
many   children, many soldiers   feet flying to a fiddle, feet   5
quick as fish fins light and fast and fleet and change up change
up   that fiddle and flick of feet   Oh I wanted to dance   wanted
to dance, but I was still   held fast   paralysed by desire and

dread and desire and dread   and I could not lift my knees to
the fiddle, my feet to fiddle, but the children kept dancing and   10
dancing and I wanted   oh I wanted to show them how I could
jig

Broadway

I am now Hastings and Main, tattooed, pierced, shaved and
dyed; the rain and rhododendrons and the Lion's Gate Bridge;
I am now the panhandlers, the junkies, the hookers, the homeless, all of them, the Vancouver city transit, crowded and crabby,
"the Drive," Film Festival and umbrellas, the lights of Grouse   5
Mountain; I am now more city than I thought the Burrard ship-
yards and the nine o'clock gun; I am too, the disquieted waters
of the Fraser, the factories and mills that fidget next to it; I am
the ferry lineups, the plum tree blossoms in March, the green
smog over Abbotsford, the blueberries, humidity, three weeks   10
of rain, and grey sky on my raincoat

scorching

1.
Scorching sun and my
        desire
              hotter than the red tips
of the burning bush
out my window   5

2.
I settle in a chair
        glowing
in full sunlight and
assflower
melts open   10
    into its hands
           imagined mouth
cupping my nectar

3.
I wait
    and wait   15
        and
               wait

for my young lover
to be at my door
his smile sweet   20

as the pinkness
of his mouth, his
teeth white
           lashes curved and
                   waiting   25
                      for me to
                             lick

them in the door

4.
I hold
    desire   30
        kindle it, carry
    one coal
          lit
into the next day

wrapping the bundle of my dream of you[1]

I am wrapping the bundle of my dream of you one frame at
a time one line at a time of your exquisite face you sailed to
North America on I am wrapping the bundle of your face one
leaf of skin on another I am wrapping the bundle of your
face   layering it   sheaf after sheaf of bright cloth   scarves   5
tissue of taste   touch   sound   smell of bodysalt sweet taste
of cardamom   on your bodyhair   soft clean curryhair   I am
bundling your face away   I am wrapping the bundle of your

1 "'Wrapping the bundle,' is a South Korean expression, which signifies a transition from one life-stage to
another." Soo-Ja Kim, South Korean Artist

face away   I am carrying the bundle of your presence, now   I
am cradling the bundle of your face   I am walking the bundle   10
of your body to its place, now I am carrying the bundle of your
face to its end   of my horizon, my vision   to its place, its
resting   I am watching the light change in my heart for you
I am watching the light fade in my hand for you, I am watching the light dissolve in my hands for you, I am watching . . .   15

throatsong to the four-leggeds

but slowly
we sniff each other's airs, noses flare
jaws drop to the shape of 'o'
in the mouth
then 'Ahhh'   5
in the throat
the other wind instrument
and we suck and blow
volley the air between us
through a long dark throatshaft   10
back and forth, back
and forth, through
a song travelling now
from my throat to your
call and response   15
call
and response to the windpipe opening and
closing the sound of elk whistling
the vibrations of moose throttle through nasal passages
stretching   20
back into the gut of ancestors, sucking and mewling
deer, moose in the muscle of our being
back into the ancestors we are
back into groin of our helplessness now
into the rhythm of our joy and pain   25
freedom to move back and forth, between and
over the pine needles of space
push through the cool dimness of spruce, fir and maybe cedar
back to the song of wind in the limbs of space
your space and mine now   30
in this era of animal tracks

in the muskeg pungent earth mixed
with droppings of ourselves and
we climb the limbs of being
into the past of bawling animals   35
in the bush we once hunted for their generous red-blue flesh
that fed us even through our own wanting and neglect
we ate all the sweetmeat of those animals
then sucked the bones white
that became our whistles when we danced and   40
the crosses when we prayed
in the Lake of St Anne and
all our sisters who gave us mercy when
we wouldn't grant it to ourselves
our bodies old   45
in recognition of what was gifted us
from those four-leggeds that mewl
far back in memory of a world
that was forever bigger and vaster than any of us
I am thankful to have eaten   50
from those beasts that feed even me
now in my occasional starvation song
I do remember it sometimes, but
only fleetingly behind shyness that hums
through my nose and larynx   55
the tune of animal remembrances
and single notes of gratitude
for those mammals that sustained me even
before I could mewl myself in my mother's belly
the chord that she struck was the chord that bore   60
both of us through all those times of want and waste
of breath that we never put to good use
in song or bellowed back refrain
of gutsong and throatsong to our relatives
now in our days of plenty   65

Marvin Francis 1955–2005

CREE

Marvin Francis was a poet/playwright/artist/ actor/director from the Heart Lake First Nation in northern Alberta. He had a Bachelor of Arts in English literature and theatre from the University of Winnipeg and wrote drama for CBC Radio and the stage. In 2003, he received the John Hirsch Award for Most Promising Manitoba Writer. Of his first book, Thomas King said, 'Marvin Francis's *City Treaty* is nasty, rude, sneaky, cranky, smart, truthful, and intelligent. Everything a good poem is supposed to be.' He was working toward a Ph.D. in English at the University of Manitoba at the time of his death.

mcPemmican™[1]

first you get the grease from canola buffalo
then you find mystery meat
you must package this in
bright colours   just like beads

let the poor intake their money take their health   5
sound familiar
chase fast food off the cliff
speed beef
deer on a bun
bury in the ground   10

special this day
mcPemmican™
cash those icons in

how about a
mcTreaty™   15

would you like some lies with that?

they line up for blocks   dying to clog mind arteries everyone has
at least one fortieth indian↓ two parts water the rest unknown

---

1 treaty manuscript

they line to see the real ↑to buy the grey owl burger
to touch the other   money did fall   20
from the sky

we had one table reserved by the window we write
the city treaty
country words   me and this clown
pencils sharp look busy act important   25
look out the window

so you have to explain who is this clown
but I won't

I can knot
will not will not   30
just like hem
ing way
instead
we found
some   35

PULLING FACES

Pull off your face
Underneath lies a Pirandello mask

And under that   Death mask lurks loudly

Colour shifty shapes edges blur   Slippery pictures delight

Pull your face in a little   Red red wagon   That you show to the world   5
One face for your friends   One for trevor   One for that job application

Now that is one helluva mask   Go paint your face hollow

Certain colours scream bright   Stripes   divide   definite
Region synthetic cool   Paint   the thinnest mask

Could be hooker red   Warrior green trickster blue   10
Paint the oldest disguise   Belladonna delight
Blinding   Fools nobody's god only Your

selves know how many layers   Pile upon skin
brown back Drop eyes light this human Stage
So pull your mind face to the Thoughts of 15
others Pull faces from history Into today
carny images Pull family faces   into
museum fodder   Art   gallery
features Acrylic dream   masks
for those to follow keep pulling 20
that face   Down the street
Down down town Down
most roads   And
Down most

Coughing 25

roads

me: my next piece is called
that most famous elizabethan
native actor or

BNA ACTOR

[PULL OUT RED SKULL (from captain america) RED
INJUN BOOK, PASS BOOK TO THE AUDIENCE]
I have many roles
treaty busting is like
a full time job, man, so 5
time for some shakey spear
[BRANDISH SPEAR]
I am most famous
buckskin role   frontier gig   fall off the damn horse too
[FIDDLE WITH SKULL] 10
They call me
Omelette!
to drink or
not to drink
that is the question 15
whether tis noble savage to
suffer the arrows and arrows
of outrageous VLTs
or to take one arm bandits

into a sea of casinos   20
and end by opposing them?
to drink
nay to party no more
and end the heartache and
the thousand unnatural shocks when you watch that   25
B movie   over and over
celluloid omelette rejects fries
bush from your brain
[BIG PAUSE]
freeway wagons circle   30
those hiways were not free
to drink or not to drink
a dime novel story
a type of stereo
typing away your 1860s   35
persona into that sunset
where wagons burn
john wayne runs out of bullets
where tonto gets a day job
hiawatha goes   40
bye—a—wa—tha
where the young man who west
goes back where he came from
where christopher columbus sails the ocean Blue
and the santa maria gets drunk and takes chris to Aunt   45
Arctica instead
think about it, man, indian pen
guins, man, red and white noble penguins, man
drunken fucken penguins, man, the only good penguin is a
dead penguin, man   50
just think what if columbus had discovered himself instead
so to drink   to drink
there's the rubbie walking down Main
doing that santa maria shuffle
elizabethan red must be tragedy where you talk to skulls   55
dead invade your living room ghosts
of dead fathers die over and over on those late
nite reruns
so the ghost of Omelette still scrambles after all these years
so let us chase those freaking   60
winnibagles off a cliff let us bury those drunken skulls
dig   up some new ones   this could be the skull of a

lawyer of the jester   a joker   a clown   a new age trickster
fooling us over and over we see through skull eyes
      [PULL APART A SKULL   FIND A POEM]   65
it is time for the dumb show the ancient legend the real
      thing written with big hair eagle
          claw
      it starts way up there
      [HAND OVER EYES, POINT]   70
one man gets to feet he sees the eagle
      he feels the feather grow
      he feels the wind rip his thoughts
      he totters on the edge of clouds
      he flaps his arms he flaps his arms some more   75
      his partner up there his buddy
      does not have to flap cuz
for the first time since they invented twist top beer
      he is sober
meanwhile flapping away he skywalks he jumps his heart   80
      soars
      I AM EAGLE I AM EAGLE I AM EAGLE
      (thank u, yuri g.)
      THUD!
      no, you are not   85
      thank you
      very much

      [TAKE OFF BONNET AND BOW]

word drummers

      so many drum sticks flash

momaday takes us to rainy mountains joy of horses joe
    (king and hiway)   break open the way   erdrich
narrative willow twists annaharte frankensquaw opens eye
while mcnickle gets surrounded maracle vancouver tears the   5
    heart   armstrong slashes   canlit within the same silko
    ceremony   jordan wheels tv   while drew some
    curve lake laughs   alexis gives us famous fistfight
vizenor theory sizzles   the bad dog trudell   crunch

bernice half bones   as duncan mixes it   10
all together in his traditionalist stew

many stubborn writers
poet playwright screenwriter
short story long novel tall tales camp fire palimpsest legends
ancient rumours novellas   petroglyph hypertext syllabics   15
prose poem
longpoem skit character sketch   first person last in line
point of view
the landscape now has city

walk in the bush narrative: up   then down   around a tree   20
sink in the muskeg   heave frost splinters   dodge a bear
so there are no linear no
straight lines in the bush
the city only thinks so
follow the word drummers to the city treaty   25

those word drummers pound away and hurtle
words into that english landscape like brown beer
bottles tossed from the back seat on a country
road shattering the air   turtle words crawl slowly from
the broken glass   30

me and the
clown caught some
well deserved sleep

fade out   *fade out*   fade out

Armand Garnet Ruffo *b.* 1955

OJIBWA

Armand Garnet Ruffo was born in northern Ontario and holds a Master's degree in literature and creative writing from the University of Windsor as well as an Honours degree in English literature from the University of Ottawa. He currently teaches Native literature at Carleton University and has previously taught creative writing at both the Banff Centre for the Arts and the En'owkin International School of Writing in Penticton, British Columbia.

Strongly influenced by his Ojibwa heritage, Ruffo's first collection of poetry, *Opening In The Sky* (1994), reveals an abiding interest in the complexities of Aboriginal identity in a multicultural society. His second book, *Grey Owl: The Mystery of Archie Belaney* (1997), is a creative poetic biography that further 'raises difficult questions about voice and identity, Aboriginal culture, human rights, and the environment'. Ruffo won the Archibald Lampman Poetry Award for his third collection of poetry, *At Geronimo's Grave* (2001), in which he uses Geronimo's life as a metaphor for resistance and survival.

In addition to writing poetry, Ruffo has written plays, stories, and essays, which continue to appear in literary periodicals and anthologies both in Canada and in the United States.

From *Grey Owl: The Mystery of Archie Belaney*

Annie Espaniel, 1923

He comes in all serious,
sits down at the table beside me and
says he's organizing an Indian War Dance
for Queen Victoria Day
Me, I smile to myself when he tells me this   5
and look at the long face he makes.
So I say Archie, What's an Indian War Dance? None
of us Indian people have had one of those recently.
For Archie that's OK.
He's going to take care of everything.   10
He'll show everybody
what they're supposed to do.

Of course he needs my help to make a special suit.
You can't have an Indian War Dance without a costume.
I agree, and he brings home some brown material   15
and red ribbons from the lumber company store.
He draws me a pattern and I make it up for him.
When I'm finished he paints on little arrows,
adds animal teeth and bones.

He does a good job.   20
It's when he makes a drum out of a cheese box
that I have to shake my head.

Why I Write

So I can live in the past,
earn a living,
protect the beaver,   25
publicize conservation,
attract attention,
sell 35,000 copies in 3 months,
give 138 lectures in 88 days,
travel over 4350 miles,   30
wear feathers,
wear make-up,
play Indian—no
be Indian,
get to go to pow wows,   35
get to tour Britain,
meet the King & Queen,
become famous,
become alcoholic,
leave a legacy,   40
lose a wife,
be lonely.

Archie Belaney, 1930–31

The current is faster than I expect.
Suddenly my articles break into demand.
Letters of congratulations come flying   45
in from across Britain and the United States
(few from Canada which I find disconcerting).
Strangers want to visit me.
Reporters want to interview me.
They announce that I'm the first   50
to promote conservation:
the beaver,
the forests, the
Indian
way of life.   55

I begin by signing my name Grey Owl,
and saying I was adopted by the Ojibway,

and that for 15 years I spoke nothing but Indian;
then, before I know it, I have Apache blood.
Finally I'm calling myself an Indian writer.   60

Fast, it all happens so fast.
At first I'm hesitant.
I'm unsure of the name, the sound of it.
(Although, do I not prefer traveling at night?
Did I not hoot like an owl in Bisco?)   65
I think of the risk, those who know me.
There are Belaneys in Brandon.
My wife Angele in Temagami—
who knew me when I still carried an accent—
not to mention all those folks in northern Ontario.   70

But the thrust of self-promotion is upon me,
and head first into it, I hear myself
convincing myself that nobody's going to listen
to an immigrant ex-trapper from England,
promote an indigenous philosophy for Canada.   75
And if this is the only way
to get Canadians to listen,
then I'll do it, and more
if I have to. I'll be
what I have to be.   80
Without hesitation.

                    *   *   *

This is my wife Gertie, an Iroquois Chief's daughter,
21 years old. Tall, slim & very strong.
A woman of great courage & a true partner.
Well-educated, talks perfect English; everybody likes her.   85

                    —Archie Belaney in a letter to Aunt Ada, 1926

How Do You Know?

Because she's the one who tells her father
she'll be gone for the day
joins you
and never returns.   90

Because she knows how to let the past go,
and encourages you to do the same,
to open yourself as you would your cabin door
to the medicine winds of spring.

Because she has wings, transparent bright wings, 95
that you want so much to hold and tame
you sit up nights watching her sleep
your arms aching with emptiness.

Because she lets you call her beautiful Insect
even though she carries her share 100
and doesn't complain
she's not used to snowshoeing 70 miles.

Because she cooks so deadly you're afraid to eat.
Drinks and plays cards.
Argues fiercely 105
and goes for your revolver
to shoot up your moosejuice party.
Stabs you
with your own skinning knife,
then cries hysterically seeing you hurt. 110

Because this is the woman who somersaults your life
who can't bear to watch you club beaver to death.
Who makes you see, as she sees,
the suffering you inflict.

How do you know 115
she's the woman? Because:
She's the only one who beats you to the draw,
and walks out on you.

Poem For Duncan Campbell Scott

(Canadian poet who 'had a long and distinguished career
in the Department of Indian Affairs, retiring in 1932.'
The Penguin Book of Canadian Verse)

Who is this black coat and tie?
Christian severity etched in the lines 5
he draws from his mouth. Clearly a noble man
who believes in work and mission. See
how he rises from the red velvet chair,
rises out of the boat with the two Union Jacks
fluttering like birds of prey 10

and makes his way towards our tents.
This man looks as if he could walk on water
and for our benefit probably would,
if he could.

He says he comes from Ottawa way, Odawa country,   15
comes to talk treaty and annuity and destiny,
to make the inevitable less painful,
bearing gifts that must be had.
Notice how he speaks aloud and forthright:
       This or Nothing.   20
       Beware! Without title to the land
       under the Crown you have no legal right
       to be here.
Speaks as though what has been long decided wasn't.
As though he wasn't merely carrying out his duty   25
to God and King. But sincerely felt.

Some whisper this man lives in a house of many rooms,
has a cook and a maid and even a gardener
to cut his grass and water his flowers.
Some don't care, they don't like the look of him.   30
They say he asks many questions but
doesn't want to listen. Asks
much about yesterday, little about today
and acts as if he knows tomorrow.
Others don't like the way he's always busy writing   35
stuff in the notebook he carries. Him,
he calls it poetry
and says it will make us who are doomed
live forever.

Creating a Country

They came to North America in search of a new life,
clinging to their few possessions, hungry for prosperity.
They'd had enough poverty and suffering to last a lifetime.
And so they believed with all their hearts
that if they laboured they would all become barons   5
in a classless society. Patriots were thus born
on both sides of the border. But the process of creating
a country took much longer than most ever imagined.

For there were a myriad of unforeseen obstacles
in this formidable new land. Like mosquitoes and Indians.   10
Undaunted, the pioneering spirit persisted.

In Canada, Susanna Moodie arrived to take notes.
After writing anti-slavery tracts in England,
she thought it only natural to document the burden
of roughing it in the bush. Susanna shied away   15
from both mosquitoes and Indians. One day, however,
quite by accident, she met a young Mohawk
whom she thought handsome and for a period flirted
with the notion of what it would be like to be swept away
by him. But she soon tired of such thoughts and nothing ever   20
became of it. Later she would say neither Indians nor mosquitoes
make good company. She did make it perfectly clear
that she bore no grudge. She believed everything has a place.

Just as she believed her place was across the ocean,
but she too had heard stories of golden opportunities.   25
Lies! She could be heard screaming. Nothing but lies!
Susanna also believed she was turning life into art
and creating the first semblance of culture
in a godforsaken land.
It was her only compensation.   30
When she spoke about her life her eyes rolled in her head
like a ship leaving port. She never gave up the dream
of returning home. Dreamed so hard
that even on her death bed she never stopped
talking to herself.   35

South of the border, Lt. Col. George Armstrong Custer
never once worried about mosquitoes.
It's said that he too was interested in culture
and for this reason carried a gun.
He was a soldier, not an artist, and made no pretence   40
about it. Custer rarely wrote and never spoke
unless formally addressed. Yet, he was a passionate man
who dreamed the same dream every night.
He fancied that he had discovered the final solution.
Each night he rounded up all the buffalo   45
in what is now Montana and shot every last one of them.

As a son of European peasantry, he had heard stories
about what it was like to go hungry.

He also knew Indians could starve
just like white people. As a patriot,   50
he believed his solution was perfectly reasonable.
He also believed American politicians
would see to it that both the buffalo and the Indian
would find a new home
on the American nickel.   55

Susanna Moodie never met General Golden Hair (as Custer
was affectionately called), she never liked Americans anyway.
She was an old lady of 73 when he died young on the plains
of Little Bighorn trying to live out his dream.
They say that Custer was singing,   60
'The Girl I Left Behind Me' the day he headed west.
We know he wasn't singing to Susanna Moodie.
We also know that after hearing what the U.S. Cavalry
was doing south of the border, Susanna thought
about the anti-slavery tracts she had written years before   65
and, for a brief moment, about what had ever become
of her young Mohawk,
if he fared any better.

Rockin' Chair Lady

Today's the day I wake up knowing I'm going to commit myself
to the memory of Mildred Bailey. To my young mother
spinning her unfashionable and unpardonable jazzy 78's
(in the land of Country & Western)
on her rigged-up gramophone. Music   5
I couldn't appreciate, let alone understand.

These days an old woman I met out west years ago
sends me tapes from her collection
spanning seventy years. The last one of Bix Beiderbecke,
the white cornet player from the 1920s   10
(they say he sounded like a girl saying yes)
who played black and died at twenty-eight. Bootlegged
booze and passion will do that.

As for Mildred, the encyclopedia says
she was 'The first white singer to absorb   15
and master the jazz-flavored phrasing, enunciation,

embellishments, improvisatory fervor,
and swinging rhythm of her black contemporaries.'
To put it plainly, 'the first non-black woman
to sing jazz convincingly.'   20

What they don't say is that she was Indian,
Coeur d' Alene to be exact,
and could party with the best of them.
In jazz things are either black or white.
Red doesn't count. Unless your name is   25
Red Norvo, the musician Mildred lived with
for twelve years, before she got too fat and too sick.
Diabetes (the Indian disease) and heart trouble,
or trouble of the heart, claimed her in '51,
before I was even born.   30

But back to Mildred's young life. Bound for the city,
she got a job with the Paul Whiteman Orchestra
(talk about ironic) and hit the jazz scene
big time, in a world of big band swing.
They called her the Rockin' Chair Lady   35
because she was one great swinger
who sang with the greats, Goodman,
            Dorsey,
            Hodges,
            Hawkins, to name a few,   40
and took over the airwaves on her own national show.

Imagine tuning into her voice
on your Motorola. Hot stuff in 1933.
Imagine being labelled Indian back then
and not wanting to be, because red is out,   45
it doesn't count,
and hearing Mildred
coming in strong, knowing she's in
all the way to the top.

In the Sierra Blanca

Geronimo sits on a cloud
heavy with rain
for the cactoid earth,
catches a shaft of light
and slides with weariness   5
down to the land
he was forced to flee.

Geronimo walks and thinks,
kicks a rusty can
lying at the roadside,   10
wonders if the assassins
still gallop to the dictate,
the only good Indian
is a dead one.

He remembers when they treated   15
his people to a gift
of piñon nuts
seasoned with strychnine,
remembers
        (this chemical warfare)   20
and grimaces
an old hate.

But now there are rumours
things have got even worse.
This he finds unbelievable.   25
How can it be so?
He's heard they are now poisoning
the earth
mother herself.

Nuclear dump site. Low level waste   30
containment. State-of-the-art
concrete canisters.
English! he shakes his head
and sees a rattler
sunning itself,   35
forked tongue
flicking the air.

But Geronimo understands
what this is really about,
because after his surrender,   40
he was invited to the 1904 World's Fair,
where he sold his photograph for 25¢
and his autograph for 10¢.
Some asked to buy his buttons
and talked investment,   45
profit.

He smiles in this knowledge.
He had learned much
about white people. Learned
what was important to them.   50
But this new thing,
as though the assassins were back
or had never left,
he has to see
for himself.   55

On the Line

Sign, sign,
on the dotted line
and you will be mine
forever and ever,
like the mountains   5
and the lakes,
sky, soil,
everything I take.

I will supply you
with all   10
your needs,
a bible,
a blanket,
rations and beads.

If you can't understand me   15
don't worry
or whine,
heed what I say,

what is yours
is mine.   20

So sign on the line,
what more
can be said,
my word is law,
you have nothing   25
to dread.

You can't resist
so don't
even try,
I have cannons   30
and armies,
cities
and spies.

Oh, yes,
I do have a home,   35
it is far
far away,
but I like what I see,
and I've decided
to stay.   40

Bear

A young woman crawls into his bed
warms it golden in the late afternoon.
He returns after a day's outing,
stealing honey, munching ants,
causing general ruckus.   5

Then, again, perhaps he's home from school.

He opens the door only to find her
scattered clothes
which he trails to her body.
She has come to be devoured.   10
Every morsel.

So he begins with toes, feet, moves to leg
up inside of thigh.
When he gets to the tenderest part,
she whimpers for him   15
to stop.

She is losing herself to his bare kiss.

But the moment he does, she whispers
to go on. And he does,
as though together   20
they were retelling
an old-time story.

Postscript

The train rattles across desert, and I find myself following you on a map written on my tongue. Dust and hot wind blowing into your face, the train roaring and belching smoke, and I am looking out of my second floor window, past the barren maple trees, beyond the faint autumn sun, looking to you and wondering what it's all about? This journey. For unlike in the before-time when your people fought and earned the name Apache, I see you chained, wrists and ankles, sweating in dismay, swallowed by the beast of progress winding its way towards doom.

I survey the high-rises and taste the word defeat on the edge of the 21st century.

Dream in the half-light of the Long Knives who hold you and have no comprehension who you are. Who they are. Where they are. On this land they are bent on speeding through. I want to tell them that the day will come when you will swallow them in the power of myth and the beauty of a galloping horse. In a power that will take their weapons and bend them like willow, change confinement to freedom, iron to feather. I want to tell them but I cannot. For I too am shut in. Today behind a glass. Tomorrow?

They say when you die you meet your fear.

This while you sit like rock, stare straight through these invaders from another world, keeping vigil over your people, who some say would be better off without you. Point the blame. This while you pray they are wrong, and the train arrives in the hot damp of Florida, and you are sentenced to hard labour for two years. Alabama for five. This is what I see when General Miles speaks of the terms of your surrender with a mouthful of promises dripping like sweet water, and you become prisoner of men who try to turn you into one of them. American.

The United States of America. Stolen land, you say.

And me, here in Canada, looking out on this heavy new millennium, seeing you see-ing them. Wondering why? Why you? Why me? This journey? When the leaves are off the trees, holding the ground for winter, and I am on my padded chair, fingers to keys, and you on a hard bench, holding on for dear life. No camera at this moment, just cold blue eyes everywhere, watching your every gesture, ready to kill something they have already lost. The moment collapses and folds into now, and choice is bound to loss, of all that might have been.

It is too easy to become lost in the self. Is that what you are trying to say?

The Sergeant shrugs and spits a gob of tobacco juice on the floor. He grins, and I know he cannot begin to know your need to go home to your land, because for him you have no land. This is the new world. The new uninhabited world. You are a prisoner, and he is simply carrying out his order to transport you. Besides you are different, danger-ous, and he firmly believes, given half the chance, you would run your knife under the skin of his scalp, clutch a clump of hair and pull. This before he would even have time to point his gun, let alone fire. He hears himself calling for help.

'Jesus, merciful father!' It is a terrible thing this fear.

It swells inside until that's all there is, and all he sees is blood red. It comes to this, and I don't want to be here any longer. I go outside for air, kick through leaves that the wind takes like birds. Back inside, I am perched on the roof of the train hauling you away. It has stopped to take on water for the boiler. You are sitting with your few war-riors in the prairie grass growing along the edge of the tracks. You are a celebrity. A photographer sets up his box camera and takes your picture. 'Smile,' he says, without thinking. And I wonder if it is really you? Some say the one we see in the photographs is merely an impersonator? Someone designated to lead away from the real trail.

Will the real Geronimo please smile.

One thing for certain: your spirit, this thing we never see, exists on the land, in the hills, grass, rock, soil, in the air itself. I breathe deep and wonder how long before the paved drive-by culture of America strips the last remnants of you off the land. Yesterday the newspaper had an article about a space station under construction. Space, the final frontier. The cliché sets off an alarm because it sounds like what they said about the Old West a hundred years ago. Sounds like murder and displacement. What makes them think it would be any different next time around? History shows otherwise. Again, I see your people fenced in under the hard labour of stone and iron.

They hunt you for your old beliefs.

The rules say that from now on you are to live under the white man's law. If you do not give yourself up to reservation life, sell your people to a life of stagnation and poverty, all the power of the United States of America will be unleashed upon you, and you will be hunted down. They warn you that its terrible ferocity will tear you to pieces. You pray to Usen but to no avail. No wind comes to blow these white men back into the great water. Their kind of power is too new and treacherous. Their Iron Serpent continues to roar over your homeland. Until finally even you are inside it. Some of your few kill themselves in despair. Jump from cliffs. Slit their throat.

It is what you get for not obeying the rules.

Later, as prisoner of war, you confront Wratton, the Superintendent of Indians, who sells your cattle (the few you are allowed to raise) and keeps the money. While your people go hungry. He shouts he doesn't care what you say. You are nothing. Your power is gone. You can do nothing to stop the greed, which has now become the American way. At this moment, your young Apache helper jumps him and manages to stab him with a homemade knife. The cut is superficial, merely muscle and fat, and Wratton recovers to have him beaten and thrown into prison. It is the young who will take over. You feel it in your bones. But to what end?

Days become an age of miracles: electricity, combustion, refrigeration, nuclear power, microchips.

There is a famous photograph of you in old age in your melon patch with your children beside you, a simple pleasure. Behind you the world is going by. And I am made to think of the Aboriginal Career Symposium I attended, watching all the young people mulling over their options, their future beckoning them like a promise. And I wondered how they will maintain their identity and survive in a society whose advertising slogan is a way of life. That tells them to consume and be like everyone else. Outside, on the telephone-computer lines, a blackbird caws to tell me we are still here. What would you say? If you saw your people now.

The statistics show few Indigenous languages will survive the 21st century.

The bird takes off and a chill runs through me in the cold dawn. The wise say that to be leader, one must know humility above all. Everyone must come before one's own interest. Every interest must be balanced against another. Geronimo, I hear your laughter when I say this aloud. 'Show me the one,' I dream you say. The sun rises brilliant, tobacco is down, and once again it is time to go indoors. Choices. Decisions. To remain passive or to act. Adapt or die. Why you chose to escape the grinding reservation poverty, the threats, I can understand. Why you killed to defend your people and the old way of life that too I can understand. And I can even understand the American soldiers whose job it was to capture you in the name of their civilization. It's the deceit and greed that boggles the mind.

Even in your whiteman's clothes, you stand for your beliefs.

From your surrender in 1886 until your death in 1909, despite your pathetic pleas for the USA to honour the terms of the treaty, your Bedonkohe never again saw their homeland. Instead you are invited by Roosevelt himself to take part in his Presidential inauguration. As though that would be enough. How much does it take to break a spirit? A friend calls and asks me what I am doing. I say your name, Geronimo. And I am greeted by silence. How to respond to such a name? A name kids and soldiers use to jump from swings or planes. A name that passes through time and place. From the desert of the southwest USA up to Canada to a tree-lined street. I think of your red earth and mention a trip to your grave.

I could say I was drawn to you.

Instead we talk about the Free Leonard Peltier rally this coming Sunday on Parliament Hill. For twenty-five years an American Indian Prisoner of War in the USA. She tells me about a recent article by a prominent Canadian journalist, comparing Peltier to Mandela. And I add Geronimo. Fort Sill. Leavenworth. It's all the same. Before hanging up, I tell her to dress warm, I expect Sunday to be dark and cold to mark the occasion. And that's it. The day now in full swing, slam of neighbours and traffic breaking through the walls. A local radio station announces the news of the day and fittingly neglects to mention the rally. Life going on in all directions, or not going on, freedom or confinement, sky or ceiling.

Richard Wagamese *b.* 1955

OJIBWA

Richard Wagamese comes from the Wabaseemoong First Nation in northwestern Ontario. He has worked extensively as a journalist, broadcaster, television producer, and writer. Among his achievements are the Native American Press Association Award for best local columns in 1989 and the National Newspaper Award for his columns in the *Calgary Herald* in 1991. In these columns he ranged from autobiographical reflections on drug and alcohol abuse and prison experience to commentary on both historical and contemporary Native people and issues. A popular element was the 'Eagle Feather', which

he awarded at the end of each column to a person or group, Native or non-Native, that he felt had made a positive contribution to the Native community. Many of his columns were collected in *The Terrible Summer* (1996).

Wagamese's columns are direct, un-flinching, and very serious—and in this way very different from his first novel, *Keeper'n Me* (1994), which is full of irony. A good example of his journalist's sensibility is a piece (not included in the collection) on imprisoned Native activist Leonard Peltier, published in the American periodical *News from Indian Country* (1991):

Peltier is dangerous. He's dangerous because he represents an image of Native Pride, Native solidarity and Native fortitude. . . . To free him is tantamount to admitting wrongdoing and recognizing the solidarity of Native groups across North America who have fought long and hard to see justice implemented.

Since publishing *Keeper 'n Me*, Wagamese has written a second novel, *A Quality of Light* (1997). Most recently, he has brought his direct voice to bear on his own life and produced *For Joshua, An Ojibwa Father Teaches His Son* (2002), a compelling memoir about personal and cultural healing.

From *Keeper'n Me*

I'm used to it now having been back five years but that first day I wondered where the hell I was landing once we approached the reserve. First there was a big sign on the side of the road with about a hundred bullet holes in it that said: YOU ARE ENTERING THE WHITE DOG INDIAN RESERVE. NO ADMITTANCE. VISITORS REPORT TO THE BAND OFFICE. NO ACCESS WITHOUT PERMISSION.

Then about a quarter mile after that was a sign that read: KEEWATIN'S GENRAL STORE! WHERE NO STOCK ISN'T A PROBLEM! GOOD FOOD! GET GAS! NO LINEUPS! BIG ED KEEWATIN PROP.

We rounded the final curve into the townsite and I swear it looked like something outta a foreign documentary. Houses were perched on toppa rocky outcroppings and they all looked about ready to tumble down. There wasn't any siding on a lotta them and it looked like most were just sitting there on the land with no basements, plumbing or furnaces. They were all about a quarter mile apart and there was a lotta dead-looking automobiles parked everywhere. Reminded me of what Lonnie described the Detroit ghettos to be like. There was scruffy kids running around everywhere, shirtless and wearing rolled-down black gumboots, and the occasional old person walking around lookin' tired and glum. Out back of all the houses was a big lake and there were lotsa shaky-lookin' docks around with boats tied up to them. There was a big red brick schoolhouse and a few modern houses all hunched together close by and further away was a buncha aluminum trailers too. First thing I noticed was the missing power and telephone poles, and I saw someone behind one of the houses walking up from the dock with a five-gallon pail with water slopping over the sides. There were outdoor johnnies behind the houses too and I worried about how I was gonna get the slivers outta my ass. It was the only time in my life I ever thought constipation might be a blessing. Everyone looked up as the cab pulled in and by the time we pulled up in front of the store there were about fifty Indians all heading towards us. Kinda reminded me of those movies I used to watch as a kid. One minute they weren't there and the next minute they were everywhere. It was true after all. Indians did just pop outta nowhere.

They were all craning their necks real good trying to get a glimpse of who it was behind the tinted glass, and it gave me a chance to check out the locals and try to see any faces I recognized from the pictures Stanley'd sent. Seeing all those brown faces craning and squinty-eyed reminded me of something you see in *National Geographic* and I laughed while I handed the cabbie his dough. I could hear them chattering in Ojibway, laughing and rustling around. When I opened the door they all stepped back in one motion like a gumbooted chorus line.

The silence was deafening. As soon as I flung one lime green spangly platform-shoed leg out the door there was a loud gasp all around the cab. And when I stepped out there was about fifty heads all leaning in gazing at my yellow balloon-sleeved shirt and you could hear the sounds of a few dozen sniffers catching a whiff of my fifty-dollar scent. Four or five sets of hands were scrunching up my Afro and I could hear giggles from the kids as everyone was pressing closer and closer towards me. When the cab pulled away in a flurry of gravel, they surrounded me. It was true after all. Indians did love to surround you.

There was another loud gasp when I took off my shades and smiled all around.

'S'app'nin'? I said, bobbing my head and reaching out for hands to shake.

'Ho-leeee!' someone said.

'Wow!'

'Ever look like Stanley!'

'Ever, eh?'

'Ho-leeee!' said about three together.

Just about then a tall guy with a long ponytail reached through the crowd all excited like and started pushing people back amidst grumbling and something that sounded like cussing. When he made it up to me he stopped and looked at me with shiny eyes and kinda reaching out with his arms then pulling back, reaching out and pulling back. Finally, tears started pouring down his face. Everyone got real quiet all of a sudden and when I looked at this guy it was almost like looking into a mirror except for there being a ponytail where the Afro should have been and a definite absence of funky threads. He stared at me for what seemed an eternity with all kindsa things working across his face, and when he spoke it was a whisper.

'Garnet,' he said. 'Garnet. Garnet. Garnet.'

He reached out and touched me finally, one soft little grab of the shoulder, and then he collapsed into my arms sobbing like a kid while everyone around us moved in a little closer too.

'Twenty-two years,' he said, sobbing. 'Twenty-two years, my brother. Twenty-two years.'

I was crying by this time too and all the faces around me went kinda outta focus through the tears but I could tell we weren't the only ones breaking down and I remember thinking I wasn't exactly being downtown cool, but right then it didn't really matter. Holding my brother in my arms was unlike anything I'd ever felt, and as we cried I could feel that lifelong feeling of wind whistling through my guts getting quieter and quieter.

He looked up finally, threw his arm around my shoulder and turned to the crowd.

'This is my . . . my . . . my brother,' he said, choking up and sniffling. 'The one that disappeared. He's home.'

People started coming up and shaking my hand and smiling and touching me and there were tears everywhere as I heard the names of aunts and uncles and cousins and just plain White Dog folk for the first time. Stanley stood off to the side looking over at me and smiling, smiling and smiling. After a while they all moved away and started looking me over again.

'Ho-lee!' said a voice.

'Wow!'

'Sure he's a Raven?' someone asked. 'Looks like a walkin' fishin' lure or somethin'!'

'Yeah, that hair's a good reminder to the kids 'bout foolin' round with the electrical!'

'An' what's that smell? Smell like that should have fruit flies all around his head!'

'Damndest-lookin' Indyun I ever saw! Looks kinda like that singer we seen on TV that time. What's 'is name now? James Brown? Yeah. We got us one James Brown-lookin' Indian here!'

'Come on,' Stanley said once people started moving away. 'There's a buncha people up at my house been feelin' kinda down 'cause they figured you weren't comin'. Seein' you's gonna make 'em all feel a whole lot better. You okay?'

'Yeah,' I said. 'Least, I think so. It's kinda weird, man.'

'Yeah,' he said, 'I guess so. Wanted to ease you in slow but you weren't on the bus. What happened?'

'Nothin', man,' I said. 'Don't matter.'

'Least you're here now,' he said. 'That's all we wanted. Took a long time to find you.'

'Tell me about it,' I said. 'Tell me about it.'

They been comin' for our kids long time now. Nothin' new. Not for us. They been comin' on the sly for years. I always thought it was us Indyuns s'posed to do all the sneakin' and creepin' around. but those white people, boy, they got us beat when it come to sneakin' through the bushes. Maybe we taught 'em too much. Heh, heh, heh.

The boy's story's not much diff'rent from what we seen around here for a long time. Sure, in them movies us Indyuns are always runnin' off with children and raisin' them up savage. Give 'em funny-soundin' names like Found on the Prairie, Buffalo Dog or somethin'. I always figured they shoulda called 'em Wind in His Pants, Plenty Bingos, Busts Up Laughing or Sneaks Off Necking. Somethin' really Indyun. Heh, heh, heh. But in the real world it's the white people kept on sneakin' off with our kids. Guess they figured they were doin' us a favour. Gonna give them kids the benefit of good white teachin', raise them up proper. Only thing they did was create a whole new kinda Indyun. We used to call them Apples before we really knew what was happenin'. Called 'em Apples on accounta they're red on the outside and white on the inside. It was a cruel joke on accounta it was never their fault. Only those not livin' with respect use that term now.

But we lost a generation here. In the beginning it was the missionary schools. Residential schools they called them. Me I was there. They come and got me when I was five and took me and a handful of others. The boy's mother was one of them. They took us and cut off our hair, dressed us in baggy clothes so we all looked the same, told us our way of livin' and prayin' was wrong and evil. Got beat up for speakin' Indyun. If we did that we'd all burn in hell they told us. Me I figured I was already brown why not burn the rest of the way, so I ran away. Came back here. Lots of others stayed though. Lots never ever came back and them that did were real diff'rent. Got the Indyun all scraped off their insides. Like bein'

Indyun was fungus or somethin'. They scraped it all off and never put nothin' there to replace it but a bunch of fear and hurt. Seen lotsa kids walkin' around like old people after a while. Them schools were the beginning of how we started losin' our way as a people.

Then they came with their Children's Aid Society. Said our way was wrong and kids weren't gettin' what they needed, so they took 'em away. Put 'em in homes that weren't Indyun. Some got shipped off long ways. Never made it back yet. Disappeared. Got raised up all white but still carryin' brown skin. Hmmpfh. See, us we know you can't make a beaver from a bear. Nature don't work that way. Always gotta be what the Creator made you to be. Biggest right we all got as human bein's is the right to know who we are. Right to be who we are. But them they never see that. Always thinkin' they know what's best for people. But it's not their fault. When you quit lookin' around at nature you quit learnin' the natural way. The world gets to be somethin' you gotta control so you're always fightin' it. Us we never fight the world. We look around lots, find its rhythm, its heartbeat, and learn to walk that way. Concrete ain't got no rhythm, and steel never learned to breathe. You spend time in the bush and on the land, you learn the way of the bush and the way of the land. The natural way. Way of the universe. Spend time surrounded by concrete and steel, you learn their way too, I guess.

Back when I was a boy there was still a strong bunch of us livin' the old way. Lot of us crossed over since then and with those of us who's left maybe only a handful still practisin' the old way. Rest are Catholic and some other whiteman way. S'okay though. They're still our people no matter how they pray on accounta prayin's the most important thing anyway. Long as there's some kinda prayer there's some kinda hope. But there's not many of us old traditional people left walkin' around. Not many for the young ones to come to no more. That's why you hear more English than Anishanabe around here. Same other places too. Other tribes, other Indyuns. S'why it's so important for old guys like me to be passin' on what we know. I'm not talkin' about bringin' back the buffalo hunt or goin' back to the wigwam. I'm talkin' about passin' on the spirit of all those things. If you got the spirit of the old way in you, well, you can handle most anythin' this new world got to throw around. The spirit of that life's our traditions. Things like respect, honesty, kindness and sharin'. Those are our traditions. Livin' that old tribal way taught people those things. That they needed each other just to survive. Same as now. Lookin' around at nature taught the old ones that. Nature's fulla respect, honesty, kindness and sharin'. S'way of the world, I guess.

But lotsa our people think that just learnin' the culture's gonna be their salvation. Gonna make 'em Indyun. Lotsa young ones out there learnin' how to beat the pow-wow drum and sing songs. Learnin' the dances and movin' around on the pow-wow trail ev'ry summer. Lotsa people growin' hair and goin' to see ceremony. Think they're more Indyun that way. S'good to see. But there's still lotsa people out there still drinkin', beatin' each other up, raisin' their kids mean. All kindsa things. That's not our way. So just doin' the culture things don't make you no Indyun. Lotsa white people doin' our culture too now and they're never gonna be Indyun. Always just gonna be lookin' like people that can't dance. Heh, heh, heh.

What I'm tryin' to say is tradition gives strength to the culture. Makes it alive. Gotta know why you dance 'steada just how. It's tradition that makes you Indyun. Sing and dance forever but if you're not practisin' tradition day by day you're not really bein' Indyun. Old man told me one time he said, the very last time you got up in the mornin' and said a quiet *prayer of thanks for the day you been given was the very last time you were an Indyun. Then he said, the very last time you got handed some food and bowed your head and said a prayer of thanks and asked for the strength you got from that food to be used to help someone around you, well, that was the very last time you were an Indyun too. And he told me he said, the very last time you did somethin' for someone without bein' asked, bein' thanked or tellin' about it was the very last time you were an Indyun. See, it's all respect, kindness, honesty and sharin'. Built right in. Do that all the time and boy, you just dance and sing up a real storm next time. Heh, heh, heh.*

That's what we gotta pass on. 'Cause tradition'll keep you goin' when you're livin' it. Us we need to remember these things. Keep 'em alive inside me. Live 'em so they stay strong. Lotsa kids comin' back nowadays really need to be shown. Tough thing to do when the kids are forty-four, twenty-five or whatever.

Nowadays the whiteman comes in lotsa diff'rent ways. Oh, they still come with their schools and their foster homes, but we got some of our own teachers and social workers now, so kinda gettin' better there. But they still come for the kids. They come with their TV, money, big inventions and ideas. They come with big promises 'bout livin' in the world, with their politics and their welfare. They come with their rap music, break dancin' and funny ways of dressin'. All kinds of shiny things. Kids get all excited, funny in the head 'bout things, wanna go chasin' after all that stuff. Tradition? Ah, it's just borin' stuff for old guys like me can't rap dance. Somethin' you gotta do when you ain't got no other choice. That's how they come nowadays. On the sly. Harder for kids to come back from these things than from them schools or foster homes sometimes.

That's why we gotta pass it on. Always gotta be someone around who knows. Always gotta be someone around to catch 'em when they land here all owl-eyed and scared, askin' questions, tryin' to find if they belong here still. If they wanna stick around. Always gotta be someone who knows the kindness built into tradition. Ease 'em back slow. Got the Indyun all scraped offa their insides, carryin' 'round big hurts an' bruises. Poke around too much you hurt 'em an' they run away. So you bring 'em back from the inside out. Nothin' in this world ever grew from the outside in. That's why I help the boy understand. He learned 'bout respect before he ever learned to sing or dance. Learned to be kind and share before he learned to tan a hide or how to hunt. Learned to be honest before I let him be a storyteller. Learned about bein' Indyun, about himself. That way he'll survive anything.

He looked funny enough when he got here wearin' all those strange things and havin' a head of hair looked like a cat been through the dryer, smellin' like fruit and talkin' funny. Guess if he could survive walkin' around lookin' and smellin' like that, learnin' to live an' learn off the land was gonna be simple. Heh, heh, heh.

The first thing most people notice about us Indians is how we're laughing most of the time. It doesn't really matter whether we're all dressed in traditional finery or in bush jackets and gumboots, seems like a smile and big roaring guffaw is everywhere with us. Used to be that non-Indians thought we were just simple. You know, typical kinda goofy-grinning lackeys riding out to get shot offa our horses by the wagon train folks. Or standing around on a corner in some city bumming smokes an' change but yukking it up anyway. But the more they stick around the more they realize that Indians have a real good sense of humour and it's that humour more than anything that's allowed them to survive all the crap that history threw their way. Keeper says laughin's about as Indian as bannock and lard. Most of the teaching legends are filled with humour on accounta Keeper says when people are laughing they're really listening hard to what you're saying. Guess the old people figured that was the best way to pass on learning. Once you stop to remember what it was you were laughing at you remember the whole story, and that's how the teachings were passed on. Guess if it was thirty below and I was hunched around some little fire in a wigwam I'd wanna be laughing too instead of listening to some big deep talk.

Teasing's big around here too. You get lotta teasing from people on accounta teasing's really a way of showing affection for someone and like me at first, a lotta people have a hard time figuring that out. Get all insulted and run away. But once you figure that out it's a lotta fun being around a bunch of Indians.

When Stanley and me got to his cabin that first day I was expecting a big warm family kind of scene like on 'The Waltons'. I figured there'd be a big spread on the table, maybe a little wine, music and a party happening. Instead there was about ten people sitting around drinking tea they were pouring out of a big black old-fashioned metal pot on a pot-bellied stove in the middle of the room. There weren't any decorations or anything unless you can call six or seven pairs of wool socks hung over the stove pipes decorations.

They all looked up as we walked in. The silence was deafening.

'Ho! Whatchu got there, Stanley?' said a big gap-toothed guy with a brushcut. 'Not Halloween yet, is it?'

'Ho-wah!' said a large fat woman with gumboots, a kerchief around her head and smoking a pipe. 'Thought he was coming from T'rana, not Disneyland!'

'Reee-leee!' said another woman. 'Who'd you say adopted him? Liberace?'

'Ahh, he's just dressed fer huntin',' said an old man with so many wrinkles he looked like he was folded up wet and left overnight. 'Wanna make sure he don't get mistook fer no deer.'

'Deer? Maybe get mistook for the northern lights but sure ain't nobody gonna be thinkin' he's a deer no matter how dark it gets,' said a tall spindly woman busy pouring herself another tea.

Stanley eased me into the centre of the room with his hand on my shoulder and I could feel the pressure of it getting a little firmer the more nervous I got. Like he wanted to hold me from bolting for the door, which was exactly the thought going through my mind at the time. He smiled at me and waved at a large round woman leaning in the doorway and staring real hard at us both.

'Your sister,' was all he said. Or at least I think that's all he said because I got swept up in her big brown arms and disappeared for about five minutes. I could feel her breathing deeper and deeper as she hugged me and when she finally let me surface for air she was crying real quiet and smiling at the same time. She was a lot wider than me, but it's kinda spooky when you look at someone you swear you've never seen before and you can see your own eyes looking back at you. I didn't doubt for a minute that this woman was my sister.

'Hi, bro,' she said. 'I'm Jane. Do you remember me at all?'

'No,' I said real quiet. 'No, I don't think I do.'

'S'okay,' she said. 'S'okay. I remember you real good. Little bigger than before but I remember you, all right.'

'Ahh, get the hell outta the way, Jane, and let us meet this boy kept us waitin' three days and twenty years anyway!' said an energetic little guy. 'How you doin', T'rana? I'm yer uncle Buddy.'

Well, they all lined up and for the next half hour or so I was introduced to my uncles Gilbert, Archie and Joe, aunties Myrna and Ella, Chief Isaac McDonald and wife, Bertha, and the wrinkled-up old guy who said his name was Keeper and who left right away with Buddy.

Two things really got my attention that day. The first was the way they just seemed to treat me like I was someone they'd always known. Like the twenty years didn't matter to them or the way I was dressed, the Afro or anything. It was like I was already a part of their lives and let's get on with it all. The second thing was the absence of my mother and my other brother, Jackie. Of all the things I was scared of, meeting my mother after all that time was the biggest and I wondered why she wasn't there. Anyway, after all the introductions were over everybody just visited with each other and it was like the excitement was over and life was back to normal for them. Me, I was pretty confused.

Robert Arthur Alexie *b.* 1956

TEETL'IT GWICH'IN

Born and raised in Fort McPherson, Northwest Territories, Robert Arthur Alexie attended the residential school in Inuvik, where he completed high school. He served as chief of the Teetl'it Gwich'in (People from the Head Waters) in the late 1980s and as vice-president of the Gwich'in Tribal Council for two terms in the 1990s, and was the chief negotiator for the Gwich'in during their land claims negotiations with Canada. He lives and works in Inuvik.

Alexie says he would like to think of himself as 'a writer who just happens to be Indian' but explains the difficulty of separating his writing from his Native background:

I have a feeling I am going to have to go through the process of being an Indian writer before becoming a writer *sans* Indian. Being an Indian doesn't hurt when

it comes to writing something like I've written, and I will take advantage of it if I can.

I began writing, during my tenure as vice-president of the Gwich'in Tribal Council, poems and short stories to spice up dry memos, letters, and reports. Most of the writing of *Porcupines and China Dolls* took place in the summer of 1999 when I was living in Yellowknife and between jobs. I saw writing, and the idea of becoming a published author, as a means to make a living and as a means to tell the story of a people, my people, who are going through a time of change in terms of losing their language and culture from the invasion of a foreign system that has a desire to help them, but that cannot do it without destroying what was.

Personally, I think, we as Native peoples cannot survive in the past. We have to take the tools of this foreign system and make it work for us and not against us. I am a good example, and I use the term 'good' loosely, of this. I have what I think is a good education: I graduated high school, went to trade school, and worked at airports as a radio operator. I also worked for Transport Canada as a Flight Service Specialist. I also have a diploma in Public and Business Administration. I do not speak, nor do I understand my language, which, according to others, will be gone in one or two generations. I do not hunt or trap or fish for subsistence, but I do buy meat and fish from those who do.

Alexie's most recent book is *The Pale Indian* (2005).

From *Porcupines and China Dolls*

CHAPTER FIVE

A Typical Night

Friday, September 24th, 1999
The old wolf watched as the pack moved into the hills. He'd seen it coming, but he'd given the younger male the benefit of the doubt. He shouldn't have. He was now alone and an outcast. He was also old and tired, but he didn't know that. He was just a wolf.

Click! Click! Click! Click!

His big, black cowboys boots hit the dirt road. His heels were well worn and his boots needed a shine. There was silver duct tape on the back of the left boot.

His steps were long, slow and deliberate, and he kept his eyes forward as if he were in deep thought. His black leather jacket, like his boots, had seen better days.

He had his hands in his jacket pockets. The two people he passed looked at him and smiled. He grinned and continued on.

He turned off the main road and walked to the large brown building. Only the sign over the large double doors gave any indication of what was inside: the Saloon.

He could hear George Jones singing one of his classics on the stereo as he walked up the steps. Boom! Boom! Boom! He stopped and checked his time—six o'clock. That meant seven and a half more hours until last call. He walked in through the first set of doors. Boom! Boom! Boom! Boom!

They all knew who it was, but they looked and waited nonetheless. They hoped it wasn't the Grim Reaper coming to kick ass. He entered the second set of doors. Boom! Boom! They all looked at his six-foot frame as if he owed them a living and wished the Grim Reaper would kick his ass, but only after he bought them all a beer.

James stood while his eyes adjusted to the light, then saw thirty or so people looking at him. They did that to everyone who came in. They were checking to see if it was their husband, wife, common-law, boyfriend, girlfriend, friend, foe, son, daughter or the one they laid last night. He was none of the above, so they all breathed a collective sigh of relief and went back to their drinks and their talk.

The Saloon was on Main Street and contained twenty tables, an old pool table, a bar and room for a hundred people. There was an old jukebox in the corner that hadn't worked since everyone converted to CDs. The forty-fives in it were already antiques, like most of the customers. There were no windows, and it was always dark, except for the last fifteen minutes of the day when the lights were turned on to scare the vampires and other blood-sucking critters back to their coffins. There was the unmistakable smell of cigarettes, beer, cheap perfume, and some strong cleanser used to clean the bathroom. The cleanser would do its job for a few hours, then the smells would re-emerge from the walls, floors and ceiling where they'd been hiding.

The Saloon would never make the list of the ten best places to be. It was an Indian bar. People came here to drink, to look for possibilities and to bitch, whine or cry in their drinks—in that order. They also came to beg, borrow, whine, cry or demand a beer, smoke or the means from anyone and everyone. But that was normal. It was a fucking Indian bar.

A couple of people waved at James. They knew he was someone they could sit and gossip with because he'd shut up and listen. He didn't talk much, and if you told him something he didn't spread it around. He spread other things, but not gossip. Sometimes they wondered if he was listening at all. Some thought he was crazy. Others thought he was nuts. Most just left him alone unless they wanted to borrow money or bum a smoke. Or was it bum money or borrow a smoke? Either way, he wasn't going to see the smoke or money again.

'Hey, James, gimme smoke!'

He pulled out his pack and threw it on the table.

'Hey, James, len' me loonie!'

He heard but didn't listen and walked to the bar. Boom! Boom! Boom!

'Hey, James, buy me beer!'

He went deaf, then opened his black leather jacket and revealed a well-worn black shirt.

'Hi, James.' *Wanna eat me?*

He looked up and saw Karen behind the bar. She was a few years older and kept herself in good shape. She was also married to an asshole and had four kids. The asshole worked here too. She smiled, then snuck a look at his crotch. He grinned and looked at her tits then at her crotch and didn't care if she saw. She wasn't wearing a bra and she was definitely not wearing panties.

'Usual?' she asked for the millionth time.

'Why not?' he answered for the millionth time and watched her pour two shots of vodka in a glass, add some water, then bend over to get his beer.

'That it?' she asked. *Wanna go in 'a back for a quickie?*

'Pack 'a smokes.' *Wanna go in 'a back for a quickie?*

She reached up and pulled down his brand. The twenty he placed on the bar barely covered the cost, but she knew she'd make twenty off him tonight in tips. *Wish he'd slip his tip into me.*

'Hey, James, len' me loonie!' *You work for the Band.*

'Hey, James, gimme smoke!' *You owe us a livin'.*

'Hey, James, buy me beer!' *Weren't for us you'd have no job.*

James made it to his table without giving away shit, but it wouldn't last. A young girl wearing a dirty denim jacket and loose-fitting pants that she hadn't changed for a few days walked up. Her hair was messy and her skin was dark from walking around all summer looking for that next drink.

'Hey, brother,' she slurred. 'Len' me twen'y bucks.' It was more like a demand.

'Ain't got none,' he said.

'Doooooon' fuckin' lie.'

He said nothing, hoping she'd leave.

'Come on,' she begged, waited. 'Gimme smoke, 'en,' she demanded. She took the smoke he gave her. 'Gimme light too.'

He lit it for her and watched her hair fall over her face. She looked forty, though she was in her late twenties. She took a deep drag, then turned and walked away. 'Asshole,' she said.

James heard but didn't say anything. He lifted his glass and took a drink. The vodka burned his throat, but he didn't taste it, nor did he smell it. He chased it with some beer and settled in.

Mutt and Jeff, the town drunks, bums and lepers all rolled into one, picked that moment to walk in looking like Mutt and Jeff: right at home. No one looked at them. Everyone just wished they wouldn't sit at their table. They ordered a beer.

'Hey, James, you ol' fart,' Jeff said as he walked over. 'Wanna buy fish?' He and Mutt were dressed in old work clothes that had seen better and cleaner days.

'Not today,' James said, and hoped they'd leave.

'Len' us some money, 'en,' Mutt asked.

'Ain't got none.'

'Doooooon' fuckin' lie,' Jeff whined with all the self-pity he could muster.

'Come on,' Mutt pleaded. After a few seconds, they knew James wasn't going to give them shit, so they left in search of other suckers.

James lifted his glass. It was empty. He wondered if they'd sucked it back when he wasn't looking, but he knew they hadn't. It still amazed him how fast he could drink when he wasn't watching. He got up and walked to the bar.

'Another?' Karen asked.

He nodded and she gave him another while he checked the time—six-thirty. He looked at her tits then at her crotch.

'Where's Brenda?' she asked.

'Home, I guess.'

'She comin' tonight?'

'Not likely,' he said. *She already came twice.*

He liked Karen, but she was too good for him. Or so he thought. He'd put the moves on her a few times, but they didn't do it. He looked around for some strange stuff and came to the conclusion that they were all strange and should all be stuffed. He looked at his drink and wondered if he drank it. He turned to Karen and smiled. 'Whatcha doin'?' he asked. 'Waterin' down 'a booze?' She laughed. 'Gimme 'nother beer while you're at it,' he said.

He took one more look at her ass before going back to his table and going off on one of his tangents. He could drink, smoke, and carry on a half-assed conversation even when he was off on one of these tangents. He'd been off on one of these tangents for half his life. He checked his watch—seven. He checked his glass, then looked around for the culprits, but no one was sitting at his table. He got up and walked back to the bar and Karen poured him another.

'Another beer too,' he said.

Back at his table, he tipped his glass back, then drifted off into the abyss. A few seconds later, he put his glass on the table and the bar was packed. He wondered where everyone had come from. He checked his watch and realized he'd time-travelled thirty minutes into the future.

He checked his glass and it was normal: empty. He walked to the bar, where Karen poured him another. He returned to his table and looked around to see if anything had changed, but nothing had. *I wish someone would shoot 'a shit with me.* Everyone looked at the door then at him. *Not her.*

Angie Lawrence floated in like she owned the place. She had on a clean pair of jeans and her own leather jacket and didn't look too bad if you didn't count her blood-shot eyes. She looked at him, then walked to the nearest man and talked to him and let loose a laugh. *See? Other men still think I'm good lookin'.* She went to the bar and ordered a beer, then joined a couple of girls who were sitting near the pool table. They were all looking for future husbands, or at least one for the night. They had come to the right place. The place was swarming with one-night stands, but no future husbands. Not unless you got knocked up, and even then it was a long shot.

James wondered how many times he'd caught the clap from her. She was ten years older and had two kids in Yellowknife. Rumour was she had two others who were lost in the system. Still, when he was high she looked good enough to eat. If she'd asked for a quickie, he might have done it. He knew there was no 'might' about it. He would've. His little head had controlled him for most of his life. It still did. *Can't do it tonight. Been fucked twice 'nd got a new woman to boot.*

He looked at his glass, then made his way to the bar, where Karen had his usual ready. He checked the time—eight. *Time's flyin'.* He saw Liz Moses and Sarah James sitting at the bar and smiled. *When 'hey get here?* He wondered where Mary and Jake were. *Prob'ly takin' care 'a business. Wish somebody'd take care 'a my business.* He smiled at his sense of humour, then at Karen.

'What?' she asked.

'Nothin',' he said, then looked at her crotch.

The next thing he knew, he was walking to his table.

'Hey, James, len' me loonie!'

'Hey, James, gimme smoke!'

'Hey, James, buy me beer!'

Karen watched his ass, then turned to Liz and Sarah. 'Might have to call Jake again,' she said.

Meanwhile, James had returned to his table and Alfred joined him. 'Hey; Al, how's it goin'?'

'Alfred was his best friend, right after Jake. They'd grown up together, and often worked together. 'It's goin',' he said.

James looked for a cigarette in his jacket. 'Got a smoke?' he asked.

Alfred opened the pack on the table and gave him one.

'Whose smokes?' James asked.

'Yours.'

'What's 'a time?'

'Eight-thirty.'

'Already?' James tried to make a joke of it.

'You okay?' Al asked.

'Fuckin' A!' James lifted his glass and drained half of it.

'Need money?'

'Everybody needs money,' he said, then stretched out.

Alfred pulled out five twenties and gave them to him.

'What's 'is?'

'You loan it to me las' week. Remember?'

'Thought I drank it,' he said. 'Wanna drink?'

'Sure, why not?'

James walked to the bar, then made his way back to his table. He put a beer in front of Alfred.

'Thanks.'

'Not a prob.'

James sat and time-travelled into the future. Someone was laughing. He looked across the table and saw two women. It took him a few seconds to place their names. *Lorraine 'nd Norma. Thirty-something going on fifty with three kids each and no husband in sight.*

'Did 'at really happen?' Lorraine asked.

He'd told them a story and it must've been a good one because they were laughing. Either that or they wanted to nail him.

'Yep,' he said.

He checked his time—ten. He looked around and saw the same people he saw a few hours ago, a few days ago and a few years ago.

He closed his eyes and concentrated, then opened them. It didn't work. Shania wasn't sitting on his lap in her tight-fitting Spandex. He reached into his pocket and gave Norma a twenty. 'Get me 'a usual 'n two beers for both 'a you,' he said.

Norma walked to the bar in her tight-fitting Spandex that left nothing to the imagination. She disappeared into the fog and emerged ten times more beautiful and with a smile that just didn't quit. It was sort of lop-sided and told him she loved him and wanted him, but she knew he had another woman. She was also ten years and three kids too late, but that didn't keep her from trying. She rubbed her leg against his. *Maybe I'll get lucky tonight?*

James felt her leg and his little head came to life. *Maybe I'll get lucky.* He picked up his drink, then looked for his beer. *She forgot it. Strike one.* He went to the bar, where Karen was waiting and watching his crotch.

'Gimme beer 'n a pack 'a smokes,' he said with a grin.

She opened the cooler and gave him a good look at what he was missing. She turned and he was eyeing her crotch. *Wanna sniff?*

He looked at her and smiled. *Lemme sniff.* He gave her a twenty, then turned serious. 'Karen?'

'Yeah?'

'Wanna go to my place?'

'For what?'

'I've always wanted to fuck you.'

'Really?'

'Really,' he said, then grinned. 'Wanna?'

'You sure?'

'Yeah.'

She looked at her husband, Gary, who was looking at Tina. 'Gary!' she shouted. Gary turned. 'I know you're fuckin' Tina so me 'n James're gonna go to his place 'n fuck!' she yelled. 'It's payback time!'

'Karen!'

She came back to reality and James was still standing there, but now he was looking at someone or something.

'Karen!'

She turned to her old man. *Asshole.*

'Gimme three Blues 'n two Canadian!'

Should give you a good kick to the balls.

James turned to see if Liz and Sarah were still there. They were and now they had company. *What's she doin' here?*

It was Louise. She was looking at him and not smiling. He looked away like he didn't see her. Then he saw the fog. He forgot about Louise and gathered his courage, then went on instinct and found his way back to his table, where Norma and Lorraine were waiting for him. *When did they get here?*

Lorraine took a sip of beer and looked around for possibilities.

Limited.

Norma wished he'd ask. *I'll show you what you're missin'.*

He was about to ask but someone had put Dwight on the stereo and he was singing like he meant business. James tipped his glass back and the fog enveloped him and he time-travelled or went comatose. He didn't know which, nor did he care. All he knew was that someone was shaking him. *Maybe Norma's ridin' me again?*

'Hey, bro, wake up.'

Jake. Am I gonna have to pack him out? Hope not, 'cause I'm drunk.

'Wake up,' Jake said again.

'Yup.'

'Where am are?' he asked as if it were a joke, but he already knew where he was.

'Same ol'.'

'Knew 'at. What am doin' here?'

'Same ol', same ol'.'

'Hey, bro, is 'at you?'

'Yeah. Let's go 'fore I have to carry you outta here,' Jake said.

He heard some girls laughing and tried to picture Jake carrying him out. He couldn't picture it. He could only picture Jake dragging him since he was two hundred pounds and that didn't include his jacket and boots. 'You 'n what forklift?' he said.

The girls laughed at that one too and he tried to collect his bearings, but they were shot to hell. 'What's 'a time?' he asked.

'Twelve.'

Still got hour 'n half to go. He saw three people behind Jake and tried to focus, but it was no use. He knew two were Liz and Sarah, but the other was a mystery. He stood, adjusted his jacket, then looked at the stranger. *What's she doin' here?* He put on his cool look and stretched to his full height and towered above them.

They had to look up to see him, but his face disappeared into the smoke and fog. He steadied himself, then looked around to see if anyone had seen him at his best, but no one had. No one would've cared if he was passed out, blacked out or croaked out. *Fuckers will roll me 'fore they check for vital signs.*

The Saloon was packed. It was payday for most, pension day for others and just another day for the rest. Angie was still sitting with the girls and she was looking at him. Doreen Aaron and Daniel Carson were sitting in the corner. She was looking at Daniel who was looking at his soon-to-be ex-wife.

James took a deep breath and almost choked. The smoke was thick up in the stratosphere. The smell of smoke, beer, piss, cheap perfume, mouthwash, Lysol, and a million other aromas burned his nostrils. There was the faint smell of weed in the air. *Did I light one again?*

He was known to light up two or three and pass them around to see how fast they'd go. They usually made it three or four tables and Karen sold a lot of peanuts and chips after that. Karen was known to con a joint from him and light up with Liz and Sarah in the can. *Wish she'd smoke my joint.* He smiled at his sense of humour and the girls wondered if he'd finally go for broke and go nuts. He didn't.

'You ready?' Jake asked.

'No, but lead way, Kemo Sabe. Me follow,' he said in his best Tonto voice, and the girls laughed at that one. *Hi ho, Silver, away!* 'Where we goin'?' he asked for the hell of it.

'My place.'

'What for?' he asked for the hell of it.

'Same ol'.'

'Good, thought it might be for same ol'. Who's comin'?'

'The girls.'

'Good, can't party 'lone. People might think we're alcoholics.'

'You're not,' Jake said. 'You're a zombie.'

'Rather be zombie 'an a drunk. Boris Karloff is my hero.'

They all laughed at that one. He might be drunk, but he still had his sense of humour.

Liz and Louise each took an arm, Sarah broke trail, and Jake picked up the rear. James wanted to walk on his own. 'I can walk,' he said.

Liz and Louise continued to lead him to the door. He felt her hand on his arm and smelled her. She smelled the same as she did the night they sat in the theatre a million years ago. He had a boner then and was getting one now. He wondered what she'd do if he turned and kissed her. *Slap.* She was beautiful and had a smile ten times sexier than Norma's. He was getting excited, but he maintained his cool. *Cool Han' Luke.*

Louise hoped Daniel saw her, then came to the sad realization that that kind of thinking was petty and childish and she was no longer a child. She was a forty-million-year-old woman with a soon-to-be ex-husband and a child to raise. She time-travelled back to that day ten million years ago when she and James first kissed. She closed her eyes, wished and opened them. *Didn' work. Maybe later. Maybe never.*

James emerged from the fog and was on the road. *Where am I?* He saw Jake and Sarah and remembered Liz and Louise were holding him. He looked at Louise but didn't smile. He just wanted to look. Even with the scar on her lip, she was still the best-looking thing around. *Why'd I let you go?*

Louise sensed he was looking and turned. *Kiss me.* He didn't. She then put on some attitude, closed her eyes and turned to show she didn't care. *Why do I do 'at? I should tell him how I feel.*

James watched her look away, and became solemn.

When he came back from the darkness, they were walking on the back road and he had to get his bearings again. He looked around, got them focused on staying with the living.

'Hey, Liz,' he said.

'What?'

'Howwwwwwww ssssssick,' he said, trying out that Fort McPherson accent. They laughed at his attempt.

'You gotta say it like 'is,' Liz said. 'Howwwwww ssssssick.'

'Gee iz bad,' Sarah said, and they all laughed at that one.

'Maybe you got 'a little Gwich'in in you,' Liz said.

'I wish I had a little Gwich'in in me,' Sarah answered, and they all laughed. She looked at Jake. *Wish I had somethin' in me.*

Liz was Beth and Isaac Moses's daughter, and therefore Jake's first cousin. She and Sarah were in their late twenties, single and enjoying life. Or whatever life in Aberdeen offered. And that was not much.

James looked up at the night sky, then walked up Jake's steps. *When we get here?* He didn't worry about it. He walked in, sat on the sofa, and the fog returned. After a few seconds or minutes, it dissipated and he was back in reality.

Liz was laughing at something or another and Sarah was looking at Jake. He leaned back and his head touched someone's arm. *What's she doin' here?* 'Sorry,' he said. He didn't really mean it. *Wish you'd put your arms 'round me 'n kiss me.* She was looking at him with no emotion. He decided to go for broke. *What 'a hell can she do 'sides slap me?* Be put his arm around her and, surprisingly, she didn't resist.

'Louise?'

'Yeah?'

'I love you.'

She started crying. 'I love you too,' she said, then leaned over and kissed him. She stuck her tongue in his mouth and searched for his tonsils. She was going to try to rip them out like she had tried so many times in their younger days.

He came up for air and looked over at Liz and Sarah. They were looking at Jake and laughing at something he'd said. He looked at Louise and she too was looking at Jake and laughing. He'd been on one of his tangents, but he didn't worry about it right then. He had other things to worry about. Like the fog that was now coming out of the walls. A few minutes later, it dissipated and she was smiling at him. *Why she followin' me?* Before he could answer his own question, the fog returned, this time for good. *Come with me, Louise. Keep 'em away from me.* He wanted to reach out for her and was seriously thinking about it, but she was gone.

'I think he passed out,' Liz said.

They picked up their cups and moved to the kitchen table while Jake stretched him out on the sofa.

Louise put a pillow under his head and smoothed his hair. She wished she could kiss him good night. She wished she could take him home. She wished she could do a lot of things. 'Think he'll be okay?' she asked.

'He'll be okay,' Jake said.

'Hey, Jake,' Sarah called. 'Got any good music 'sides Elvis?'

'There is no other good music.'

'Yeah, right,' she said. 'Hey, Liz, where's your Vince Gill?'

Liz reached into her handbag and threw a tape to Sarah, who put it in the tape deck and Vince Gill started crooning.

'Vince can shack up with me anytime,' she said. 'Be skin 'n bones when I get through with him.'

Louise went to the washroom and looked in the mirror. She was forty-something, dark skinned with a daughter and a worthless husband. She had scars, false teeth, and lines around her eyes. *Where'd they come from? They weren't 'ere yesterday.*

She closed her eyes and time-travelled back to the day she and James first kissed in that crowded theatre in Helena. She thought it would be forever. It wasn't. She thought about Michael Lazarus and silently cursed him and hoped he was burning in hell. She remembered the many times she wanted to make things right. She would never get the chance now. She remembered the many times she hoped he'd call.

'Louise?'

James? It was Liz calling her back to reality and it still sucked. She looked in the mirror. *Twenty-seven years ago next month we went out. Was it 'at long ago?* She fixed her hair and walked into the living room.

'What was you doin' in 'ere?' Liz asked.

Thinkin' 'bout killin' myself. 'Nothin',' she said, then looked at James. *He looks dead.* She looked at his crotch, then at his eyes. *He's dreamin'.*

James was not dreaming. He was having a nightmare. He was quiet on the outside, but on the inside some serious shit was starting to happen and he didn't want to be there. He wouldn't remember it tomorrow, but that was the least of his problems. He was here and now and it was as real as it could be.

He was in a room that looked familiar. Even the smell was familiar. *What is it? It smells like. . . Oh fuck, it's his room.*

He tried to turn, but he couldn't. Someone or something was keeping him there. He knew what it was. He knew who it was. He tried to move. He couldn't. He didn't want to look, but he had no choice. *Oh fuck, it's his hand!* Soft, warm, white and hairy. *Oh fuck, le' me out!* He was being led over to the bed. *Oh fuck!*

Paul Seesequasis *b.* 1958

CREE

Paul Seesequasis was born in Melfort, Saskatchewan, into a family that blended Plains Cree and Dakota with Ukrainian and German ancestry. 'I like the idea of mixed blood existing between cultures and not being easy to place,' he explains.

> That hybrid existence is the direct result of the meeting of different people and it can create new imaginings of self, which I think are reflected in my writing. I'm fascinated with the creative potential of miscegenation. My identity as a Native person is real in terms of family and lived memory, but not in any pan-tribal or pan-spiritual sense. My grandfather and my mother are the two Indian people who have had the greatest impact on my life and I can't remember either of them ever talking about 'being Indian'. They are simply people who dance through life with humour and gentleness.
>
> I want my writing to deal with transformation and crossing boundaries. I hope my writing contains a 'trickster spirit' in that it challenges the reader as much as it entertains them. . . . I think we are entering a new nomadic age where, especially in the urban wilderness, there are cross-breeding, cross-gender, and cross-culture things happening. Nothing is pure and the only two constants are love and change. In these new meetings I think the trickster can thrive.

Seesequasis's stories and essays have appeared in *All American* (1997) and the Banff Centre's *10 Years of Arts Journalism*. He worked as an editor for *Aboriginal Voices Magazine* and is now working for 7th Generation Books in Toronto.

The Republic of Tricksterism

We were urban mixed-bloods. Shopping malls and beer parlours were our sacred grounds, reaching adolescence in the 70s, the Sex Pistols and the Clash provided the tribal drums. Fallen between the seams and exiled from the reserves we were the prisoners of bureaucratic apartheid, of red tape and parliamentary decrees.

Our tribal links were obscure, our colonial banishment confirmed by the Indian Act. White bureaucrats and tribal politicians alike were our oppressors. 'We are heading toward self-government,' proclaimed Tobe, the Grand Chief of the Fermentation of Saskatchewan Indian Nations (FSIN) as he shook the hand of then Saskatchewan Premier Allan Blakeney.

In his hands Tobe, the Grand Chief, held a paper promising tens-of-millions of dollars, but that money and power were destined only for a select few. The Grand Chief's vision was obscured by power and long-legged blondes. He denounced Indian women who had married white men, while at the same time blonde secretaries and assistants crossed their legs in his plush office at the FSIN.

Mary Seesequasis, aka Ogresko, was born on Beardy's reserve on January 20, 1934. The first child of Sam Seesequasis, of Beardy's reserve, and Mary Rose Nahtowenhow, of the Sturgeon Lake band. Sam, my *nimosom*, danced through life with gentleness and humour and became a leader in the community. Mary Rose, my *nohkom*, was large and became a bear when she laughed. She hunted rabbits, decapitated chickens, and farted in the direction of bureaucrats and posers.

They made love, had nine children, and seven lived to adulthood.

The grand-chief-to-be and his family lived downwind from my grandmother's farts. He was born the same day as my mother but their lives were destined to take far different paths. Tobe was born mixed-blood, his father Cree, his mother white. But the irony and humour of being mixed-race was lost on Tobe. He would grow up as mixed-race pure-blood, purer than thou and given to exaggerating the quantity of his half cup of tribal blood. Tobe lived in denial of his white parentage.

Being the same age, Tobe and my mother played together as children, they fell asleep infused with dreams of *Wesakaychuk* and *Pakakos*, they hid under the covers from the wetigoes and the hairy hearts.

But The Indian Act enabled Tobe to imagine himself the pure-blood. With Indian father and white mother he was allowed to stay on the reserve. In 1950 my mother met and fell in love with a white man, Dennis Ogresko, and because she was in love with a white man and she was *hisqueau*, a woman, she had to leave the reserve.

The hairy hearts ran amuck in 1950s Saskatchewan. Cannibal spirits plagued the small towns and hid in the grain elevators. It was open season on squaws, wagonburners, and breeds. By courageously proclaiming brown-white love my parents challenged the humourless segregational values of the time.

Unable to hide on the reserve they weathered taunts and jeers with laughter. That love could exist between races offended all the pure-bred breeders; and in making love Dennis and Mary parented two cross-breed mutts, my brother and I.

We experienced childhood between the seams, spending summers on the reserve, winters in the city. We played without leashes, without pedigree we learned to live with our genetic-mixture coats and our lack of papers. We lived in a no-man's land between Indian and white. At school we quickly learned to stick together to avoid the beatings of the pure bred-breeders. We found delight in the repulsion others felt for us. We pissed on the city trees, marked our traditional urban territories, and barked ferociously at the white poodles.

It was the 1960s and my mother, now a registered nurse, worked in the Community Clinic in Prince Albert where she healed the urban orphans and mixed-bloods who were now entering the cities in increasing numbers.

Tobe, the mixed-blood/full-blood too had grown up. He became a tribal politician, a Chief of the reserve and a wearer of suits and ties. His hair was short and his speeches were long. He spoke of self-government and economic development but his mind was on attending conferences and getting laid in hotels.

With enthusiasm he joined Wild Jean's Indian Affairs Bandwagon and Wild West Show and with conferences here and there and blondes to his left and right, it was the modern-day chief's delight. Tobe sold his Pontiac—*the Poor Old Nechee'd Thought It Was A Cadillac*—and actually bought a real Cadillac, and a blonde chauffeur. But while Tobe played the colonial game a revolution was brewing in Prince Albert.

Uncle Morris was a *rigoureau*, a mixed-blood shape-shifter. He often came to visit our home on the east side, the poor side, of the city. My uncle was a co-founder of the Metis Association of Alberta in the 1930s, and an urban activist who cut through the lies of white bureaucrats and tribal politicians alike. His mission was to liberate the urban reserves from the cannibal spirits and the hairy hearts. He told my mother of his vision and Mary laughed and agreed to help him. Uncle Morris wanted to take over the Prince Albert Friendship Centre and remove the metal detectors from the door. Those detectors beeped a warning anytime someone without a status card tried to walk in.

Malcolm spoke passionately about uniting all urban skins, mixed or full. 'Burn your status cards!' he proclaimed, 'and throw away your colonial pedigree papers. Don't let the white man define us. Let's define ourselves.'

Uncle Morris knew how to respond to taunts and jeers with trickery. When he laughed he became a bear and his joyous chuckles reverberated from deep within. My mother would prepare dinner and then we would sit, expectedly, waiting to hear of his latest exploits.

As a *rigoureau* Morris was hated by the hairy hearts and the cannibal spirits. They envied his power, his ability to turn into a dog, a bear, or almost any kind of rodent he chose. I remember once his turning into a red squirrel, jumping from his chair and scurrying around the kitchen floor while my parents cried with laughter and said 'Enough! Enough!'

From Morris I learned to see the evil spirits around me. I saw them in the frowns and looks of scorn us mixed-bloods received on the streets. I felt the disapproving glares of the police, farmers, tribal politicians and store owners. They were everywhere in the city and their numbers were increasing.

The cannibal spirits and the hairy hearts ruled the cities and reserves. They fed on both Indians and whites. 'There just aren't enough of us *rigoureau*'s left to stop them,' uncle once told me. 'These evil spirits,' he explained, 'feed on souls that are empty, rub against their bodies and penetrate the skin. Sometimes a person can repel them if they are strong enough or if they can call on a *rigoureau* to drive the spirit away. But most people succumb and the cannibal spirits continue in their goal to create a world of hate. A world in which they can proliferate.'

Morris would often go to the clinic where my mother worked to watch and to offer humour to those who were forgetting how to laugh. He played the compassionate trickster, upsetting the plans of the cannibal spirits, and frustrating the violent emotions of the hairy hearts. Many a body was purged of poison.

Then, one day, Uncle Morris went missing. Search parties were organized and the mixed-bloods and urban orphans looked everywhere but it was the squirrels, the rodent friend of the *rigoureau*, who led us to him. He had been dumped into a grain chute and his body was badly beaten. We lowered ropes and a canvas stretcher. My mother was among those selected to gently retrieve his body from that dark cavern.

While the crows cawed mournfully and the stray dogs howled their lament, our procession carried Morris back to our house. He was laid in the guest room and a group of women healers worked with him. They washed his bruised body, set his broken bones, removed all the grains that had been shoved down his throat and nostrils, and, after a few days, his heart began to beat again.

Time passed and Morris cracked a smile and we rejoiced, knowing he would live. 'My spirit has tasted life again though parts of my body probably never will,' he confessed. True he was now paralysed from the waist down. We pooled our meagre resources and had made for him a cedar wood wheelchair with wheels of rounded stone. Being confined to a wheelchair didn't slow Morris down. Rather he called for a gathering of mixed-bloods and urban orphans.

I remember that day. We met at an old skating rink. Long benches had been set up for the occasion. The building was packed. Uncle Morris's life history was in that building and each person had a story to tell. Some kindness, some help from trouble, some funny story. There were trappers from the north, none more than three feet tall, with bristled faces and wooden pipes. I remember how they stamped their fur-covered feet in applause when Morris was wheeled into the arena. There were *kokums*, grandmothers, with shawls wrapped tightly around their heads and their aged but strong fingers beading leather. There were young street girls who took the day off from work. I recall the smell of perfume, their make-up, and the candy they gave to the children who ran up and down the aisles. And there were nurses, construction workers, loggers, teachers, drunks, and others and they had all come to hear my uncle.

'The main cannibal spirit has arrived in town,' Morris roared in his bear voice. There was silence in the hall. 'He has come for me. I have frightened him and he seeks to destroy me with violence.'

'Shame!' cried the audience.

'He has come in the guise of an Indian. A Chief. A person you know well. He is Chief Tobe, the plains warrior wearer of chokers and ties, the politician without humour. The one whose ideas are short and his speeches are long.'

The crowd laughed.

'You remember Tobe. He speaks of purity and his heart is cold. He has chased the mixed-bloods from the reserves and he has created a world of urban orphans. I shall trick him with humour. With your help we will create a story. A myth. That is something that cannot be destroyed by violence. It will annoy him immensely because we will create a world he cannot shatter with hate, for it exists here,' Morris said, pointing to his head.

Uncle told of his plan to establish the Republic of Tricksterism, a place where humour rules and hatred is banished, where love's freedom to go anywhere is proclaimed. 'Our headquarters will be the Indian Friendship Centre which, as you know, has been controlled by the hairy hearts. We don't seek permanence for our republic but a moment of time that lasts forever.'

We cheered and with Morris's wheelchair at the head, we marched downtown on our mission of liberation. We marched into the Friendship Centre as the hairy hearts, panic-stricken, climbed out the back windows. They left in a rush, not having the time to shred their Indian Affairs hit list of their sacred status card membership rolls. We took their defining documents, turned them upside-down, and wallpapered the building. The children, myself included, were given crayons and told to draw freely. We created a world of merging colours, a world without paint-by-numbers.

The Republic of Tricksterism was proclaimed. All skins are equal was the first constitutional decree and a pair of red drawers became the new flag. Skins from the street came in to help the social workers heal themselves and tribal lawyers were deprogrammed.

Chief Tobe was soon in a fury. He roared with anger and dark clouds pelted the city with hail. He smashed his fists on the ground and the streets cracked and the sewers overflowed. He called loudly and the poisoned souls congregated outside the offices of the Prince Albert Regional Tribal Council to hear his message of hate. The Tribal Council was in an uproar, they passed resolutions and sent ultimatums to the Republic of Tricksterism demanding they abdicate power. 'We are the Chiefs!' they proclaimed. 'The big white men in Ottawa say so.' 'Ah—go on,' replied the Republic of Tricksterism. When even memos from the Minister of Indian Affairs failed to dislodge the trickster-upstarts, Tobe went into action.

A hundred tribal goons were summoned. They were armed with baseball bats, dog repellent and mace. 'We shall disperse these mixed-bloods. These defilers of our traditions. These people without status!' The goons chanted their approval in unison. The Tribal Council Chiefs smiled, patted their beer bellies, and licked their fat lips in anticipation.

The assault came at dawn. Calling in the mounties, who in honour of the chiefs donned full regalia and did a musical ride, Tobe, the goons and the mounties marched in a column toward the Friendship Centre. But the urban animals, the squirrels, raccoons and foxes, ran out ahead of the approaching army and barked out a warning to the citizens of the Republic of Tricksterism.

'We must avert bloodshed,' Morris observed to the citizens. 'Violence is the tool of fools. It is with humour and irreverence that us urban animals must survive. Let them have their building back, let them issue their proclamations with dead trees, let them have their dubious titles like national chief, let them become the media stars. We'll find our humour back on the streets.'

And so it came to be that Tobe and his goons recaptured the Prince Albert Friendship Centre without bloodshed. 'These mixed-bloods are cowards,' Tobe proclaimed, in disappointment.

Uncle Morris was captured by the tribal goons and brought before the Prince Albert Regional Tribal Council. 'He must be punished as an example,' proclaimed Tobe. 'He has committed blasphemy and challenged our noble and sacred institutions.'

'Spare him!' yelled the urban orphans and mixed-bloods but, as always, the chiefs were deaf to the sounds of the streets. On a Sunday, surrounded by a procession of goons, Morris was forced to wheel his chair to the highest hill in Prince Albert.

There he was nailed to a metal medicine wheel, his arms and legs spread in the four directions. Morris died soon after and his body was taken by the goons and buried in an unmarked grave. The mixed-bloods and urban orphans mourned. Crows flew high and cawed his name to the clouds. A wake was held and for four days the memory fires burned from street corner garbage cans. On the fifth day the crows told the people that my uncle had been resurrected but that he had come back as a termite.

The urban people rejoiced and Morris, in his new life form, moved into the regional Indian Affairs building and gnawed at the bureaucrats' desks until they dissolved into sawdust. Meanwhile Tobe, sporting the retaking of the Friendship Centre as another dishonourable feather in his war bonnet, ran for national leader of the FSIN and won the big chief position at that fermenting organization.

'Who better to speak the politicians' garble? Who better to hide the truth between platitudes of self-government and economic development than Tobe?' proclaimed the FSIN in their press release announcing his victory.

Then, one day, despite the opposition of the FSIN, C-31 became law. At the stroke of a bureaucratic pen, status was restored to those long denied, a government decree pronouncing the end of a hundred years' damage. 'Hallelujah, we're Indians,' responded the mixed-bloods. Our hearts soared like drunken eagles. We donned our chicken feather headdresses, our squirrel tail bustles, and fancy-danced around the Midtown Plaza.

My mother, a full-blood Cree woman, could only laugh at the gesture. Meanwhile in the FSIN offices Tobe, the mixed-blood/pure-blood, and his Indiancrats, were having a bad day. They grumbled, drank double shots of rye, and hit their blonde secretaries.

But C-31 was only a temporary irritation for Tobe. His vision remained focused on careerism and playing the colonial card game. He wore blinkers whenever he entered the city to avoid seeing the urban orphans. He talked about first nations as if the cities did not exist. He became bloated with his power and gained weight by the hour. As the Honourable Heap Big Chief he increased his salary and his belly respectively. Mary Seesequasis moved to Saskatoon and worked at the 20th Street Community Clinic where she administered to the mixed bloods: the whores, dykes, queers, street people, everyone. My uncle's words, 'We are not victims. We are survivors,' was the motto she lived by. Tobe also was a survivor but in a more dangerous game. My mother saw the Indian Act as a bad joke. Tobe embraced it as a career. His sense of humour was lost in the shuffle of colonial cards and his heart was hardened by the cannibal spirits.

Meanwhile Uncle Morris, having completed his job in Prince Albert, found his way into a chief's pocket and made it to Ottawa. Rumour has it that even today he has led an army of termites into a certain national chief's organization where he is currently munching away at the legs of that chief's chair.

Joanne Arnott *b.* 1960

MÉTIS

'I do think of myself as an artist,' Joanne Arnott writes, 'crafting with words to create portraits, recreate experiences and places, using rhythm and sound for evocative effect. I identify primarily as a Métis writer, less formally as an Indian. This is important for me personally, to counter the pull to integrate/disintegrate into the mainstream, and professionally, so that my work is marketed in such a way that I am connecting with people of common experiences and history, rather than only on display as some form of multicultural window dressing.'

Born in Winnipeg, Manitoba, Arnott studied English at the University of Windsor in Ontario. She moved to Canada's west coast in 1982.

'My community is very much one of individuals, of insecure identities,' she says. 'Whether we've arrived in the borderlands between nations through intermarriage, misce-genation, and migration, or as a consequence of government removal of indigenous children from indigenous homes and communities, or by other means, there is a commonality of insecurity and isolation that marks membership in this community. My writing rises out of this community.'

Arnott worked for many years as an Unlearning Racism facilitator. She has read her work and given writing workshops across much of Canada and in Australia. Her publications include three volumes of poetry—*Wiles of Girlhood* (1991), which won the Gerald Lampert Award; *My Grass Candle* (1992); and *Steepy Mountain: love poetry* (2004)—as well as a work of nonfiction, *Breasting the Waves: On Writing and Healing* (1995), and a book for children, *Ma MacDonald* (1993).

Arnott lives with her husband, a visual artist, and her children—five sons and a daughter, all born at home—in Richmond, BC.

Wiles of Girlhood

GARBAGE

White paper, waxed stiff and shaped into a flat-bottomed cup, and used once, and crushed. Nearby, a lid, a cracked straw, mysteriously forged, equally abandoned. The eleven-year-old with her pain-hollowed face, her weedy dark hair, passed down the street with her eyes focusing inward.   5

ELEPHANT PANTS

She wore a very large pair of very bright pants, peacock blue, roped in at the waist so that uncomfortable bunches alternated with hanging crevasses, the whole shifting about with each step as her toes pulled the hems. Elephant pants. When anyone said, "What's that?" she ignored the laughter and answered, "These are my elephant pants." 5

THE FIGHT

They were halfway down to Dennis's, by the big hedge where she sometimes stopped to eat flowers. Small yellow flowers, honeysuckles she called them, with a tiny taste of sweetness among the petals. Or maybe the bush with the hard purple berries, said to be poison. Sam was with her, and when the large angry Prince bolted across the street toward them Sam stiffened and moved in a kind of pleasure to meet him. Their lips curled and their tails twitched in formal gestures, then both broke and lunged and they whirled fiercely together. 5

She waded in, telling them to stop. Their backs fell against her legs and launched forward again, totally absorbed, not listening. 10

Someone told her to move away, threw a bucket of water on them, shocking.

FLYING

She walked down the street to school, tasting the rain and its relative freshness. On the way back up in the afternoon, she felt the wind at her back, and lifted her arms, arched her body. She knew there was a special way to do this, to send herself into the sky. She tried to, for it had a delicious sensation. 5

PHANTOMS

At night she was very concerned with a particular corner of the room. She threw all her concentration there, heard voices warbling in from another dimension. Wicked, angry voices, indistinct. Also a wee child's voice, she strained to hear it. None of these voices had bodies, faces. Invisible lives that would emanate from the blank shadows. 5

THE FIRE

She awoke to see the whole sky vivid and beautiful, and she could hear the operatic voices of the legions of angels. She ran to the window, with her sisters, and the eldest announced that it was a housefire down the street. "But what about the angels?" She shook her head, trying to shake the sound. But it remained, real, the singing. 5

DYSFUNCTION

They were yelling in the kitchen, she had a bad sense of it, a foreboding. She moved past the tv set, along the wall where the guitars, ukelele, tambourines and drum were hung high, into the doorway as she heard the loud steps and the banging of the back door. Her father stood wiping the grease from the 5 automobile from between his fingers. Her younger brother and sister stood separate before him.

His look of anger was overwhelmed with purest hatred, and he picked up a child and threw it against the wall, picked up the other and threw it at the same spot so that it fell on top of the 10 other. Then he kicked and kicked the whole mess, shouting his fury.

ENCHANTMENT

There was a ghost that came in at night and tried to suffocate her older sister. It put a large hot hand that she said she could actually feel, right on her mouth, and a great weight pressing down all over her body. This was a very evil spirit, very frightening. Though it left, it might still come back to haunt 5 her.

If Honour is Truth

If I were a rat in a bucket
instead of your daughter,
would you take up the shovel just once,
killing me outright?

Few are the people whose smiles   5
I have sought with such rigour,
soaked in, treasured, like the rare
pure smiles alighting your face. And now

this long decade later, the distance
between us is finally a comfort,   10
not devastation. Bad boy, kicking his toy-like
offspring around rooms, into corners,

opting for tyranny in the home
instead of the harder inward struggle

that ends at peace. Your mistake lay   15
in thinking you could escape

dealing directly with your pain.
A bad boy, pushing his fears
and rage onto children, and *mastering*
them.   20

For children grow.
Having escaped the confines
of your psyche, and becoming the terrifying
outside world, we are approaching.

If you were a wild dog   25
instead of my father,
how many times would I try to befriend you,
before shooting you down?

White Belly

Once upon a time there was a young man, tall and thin and boney. He was born into a farming family, his people were prairie people. His mother was an Indian woman, She Who Hides. His father was a Gaelic man, He Who Breaks Away (Then Regrets). First named for his father, the boney youth eventually earned a second name: White Belly.

She Who Hides and He Who Breaks Away (Then Regrets) suffered both poverty and poor health. They had a small brood of children, one daughter and five sons, and as the eldest moved off the land and the youngest were suckling still, they decided to sell their failing farm and move to the big city. White Belly, a middle child, was dismayed, heart-broken, pleased and enthusiastic about the great change. A guitar-playing youth, he carried his refuge with him.

In the city they bought a big house and took in boarders. The work changed but barely diminished, the poverty continued and the poor health of She Who Hides and He Who Breaks Away (Then Regrets) continued, worsening. White Belly and his brothers made friends, at school and in the neighbourhood, and White Belly fostered dreams of gigs and do's, of flying away on the magical strings of his guitar.

White Belly met a young woman, one in particular whom he teased and sang to. She Sang Back sang back, laughed at his bravado and leaned into his long boney body with pleasure. They married. He Who Breaks Away (Then Regrets) was furious, White Belly took sick and nearly died, and She Who Hides braved her husband's rages to visit her son on the sly. She Sang Back was frightened by it all, and pregnant.

As He Who Breaks Away (Then Regrets) softened, and wordlessly revoked his banishing of his son, White Belly's health improved, She Sang Back's baby was born, and She Who Hides' health crumbled and withered, and she died White Belly and his new family moved in with his father and brothers. She Sang Back had another baby, tended He Who Breaks Away (Then Regrets) and his sons, until He Who Breaks Away (Then Regrets) died also.

White Belly moved from job to job, singing at night while the children cried and slept. White Belly and She Sang Back, his youngest brother and the three new children, took over a small house built by She Sang Back's grandfather. More children came.

White Belly wanted a job that would feel good. He wanted a job that he could do as well as he did finger-picking, plucking sweet music from the six metal strings of his guitar. He sold sewing machines. He delivered laundry. Each time he tried to make a break, to try a job that was new or different or better, She Sang Back cried out. With a rising tide of children flowing from her womb, she expected just food, shelter, clothing, and not to worry. Each time White Belly made a change, everything she expected was threatened, and she cried out in pain.

She Sang Back wanted more than she expected. She wanted more than children and chores, more than worries. White Belly taught her to play the guitar, and she loved it more and more as she loved him less and less. Across the rooms of children and worry, she could not see him anymore. He was angry, trapped, and afraid to reach out. She was angry, trapped, and deeply, deeply disappointed.

When White Belly went for a job interview, they looked at his black hair and brown eyes and his redbrown skin They saw his fear and his pride and his poor man's clothes, and again and again they made the same decision: I can trust you with my truck. I can trust you with a load of bread, a load of milk, a load of laundry.

She Sang Back earned a second name, and both were used: She Sang Back (Then Left). White Belly saw himself again as his father's son, and he called himself He Who Breaks. He put the memories of his dead mother and gone wife, his hopes and dreams of gigs and do's behind a wide fence and left them He took his five youngest children and returned to the vestiges of his childhood home.

White Belly knew what those job people were thinking. He could see his redbrown face and arms, his raven black hair. He would look down at his white belly, knowing that they couldn't see this, knowing that if only they could see this it would be his ticket out.

So, he fed it. He fed his white belly until it grew and grew and grew, until it was a major presence in life. Embarrassed by its size, still he took its name as his own:

Hello, I am White Belly.

White Belly's white belly peeked out of his poor man's clothes. It winked at his children, jostled with his co-workers, and even though he tried to look his best when the bosses came around, White Belly's white belly slipped out to flag down his bosses and beg for promotion. White Belly's white belly said one thing, meant for everyone to know:

I am a white man.

    Out of the sea of children one from the
    middle arose, I Am Brown All Over.

    I Am Brown All Over loved White Belly
    as much as she feared him, she put

    nearly everything she knew   5
    behind a wide fence, so she could say

    I am safe in my home.
    One day while the fence was secure

    her love for White Belly seeped up
    and flooded her being   10

    and she danced to her father in the kitchen
    singing I Am Like You!

    You are a redbrown man
    and I am your daughter, I Am

    Brown All Over!   15

    White Belly leaned back
    uncertain for a moment

    then his redbrown fingers reached down
    and grasped the bottom of his shirt

    and pulled it up to cover his heart.   20

    I am only redbrown from the weather,
    you see I have a white belly.

    LOOK
    I AM

    WHITE   25
    BELLY!

He thundered.

And the girl fell back
back into the sea of children

painting the wide fence white   30
as she fell

putting her
I AM LIKE YOU DAD

behind it
dropping into the motley   35

sea of children
falling

like a stone
I Am Brown All Over

Like No One Else   40
falling

Steepy Mountains

all that has so
perturbed us these years
unperturb us

all shining dreams
all shadowy conflicts   5
out on the ground

the painter loves the poet
the drugstore clerk eyes
the welfare mom:

call security?   10
watch her moving slowly
down the aisle

the soda fountain is gone
like so much else, still
he might make an honest   15

woman of her
finally

the sun is always on your hair
you are always standing
at roadside   20

smiling at me
while flowers, grasses, and trees
bob gently

beautiful vales beckon
towns call out their names   25
steepy mountains rise, and yield

the poet loves the painter
the Metis woman eyes
her German-Irish lover

the road allowance people   30
play guitar and tune fiddles, watching
another roadside attraction

as the mist leaves no scar
on the dark green hill
so the sea waves surge   35

upon the shore
and always will

at university
I understood how all of life
could be gathered into   40
one poem

in the school of hard knocks
with a long row to hoe
I thought about you now and then

served warm drinks to 45
small children, wore
your striped shirt

grew my hair to my waist
and cut it short again
saw the grey come in 50

all that has so
perturbed us these years
unperturb us

all shining dreams
all shadowy conflicts 55
out on the ground

beautiful vales beckon
towns call out their names
steepy mountains rise, and yield

the shepherd calls to 60
his mistress
promises to decorate her world

one catholic boy
one catholic girl
prepare to receive a sacrament 65

they do not understand
two middle age strangers
holding keys and deep knowledge

sift through their sweet hearts
of rainbows and rubble 70
and tentatively

hold out their hands

all that has so
perturbed us these years
unperturb us 75

all shining dreams
all shadowy conflicts
out on the ground

beautiful vales beckon
towns callout their names   80
steepy mountains rise, and yield

standing under constellatians
we may build a big fire, together
while tree frogs creak and

birds sing   85
madrigals

and from the comfort of our
old porch swing, star blanket
pulled across our knees

we may   90
deep into evening
watch it

burn down

Dog Girl Verse

1. 1967

uplifting the dog: the dog: the dog:
so small am i: the dog
is smaller still: cold winter
air and coarse red hair:
bear the dog up up up   5
in my two winter arms

2. 2000

my spaniel ears are long
and soft: i open my mouth:
a gold ring drifts out:
i open my mouth: a puppy   10
drifts out: we drift up up up
through the autumnal stars

when you

when you were adam
and i was eve
when i sought consolation
with the serpent
when i sought to nourish you   5
not with the milk of my breast
but with fresh fruit
when i had plucked
all of the flowers
from the garden   10
made you a bed
garlanded your pale thighs
your pink nipples peeking through
love-strewn petals

when you were a young prince   15
when i was rapunzel
when i had grown through girlhood
in the doorless tower built
by my parents' neighbour
my mother   20
biting her tongue
for guilt
my father's heart
crusted over
from all that breaking   25
when you heard my lovely song
and found the way to
trick your
way in
and made love to me   30
and suffered the con
sequences
and when in the fullness of time
only my tears
healed you   35

when i was the great goddess
and you were my king
and each spring
i sang to you, my back
pressed to the sapling   40

and you came
and i praised you
and i loved you
and you loved me
when you annoyed me   45
or you betrayed me
or you abandoned me
each time
i put you to death
and you died fully   50
and then i called you
and then you came to me
again

when i was a small mouse
and you were a farmer   55
you stopped the plow
and crouched beside me
took me up
in work-roughened fingers
and palm   60
you carried my small and
quivering self
high to your pink
angelic lips
and kissed me   65

when i was a leaf
of grass, a plant
at your window
when you were the burning
summer sun and the deep   70
taste of rain
when we turned the house
inside
out
and were captured   75
we wondered at
the hidden landscapes
we contained

when you were the wildfire
when i was the forest   80
you ran through me

crackling with joy
my leaves my twigs my needles
and low brambles
flamed up in hot desire   85
then died
devoured, limbs blackened
i stood empty
as you became the winter sun
so weak and low   90
slowly, slowly warming, my
hesitant greening
coyote prowling through the last
thin patches of snow

Lorne Joseph Simon 1960–1994

MI'KMAQ

Lorne Simon died in a car accident on 8 October 1994. He was heading home from his Bachelor of Education studies at the University of New Brunswick to the place where he was born, Big Cove Reserve. Fluent in Mi'kmaq, Simon had been well educated in traditional culture and had also attended the En'owkin International School of Writing in Penticton, British Columbia, where he was the top graduate in 1992. *Stones and Switches* was about to become the first publication by Theytus of a book by an En'owkin graduate.

Stones and Switches is dedicated 'With love to my mother, Sarah, who told me the story—and knows better than I do what really happened to Megwadesk.' In the book, Jeannette

Armstrong quotes from a letter the author sent to her:

> You recently spoke to the public on the excitement you felt about the work Native writers will be doing in the future in reclaiming and revitalizing our past and our cultural heritage. I feel that I am part of this. . . . Currently there are hardly any Mi'kmaq writers who are vigorously taking part in this effort, yet I am sure that I will be setting an example and that others will follow. What I am doing is a ripple emanating from a pearl thrown into the pool of talent. Keep throwing pearls into the pool, for they are not wasted.

From *Stones and Switches*

THE SECOND COMING

'I was just getting ready to check my net,' Skoltch hollered at Megwadesk, as they stamped the mud off their boots and hung their jackets, 'when I heard you yelling! Gisúlk, Máli! I thought somebody was killing you! The way you were going on, I almost ran into the house to get my rifle! And then to find out it was just my dog—

well, I didn't know who to throw into the ditch—the dog for playing with you or you for screaming like it was the end of the world! Nisgam nuduid, I'd hate to see you in a war! Here! Take a seat!'

'Boys oh boys, I'm telling you,' Megwadesk replied, 'if that bitch comes at me again, eh, I'm gonna slit its throat from ear to ear! Cut its damn head right off!'

Megwadesk kept his navy-blue cap on. He scratched his left arm through his shirt. It felt swollen but he could not tell for sure.

'How are you, anyway? Did it bite you anywhere?' Skoltch asked.

Megwadesk rolled up the sleeve and they looked at his arm. It didn't appear to be cut anywhere but it was swollen. Skoltch offered to bind it up but Megwadesk insisted that he was fine.

'Well at least have something to drink!' Skoltch said. 'What will it be? Tea or coffee?'

'Tea, if you got some,' Megwadesk replied.

'Sure we got tea, boy! We got bologna, too!' Skoltch bellowed. Megwadesk noticed a large scab on Skoltch's brow and he guessed rightly where it came from.

'You know what the Maliseets say about us, don't you? "What's a Micmac breakfast? Tea and bologna!" '

Skoltch laughed at his joke as he struck a match and lit a kerosine lamp. Beside the lamp stood a jar of pickled babycorn. Megwadesk could hear Skoltch's wife snoring through the open bedroom door. Skoltch poured some water from a bucket into a kettle and set the kettle on the stove.

He put a cigarette in his mouth and added, 'Say, you sure looked woebegone checking your net a few days ago! Your jaw just about dropped to the water! Whoa, there! I almost told my son to reach over with a bucket to catch your jaw before you lost it in the water! But you caught it in time! Nisgam nuduid! You had your empty net pulled out of the river and up over your head and you kept looking this way and that, and up and down, and shaking your head, and staring! Ho! I told my son, "Get your handkerchief out because he's going to start bawling any minute now!" Ho, boy, you sure were a sight!'

That's Skoltch all right, Megwadesk noted. *He gets a little lucky 'n' he loses no time 'tall getting up there on his high horse 'n' he forgets how to talk to people in a sensible way! He's got to shout at the top of his lungs, eh, like he's talking to his lessers 'n' he's got to exaggerate everything, too, eh!*

'Since then, though, I haven't seen you check your net!' Skoltch shouted as he stood by the counter, his arms crossed over his chest. It seemed he forgot the cigarette. The tip of it constantly bobbed up and down as he spoke. 'Is this your seventh day, or what? You've made the world and you've set the lamps in the sky, right, and now it's time to rest, huh! Ah, ha, ha! Or is your girlfriend keeping you in bed? What is it? Too much of that and you'll soon start to waste away! You won't want to do anything else! That's what my father told me! Gisúlk, Nisgam, he should have knowed! He got ten kids out of my Mum alone! That's before he took off to Cape Breton to start another brood! And, you know, come to think of it, that old geezer must have been right! He never did do much else! I had to learn fishing from my uncle! That's where my son is now—with my uncle. They went out to the breakwaters yesterday to spear eels! I miss my boy already! Anyway, he'll learn from the best—he'll be learning from Uncle Noel! Like I said, Dad could talk fishing but I never seen him so much as bait a hook or haul a minnow! So don't tell me your new little lady is getting you to be like he was! Whoa, there, big fella! Ho!'

Skoltch had acquired his nickname, which meant frog, because of his double chin. It was so enormous it seemed pendulous. The great width of his mouth and the thin, flat lips that lined it further enhanced his resemblance to a frog. The size of his mouth had never pleased Skoltch. In his youth he had spent many hours before the looking glass puckering his lips, trying to make his mouth smaller. Years later, he hit upon the idea of letting his facial hair grow to cover up his mouth but there must have been only a thimbleful of French blood in him. His beard was sparse.

'I should say it's your woman who's keeping you in bed,' Megwadesk replied. 'You don't see me check my net, eh, 'cause you don't get up early 'nough no more.'

And Megwadesk slyly winked and quickly pointed by jutting out his bottom lip to Skoltch's bedroom door. Skoltch's wife kept snoring. Skoltch laughed heartily. Any comment ascribing virility to him, easily flattered him. Between hoots of laughter, Skoltch blushed and cried, 'Nooo!' in a faint attempt to put the matter into sober perspective. At length, Skoltch regained composure.

'Nugú!' Skoltch announced, his face red. 'Let's not talk about our better halves no more, huh!'

'Oh, come on.' Megwadesk pretended disappointment.

'No, no, no! We'll save those stories for when we're out of ear shot! You're an eager young buck and all that, I know, so there are things you want to learn from an old nabéw like me! Ho, I can tell you stuff! But in due time, boy! In due time!'

Skoltch took a match out of the matchbox, struck it, and lit his cigarette. He inhaled peacefully. Skoltch's compressed eyes gleamed and dimples formed in his fleshy round face as he stood looking at the stove, impatient to hear another protest— another, 'Oh, come on'—certain that Megwadesk had not taken his injunction to heart. Skoltch was reluctant to leave so soon, the laudable subject of his manly ardour, but he had felt it was only proper to show some degree of modesty, which was why he had feigned insistence on waiving the matter. Now he stood grinning at the steaming kettle, a suitable epic about his virility set to course from his mouth, just waiting for another protest and a chance to roar with bogus reluctance, 'Well, all right! If you insist! I'll tell you a little something I know about women!'

Megwadesk, however, missed his chance to humour Skoltch. He shrugged his shoulders and said, 'Whatever you say.'

Skoltch found something suspect in this sudden indifference. To make matters worse, Megwadesk made Skoltch positively hostile by pointing out the sizable scab over his left brow and asking, 'Is that cut on your head from a rock, eh? Are they still throwing rocks from the bridge?'

'Do you really care to know?' Skoltch growled. Then he sucked on his cigarette three times.

Megwadesk was taken aback. After a long pause, Megwadesk said, hoping to break the hostile silence, 'I heard you're going to get a new sail-boat.'

Skoltch ignored the question and said, 'Well, if you really want to know, I did get hit with a rock! Now what do you want?'

'What do you mean?' Megwadesk asked. He thought Skoltch was asking him what he wanted that information for but that made no sense.

'What do you want? Why are you here?'

'Oh, that! I'm here to find out what's been going on at the bridge, eh. I haven't gone past it 'tall in six days now.'

'Humph! Don't look like you'll be going past it any time soon either, so why are you worried?'

'I'm thinking of going to ykdánug, spearing eels, eh. Ain't had no luck 'tall this far upriver for too many days.'

'Spearing eels, eh! I should head out there one of these nights, too, just to do some spearing with my boy! Nisgam! Kids sure grow up fast, eh?'

Skoltch didn't expect an answer. He was still feeling surly. He took a deep drag from his cigarette and then he said, 'Yeah, I'm looking at a twenty-footer with a twenty-four foot mast!'

'A twenty-footer!' Megwadesk said, with the proper measure of wonder in his inflection. 'Man oh man, that'll hold quite a load, eh, an' with a good breeze them wardens'll never catch you 'tall!'

Nobody owned a twenty-foot-long boat in Messkíg. Sixteen-foot sail-boats, mostly scows equipped with centre-boards, were standard. Still, Megwadesk was not spontaneously expressing his surprise for he had already heard about the details of Skoltch's proposed purchase some time ago. Skoltch, however, found his visitor's calculated response flattering. 'It's lapped hardwood!' Skoltch said. 'It's a fancy sloop, a real cutter, complete with a jib and a centre-board as deep as I am tall! I can set three nets if I want to! It'll easily hold that much catch! A twenty-foot cutter with high gunwales! Nisgam! That's a lot of space!'

'Man oh man, that'll be a wonder,' agreed Megwadesk.

Skoltch smiled indulgently and then, for the sake of modesty, he redirected the conversation again, deciding it was time to offer some friendly advice.

'Well, anyway,' he said, 'if you're going to ykdánug just make sure to go past the bridge by night, if you wanna avoid trouble! Even a mere stub of a mast'll slip you by fast enough! But then you have to hope the wardens don't see you, either! Jumping Moses, it's like we're a bunch of criminals, eh! It's like we're the newcomers instead, huh! Can't touch the animals! Can't touch the fish! Nisgam! We can't even touch the trees! You see a good stand of ash, perfect for axe-handles, and you go take a couple down—one or two, that's all—and some milky-eyed madman's gonna run out with his rifle and tell you to get away from his trees! Everything's theirs now! Gisúlk, Máli!'

'Pretty soon they'll be telling us we can't keep time by the moon 'cause that's gonna be theirs too! You know what really gets me, though, is how they point the finger at us when the fish stocks go down! Isn't that something, huh? They've had them great big boats fishing off the Grand Banks and shipping millions and millions of tons out to every corner of the world since before the time of Christopher Columbus! When they blame us, it sounds like this to me: like one kid, who has taken and eaten most of the cookies in the cookie jar, blaming a smaller kid for eating all the cookies just because that smaller kid took one cookie, which so happened to be the last one! See? For thousands of years we've been taking that one cookie every year, but when all that's left is our one cookie and we still take it like usual, well, we get called gluttons! And a lot worse things, too! Anyway, it's boiling! You like your tea strong?'

'Éq! Black as crow's butt, eh,' Megwadesk answered.

'Six tea bags, then! I like mine strong too! One, two, three, four, five, six, and pick up sticks! Or, around here, pick up switches! There we go! Hey, look at that!'

Megwadesk looked out the window above the counter. Hazy sunlight filtered through the clouds.

'You can stop shaking in your boots now, boy, 'cause it looks like it's gonna clear, after all!' Skoltch roared, as if Megwadesk had fled like a child to the security of Skoltch's house in fear of the storm.

'I didn't even notice 'tall that the thundering had stopped, eh,' Megwadesk said.

'Oh, I know you didn't! But I did! I noticed right away—as soon as that last rod of lightning flashed four miles away! Nadóq, I said to myself, it's over now—that last one sounded like no more than a fart! It's over all right! I'll set the teapot right here on the table!'

As he put the teapot down, there followed a faint flash and several seconds later, another distant rumble.

'Humph!' was all Skoltch voiced. He took the butt out of his mouth and squashed it in a clay ashtray and he turned to the cabinets.

While Skoltch thrust his meaty arms into the cabinets to retrieve two cups and two saucers, a bowl of sugar, and a bag of home-made doughnuts, Megwadesk thought about the storm. Storms, especially very windy ones, used to be explained by his people as the doings of Wejúsyn, a giant bird, whose great beating wings moved the air. This, in turn, made him think again about the man in white and about spirit stories. Spirits, as far as he was concerned, were nothing more than tricks of nature, tricks that people misunderstood.

He had been mulling over this idea for several weeks but he could not share it with anyone. It was still too fuzzy in his head. He felt he had to bring together many examples before he could say clearly what it was he meant. And he knew that to talk about any idea before it had fully matured in his head was the worst thing to do, because people wouldn't understand it and they would only muddy up the water some more. Besides, Mimi often got impatient with his speculations. Megwadesk had learned that, with most people, it was best to skirt around an idea first just to see how they felt about things by slightly touching on the question.

Megwadesk thought about how he enjoyed talking to Mr Severman because the preacher enjoyed talking about things that most people considered foolish, strange or dangerous. During their talks once, Megwadesk had told Mr Severman that maybe what people sometimes called goodness was just the outcome of weakness and, to his surprise, the preacher had answered, 'William Blake, the prophet-poet of England, would have agreed with you, my friend. He wrote that people who bridle their desires can do so because their appetites are naturally small to begin with. No virtue in temperance from that perspective—is there?'

Skoltch set the cups and saucers, and the sugar and doughnuts, on the table. Then he opened a drawer and took out two spoons and set those on the table as well.

'Help yourself!' Skoltch ordered. 'I don't put up with timidity in my house! Go on, boy! I'm not serving anyone! If you can't fend for yourself, you'll starve—that's all!'

'Thank you,' Megwadesk answered, as he poured the tea into his cup. He drank it black.

'Oquetédud! This is a man's tea, eh, a Micmac's tea, all right!'

'Oh, yes!' Skoltch answered and he sat and poured himself a cup too, adding three heaping spoons of sugar.

The two men quietly sipped their tea for several minutes.

Skoltch pushed the doughnuts to his guest and said, 'Here! Try some! They're good!'

Megwadesk took a doughnut and swallowed a bite and then washed it down with tea. Skoltch dipped his doughnut into his tea and chewed on it. Megwadesk noticed the rain had stopped. He looked out the window to the east and saw a pair of rainbows, one fainter than the other. The rainbows reminded him of a promise of some kind—he couldn't remember exactly what it had been about—a promise anyway—that God had made to Noah after the flood.

Suddenly Megwadesk asked, 'Do you believe in that Bible stuff, eh? You know, all the miracles like Jesus raising the dead?'

'Sure, I believe in Jesus,' Skoltch answered, not at all surprised by the question. He had been expecting something like this from Megwadesk. For such an uncanny fisherman, Skoltch thought, Megwadesk still asked the foolish questions of a youth.

'Can you believe in a god who'll make everybody rise stark naked 'n' all rotted on judgement day, eh?' Megwadesk continued. The growing sunlight made him bold. He could voice his secret horrors now.

'Sure, sure,' Skoltch answered with forced impatience. He was pleased actually, for this opportunity to wax philosophical. A conversation with Megwadesk was always good for that. 'But you shouldn't worry about them details! Let the white people worry about all that stuff! Nisgam gejidoq! We didn't have nothing to do with his murder! As far as I see it, on judgement day Jesus will come down on a cloud and he'll go to all the reserves first and tell all the Indians to just keep right on fishing, that's all! Then he'll get back on his cloud again and fly off to Trenton and go deal with the white people there, and everywhere else there's whites—and, by God, they'll pay for killing him all right, and for killing all the land and all the rivers and all the fish and leaving none for us! Amudj! They'll pay! Jesus was a fisherman! And don't you forget it! He knew where to set his nets, too—even better than you, I'm sure! He understands us! So don't you worry!'

Skoltch's comments annoyed Megwadesk. He told Skoltch, 'You make Jesus sound like Glúskeb almost, eh, the way he'll help us and all.'

'Well, they're cousins, I think,' Skoltch declared. 'Or maybe step-brothers! I forget right now how it was my dad put it! My dad was only good for stories, you know!

But anyway, Glúskeb took care of us for a long time till he got tired, 'cause we were always making trouble for him, going to war with all kinds of tribes and everything like that! Gisúlk, Máli! So Glúskeb needed a rest! Before he left, he called his cousin, Jesus, and told him to come on over and take care of us for a while! Sort of like babysit, I guess! So Jesus said, no problem, jínym! Remember, Malsum still had to be watched or else that devil would take over the world again! So Glúskeb knew somebody like Jesus had to be here while he went out west to sleep a bit!

'But Jesus was kinda lazy, see! He liked his wine too much, I think! Anyway, he stayed home and only sent his messengers to look after us! That's the priests and stuff! But you know how messengers are! Glúskeb never could leave anything up to his messengers, loon and rabbit! Nisgam gejidoq! If he did, they would make a mess of things! Éq! Bana total mess! So it's the same with these messengers from Jesus! Instead of just taking care of us and baptizing us and giving us decent burials, these priests turned around and invited all kinds of other people with them, see! Bana foolishness!

'So judgement day's going to come around just after Glúskeb wakes up and just before he gets back here! Glúskeb is going to shoot his arrow ahead of him and it'll land in the Minas Basin, see, to tell Jesus he can pack up his stuff and get ready to go back to his home! And Jesus'll get scared, see, 'cause he's let his messengers make a big mess of things here, and it's really all his fault 'cause he's been so lazy, see! Gisúlk, éq! That's when he'll come around on his cloud and tell us to keep right on fishing and then he'll take all the other people together, even the dead ones—he'll call them right up from their Loyalist graves and all—and tell them, "Listen here," Jesus will say, "either you go back with me or you go to hell!"

'Of course, you know how stubborn white people are! Many of 'em'll stand around their farms with their shotguns in their hands! Nisgam! They'll be just ready to kill Jesus all over again, if he so much as steps near their potato gardens! So poor Jesus'll have no choice but to send Satan after them! Satan'll come out of the water with his red cape and red whip and flog the laggards! Some clever ones'll manage to run away and hide in the swamps, though! Then Glúskeb'll come back and if there's any left over—shotgun or not—he'll take them by the scruff of their necks and throw them across the ocean, and tell them to stay there! They can hide from Jesus and Satan but they won't be able to hide from Glúskeb, that's for sure!'

Megwadesk did not find the story helpful. In his mind, either one believed in the old ways or one believed in the white man's Christian ways and yet there were many stories around which were a blend of the two.

'I've heard stories where Glúskeb and Jesus had contests and Glúskeb always won, eh,' Megwadesk said. 'First time I heard this one, though.'

'Oh, yeah, Glúskeb always wins!' Skoltch said very seriously. 'Dad told me them stories, too! Oh, there's hundreds of them! One time, some white guy came around here and wrote a couple down, but the old timers pulled his leg! Instead of telling him all the Glúskeb stories, they told him fairy tales, with Indians in them though, just to see if he'd write those down, too, and call them legends! Nisgam! And he did! So that's how much some people know! Ho! We're always pulling people's legs—and looking pretty serious when we're at it, too! But, anyway, about this Jesus and stuff! Meantime we got to go to church and all that just like a kid has to listen to a baby-sitter! But don't worry about all that judgement day stuff! It's just for white people really! That's why the priests are always going on about it, because they're guilty and they know it and it's always on their minds, bugging them like! So they go on and on about it! Me and you, we're okay and we'll keep right on fishing, either way! Personally, I wouldn't blink an eye if judgement day happened this afternoon!'

Skoltch coughed and then fell silent. His voice was hoarse from all the shouting. Talking down to people was exhausting sometimes.

'Oh, I'm not scared of that stuff, either. Don't get me wrong, eh,' said Megwadesk. 'I'm just curious 'bout what you think, that's all. But you don't really believe that silly story, eh? That's the matter with our people!'

'What's the matter? What're you talking about? Don't you know a good story when you hear one?'

'Too many of our stories are like that, that's all.'

'Like what?'

'They're just like wishes that we keep holding tight to, eh, an' after a while alls we got's is wishes.'

'What do you mean, "wishes"? I'm telling you what my elders told me! It's like a story the prophets tell! It talks about what's gonna happen one day!'

'An' I say instead of wishing the white people'll just disappear one day and we'll all live happily ever after, we gotta start dealing with the facts, eh. Geez, we keep acting like we can just go on ignoring the real world, like we don't have to change someday 'n' start picking up ways of surviving in the white world!'

'That's not—'

'Sure it is! Sure, that's what it's about! Boys oh boys, just look at the story they tell about Old Set-Ból coming back to haunt the priest. They just wish the old priest could be scared by something the way he can scare the people, eh, so they make this story up 'n' it makes 'em feel good—like it really happened. That's like justice for them. But, really, eh, it's just a fill-in for justice. It's all really 'bout wishful thinking, and nothing 'tall else! Nisgam nuduid, why do you think people believe in spirits and witches for, eh? It's 'cause they feel like they got no real power. So they need this magic power. If they can't get back at the whites for stealing all the land, then they'll say that the spirits like Jesus or Glúskeb or whatever'll get back at them one day! That's no different than anything else, either! If you do something wrong to another fellow in Messkíg, 'n' you get away with it, like you don't pay a fine or go to jail or nothing, eh, then that fellow'll tell himself, *Well, maybe I can't do nothing but the spirits'll get 'im back 'cause what goes 'round comes 'round.* Then he'll feel a little better. See what I mean? All these stories 'bout spirits 'n' medicine 'n' stuff is just a way of keeping our blinders on! We don't even see half—'

'So that's all you see in them stories, huh?' Skoltch cut in. 'Then it's you who don't even see half of what them stories are for! First off, let me tell you that I don't act like I don't have to deal with the white world! I have to deal with them people all the time and some of them are real nice but lots of times they get away with things like throwing rocks at people and stealing land left and right! Okay, then! This story I told you tells me that we're not like them! We never went across the ocean and stole their land and told them they couldn't do this or they couldn't do that! So who's right? We're right! Now if we're right, does it mean that we should forget about our honest ways just because we're in a weaker position now? No, sir! I don't think so! Like I said in the story, we keep right on fishing and living the way God wants us to! We don't just turn around and be like them, stealing land, hurting people, taking kids away from their parents, breaking up families, destroying all the trees, being greedy, greedy, greedy! If they're right, then I'd rather be wrong! You see now what you missed in that story?'

'Well, let me put it 'nother way—' Megwadesk said but just then, the door opened and a brutal-looking middle-aged man with a twisted nose, a chipped eyebrow and a lopsided grin swaggered in. His hair was dishevelled and there were branches stuck to his clothing in a manner that hunters sometimes wore to camouflage themselves in the woods.

'Here to see godmother Molly!' the fellow demanded, banging the door shut behind him. Megwadesk glared at him. Even from seeing only his back, he knew it was Rancid.

Connie Fife *b.* 1961

CREE

In her biographical entry for *Piece of My Heart: A Lesbian of Colour Anthology*, Connie Fife says, 'I am a Cree woman who writes in the hope that my words find their mark. I offer them healing, pain, and ways of making radical change in a confused world. Meegwatch to my sisters. They know who they are.'

Originally from Saskatchewan, Fife has been published in many anthologies and has published three books of poems, including *Speaking Through Jagged Rock* (1999). Her first poetry collection, *Beneath the Naked Sun* (1992), was acclaimed by Chrystos, Joy Harjo, and Beth Brant. The latter asserts, 'Connie Fife has made music out of the chaos and pain of being indigenous and lesbian in a culture that respects neither.' As editor of an issue of *Fireweed* dedicated to Aboriginal women's issues and of the anthology *The Colour of Resistance*, Fife sees herself as very much a part of a larger movement. In the introduction to the anthology she states:

Whether oral or visual, Indigenous literature has always existed throughout the Americas. Our collective memory remains intact regardless of any attempt to separate us from its origins. No matter the authors or their skills in the written word, European writers have failed miserably at conveying the essence behind our words; they have failed to transport the life we find in language onto the page. This is our struggle as Native writers, as women who inherently know the nature of birth: to bring to life a language that is at times lifeless.

A graduate of the En'owkin International School of Writing in Penticton, British Columbia, Fife now lives in Victoria, although she travels widely, as when she was Barker Fairly Distinguished Visitor at University College, University of Toronto. Her most recent collection of poetry is *Poems for a New World* (2001).

Dream

last night you drummed me Azania
i heard her shores and felt her lap against my heart
beating
      beating
            deep into the night   5
you brought me to the edge of her forests into
a clearing down into the opening   i walked towards
women gathered in a circle   renewal of spirits   a
dance to celebrate your survival   a dance of masks
you drummed me Azania on a taut skin   10
the colour of my own   down from the mountains your
voices travelled on bolts of lightning   touching
down on moist earth
beating
      beating   15
          and you raise your arms to the sky
your chanting grows stronger as your bodies move to
and fro   colliding with the old women you honour
through your struggle
beating   20
   beating
          and your hands touch one another
          touch the earth
          touch me
last night you drummed me Azania deep into the night   25
taking me to her hills and a circle of women whose
outstretched arms embraced me and
   beating
   beating
          your spirit met mine and   30
          we celebrated

beating
   beating
          you drummed me Azania

dedicated to Thato Bereng   35

Driftwoodwoman

buried under a mountain of her own victimization
grabbing at sun covered by her distorted thought
caught by her reflection in a cracked mirror
veiled in drifting spiderwebs
unable to hear the voice of spiderwoman   5
unyielding to the rhythm of thoughtwoman
a prisoner by her own conviction
beyond her cement walls
a gathering of women tend the fire
calling her home   10
calling her home

i have become so many mountains

standing on the shoreline of history
pondering the forthcoming sunrise
or the very impossibility of it
i have become so many rivers
not a single current but many   5
leading to a whirlpool of countless places
i have become so many women
waking each morning with jaws clenched
determined to bite down on the impending day
i have become so many men   10
wondering which mask to remove
afraid of flailing skinless in the wind
i have become so many forests
whose tears slide down hillsides
then come to rest in shimmering pools of ice   15
i have become so many ancestors
who dance through empty houses
windows blown out by our laughter
i have become so many photographs
framed and frozen behind glass made of lies   20
whose eyes hold the truth despite the distortion
i have become so many songs
slipping off the tongues of entire nations
who sing me into the existence of memory
i have become so many landscapes   25

scarred by the hands of the uncivilized
whose open wounds now swallow them whole
i have become so many poems
whose fingers caress me with their desire
while fighting for our lives breath by breath   30
i have become so many mountains and rivers
so many women and men singing
so many ancestors
so many photographs carried in my lungs
so many landscapes acting in revolutionary fashion   35
i have become so many movements
without having made the slightest motion
standing in solitude on the shoreline of history

the knowing

the re-invention of oneself
through the tongues of whispering mountains
the re-arrangement of the universe
because a spider wrapped her legs around a star
the knowing   5
the remembering of stone's story
while walking down a dried riverbed
being serenaded by crickets singing the blues
because everyone except them has forgotten
the knowing   10
which trail to follow through clear-cut forests
which scent will lead you home
because a thousand-year-old bear still lives
amongst the dead bodies feeding off their memory
the knowing   15
the recollection of the loudness in silence
the clarity of unspoken words while sound crashes earthbound
because it is in what is not said that the truth sits
the knowing
the peeling back of ones own skin   20
to discover that the lizard sleeping against your spine
was born the same moment as you
because she knew that one day you
would need her sharp tongue to survive
the knowing   25

the rediscovery of crow perched on your shoulder
her claws leaving scratch marks against your heart
because you need to be reminded that you are alive
on days when you are numbed into speechlessness
the knowing   30
the glimpse of your reflection in the eyes of a stranger
who is leaning against the chest of a cedar tree
while cars spit at her then mock her existence
because she refuses to roll over on the sidewalk
and you need to be reminded of why you were born   35
the knowing
the recreating of ceremony at the hands of change
while wandering through unknown places
because history has turned us into our own lodges
when it tried to bound our mouths and tie our words   40
the knowing
the acknowledgment of ones ancestors
must become an ordinary event taking place with each breath
keeping them alive so their voices touch our skin
with urgency and desire in our ribcages   45
because it is their shadows that protect us
the knowing
the importance of embracing our places of remembering
because inside their bodies live our beloved
through their existence we are fed love on a plate of resistance   50
while we swallow stars dropped down our throats by spider

dear walt

it must have been difficult
to be caught in the grip
of strong willed metaphors
who dictated that you
live as an outsider   5
in a country you so
wanted to breathe into
dear walt
i imagine you actually
believed that poetry can   10
make a democracy smeared
with the blood of others
into some kind of beauty

now you have become the dust
you wrote about us being   15
so little has changed
we who are poets
still believe we shift hearts
while speaking through the voice
of stone and water   20
not even paralysis drove
your spirit away
nor the illness of a brother
in a world without compassion
dear walt   25
is it ever possible to escape
metaphor or change a democracy
whose foundation digs into the bones of her original people
i would like to know walt
if there is a place for dead poets   30
where we can lie among leaves of grass
then laugh at how little has changed

speaking through jagged rock

i will take you
amongst jagged rock
lick you smooth
beneath a naked sun
(she remembers the   5
birth of every constellation)
we will bask
amongst tall grass
who will stroke
our backs until sunset   10
the red of the evening
will dance across
our breasts until
moon begins to sing
we will become darkness   15
together with the stars
who will laugh into the wind
(they will dance
a stomp song for us)

under the cover of clouds   20
we will re-arrange the lining
of the universe so that
she will know we existed
i will take you
amongst jagged rock   25
witnessed by a naked sun
stroked by tall grasses
the moon will dance
across our breasts
while stars laugh our   30
memory into the wind

poem for russell

if a life could be sustained in
the arms of a poem
let this one be for you
a companion on your journeying
toward the sun and her laughter   5
she will accompany you
your hand grasped in hers
during those treacherous moments
when you stand on the cliffs edge
balancing between two worlds   10
this poem will love you
whether or not you remember
the taste of sunlight and mountains
or the trail you followed through
a forest fading behind your heels   15
it will be left in your footprints
for others to place their ear against
the cool dark earth of your story
this poem will wait for you if
she has to because it is your   20
tone singing in her throat
and you are always standing
in the doorway arms outstretched

For Matthew Shepard

had i found your body
draped across that barbed wire fence
i would have buried you
in the tradition of my own
    off the ground facing the sky   5
    surrounded by stone and wood
a fire for your freedom would be lit
you would become wind and star
your life remembered through flame and ash
in your memory a mourning song   10
in your name an honour song
for you a celebration among the constellations
a dance for you
a dance for your loved ones
weaponry for each of us   15

Exiled

Shadows cast your image across sleeping mountains.
Your face flashes from within the gaping mouth of my
    television,
wordless, homeless, exiled into the unknown.
The world decides the degree of self-righteousness   5
by which to exorcise their guilt.
I want to rebuild your home,
bring your husband and children back,
redeem their needless deaths
then change the robes of history—   10
replacing all this with blossoms growing in spring fields
watch as your family falls into stride beside you.

Politics

unchained
you are broken
and this thing
called freedom
is not   5
what it seems
she cannot fly
as was promised
so back to earth
she must fall   10
while others speak
revolution
without ever having tasted
the blue of her skin

san francisco, february 1999

For James Byrd Jr

3 a.m. poems cling to the walls
they pace from corner to corner
watching me as i think of you
your body dragged behind a truck
in the deep south of your history   5
dismembered and decapitated
a leg for slavery
a leg for the underground railroad
your head for harriet tubman
your heart for your grandmothers   10
an arm for malcolm x
an arm for martin luther king
cartilage and tendons mapping your journey
while three men gun their way
into the darkness of white america   15
claiming us as equal
  i know your children cannot sleep tonight
  that when exhaustion finally leaves them no choice

their dreams will be full of you
they will be woken to your absence   20
as history screams in their faces
while liberty froths at her mouth

Witnessing

we bear witness to the changing of history
remembering places where we were born
to which we can never return

we bear witness to shifting movements
remembering moments etched on cave walls   5
buried in our past

we bear witness to memory housed in stories
whispered through tongues of laughing stones
their voices quiet with indiscretion

we bear witness to change   10
remembering our original being
her journey from here to now

knowing that in our fingertips
history sleeps yet to be formed

vancouver, september 1999

Drew Hayden Taylor *b.* 1962

OJIBWA

Drew Taylor, from the Curve Lake Reserve near Peterborough, Ontario, is known for his humour: 'My mother says I was eleven pounds twelve ounces when I was born. That's probably why I'm an only child.'

After receiving an Honours Diploma in broadcasting from Seneca College in 1982, Taylor worked in media journalism and contributed to documentaries on Native culture. He also 'spent time working in the television mines', writing scripts for *The Beachcombers*, *Street Legal*, and *North of Sixty*.

Taylor's work in theatre has earned him a Chalmers Award, for *Toronto at Dreamer's Rock* (1989); a Canadian Author's Association Award, for *The Bootlegger Blues* (1990); a Dora Mavor Moore Award, for *Only Drunks and Children Tell the Truth* (1995); and first prize in the

University of Alaska Anchorage Native Playwriting Contest, for *The Baby Blues* (1996).

A prolific writer, Taylor's publications include plays for adults (*Only Drunks and Children Tell the Truth*, 1998, and *alterNatives*, 2000) and plays for young people (*The Boy in the Treehouse/Girl Who Loved Her Horses*, 2000), as well as short stories (collected in *Fearless Warriors*, 1998) and several volumes of humourous commentaries, including *Funny You Don't Look Like One, Observations of a Blue-Eyed Ojibway* (1996) and *Further Adventures of a Blue-Eyed Ojibway, Funny You Don't Look Like One Two* (1999). On the diversity of his writing he comments, 'I have written practically everything under the sun, in one form or another, except for a novel or poetry. Maybe someday I'll combine the two and write a poetic novel.'

Pretty Like a White Boy:
The Adventures of a Blue Eyed Ojibway

In this big, huge world, with all its billions and billions of people, it's safe to say that everybody will eventually come across personalities and individuals that will touch them in some peculiar yet poignant way. Individuals that in some way represent and help define who you are. I'm no different, mine was Kermit the Frog. Not just because Natives have a long tradition of savouring frogs' legs, but because of his music. If you all may remember, Kermit is quite famous for his rendition of 'It's Not Easy Being Green'. I can relate. If I could sing, my song would be 'It's Not Easy Having Blue Eyes in a Brown Eyed Village'.

Yes, I'm afraid it's true. The author happens to be a card-carrying Indian. Once you get past the aforementioned eyes, the fair skin, light brown hair, and noticeable lack of cheekbones, there lies the heart and spirit of an Ojibway storyteller. Honest Injun, or as the more politically correct term may be, honest aboriginal.

You see, I'm the product of a white father I never knew, and an Ojibway woman who evidently couldn't run fast enough. As a kid I knew I looked a bit different. But, then again, all kids are paranoid when it comes to their peers. I had a fairly happy childhood, frolicking through the bullrushes. But there were certain things that, even then, made me notice my unusual appearance. Whenever we played cowboys and Indians, guess who had to be the bad guy, the cowboy.

It wasn't until I left the Reserve for the big bad city, that I became more aware of the role people expected me to play, and the fact that physically I didn't fit in. Everybody seemed to have this preconceived idea of how every Indian looked and acted. One guy, on my first day of college, asked me what kind of horse I preferred. I didn't have the heart to tell him 'hobby'.

I've often tried to be philosophical about the whole thing. I have both white and red blood in me, I guess that makes me pink. I am a 'Pink' man. Try to imagine this, I'm walking around on any typical Reserve in Canada, my head held high, proudly announcing to everyone 'I am a Pink Man'. It's a good thing I ran track in school.

My pinkness is constantly being pointed out to me over and over and over again. 'You don't look Indian?' 'You're not Indian, are you?' 'Really?!?' I got questions like that from both white and Native people, for a while I debated having my status card tattooed on my forehead.

And like most insecure people and specially a blue-eyed Native writer, I went through a particularly severe identity crisis at one point. In fact, I admit it, one depressing spring evening, I died my hair black. Pitch black.

The reason for such a dramatic act, you may ask? Show Business. You see, for the last eight years or so, I've worked in various capacities in the performing arts, and as a result I'd always get calls to be an extra or even try out for an important role in some Native oriented movie. This anonymous voice would phone, having been given my number, and ask if I would be interested in trying out for a movie. Being a naturally ambitious, curious, and greedy young man, I would always readily agree, stardom flashing in my eyes and hunger pains from my wallet.

A few days later I would show up for the audition, and that was always an experience. What kind of experience you may ask? Picture this, the picture calls for the casting of seventeenth-century Mohawk warriors living in a traditional longhouse. The casting director calls the name 'Drew Hayden Taylor' and I enter.

The casting director, the producer, and the film's director look up from the table and see my face, blue eyes flashing in anticipation. I once was described as a slightly chubby beachboy. But even beachboys have tans. Anyway, there would be a quick flush of confusion, a recheck of the papers, and a hesitant 'Mr Taylor?' Then they would ask if I was at the right audition. It was always the same. By the way, I never got any of the parts I tried for, except for a few anonymous crowd shots. Politics tells me it's because of the way I look, reality tells me it's probably because I can't act. I'm not sure which is better.

It's not just film people either. Recently I've become quite involved in Theatre, Native theatre to be exact. And one cold October day I was happily attending the Toronto leg of a province-wide tour of my first play, *Toronto at Dreamer's Rock*. The place was sold out, the audience very receptive and the performance was wonderful. Ironically one of the actors was also half white.

The director later told me he had been talking with the actor's father, an older non-Native type chap. Evidently he had asked a few questions about me, and how I did my research. This made the director curious and he asked about the father's interest. He replied, 'He's got an amazing grasp of the Native situation for a white person.'

Not all these incidents are work-related either. One time a friend and I were coming out of a rather upscale bar (we were out YUPPIE watching) and managed to catch a cab. We thanked the cab driver for being so comfortably close on such a cold night, he shrugged and nonchalantly talked about knowing what bars to drive around. 'If you're not careful, all you'll get is drunk Indians.' I hiccuped.

Another time this cab driver droned on and on about the government. He started out by criticizing Mulroney, and eventually to his handling of the Oka crisis. This perked up my ears, until he said 'If it were me, I'd have tear-gassed the place by the second day. No more problem.' He got a dime tip. A few incidents like this and I'm convinced I'd make a great undercover agent for one of the Native political organizations.

But then again, even Native people have been known to look at me with a fair amount of suspicion. Many years ago when I was a young man, I was working on a documentary on Native culture up in the wilds of Northern Ontario. We were at an isolated cabin filming a trapper woman and her kids. This one particular nine-year-old girl seemed to take a shine to me. She followed me around for two days both annoying me and endearing herself to me. But she absolutely refused to believe that I was Indian. The whole film crew tried to tell her but to no avail. She was certain I was white.

Then one day as I was loading up the car with film equipment, she asked me if I wanted some tea. Being in a hurry I declined the tea. She immediately smiled with victory crying out, 'See, you're not Indian, all Indians drink tea!'

Frustrated and a little hurt I whipped out my Status card and thrust it at her. Now there I was, standing in a Northern Ontario winter, showing my Status card to a nine-year-old non-status Indian girl who had no idea what one was. Looking back, this may not have been one of my brighter moves.

But I must admit, it was a Native woman that boiled everything down in one simple sentence. You may know that woman, Marianne Jones from 'The Beachcombers' television series. We were working on a film together out west and we got to gossiping. Eventually we got around to talking about our respective villages. Hers on the Queen Charlotte Islands, or Haida Gwaii as the Haida call them, and mine in central Ontario.

Eventually childhood on the Reserve was being discussed and I made a comment about the way I look. She studied me for a moment, smiled, and said 'Do you know what the old women in my village would call you?' Hesitant but curious, I shook my head. 'They'd say you were pretty like a white boy.' To this day I'm still not sure if I like that.

Now some may argue that I am simply a Métis with a Status card. I disagree, I failed French in grade 11. And the Métis as everyone knows have their own separate and honourable culture, particularly in western Canada. And of course I am well aware that I am not the only person with my physical characteristics.

I remember once looking at a video tape of a drum group, shot on a Reserve up near Manitoulin Island. I noticed one of the drummers seemed quite fairhaired, almost blond. I mentioned this to my girlfriend of the time and she shrugged saying, 'Well, that's to be expected. The highway runs right through the Reserve.'

Perhaps I'm being too critical. There's a lot to be said for both cultures. For example, on the left hand, you have the Native respect for Elders. They understand the concept of wisdom and insight coming with age.

On the white hand, there's Italian food. I mean I really love my mother and family but seriously, does anything really beat good Veal Scallopini? Most of my aboriginal friends share my fondness for this particular brand of food. Wasn't there a warrior at Oka named Lasagna? I found it ironic, though curiously logical, that Columbus was Italian. A connection I wonder?

Also Native people have this wonderful respect and love for the land. They believe they are part of it, a mere chain in the cycle of existence. Now as many of you know, this conflicts with the accepted Judeo-Christian, i.e., western view of land management. I even believe somewhere in the first chapters of the Bible it says something about God giving man dominion over Nature. Check it out, Genesis 4:?, 'Thou shalt clear cut.' So I grew up understanding that everything around me is important and alive. My Native heritage gave me that.

And again, on the white hand, there's breast implants. Darn clever them white people. That's something Indians would never have invented, seriously. We're not ambitious enough. We just take what the Creator decides to give us, but no, not the white man. Just imagine it, some serious looking white man, and let's face it people, we know it was a man who invented them, don't we? So just imagine some serious looking white doctor sitting around in his laboratory muttering to himself, 'Big tits, big tits, hmmm, how do I make big tits?' If it was an Indian, it would be 'Big tits, big tits, white women sure got big tits' and leave it at that.

So where does that leave me on the big philosophical scoreboard, what exactly are my choices again; Indian—respect for elders, love of the land. White people—food and big tits. In order to live in both cultures I guess I'd have to find an Indian woman with big tits who lives with her grandmother in a cabin out in the woods and can make Fettuccini Alfredo on a wood stove.

Now let me make this clear, I'm not writing this for sympathy, or out of anger, or even some need for self-glorification. I am just setting the facts straight. For as you read this, a new Nation is born. This is a declaration of independence, my declaration of independence.

I've spent too many years explaining who and what I am repeatedly, so as of this moment, I officially secede from both races. I plan to start my own separate nation. Because I am half Ojibway, and half Caucasian, we will be called the Occasions. And I, of course, since I'm founding the new nation, will be a Special Occasion.

Joseph A. Dandurand *b.* 1964

KWANTLEN

Joseph Dandurand is a poet and playwright from the Kwantlen Reservation of the Fort Langley band in British Columbia. He received a diploma in performing arts from Algonquin College and a Bachelor of Arts in theatre and direction from the University of Ottawa. His produced plays include *Crackers and Soup* (1994), *No Totem for My Story* (1995), *Where Two Rivers Meet* (1995), and *Please Do Not Touch the Indians* (1998), which has had productions in Chicago, Connecticut, and most recently in Los Angeles (2004).

I came out of university telling myself: I am a writer. I even had some work posing as a writer. But the flavour soon lost its sweetness. . . . I . . . headed west with a plan in my head to fish the summer and then drive down and live and write in Mexico and live a poet's life. That was near ten years ago now and I have been on this little island in the middle of the Fraser River where my ancestors have lived since time began. . . . I have found my spiritual place. . . . I am talking about tradition and ceremonies that are as old as the river that flows by my house, spiritual things that I cannot and will not write about. . . . When I first thought I was a writer I wrote constantly, thirteen plays and numerous books of poems. Since I have been home I have only written two manuscripts of poetry and have a couple of unfinished plays on my desk. . . . I have started a family and my role in life is to be a father for my children, a husband for my wife, and a man for my people. I know that sounds corny and even in this day and age a little unbelievable. I even pinch myself someitmes. This is where I am and this is who I am. I am a father, a husband, a Kwantlen man.

Dadurand's poetry collections include *I Touched the Coyote's Tongue* (1994), *burning for the dead and scratching for the poor* (1995), *looking into the eyes of my forgotten dreams* (1998), and *SHAKE* (2003).

dirt of the old ones

i see faces singing in the dirt
old shoe prints form near perfect images of the old ones who used
to walk this earth.

the earth beneath me is older than any thoughts i may have come
up with.

its stories compressed by footsteps of the present day
we just walk now and listen
and we do not know much other than we should have listened to
the old ones.

the rains come   10
as they always do
washing the dirt and cleansing our past.

i watch my daughter run and play and pick at the dirt
this pure act of play
gives her what we all need: 15
     innocence.

to be born again
to know what we now know
if we only knew this when we first felt the songs coming from the
dirt   20
our lives would've been
better.

drunks, drifters, and fat robins

he wears his 3-dollar sweater bought from value village
his 2-dollar shoes stolen from a party long ago
as he stumbles up our one road.

this drunken drifter squeezing some life out of his sore eyes
as fat robins feast on big worms nearly pulling their heads off as   5
they tear them
from the wet ground.

past the old church that no one uses anymore he makes the sign of
the cross
and nearly falls and nearly lands on a fat robin that just won't let   10
go of a 6-inch worm
they both
the drunk and the robin
look at each other with sore eyes and squawk
their displeasure for the other   15
regain their balance
and move on.

the church sits quiet
no more prayers or salutes to a false god
a god who preys upon small boys through the skin of men in   20

clergy clothes.
the windows are all broken
the pattern of them now reflects some sort of eerie
message that only drunks and robins could comprehend.

shards of prayers follow him as he stumbles forward   25
never looking back at the old white church
its paint folding and falling away and landing on the ground
this sacred ground where little boys used to be touched and used
by men in clergy clothes
their rotten breath floats throughout this place causing even the   30
drunk
to stop and choke it out of his already dead body.

then he falls down
spread out as if catching himself would help
his arms and legs spread   35
not like jesus on the cross
but like a defenseless worm about to be pulled up out of the warm
earth below him
he breathes in that rotten breath
and he stays there like the church with its broken windows and   40
falling paint.

rain falls as the drunk does not move
robins eat big worms and become too fat to fly so they hop
around the dead drunk
his sore eyes opened   45
if only for the
last
time.

Jordan Wheeler *b.* 1964

MÉTIS

Jordan Wheeler was born in Victoria, British Columbia, of Cree, Ojibwa, Irish, English, Scottish, and French descent. Educated at St John's Ravenscourt School in Winnipeg, he began writing at the age of seventeen. In 1985, three of his stories were published in the anthology *Achimoona*. *Brothers In Arms*, published in 1989, is Wheeler's collection of three novellas about Native brothers. He has also written two books for children: *Just a Walk* (1998) and *Chuck in the City* (2000).

Wheeler now lives in Winnipeg, where he works in video, film, and popular theatre, writing plays with inner-city youth. He has written extensively for such television shows as *North of Sixty* (where he was senior story editor), *Black Harbour*, and the children's show *Tipi Tales*.

A Mountain Legend

The school bus drove into a small summer camp at the base of a towering mountain. Boys and girls between the ages of eight and twelve, who had signed up for the three-day camping trip, poured out of the bus. Following instructions from counsellors, they began hurriedly preparing their camp as the sunset dripped over the rock walls towering above them. For many, it was their first time away from the city, which they could still see far off in the distance. Tents were put up and sleeping bags unrolled before the last of the twilight rays gave way to the darkness of night.

Roasting marshmallows around a large campfire, the young campers listened intently to stories told by the counsellors. Behind the eager campers, the caretaker of the camp sat on the ground, himself listening to the stories.

As the night grew old, the younger children wearily found their way to the tents, so that by midnight only the twelve-year-olds remained around the fire with one counsellor and the caretaker. Their supply of stories seemingly exhausted, they sat in silence watching the glowing embers of the once fiery blaze shrink into red-hot ash.

'The moon is rising,' announced the caretaker in a low, even voice. All eyes looked up to the glow surrounding the jagged peaks of the mountain. The blackness of the rock formed an eerie silhouette against the gently lit sky.

The caretaker's name was McNabb. He had lived close to the mountain all his life and knew many of the stories the mountain had seen. He threw his long, black braided hair over his shoulders, drew the collar of his faded jean jacket up against the crisp mountain air, and spoke.

'There is a legend about this mountain once told by the mountain itself,' he said, paused for a moment, then continued. 'People claim that long ago it told of a young boy who tried to climb up to an eagle's nest which rested somewhere among the many cliffs. He was from a small camp about a day's journey from here and when he was twelve years old, he thought he was ready to become a warrior. His father disagreed, saying he was too young and too small. But the boy was stubborn and one morning before dawn he sneaked out of his family's teepee and set off on foot toward the mountain. There were no horses in North America in his time. They were brought later by the Europeans.

'It took most of the day for him to reach the mountain. The next morning, he set out to find an eagle and seek a vision from the mighty bird, as that was the first step in becoming a warrior. But as he was climbing up the rock cliffs to a nest, he fell to his death, releasing a terrible cry that echoed from the mountain far out across the land. The legend says the boy's spirit still wanders the mountain today.'

A coyote howled in the distance and the campers jumped.

'Is it true?' asked one of the boys, with worry and fear in his voice.

'Some people say so, and they also say you can still hear his scream every once in a while.'

All around the dying fire, eyes were straining up at the menacing rock peaks. The caretaker McNabb, however, wasn't looking at the mountain, he was watching one of the young campers. He was an Indian boy, smaller than the others, with short braided hair that fell down his back. The boy was gazing up at the mountain, his curiosity obviously blended with fear. Turning his head, his eyes met those of McNabb. For a fleeting moment, they locked stares, then McNabb relaxed, a knowing expression spreading over his face, while the boy continued to stare at him, wide-eyed and nervous.

There were small discussions around the fire, debating the story's truth before the counsellor told them it was time for sleep. Both tired and excited, they retreated to their tent and crawled into their sleeping bags.

The boy Jason lay in a tent he shared with two other boys, who lay talking in the dark. As Jason waited for the heat of his body to warm his sleeping bag, he thought of that long ago boy. He felt a closeness to him and imagined himself in his place.

'Hey Jason, why don't you climb up that mountain tomorrow morning and try to catch an eagle?' It was Ralph, who was against the far wall of the tent on the other side of Barry.

'Why?' asked Jason.

'You're Indian aren't you? Don't you want to become a warrior?'

True, Jason was Indian, but he knew nothing of becoming a warrior. He had spent all his life in the city. All he knew of his heritage was what his grandmother told him from time to time, which wasn't much. He had been to three pow wows in his life, all at a large hall not far from his house, but he never learned very much. His time was spent eating hot dogs, drinking pop, and watching the older boys play pool in the adjoining rooms. Little as he knew though, he wanted Ralph and Barry to think he knew a lot.

'No. It's not time for me to be a warrior yet,' he told them.

'Why not?' Barry asked.

'It just isn't, that's all,' Jason said, not knowing a better answer.

'You're chicken, you couldn't climb that mountain if you tried,' Ralph charged.

'I'm not chicken! I could climb that mountain, no problem. It just isn't time yet.'

'You're chicken,' Ralph said again.

'Go to sleep!' boomed a voice across the campground.

Ralph gave out three chicken clucks and rolled over to sleep.

Jason lay there in mild anger. He hated being called a chicken and if the counsellor hadn't shouted at that moment, he would have given Ralph a swift punch. But Ralph was right, the mountain did scare him.

With his anger subsiding, he drifted into a haunting sleep, filled with dreams. Dreams the wind swept through the camp, gently spreading the mountain spirit's stories throughout. A coyote's piercing howl echoed down the rocky cliffs, making Jason flinch in his sleep.

The following morning, Ralph, Barry, and Jason were the first ones up. As they emerged from the tent into the chilled morning air, their attention was immediately grasped by the huge rock peaks looming high above. Ralph's searching eyes spanned the mountain. A light blanket of mist enveloped its lower reaches.

Pointing up he said, 'See that ledge up there?' Jason and Barry followed Ralph's arm to a cliff along one of the rock walls just above the tree line. 'I bet you can't get to it,' he dared Jason.

'I could so,' Jason responded.

'Prove it,' Ralph said.

Jason was trapped and he knew it. If he said no, he would be admitting he was scared. And there was another challenge in Ralph's voice, unsaid, but Jason heard it. Ralph was daring him to prove himself an Indian. Jason had lived his whole life in a city on cement ground and among concrete mountains where climbing was as easy as walking up stairs or pressing an elevator button. To prove to Ralph and himself that he was Indian, Jason had to climb to that ledge. He knew that mountain climbing could end a life. And there were wild animals he might have to deal with. How was he supposed to react? How would he react? He was afraid. He didn't want to go. But if he didn't?

'What's the matter?' Ralph taunted. 'Indian scared?'

At that point, Jason decided he would face the mountain and he would reach that ledge. 'Okay,' he conceded.

At first, the climbing was easy, but his progress became slow and clumsy as he got higher up. Struggling over uneven ground and through trees, he came across a large flat rock. In need of a rest, he sat down and looked down at the campground he had left right after breakfast an hour ago. He could see bodies scurrying about. If they hadn't noticed by now that he was missing, he thought, no doubt they would soon.

Looking up, he could just see the ledge above the tree line. It wasn't much further, he thought. He could get to it, wave down at the camp to show he had made it, and be back in time for lunch. Raising himself up, he started to climb again, marching through the trees and up the steep slope, over the rough terrain.

A few moments later he heard a loud howl that seemed to come from somewhere above. At first, he thought it was a coyote, but it sounded more like a human. Nervously, he kept going.

In the camp, Ralph and Barry were getting ready to help prepare lunch. McNabb was starting a fire not far away. They, too, heard the howl.

'I never knew coyotes did that during the day,' Ralph said to Barry.

Overhearing them, McNabb responded. 'That was no coyote.'

Half an hour later, Jason stood just above the tree line. The ledge, his goal, was thirty feet above, but what lay ahead was treacherous climbing, nearly straight up the rock wall. He scrutinized the rock face, planned his route and began to pick his way up the last stretch.

The mountain saw the boy encroaching and whispered a warning to the wind sweeping strongly down its face as it remembered a similar event long ago. Jason felt the wind grow stronger, driving high-pitched sound into his ears. Gripping the rock harder, he pulled himself up a bit at a time. The wind seemed to be pushing him back. But he felt something else, too, something urging him on.

When he was about twenty feet up the rock face, with his feet firmly on a small ledge, he chanced a look down between his legs. He could see that if he slipped, he would plummet straight down for that twenty feet and after hitting the rocks below, he would tumble a great distance further. He knew it would spell death and for a split second, he considered going back down. But once again he felt an outside force pushing him to go on. It gave him comfort and courage. His face reddened, his heart pounded, and beads of sweat poured from him as he inched his way higher. Straight above, an eagle flew in great circles, slowly moving closer to Jason and the ledge.

Far down the mountain the search for Jason was well underway, but the counsellors had no way of knowing where he was, as Ralph and Barry hadn't told. McNabb also knew where Jason was, but he, too, remained silent.

An eight-year-old girl in the camp lay quietly in her tent, staring up through the screen window at the sky. The search for Jason had been tiring and she had come back for a rest. She was watching a cloud slowly change shape when a large black bird flew by high above. Out of curiosity, she unzipped the tent door and went outside to get a better look. She watched the bird fly in smaller and smaller circles, getting closer and closer to the mountain. She took her eyes off the bird for a moment to look at the huge rock wall, and there, high above the trees and only a few feet below a ledge, she saw the boy climbing. Right away she knew the boy was in danger. After hesitating for a moment, she ran to tell a counsellor.

Jason paused from climbing, just a few feet before the ledge. He was exhausted and the insides of his hands were raw, the skin having been scraped off by the rough rock. The ledge was so close. He pulled himself up to it, placing his feet inside a crack in the rock for support. Reaching over the edge, he swept one arm along the ledge, found another spot for his feet, hoisted his body up, rolled onto the ledge and got to his feet. There, an arm's length away on the ledge, were two young eagles in a large nest. For several minutes he just remained there looking at the baby eagles. He had never seen an eagle's nest before. He was so interested in the two young eagles he didn't notice the mother eagle circling high overhead, nor did he hear her swoop down towards him and her nest. She landed in front of him, spread her wings, and let out a loud screech. Jason was so terrified, he instinctively jumped and in doing so, lost his balance. Both feet stepped out into air as he grabbed the rock.

His hands clung desperately to the ledge as the sharp rock dug into his skin. He looked down and saw his feet dangling in the air. The wind swung him, making it impossible to get his feet back on the rock where they had been moments earlier. A coyote howled and Jason's terror grew. Again he looked down at the rocks below. Tears began streaming down his face. He didn't want to die. He wished he had never accepted Ralph's dare. He could picture them coming up the mountain, finding his dead body among the rocks, and crying over him. He began crying out loud and heard it echoing off the rock. Or he thought it was an echo. He stopped and listened. There was more crying, but not from him. Again he felt the presence of something or someone else. The wind swirled in and whispered to Jason the mountain's legend.

Though running swiftly, the boy Muskawashee had paced himself expertly for the day's journey. He would arrive at the base of the mountain far earlier than he had expected and would have plenty of daylight left to catch his supper and find a spot for a good night's sleep. Though small and having seen only twelve summers, his young body was strong. He would be able to reach the mountain in only two runs, pausing in between to catch a rabbit for lunch.

As his powerful legs moved him gracefully across the prairie, he thought back to the conversation with his father the day before. He had explained how most of his friends were already in preparation for manhood and he felt he was ready also. He did not want to wait for the next summer.

When some of his friends came back later that day from a successful buffalo hunt, he decided he would go to the mountain alone and seek a vision from the eagle.

He knew he would have to rise before the sun to get out of camp without being seen.

When he reached the base of the mountain, the sun was still well above the horizon. He sat down in a sheltered area for a rest. He decided this was where he would sleep for the night.

After a few minutes, he got up and made himself a trap for a rabbit and planted it. After laying the trap, he wandered off to look for some berries to eat while preparing his mind for the following day when he would climb the mountain. After some time, he returned to his trap and found a rabbit in it. He skinned it with a well-sharpened stone knife he had brought with him, and built a fire to cook his meal. He would keep the fire burning all night to keep away the wild animals while he slept.

Finishing his meal, he thanked the creator for his food and safe journey and prayed for good fortune in his quest for a vision. Then he lay down in the soft moss and fell asleep to the music of the coyote's howls and the whispering wind.

The next morning, he awoke to the sun's warming shine. The still-smouldering fire added an aroma of burnt wood to the fresh air. He again prayed to the creator for good fortune in his quest for a vision and for a safe journey up the mountain. When he finished, he looked up, high above, and saw eagles flying to and from a rock ledge. This would be his goal.

Half an hour later, he stood where the trees stopped growing and the bare rock began. His powerful body had moved steadily through the trees even though he wasn't used to uphill running. Without resting, he continued his climb, knowing he would have to be careful ahead. The mountain could be dangerous and its spirit could be evil.

As he pulled himself up the face of the rock, he heard the mountain spirit warning him to stay away. Its voice was the whispering wind, which grew stronger and seemed to be trying to push him back. With determination, Muskawashee climbed. High above, the powerful eagle circled its nest.

Just five feet below the ledge, Muskawashee paused. He was dripping with perspiration from fighting the wind and the mountain. Though scared, he would not let fear overcome him. His desire for manhood was stronger. His hands were hurting and covered in blood from the climb, but he reached out again. After several scrabbling attempts, he was able to grab hold of the ledge and pull himself up onto the narrow, flat edge. Eye to eye with two baby eagles, he stopped. He felt great pride and relief in having reached his goal and stood there savouring those feelings. He didn't hear the approach of the mother eagle. As she landed on the ledge in front of him, she let out a loud screech and spread her wings wide. Muskawashee was startled, stepped back and lost his footing. A gust of wind shoved him further and he could feel his body in the air as he tried to get a foot back on the rock. He grabbed the edge, but his arms were trembling and he could not pull himself back up. His fingers ached and began slipping from the edge. Knowing he would soon fall, he began whimpering. He looked up, into the eyes of the eagle. One day, he thought to himself, he would be back.

His fingers let go and he fell, releasing a loud terrifying scream that echoed from the mountain, far out across the land, and down through time.

McNabb and one of the counsellors left the camp when the eight-year-old girl told them what she had seen. Both experienced hikers and mountain-climbers, they were able to cover the distance in a third of the time it took Jason. When they heard the scream they quickened their pace. Minutes later, they reached the edge of the tree line and looked up at the ledge.

Jason, who had been hanging there for several minutes, also heard the scream and looked down into the eyes of Muskawashee as he fell. Jason felt the tension in his fingers, but sensed there were greater forces keeping him hanging there, perhaps the mountain itself was hanging on to him. Whatever it was, Jason remained high above McNabb and the counsellor, who were watching from the tree line. The wind died down and the eagle stepped back, making room for him on the ledge. Jason hoisted a foot back onto the ledge and tried again to haul himself onto the shelf.

Suddenly, he saw Muskawashee standing on the ledge, extending a hand down to him. Jason grabbed his hand and Muskawashee pulled. The two boys faced one another, looking into each other's eyes. The descendant gaining pride in being Indian, and the ancestor completing the quest he had begun hundreds of years earlier. A powerful swirl of wind swept Muskawashee away, leaving Jason alone before the eagle's nest. Jason reached down and picked up a feather out of the nest.

Below him stood the counsellor and McNabb. They had witnessed Jason's rescue. 'Who was that other kid up there?' asked the counsellor in disbelief.

McNabb smiled and answered. 'Muskawashee. He will wander this mountain no more.' Then, unravelling a long line of heavy rope he said, 'Come on, let's get Jason down.'

kateri akiwenzie-damm *b.* 1965

ANISHNAABE

kateri akiwenzie-damm is a 'mixed-blood' member of the Chippewas of Nawash First Nation, based on the Cape Croker Reserve on the Saugeen Peninsula in southwestern Ontario. She received her Bachelor's degree from York University and her Master's degree from the University of Ottawa. She currently works as a communications consultant with First Nations groups internationally and is the publisher of Kegedonce Press, a small company dedicated to the works of Indigenous writers. She has published her own writings across Canada, the United States, Aotearoa (New Zealand), Australia, and Germany. 'I write because I need to write,' she explains, 'because for me writing is ceremony. It is a spiritual practice, a way of connecting with others, a way of contributing back to my community and to all of creation. It is a form of activism, a creative, positive, giving, true way to maintain who we are as indigenous people, as Anishnaabe, and to protest against colonization in its many forms. It is a way to share, to reaffirm kinship, to connect with the sacredness of creation. I write because I believe love is medicine, love is the strongest power in creation, and writing is a way of expressing and experiencing this.'

With Kegedonce Press, akiwenzie-damm's most recent publication, as editor, is *Without Reservation, Indigenous Erotica* (2003). Her critical writing has appeared in *The Journal of Canadian Studies* (1996) and *Looking at the Words of Our People: First Nations Analysis of Literature* (1993). Her poetry has appeared in many journals, anthologies, and audio recordings, including *Rampike* (1997), *Sweetgrass Surrounds Her* (1997), *Returning the Gift* (1994), and *Your Silence Will Not Protect You* (1989). Her collected work is represented in *my heart is a stray bullet* (1993).

kegedonce

i thought about you all last night
now here you are
when my eyes are cloudy
and my tongue is swollen
giving me words as if tomorrow depends on them   5
you say
nniichkiwenh this morning i heard a bird's voice calling to the sun
and i was that bird
i was a swallow swooping into forest
then i was that forest turning my leaves towards the warmth and light   10
i say nothing
then you sing me your swallow song until my words are loosened
and come pouring out like a dammed river bursting in spring
i say
words are heavy with meaning   15
they are the true survivors
echoing into infinity when we have become bones cradled by the earth

you say
we belong to them and they belong to us
i say to you   20
words are my manitouwan my conjurors
with their magic the spider can be set in her web
the old people can live in the memory of generations
people from every direction can be made kin
the world can be recreated out of a fistful of clay   25
then
i pour my words over you smoothly
you give your words to me in song
i throw my words like poisoned arrows
but you steal the venom and give me back to myself   30
together we are healed with words
so we open our ears and take the scales from our eyes
letting our words shine like silver in the sun
together we are different yet one
speaking a language of true people   35
then you say in my voice
we are joined to each other as we are joined to this land
and i say in your tongue
i do not know how we came to this spot
but maybe it is enough to know that we are here   40
we are safe
and we are together

the resurrection of desire

the craft of devotion
is the passion of saints idiots lovers
and abusers of every kind
those whose heads of filled reflections and suffering
float slowly downstream   5
while their lips move as if in prayer
counting branches waving from the shore

homeless
forgotten sailors
swept in a tidal wave of their own creation   10
destroyers of flesh
worshippers of forever

mapping the way to heaven
across feet and hands and heads and torsos
rejecting the beautiful mortifications that haunt the minds of perverts   15
the guilt of sinners three scalps hanging from their belts
starkly insanely lovely

delicate in flight these wingless birds
transform into sweet bloody joyous messiahs
noiselessly stripping themselves of flesh   20
to the envy of those who sing of pain and make love in the dark

manitouwan oh manitouwan
earthy earthly exalted exiles
where is the raven
or those strange ancient monsters of the waterways   25
who would drag an innocent to that other world
where death sleeps

tell us
what ceremony or madness will safeguard their return?

words for winter

i cannot touch you
but i know how you dream
about a country
where snow falls in sacred secret places

i picture you   5
       standing out
against the whiteness
       tall
breathing life into the air around you
while the world rushes headlong   10

   i sigh
cloaking myself in the darkness of a january night
   watching the snow fly
safe from the howling storm outside

Grandmother, Grandfather

i carry a picture of you
in my head
i carry your blood in my heart
like a secret
i carry a cross   5
since you went away

i lost your words
i lost the sound of your voice

my skin is made of spirits
at night i feel them dance   10
my hair is a thousand feathered arrows
my face a dull moon

i carry a picture of you in my head

Why This Woman

For Jo-Anna and Pietra Anna

why this earth
in solemn patterns
turns
why this sun
circles nightly   5
casting shadows across the sinking front porch
swing
why this woman
in holy wonder
repeats the human story   10
why this child
grows in beauty
laughs and cries
lives
turning never escaping   15
this simple narrative spins us
into reflections
versions of each other

turning turning
we watch   20
as brightly shines the moon

sturgeon

i twist and gasp
open and close my mouth
searching for air
whenever a sturgeon is caught in the rainy river
i know   5
the feel of strange hands touching my body
the struggle
to be free
the longing
to go where i want to go   10
i feel
the impact of stick or rock on bone
the splash of colour
then the emptiness that is my head
my head like a midnight sky if the stars and moon were captured   15
by another heaven
i know
even when i am awake again
sitting at the kitchen table
staring at my plate with its bramble design   20
and rough chipped edges
i know

that is why i do not eat sturgeon
because i know
when a sturgeon is caught in the rainy river   25
i am a sturgeon
and i dangle on hooks

river song

take me down to the river's edge with a rush of tears and the sound of
　　angels' wings
give me breath with a host of desire and a single touch lifted from
　　despair
wash my fears at the martyrs' grave with the blood of saints shouting
　　holy names
sing my pain in mid-summer rain with forgotten words and a tongue
　　of fire
dance my heart like a laughing child like a drunken man with sallow
　　cheeks lash　　　　　　　　　　　　　　　　　　　　　　　　　　5
my burdens to another cart with ropes of your hair and no mercy
　　feed my head
with beauty and stories collected like shells from old women
　　in kerchiefs
and storm whipped beaches forget my ugliness and the imperfections
　　large
and small that make me ashamed but human carve my name in the
　　dead of night
beyond all stars and forgiveness　　　　　　　　　　　　　　　　10

desire

i want you
inside me
i want to be
inside you

i want your love　　　　　　5
your babies
your breath rhythm
against my cheek

i want skin touching
my name on your tongue　　　10
i want to shake the earth
with you

Gregory Scofield *b.* 1966

MÉTIS

Gregory Scofield was born in Maple Ridge, British Columbia, of Cree, Scottish, English, and French ancestry. He spent much of his childhood in 'the bush' in the northern parts of Manitoba, Saskatchewan, and the Yukon. He found public school 'extremely disastrous' and left at the age of fifteen, later completing grade eleven at Vancouver's Native Education Centre before enrolling as a mature student in the Native Human Justice Program of the University of Regina's Gabriel Dumont Institute. In 1988 he returned to the West Coast, where he began working with young offenders. In 1993 he attended the Native Youth Worker Training Program at the Vancouver Community College and is now an alcohol- and drug-addiction counsellor and outreach worker.

I am called a poet—a political poet, an angry poet, a Métis poet, an ex-street-involved poet, a gay poet—yet I think of myself as a community worker, a teller of stories, a singer of songs. . . . My voice is the voice of many communities, the voice of ancient speakers, the voice of contemporary nomads—though always it is the voice of my 'Grandmothers and Grandfathers', a voice that sings one small song in a community of powerful singers.

Scofield's poetry is collected in *The Gathering: Stones for the Medicine Wheel* (1993), *Native Canadiana: Songs from the Urban Rez* (1996), *Sakihtowin-Maskihkiy Ekwa Peyak Nikamowin / Love Medicine and One Song* (1997), and *I Knew Two Metis Women* (1999). His autobiography, *Thunder Through my Veins, Memories of a Metis Childhood*, appeared in 1999.

Nothing Sacred

Excavate: uproot a granny
gets a new resting place   pay
five bucks to view her in a
plexiglass tomb

New Age Movement: b & e our healing lodge   5
making off with our medicine
bird   so much for your
exhausted Buddha on the altar

Fashion: Pocahontas makes Vogue in
that two-piece buckskin   10
trim your fantasy with fringe
and beads   feathers tacky

Tourist Traps: only place to get a genuine
Wong & Sons totem pole
deciphering clan designs   15
extra

Read All About It: Pigeon Park Indians make
                              Premier an honorary drinking
                              chum   big powwow
                              scheduled after party   20

For Now: steal our spotlight   his high
                              profile   mixing promises
                              and Lysol

Âyahkwêw's Lodge

for Garry G.

êkwa êkosi, nikîwêhtatânân ôhi mistatimwak
and gave them to our women
who in turn
gave them to our men.
That night a baby was born in camp,   5
eyes clenched shut,
fist in his mouth.

In the lodge
there was an old woman
who had woken in the night   10
to a lightless presence.
She was instructed
to make offerings,
bring water and blood
from the sacred woman's belly.   15

These she took to *Âyahkwêw*.

In the blood
a twinning spirit was seen.
The water
was marked by thunder.   20
Âyahkwêw prepared the rattle,
placing inside
the child's umbilical cord.

At dawn, the time of prayer
they brought the child   25
to our lodge to be named—

and so we named him twice,
Mistatim-awâsis /
He Who Calls *Piyesîwak-iskwêw.*

êkwa êkosi, nikîwêhtatânân ôhi mistatimwak: And so, we brought these horses home
Âyahkwêw: loosely translated as a person who has both male and female spirits; also known as Two-Spirited
Mistatim-awâsis: Horse-child
Piyesîwak-iskwêw: Thunder-woman

Promises

not always did I have an aversion
to shiny objects, convenient arrangements

beneath the buffalo robe

snuggle into him   temporary
the famine his doeskin fingers snail   5
across my lips of strawberry pleasure

beneath the buffalo robe

spread my arms, my legs
I offer moose tongue and berries
generations he devours in seconds   10

beneath the buffalo robe

I don't get sweet-talked easy
his hands know what to do
in the dark / light of day

beneath the buffalo robe   15

promises he whispers   temporary
the taste his foreign tongue snakes
through ravines, over valleys

beneath the buffalo robe

each kiss   20
history
lolls on the tip of my tongue

Cycle (of the black lizard)

It was a priest
who made him act that way
so shy he wouldn't say shit
if his mouth was full of it.
At least that's what his   5
old lady said
each time her face got smashed
with his drunk fist.
The last time
he just pushed her around   10
then passed out.
Later, her *kôhkum* said
a lizard crawled inside his mouth
and laid eggs.

It was a black lizard, she said   15
the kind who eat the insides
feasting slowly
until their young are hatched.
Already his tongue was gone
from so much confessing.   20
Other boys at the boarding school
never talked out loud
for fear the lizard
would creep into their beds.
At first it just moved around   25
inside his head
manoeuvring serpentine
like a bad dream.

Then one night
his brain caved in & oozed out   30
his ears, nose and mouth.

It was his mouth
that caused him so much trouble.
In there was rotten teeth
and stink breath   35
made by that gluttonous lizard.
Morning Mass
he swallowed hard to rid the slime
but nighttime it just returned
and slithered around.   40

Another boy, only older
had the same trouble.
Recess
they eyed each other's dirty holes
and spit, spit, spit.   45
Once they got caught
and had to scrub the stairs—
and neither said shit about it.

At school, the teacher
noticed his kids had dull eyes   50
and never spoke or laughed.
The girl was ten
and developed for her age.
When asked in class to tell an Indian story
she went crimson in her face   55
and cried.
Every few days
her brother got sent
to the principal's office.
They thought he was just naturally rough,   60
like all Indians.
What they didn't know
was in her pee-hole, his mouth
a lizard crawled around
leaving eggs   65
during the Lord's prayer.

kôhkum: grandmother

Warrior Mask

This face
wasn't always
a concrete mask
littered in neon
to be spit, frowned   5
or pissed on.

In puberty
my *Âyahkwêw* eyes
followed strangers

and saw the black junk   10
squishing
around inside.

The face
came one night
when a grandfather   15
worked his medicine
in a dream.

'*Sâwanohk*,' he said
softly, mixing pollen and spit
he covered the right side   20
completely and
gave me summer songs
to sing.

A black line divided.

'*Pahkisimotâhk*,' he continued   25
grinding charcoal, spitting
and mixing and
marked four black dots
on the left.

'*Â*' he clapped,   30
'your path to the spirits.'
'*nikamow*,' *itêw*, '*nikamow*.'

Âyahkwêw: loosely translated as a person who has both male and female spirits; also known as Two-Spirited
Sâwanohk: south
Pahkisimotâhk: west
Â: exclamation or acknowledgement
'*nikamow*,' *itêw*, '*nikamow*' : 'Sing,' he said, 'sing.'

Ôchîm ◆ His Kiss

his mouth brushing mine
is a flat stone
skipping the lake's surface
and oh his tongue
a spawning fish jumps   5
over and over the waterfall

is maskwa pawing
all his winter hunger
so I yield up roots and berries
and lie back   10
my whole abundant self
curling fingers in his hair
while he nudges and strokes
the earth of me weightless
firefly in his ear   15
humming and buzzing higher and
higher yes yes yes
beating his rhythms
through my body,
a low water moon drum   20
till my mouth is dry of song.

maskwa: bear

Morning in the White Room

In the white room
we had joined
the way two rivers meet;
swollen from days
of endless rain, overflowing   5
our opposite banks which met
here, in the middle
flooding the floor
with our lips and limbs
like so many gasping fish.   10

We had made it
our celebration, a holy gathering
of the empty walls
and all that haunts them.
Take for instance,   15
your aqueous silhouette,
how it danced
to my mouth's sacred song.
And our bodies,
painted black and clinging   20
to invisible horses

galloped across the walls,
overtook the room like warriors
whooping our victory.

And in the morning   25
when the sun spoke up,
scolded clean the walls
we laughed like children,
shy in our nakedness,
scheming like raven   30
the last meddling rays.

Hunger

This is the mouth's madness.
This is my tongue, my plaything
collecting dew,
drinking with all its senses;
air spiced with rain   5
and you, unbathed,
sweet swamp, muskeg in June.

This is the tongue's madness.
This is the ruby
in all its precious forms.   10
It moves
on the wet floor in the Amazon.
A slow, lazy species,
shy as gecko.
Not meaning elusive but hypnotic,   15
and charming
a basket of cobras.

This is the night's madness
and the mouth's great sorrow.
This is the hour   20
I drift up and out of bed,
all of its space
whirling in my eyes
as the moon floats teasingly by,
she, looking rather full.   25

My Drum, His Hands

over the bones, over the bones
stretched taut
my skin, the drum

softly he pounds
humming   5

as black birds dance,
their feathers
gliding over lips, they drink
the stars
from my eyes   10
depart like sun
making way for moon
to sing, to sing
my sleeping

my sleeping song   15
the sky bundle

he carries me to dreams,
his hands wet
and gleaming

my drum aching   20

Unhinged

Sure
I've imagined you,
my unkempt soldier
alone in your room
pulling up all your heated secrets,   5
coming unglued
like the dovetail joints
of my antique dresser.

You are exquisite at this hour,
pure milkweed,   10
opalescent as the moon
turning down her blind eye.
And always, dangerous.

Sure
I've slipped the curve   15
of your backside, slipped between
your thighs,
my seasoned lips mouthing
the peach song
beneath your scrotum.   20
So, sing my breather, play me
the whole black night.
Sing me, anoint me
with your musk, ear wax,
your navel dew.   25

Sure
I've imagined you
alone in your room,
alone with me
in a phone booth, a theatre,   30
the back seat of a bus
travelling somewhere so solitary
the landscape has no memory.

Sure, my unkempt soldier
I've dreamed you unhinged   35
and raging,
your seed exploding like a bullet,
my death
merely a fading pulse.

Wâstêpakâwi-pîsim

SEPTEMBER ◆ THE AUTUMN MOON

Our bed of grass has turned brown
and leaves are changing
burnt red
and flecked gold
before breaking from the trees   5
and kissing the river
in separate hungers.

Last night
you bloomed to my touch,
called the birds together   10
with only a whisper.
We were driving south
on a stretch of road
so endless and smooth
it flowed like water, disappearing   15
beneath the wheels.

And, looking at you
peering into the limitless night
my thoughts passed over
your precious mouth   20
where I'd come to plant
my most sacred seed. Love . . .

It will be cold soon, you said
clasping my hand,
cupping it between your thighs   25
where you are always warm.

And we drove, bound by the silence
and behind us, a thousand miles
wrinkled moon's face.

And weasel and rabbit, I said,   30
will turn their winter white,
my hand squeezing the last blue
from the sky,
pulling you to a warmer climate.

Night Train

Tonight
I am in dual love.
Praise all! Praise
the slippery eye, praise to
the transient night, my weary travellers.   5

Praise
to this narcotic hour
fleeing so quickly
like sparks
whistling down the track.   10

Tonight
I am in dual love, no
I am in love double: 1 + 1 = 3
counting him, her and me, and

if you added   15
his perfect lips, her perfect arms
multiplied my heart, counted
all the sensations
I subtract and divide and
put together like so many railcars   20
my skeleton would stretch
a love song from here
to eternity.

And praise
to all this motion, the eyes trailing   25
their week-long bags,
praise to the bed
and the loveliness we'll make.

Tonight
I am in dual love. Praise!   30

She will carry his song
sing it for days,
and he, my shadowed engineer
will ride straight through,
whistle me   35
a slow beat against the night.

Randy Lundy *b.* 1967

BARREN LANDS FIRST NATION

Randy Lundy, a member of the Barren Lands First Nation in northwestern Manitoba, was born in Thompson, Manitoba, and grew up near the confluence of the Etamomi, Fir, and Red Deer rivers just south of Hudson Bay, Saskatchewan. His poetry draws from this landscape recurrent with recurrent images of water, stones, birds, animals, the earth, the moon, and the stars. 'I think the relationship between my poetry, the land, and its creatures is one that many First Nations peoples might understand and identify with,' he suggests. 'I think the poems dwell, as we all do, in an animistic/polytheistic world of living and breathing creatures, including what some others might call the inanimate'.

After attending the University of Saskatchewan, in Saskatoon, Lundy moved in 1999 to Regina, where he was awarded an MA in Native Canadian Literature in 2001. He is currently an assistant professor in the Department of English at the First Nations University of Canada.

Commenting on the diversity of his subject matter, Lundy says, 'At polite dinner parties, we're not to talk about death, sex, religion, or politics, or so says some old adage. But really, what else is there to talk about? What else is there to write about? So I write about these things, and the imagery that anchors all the meanderings is imagery drawn from the (so-called) natural world, although, of course, the human is always immersed in that.'

Lundy's poetry has appeared in anthologies such as *Sundog Highway: Writing from Saskatchewan* (2000), *Native Poetry in Canada: A Contemporary Anthology* (2001), and *Without Reservation: Indigenous Erotica* (2003). His first collection, *Under the Night Sun,* appeared in 1999 and his second, *The Gift of the Hawk,* in 2004.

Geography

Take away the corn, the sun-filled fruit of the fields, and all the roots, the water that they hold. Take away the hoofed animals that have given, reluctantly, their flesh. Take away air, sun, the moon and stars. Take them all away.

I depart into the dark, tangled forest of your hair and make a home there. I dwell alone in that night, live as an ascetic, one seeking his vision in the body of the crow, in the eye of the owl. But I come out again, travel past the two new moons of your eyes, and along the gentle ridge of your nose. I pause at, but pass, the dreadful chasm of your lips, and I fall off the edge of the known world as I traverse the incline of your chin down to the hollows of your neck, where willows grow and deer have come to graze. I travel the valley between your breasts, never reaching those peaks, capped by the fading light of day. Onto the plains of your belly my wanderings go, and I pitch a tent there, to study how the cacti grow, to await the sandstorms that blow from the peaks farther north. Deaf and blind, I remember what I know.

One day, I take the long journey to the south, find the sinuous rivers of your thighs, the hummocks of your knees, and the thin passages of your shins. Climbing, at last, the incline of your feet, I discover the many paths of your toes, and, beyond them, the thundering seas.

Heal

Love descended upon me,
a sickness, a disease that insisted
it would never leave; it descended upon me,
a fever, a plague upon a delirious city;

I have languished   5
without hope of survival, with no desire
to remain alive.

Now the fever is broken,
and I rise with clear eyes

—but I find love   10

a steady rain falling
over a drought-dry plain, every morning
some new plant is in bloom—

the prickly pear spreads its blossom
a translucent, earth-bound moon—   15

and standing, I spread my hands
to gather the medicine that will heal.

Old Man & Old Woman in the Garden

It was that other one, that damned
silly husband of hers. See,
he didn't know the joke.

You know the one
—red on the outside,   5
white on the inside.

She saw the buds on the trees
watching her with thin green eyes.
Her, she just winked at them and danced.

Later, they became friends, her and the leaves.   10
When they laughed, she laughed, their voices
rising from inside the same deep belly.

Meanwhile, her husband, he was always busy
whispering with that bearded one,
whispering and looking at her, giggling   15
like a coupla hormonal schoolboys.

Her, she would just wink and dance
flash a bit of thigh or breast.

See her, she talked with all the animals.

Sometimes even with that one,   20
that long, skinny, twisting one,
the one with the eyes like the budding leaves.
He was all slurs and spit that one.

But sometimes, she would wrap him
around her dancing body   25
and teach him to use his tongue properly.

One day her husband, that damned
silly one, he bites the apple
and then they have to leave.

Her, she didn't eat no apple.   30
Cuz see, she knows, she knows
you are what you eat.

Migrations

(St. Peter's Abbey)

In this season, the sun meditates
naked, shivering low on the horizon.

She is a nun with empty palms
someone who has let go of everything.

She lives back in the trees where the bare   5
branches creak, the song of the ascetic.

She keeps company with the crows
whose silence will be the invocation of cold.

She sees their eyes are new moons
their feathers an eclipse of the weakening light.   10

If she dreams of death and loss, its cause is
the absence of these birds.

She

She is twig-fingered. Cedar-skinned. Sweetgrass-braided hair. She is open-eyed, onyx-eyed dreamer, dwelling deep in the moonless, forested cavern of your skull. She does both what you can and what you cannot do. She is companion of bat, consort of owl. In your hand, she places raven feather, bear scat—and his hand.

That man you had forgotten, had tried to forget.

She leads you to the slow flow of river. She says, *Sit. Sit here. See how it moves. See how it all moves.* You think the dark water is sky. You think it is earth, but *No,* she says. *This is old water, and you must sit here. Be as stone, the two of you, as full and as empty. Be as one stone, moved by water, moved by ice. Rubbed by wind and the heavy-shouldered buffalo. Sit here, on this old lakeshore. What you seek is here. It is here. Deep in the sediment, you will find what you seek.* The moon, she lies buried here like some slow creature of the sea.

Dawn

In the grave, my father's bones
brittle as starlight just before dawn—

the stars reach out to embrace the night
and break beneath its weight—

just before birds begin to sing   5
a silence grows and holds—

bones and stars and moon.

The Gift of the Hawk

The silence you must find
is not the near silence
of the deer mouse, a rustling
in a fallow field.

The silence you must find   5
is like the wing of a red—
tailed hawk, riding a late afternoon
updraft, until it almost touches
the sun.

A silence like that wing—   10

slicing through air
cleaving sunlight in two
devouring the distance to earth.

But this is not enough.

The silence you seek   15
is a darkness and a stillness
bestowed by the perfection of talons.

Bear

for Susan G.

Late-summer sunlight, reflected off the river's slow flow
afternoon aurora on patient river stones;

when the bear emerges onto the bank
to dip its muzzle and drink

stones exhale warm breath into dusk   5
sigh in wet, clay-heavy sleep;

the animal lifts its heavy head in a broad-nostril flare
its senses leaning to the far-bank stir of leaves;

your breathing   hesitates
while the bear's mouth spills mist, and he snorts   10

the first stars into the darkening eastern sky.

Eden Robinson *b.* 1968

HAISLA/HEILTSUK

Eden Robinson was born on the Kitamaat Reserve of the Haisla Nation's traditional lands in the rainforests of northern British Columbia. She earned a Bachelor's degree from the University of Victoria and a Master's degree from the University of British Columbia, both in creative writing.

Robinson's first collection of fiction, *Traplines* (1996), was well received. An admitted fan of Stephen King, she describes the collection's four stories about adolescents confined by their age and class as 'dark fairy tales'. 'I love grim stories. They just make your own life seem so much better.'

Robinson's second book, *Monkey Beach* (1997), is a novel set in her home community.

Explaining the difficulty of situating her work closer to home, she says,

> 'It's a tougher book for me to write because I'm not hiding behind these flamboyant psychopaths. None of the characters are bad. They're just reacting like everyone else to situations of loss and death. . . .
>
> It's a balance between my artistic freedom and the privacy of the community I come from. That's a scary balance for me. I find it hard. I want to get it right before I do it. It really feels rude in some ways to write about people who can't write back at you.

Robinson's most recent novel, published in 2005, is *Blood Sports*.

Terminal Avenue

His brother once held a peeled orange slice up against the sun. When the light shone through it, the slice became a brilliant amber: the setting sun is this colour, ripe orange.

The uniforms of the five advancing Peace Officers are robin's egg blue, but the slanting light catches their visors and sets their faces aflame.

In his memory, the water of the Douglas Channel is a hard blue, baked to a glassy translucence by the August sun. The mountains in the distance form a crown; *Gabiswa*, the mountain in the centre, is the same shade of blue as his lover's veins.

She raises her arms to sweep her hair from her face. Her breasts lift. In the cool morning air, her nipples harden to knobby raspberries. Her eyes are widening in indignation: he once saw that shade of blue in a dragonfly's wing, but this is another thing he will keep secret.

Say nothing, his mother said, without moving her lips, careful not to attract attention. They waited in their car in silence after that. His father and mother were in the front seat, stiff.

Blood plastered his father's hair to his skull; blood leaked down his father's blank face. In the flashing lights of the patrol car, the blood looked black and moved like honey.

A rocket has entered the event horizon of a black hole. To an observer who is watching this from a safe distance, the rocket trapped here, in the black hole's inescapable halo of gravity, will appear to stop.

To an astronaut in the rocket, however, gravity is a rack that stretches his body like taffy, thinner and thinner, until there is nothing left but x-rays.

In full body-armour, the five Peace Officers are sexless and anonymous. With their visors down, they look like old-fashioned astronauts. The landscape they move across is the Surreycentral Skytrain station, but if they remove their body-armour, it may as well be the moon.

The Peace Officers begin to match strides until they move like a machine. This is an intimidation tactic that works, is working on him even though he knows what it is. He finds himself frozen. He can't move, even as they roll towards him, a train on invisible tracks.

Once, when his brother dared him, he jumped off the high diving tower. He wasn't really scared until he stepped away from the platform. In that moment, he realized he couldn't change his mind.

You stupid shit, his brother said, when he surfaced.

In his dreams, everything is the same, except there is no water in the swimming pool and he crashes into the concrete like a dropped pumpkin.

He thinks of his brother, who is so perfect he wasn't born, but chiselled from stone. There is nothing he can do against that brown Apollo's face, nothing he can say, that will justify his inaction. Kevin would know what to do, with doom coming towards him in formation.

But Kevin is dead. He walked through their mother's door one day, wearing the robin's egg blue uniform of the great enemy, and his mother struck him down. She summoned the ghost of their father and put him in the room, sat him beside her, bloody and stunned. Against this Kevin said, I can stop it, Mom. I have the power to change things now.

She turned away, then the family turned away. Kevin looked at him, pleading, before he left her house and never came back, disappeared. Wil closed his eyes, a dark, secret joy welling in him, to watch his brother fall: Kevin never made the little mistakes in his life, never so much as sprouted a pimple. He made up for it though by doing the unforgivable.

Wil wonders if his brother knows what is happening. If, in fact, he isn't one of the Peace Officers, filled himself with secret joy.

His lover will wait for him tonight. Ironically, she will be wearing a complete Peace Officer's uniform, bought at great expense on the black market, and very, very illegal. She will wait at the door of her club, *Terminal Avenue*, and she will frisk clients that she knows will enjoy it. She will have the playroom ready, with its great wooden beams stuck through with hooks and cages, with its expensive equipment built for the exclusive purpose of causing pain. On a steel cart, her toys will be spread out as neatly as surgical instruments.

When he walks through the door, she likes to have her bouncers, also dressed as Peace Officers, hurl him against the wall. They let him struggle before they handcuff him. The uniforms are slippery as rubber. He can't get a grip on them. The uniforms are padded with the latest in wonderfabric so no matter how hard he punches them, he can't hurt them. They will drag him into the back and stripsearch him in front of clients who pay for the privilege of watching. He stands under a spotlight that shines an impersonal cone of light from the ceiling. The rest of the room is darkened. He can see reflections of glasses, red-eyed cigarettes, the glint of ice clinking against glass, shadows shifting. He can hear zippers coming undone, low moans. He can smell the come when he's hit into passivity.

He wanted to cut his hair, but she wouldn't let him, said she'd never speak to him again if he did. She likes it when the bouncers grab him by his hair and drag him to the exploratory table in the centre of the room. She says she likes the way it veils his face when he's kneeling.

In the playroom though, she changes. He couldn't hurt her the way she wanted him to; she was tiring of him. He whipped her half-heartedly until she told the bouncer to do it properly.

A man walked in, one day, in a robin's egg blue uniform, and Wil froze. When he could breathe, when he could think again, he found her watching him, thoughtful.

She borrowed the man's uniform, and lay on the table, her face blank and smooth and round as a basketball under the visor. He put a painstick against the left nipple. It darkened and bruised. Her screams were muffled by the helmet. Her bouncers whispered things to her as they pinned her to the table, and he hurt her. When she begged him to stop, he placed the painstick against her right nipple.

He kept going until he was shaking so hard he had to stop.

That's enough for tonight, she said, breathless, wrapping her arms around him, telling the bouncers to leave when he started to cry. My poor virgin. It's not pain so much as it is a cleansing.

Is it, he'd asked her, one of those whiteguilt things?

She'd laughed, kissed him. Rocked him and forgave him, on the evening he discovered that it wasn't just easy to do terrible things to another person: It could give pleasure. It could give power.

She said she'd kill him if he told anyone what happened in the playroom. She has a reputation and is vaguely ashamed of her secret weakness. He wouldn't tell, not ever. He is addicted to her pain.

To distinguish it from real uniforms, her uniform has an inverted black triangle on the left side, just over her heart: Asocialism, she says with a laugh, and he doesn't get it. She won't explain it, her blue eyes black with desire as her pupils widened suddenly like a cat's.

The uniforms advancing on him, however, are clean and pure and real.

Wil wanted to be an astronaut. He bought the books, he watched the movies and he dreamed. He did well in Physics, Math, and Sciences, and his mother bragged, He's got my brains.

He was so dedicated, he would test himself, just like the astronauts on TV. He locked himself in his closet once with nothing but a bag of potato chips and a bottle of pop. He wanted to see if he could spend time in a small space, alone and deprived. It was July and they had no air conditioning. He fainted in the heat, dreamed that he was floating over the Earth on his way to Mars, weightless.

Kevin found him, dragged him from the closet, and laughed at him.

You stupid shit, he said. Don't you know anything?

When his father slid off the hood leaving a snail's trail of blood, Kevin ran out of the car.

Stop it! Kevin screamed, his face contorted in the headlight's beam. Shadows loomed over him, but he was undaunted. Stop it!

Kevin threw himself on their Dad and saved his life.

Wil stayed with their father in the hospital, never left his side. He was there when the Peace Officers came and took their father's statement. When they closed the door in his face and he heard his father screaming. The nurses took him away and he let them. Wil watched his father withdraw into himself after that, never quite healing.

He knew the names of all the constellations, the distances of the stars, the equations that would launch a ship to reach them. He knew how to stay alive in any conditions, except when someone didn't want to stay alive.

No one was surprised when his father shot himself.

At the funeral potlatch, his mother split his father's ceremonial regalia between Wil and Kevin. She gave Kevin his father's frontlet. He placed it immediately on his head and danced. The room became still, the family shocked at his lack of tact. When Kevin stopped dancing, she gave Wil his father's button blanket. The dark wool held his smell. Wil knew then that he would never be an astronaut. He didn't have a backup dream and drifted through school, coasting on a reputation of *Brain* he'd stopped trying to earn.

Kevin, on the other hand, ran away and joined the Mohawk Warriors. He was at Oka on August 16 when the bombs rained down and the last Canadian reserve was Adjusted.

Wil expected him to come back broken. He was ready with patience, with forgiveness. Kevin came back a Peace Officer.

Why? his aunts, his uncles, cousins, and friends said.

How could you? his mother said.

Wil said nothing. When his brother looked up, Wil knew the truth, even if Kevin didn't. There were things that adjusted to rapid change—pigeons, dogs, rats, cockroaches. Then there were things that didn't—panda bears, whales, flamingos, Atlantic cod, salmon, owls.

Kevin would survive the Adjustment. Kevin had found a way to come through it and be better for it. He instinctively felt the changes coming and adapted. I, on the other hand, he thought, am going the way of the dodo bird.

There are rumours in the neighbourhood. No one from the Vancouver Urban Reserve #2 can get into *Terminal Avenue*. They don't have the money or the connections. Whispers follow him, anyway, but no one will ask him to his face. He suspects that his mother suspects. He has been careful, but he sees the questions in her eyes when he leaves for work. Someday she'll ask him what he really does and he'll lie to her.

To allay suspicion, he smuggles cigarettes and sweetgrass from the downtown core to Surreycentral. This is useful, makes him friends, adds a kick to his evening train ride. He finds that he needs these kicks. Has a morbid fear of becoming dead like his father, talking and breathing and eating, but frightened into vacancy, a living blankness.

His identity card that gets him to the downtown core says *Occupation: Waiter*. He pins it to his jacket so that no one will mistake him for a terrorist and shoot him.

He is not really alive until he steps past the industrial black doors of his lover's club. Until that moment, he is living inside his head, lost in memories. He knows that he is a novelty item, a real living Indian: that is why his prices are so inflated. He knows there will come a time when he is yesterday's condom.

He walks past the club's facade, the elegant dining rooms filled with the glittering people who watch the screens or dance across the dimly-lit ballroom-sized floor. He descends the stairs where his lover waits for him with her games and her toys, where they do things that aren't sanctioned by the Purity laws, where he gets hurt and gives hurt.

He is greeted by his high priestess. He enters her temple of discipline and submits. When the pain becomes too much, he hallucinates. There is no preparing for that moment when reality shifts and he is free.

They have formed a circle around him. Another standard intimidation tactic. The Peace Officer facing him is waiting for him to talk. He stares up at it. This will be different from the club. He is about to become an example.

Wilson Wilson? the Officer says. The voice sounds male but is altered by computers so it won't be recognizable.

He smiles. The name is one of his mother's little jokes, a little defiance. He has hated her for it all his life, but now he doesn't mind. He is in a forgiving mood. *Yes, that's me.*

In the silence that stretches, Wil realizes that he always believed this moment would come. That he has been preparing himself for it. The smiling-faced lies from the TV haven't fooled him, or anyone else. After the Uprisings, it was only a matter of time before someone decided to solve the Indian problem once and for all.

The Peace Officer raises his club and brings it down.

His father held a potlatch before they left Kitamaat, before they came to Vancouver to earn a living, after the aluminum smelter closed.

They had to hold it in secret, so they hired three large seiners for the family and rode to Monkey Beach. They left in their old beat-up speedboat, early in the morning, when the Douglas Channel was calm and flat, before the winds blew in from the ocean, turning the water choppy. The seine boats fell far behind them, heavy with people. Kevin begged and begged to steer and his father laughingly gave in.

Wil knelt on the bow and held his arms open, wishing he could take off his life-jacket. In four hours they will land on Monkey Beach and will set up for the potlatch where they will dance and sing and say good-bye. His father will cook salmon around fires, roasted the old-fashioned way: split down the centre and splayed open like butterflies, thin sticks of cedar woven through the skin to hold the fish open, the sticks planted in the sand; as the flesh darkens the juice runs down and hisses on the fire. The smell will permeate the beach. Camouflage nets will be set up all over the beach so they won't be spotted by planes. Family will lounge under them as if they were beach umbrellas. The more daring of the family will dash into the water, which is still glacier-cold and shocking.

This will happen when they land in four hours, but Wil chooses to remember the boat ride with his mother resting in his father's arm when Wil comes back from the bow and sits beside them. She is wearing a blue scarf and black sunglasses and red lipstick. She can't stop smiling even though they are going to leave home soon. She looks like a movie star. His father has his hair slicked back, and it makes him look like an otter. He kisses her, and she kisses him back.

Kevin is so excited he raises one arm and makes the Mohawk salute they see on TV all the time. He loses control of the boat, and they swerve violently. His father cuffs Kevin and takes the wheel.

The sun rises as they pass Costi Island, and the water sparkles and shifts. The sky hardens into a deep summer blue.

The wind and the noise of the engine prevent them from talking. His father begins to sing. Wil doesn't understand the words, couldn't pronounce them if he tried. He can see that his father is happy. Maybe he's drunk on the excitement of the day, on the way that his wife touches him, tenderly. He gives Wil the wheel.

His father puts on his button blanket, rests it solemnly on his shoulders. He balances on the boat with the ease of someone who's spent all his life on the water. He does a twirl, when he reaches the bow of the speedboat and the button blanket opens, a navy lotus. The abalone buttons sparkle when they catch the light. She's laughing as he poses. He dances, suddenly inspired, exuberant.

Later he will understand what his father is doing, the rules he is breaking, the risks he is taking, and the price he will pay on a deserted road, when the siren goes off and the lights flash and they are pulled over.

At the time though, Wil is whiteknuckled, afraid to move the boat in a wrong way and toss his father overboard. He is also embarrassed, wishing his father were more reserved. Wishing he was being normal instead of dancing, a whirling shadow against the sun, blocking his view of the Channel.

This is the moment he chooses to be in, the place he goes to when the club flattens him to the Surreycentral tiles. He holds himself there, in the boat with his brother, his father, his mother. The sun on the water makes pale northern lights flicker against everyone's faces, and the smell of the water is clean and salty, and the boat's spray is cool against his skin.

David A. Groulx *b.* 1969

OJIBWA

Marilyn Dumont has said of David A. Groulx: 'He has a keen sense of the contradictions that being native means in a nation that still distrusts its cultural/historical existence.'

Born in northern Ontario, Groulx obtained a Bachelor of Arts degree from Lakehead University and studied creative writing at the University of Victoria and the En'owkin International School of Writing. He published his first book of poetry, *Night in the Exude*, in 1997. Of his second collection, *Long Dance* (2000), from which the selections offered here are taken, Lee Maracle said 'this "long dance" is our dance. It is the pathway we have travelled for over 100 years now. . . . We all got through it and we have this dance, this song, to mark it, to remember it, to experience the beauty of it—the terrible terrible beauty.'

Groulx currently lives in Thunder Bay, where he works for the Ka-Na-Chih-Hih solvent abuse treatment centre.

In the Cold October Waters

In the cold October waters I stood
up to my thighs
the waves bounced against my back
as I held my tobacco up to the skies

The smoke rose to a cold Autumn moon   5
and over my body bare
the water splashed droplets
into my long black hair

It was there in that place
I knew I'd belong   10
as I stood in the cold dark water
singing my sacred song

Victims of Lashing Under the Hanging Sky

Your father was a good man
who relocated my father

    to

Resolute Bay

Your father was a good man   5

like steam rolling
off the mountains
in to the blue sky

to a job out in Battleford Sask.
rode out with   10

Middleton

and took my father's hungry bullet

Your father was good man

Your father took a job in Ottawa
with his bullet in his head   15

with Victorian rule

My father carried firewood
into brick buildings
his bleeding lungs
spitting on the wooden floor   20

as the sun

went down

he carried it all home

to his wife
My father grew up with   25
broken legs
spoke Red to God
grew old
and gave his children
away   30

My father was a good man

like yours
he danced in the earth
his bones-a rattle

his bones in a   35
rusted
wheelbarrow

Wouldn't We Be Fucked

Wouldn't we be fucked

if God

didn't have a plan   5

Oh

We are a plan

a good plan

a mission

A whole reservation   10

protected

by dead angels

working Yonge St.

The Long Dance

To the girl who wore the jingle dress

behind the glass

with the small pox

that I could not touch

but only with my eyes   5

in these sunless galleries
in these hallways
where the wind doesn't whine

tonight your grand-daughter
is in San Francisco   10

speaking to the hearts of the people

with the smallpox

Let me hold you like a banister
let me hold you like a deadman

with dancing rage   15

with smallpox

that I could touch

but only with my eyes

Nootka woman with echoes
of gunboats in your ears   20

show me the place

where Raven was shot to pieces

and taken away

to the industrial schools

where he danced with the rage   25

and showed it to you

Nootka woman
show it to me

and I'll show you

Coyote's leg   30

that he left in a Bear trap

left by a Whiteman

who left for Saint Mary's river

with my Algonquian grandmother

who could paint   35
play the squeezebox
and sew.

Tell it to me Anishnabikwe

when

Nanabush snatched some children   40

away from there

in a big boat that was left
by the river

And none of them
were ever seen again   45

Tell me Cree woman
where Whiskey jack

was shot by some

Moose hunters

and died   50

in the fall

with his hands clenched

around another dream-hunt

and I'll show you my daughter

who ran away from sleep   55

to finish building this body

I'll show you where

the Daybreak people died

and why

we danced with the rage   60

and speak of dreams

no one has seen

for five-hundred years

Philip Kevin Paul *b.* 1971

W̱SÀ NEC'

'After writing "Still Falling", which is really a thought in progress, I began defining what I called "The Weight",' recalls Philip Kevin Paul.

Since so much has been taken away from my people in the last 150 years, most that was good about W̱SÀ NEC' seems only to be a memory. My grandfathers and grandmothers on both sides heard the stories of W̱SÀ NEC' in sadness, because their parents lived in the generation that truly made the transition from one way of life to another. Thankfully, my grandparents lived in and remembered the old ways, but they also remembered (without knowing it, I think) the sadness that the stories were told in. That sadness, or weight, has been passed from one generation to the next along with each story. As the sadness gets farther from its original generation, the weight of it gets heavier, because it becomes less comprehensible. To my generation, the weight is very heavy, but to the generations behind me, it is crushing.

Philip Kevin Paul received a degree in writing and English from Camosun College and the University of Victoria, British Columbia. At Camosun he won awards in creative writing and in English. One of his plays has been given a staged reading at Kaleidoscope Theatre in Victoria, and he did a report for the Institute of Ocean Sciences on correlations between Saanich place names and modern scientific research. His poems are collected in *Taking the Names Down from the Hill* (2003).

Though I have a somewhat limited vocabulary in my own language, I grew up hearing my language, especially when referring to the ideas that do not translate into English. All the poems, in the collection of poems that I am working on, are based on the discovery of a map hidden within the language itself (meaning my language, SENC'OTEN). Since writing will never be central to my life, but will be used to express what *is* central, many of my poems could be considered translations; I am trying to express the feeling of a tradition that has always contained me.

The Bare Story of My Life

I was born in a time when the heart wasn't well
understood. My mother was alone with me
in the hospital most of each day,
though whenever he could, my father came
to be with his dying son-after work,   5
through visiting hours
and more. He would lift me, as though
practicing something new and ceremonial,
away from the machines I was connected to
with wires the colour of blood. In his story   10
of this time, he mentions it twice—
they were the colour of blood.

And the circular pads stuck to me
to monitor the patterns of my deformed heart,
they were a sickly grey, *cold and hopeless.*   15
My mother and father took turns cradling me
alone at the quiet end of the hospital.
How odd to think of it now—that in
their stories about this time they are
never together with me in that room.   20

A few days before I was released
from the hospital, and after it had been
determined I wasn't going to live long,
a stranger arrived in the doorway
of the quiet room. My father would   25
often recall beholding a man
whose *simplicity lives with him*
like a great gift.

'I wish for this child a great life'—
the stranger's words called a tear to his eye,   30
which he captured with his index finger
and placed with no small sense of grace
at my right temple. Then he turned to leave,
barely acknowledging my father sitting there,
holding me with an awkward beauty.   35

When I think of my life before conception,
how difficult my decision to come here
must have been, knowing the pain I would
cause my mother and father in those early
months. Knowing how much later when   40
my brothers and I were left alone here
together, I would trouble them by being lodged
so deeply in my own story. My mother

never forgot, despite the going on of my life,
that I was her ill child. And my father   45
eventually told me that in the days after my birth
he must have appeared to be celebrating—but
he was lifting his glass as though at a wake,
in tribute and praise to his dying son.

The Cost

a song

Outside night and morning are shaking hands.
Night says *Good morning,* morning says, *Good night*
and under the oak tree where my father used to stand
the snow is rotting. It's just a matter of time.

I hope of all the things that remain,   5
we don't dwell too long on what we've lost
and when we truly know what has been gained,
love outweighs the cost.

Outside the wind is scratching her back
on the leafless trees whose ancient hands are strong.   10
The wind sings praise for the things that pass,
and I swear she's singing my mother's song.

I hope of all the things that we've gained,
we don't pine too long for what we've lost
and when we look back up to see what remains,   15
we see love outweighs the cost.

So the leaves get dropped and then they're kicked around,
by Wednesday they'll be ash.
Funny how the rain turns all our faces down,
till all the world seems at mass.   20

I hope of all the things gone strange,
we don't believe we will always be lost,
please let me hold you completely for a change
and let our love outweigh the cost.

Taking the Names Down from the Hill

What is Saanich to me now?
Merely the sheer promise
of Matthew before his death,

merely my father's suffering fight
against *his own* death,   5

merely the painful pierce of doubt
through to my mother
before her death,

and forever the wisdom
we need and will continue to need   10
rotting out in hollows
in Uncle Gabriel's bones,
under pounds of earth.

It pleases me to be angry,
to be angry and to speak and to write it.   15
I'm glad, finally,
to have shrunk down Saanich
—what I imagined to be Saanich—
and put it away.

What I imagined was my only home   20
lost forever under tons of concrete
and vulgar electric houses humming
the sickness into us.

What I imagined to be the only rightness
worth striving for or dying for and making   25
their deaths right.

Sorrow was pathetic and laden
with a silence so vast that
the drummer could not wake us.

The people went into the hills.   30
They went there together as one body
knowing who they were
to bring the names home.

Where are the ancestors
we keep calling ourselves?   35

And while the roadways were being imposed,
the crowns were cast aside and tangled
and will never be brought home
and never properly given.

However, sorrow has had its time.   40
The mourning must break

at last. I will tell you
what they really left us.
They left us
magic in everything,   45

the *beautiful way*
in everything. But what
we truly own has never left us:

magic in word,
magic in thought,   50
magic in song,
magic in touch,

and, yes, magic in the breath
that joins them.

I went to the hills alone   55
with what I'd shrunk Saanich to
in a few measly pores of the lifeline
of the palm of my hand.

From there,
where it was unceremoniously cradled,   60
I blew it out over the cobwebbed underbrush
four paces off the footpath
and felt that my work was done
without even singing a song.

On the way back down I stopped   65
and touched the road but twenty paces
from someone's house,
someone I've never even met
and breathed out *Saanich,*
this is Saanich.   70

I began to dance. I danced
at least as foolishly as a Scotsman
gone Indian, naked in the woods!
(Or an Irishman for that matter.)

I named and renamed everything   75
that I spied with my little eye:
Saanich. And my dance?

When I figured I had it down,
that I had it just right, I knew
it was time, as it is for us all.   80

So by the gift of this
old unapologetic magic
I called it the *Dance of Forever,*

our newest tradition.

Richard Van Camp *b.* 1971

DOGRIB

Richard Van Camp was born in the Northwest Territories, in Fort Smith, which he calls 'the greatest town in the whole wide world'. The multiculturalism and general sense of community found there are central to his work: 'Dogribs are rare here. My being born outnumbered and having friends from every spectrum of the rainbow has given me the gift of, I believe, an open mind and an open heart. I write about Northerners, people who have decided to spend their lives and their love up north.'

Van Camp was educated at the En'owkin International School of Writing in Penticton, British Columbia, and at the University of Victoria, but he describes his desire to become a writer as rooted in his friendship with Lorne Simon: 'I became a writer the day I heard he died. When I write now I feel him around me. We still talk, Lorne and I. I know he guides my hand. He taught me more about writing than any school. Writing is about feeling. It's about gut. It's raw. It's sexy. It's impact.'

Van Camp's varied publications include the novel *The Lesser Blessed* (1996); two children's books, *The Man Called Raven* (1997) and *What's the Most Beautiful Thing You Know About Horses?* (2003), illustrated by George Littlechild; and a collection of short stories, *Angel Wing Splash Pattern* (2002). As he explains, 'I write everything from poetry to children's stories to graphic scripts to transcriptions of elders' stories to novels.' In 1997 he received the Canadian Authors Association Air Canada Award, presented annually to young writers of 'outstanding promise'.

Mermaids

Come flying out of the Range Hotel. Elbow's busted. Bleeding through my sock. Gotta find those sisters. Right rump is sore. Took the fall so I wouldn't go through the TV. Yellowknife. I hate this town. Cabbies everywhere. The little Native girl I saw waiting earlier is still there. Waiting. Still waiting. For who—her folks? She's got those yellow gumboots on. Christ, she's gotta be cold. It's late. What time is it? Gotta make that bus. I feel my blood drain and pool in my boot. I head towards her. Her face is filthy. She's shivering. I gotta make that bus.

'You're bleeding,' she says.

I lean hard against a parking meter. 'You should be inside.'

'I can stay out late as I want,' she insists.

My throat. Everything starts spinning. My mother was cursed. I swallow blood. The day she bore me. I stare at the little girl and I am faint with envy of the dead. 'Did I ever tell you why God killed the mermaids?'

That's when I black out.

When I come to, I'm in an apartment. Awful little apartment. Black velvet paintings on the wall. Sticky beer on the kitchen floor. Something sticky all over me. Band-Aids. I got Barbie Band-Aids on my arms and hands. All over my throat and face. There's a party next door. We hear it. I'm sitting down with my sock off. Did she drag me here? She comes around the corner holding something.

'What you got there?'

'My last Band-Aid,' she says, 'for your foot.'

I look down. The skin on the back of my foot is torn absolutely off. It's stopped bleeding. Lint and hair on my pink wound.

'Okay,' I say.

She rolls the Band-Aid on while I wiggle my toes. 'Don't pick it,' she says.

I look around. I'm sitting on urea foam furniture. Christ, these people. Don't they know anything?

'Don't pick it,' she warns. 'Don't pick it. Don't pick it.'

'Where's your mom?'

'Working.'

'Yeah right,' I say. 'This late?'

She crosses her arms. 'My mom's working.'

'Okay, kid, okay. You're the boss. Does your mom have any smokes around here, or what?'

Shakes her head. What kind of Indian is she? 'Are you Cree, Chip, or Slavey?'

'I'm Dene. Why did God kill the mermaids?'

'Come on,' I say. 'You don't want to know why God killed them.'

'Sure I do,' she says. Before I know it, she sits on my knee. I think I chipped the blade of my elbow off. I can't seem to move it. Legs are tightening up too. Who would have guessed I could kick them so far forward?

'How old are you?' I ask.

'Nine,' she says.

My meds. Good thing I take my meds. I can miss two meals and never feel it cuz I take my meds.

'What happened to your arms?' she asks.

My tattoos. She's covered my tattoos with Barbie Band-Aids.

I smoldered them off with a car lighter after Sfen died. They were home-grown crosses Sfen gimme, one on each arm. 'Accident,' I said. 'What's your name?'

'Stephanie. What's yours?'

'You never heard of me?'

She shakes her head. She's gonna be pretty with those dark eyes of hers. She's gotta be Slavey.

'You sure?' I look around. 'My name's Torchy.'

'That's not your name,' she says.

'Sure it is.'

'What's your real name?'

I look around again. No one here but us. 'Hazel,' I said. 'But I hate that name. Call me Torchy.'

'Why do they call you Torchy?'

'You don't want to know.'

Her eyes light up. 'Sure I do.'

'Because I like to burn things down,' I say.

'Why?'

'I got a gene variant.'

'A what?'

'A cocaine gland in my brain. It spills sometimes.'

She frowns. 'Don't lie.'

'Hey. How does God clean?'

'With his hands.'

'No. He cleans with fire. And I would rather unleash fire than have fire unleash me.'

She didn't get it. She didn't even hear me. She pouts her lips. 'But firebugs pee their bed.'

'What?'

'My daddy told me firebugs pee their bed.'

I laugh for the first time in months. 'Where's your old man?'

She doesn't answer. Looks down. I shoulda known better.

'Why did God kill the mermaids, Torchy?'

'God killed the mermaids,' I say. 'He did, you know.'

She looks at me with a filthy face. Rests her little head on my bony shoulder. 'But why?'

Jesus, this kid trusts me. Doesn't she know who I am? Eleven o'clock at night. Her folks are drinkin' and she's here with me. Okay. She saved me so maybe I owe her. I need time. Need to power up. It's eleven now. I gotta make that midnight bus.

'Well,' I say, 'this is a story. It's not an old time story. It's not a "Once upon a Time" story. It's a Torchy story and-Christ—I wish your mom had a smoke around here. I can feel my brain swelling.'

'Torchy—'

'Okay. Okay. The best I can figure is when sailors saw the mermaids, they leapt from their boats and swam to them. They forgot about their houses, their mortgages, their ol' ladies, they forgot about all that. They saw such beautiful women. They just wanted to be with them. And if they died swimming across, they died with glory in their eyes. Then they saw the mermen. While they were swimming. These mermen were so beautiful they fell in love with them, too. They became bi-sexual.'

I look at the little girl for her reaction. She's listening but she's got sleepy eyes.

'You know what that means?' She shakes her head. 'That means you love everyone and everything around you. You love men. You love women. You love puppies and you love Country and Western music. You just love everything. And everyone. The mermaids and mermen were so beautiful, the men wanted to stay there forever until they died. They carved temples out of Chinese jade for them, so the mermaids and mermen could sit on altars. The mermen would have to remind the men to eat. They were so in love they forgot to eat. Like the bison when they're rutting. They forget to eat, eh? They just wanted love.'

I look. She's almost asleep. 'God killed the mermaids because they were more beautiful than God. Men worshipped mermaids and mermen. They forgot about God and anytime men forget about God, He reminds them that He's still there. That's why he brought AIDS. Because we forgot.'

I flex my fingers. Make a fist. Oh, I'm gonna feel this all tomorrow. I lean back in the chair. I hope my throat doesn't close. I hold Stephanie close. She's still got those gumboots on. I hug her and hold her close.

'Where do fish sleep?' she asks suddenly.

'I thought you were sleeping. What?'

'Where do fish sleep?'

'I don't know.'

She smiles. 'On river beds, silly.'

'Oh,' I say. Then we burst out laughing.

She studies me deep. 'Are you a bad man, Torchy?'

I think about this long and hard. 'Am I a bad man?' I ask. 'I'm not a bad man. I just leave for a while and let the bad man in.'

I think of another logo me and Sfen could have done if he would have met this little girl. It would say, LAUGHTER IS THE BEST MEDICINE and under it we could have little kid's handwriting that says: AND HUGS HELP TOO.

They used to call my brother 'the idea man.' He was a logo artist by trade, but I couldn't think about that. I lift Stephanie and place her on the sofa. Where's Stephanie's mom? Doesn't she know guys worse than me walked the streets? Some guys right now would be pullin' their junk lookin' at her.

How much money do I got left? Four hundreds. There's a red crayon. Good. I take it and write with on each bill, 'My mother was cursed the day she bore me. I am faint with envy of the dead.'

I look out the window to the Yellowknife sky. I love how clouds here fold themselves and burn for sunsets. I pray, I guess, in my own way. Bless these bills, someone. May each of these bills burn to sunlight. May each of these bills change lives forever, for good.

How'm I gonna explain this to Snowbird? The old man who blessed my hands and warned me, 'Grandson,' he said, 'make sure you drop some tobacco when you get to

Yellowknife. Say your name out loud after you land so your soul can catch up with you and don't forget to wash your hands after you win.'

It was only yesterday when I worked up the courage to go see him.

'Old man?' I called as I walked into his porch.

'A-mi-nay?' he asked. 'Who's there?'

'Maybe I'm your long lost grandson, and maybe I want to make my long lost grandpa rich.'

The medicine man called Snowbird studied me with glassy, filmy eyes. It looked like someone had emptied an egg into each of his eyes. We were quiet for a bit. I recognized the music on the radio. It was Van Morrison's 'Sometimes I feel like a motherless child'. It was a hurtin' song so we listened hard.

He opened the door of his wood stove with a piece of fresh kindling, and popped a large spruce in before closing the door with the same stick. He waved the glowing stick around in the air and I could smell its beautiful sweet smoke.

'I remember you when you were this high,' he lifted his brown hand to his knee. 'Hey-ya-hay!' the old man smiled, 'I better put on some tea so me and my long lost grandson can catch up. Also, we should pray now that we have found each other after all these years.'

Snowbird must have been the loneliest man in the world, the way he moved. He pulled out a pouch of Drum and opened his woodstove. He threw in a pinch of tobacco and began to pray in Dogrib. I was disgusted with how lonely he was. He was starving for someone to talk to. I watched him pray and didn't understand a word. He then switched to English: '. . . and this is for my adopted grandson,' he said. Then he handed the pouch to me. 'Now you, Grandson.'

I pinched some tobacco and pulled it out. 'For everyone with AIDS,' I said.

'Ho,' he said.

I threw the tobacco to the naked fire. It smelled sweet. 'For my brother Sfen.'

'Ho.'

I was just about to cross myself but suddenly remembered: 'For all my enemies.'

'Ho!' he said really loud. Maybe I was praying for us both. 'I'm sorry to hear, Grandpa,' I said, 'that your wife died.'

'Yes yes,' he answered sadly, 'but that is God's plan. Not ours. It's up to the boss upstairs.' He pointed with the piece of kindling to the ceiling. 'Jesus was a medicine man.'

'Here are the signs,' he said as he sucked on his pipe. 'There are three wolves running outside of town. Three wolves. One is white. One is gray. One is black. Wolves are how the Creator moves over the snow.'

I thought of lepers and tornadoes touching down.

He was quiet for a while before he said, 'There is talk of a midnight burial outside of town, by the lake.'

I cleared my throat but couldn't speak. Don't ask about my brother, I was thinking. Don't you dare ask about my brother.

He waited a long, long time before saying with a soft voice, 'That's all right, grandson. We do what we have to, don't we?'

I nodded, waited for the tears to stop burning my eyes. How did he know? I waited, nodded again, looked away. How did he know? He poured us some tea and turned the radio off.

'Why have you come here, Grandson?'

I took a big breath. 'I want the jackpot in tomorrow's Bingo in Yellowknife. Eighty grand cash. I'll give you half if you bless my hands with your medicine.'

He thought about it. Nodded. 'Come visit your grandpa tomorrow before you leave,' he said.

Great! 'But I have to get on the plane. Will it last until Yellowknife?'

'Yes. Just don't touch any cards or Bingo dabbers until you get to the game you want to win.'

'What if we have to share the pot with someone in Y.K?'

'You won't.'

I waited. 'What will you do with your half, old man?'

He was Quiet for even longer. It was like he was listening to the fire and remembering the words of the song and each instrument in the band and maybe the thoughts of each band player and mister Van himself. It was as if he realized again how pitiful he was hugging such loneliness every day. 'Do you know what I wish?' he asked. 'I wish someone were to visit me and read to me the Bible. It is such a beautiful song sung with so many voices. I could make tea and we could talk after. That's what I wish, grandson.'

I stood up. Me? He was talking about me.

'I don't want money,' he continued. 'You're young. You keep it. But please remember your Grandpa.'

A medicine man saying please to me. I couldn't believe it. He held out his small, brittle hand. I took it. It was almost like his fingers were made with the same tiny hollow bones in sparrow wings.

'Is there a woman in your life, Grandson? Where are all my grandchildren?'

I remembered me and Sfen sneaking out to the highway at night to hunt ptarmigan sitting high in the poplars. 'There's no such thing as '90s love,' I said and pushed away. 'The earth is burning, Grandpa.'

'Why do you talk like this?'

I looked into his blind eyes. 'It's gonna take hell for me to find another heart that beats like mine.'

He nodded. Didn't know what the hell I was talking about.

'I have to go, Grandpa.'

'Come visit me tomorrow,' he said. 'I'll bless your hands.'

I coughed I would. 'Grandpa,' I said. 'Can I ask you a Question?'

'That's what grandpas are for.'

'Why don't you cure yourself? Your eyes, I mean.'

He worked his tight little lips around his fake teeth. 'I would have to kill a man and take his eyes,' he said. 'Then where would I be? I just have to tap my cane and children take me where I wish to go. If I could see, they would not help me anymore. I am already in heaven, Grandson. You were the one who could smell the fireweed roots, weren't you?'

That's right! I had forgotten. I remembered taking the old man's cane and leading him to the Bay when I was a child.

'What do you smell, Grandson?' he would ask.

'Fire,' I'd answer. 'I smell fire.'

He would chuckle deep into his chest. I could smell fire even when I was a little boy, and I could smell cancer in trees. So how did I end up bloody in Yellowknife with blessed hands? I won the Bingo game, all right, just like the old man said I would. I had eighty thousand dollars cash in two duffel bags. I should have put it in storage, but I ended up taking a taxi right to the top of the Gold Range. I figured the old man's medicine could win me more. It did. I won every hand I played: Blackjack, Poker. I got the Gook who ran the place to bring me some ginger pork and rice. And then I saw the hookers, two Gook sisters who wanted me, so I bought a room, but I forgot to wash my hands.

I woke up choking after throwing fire into both twins. I was being choked. I looked for someone to kill. No one. There was no one I could see, then I realized they were my own hands choking off my windpipe. The twins shot up screaming. My own hands were killing me. I couldn't breathe. I was gagging so I charged to the bathroom.

I knew what was happening. The old man's medicine ran out and turned sour. I sat down and pulled my legs back and kicked my arms loose. That's when I saw them. I had claws instead of hands. The devil's claws were on me. The same hands that won me eighty grand plus were digging through my throat. But I got the tub going. I got it going and I put those claws under the bloody water for a long time until they turned back to my hands. When I went back to the room, the twins had vanished with all my money.

I remembered the night Sfen told me everything. We were at the Lake. It was such a pretty night for sin. We were relaxing after kicking in the door and looting the Warden's house. Sfen knew the Warden was in the city with his ol' lady. And just like the song, there was a smoke on the water. There were parties rocking hard across the lake. Sitting around our fire, counting stars, trying to make out the voices, we strained to hear what they were talking about.

'This is my favorite place in the whole world, brother,' he said.

I thought about it. 'Mine too, I guess.'

We could hear ducks laugh with wooden throats somewhere not too far away. A few mallards whistled by overhead. There was a breeze then, the first breeze of summer. It was cool and it whispered through the hair on our arms. We shared the Warden's smokes, passed the Warden's bottle. That's when Sfen told me everything.

But I had known a long time ago. The way his skull sucked his face in. The night sweats that drenched his mattress.

I should have asked the old man if he had medicine for AIDS.

What animal would know which part of itself to give? The caribou? I heard the cure for cancer is in the root of a bear's tongue. But which part, and which cancer? There are so many now.

'What am I gonna do, Torch?' Sfen asked. He had lost so much weight the last year. He couldn't stop his hands from shaking and he wiped his tears away with his sleeve. 'It's getting worse every day. I can't take it anymore and I don't want to take it anymore.'

I tried so hard to think of the perfect answer and it suddenly hit me we were sharing the same bottle and the same cigarette. Could you get AIDS from that?

'What would a wolf do?' I asked Sfen.

'That isn't the question,' Sfen said. 'What would a sick wolf do? I have AIDS, Torchy. I'm dying. I ran outta my pills yesterday and I ain't going to the drug store in town. If anyone finds out, Torch, we're both dead and you know it. We ain't exactly town heroes.'

'You're out of meds? Sfen, you need those. What are we doing here then? Christ, we should make a run to the city and get some more.'

I started shaking. Something was up. That's when he said, 'You know, Torch, I been thinking. All my furniture is stuffed with that urea foam. You told me once it releases cyanide gas when it burns.'

I stood up and yelled, 'What are you talking like this for!?'

'I'd sit up when I heard the fire alarm,' he continued. 'You'd have to do it when I was asleep. I'd sit up and breathe two lungs full. It'd be painless, wouldn't it? You'd do that for me wouldn't you?'

'No!' I said. 'Never! Sfen don't talk like that!' And that's when I ran. I ran all the way up the road as far as I could. I ran until I puked. I was thinking this wasn't happening. I kept waiting for someone to tell me this wasn't real. I was thinking until I couldn't think anymore and that's when I heard the shot.

The Warden's gun.

The one we found under the bed. The one I was gonna take back to town and stash.

On the beach. There was blood everywhere when I found him. My brother's eyes were still open. I never seen blood so red. The Warden's rosary braided through his fingers. Sfen's eyes wide open. Looking at the lake. I never seen blood so red.

And there was his cigarette. Still smoking. Blowing itself away.

I picked it up, finished it all by myself. The party didn't even stop across the lake. People just hooted and cheered when they heard the shot.

Now Sfen is where the fish sleep. At the lake, by the river bed. My brother who loved mermen.

'Torchy? Torchy!' Stephanie is shaking me. 'Torchy? You were having a nightmare.'

I look around, covered in sweat. 'I was?'

'You were calling for Sfen. Who's Sfen?'

I look down. 'My brother.'

'Where is he? Is that who you were looking for?'

'Yeah,' I wipe my sleeve across my eyes, 'but he's gone.'

'Just like my daddy's gone,' she says. 'My mom says he was fast. Faster than the wind. He froze to death, she says. Maybe the wind caught him.' She looks at me and says, 'I'll be your sister, Torchy, if you'll be my brother.'

I can feel it build. I don't want to scare her so I move fast and picked her up. I hug her and I start to cry. I have to keep it quiet but I can't stop.

'Take me with you, Torchy,' she says. 'I don't want to stay here anymore. I'm scared all the time. I'll wash floors. I'll cook. I'll clean . . .'

I think of the old man and I look at my hands. 'Do you want to come with me? To where I live?'

She looks around. 'What about my mom?'

'We'll call your mom when things get better, okay? There's a bus leaving in half an hour to Simmer. There's an old man I want you to meet—my grandpa. He really wants to meet you.'

She scratches her head and smiles. 'He does?'

'Yeah,' I say. 'He does. Can you read?'

She nods. 'Let's go, Torchy. Let's go to your home.'

I remembered Sfen, when we were kids. One of my mom's boyfriends felt guilty, I guess, for beating on all of us. He took us to the lake after for a picnic of chips and beer. He also bought one pair of flippers for me and Sfen.

Mom needed shades to hide the love he put on her. 'You're gonna have to learn to share,' she called weakly as we ran from the car. 'You two are brothers and brothers share.'

'It's okay, Torchy,' Sfen whispered. 'Don't look at him.' Sfen's left eye was swollen shut. He had to help me with mine because my arms were so sore. I got the right flipper because I had smaller feet. He took the left, though it was too tight for him. We held hands and ran to the water. The same lake I buried him beside. We ran together, my big brother and me, never letting go, laughing, free . . .

the uranium leaking from port radium and rayrock mines is killing us

and the girl with sharp knees sits in her underwear. She is shivering. The bus is cold. The man at the gun store has seagull eyes. Freckles grow on the wrong side of his face. This town has the biggest Canadian flag anywhere. It is always tangled and never waves. For grass this playground has human hair. It never grows on Sundays. The kids that play here are cold and wet. They are playing in their underwear. They are singing with cold tongues. They have only seven fingers to hide with.

Those are rotting clouds. This is the other side of rain. The band plays but there is no sound. I snap my finger but there is no sound.

There is someone running on the highway. There is no one in the field. Nobody knows the cats here. No one knows their names.

They are letting the librarian's right eye fuse shut. There is a pencil stabbed thru her bun. She can read 'I didn't pop my balloon the grass did' in my library book. She looks into me. One eye is pink. The other is blue.

My father said take the bus. There is yellow tape around my house. A finger is caught in the engine but they only rev it harder. There are cold hands against my back. I want to kiss Pocahontas before she dies at age 21. Someone is stealing the dogs of this town while doctors hold babies high in black bags. My mother's voice is a dull marble rolling down her mouth, stolen to her lap, not even bouncing, not even once. She has sprayed metal into her hair. I am sitting on a red seat. My hands open with rawhide.

This is the ear I bled from. There is a child walking in the field. He is walking with a black gun.

In my girlfriend's fist is a promise. She does not raise herself to meet me. Her socks are always dirty. She is selling me a broken bed so she can lie on plywood. Her feet are always cold. The coffee we drink is cold. The bus driver does not wave goodbye. Why are there only children on this bus? Why are we wet and cold? Why are we only in our underwear?

I want to run but I have no legs. The tongue that slides from my mouth is blue.

Friday is the loneliest day of the week she says. The blanket she knitted this winter is torn upon us. She laughs at me with blue eyes. She says if you walk in the rain no one can tell you're crying. The soup we drink after is cold. The popcorn we eat after is cold. Someone is crying in the basement. Someone is crying next door.

The dream we have is something running on four legs, running on pavement towards us. It is running from the highway. It is a dead caribou running on dead legs. I meet its eyes but there are only antlers. In between the antlers is an eye. It too is cold and watching. Its eye is the color of blue.

The plants here have no flowers. The trees themselves are black. The fish are rolling sideways. Rain has started to fall.

The child with the black gun sees my house. He is walking backwards towards me. He swings his head. His eyes are blue. *Can you please sing with me?*

The bus driver does not wave goodbye.

The band is playing but all I hear is galloping.

I snap my finger.

My eyes are blue.

All I can hear is galloping . . .

My Fifth Step

This is my fifth step. I miss you. I'm sorry. I miss you and I'm sorry.

Do you think about me sometimes? I sure think about you. I think the hard feelings between us would go away if we just went for coffee sometime, just to check up on each other and see that the wounds weren't so deep anymore, but I don't think that will happen.

You'll always be with me you know. No matter what. What we had was good and I'm sorry for any bad between us. Really I am.

I think about you mostly when I'm around fire or when I hear a sad song. I start to feel hollow and I have to turn away. I look away and remember the nights we shared, the laughter—there was laughter. Remember? Before the battles, before the pissing contests between us about who was hurt more, who had done more, who had lied and betrayed more.

I'd love to see you again in the best way, your way. No power, no overwhelmance, no control, just a soft hug and a smile. I'd love to hear how you're doing and where you've gone. I'd love to watch you talk about your friends, your job, your boss, what you do alone, where you go to gather strength. Do you still love to swim? Do you have children? Is he good to you?

I was thinking the other day on a long drive with all my nephews and nieces that all we have—really have in this life—is our family and friends, and I'm glad you and I had some time together. I hope all your dreams come true—I really do. Lord knows, you deserve all good things that come your way.

Have I softened over the years? Well, for one, I quit fighting. I don't got the poop anymore, and, really, I can talk anyone down, and I think folks know I play for keeps so if you want to go, you're taking on a bull (in the sheets and in a fight ha ha!). So, I quit all that. Assholes are assholes. Lord knows it's not my job to bust 'em or try to change 'em. There's man's way and there's God's way and I have learned to let go. I don't think I told you I love you the way you should have heard it. Sure, I said it when things were going good, but when things soured I never said it when you needed to hear it most, or maybe when I needed to. I'm sorry about that. I thought crying was a weakness, but I know now that it's a strength and that it takes something I always wanted: courage.

It's funny and sad but you said you never really got to know me all those years, but if you think about it I showed you more than anyone who I really am. When I brought you to the field behind the highway, I was showing you the innocence inside me, the place that's me, and when I took you to the lake, I was showing you the possibilities inside me, the freedom I feel all the time, and when I let you meet my grandparents, I was showing you the royalty of my family, the richness of my blood and what we could share if we had a baby. Remember when I showed you how to call the northern lights? I hope you teach that to your children one night and that you tell them 'a great man taught me this many moons ago.'

I was surprised when you used how I communicate against me. Men are single-minded and women are emotional and can do way more at once. This is how we may help and balance one another. You wanted me to cry with you and I don't know any man who would or even could. You said I was capable of two emotions: anger and happiness, but that wasn't true either. I felt every emotion possible. Couldn't you read it in my eyes or hear it in my voice? My silence was never anger. It was meditation on everything you said, and sometimes I needed more time to answer than you would give me.

Courage. I have it now because I did go for counseling. When you left, you took the two most sacred words I know with you: HOME and FAMILY. That's why I got so crazy and that's why I never came back. The man inside me felt betrayed. The little boy inside me felt abandoned. The elder inside me was heartbroken with all the dreams I had for us. My spirit split when you left and it took oh about four years to get back to me. I fell down. Sure I did. I'm not going to talk about it but some of the rumors about me are true. . . I know about shame and doubt and embarrassment, but I'm a better man for it. I am more compassionate now, more giving, not willing to judge (try not to!). I give freely and have learned that the joy is in the giving. I treasure my friends and family every chance I get. 'Affirmations are friends.' It's true! There is help out there if you ask and look for it.

We're both so bloody proud and stubborn, and that was our downfall. I'm sorry family got involved on both sides and I'm sorry this town can be so cruel with its talk. We were the flavor of the month and things got out of control so fast. People need things to gossip about so they don't have to look at their own lives. They feed on misery to feel better about where they're at and we should have worked things out together-away from town. We should have gone camping for as long as we needed together. The land would have welcomed us home.

You'll never guess it but I'm softer now. Yeah, I love country music (now I know we'll never get back together—just kidding!). Well, maybe you like it now too. Yeah, it calms me, makes me feel. I'm actually a good little two stepper. I learned how at treatment and two steppin's where I got my wings back. Remember how I used to groan about how much cocoa butter you used on your feet at night? Well, I have a confession. Sometimes, when the day's been hard or I'm lonesome, I have some and I rub it on my feet and I wear my softest shirt and I fall asleep right away. I also remember how you used to take baths at night. Well, I do that too now and I wish I would have said yes to you every time you asked me to join you. I can't, for the life of me, imagine why I would have said no all those years.

Anyhow, I called your place a few times but some guy keeps answering. The fifth step teaches that if you think you may get someone in trouble or beat up by contacting them, then it's okay not to, but I figured that if I sent this here and it got published it would somehow find its way to you and you'd know that it was me and you'd know I was sorry.

I pray to God you're not getting hit or pushed around. There was this one elder at the lodge who said, 'When a man hits a woman, he breaks something not even God can fix.' He's right. I may have swore. I may have yelled, but I never hit and I never will. I'm proud of that.

I loved the way you pulled me into the tea dance every time. I waited for it. I loved the way you led me into the bush when I first came back to town. You saved my life that night. I loved making love to you and I miss your cooking. Most of all, though,

I miss how when we slept together, you wrapped your arms around me and never let go. I never thanked you enough for all you did for me and I want to thank you for trusting me when we first met. You never held back and I did, and I never wanted to become the biggest disappointment in your life. I loved my coffee in the mornin', and I loved you in the afternoon . . . remember that? I also miss listening to you talk in your sleep and making you smile with a joke or a story or just a look between us. You have such pretty eyes . . .

My family still asks about you, and I tell them you're happy and doing what gives you the most joy. I hope I'm right. I also hope whoever that guy is who answers your phone knows what a queen you are.

Take care of yourself and thank you again for all your love. You made me feel so special. I'm a better man because of you and I know now what's possible. Be gentle with yourself, my friend . . . now and forever . . . I miss your love and friendship . . .

Walk in beauty . . .

Acknowledgements

KATERI AKIWENZIE-DAMM. 'kegedonce', 'the resurrection of desire', 'words for winter', 'Grandmother, Grandfather', 'Why This Woman', 'sturgeon', 'river song', and 'desire' are reprinted by permission of kateri akiwenzie-damm.

ROBERT ARTHUR ALEXIE. Excerpt from *Porcupines and China Dolls*, by Robert Arthur Alexie, copyright © Robert Arthur Alexie, 2005, is reprinted by permission of Penguin Group (Canada), a division of Pearson Penguin Canada Inc.

ANNHARTE. 'Got Something in the Eye', 'Exercises in Lip Pointing', 'How to Write About White People', 'Saskatchewan Indians Were Dancing', 'I Shoulda Said Something Political', 'Me Tonto Along', and 'Dad's Zipper', from *Exercises in Lip Pointing* (New Star Books 2003), are reprinted by permission of the publisher. 'Coyote Columbus Cafe' and 'I Want to Dance Wild Indian Black Face' are from *Coyote Columbus Cafe*. 'Coyote Trail', 'Penumbra', 'Raced Out to Write This Up', and 'One Way to Keep Track of Who Is Talking'.

JEANNETTE C. ARMSTRONG. 'History Lesson', 'For Tony', 'Sketches', 'Indian Woman', 'Threads of Old Memory', 'Fire Madness', 'Wind Woman', 'Keepers Words', 'The Disempowerment of First North American Native Peoples and Empowerment Through Their Writing', and 'Blue Against White' are reprinted by permission of Theytus Books.

JOANNE ARNOTT. The following are reprinted by permission of Joanne Arnott: 'Wiles of Girlhood' and 'If Honour is Truth', from *Wiles of Girlhood*; 'White Belly', from *My Grass Cradle*. 'Steepy Mountains', 'Dog Girl Verse', and 'when you', from *Steepy Mountain Love Poetry* (Kegedonce Press 2004 <www.kegedonce.com>), are reprinted by permission of the publisher.

BETH BRANT. The following are reprinted by permission of Canadian Scholars' Press/Women's Press: 'A Long Story', from *Mohawk Trail* © 1990 CSPI/Women's Press; 'Grandmothers of a New World', from *Writing as Witness: Essays and Talk* © 1994 CSPI/Women's Press. 'Swimming Upstream' is from *Food & Spirits: Stories by Beth Brant (Degonwadonti)*.

MARIA CAMPBELL. 'Jacob' and 'Joseph's Justice' are reprinted by permission of Theytus Books Ltd.

HAROLD CARDINAL. 'A Canadian *What the Hell It's All About*' is from *The Rebirth of Canada's Indians*.

JOAN CRATE. The following are reprinted by permission of Brick Books: 'The Poetry Reading', 'Story teller', 'Encounter While Fishing', and 'Wife of Son of the Sea', from *Pale as Real Ladies*; 'The Year of the Coyote', 'Heirlooms', 'Sentences: At the Culls', 'Loose Feathers on Stone', 'The Fly and I', and 'Thank-you Card', from *Foreign Homes*.

BETH CUTHAND. 'Shake 'N Bake', 'Zen Indian', 'He Told Me', 'Four Songs for the Fifth Generation', and 'Post-Oka Kinda Woman' are reprinted by permission of Beth Cuthand.

JOSEPH A. DANDURAND. 'dirt of the old ones' and 'drunks, drifters, and fat robins' are reprinted by permission of the author.

MARILYN DUMONT. 'Squaw Poems', 'Let the Ponies Out', 'Horse-Fly Blue', and 'Circle the Wagons', from *A Really Good Brown Girl*, are reprinted by permission of Brick Books. 'monuments, cowboys, & indians, tin cans, and red wagons', 'the dimness of mothers and daughters', 'jig dream', 'Broadway', 'scorching', 'wrapping the bundle of my dream of you', and 'throatsong to the four-leggeds', from *green girls dreams Mountains* (Lantzville, BC: Oolichan Books, 2001), are reprinted by permission of Oolichan Books.

CONNIE FIFE. 'Dream' and 'Driftwoodwoman' are from *Beneath the Naked Sun* (Sister Vision Press, Toronto 1992). 'I have become so many mountains', 'the knowing', 'dear walt', 'speaking through jagged rock', and 'poem for Russell' are reprinted from *Speaking Through Jagged Rock* (Broken Jaw Press 1999) by permission of the publisher. 'For Matthew Shepard', 'Exiled', 'Politics', 'For James Byrd, Jr.', and 'Witnessing' are reprinted with permission from Connie Fife's *Poems for A New World* (Vancouver: Ransdale 2001).

MARVIN FRANCIS. 'mcPemmican', 'PULLING FACES', 'BNA ACTOR', and 'word drummer', from *city treaty* by Marvin Francis, copyright © 2002 Marvin Francis, are reprinted by permission of Turnstone Press Ltd, Winnipeg, MB.

GHANDL. 'In His Father's Village, Someone Was Just About To Go Out Hunting Birds', from *Nine Visits to the Mythworld*, copyright © 2000 by Robert Bringhurst (Douglas & McIntyre Ltd), is reprinted by permission of the publisher.

RICHARD G. GREEN. 'The Last Raven' is reprinted by permission of Richard G. Green.

ALMA GREENE. Excerpt from *Forbidden Voice: Reflections of a Mohawk Indian* is reprinted by permission of Green Dragon Press.

DAVID GROULX. 'In the Cold October Waters', 'Victims of Lashing Under the Hanging Sky', 'Wouldn't We Be Fucked', and 'The Long Dance', from *The Long Dance* (Kegedonce Press 2000 <www.kegedonce.com>), are reprinted by permission of the publisher.

LOUISE HALFE. 'Pāhkahkos', 'She Told Me', 'Body Politics', 'Fog Inside Mama', 'Stones', 'Idlywyld Crow', 'My Ledders', 'for Omeasoo', and 'The Heat of My Grandmothers', by Louse Halfe, from *Bear Bones & Feathers* (Coteau Books 1994), are reprinted by permission of the publisher.

TOMSON HIGHWAY. 'The Lover Snake' and 'Aria' are reprinted by permission of the playwright Tomson Highway and Playwrights Canada Press.

ALOOTOOK IPELLIE. 'Summit with Sedna, the Mother of Sea Beasts', 'Waking Up', 'Journey Toward Possibilities', and 'Walking Both Sides of an Invisible Border'.

RITA JOE. 'Today's Learning Child', 'I Lost My Talk', 'Micmac Hieroglyphics', 'Shanawdithit', and 'The Lament of Donald Marshall Jr.', from *Song of Eskasoni* (Women's Press, Toronto 1988), are reprinted by permission of Women's Press.

BASIL H. JOHNSTON. 'The Prophecy', 'One Generation from Extinction', and 'Is That All There Is? Tribal Literature' are reprinted by permission of Basil H. Johnston.

MARGO KANE. 'Moonlodge' was developed and performed by Margo Kane.

LENORE KEESHIG-TOBIAS. 'After Oka—How Has Canada Changed?' is reprinted by permission of the author. Excerpt from 'Trickster Beyond 1992: Our Relationship', by Lenore Keeshig-Tobias, from *Indigena: Contemporary Native Perspectives*, Canadian Museum of Civilization © 1992.

WAYNE KEON. 'heritgae', 'howlin at the moon', 'for Donald Marshall', 'I'm not in charge of this ritual', 'if I ever heard', 'my sweet maize', 'the apocalypse will begin', 'replanting the heritage tree', 'back in therapy', 'on studying ojibway (the people)', 'on studying ojibway (earth mother)', and 'on studying ojibway (great mystery)' are reprinted by permission of the author.

THOMAS KING. 'The One About Coyote Going West', from *One Good Story, That One* (HarperPerennial 1993) copyright © 1993 Dead Dog Café Productions Inc., is reprinted by permission of the author.

RANDY LUNDY. 'Geography', 'Heal', 'Old Man and Woman in the Garden', 'Migrations', 'She', 'Dawn', 'The Gift of the Hawk', and 'Bear', by Randy Lundy, from *The Gift of the Hawk* (Coteau Books 2004), are reprinted by permission of the publisher.

JOHN MCLEOD. 'The Shivering Tree'.

LEE MARACLE. 'Yin Chin' and 'Sojourner's Truth'.

MARTIN MARTIN. 'We, the Inuit, Are Changing', from *Them Days*, Vol. 2, No.1, September 1976.

DUNCAN MERCREDI. 'could be anyone but i call him syd', 'statue', 'god shrugged and turned his back', 'big bear', and 'kiskisin (i remember)' are reprinted by permission of Pemmican Publications Inc.

MONIQUE MOJICA. Excerpt from *Princess Pocahontas and the Blue Spots* © 1991 Canadian Scholars' Press Inc/Women's Press is reprinted by permission of CSPI/Women's Press.

DANIEL DAVID MOSES. 'The Sunbather's Fear of the Moon', 'Inukshuk', 'The Persistence of Songs', 'The Line', 'Hotel Centrale, Rotterdam', 'Report on Anna Mae's Remains', 'Some Grand River Blues', 'Party Favour', and 'Witch of Niagara' are reprinted by permission of the author.

BEATRICE MOSIONIER. Excerpt from *April Raintree* by Beatrice Culleton © 1984 is reprinted by permission of Portage & Main Press, 800-667-9673, <www.portageandmainpress.com>.

PHILIP KEVIN PAUL. 'The Bare Story of My Life', 'The Cost', and 'Taking the Names Down from the Hill' are from *Taking the Names Down from the Hill*, by Philip Kevin Paul (Nightwood Editions 2003).

SHARRON PROULX-TURNER. 'a horse's nest egg is very large' © Sharron Proulx-Turner is reprinted by permission of McGilligan Books from *What the Auntys Say*.

DUKE REDBIRD. 'I am a Canadian' and excerpt from *We Are Métis* are reprinted courtesy of Duke Redbird.

EDEN ROBINSON. 'Terminal Avenue', by Eden Robinson, copyright 1996 by Eden Robinson, is reprinted by permission of the author.

HARRY ROBINSON. 'Captive in an English Circus' is from *Write It on Your Heart: The Epic World of an Okanagan Storyteller* © Harry Robinson and Wendy Wickwire (Talonbooks, Vancouver 2004).

ARMAND GARNET RUFFO. Excerpt from *Grey Owl: The Mystery of Archie Belaney*, 'Poem For Duncan Campbell Scott', and 'Creating a Country' are reprinted by permission of the author. 'Rockin' Chair Lady', 'In the Sierra Blanca', 'On the Line', 'Bear', and 'Postscript', by Armand Garnet Ruffo, from *At Geronimo's Grave* (Coteau Books 2001), are reprinted by permission of the publisher.

BUFFY SAINTE-MARIE. 'Universal Soldier'. Words and music by Buffy Sainte-Marie. Copyright © CALEB MUSIC. Copyright renewed. All rights in the US and Canada controlled and adminis-tered by ALMO MUSIC CORP. All rights reserved. Used by permission. 'My Country 'Tis of Thy People You're Dying'. Words and music by Buffy Sainte-Marie. Copyright © 1966 GYPSY BOY MUSIC, INC. Copyright renewed. All rights in the US and Canada controlled and administered by ALMO MUSIC CORP. All rights reserved. Used by permission. 'Now That the Buffalo's Gone'. Words and Music by Buffy Sainte-Marie. Copyright © 1965 GYPSY BOY MUSIC, INC. Copyright renewed. All rights in the US and Canada controlled and administered by ALMO MUSIC CORP. All rights reserved. Used by permission.

GREGORY SCOFIELD. 'Nothing Sacred' is from *The Gathering: Stones for the Medicine Wheel* (Vancouver: Polestar, an imprint of Raincoast Books, 1993). '*Ayahkwêw's* Lodge', 'Promises', 'Cycle (of the black lizard)', and 'Warrior Mask' are from *Native Canadiana: Songs from the Urban Rez* (Vancouver: Polestar, an imprint of Raincoast Books, 1996). 'Ôchîm ◆ His Kiss', 'Morning in the White Room', 'Hunger', 'My Drum, His Hands', 'Unhinged', 'Wâstêpakâwi-pîsim', and 'Night Train' are from *Love Medicine and One Song* (Vancouver: Polestar, an imprint of Raincoast Books, 1997).

PAUL SEESEQUASIS. 'The Republic of Tricksterism'.

LORNE JOSEPH SIMON. Chapter Four, 'The Second Coming', from *Stones and Switches*, by Lorne Simon, is reprinted by permission of Theytus Books.

RUBY SLIPPERJACK. 'Blueberry Days' is reprinted by permission of Pemmican Publications Inc.

MARY AUGUSTA TAPPAGE. 'Tyee—Big Chief', 'The Lillooets', 'Christmas at the Mission', and 'At Birth', from *The Days of Augusta* copyright © 1973, 1992 by Augusta Evans and Jean E. Speare (Douglas & McIntyre Ltd), is reprinted by permission of the publisher.

DREW HAYDEN TAYLOR. 'Pretty Like a White Boy: The Adventures of a Blue Eyed Ojibway' is reprinted by permission of the author.

ANTHONY APAKARK THRASHER. 'Playing with Girls is a Sin' is from *Thrasher . . . Skid Row Eskimo*.

MARION TUU'LUQ. 'A Story of Starvation' is from *Inuit Today*, 1977.

RICHARD VAN CAMP. 'Mermaids', 'the uranium leaking from port radium and rayrock mines is killing us', and 'My Fifth Step', from *Angel Wing Splash* (Kegedonce Press 2002 <www.kegedonce.com>), are reprinted by permission of the publisher.

RICHARD WAGAMESE. Excerpt from *Keeper'n Me*, by Richard Wagamese, copyright © 1994 by Richard Wagamese, is reprinted by permission of Doubleday Canada.

EMMA LEE WARRIOR. 'Compatriots' is reprinted by permission of the author.

JORDAN WHEELER. 'A Mountain Legend' is from *achimoona* (Fifth House Publishers 1985).

ALEXANDER WOLFE. 'The Last Grass Dance' reprinted with permission from *Earth Elder Stories.* Copyright 1998 by Alexander Wolfe. Published by Fifth House Ltd, Calgary, AB.

Index